ALEX HALEY'S QUEEN

Alex Haley is the author of the Pulitzer Prize winning masterpiece *Roots*. He also collaborated with Malcolm X on *The Autobiography of Malcolm X*. He died in February 1992.

David Stevens worked closely with Alex Haley on both book and screenplay for *Queen*. Among his other works, he co-authored the screenplay of *Breaker Morant* and wrote and directed the PBS miniseries *A Town Called Alice*.

D1331476

ALEX HALEY'S

QUEEN

The Story of an American Family

ALEX HALEY
AND
DAVID STEVENS

PAN BOOKS
in association with
MACMILLAN
LONDON

First published 1993 by William Morrow and Company, Inc.
First published in Great Britain 1993 by Macmillan London Limited
This edition published 1993 by Pan Books Limited
a division of Pan Macmillan Publishers Limited
Cavaye Place London SW10 9PG
and Basingstoke

in association with Macmillan London Limited

Associated companies throughout the world

ISBN 0 330 33307 0

579864

A CIP catalogue record for this book is available from
the British Library

Typeset by CentraCet Limited, Cambridge
Printed by Cox & Wyman Ltd, Reading

Dedicated to the memory of Alex Haley

And to the African, Kanyuro, of the Kikuyu, who saved my life during a small skirmish in an obscure war on the Kenya/Uganda border, and gave me the priceless gift of the years since then.

ACKNOWLEDGMENTS

The role played by David Wolper in Alex's career, and, latterly, my own, is remarkable, but I would also like to record my gratitude to Bernard Sofronski, who first had the idea of associating me with Alex and this project.

My thanks also to Mark Wolper and John Erman. To Jeff Sagansky, John Matoyan, and Larry Strichman. To Paul Bresnick, and everyone at William Morrow.

To Louis Blau, and to George Haley, Alex's brother, and William Haley, Alex's son.

To my agent, Irv Schwartz, who is the best, a pillar of support and a valued friend. To Fiona McLauchlan and Daniel Donnelly, for their help in research. To the staff at Alex's farm, who adopted me and nicknamed me The Moonshine Kid, and especially Gertie Brummitt, who first let me into the secret.

To Bubby, with love. And Rooney, Myrtle, Maggie, and Dudley. And Morgan, whom we miss.

On Alex's behalf, it is incumbent on me to record his gratitude to Myran E. Haley, his wife and valued associate, and to George Sims, his lifelong friend and master researcher.

PART ONE

BLOODLINES

Hurra for the Hickory Tree!
Hurra for the Hickory Tree!
Its branches will wave
O'er tyranny's grave
And bloom for the brave
And the free.

Presidential Campaign Song, 1832

1

On a cold and rainy April night, in a guarded garret somewhere in Dublin, James Jackson II, known as Jamie, swore a most sacred, solemn oath.

"In the awful presence of God, I, Jamie Jackson, do voluntarily swear and declare that I will form a brotherhood among Irishmen of every religion, for equal, full, and adequate representation of all Irishmen. Not hopes, fears, rewards, or punishment shall ever induce me to inform on, or to give evidence against, any member of this society. So help me God."

It was the year 1797. Jamie was barely fifteen. There were eleven other men in the room, for no cell of the illegal association could be larger than twelve. He had been sponsored into the group by his uncle Henry. Partly because of the eloquence with which young Jamie voiced his convictions, partly because they needed every man they could get in the fight against the occupying British, but mostly out of respect for his uncle, not one black bean was cast against him.

Three months previously, a fleet of forty French ships carrying twelve thousand men had sailed toward Bantry Bay, in southern Ireland, to drive the British from the country. On the flagship, *Indomitable*, was Wolfe Tone, who had persuaded Napoleon that the British could be defeated. The weather went against them, and high winds and heavy rainfall frustrated the landing of men from the French fleet. The storm raged for six days, forcing the ships, one by one, to cut cable and seek safe harbor, until the *Indomitable* stood alone. Then she too turned about and limped back to France.

When news of the retreat at Bantry Bay reached Dublin Castle, Lord Clair, the Lord Chancellor of Ireland, personally appointed by King George III, made a jubilant proclamation.

"It was a Protestant victory! It saw God on our side!"

He intensified the suppression of the United Ireland movement, he ordered massive recriminations against the intransigent Irish peasants, and finally he declared martial law.

The ferocity with which the British troops enforced his orders shocked even the most moderate of men, and Jamie, appalled by what he saw, made his decision and formally cast his lot with the Irish cause.

He was not the only member of his Protestant family to have made such a dangerous commitment.

His older brother John had abandoned Ireland and gone to America with three of his brothers, but his older sister Eleanor was married to Oliver Bond, a leader in the secret association. His sister Martha had married Hugh Hanna, whom Jamie believed to be a "Peep O' Day Boy," a vigilante group mostly from the peasant class. Under cover of night, toward dawn, the Peep O' Days took what small vengeance they could against the occupying British troops.

His sister Sara was engaged to Jimmy Hanna, Hugh's brother, who had been tutor to Jamie when he was a boy in Ballybay, and had helped to awaken his social conscience. Jamie's uncle, Henry Jackson, with whom he lodged while he was at school in Dublin, was leader of the small cell that Jamie had joined.

Yet Jamie was an unlikely revolutionary. The eleventh of twelve children, he was born to comparative wealth, and grew up in an atmosphere of privilege and security. His father, James Jackson, owned many acres of land and a linen mill at Ballybay, near Carrickmacross, in County Monaghan. The British were well disposed to those native-born Irish who espoused their religion and respected their authority, and James Jackson had flourished under their colonial dominion.

4

A stern, intolerant man, James Jackson loved the English way of life, and had little sympathy for the Catholic peasants. It appalled him that so many of his children had chosen to embrace the nationalist cause, and thus put everything he had worked for and achieved, and their own inheritance, at risk. He could not understand that it was the bloodless austerity of his heart and manner that had driven his children to seek love and companionship in the camaraderie of political passion. He was dispassionate toward his family and, except in matters of procreation, detached from his wife. Other than the marital bed, his only passion was his hobby, the breeding of champion racehorses.

When Jamie was eighteen months old, his mother gave birth to another boy, Washington, and died four months later, at thirty-five, worn out from childbearing and a loveless marriage. Jugs, the family housekeeper, became surrogate mother to Jamie and his infant brother, and she came to love Jamie as the son she had never had, and he basked in her affection.

Gravel-voiced, toothless, bosomy, and superstitious, the Catholic Jugs had served in the Jackson household as loyal friend and confidante to Jamie's mother, Mary Steele Jackson, whom she had nursed from infancy. After Mary's death, she ran the house with peasant discipline, faced trouble by first crossing herself and then wielding a big stick, and tended toward earthy language after a few nips of her master's brandy. She knew every Irish superstition in the book, and practiced most of them, especially those that were said to placate the fairies.

It was she who introduced Jamie to the world outside his father's bleak and loveless estate. Several times a week, Jugs went to visit her sister, Maureen, and her husband, Patrick, a tenant farmer on the neighboring Hamilton land. Maureen had a son, Sean, of Jamie's age and Jugs took Jamie with her on these visits because she thought the boy needed a companion. They became more than playmates. From widely diverse backgrounds, Jamie and Sean quickly became fast friends, and grew up in each other's company.

Maureen's simple home was paradise for a young boy whose own was cold and formal. The cottage had a thatch roof, mud walls, an earthen floor, and a vibrant sense of life, of passion and laughter and anger. The loom was the largest piece of furniture, and in the winter the cow lived inside with the rest of the family.

Jamie loved the simple formalities of peasant life. Whenever he went in through the door he would say, "Blessings upon all I see," as Jugs had taught him. He learned some words of Gaelic. When Maureen churned butter, she recited to him the legends of it. If milk splashed during the churning he would be doomed to marry a drunken spouse. If someone "blinked" your cow, he learned how to break the curse. When the butter finally broke, he twisted the staff three times, and placed it over the mouth of the churn, and he helped her smear a little of the butter on the wall of the cottage as an offering to the fairies.

He loved the stories that the shanachies, the traveling storytellers, recited of the leprechauns and the little folk, and he believed in the fairies, who lived on the mist-shrouded Crieve Mountain nearby. He loved the great history of the Gaelic people, and of the blessed Saint Patrick who had converted them to Christianity, and had rid the island of snakes by tapping with his staff upon the earth. He learned of the glories of the time of kings and poets, and of the Viking raiders, who were defeated at Clontarf by Brian Boru. He heard the long history of invasion by the British, who were determined to subjugate the Emerald Isle, from Henry II to the ruthless, hated Oliver Cromwell. Of the Protestant settlers brought from England and Scotland to be settled in the north, to reduce the influence of the Catholics. He heard of repression and rebellion, evictions and retaliations, and the suppression of the Cath-

6

olic religion that followed the Irish defeat at the Battle of the Boyne.

He gasped at the stories of the White Boys, who refused to pay tax, and rode through the night cutting off the noses and ears of tax collectors, but never harming the innocent.

He wept again at the tales of the reprisals against the White Boys, how they put the tar cap of molten, burning pitch on the peasant's head, and mocked him while he screamed in agony, unable to remove the fiery mess.

His blood ran hot at the stories of indiscriminate flogging and looting and rape, or the British soldier's sport of setting fire to the hay in a peasant's cart and ramming the flaming cart into the man's house, laughing while the cottage burned.

Most of all, he loved Sean, and tried to emulate his hero in every way. A moderate and studious boy, who grieved for the mother he had never known and sorely missed his father's affections, Jamie found in the rollicking, boisterous Sean a friend who filled the emotional void in his heart. Through the days of their childhood they were inseparable, roaming the lanes between Ballybay and Carrickmacross, the daring Sean leading the wide-eyed Jamie into scrapes and adventures and pranks.

Sean taught Jamie to play the wild game of hurley, and how to cut turf from the peat bogs, stack it in barrows, and take it back to the cottage to dry, to be used as fuel for the fire. They visited Sean's father at the Jackson linen mill, and Jamie watched in amazement the arduous labor, as the flax was hackled and scutched, and the peasant women toiled over great steaming kettles boiling the spun thread to purify it. They went to the annual Ballybay Fair together, and reveled in the fun of it, the tinkers and fiddlers, and the increasingly drunken peasants dancing increasingly drunken gigs. They giggled at the man with the shillelagh and long tailcoat who earned his living by challenging stalwarts to "step on his coat" and fight with him. They watched the races, dazzled by the bright colors of the silks the jockeys wore, and cheered the winners until their throats were sore, and, at the subsequent auction, pretended to bid for horses they could not afford.

When they grew older, and Jamie's father took a mistress, Sarah Black, who lived in Carrickmacross, it was Sean who taught Jamie about girls, and the great mysteries of sex, and it was Sean who first introduced Jamie to the wonders of beer and poteen, for the boy could not understand his father's faithlessness to the memory of his dead mother.

In all things they were as brothers, but although their ages were similar, it was Sean who led and Jamie who followed. They bridged, with the easy bond of youth, the many chasms that their different positions in society created for them, and they nurtured each other in spite of these differences, and drew strength from them. Once Jamie had Maureen crop his hair short, in the peasant-boy manner, the more to identify with his sunshine friend. When he went home, his father whipped him, and forbade him to leave the house until his hair had grown out, and Jamie kept his hair long after that.

So Jamie grew up with an appreciation of the life and hardships of the mass of the people. His other world of his father's ambition, and of class and privilege, bored Jamie, and made him long to be back with his peasant friends. Yet he could not avoid that other life.

Much of Ballybay was owned by the Leslie family, impoverished minor English aristocracy, who, lacking funds, were happy to accept the sometime friendship and occasional loans of James Jackson, whom otherwise they regarded as a man of trade and not of their social quality. For a while they were prepared to consider the possibility of an acquaintance between James Jackson's

8

children and their own, and invited Jamie and Washington to spend an afternoon with their own children. Dressed in their best and sworn to good behavior by Jugs, they were driven by old Quinn, the hostler, in a fine gig with handsome horses.

Jamie and Washington took a stiffly formal tea with the Leslie boy and girl, attended by their governess, whose manners were as starched as her dress and high collar. Afterward, they were taken outside to play in the formal gardens of the small castle. They strolled politely through the grounds until they came to a fence that bordered a cow pasture. Young Jamie, the devil in him, dared the Leslie girl to run through the pasture with him. She accepted.

The governess, furious, raced after them, calling on her charge to watch her step, but it was too late. The girl slipped on a cow pat and fell to the ground. When Jamie went to help her up, he slipped too, in the same pat. The girl began to cry, and the governess berated Jamie for what he had done. He was suitably contrite at first, but the sight of the primped girl covered in cow dung was too much for him, and he started to laugh. This infuriated the victim.

"Go away, you bloody Irish ass!" she cried. The governess boxed her ears for her language but not her sentiments, dragged her away, and told Jamie he was a horrid little boy, who was never to come near them again.

Old Quinn drove the boys home, his nose wrinkling at the smell of cow manure coming from the seat behind him, but his eyes twinkling with delight at the cheek of his young master. Washington was in awe of his slightly older brother, and Jamie could not wait to tell Sean.

That afternoon caused something of a change in Jamie's relationship with old Quinn. Previously, the stable master had regarded him as a bit of a nuisance, a bothersome boy who had to be taught to ride, and whose presence in the stables distracted Quinn from his true passion, and disturbed his precious thoroughbred mares. Following the incident at the Leslies', Quinn, who detested everything British except racing stock, took more time with Jamie, and found in him a natural talent for riding. He encouraged Jamie's interest in horses, and astonished the boy with the breadth of his knowledge. He could recount the bloodline of every horse in his stable, their ages, sires, and dams, back through several generations. He instructed the boy in their care and management, he advised him of the potential of any new colt, and by the time Jamie was a young man, he had acquired much of Quinn's knowledge, as well as his passion. All the animals were divided into separate stables, the racing horses in one, the riding horses in another, and the workhorses in a third, because, Quinn insisted, the bloodlines could not be mixed.

Jamie's father, James, was often away, on business in Belfast or Dublin, but sometimes Jamie was allow to accompany him to races in which a Jackson horse was entered. Then his father was a different man to him. Free of the burden of being a parent, free to indulge his love of the track, James Jackson was attentive to his son, and taught him something of the ownership of racehorses, and the special skills that racing required. If his horse won, which his favorite, Crazy Jane, often did, James was expansive and bought his son gifts. If their horse was not placed, father and son traveled home in mutual, depressed silence.

Occasionally, his father would entertain, and the breakfast for the hunt club would be held at the mansion. These social events were used by James to extend and develop his social and business connections with the ruling class, with the Leslies and especially Dacre Hamilton.

Hamilton was the major English presence in the county of Monaghan, and served as sheriff. He was a strict Protestant, with no sympathy for Catholics. He took pleasure in rigidly enforcing all the penal laws against the peasants, whom he regarded as illiterate idolaters. These laws, instituted after the British victory at the Battle of the Boyne, were used to keep the defeated Catholics out of money, land, and power. The laws encouraged religious conversion and informing on neighbors—and even families, for only a Protestant in a Catholic family could inherit the land.

James expected his children to attend these functions, which they did unwillingly, for Dacre Hamilton was not loved by any of them. He had once briefly imprisoned their brother and sister, John and Eleanor, for some youthful high jinks. John had defended a hedge-school teacher against an irate landlord, and Eleanor had announced in public that she thought the religious persecution of the Catholics was obscene. Dacre Hamilton also protested to James Jackson, and warned him to exercise greater control over his children's opinions and actions. James had taken a riding crop to John, and locked Eleanor in her room for three days. It was this that persuaded John to emigrate to America and Eleanor to move to Dublin. The other Jackson children were wary of Hamilton, and while they enjoyed the sport of the hunt, they disliked the overweening sycophancy to England of the hunters. Encouraged by Sean, Jamie began to believe that most of the club would rather be in pursuit of Irish peasants than foxes or hares.

Nothing was more indicative of the social gap that existed between Jamie and Sean than the manner of their formal education. A tutor was engaged for Jamie: Jimmy Hanna, an impoverished young man of good learning, from Dublin, who had recently graduated from Trinity College and was looking to make his way in an unfair world. The classroom was the music room of the Jackson house, and they would sit together in isolated splendor, the teacher and his only student, and

11

Jamie was introduced to the classical world of Latin and Greek, of mathematics and history. As he got to know his student better, and trusted him more, Jimmy introduced him to the glories of Irish literature. Jamie loved the beautiful words, and the worlds they evoked of rain-washed fields and white-walled cottages, of lowering skies and breaking sunlight. Of heroes and rainbows.

With poetry as a foundation, Jimmy gently led his student to Ireland's present troubles, gave him a clear appreciation of the battle that lay ahead to rid their country of foreign rule, and taught him that freedom was the most precious word in any language.

Sean's school was behind a hedge. The British authorities were fearful of education for the peasants. History, presented in the wrong light, could lead to sedition, and many of the hedge-school teachers were deeply involved in the liberation movements. The teachers taught where they could, in ditches and behind hedgerows, with some lucky few having access to a shed or shack. They were paid in kind, with peat for their fires, or food for their stomachs—small slabs of bacon, or some potatoes, a bag of meal, a pound of butter or a few eggs. Textbooks were few, and those the teachers did have they had usually copied themselves, from printed books they could not afford to buy. Often a young man of the village would be posted as lookout, for many landlords kicked teachers off their properties, and burned their precious books, or charged them with sedition.

Sean's classes lasted only two or three hours, and he could go at all only when Maureen had something to give the teacher, but Jamie studied morning and afternoon. His older sister Sara was a frequent visitor to his classroom, for she was smitten by the tutor.

Jimmy Hanna had come to them through a family connection. The Irish Protestants were few in number, and even fewer owed their first allegiance to Ireland rather than England. Jimmy's brother Hugh was a friend of their sister Martha, who was completing her studies in Dublin. Both brothers were handsome, educated men, dedicated to the Irish cause, and both sisters, Martha and Sara, were headstrong and willful. Lacking parental affection and guidance, they longed for love, and followed the example of their older sister, the firebrand Eleanor, by challenging their father and all he stood for, if only to try to make him appreciate them more, or at least play some active role in their lives. Their patriotism was genuine, and deeply felt, and they saw in their own lives the greater cause. Like Ireland, they were unloved by him who governed them and had dominion over them, so they identified with the larger community, and dedicated themselves to its well-being, for at core they were deeply lonely. When a handsome young man who shared her convictions rode into Ballybay and into her life, and encouraged her to have faith in herself, Sara fell hopelessly in love. She would sit for hours in the classroom watching him teach, learning from him herself, and about him.

It worked to Jamie's advantage, for sometimes, on a dreary, drizzly afternoon or a pretty spring day, Jimmy, anxious to be alone with Sara, would curtail the lessons, and Sara's eyes would sparkle. She would send Jamie off to old Quinn in the stables, or to Jugs for some food, or to play with his croppy friend Sean. Then she would sit with Jimmy and hold hands with him, or sometimes they would kiss, and the warmth and reassurance of his presence, the strong beliefs that they shared, and the generosity of his nature persuaded Sara that she was loved.

When she found out that Sarah Black had become more than a friend to her father, although less than a wife, Sara was bitterly hurt. She could not understand why her father would not marry the woman, and bring her to his house so she could fulfill some of the functions of mother—or older woman friend at least. In

13

her distress, she turned to Jimmy for comfort, and, lacking any moral conviction or example, she surrendered herself to him. They took their pleasure secretly, covertly, in places where they thought they would not be discovered, but they were not discreet enough. Jamie, returning to the house one day because Sean was sick, saw them coupling together in the classroom. He did not announce his presence, for he was at puberty himself, and fascinated by the things Sean had told him. He watched Sara and Jimmy for a while, through the slightly open door, but then became embarrassed and excited, and crept away to his bedroom, to caress his own adolescent need.

He could not keep quiet about what he had seen for long, for it gave him some ascendancy over his sister, which was important to a boy of his age. Sara blushed and flared, and slapped his face for a peeping Tom, and then cried, and swore him to secrecy. When she had his promise, she giggled, and began to treat him as a young man from then on, and no longer as a boy.

Thus the Jackson children grew up effectively left to their own devices, and found love where they could. They were not unhappy, for each child had developed a keen self-reliance, and each tried to give his brothers and sisters something of what they lacked. These sibling bonds, woven in youth, stayed with them, and were a source of comfort and support to them all their lives, though never constraining.

But Jamie determined to create a family that would supply to his own children what he had never had. His father's house was not his home, merely the house in which he lived.

For home, he had learned from Sean, is where you are loved.

2

Jamie was fourteen when he had his first experience of violence by the soldiers. For years he had known that the local priest, Father Moran, forbidden to practice his religion in public, still tended the spiritual needs of his peasant congregation in a small cave on Crieve Mountain. Jamie knew very little about the Catholic religion, but was told by his father and other Protestants that it was a pagan cult of cannibalism, venerating a priest in Rome, and worshiping graven images. Its followers believed that in the communion they were eating the actual flesh of Christ. Jamie had never seen the priest, but knew of him from the peasant whisperings. He became a legendary figure in Jamie's mind, a secret, superstitious man of magic, who lived with the leprechauns on the misty mountain, and practiced strange and ancient rituals, spoken in Latin, that were to do with birth, and marriage, and death, and the life to come.

He was with Sean at the cottage when the messenger came by. The messengers carried poles, to help them vault over hedges and ditches, and brought important news to the villages of Ireland. This messenger, wary of the longer-haired Jamie, whispered to Patrick in Gaelic, which Jamie hardly understood. Patrick spoke to Maureen and Sean, also in Gaelic, and Jamie could feel a sudden excitement among them, and a sense, for the first time in his life, that he was an outsider to them. When he and Sean went fishing the next day, Jamie badgered his friend about the messenger, and eventually Sean swore him to secrecy and told him the news. It was Easter, and Father Moran was going to say a public mass in the village square the following Sunday.

Jamie was thrilled and appalled. The saying of mass

15

was proscribed, and if the soldiers or any English sympathizer knew of it, the priest would be imprisoned. At the same time, Jamie itched to know about the secret religion, and what it was that made its persecutors so angry. Reluctantly, Sean agreed to take Jamie to the mass, but made him swear, by all he held holy, by his mother's grave, that he would tell no one. They met at the cottage on Sunday, ate soda bread and cheese, and then Sean walked with Jamie to the village. Maureen and Patrick went on before.

Jamie was not sure what he expected to see, but certainly had not expected what he saw. In the village square, an old man in black was holding a simple cross and chanting in Latin to the fifty or so kneeling villagers assembled there. He saw nothing subversive, nothing pagan, nothing that might destroy the fabric of the society in which he lived, only a deep and simple faith, and an adoration of the cross and what it symbolized.

It was Easter Sunday and Christ was the risen king, he understood from the Latin words, and his Protestant soul could not argue with that, for it was what he was taught and what he believed. He found the rituals odd but oddly beautiful. He marveled at the true belief of those assembled, and at their stubbornness and bravery for resolutely following a faith that was so viciously circumscribed by the authorities.

Then the soldiers came.

A troop of red-coated British soldiers marched into the town, their officer on horseback. The officer rode to Father Moran and accused him of sedition. Fury and resentment ran through the congregation, but the priest held up his cross.

"Go peacefully about your ways," he called to his flock. They fell silent, but stayed to watch for the safety of their shepherd. Jamie, standing with Sean, was aware of a deep and awful anger in his friend, and Sean glared at Jamie.

"Was it you who told?" he whispered furiously. Jamie swore not, but Sean was not convinced.

"You knew," he said. "And someone told."

Father Moran was arrested and tied to the posts of the village well. The old priest was flogged mercilessly in front of the people, and then dragged away. A palpable fury ran through the crowd as they witnessed the flaying, and they jeered the soldiers, but the time was not right for rebellion. Some few lads threw stones and clumps of earth at the soldiers, but were chased and beaten for it.

As they walked home, Sean kicked the ground in his fury and frustration. Jamie tried to say something to comfort him, but Sean rounded on him, and asked him if he was proud of his rich, Protestant ruling class now. Jamie protested. He had been horrified by what he had seen, but did not know what they could have done to prevent it.

"We must fight," Sean said. "We must be rid of them."

Jamie could not see how they could win. The soldiers had guns. The peasants had only pitchforks.

"It is enough," Sean insisted. "We are many and they are few, and it is better to die for what you believe in than live in bondage."

He looked at his friend, who was not, at that moment, his friend.

"Would you die for what you believe in?"

Jamie felt guilty, because he was not sure that he would. The violence of the soldiers, and their blatant abuse of their power, had frightened him.

Sean saw the fear and doubt in his eyes. "Living up there in your fine mansion, born with a silver spoon in your mouth, you don't even know what you believe," he said disgustedly, and turned away.

It was true, Jamie thought. He loved Sean and his family, and Jugs and old Quinn, and his heart bled for their Ireland. He loved his sisters and brothers, and respected his father and what he had achieved. Above everything, he knew he loved being alive, and shuddered at the prospect of laying down his life for a cause he did not believe could triumph. The temporary souring of his friendship with Sean made him examine his heart, and he was shocked to discover that there was nothing he believed in that was worth his life. And not having such a cause, and lacking his friend, he was lonely, and sought for some passionate faith.

Jamie returned home to be greeted by his father's wrath. James knew his son had attended the mass, because Dacre Hamilton had told him. He knew that a visiting English business friend had been assaulted, on leaving the Jackson mansion, by some peasants as a reprisal for the beating of Father Moran, because Dacre Hamilton had told him. He knew that his standing within his small privileged community was threatened by the various actions of his children, because Dacre Hamilton had told him.

James Jackson also knew that his business could not survive without the patronage of the British. He didn't need Dacre Hamilton to tell him this; it was the law of the land. There was an embargo on all Irish commerce and trade unless a British agent was involved. If it was decided that James was a Catholic sympathizer, or an Irish collaborationist, the agents would find other sources of supply for linen, and James could not sell his except on the local market, where the prices were meaningless. All because of his foolish children.

He was hurt and angry. He had tried to give his offspring every advantage, and, one by one, they had rejected him, and all he had done for them.

"All this could be yours," he shouted at Jamie, waving his hand at the estate, pointing to the mill. "But only if you have the good sense to protect it!"

Obviously, the boy had no sense, and was in sore

need of discipline. For reasons that were as much political as practical, James did what he had done for each of his other children. He enrolled Jamie in a school in Dublin, and wrote to his brother Henry asking if Jamie might board with him there.

All the Jackson children had boarded with Uncle Henry when they went to school in Dublin. He was all the things their father was not—a warmhearted and generous man, and dedicated to Ireland. He had a fine house in the best part of the city, but was living on yesterday's income. He owned an ironworks that had been successful, but the more he announced his sentiments against the British, the more his business declined. He still had loyal clients, but none of the large orders from the British Commissioner or the military came his way anymore. His financial fate was exactly what James Jackson was trying to desperately to avoid.

The prospect of Dublin thrilled Jamie. He had never been there, but knew from his sisters, when they came home to visit, that it was a vibrant and exciting city, full of adventure and teeming life. He was sad to leave Washington and Jugs and old Quinn, and said many fond farewells to them, and assured Jugs he would change his linen frequently, and eat well, and not get into trouble. On his last day in Ballybay, he walked to Maureen's cottage, and said his good-byes to her and to Patrick, and thanked them for their many kindnesses to him.

Then he turned to Sean, whom he had hardly seen since their argument. To his surprise, Sean had tears in his eyes, and embraced Jamie, and wished him well, and Jamie clung to his friend, and felt, for the first time, that he was leaving home.

The following morning, when Jamie set off in the trap with Quinn, on his new adventure, Sean was sitting at the gate, and rode with them to Carrickmacross. He told Jamie it was as well he was leaving. The country was in turmoil, and the long-promised battle was looming. It was better that Jamie be out of it, comparatively safe, in the big city. At Carrickmacross, Sean jumped out of the trap, shook hands with Jamie, said a gruff good-bye, and wandered away into the crowd.

Sean's cautionary farewell distressed Jamie, for he realized that his friend did not think him brave. But he was brave, and he would prove it, and make Sean proud of him.

He loved Dublin. It was everything his sisters, especially Eleanor, had promised him it would be. He loved the elegance and graciousness of Merrion Square, where his uncle Henry lived, and he was shocked by The Liberties, where the tattered poor squatted in mansions that had once been the homes of the rich. He strolled on the banks of the meandering river, the Liffey, and stood in awe before the imposing Dublin Castle, the grandest he had ever seen. He thrilled to ride with his uncle through the grinding slums of Whitechapel, and wept at the poverty he saw there, and did not know that his uncle was carefully appraising his reactions. His ears were enchanted by the strange music of the city, the perpetual noise, out of which came chants that he began to recognize, the street vendors announcing their wares, the tinkers and apple sellers, the muffin men and costermongers and herring women.

He loved the sense of unity that prevailed among the governed Irish, and he shared the general hatred of the governing British. His blood boiled when he saw the red-coated soldiers marching through the streets, pushing the poor and the beggars out of their way, and arresting or beating any who offended them, no matter how slight the cause. His mind raced at the conversations in his uncle's house, at the dinner parties, where he was allowed to sit and talk with the older guests, and was included in their conversations. His nerves tingled at the sense of revolution and rebellion that was the undercurrent of all their talk, however guarded they might be in front of him.

He came to love and respect Eleanor, whom he had never known well. The red-haired passionate young woman and her wealthy, deeply committed husband, Oliver Bond, were frequent visitors to his uncle's house, and brought with them a sense of danger and glamour and excitement.

It was Eleanor who questioned James about his political beliefs, for she had heard something of his adventures with Sean, in Ballybay, and it was she who cautioned him.

"I must warn you to keep in strictest confidence whatever you see and hear in this house," she said, when they were alone together.

Jamie, in awe of his sister, swore that he could be trusted with any secret, and told her how he had kept to himself the information that Father Moran would say mass. Eleanor nodded, and seemed satisfied, and gave him books to read by Rousseau and Thomas Paine.

The books introduced him to concepts of democracy, and of the equality of all men, and he began to sympathize with the plight of the poor as he had sympathized with the peasants. He cheered as lustily as any when Lord Edward Fitzgerald and his beautiful wife, Lady Pamela, rode by in their carriage.

Lord Edward was now the commander of the revolutionary forces. The British knew this, but were loath to touch him, because of his title and position, and because he had not yet given them any great cause. But the very sight of him offended them, just as it enthused the masses, for he wore simple clothes, his hair was close-cropped in the peasant style, and his lovely wife was dressed in peasant linen with a muslin apron.

With a young man's zeal, Jamie had mistaken the function of revolution; he saw virtue in poverty and felt guilty because he was not poor. The appalling contrast between the desperate masses and the few rich was so overwhelming that he thought he had found the cause he had been looking for. Again, it was Eleanor who instructed him.

"It is not just for the poor and the peasants," she told him. "It is for all of us. It is for Ireland. When we are free of foreign domination, when we rule ourselves, then we can address the problems of the masses."

Jamie knew he was teetering on the very edge of tumultuous times, and longed to be closer to the center, although he was, by his relationships, nearer than many. He spoke to his uncle Henry, and begged to be allowed to join his association.

"It is not altogether your youth," Uncle Henry said, shaking his head slightly. "It is that you are so new to the idea."

But Henry saw the potential of the young man, and did not dash his hopes entirely.

"But I would say you are a fair possibility," he said, and smiled.

Soon after Christmas, Oliver Bond and Eleanor came late at night to Henry's house, and whispered the depressing news. A great French fleet, led by Wolfe Tone, had sailed into Bantry Bay to invade Ireland and begin the conquest of the British, but had been forced back by foul weather.

Oliver correctly predicted the bloodbath that was to come, but looked to the future. They would strive for the revolution, and they would succeed, but without French help. The disappointed nationalists retired and licked their dashed hopes for a while, but the violence of the British reprisals against the people stirred them, and the coming spring brought them renewed vigor, renewed hope, and renewed determination. But they needed more men.

So on a cold and rainy April night, Jamie went with his uncle Henry to a guarded garret in the slums of Whitechapel and was admitted to the association of United Irishmen, and swore his solemn oath. Jamie's

22

youthful soul thrilled to this new world of whispered plots and plans and secret passwords, and the inclusion in the company of men.

That summer, Jamie went home to Ballybay for Sara's wedding to Jimmy Hanna, who was now tutoring Washington. Jamie was a hero to Washington as Sean was a hero to Jamie, and Washington reveled in his company. His father was surprisingly affable, perhaps because, with most of his children living in Dublin or America, his position was more secure. Jugs wept, and overfed Jamie, convinced he had lost weight, when he was merely growing taller. Quinn shared a welcoming mug of poteen with him, and Sean welcomed him as if there had never been a difference between them. Sean was aware of some change in Jamie, and obviously approved of it, but did not question him closely, nor could Jamie have told him of his new political associations, because of the binding secrecy of his oath. But now it was summer and they were young men, anxious to test their burgeoning manhood and growing muscles, and they passed a pleasant season, fishing, and boxing and wrestling, and getting into young men's trouble. Jamie gave his virginity to a buxom peasant girl, who had long had Sean's, under a hayrick, drunk on cider.

Of all the good summers of Jamie's life, this was golden, for underlying their pastoral idleness was the growing whisper of rebellion.

Still the call to arms did not come, and, back in Dublin, Jamie chafed at the lack of activity. They seemed to be doing nothing, getting nowhere, and the British were still riding roughshod over the Irish community. He poured out his frustrations to Eleanor, and she listened, and nodded her head gravely.

"When?" he cried, for if anyone knew, it was Eleanor.

"When Ivers or Carlow is come," she told him, and he could see the twinkle in her eyes.

23

It was the whispered password that got them into their meetings: "Is Ivers or Carlow come?" The two names were changed frequently, for fear of traitors, but the substance remained the same, and one day, when the given answer would be yes, Ivers or Carlow is come, the revolution would begin.

Ivers, or Carlow, came the following March, but not in a way that any of them expected or wanted. Rioting by peasants farther to the south, in County Wexford, persuaded the British that it was time to destroy the leadership of the United Irishmen. A traitor came to them, Thomas Reynolds, a silk merchant, who had been in Paris during the Terror, and was appalled by the mob rule. After the debacle of Wolfe Tone and the French fleet, he was persuaded by his wife that perhaps they should reconsider their commitment to the Irish cause. Both were social climbers, both realized what patronage from the British could do for them, and as the possibility of Irish victory receded in their minds, Reynolds turned his coat to the British.

Oliver Bond himself opened the door to the three burly men whose faces he did not recognize.

"What do you want?" he demanded.

"Is Ivers or Carlow come?" the first man said, smiling. It was the proper password, but still Oliver was confused, and hesitated a fraction too long. The men burst into his house, and arrested all who were gathered there. United Irish guards keeping watch on the house from the Brazenhead Inn, across the street, were astonished to see the reinforcing British troops that now arrived, and, knowing the game was lost, some scattered into the night to warn the others. Those remaining saw Lord Fitzgerald's coach arriving, and rushed to head him off. He needed no second bidding but whipped his horses, and drove, hard as he could, toward Whitechapel. The troops gave chase, but as they came to the slums, word spread like wildfire, and the poor people thronged into the streets behind Lord

Edward's carriage, and blocked the passage of his pursuers.

A lookout got to Henry's house just before the soldiers, and raised the alarm. For himself, Henry saw no point in flight, but worried for his nephew. He gave Jamie a little money, and told him to get to Ballybay, where he would be safe. Jamie was reluctant. He had a young man's need to prove himself.

"This is just a skirmish, not the battle," Uncle Henry urged him. "You are more useful to us free than in prison. Go free and fight."

He pushed Jamie out of the back door, and returned to the hallway, where the soldiers were already battering their way inside.

Jamie crept through the back alleys and lanes to the slums, where he used the password to find friends. He was sheltered for the night, and in the morning they guided him to the outskirts of the city. They cropped his hair and put him in peasant clothes, and found a friendly farmer, who hid him in his cart and took him to his home county. Along the way they heard the news. The conditions of martial law were to be made stricter, harsher. British troops would now be dispersed throughout Ireland, and free-quartered wherever they chose. It was Crown-ordered that the association of United Irishmen be crushed by whatever means necessary, and many of the leaders were now in Newgate Prison, following the arrests in Dublin. The Sheares brothers and Oliver Bond. Uncle Henry, although not a ringleader, was with them. Lord Fitzgerald, who had not been caught, was in hiding somewhere in the city, and Lady Pamela. Eleanor had not been arrested, as women were not considered dangerous.

At Rockfield, Jamie bade farewell to his farmer friend, and made his way on foot, under cover of night, to Carrickmacross and thence Ballybay. He avoided the towns and villages, slept in the hedgerows, and used the money his uncle had given him to buy food at peasant cottages.

On a moonlit evening, he reached his father's house, and saw half a dozen British soldiers gathered around a campfire on the front lawn. He sneaked through the grounds, made his way to the stables, and scraped his nails on old Quinn's door. The hostler, rubbing sleep from his eyes, was immediately awake when he saw Jamie. He dragged the boy inside, shushed him to silence, and closed and barred the door.

"The sodyers are after ye," he said. He hid Jamie under the bed, and went to find Jugs. She came to him in dead of night, and held him to her, and wept for him. The soldiers had come for him, and were waiting in case he should come home. His father was practically a prisoner in his own house, a suspect despite his past record because of Henry and Eleanor, and their known association with the United Irishmen. Jamie's membership was also known, and, despite his youth, a warrant was out for his arrest, as brother-in-law to the traitor Oliver Bond, and nephew to Henry Jackson. Jugs had a message from his father, given in case he should come home.

"Don't come here, and I may yet be able to get us out of this."

Jamie was touched, for these were almost the kindest words he had ever had from his father. But he despaired. He could not stay in his father's house, and had nowhere else to go. Jugs came to his rescue again. Quinn created a distraction with a horse, causing it to bolt in its paddock, and the soldiers mocked and jeered the old man's apparently feeble efforts to calm it down. Jugs led Jamie through the night and took him to a small, abandoned barn on a nearby property.

Sean was there, in hiding from the soldiers.

Jamie smiled in relief when he saw his old friend, and Sean was astonished at the muddy, peasant-clad, crop-haired young man who stood before him.

"Is Ivers or Carlow come?" Jamie whispered with a grin, and Sean grinned too, and hugged Jamie hard.

"Yes," Sean said. "He is come."

3

They talked until dawn, and made their plans. They were not safe in Ballybay, and they needed to fight, for they were young, and their blood ran hot for their cause, and they were men of Ireland, and their country was bleeding. Sean had heard, as Jamie before him, of the riots to the south, in County Wexford, and they looked at each other, and nodded their heads, and knew, without voicing it, where they would go.

Maureen and Jugs made food for them, and wept in their hearts, but would not show their tears to their sons, for they were women of Ireland. Old Quinn gave them two nags from the stables, workhorses too old to work, who would otherwise have been sent to the knacker's yard, and justified it, not as stealing, but as a contribution to his young master's need. Under cover of night, Washington and Sara stole to the barn to greet their brother and wish him Godspeed.

There was no moon to guide them south, but they knew the way, for they knew all the byways of their county, which was their own, their native land. Maureen and Jugs waved them on their journey, and took comfort from each other, and wept, for that was the way of it.

And their country was bleeding. On the morning of the second day, they saw the bayoneted corpses hanging from trees, and then more dead, peasants shot in a field. They came upon a father, wounded himself, carrying his dead son.

"Bastards wiped 'em out," he gasped to no one, or to

27

anyone who might hear his piteous rage. "Just boys, armed with sticks, all gone, gone."

He staggered on with his awful burden, to take his dead son home to his mother, who would weep for her lost boy, her only son.

A little farther down the road they saw the bodies of the boys, similar in age to themselves, white-hooded heads almost severed from their shoulders, and left for carrion.

They aged, not in years, on their short journey south, but with experience of the world, and a new kind of passion engulfed them, the need for revenge.

As they rode into the county of Wexford, they stopped in taverns in all the villages they passed through, listening for rumors of rebellion, but the fight they were looking for, the war that they needed, eluded them, until they came to Boulavogue. They rode toward the town and saw a platoon of red-coated soldiers marching in that same direction. They looked at each other and thrilled, and spurred their horses.

In Boulavogue, the people were gathered in the town square, listening to two priests, brothers, who held carved wooden crosses and a paper.

Father John Murphy and Father Michael Murphy might have been twins, but were not. Dedicated to the welfare of their parishioners, they had spent their lives as priests in search of peace, practiced their religion covertly, and bridged, when they could, the awful gap between the rulers and the ruled. The local British Commissioner knew of their existence, but the brothers were useful to him, as mediators between himself and the people, and on many occasions the priests had been able to calm angry crowds, and bring order and reason to a disordered world. The riots and the subsequent bloodshed in the county had shocked the Commissioner, and he believed that the actions of the military were fomenting rebellion rather than suppressing it. He had suggested to the brother priests that if all the citizens signed a petition of loyalty to the Crown, Boulavogue would be left in peace.

Father John and Father Michael stood before their flock now, and urged them to sign the petition, for they had seen the disastrous aftermath of earlier riots, and could not believe that any good could come from the use of force, if only because the soldiers, although fewer in number, were superbly trained and armed. The priests were peaceful men, who believed that there was nothing that a fight could achieve that a smile could not, except blood and death and anguish.

Jamie and Sean resisted the powerful simple urgings of the priests. This was no place for them, and it disgusted them to see that several of the peasants had already stepped forward and made their mark on the petition. As they were about to leave, they saw a messenger come gasping into the town. He shouted out his news. The Commissioner had been replaced; martial law prevailed. At nearby Dunvin, twenty Catholic peasants had been mercilessly shot for refusing to denounce their religion. At Carnew, twice that number had died.

Father Michael stared at the man, dumbstruck with pity and horror, and crossed himself, and murmured prayers for the souls of the dead. His brother, Father John, lifted the parchment that was the petition high in the air, and tore it to shreds, to the silent appreciation and deep-rooted fear of the people.

Then they saw the flames, and the redcoats.

The church at Boulavogue had been boarded up for years, unused by the clergy since the religion was proscribed. Father John and Father Michael held their services in barns, or milking sheds, or ditches, believing that the Holy Spirit was with them wherever any number, no matter how few, were gathered together. But the church building, abandoned and rotting, had been a powerful symbol for the community, and they lived in the hope that one day the edict against their

29

religion would be repealed, and they could take down the boards, and open the church, and let the sweet light of day come flooding in.

Now it was burning, torched by the soldiers, who were marching toward them. There was no doubt in anyone's mind that a fate similar to that of their cousins in Dunvin and Carnew awaited them unless they renounced their religion, and this they would not do. They would fight and die if necessary, and preferred this to abandoning their God.

To everyone's surprise, it was Father John who led the charge. The sight of his beloved church in flames, the news of the death of so many innocents who had done nothing more than worship God in their own way, and defended that right to worship to the death, enraged the gentle priest. With a cry that came from the very pit of his soul, he grabbed a stout staff from a man standing near, and ran screaming at the soldiers.

Where Father John went, Father Michael went, and where the priests went, the flock followed. All the men in the square grabbed whatever weapons came to hand, pitchforks and sticks, spades and cart whips, and followed the priests into the fray.

Sean looked at Jamie in triumph, and both cried out in exhilaration, Sean in Gaelic and Jamie in English.

"Erin go bragh!"

"Ireland forever!"

They leaped from their horses and ran to the thick of the fight, punching, kicking, wresting guns from soldiers. The women of the town stood and cheered their men to battle.

The soldiers were surprised by the speed and ferocity of the attack, and its very unlikeliness, and for the first few minutes, the peasants had the advantage. But, better trained and better armed, the troops recovered their wits, and fought back. In hand-to-hand combat, the peasant band slowly retreated toward the square.

A man fell to the ground, his head cracked open by

the butt of a musket. His wife, who had been praying for him, ran to him, and saw that he could not live, or perhaps was already dead. Years of repression and anger, years of hardship, years of brutality by the soldiers now welled up in her. A banshee cry came from her, and she threw herself at the soldier who she thought had killed her man, kicking and screaming, tearing out his hair, gouging at his eyes.

It was a clarion call to the other women. The primal scream that they heard from the now widowed woman woke the animal in all of them. Like their men before them, they grabbed anything they could find to use as weapons—pots and pans, sticks and stones, or just their bare hands—and they descended on the soldiers like lions in defense of their lair.

The soldiers were astounded. They were trained to fight men, other soldiers, in formal ranks of order. They were trained to kick and crucify docile peasants. They were trained to whip and mutilate untrained youths. But they were not trained to face a screaming, cater-wauling mob of rampant women out for blood.

It was a rout, and the soldiers fled, to the cheers and jeers of the people. They fled to regroup, and nurse their wounds, and be harangued by their officers for letting a pack of women get the better of them. Most of them lived to fight another day, and would never underestimate the ferocity of females again.

Not all of them lived. One soldier's neck was broken. Another had a pitchfork through his heart. Five peasants were dead.

When the soldiers were gone, the cheering died to nothing. The women, as if appalled by the forces that had been unleashed from inside them, became docile, and wept for the dead, and for themselves. Their husbands and sons came to comfort them, and stood with them, thrilled but apprehensive, for they feared what the soldiers would do in retaliation.

The brother priests stared at one another, and then

31

each looked at his bloody hands. They whispered together, and began to make plans, for they had entered, or been dragged into, a strange and frightening new world, but they knew there was no going back.

Jamie sat on the ground and tended his bloody nose and a gash on his arm, while Sean sat beside him, and put a wet cloth to his blackening eye, and looked at the scratches on his arms and legs. It had been a good fight, but they felt no sense of jubilation. It was only a skirmish, and the real battle was yet to come.

The messenger ran. He had seen the fight and bashed a few British heads with his long, thick pole, and felt a swingeing surge of excitement, for this was something that was worth the telling, and it was his alone to tell.

He raced from the town, and pole-vaulted ditches and hedges with breathless, careless speed, to the villages nearby and gasped his news. Other messengers took up the cry, and soon the county rang with the glad tidings, that a small group of unarmed peasants, led by two priests, had defeated the might of Britain.

They left their homes, taking with them what weapons they had, and came in a trickle at first, and then a flood, to Gorey Hill, not far from Boulavogue, where the fathers, Michael and John, had made their camp. Within two days their number was a thousand, and within a week, three times that.

But on that first night they were only a dozen, the priests and Jamie and Sean, and eight more, young men eager for battle. The soldiers could have struck them down with ease, if they had found them, but they did not bother. They contented themselves with setting fire to a score of peasant cottages, as vengeance for their defeat. Several of the women who had fought, and a few who had not, were raped.

Jamie and Sean had cast their lot with the priests because there seemed no better place to be. The fathers

32

had thanked them, and accepted, unwillingly, their congratulations. Father John looked at his hands again.

"With my own hands I choked a man almost to death," Father John said. "I am in fear for my mortal soul."

"But he didn't die," Jamie said, puzzled by the priest's grief.

"No." Father John nodded, but mournfully. "But others will, and I believe that I will do some of that killing."

He looked at his hands again, as if continually astounded by what they had done. "I have devoted my life to the healing grace of God, but it seems He has other plans for me."

Sean took charge, for the priests were not practical men of war.

"They will come again," he said. "We had best find a hiding place."

"Yes," Father Michael agreed. "Are you with us?"

He was only offering shelter, but he had the first two recruits of his army. The priests led Jamie and Sean to Gorey Hill, avoiding the soldiers' camps, and to a small shack that they used when the town was unsafe for them. As the four men wended through the dew-soft evening, other young men joined them, and made camp on the hill, and, safe in the night, celebrated, at last, their victory. Some had beer, which they had stolen and shared, and food given them by their families, for all understood that it was only the beginning. But it was something. After years of servility, it was a start on a long road to freedom.

The little group of unarmed, unlikely soldiers who had priests as their generals sat around the campfire, as soldiers do, after battle, and recounted the stories of their day and their fight. They relived every moment of the small battle, and exaggerated their roles in it, and their own valor, and laughed with love at the reckless women who had probably saved their lives, although none would admit that.

Jamie had never known such a sense of companionship and, sitting in Sean's company, felt that he had proved his bravery to the world, and, most important, to his friend. At that moment, he wanted no other life than this, to do daring, foolish things in a great cause, in the company of like-minded fellows, and to sit with them afterward and revel in the memory of it.

Then they saw fires, and stood and looked at the burning cottages around Boulavogue, and knew what the soldiers had done.

"Damned British Protties!" a young man said, tears in his eyes. His name was Liam and his home was in flames.

Jamie was silent for a moment, but had to tell them, whatever the consequences might be.

"I am not Catholic," he said.

There was an awful silence, and then Liam, who had damned the British Protestants, damned him too, and spat at him.

"Then go to your heretic mates," Liam cried, ready, at that moment, to kill Jamie.

Jamie knew it was a test, and the moment was his. Others might defend him. He had to defend himself.

"I did not think to fight with God," Jamie said softly. "I thought our cause was Ireland."

The moment passed. Liam leashed his anger, and looked away. Father John made a joke, which voiced what most of them felt.

"It doesn't matter,' he said, "if he's a good Catholic, or a wretched, fornicating Protestant—he is a good Irishman."

They laughed to break the tension, but Sean did not. Proud of Jamie, he said something simpler, and, to Jamie, so much more important. He stared at Liam.

"He is more," he said. "He is my friend."

It was said quietly, just as it was, a simple statement,

but it communicated to Liam and to them all the sure and certain conviction that anyone who challenged Jamie also challenged Sean.

They lay side by side, on the soft Irish grass, under blankets the women had brought them, and stared at the stars.

"It was a good day," Sean whispered, and turned his head to sleep.

"It was a good day," Jamie whispered. He stared at the moon and shivered for his life.

It had been the most wonderful day of his life. The cause was just and the fight was good. But he had discovered a terrible secret within him. He did not want to die, because living was infinitely precious to him.

4

For ten days they camped on Gorey Hill until they were three thousand strong. The volunteers brought hope and conviction, and a crusading dedication to their holy cause. All had weapons, pikes and pitchforks; some had horses and a few others guns. They sustained themselves with faith and ancient battle songs.

Very few brought any food.

"God will provide," Father Michael told them, but there was little to eat, and in private the priests prayed for manna from heaven, or a miracle of loaves and fishes.

Jamie was in despair. Cursed with a rational mind, with every increase in their swelling numbers he felt his belief in their ultimate victory diminish. He could not make anyone else understand the proportions of the coming disaster.

"It is pointless, we cannot feed them!" he whispered angrily to Sean, who shrugged.

35

"They are starving anyway, and prefer to fight," Sean said, irritated by his friend's practicality, for it dampened his own optimism.

Before them, on the plain, the British assembled a formidable army. Although few in number, less than a thousand, the Ancient Britains had a fiercesome reputation as a ruthlessly successful fighting unit. Their very name carried with it the frightening ferocity of their ancestors, naked savages painted blue, whose primitive religion called on the sun itself as their ally, and whose battle skills had been honed against the unconquerable forces of Rome. Eventually, they believed, they had conquered those invincible legions, and driven them from their shores, and the noblest days of their history came to them—Arthur, and his heroic knights, whose quest was holy—and even if the legends of that history were not true, they were believed. They were ruled by formidable monarchs, whose achievements propelled and nourished them, and they had conquered, on land and at sea, half the known world. It was this unshakable faith in their own invincibility that had given them an empire the like of which the world had never seen, and earned their country the title "Great." A bunch of rowdy Irish peasants were nothing to them.

The flawless order and discipline of the red-coated army arrayed before them struck fear in the Irish hearts, and hunger brought dissension to the ranks. They were not afraid to die for their cause, but they would rather die in battle than suffer the slow death of starvation. Their generals, however, the priests, seemed reluctant to fight.

Yet fight they must, and perhaps succeed, for if they did not fight they could not win.

It was a warm night, and a fine, soft rain was falling. Sean came to Jamie, who was lying against a tree, trying to sleep. His clothes were wet, his blanket was soaked, and he had not eaten anything other than some oatmeal for days. But Sean had a smile on his face.

36

"It is tomorrow," he whispered. The words hardly gladdened Jamie's miserable heart, and he tried to come to terms with the fact that tomorrow he might die.

"If I should die," Sean said softly, "and you should live, do your old friend one last favor."

"Anything," Jamie answered.

"Bury me decent, in some quiet place," Sean said.

Jamie did not react for a moment, for Sean's simple acceptance of his possible fate disturbed him. Nor was he puzzled that he did not ask the same of Sean, for he was determined not to die.

"Swear it to me," Sean insisted.

Jamie swore his vow, which seemed to satisfy Sean. They lapsed into silence for a while, each man considering the morrow.

"Are you scared?" Jamie asked him, when he found the courage to voice his own fear.

"Oh, I expect so," Sean laughed. "But anything's better than living as we have."

He stared at the drizzling rain and was glad of it, for the resulting mud would hamper the formally uniformed British, and give the peasants some small advantage. They were used to mud; it was the stuff of their lives. They built their houses from it, and burned it to warm them, and its clover fed their cows. He looked at Jamie, and saw, not for the first time, fear in his friend's eyes. He laughed, put his arm round his friend, and took a small flask of poteen from his pocket.

"And it's better than being bored to death," he said. He held up the flask.

"Erin go bragh," he whispered, excitement in his eyes, for he had been chafing for action. He passed the flask to Jamie.

"Ireland forever," Jamie agreed, and drank deep of the harsh liquor, and felt better as the warm fire raced through his body, and calmed his raging fear.

*

37

They attacked at dawn, hoping for the benefit of surprise, but the Ancient Britains were ready. They had been trained on the battlefields of India and America, and always stood to just before dawn, for that, experience had taught them, was when savages attacked.

The mud was not the peasants' ally because they had to run through it, down the hill, and slipped and slid toward the waiting muskets of the British, who stood in formal ranks, picking them off as they presented themselves. Jamie believed it must be a rout. They could not possibly win. The sound of gunshots and the screaming of wounded and dying men deafened him; the riotous energy, the flashing of colors, and the sight of spurting blood almost blinded him. He saw the standard-bearer shot from his horse, and all hope deserted him.

He saw Father Michael caught in the dichotomy of priest and soldier. As men died, his faith asserted itself, and he ran to give them the last rites, which were more important for their immortal souls than any earthly victory. He had hardly begun to say the precious words of redemption when a bullet blasted into his heart and he fell to the ground to die beside his brothers, and went unsung and unshepherded to heaven.

Still the peasants charged, for they could not go back, only forward. Sean, riding by on his horse, saw the tattered rebel flag, green with a golden harp, trampled in the mud. Fury invaded him, and reckless abandon. He snatched up the glorious banner, waved it defiantly at the redcoats, and galloped to his gunfire death screaming, "Erin go bragh!"

As in an awful dream, Jamie saw Sean reach down from his horse, gather up the flag, and gallop toward the British lines. Then he saw something else, and it was something he envied all of his days. The vision of Sean riding to certain death was so heroic in his mind that Jamie stared at him in wonder, and thought his friend triumphant.

38

He saw Sean fall from his horse, and raced to him. He jumped down and gathered his friend in his arms. Blood was pumping from Sean's chest, and gurgling up through his mouth, and his face was contorted in pain. Jamie held Sean to him, crying on him to live, but knew he could not.

Then Sean looked at him, and a sweet smile suffused his face, for behind Jamie he saw a pure, golden light, brighter than any sun, that warmed his soul, and then there were all the dazzling colors of a rainbow, and a deep and abiding sense of peace swept over him.

Jamie knew nothing of this. The futile battle raged around him, unseen and unheard by him, because all he saw was that sweet smile on Sean's face, and then the body relaxed in his arms, and Sean was gone from him. But Jamie could never define, with any certainty, the moment of his going. He clutched his friend to him and screamed his name, but Sean could not hear him.

He scrambled to his feet, Sean's body in his arms, and staggered through the blood and the mud and gunfire and the bodies to find some quiet place to fulfill his promise to his friend.

He could not escape the deafening roar of the battle, but the place he found would be quiet enough, he knew, tomorrow, when the soldiers were gone. There was a large oak tree by a little brook, and Jamie set Sean down, and waited to gather his strength, to dig, with his bare hands, some form of grave.

Soldiers found him, far from the battleground, and were puzzled by him. A crop-haired lad, with blood all over his rough clothes but otherwise unharmed, sitting beside the body of another and keening for what he had lost, he did not have the manner or bearing of a peasant. They surrounded him, guns drawn, and dragged him to his feet, punching him a few times.

They demanded his name, and when he told them, his accent did not have a thick brogue. Thinking him a possible ringleader, they did not kill him there, as they might have done, and had done to others, but took him away, to be questioned by their officers.

Jamie stared at them with vacant eyes, but when they kicked the body of Sean into the brook, his anger raged, for he knew he had broken a most solemn vow. With a furious cry, he launched himself at his captors, who laughed, and hit him on the head with a musket butt. He fell to the ground, but the blow, although painful, had not been hard enough, and he was conscious of all that they did to him as they dragged him away to whatever his fate might be.

What Jamie did not know was that the British spared him because the Irish had won. Father John had led a foolhardy charge to the British artillery, had taken it, and turned it on the astounded Ancient Britains. The soldiers who found him were looking for stragglers or runaways who might give information about the Irish numbers and intentions.

The officers of the Ancient Britains knew his name. He was on a list of wanted men, because of his family connection to the traitor Oliver Bond. They marched him to Dublin and delivered him to Newgate Prison, to be hanged, or to rot with his fellows for his treachery.

Jamie felt none of their wrath and was insensible to their scorn. Battered and bruised by his captors, he walked in chains to Dublin, lost in a limbo of present grief and the expectation of coming execution. As they marched him through the towns and villages, the people lined the roadway, but not to cheer him or jeer the soldiers, for he was only another victim of their revolution, and the soldiers were the victors. Father John had won the battle of Gorey Hill, but the war was being lost.

They took him to the forbidding prison and released him from his manacles. There was no need of them here, because escape was impossible. His new guards, rougher than any soldier, kicked him below, and locked him in a small, dark cell.

Alone in a dank and musty cell, and without any light, Jamie felt his way along the wall and found a bunk where he lay down and stared at the blackness that engulfed him.

5

Newgate Prison was a hellish place, but no worse than Jamie's imaginings, and perhaps somewhat better. In the morning they let him out of his cell, to empty his bucket and wash his face, as best he could, at the communal well in the yard. Bread and oatmeal were the only foods his captors supplied, but many prisoners had plentiful nourishment, provided by relatives on the outside, or bought with bribes to the venal guards. They ate and spent their days in the great hall of the prison, and Jamie found several he knew there, United Irishmen, and many acquaintances. They cheered him, as a new arrival, and were kind to him, and those with food shared some with him, and begged for news of the outside world.

Then he heard a familiar voice.

"Jamie? Is it you?"

He turned and saw his uncle Henry, pale, thin, and scruffy, but with a welcome smile and open arms. The sight of the loved and loving man broke the dam of Jamie's reserve. He went to his uncle and wept, for the first time since Sean's death, and poured out his distress. Henry was gentle with him. He sat Jamie down and listened to his sad story, and said nothing of his own.

He tried to find words of solace, but he had no good news for his nephew, Jamie's small war at Gorey Hill was a tiny fragment of the larger whole. In one battle, thirty thousand Catholic rebels had died, for the loss of only two thousand British. Father John was dead: caught, imprisoned, and hanged. Wolfe Tone was dead. Caught after a futile landing with a token French force in the south, he had been imprisoned and condemned to death, and had slashed his neck with a penknife smuggled in by a friend. The Sheares brothers had been hanged. Oliver Bond was condemned to a similar fate. Lord Edward Fitzgerald had lost his reason. Captured when sick in a tiny garret, he was beaten about the head by arresting soldiers, and his brain was damaged. Unable to comprehend or accept the failure of their enterprise, or the coming execution, not only of himself but of so many he held dear, his mind had wandered into happier pastures, from which no doctor could reclaim him. The rebellion was a failure. The noble cause for which they had fought lay about them in ruins.

Jamie listened to the litany of woe in silence, and when his uncle was done, he asked the question that dominated his thinking.

"What will happen to me?"

Then he corrected himself.

"What will happen to us, I mean?"

Henry nodded again, but did not smile. Most men's thoughts were selfish when faced with the prospect of their possible demise, and it was the question that every prisoner asked when first delivered to the place of his captivity. There was a similar question that all condemned men asked at some point before their coming execution: "Will it hurt?"

"They might hang us; they say they will," he said, with a cheerfulness that surprised Jamie. "But then again, they haven't yet, and while there's life, there's hope."

It was an old cliché, but clichés often brought comfort to hopeless men, and he had no better words to say.

Jamie did not believe him then, but the simple, reassuring presence of his uncle made his burden somewhat easier to bear. Over the weeks, he was questioned, sometimes with brutal force, about what he knew, but it didn't matter if he gave his interrogators the names of subversives, for all those he knew were already behind bars. As the months wore on and no hint was given of a trial, Jamie relaxed, and almost began to enjoy the rough companionship of prison life.

They were taken out into the prison yard one day, and lined in ranks. Nothing was said to them, no reason was given for this change in the daily pattern of their lives, and several believed they were to be shot, or hanged, although there was no gallows. They were kept at attention for half an hour, and any man who spoke or asked a question was hit with a truncheon.

A big metal door on the opposite side of the yard scraped open, and two guards came through, with another man between them. It was Lord Edward Fitzgerald, now a babbling idiot. His hair was wild and unkempt, his eyes were glassy. Spittle dribbled from his chin. They paraded him past his fellows, so that all could see the degradation of the man who had been their leader. Nothing was said, nothing was spoken, except by Lord Edward, who chattered to himself throughout, in a language no one but he understood. He did not recognize any of those who had been his brothers-in-arms.

They took him back to his cell, left the assembled men in the yard for another half hour, then ordered them back inside.

Jamie saw Eleanor once, on a high walkway, taking food to her husband's call, for he was a condemned man, and kept apart from the others. Eleanor saw Henry and waved at him, and then Jamie, and a smile lighted her face. She called words of encouragement, and threw some food from her basket to him. Jamie found it hard to imagine that she could be so caring for him and others, and so cheerful of manner, when Oliver was to die.

Eleanor's grief at her husband's conviction was real and deeply felt, but she saw no point in dwelling on it, especially with him, who was already keenly enough aware of what lay in store. She tried to make his final days on earth as bounteous as possible, kept him well supplied with good food and the gossip of the city, and liquor when she could, and talked of his coming execution only when he raised the subject. She took advantage of the penal laws to arrange a party for him, some few days before his appointed date with the hangman, for she thought he would enjoy being with all his old friends. She bribed the guards, as was necessary, and brought in food and drink. Oliver was allowed out of his solitary confinement for the afternoon, although several other guards had to be paid handsome sums to keep watch on him during the festivity.

Jamie, when he heard about it, thought it was morbid, and could not imagine how the revels could be anything other than gloomy, but Oliver, and Eleanor, surprised him, and he had forgotten the Irish capacity to enjoy themselves, and laugh, even in the teeth of death. They sang songs and swapped yarns, and relived the dreams of what might have been if their rebellion had succeeded. They swore eternal friendship, and told dark jokes of the gallows.

Oliver stood up to speak. Visibly overcome with emotion, he called them his brothers, and thanked them for their loyalty and friendship. He stopped speaking, and seemed to be struggling to control his emotions. Eleanor took his hand and held it, and he looked at his wife with a curious amazement, as if he needed to tell her something of utmost importance, that he had never known before.

He stumbled and slumped to the floor. Eleanor gave a little cry and ran to him, calling out his name. Others came to her help, but there was nothing they could do for Oliver, who had suffered a stroke. He died in Eleanor's arms.

"Glory be, the ould bugger's dead," a man said gently to Eleanor. She clutched Oliver to her, and then remembered her duties as a hostess. She laid her husband on the floor, went to the table, and raised a mug of ale.

"To a glorious son of Ireland," she shouted defiantly.

They cheered and drank to his memory.

Eleanor looked at the guards, who were jolted, and not sure what to do in the face of this unexpected crisis.

"To Oliver," Eleanor cried again, "and home rule for Ireland!"

The others cheered and drank with her again.

"To Ireland," she said softly.

"To Ireland," they all agreed, as softly as she.

Eleanor knelt on the floor beside her dead husband, stroked his face, and keened a gentle threnody for her lost love.

The death of Oliver Bond provided the British authorities with the catharsis they needed. The rebellion had been crushed; the leaders were dead, or, in the case of Lord Edward, mad. The assocation of United Irishmen was broken. There was little point in further persecution, because that might inflame the populace anew, and Britain wanted a settled colony and simply could not afford the men to police an Ireland of continuing turmoil. The empire was expanding rapidly, and the troops were needed in other trouble spots.

But they could not set the prisoners entirely free. Those convicted or suspected of only minor treason were offered the chance to sign a confession of all their misdeeds, and would then be released on the condition that they leave Ireland forever.

It was exile, or banishment, Jamie understood, but it

45

was preferable to a lifetime behind bars, or a possible death by hanging. In any case, there was nothing for him in Ireland now. He talked with his uncle Henry, who was of a similar opinion.

"I've fought the good fight all my days," he said, "and I do not think I have lost, for it will go on. But I'm getting old, and I want a settled life, before I am too old to enjoy it."

"Where will you go?" Jamie asked him.

"America, of course," Uncle Henry replied, slightly surprised that his nephew had the need to ask. "Where else is there?"

Jamie laughed. It was so very obvious, and it had probably been in the back of his mind, but buried beneath a mountain of worry.

"Half of Ireland is already there, and your brothers," Uncle Henry reminded him. "John is doing well in Philadelphia. I shall join him there."

He wondered what his nephew would do, where he would go.

"America, I guess." Jamie shrugged, because he couldn't think of anywhere else. He wasn't very good at languages, and he didn't want to live among foreigners all his life, so there was nowhere in Europe for him. He wasn't allowed to live in Britain. So he chose America, if only by default. And having chosen, he felt his soul tingle a little, for America represented a great, new adventure, free of danger, free of the complications of having to choose between his Irish people and his English masters. A place that now, in his moment of direst need, at the time of his banishment, at the start of exile, gave him a haven. He did not choose America just to save himself from prison, but he did choose America because it would give him freedom.

They were released in rough order of their imprisonment, Henry some weeks before Jamie. When his time came, Jamie answered their questions and signed his confession. His papers were put in order by the prison officers, and he was provided with a warrant that allowed him time to get his affairs in order, and, if necessary, pass through an English port on the way to his destination. It was assumed he could support himself financially because his father was known to be wealthy. He was released on a cold autumn day. He had been in prison for nearly two years.

He went straight to his uncle Henry's house and was warmly received. His first priority was a hot bath, to rid his body and hair of dirt and lice, and his uncle burned his old clothes, and gave him new ones. Henry was leaving for America within the week. He had sold his house and his ironworks at rock-bottom prices, but he had enough for a good start in the new world.

"A new start at my age," Henry said wryly. "But then, all things are possible."

He offered money, but Jamie, whether from pride or foolishness, would not take it.

He moved to Eleanor's and spent a quiet Christmas with his sister. For the first time since Oliver's death, they talked of him, but Eleanor, although she wore the formal black of mourning and grieved for her husband, was more concerned about the future. At midnight on the last night of the year, she gave him champagne, and they drank to the challenges ahead. It was the end of the old century, and the beginning of the new.

"I had wonderful times with Oliver," she said, "no matter how short. But he is gone from us, and we must look forward."

She had few plans of her own, but as yet she was still coming to terms with her widowhood, and asked what Jamie would do.

"America," he smiled, and Eleanor laughed.

"Of course, a new land for a new century," she said. "It is the proper place for a young man to be. This old world is too decadent."

She folded her hands neatly on her lap, and looked at her young brother coyly.

"It is not beyond the bounds of possibility that I might go there myself," she smiled.

"But how could you leave Ireland!" he cried, both thrilled and shocked. Oliver was already perceived by the people as a martyr to the Irish cause, and she, as his widow, a heroine.

"Tush," she said. "As easily as you will do."

She looked sad, and Jamie thought she might cry, and he knew that if she ever did leave Ireland it would not be as easy for her as she pretended. But she shook her head, and busied herself with his business. She asked if he had any money, and Jamie lied, but she knew that. She gave him a small purse of coins, and when he protested told him not to be a romantic fool.

"You have to eat, boy," she said. "You have to live."

He took the purse, and she hesitated for a moment before asking her next question.

"Shall you go and see Father?"

Jamie nodded. He had no alternative. His father was his only possible source of money for his passage, and he wanted to make his peace with the man who had given him birth, and whom he might never see again.

He stayed with Eleanor until Washington came from Ballybay, to return to his school in Dublin. Washington was thrilled to see his daring brother, and they pumped hands and slapped each other on the back, and sparred with each other, laughingly, as brothers do. When he heard of Jamie's plans, Washington let out a yell of jealousy, because America was his dream; he longed to go there, and fight Indians. He swore he would join Jamie as soon as he had finished school, and they would have a rollicking time together. The brothers shared a room in Eleanor's house, and talked themselves to sleep each night with plans for the future. And they talked of Ballybay.

Things had improved for their father, Washington

told him, since the rebellion was put down. The local British had shown tokens of desire to make amends, and pretend they had no hard feelings. The linen mill was too valuable to them to do otherwise.

Jamie bought new clothes with some of the money Eleanor had given him, and a cheap horse from the livery stables. He rode toward Ballybay, and saw the country with adult eyes, and not those of an impetuous boy. He loved it still, but it seemed dank, and a little dirty to him, and the grinding poverty of the peasants depressed him. The white-walled cottages that had once represented home to him looked small and shabby now, and he began to despise the superstitious, docile peasants who had not been able to rid their land of a governing power, despite their greater numbers. Bands of homeless trekked the road, looking for shelter, and ignored him, or turned away from him, for he was better dressed than they. Beggars were not so fearful of him, and accosted him. Red-coated soldiers tramped the highways, and would stop him, and ask for his papers, and snigger when they saw he was banished. He despised being a marked man, and looked forward to the new life that awaited him, not so far away, just across the ocean.

The song of America sang in his ears, and he was already casting off the shackles of his old country.

On reaching Ballybay, he went to Maureen and Patrick's cottage, to tell them the details of Sean's brave death and lie about his burial. They greeted him politely, but suspiciously. They knew their son was dead, and Jamie's tales of his bravery hardly comforted them, for their hearts were empty. They were glad he died as a hero, but they did not want him dead. Jamie could not resist the feeling that they resented him, because he had survived.

He rode to his father's estate, and looked at the linen mill beside the river. From before his birth, hundreds of peasants had toiled there, earning a pittance from his wealthy father, whose sympathies lay not with them, but with himself, and the British. For a moment he was not sure which made him more angry, the blind acceptance by the peasants of their lot, or the exploitation of them by the ruling class.

"They could get out, get away," he shouted to the wind. "Like me, to America!"

The call of his new land, his new life exhilarated him, and he galloped up the drive to his father's house, loving the clean fresh air of freedom. Jugs might have been waiting for him, for she ran from the house when she heard his horse, and cried out his name. She threw her apron over her head, and sat on the steps weeping, because he was safe, and home again.

He turned her tears to laughter by picking her up and swinging her round, gasping good-naturedly with the effort.

"Put me down," she cried. "I'm too heavy!"

"Yes, you are!" he laughed, and put her down. She held his face in her hands and looked at him closely, as if inspecting every pore of him, to see what the world had done to her boy. Satisfied that there were no visible scars of his wars, she hugged him, and old Quinn came by, looking older now, and walking with a stick. He shook Jamie's hand, and winked that he would hear all his news in the stable, when old Jugs was done with him.

She took him to the kitchen, and fed him mugs of thick sweet tea, and oatcakes, and begged to hear all he had done.

He told her of his adventures, but briefly, because he could tell Jugs did not want the details, they were too distressing for her. She crossed herself when he described how Sean died, and she cursed the British when he described Newgate Prison.

He told her he had to leave Ireland, and where he

50

would go. Jugs turned her head away, to compose herself.

"'Tis proper that ye go," she said. "There's nothing for ye here."

She tried hard to look on the bright side.

"And half of Ireland is there afore ye. Ye'll not lack for friends."

But she could not hide her fear.

"But, oh, Master Jamie," she cried. "Be careful of them Injuns. They's awful fierce, the heathen savages."

He laughed and said he would be very careful, and then asked after his father.

"In his study," Jugs said. "He's waiting for ye."

Jamie went to his father's study, rapped on the door, and went in when called.

James Jackson was writing at his desk, and finished his signature before he looked at his son. He stared at him for a few moments, and nodded his head, as if in approval.

"You look none the worse for your misadventures," he said. "In fact, you look positively healthy."

"Good evening, sir," Jamie smiled. "I trust you are well."

His father nodded again. "Things have come to a sorry pass," he said. "I told you no good would come of mixing with croppies."

Jamie felt a flash of anger, but controlled himself.

"I blame myself, of course," his father continued. "I should have been stricter with you. I'm sorry if you found me wanting as a father. I tried to do my best by you."

Jamie struggled hard to control a smile. It was hard for him to imagine how his father could have been stricter with him.

"To make some small amends I have booked you a passage to America. It is not until April—it seems it is a popular destination. I suppose you will want to stay here until then."

51

It was not a gracious invitation, but Jamie was pondering something else. How did he know about America? Had Eleanor told him?'

He accepted the envelope his father gave him. "Thank you, sir," he said, but his father did not smile.

"I have also made arrangements for some portion of the family funds that would have come to you to be sent in letters of credit for your use in Philadelphia."

Uncle Henry had told him, Jamie guessed. He had not talked to Eleanor about Philadelphia.

"After that," James Jackson said, "you may not expect another penny from me, during my life, or in my will."

Jamie's cheeks flushed with angry shock. He had not expected much from his father, some few words of comfort, perhaps a little well-intentioned advice, or even a scolding. But he had not expected this. Banished and disinherited. It was a cruel world. He was being treated as an errant, headstrong boy. But he was not a boy anymore, he was a man, and he would show his father how much of a man he had become.

"I will make my own way in this new world," he murmured, and could not stop his voice from rising. "I will be richer than you ever imagined, and more powerful than you have ever been. And I will use my money wisely, like Lord Fitzgerald and Oliver Bond, in the people's interest—"

"The people," his father sneered. "The common rabble, you mean."

Jamie was close to losing his temper and struggled to control himself.

"I take this because I must," he said, holding up the envelope. "But I do not want one penny more of your money, or your damned letters of credit, in your life or when you are dead."

But he could not make his father believe him.

"You will never amount to anything," James Jackson said to his son.

Jamie wanted to cry out or to hit him, but he did

neither. All the hope of all the love he had ever wanted from his father came to nothing, and he believed that his father had never cared one whit for him, for if he cared, how could he disparage him so?

"I will make a liar of you yet!" he shouted. Fists clenched in rage and bitter disappointment, he walked out of the room.

Jugs was waiting for him in the hall. She had heard the shouting through the door, and tried to make amends.

"He didn't mean it," she said. "He's been worried about ye."

"He never cared about me for one day in his life," Jamie replied. "But I will show him—you wait and see. I'll prove him wrong."

James Jackson sat at his desk, his face livid with rage, his hands trembling with anger. He had done his best by the boy, had offered him his portion, and it had been thrown back in his face. He had tried to do his best by all his children, and all were ungrateful, and had turned on him. All had been given every possible benefit when young, but their wretched flirtations with the nationalist movement had almost destroyed his life, his business, and their inheritance. He could not understand their stupidity and ingratitude.

He poured himself a brandy, and tried to calm down.

He had not wanted children, except a son, to inherit what he had created. Sadly, children went hand in glove with what he did want, for he loved women, and needed their physical company. Since in order to have that physical companionship he must have children, and since because of his standing in the community he should have children, and because without an heir everything he worked for would die with him, he had raised a family. He was quite fond of each of them when they were little, but intolerant of their demands on his time. The difficulty of running and expanding a

53

business such as his in these troubled times had taken all his energy. He had provided his family with everything they needed, had employed nannies and teachers for them, and had asked, in return, simply that they behave themselves and not trouble him. Surely that was not selfish? But they had troubled him, to distraction, and when he could not accommodate the demands they made on him, they had turned against him. He did not mind the behavior of the girls so much, for they, at least, were pretty and womanly, and he actually admired and defended Eleanor, despite his opposition to her marriage. It was the boys who were truculent and troublesome, and he wondered if there was too much of himself in them, or if he simply envied their strength and youth and vitality. Most of all, he was disappointed in Jamie, who shared his love of horseracing, and who, he thought, might have been his true heir. In the end, even Jamie had let him down, and was off to America to join his wastrel brothers.

The sense of complete failure of his domestic life was shocking to him, but he did not blame himself. Matrimony, he decided, was an archaic institution, of peasant origin, and worthless to the modern man. He had refused to marry his mistress, Sarah Black, because he did not want to be disappointed by marriage again, but she was content with the hours he could give her, and he had two fine boys by her, who appreciated him and never asked for more than he could give. Why could not his legitimate children be the same?

But still Jamie was his son, and he could not send him out into the world without some provision for his welfare. He wrote to his lawyer advising that Jamie should be excised from his will, but he did not cancel the letters of credit. Whether the boy chose to use the money or not was up to him. He had done his duty as a father. In the morning he went to Belfast on business, and never made contact with Jamie again.

*

54

Jamie spent a day with Sara and Jimmy at their cottage, and they envied his plans. With Washington at school in Dublin, Jimmy was no longer employed as tutor, but had found some few hours of part-time work, with other families, but was hard-pressed to make a living. They had often talked of emigrating, and Jamie's plans gave their own fresh impetus. Jamie laughed that soon the whole family would be there.

"And why not?" Sara asked. "What is there for us here?"

Jamie was anxious to be gone from his father's house. He planned to return to Dublin and to find work for a month, to give him some spending money, or to ask Eleanor for a loan. He spent a happy evening with old Quinn in the barn, talking of racehorses and getting drunk on poteen, and said a tearful farewell to Jugs, when he staggered into the kitchen late that night.

She saw the moment she had been waiting for, and pressed a small bag of money into his hand. It was not much, but as much as he needed. He looked at it in surprise, and sobered up fast.

"It is some part of my savings," she said. "And ye have need of it."

"I can't take this, Jugs," he protested, for her generosity embarrassed him. She was a poor woman, and he could have been rich.

"Oh, tosh," she said. "Put it in your pocket, for I know ye have none. Ye think I could rest easy with you going off to that savage land and not a penny to bless yourself with?"

He would not take it.

"I have no need of it," she cried. "I have everything here." And, sensibly, she gave him a way out.

"It is a loan," she said. "Ye can easy pay me back when ye've made your fortune."

That, and his need, convinced him, and he swore that he would pay back every penny of it. He kept his word. From the first few dollars he earned in America, he sent small sums back to Jugs until the loan was paid off, and he continued to send her money for the rest of her life.

The following morning, at dawn, Sara and Jimmy came to the house to wish him Godspeed, and they stood with Jugs and old Quinn, and watched him trot down the drive and away, out of their lives. Then they went inside and sat with Jugs, who wept for the boy she had raised and would never see again.

The sadness and many tears of the leavetaking depressed Jamie, and halfway down the drive he spurred his horse to a gallop. The sudden energy and easy motion of the horse broke him from melancholy, for he was on his way at last. He galloped through the chill morning, the crisp wind biting his hands and ears, and felt an extraordinary power of masculinity within him, for he was taking on the world.

He stayed with Eleanor in Dublin again, and said his good-byes to his sister and Washington, and in late March he took the ferry to Liverpool.

As the boat sailed out of the harbor, he looked back on his native land with little regret, for his father's insult still rang in his ears.

"You will never amount to anything."

He would amount to something, he swore to himself. He was casting off his old life and taking on a new. He was not a boy anymore, he was a man, hardened by life, blooded in war, forged in prison.

He was not young Jamie either. The diminutive always made him feel little, if loved, and not quite a man. It had been used to distinguish him from his father, but there was no need of it now, for he had no father. A new name for a new life seemed fitting, and anyway, it was not a new name, it was his true name, and his father's name, and perhaps to spite the man who had sired him, he called out his name.

"James," he shouted at the seagulls.

And again, to convince himself.

"I am James."

In May, when he sailed from Liverpool on the good ship *America*, under the command of Captain Silas Swain and bound for Philadelphia, the passenger manifest listed him simply as James Jackson.

6

The ship pitched and rolled, and mountainous waves endlessly broke over the bow. The storm had raged for two days, and the passengers had come to believe that the ship could not withstand the tempest, and must break apart. Most of the passengers, apart from James and some of the crew, were wretchedly ill, and spent their days in their cabins, moaning their fear and their distress. To a few of those who had never been to sea, the sickness and fear were worse than death, and they begged the good Lord for deliverance, and if that meant the ship would be smashed apart and plunge them to a watery grave, it was preferable to their present plight. There was talk of mutiny among some of the men who had no experience of the sea, of forcing the captain to return to port, but he, an old sea dog, only laughed at them.

"Would you have me go back into the teeth of the gale when we have nearly ridden it out?"

They were hardly convinced that an end to their suffering was in sight, but it gave them a small hope, and they could not countenance going back and into the storm again.

The missionary Reverend Blake and his good wife spent hours on their knees, when they were not on their bunks being ill, praying to their Savior to calm the seas, as at Galilee, and on the third day, when the waves subsided and the wind abated, they believed He had wrought a miracle.

Jamie found his sea legs early. The Irish Sea had been choppy, but he soon got used to the rolling motion of the ship and spent happy hours on deck, watching the sailors clamber up the ropes with the agility of monkeys, furling or unfurling the vast sheets of canvas to mysterious commands, or singing sea chanteys when, as if on their knees in a pagan temple to the sea, they holystoned the wooden decks to a pristine whiteness. He loved the salty, briny wind, and the companionship of his fellow passengers, who shared, in varying degrees, a fear of their formidable voyage, but were united in a common optimism that their destination would be the earthly paradise they sought.

The great port of Liverpool had excited and frustrated him. He was overawed by the huge numbers of ships in the harbor, which had journeyed from every corner of the earth, bringing with them strange and exotic cargoes. He smelled the scent of spices he had never known, and watched in wonder the unloading of the chests of tea from India and silks from China and cotton from Madras, sheets of raw cork from Portugal, and oranges from Spain. He loved being among the community of seafaring folk, the hardy and colorful sailors, rings in their ears and tattoos on their arms, who walked with a rolling gait, as the rolling sea had taught them. He saw small brown men from the Malacca Straits, and blond descendants of the Vikings, giants to him, and heard strange languages that were beautiful and others that grated on his ears. He loved the women of the dockside, raw and lusty creatures, who cheered when the ships docked and wept when they left, and he spent days in tiny smoky taverns by the water, hearing tall tales of the seven seas, and Africa and Madagascar, the Azores and the Caribbean, Araby and Siam.

And he saw a black boy, the first he had ever seen.

A well-dressed woman came to the docks to greet her returning husband, a captain. Behind her trotted a little black boy, elegantly appareled in velvet and a turban, and around his neck was a long silver chain, with which his mistress led him. Like a pet dog, James thought, and watched as they passed by, fascinated by the ebony child. He had heard of these African creatures, niggers as they were called, heathen savages, who ran around naked in their native jungles, bloodthirsty warriors, licentious animals.

He heard of the slave ships that sailed from England to Africa with cargoes of iron or manufactured goods, and from Africa to America with cargoes of naked savages, and from America back to England with raw cotton, or tobacco, or rice. He had heard of the calls for abolition of the slave trade from some of the church people, and the furious opposition to that abolition, for the slaves were apparently the most lucrative of all cargoes, and some of the planters in America claimed they could not survive without the labor. He had no special feelings about it, for it was not part of his life. The fate of these odd and alien creatures did not matter to him, one way or the other.

He grew impatient as his days of waiting wore on, for he longed to be at sea himself, to experience some of what he had heard about, off on his own great adventure. He lost a little money to a prostitute and a little more to a pickpocket. He avoided the city itself and stayed near the docks, for he quickly discovered that his Irish accent caused him to be disparaged among people whose own dialect seemed primitive and guttural to him.

When he boarded his ship at last, the cramped spaces belowdecks surprised him, and he banged his head several times on overhead beams, before learning to duck, as the sailors did, as naturally as breathing. He shared his cramped and crowded cabin with five others, Englishmen who loved their country and couldn't wait to leave it. Good-humoredly, they denigrated the Americans as ungrateful and troublesome colonists, but were anxious to be of their number. They baited him for a bog-Irish peasant, and he took their jokes in good part, but they wearied him, and sometimes he had trouble controlling his temper. The tiny cabin was claustrophobic, and the natural human stench of his fellows reminded James of his time in prison. He talked with the first officer, and they gave him a hammock, and on the pleasanter nights, he slung that hammock up on deck, with the sailors, and slept pleasantly, rocked by the gentle wind.

The food was awful but edible, pickled pork and potatoes for the first few weeks, dried beef and hardtack later. The lore of the sea fascinated him, the defined but easy hierarchy, the absolute power of the captain, the endless, easy grumbling of the tars, and the constant cheerful resentment by all the seamen of their tantalizing, temperamental bitch goddess, the sea, which they loved with all their hearts.

They talked with him about their country, for which they had a deep and abiding affection, and gave him some sense of the awesome size of it. James had always known that America was a large country. Now he learned that the United States was but a small fraction of that continent. The physical land itself ranged from the ice-ridden north to the tropical south, encompassing mountains and deserts, forests and wilderness, and some of the finest farming land in the world. The British still ruled the northern part, Canada, the Mexicans controlled the arid southwest and the legendary California, and the French, under Napoleon, had assumed from the Spanish the great southern region of swamps and jungle that was known as Florida.

"Go west," they told him. "A man can find his true

self there, and own land beyond his imagining, just for the taking."

For themselves, they had found their fortune at sea. So many of the young men of America went west, to settle the vast new territories, that sailors were in short supply, and well paid because of it. They cursed the British, who ruled the seas, and frequently stopped and boarded American ships, and pressed into service any of the crew who still maintained British nationality. They nodded their heads wisely at the stories of the savage Indians, but dismissed them as any threat to the settled colonies. The Indians were retreating, to the west, before the settlers' advance, and soon must stand with their backs to the great Pacific Ocean, and then where would they go?

As they sailed on, he began to understand something of that love, for there was only the sea, always the sea, endlessly the sea. He was lost in a world of water and sky, on which the sun rose each morning, and the stars and moon each night, and always, the crew told him, where they were supposed to be. The small ship became their only world, and each aboard it was joined to the others by a strange and powerful sense of community, united before a common foe, a common love, that was awesome in its breadth and power.

The storm came, and frightened James at first, for he could not imagine that they could survive it. He was forced to sleep in his cabin, when he could sleep, and the men with him were as scared as he.

"Surely America must be heaven," one said. "For you have to go through hell to get there."

He preferred the attitude of the sailors, for they respected the wrath of the tempest, and were not overawed by it. They believed in their survival because of their skill and seamanship, their stoutly built craft, and because they had weathered worse, much worse, before.

Then winds abated and the seas quieted, and for the next few weeks they sailed through calmer water, blue skies, and sunny weather. Flying fishes tripped through the whitecaps, and landed sometimes on the deck, and were good eating. At night the tars would gather round the capstan and sing chanteys, and dance strange steps that were, James guessed, centuries old, and known only to men of the sea. He laughed with the others when the two apprentices had their ears pierced with hot needles against cork, and wore the small threads of blue wool proudly, for days to come, as symbols of their initiation as mariners.

He learned the map of the stars in heaven, and the directions of the wind. He saw whales, enormous creatures that spouted water from their backs like fountains, and could not believe what his eyes told him. He began to believe all the legends of the sea, of mermaids and sirens, and strange monsters from the deep. He lay in the bow for hours, in the sunshine days, delighted at the dolphins as they frolicked at the prow, and believed, as the sailors did, that these joyous creatures were guardians, guiding them safely to haven.

He felt safe in their company, and as he watched them, following where they led, he dreamed of the life that would soon be his, on the distant shores that the dolphins knew.

Born to money, born to a secure station, his father's friends were oriented toward England, and many regarded the former colonies of America still as colonies, a hostile land of former convicts and the dregs of Europe, governed by unscrupulous merchants and planters, and constantly threatened by wild Indian savages. None denied the riches that could be made there, but all disparaged the way those riches were made, and the resulting lawless, classless society, in which Mammon was the only God.

Yet the sailors told of a different America, of freedom and peace and a settled life. Go west, they told him, where a few dollars will buy a thousand acres, and a man could be a king in his own castle. If he could survive the Indians.

From his Protestant teachers at school in Dublin, he had heard of a different America again, of a land free of religious intolerance, a land where idyllic, Godfearing communities could flourish in peace and tranquillity. If they could survive the Indians.

From his school friends, he had heard of an untamed paradise, where wild animals roamed the wilderness, and a man could test himself against nature, and find undiscovered territories, and be hailed as an exploring hero. If he could survive the Indians.

His rebel friends had told him of a utopian society of political freedom, whose brave, pioneering citizens had risen up against the colonial yoke, and broken the shackle of it, had triumphed over Britain, and had spat in the face of the mad king. A land where all men were regarded as equal, and all had equal opportunity—to be a simple farmer or leader of their fledgling democracy, as they chose. If they could survive the Indians.

From his peasant friends he learned of a different America yet, a new Erin that had cast off its colonial shackles, and become a safe haven for all who sought refuge there, a land of boundless opportunity, the streets of whose small cities were paved with gold, and whose black soil was the richest anywhere in the world. A land where simple peasants could find shelter, and be respected as human beings, and could own their own land, beholden to no one, paying rent to no absentee landlord across the seas, and where they could grow old in security and leave something for their children to inherit. If they could survive the Indians.

From Jimmy Hanna, he had learned of the Founding Fathers, and the Declaration of Independence, which was, according to Jimmy, the simplest, most eloquent foundation for the creation of an idyllic country that had ever been written, the culmination of three thousand years of human reason. Jimmy Hanna was not as concerned about the Indians as the others. They are heathen savages, he said, and they will come to God or they will perish, for America is God's gift to us, a reward for all our labors.

He realized something that came as a sweet surprise to him. All his life he had sought a cause to believe in and to fight for. He had thought it was the Irish peasants, but he was not of their number, and so that cause was adopted, false, and not of his true soul. For a time he had thought it was the nationalist cause, of being a foot soldier in the glorious war of ridding Ireland of foreign domination, as the Americans had done, but now he believed that cause hopeless, and Ireland lost.

America.

The word, the name, kept ringing in his ears. America, land of freedom and liberty. America, land of promise and fulfillment. America, where all men were equal, and could lead pleasant, fulfilling lives in the pursuit of happiness.

America.

America was his cause, he knew, America was his passion, America was his creed. He would become a good citizen of his new country, and work to take advantage of the boundless opportunity it afforded. He would go west, and build an estate of such magnitude that his father must apologize, and stand in awe of him, for he would be magnificent. He would not forget the experiences of his youth; he would dedicate his life to his fellow men, and strive for the ideals of America, of liberty for all and the equality of all men, and if necessary, he would die in defense of what he believed. He could not think of a nobler cause.

They had been at sea for weeks, and for a time all had been bored with their journey and with each other, but they knew they must be nearing their destination, and they began to forget the quarrels they had with their temporary traveling companions, and looked forward to the new life. Progressively, with each meal, with each conversation, the subject turned more and more to what they hoped to achieve after landfall, and James discovered his passion was shared, to a greater or lesser degree, by them all, and it reinforced his own.

He was dozing in the prow one sunny afternoon, and woke to a strange cry he had never heard before. A sense of anticipation and excitement buzzed through the crew and the passengers, and they ran to the side of the ship.

The cry came again, from the lookout, who had a better vantage point high in the crow's nest.

"Land ho!"

It was Newfoundland, the land so newly found, and although they could not see it, they knew it was there, for one of their number had seen it, and it would appear to all of them soon. Gulls appeared, as if from nowhere, the cawing heralds of their arrival.

"I see it!" Reverend Blake cried. He pointed to the horizon, and then fell to his knees, his wife beside him, to pray for whatever it was he wanted to find, or give thanks for what he had endured.

James, from his vantage point in the bow, climbed onto the bowsprit and saw it now, a thin, dark sliver of something, between the sea and the sky. He cried out in joy, and his soul sang. As they sailed on, the sliver got larger and longer, and changed from black to a deep and misty blue.

The land shimmered before them, lazy, hazy, repository of all their dreams and aspirations. They had left unsatisfactory lives behind them for the promise of untainted opportunity; they had cut themselves adrift from all they held dear, from the soil of their birth and the bonds of their families. They had escaped from rigid and unyielding societies in search of something better, fairer, and had put their faith in a small and fragile

65

boat, and a dream that was intangible and glorious, the right to carve out their own lives, according to the destiny they perceived for themselves, and a dream of freedom, in whatever form they desired that freedom to be.

They had found what they sought.

America.

7

Philadelphia was almost everything he hoped it would be, but not quite in the way he had imagined.

His very first impressions of the city had confirmed for him, if he needed such confirmation, that he had arrived at a place that was quite unlike anything he had known. The streets were wide and straight, and well ordered. The houses were clean, brightly painted, and built of red brick or wood, unlike the stone buildings of Dublin, or even Liverpool, and the people who dwelt in those houses were a different breed. There was a sense of bustle and purpose about them, tempered by an evident enjoyment of life. They seemed to be constantly going somewhere or doing something, always on the move and yet never too busy to stop and bid a cheery greeting to friends. They were casual in their language and relationships and dress. Many of the men, and some of the women, had adopted trousers, rather than breeches, and tricorns instead of top hats. Their language shocked him. They cursed and swore commonly, and yet there was an abundance of churches. It was a town of immigrants, and he heard the Irish brogue often, but German and French as frequently. The summer weather was hot and humid, but it had little effect on those who were used to it, and they bustled about their business as if it were a mild spring day.

Everyone had an opinion as to how money could be made, and everyone had an opinion as to how best their country could be run, but these opinions were divergent and often contradictory. The only common certainty was the passion of their belief in their country, and of their own ability to prosper. That they prospered was beyond question. James had never seen such general well-being, and while there were poor, their poverty would have been riches to an Irish peasant.

Suddenly, the reason for this casual vibrancy occurred to James. Americans said what they liked because they could, and did what they liked because they could. For the first time in his life he was living in a place that did not have a sense of oppression. No one had any need to look over his shoulder before whispering a complaint of the ruling class, because there was no ruling class. Those who governed were elected by the people, and were beholden to them.

At that moment of realization, so simple and yet so profound, James's soul took wing, and he understood the enormity of freedom, and knew that he was free. He was humbled by it, and his sense of gratitude to America was unbounded.

His brothers had prospered along with everyone else, and were generous with their success. They had welcomed Uncle Henry to their business when he arrived, just as they welcomed their brother James. They had a large provisions store, and supplied to and bought from farmers as far away as Tennessee. The arrival of Henry had enabled them to expand, and Hugh and Alexander had gone to Baltimore, to open a branch there, while John and his uncle supervised things in Philadelphia. They took James into their hearts and their affairs, employed him immediately, and, because he had a natural aptitude for accounting, within a year they had made him a full partner.

Thus James prospered with America, and learned the

contradictions that came with that prosperity. He lodged in an elegant boardinghouse in High Street, run by the formidable Mrs. Bankston. The rooms were spacious and high-ceilinged, and adequately, if simply, furnished. There was a large ballroom, with columns grained in imitation of marble, wide-board, immaculately polished floors, and intricate Oriental rugs. The house had been the home of George Washington when Philadelphia had been the capital, and it amused James, and gave him no small sense of triumph, that he lived in what had been a presidential palace. Several of the staff were black, and James assumed that they must be slaves until Mrs. Bankston disenchanted him.

"They are free men," Mrs. Bankston sniffed. "I do not hold with slavery."

Mrs. Bankston didn't hold with a lot of things. She ruled her staff with a rod of iron, and didn't hold with her niggers getting uppity.

"They are prone to it," she sniffed. "Because they are so recently from the jungle, and civilization has gone to their heads."

She didn't hold with her gentlemen guests receiving ladies in their rooms. She didn't hold with drunkenness; she didn't hold with atheists; she didn't hold with taxes.

"I had to board up many of my windows," she sniffed. "Because the property tax is based on the size and number of one's windows. It is iniquitous. It is atheistic heresy to tax God's daylight."

She didn't hold with politicians, who were intent on accumulating the powers of monarchy unto themselves, and were building palaces in the dismal swamp that was Washington, the new capital.

"I bless my cotton socks that the good Lord sent Thomas Jefferson to us," she sniffed. "He is a man of the people, unlike that Mr. Adams, who wanted to be king."

She didn't hold with the fact that the new president

kept slaves on his estate in Virginia, but forgave him for it.

"He is good to his niggers," she sniffed, and then lowered her voice. "Much too good to one of them, if rumors are to be believed, and even had children by her, if you take my meaning."

She didn't hold with Indians, who were nothing but bloodthirsty savages, she didn't hold with anyone who lived in New York, which was a cesspool of vice, and she didn't hold with New Englanders.

"They believe that God speaks only to them, and that only they know what is ordained for the country," she sniffed. "They are plain folk, but arrogant in their humility. The sooner we are rid of them the better."

Most of all, she didn't hold with the British.

"They have never forgiven us for trouncing them," she sniffed. "They regard us as disobedient children. Mark my words—they will try to smack our naughty posteriors for it yet."

James understood that well, because he remembered his own father, but some of the things Mrs. Bankston didn't hold with confused him. He went to his brother John for clarification.

John laughed. "It is the great flaw of equality," he explained. "For it means that everyone believes that only they know what is best for the others."

The United States, he told James, was not one country but a collection of independent, sovereign countries, which had forgotten their differences and banded together to defeat the British. Once they had achieved their aim, they were not quite sure what to do next. They had a federation but no common purpose any-more, other than an idea. Some wanted a return of the monarchy in some form; others wanted a true democ-racy; some wanted to break away from the loose feder-ation and form confederations of smaller numbers of states, or go it alone. The states fought and bickered and argued among themselves, and somehow held fast. Many in New England, with Boston as its capital, were resolutely opposed to any expansion of the original thirteen states, believing the result would be unwieldy.

"What they really mean is that their own power and influence would be reduced," John said.

Many in the South, the slaveholding states, wanted to break away and form their own country, a slave country, or to extend the number of slave states so that their own influence would be increased.

Virginia was the glue that had kept the country together. Although it was a slaveholding state, it was balanced between the two major factions, North and South, slave and free, and it had produced giant men and giant minds, who had a dream of America and the ruthless will to make that dream a reality.

"I don't know how long it can last as it is," John said. "But it will survive in some form or another. America is inevitable."

The issue of slavery confused James most of all. The few blacks in Philadelphia were free, but were largely disparaged and despised by the whites. Jungle bunnies, they were called, who were lucky to be allowed the crumbs from the white man's table. Yet they were not enslaved. Again, John provided clarification.

"It is New England again. The great argument of the federation was that the Puritans and Calvinists and Quakers would not tolerate slavery, and the Southern states would not abolish it. A compromise was reached, but, like all compromises, it is hardly satisfactory, because it leaves the issue unresolved."

The compromise was that the Northern states would be free states and the Southern states slave states, but neither side was happy with the status quo. The Southerner wanted new, slaveholding territories admitted to the Union, thus increasing the power of the South, and the North as strongly resisted the expansion of the Union under those terms.

70

None of this helped James's confusion. He did not know what he thought of slavery because he had not yet encountered it. He knew of free blacks in Philadelphia who were doing extremely well. One, a sailmaker called Fortan, was reputed to earn over one hundred thousand dollars a year. At the other end of the scale, Mrs. Bankston's blacks were hardly literate.

"They were not meant to read or write," Mrs. Bankston sniffed. "They are put here to serve us, to atone for the sins of their ancestor, Ham, who mocked his father, Noah. God cursed them for it. That is why they are black."

Certainly, the black staff served James well, and he heard that during a recent outbreak of yellow fever, when many whites had fled the city, the blacks had stayed, and volunteered to work in the hospitals.

He felt inadequate to argue with Mrs. Bankston because she claimed the Bible as her authority. James had only a superficial acquaintance with the Good Book. So he shrugged his shoulders on the matter of niggers and slavery, because it did not directly concern him, and went about his business.

In the first flush of his flirtation with Philadelphia, he had abandoned his intention to go west, to find some idyllic spot and build a simple country life for himself, but his growing confusion at the contradictions of the city rekindled his earlier dream.

He had thought America to be a classless society, but quickly discovered he was wrong. If there was no ruling class as such, there was certainly a form of aristocracy, with wealth as its bloodline, and its members could be at least as arrogant as their more illustrious counterparts in Europe.

John was a citizen of some standing, and invited to many fine houses. He took his brother with him sometimes, to introduce him, because James was young, and handsome and eligible. James discovered that he enjoyed being the center of attention for the many charming young ladies of the elite. He flirted with them outrageously, to their delight, and the greater, evident pleasure of their mothers, who saw him as a potential suitor for their daughters. Invitations flooded to him, and he was invited to the annual Pemberton ball, the finest evening on the Philadelphia social calendar.

The display of wealth was almost too gaudy. He had never seen such opulence and extravagance. The tables were heaped with food, hams and lobsters and crabs and pheasant and venison and tempting cakes and trifles, and fruits he had never before seen.

The men were simply but handsomely attired in dark velvets, as if they did not want to distract from the beauty of their female companions. The women were gorgeous. The younger wore elegant, simple gowns, cut low to reveal their breasts in a way that James found delightfully shocking. Their mothers and aunts were more cautiously dressed, but still the rainbow colors of the silks and satins and velvets enchanted him, and the clusters of jewels on necks, fingers, arms, and ears dazzled his eyes.

The splendid musicians played lively gigs, black servants dressed in white kept his glass filled with champagne, and he danced as heartily as ever in his life.

Giddy with happiness, he was introduced to his hosts and their daughter, Lucy Pemberton. He smiled his most mischievous smile, told Lucy how pretty she was, and begged to be allowed the honor of a dance.

Somewhat to his surprise, Lucy found a place on her card for him immediately, and accepted his arm. To his further surprise, many of those watching applauded as the couple stepped to the dance.

"You will never amount to anything."

James wished his father could see him now, for he had already amounted to something, an eligible young bachelor with money in his pocket, dancing with the most desirable young lady in the city. He had been in

America for only a year, was hardly on his way, and yet he was already more than his father had been.

Lucy's dress was in the French Empire style, and exceedingly low cut. James could hardly take his eyes from her delicious breasts, which must bounce from their muslin restraints, he was sure, if she danced too energetically.

"We haven't seen you before," Lucy said sweetly, and James turned on his most charming, self-effacing smile.

"No," he laughed. "I just got off the boat."

Lucy trilled a silly laugh and told him how worried she was about the conditions in Ireland.

"Indeed, they are terrible," James agreed, his eyes drifting to her bosom.

"With all those peasants dying, how will we ever get our supplies of linen?" Lucy twittered.

James said nothing because he could think of nothing to say. He tried to keep the smile on his face, and concentrated on Lucy's breasts, but they had lost their attraction for him. He finished the dance and delivered Lucy to her parents, and shortly afterward he left the party without telling John of his departure.

He walked home with a dull and simmering anger churning in his stomach. He was appalled by Lucy's callousness. Peasants, his friends, were dying, and all she could think about was her precious linen. He couldn't blame her, she was just a silly, vapid girl who didn't know what she was talking about. He directed much of his anger at himself, because he did know better, and he began to question his goals. Although he had worked hard, he had been idle in the pursuit of his dream since he had come to America. He had taken what he had been given by his brothers, but had created nothing for himself. He was doing well by other people's standards, but not nearly well enough by his own. He had been sidetracked by his need to be accepted as a member of this new society, but it was all glitter and frippery. He had not earned his invitation to the Pembertons'; it had come to him for superficial reasons—because of his looks, and his family, and his bachelor state.

He was not his own man; he was other people's toy. He had abandoned his principles to pursue social acceptance; he had allowed himself to be seduced by wealth and glamour and—that word that he hated—class. In his depression, other aspects of life in Philadelphia became distasteful to him. He was tired of the interminable political arguments about what America should be. America was America, and that was enough. He was bored with the constant raging against Britain and France; he had fought that battle in his youth, and had come to America to be free of it. Yet he was angry at the way both Britain and France seemed to be playing games with the new country, the British Navy harassing American ships, and the French emissaries trying to seduce America into the Napoleonic cause. He wanted a simple life, with no great, moral issues to consider.

John and Uncle Henry had eased him into this new world and he was grateful for it, but it was time to strike out on his own.

He had money. Quite apart from what he earned, the sum that had come to him from his father was sitting in the bank, earning interest. When he first heard of it, James refused to touch it, determined to keep his vow that he would take nothing from his father, but Uncle Henry had called him a fool.

"It's your money, boy," he said. "Will you send it back?"

James didn't send it back, but neither did he use it. He decided to save it, in case he ever had need of it.

His problem was that he didn't know what to use it for. Or where to go. Or what to do.

He was distracted from his new melancholy by the arrival, as promised, of his younger brother.

Washington bounded off the boat and into America with a zest and energy that left James breathless. Unscarred by life, full of Irish blarney, bright-eyed and apple-cheeked, Washington ripped into life with careless abandon. Women adored him, men shook their heads in wonder, and everyone envied his joyous youth. Mrs. Bankston mothered him, John and Uncle Henry took him into the business, and James found in him the same rapture of companionship that he had found with Sean.

He brought them family news. Eleanor had married again, to an older merchant, Thomas Kirkman, and they had a daughter, Mary. Sara and Jimmy also had a daughter, another Mary, and a second child on the way. Martha, their other sister, was grievously ill, and Eleanor was taking care of her two girls.

He brought no news for James from his father.

Jugs was pining for James, but did not want him to return. The social and political situation had got worse since the so-called Act of Union with Britain. The persecutions of the Catholics continued with unabated ferocity, and mass evictions of the peasants had turned half the country into homeless wanderers.

"But to hell with Ireland," Washington shouted in glee. "We're here now!"

He could find nothing bad to say about the country. When it snowed and others grumbled of the cold, he built snowmen. When it rained, he said it reminded him of Ireland, and when the sun shone, he turned his face to it, and said home was never like this. In the stifling summer he said it made him appreciate winter more, and in the winter he said how much he would enjoy the summer. In the spring he was the first to cast off his heavy clothes, and in the fall he stood before the changing leaves and applauded them for their fabulous display.

"If this is good," he said to James, "how much better is it in the wilderness?"

James couldn't tell him. He'd never been farther than Baltimore.

"Man, what are we waiting for?" Washington urged. "There's a whole world out there."

He was the stuff of pioneers, ready to take on anything with a laugh and a smile, ready to put his muscles to any task, ready to carve out his own life.

He had wild dreams of becoming a hunter and living in a log cabin by a brook in some sylvan glade. He wanted to catch a bear. He wanted to watch beavers build dams. And he wanted to see an Indian.

"Nashville," John said, tapping a letter with his fingers. Uncle Henry nodded.

James was uncertain. He hardly knew where Nashville was, although they did a fair business with the settlement.

"Isn't that a long way away?"

"Out west," John agreed. "Hundreds of miles."

"Thirty days traveling if you make good speed," Uncle Henry concurred.

Nashville was almost the frontier of the settled world. Beyond it was only the territory of Missouri, a wild Indian land, and the Mississippi River, and beyond that was a foreign country, the Mexican province of Texas. To the south was Louisiana, which Jefferson had just purchased, against the strident opposition of the New Englanders, from Napoleon.

John believed that the Purchase would open up vast new territories for settlement, and that Nashville would be the gateway, for it was the junction between the East Coast and New Orleans. If James and Washington wanted to go to Nashville and open a store, John would provide them with credit and supplies.

"What are we waiting for?" Washington cried, already chasing bison in his head.

"Be careful," John said with a smile. "They're rough men there."

He looked at the letter he was holding and passed it to James. It was from a customer in Nashville, Andrew Jackson—who was not related to them—and was full of complaints about the supplies he had received from them, and their prices.

"He's a crusty curmudgeon," John grinned. "He's cross because he sold his cotton early, and the prices have gone through the roof since. I warned him, but he wouldn't be told."

He grinned again.

"Nobody can tell Andrew anything," he said. "He's as likely to fight a duel with anyone who tries."

James had seen some of Andrew's correspondence before, voluminous, irate, and eloquently phrased. He felt a stirring in his soul, a call to something extravagant, a feeling he had not known since he first saw the land of America from the bow of the ship. This was the challenge he had been seeking, not just of the land, but of the men who inhabited the land. If his customers, frontiersmen, were all as cantankerous as Andrew, and if he could survive, and even win, against them, then he would have reason to be proud of himself. That would be an achievement, and of his own making, of his own doing.

"He's a good customer," he said. "We'll do well by him."

"Let's go!" Washington yelled, dancing about the room, shadow-boxing an imaginary Andrew.

They laughed, and drank a toast to the new venture. It was three months before they were ready to leave, but those weeks flew by in a welter of preparation and planning.

"And watch out for yourselves," Uncle Henry cautioned them, as they were ready to leave. "There's Injuns there."

77

Washington whooped, and James tingled with excitement. In all his time in Philadelphia, he had not seen an Indian. There were a few half-breeds, shabby, dispirited men mostly, often drunk, and with vacant eyes, as if they were looking for something they had lost.

But they were not the real thing to James. They were not the warriors of the legends. Soon he would see them, the noble red-skinned savages on fine horses, naked but for paint and brilliant feathers.

Soon he would know the real America.

Soon he would be a true pioneer.

It was so close. Just a few hundred miles away. Just on the other side of the mountains.

8

The simple thrill of being on the road kept their spirits up for the first few days, and Washington took unalloyed delight in everything he saw. It amused James to be guide to his younger brother on their journey of exploration, for he knew the way, as least as far as Baltimore. They stayed with their brothers Hugh and Alexander, who were doing well in business, and organized the supplies to be delivered, at appropriate intervals, to them in Nashville.

"Land," Hugh told them. "Buy every scrap of land you can, be agents for others' purchases, accept land as guarantee for credit, but get yourselves into land as fast as you can."

From Baltimore, they were in virgin territory for both of them, but the road was well traveled by others, and they headed inland, to the new capital, at Washington. The days were warm and sunny, the villages they passed through charming, and they spent the night in an inn where German was the first language. They arrived at their destination the following afternoon, and

Washington laughed out loud when he saw the capital, a small village in the middle of a swamp with a few extravagant buildings rising out of the marsh. There were no rooms to be had at any of the few inns, so they slept in their wagon, delighted in the fireflies in the bushes, which they had never seen, and were attacked by mosquitoes all night long. They played sightseers for a day, gawking at everything, and stood outside the presidential mansion for half an hour hoping to see Mr. Jefferson, but he did not appear. They loaded their wagon onto a barge and crossed the Potomac, to Alexandria, and suddenly found themselves in another country.

They could not define why Virginia was different at first, but quickly realized it was because of the slaves. There was nothing else odd or unusual—Alexandria was a lovely city, of gracious red-brick buildings, built on a little hill that rose up from the river, but with more black people than they had seen anywhere else.

"Slaves," Washington whispered in wonder. "They are all slaves."

They had seen a few slaves in Maryland, which was also a slave state, and a slave ship in Baltimore, but it was empty, as was the auction house, and they felt a little cheated. None of the blacks they saw on the streets there looked any different from those who were free, in Philadelphia, but they knew that here almost every black they saw was in bondage.

They felt cheated again in Alexandria. Everyone, black or white, was simply going about their business, whatever that might be, and they saw nothing to justify the sermons they had heard denouncing the trade. Still, there was something different, some different manner or attitude between the races, or perhaps it was only a different accent, or perhaps it was simply that they knew they had crossed an invisible line, and were now in unknown territory, where the rules were changed.

They found an inn for the night, and talked freely

between themselves about the slaves they had seen, who were not in any way remarkable, until they realized that no one else, in conversation, ever used the word *slave*. *Darkies*, *nigras*, *niggers* occasionally, if women were not present, or simply *our people*, but never *slaves*. They knew the servants at the inn must be slaves, but they seemed no different from servants on the Northern side, and the owners treated them no better or no worse than servants were treated in the grander houses in Dublin. Again, they were disappointed that the country they were in, which was exotic, was not exotic enough. James thought it was rather like going from Dublin to Liverpool: The accents and manners were different, and the laws, and you realized you were in a foreign country, but everything else was much the same.

The following morning, as they were loading their wagon, they saw something that jolted them.

A young black man was staggering down the street carrying a large box of something, and could hardly see over the top of it. Walking directly toward him were a couple of well-dressed white businessmen, deep in conversation. They were on a collision course with the black youth, who, peering over his burden, saw them in time and, at the last possible moment, swerved out of the way. But a corner of the box clipped the arm of one of the whites. Without breaking his stride, or even seeming to look at what he was doing, the white man raised his cane and smashed it on the black youth's shoulders. The youth fell to the ground, and there was an awful crash of breaking glass inside the box he was delivering. The two white men walked on, and the black youth, after catching his breath, picked up his box and staggered on. He was weeping, but whether it was from the pain of the blow or because of the damage to his cargo, James and Washington could not tell.

No one paid any attention to the incident but themselves. They said nothing to each other, but climbed into the wagon, flicked the horses, and drove away.

They rode in silence for a while, each trying to come to terms with what he had seen, until Washington spoke.

"I've seen as bad or worse in Dublin," he said. "The British treated the croppies no better."

James nodded, for he had seen worse, but the incident soured their pleasure in their travels, until the countryside, the loveliest they had ever seen, worked some magic on them, and they thought themselves in Arcady. They rode through arbors of walnut and oak that bordered pretty farms, where horses grazed on flawless grass. The farmhouses were neat and ordered and painted white, and babbling streams and creeks called runs—Four Mile Run, Holmes Run, and Bull Run—fed into lazy rivers.

As the days passed by, they had the sense that they were climbing upward, higher into the mountains, and daily the scenery became more beautiful—grand but placid and peaceful. They saw snakes sunning themselves on the roads, but they slithered away when they heard the wagon. They heard birdsong that was beautiful, and saw squirrels and deer and possum. They learned to be careful when they had to go into the bushes, because of a nasty little creature called a chigger, an insect that burrowed into skin and itched like blazes. Kindly innkeepers gave them a cure for it, a pungent oil based on turpentine, and everywhere they stayed they were treated with extraordinary civility, and a lazy, casual courtesy that was overtly friendly, yet curiously reserved.

They never talked about slavery again, did not discuss it even between themselves, but came to accept the practice as the tradition in this part of the world. They did not see anything they considered as unfair or harsh treatment of the blacks, but their standards had adjusted since Alexandria, and things that might once

81

have set their teeth on edge became an accepted fact of life.

Each town or village they came to seemed prettier than the one before. Almost always there was a well-tended square, surrounded by churches with spires and lovely, white-painted houses, but after Charlottesville the villages became less ordered, less formal, newer in construction, and with an increasing abundance of log cabins.

They crossed a small mountain range, and gasped at the splendor of the valley that lay before them that was called Shenandoah, and found themselves in another country again, a different and exciting country, for if eastern Virginia had been Arcady, then this, surely, was Eden.

Their most extravagant dreams came true. They climbed the mountain range on the other side of the vast valley, and the people were rougher, if still as hospitable, and pleased to see the strangers, and desperate for news of the outside world. They had a sense of wilderness only recently tamed, and while they saw many farms, they also saw true pioneers, clusters of families who lived in log cabins, miles, it seemed, from anywhere, even their nearest neighbors. Then they would come to a small town, and the wilderness would recede for a while, only to open up before them again as they traveled on.

In the evenings they heard fiddlers more frenetic than any they had known in Ireland, and drank a clear white liquor called moonshine—for it was made by the light of the moon—that had the kick of a mule and produced a wondrous, dreaming drunkenness. They saw a revival meeting, the preacher on a wagon outside a church, practicing a brand of Christianity that provoked his congregation of simple hardy souls to an ecstatic fervor that was moving and slightly frightening.

Sometimes they saw a few Indians, still not the naked, noble savage, painted and feathered, but a far

82

cry from the drunken half-breeds of the city. Calm and self-possessed, they came to the little villages or simple trading posts to sell soft animal hides, or fish they had caught in the river, or trinkets of beads, and took in return the supplies they needed instead of money.

They came down from the mountains through stands of magnificent pine or cedar, past gushing waterfalls and some small mountains that were perpetually shrouded in a mist that looked smoky. Now they came to rolling gentle hills, of grass so sweet that in the distance it looked blue. Up again into the hills, through woods that slowly gave way to farms, and they saw fields of cotton and wondered at it, and played with some bolls of it, although they got prickles in their fingers. The weather was hot but it suited the land, and they saw slave gangs out picking the cotton, chanting work songs as they picked, and they thought it idyllic. Even the overseer flicking his whip occasionally, lazily, at the blacks, appeared to them to be a necessary functionary. They came to a river running through a deep gorge and were told it was called the Cumberland, and that they were close to their journey's end.

After thirty-five days of traveling, they arrived in the thriving settlement of Nashville. Dirty, disheveled, and unshaven, skins browned and necks reddened by the sun, they beamed in delight for they had arrived almost at the edge of the world, and were happier than they could possibly have imagined.

9

As far as James was concerned, Nashville was America, and the rest of the country could go hang. From the moment they rode into the town, he was so captivated by its simple vigor and pleasant aspect, its sense of isolation and independence, that he could not imagine he would ever want to live anywhere else. It was Tennessee's oldest town, but established almost within the span of his own lifetime, so that he could feel part of its growth, and would be able to tell his children that he had been there from the beginning. It was a thriving community, with half a dozen brick houses already replacing the log cabins, and another hundred dwellings of clapboard. There were a dozen small shops and stores, which drew their supplies, as James and Washington would do, from Philadelphia and Baltimore to the east, and New Orleans to the south. The local cotton farmers sent their crop to those same cities, for export to Europe.

The land around Nashville had been settled by an early pioneer, John Donelson, who had made a treaty with the Indian tribes, Cherokee, Creek, Choctaw, and Chickasaw. To the south and southeast were immense tracts of Indian land, mostly Cherokee in Tennessee and Creek in Alabama, which were sacred to their traditional owners, and exempt from white settlement. Constant encroachments were made onto this land in violation of the treaties, and then the Indians retaliated. The Tennessee Militia, now under the command of Andrew Jackson, would trounce the raiding parties, and the usual result was that more Indian land would be ceded to whites. For the most part, the Indians near Nashville who lived on white man's land dwelt in uneasy alliance with their conquerors, but resentment simmered among the younger men, the braves.

In the early days, the main route south from Nashville had been the river, which connected briefly with the Ohio and then flowed into the mighty Mississippi, and down into Louisiana. There was still considerable river traffic, but a new road, the Natchez Trace, a mere remnant of an old Indian path, led from Nashville, twisting and turning through the forests and beside the gorges, skimpy wooden bridges fording the streams, to Natchez. With the influx of settlers and merchants and

84

speculators, the path became broader and well traveled, linking Philadelphia to New Orleans, a distance of two thousand miles.

There was a plentiful water supply from the Cumberland River, good rain, sharp, snowy winters, and high, hot summers. A printing office published a weekly newspaper. There was no hotel or inn as yet, no industry of any kind, and the ambience of the town was pastoral, uncluttered by machinery or factory.

Of the many settlers who had come to the district, to stay and farm, or move on in search of that elusive, ultimate, perfect pasture, many had prospered mightily. Land was abundant and cheap, and fortunes had been quickly made by some. Not all had been so lucky. The adventurers and speculators, the entrepreneurs and the farseeing, had taken the best of the land, and those less fortunate immigrants who had stayed had found what few acres they could on less productive soil. Dour, hardy, weatherbeaten folk, worn out by wandering, had pitched tents on rocky plots which could be had for a cent an acre, or squatted on Indian borders. They scratched out an existence raising tobacco or corn, and, the women more fertile than the land, swarms of children. Many of these children did not live beyond their first few months or years, and those who did were condemned to a life at least as harsh as their parents', unless they got lucky, or moved on.

West, always west. It was the anthem of the frontier. Somewhere out west was the elusive crock of gold at the end of the rainbow, and few looked back to the East, or to Europe, for what they had now, no matter how little, or how much, was almost always more than what they had left behind.

These white poor gave spice to James's appreciation of his new environment, for without the less lucky, how could the fortunate appreciate what they had achieved? While he believed that all men were created equal, and believed in equal opportunity, he did not believe in a leveled society, with no rich and no poor. It was the duty of the strong to protect the weak, but not to become weak themselves.

The population of the town was cosmopolitan, reflecting America. English and Scottish and Irish and Welsh, German, Huguenot, and Scandinavian, and a few from the Caribbean Islands. There were blacks—a few free tradesmen, and enslaved laborers. Some Indians, like the Cherokee chief Doublehead, had adapted to the white man's ways, and had successful farms. Others lived in the forest, tribally, in small communities, some in log cabins, some in wigwams or tepees.

Already there were settlers in the neighboring, less peaceful, territory of Missouri, and some had gone farther west, and crossed the Sabine River, into the Mexican province of Texas.

Nashville was the crossroads, and James was wise enough to understand that fortunes can be made more easily at crossroads than at destinations.

James and Washington found a boardinghouse and settled in. Their letters of introduction served them well, and they were welcomed to the community. Being Irish was no disadvantage here; it was sufficient, they quickly discovered, that they were white gentlemen. The manners and modes of the town were no different from any other they had known, if more open and informal, though both James and Washington were amused that almost all white men, rich or poor, had constant dribbles on their chins, from chewing tobacco. James never took to the practice. The few free blacks were regarded dubiously by the majority of whites, if not with open hostility, and the slaves were a simple fact of life, harshly treated or otherwise, depending on the whim of their Massas. The Indians, of whatever tribe, were mostly shunned and avoided, and half-breeds despised, even by other Indians.

Within two weeks, James and Washington had

found, and arranged to buy, a spacious wooden store in the main street. Washington had his portion from his father and was ready to pay cash. James had wrestled with his conscience. Ultimately, not wanting to be indebted to a bank or his younger brother, he used his own portion that he had vowed he would never touch. He justified the breaking of this oath by his need for a start in life.

Their supplies began arriving by flat-bottomed barge from Philadelphia and Baltimore, and soon their shelves were stacked with clothing, and cloth—calico, linen, wool, and woven cotton—hats and boots, cases of candles, tins of tobacco, bags of loose coffee and tea, flour and oatmeal, dry beans and maize, crockery and cutlery, pots and pans, and racks and spades and hoes. Even before the shop opened, they had begun business, making contact with the farmers who dealt with their brothers in the East, offering their services in any and every capacity, as mailmen and post office, as agents and suppliers, and as accountants and bookkeepers. They preferred cash money, specie, as their payment, but were prepared to take signed notes or paper; they offered credit, provided there was collateral, they would even barter, and they accepted deeds to land, the common currency of the frontier.

They hung up their shingle, JACKSON BROTHERS, DRY GOODS, and on the day the store was ready, they looked at each other, both in serviceable trousers, with blousy shirts and clean linen aprons, shook hands, wished each other good luck, and opened their door.

They did better than they had hoped and were busier than they could have imagined. At the end of the first day, they knew they needed some help, if only an errand boy, to run messages, clean the store, and load wagons. They put a sign in the window, confidently expecting a number of applications from the poor white boys in the district, keen to earn pocket money, but to their surprise, no one came for the job. Had they been more attuned to the town and the times, they might have noticed that some of their customers looked at the sign suspiciously, but they were new to the district, and naive.

James ran the store on his own, for Washington was always out making deliveries in the wagon. He was toying with putting an advertisement for the job in the local newspaper, when the door burst open, and an angry white man came in. He snatched the job advertisement from the door and marched to the counter, interrupting two women who were debating the merits of different brands of linseed oil with James.

"What is the meaning of this?" he demanded.

James was irritated, and glared at the intruder. A tall, lanky man, with a shock of unruly red hair and startling, sapphire eyes that were dancing with anger. A slender, well-dressed black man had followed him into the store, and stood behind him, like a shadow.

The ferocity of the man's approach unnerved James. The two women drifted away to inspect bags of white beans.

"I need a boy for the store," James said. "To run errands, and keep the place clean—"

"Nigger work," the man shouted, interrupting James. He turned to his shadow. "Nigger work, eh, Alfred?"

The shadow nodded, and his Massa turned back to James.

"No decent white boy would do this."

James's temper was rising.

"But I need help, and I'd pay well," he said, with an edge in his voice.

The man laughed, and James wondered what was so funny.

"Then get a nigger," he said.

"I don't know how," James countered. "None have applied."

The man laughed again, and the shadow chuckled. "Nigger boys don't apply for jobs; they don't have a choice in the matter. You buy 'em."

James felt foolish now. The concept of owning slaves was no longer shocking or exotic to him, but he had never imagined he would have the need to purchase one. He was not sure he wanted to own a slave.

An image popped into his mind of a well-dressed woman in Liverpool leading a beautifully attired Nubian boy, on a silver chain. The boy had not seemed unhappy.

"How?" was the best he could manage.

The man's anger had dissipated, and he looked at James almost pityingly, and shook his head.

"I thought your brothers would have equipped you better for the frontier."

It dawned on James who he was. Some cadence in his speech matched the phrases he had read in irate letters.

"Mr. Jackson?" he wondered, and Andrew laughed, and shook his hand.

"Andrew will do," he said. "And you're the greenhorn. James or Washington?"

"James," James murmured, feeling very like an errant boy before his father.

"Well, James," Andrew said. "You've already set a few tongues wagging in Nashville with this advertisement. Everyone took pity on you because you are new, but no one had the guts to tell you. Except me."

He tapped the advertisement on the counter.

"We'll find you a boy."

He turned to his shadow. "See to it, Alfred. Get him a good 'un, but not too pricey. We may have one at the farm."

"Yes, suh, Massa," the shadow, Alfred, murmured.

Andrew turned back to James.

"Irish," he barked. "Horses?"

89

James didn't understand the question.

"Horseracing!" Andrew snapped impatiently. "Are you a gambling man?"

"Some," James admitted. The truculent manner of his visitor was annoying him again. He wanted to say something to put him in his place, but was already slightly in awe of him.

"My father bred steeplechasers," he said, with a tinge of pride. "Crazy Jane, among others."

Andrew nodded in appreciation, and James was surprised again, for he could not imagine that anyone here had heard of his father's prize mare.

"We'll make a frontiersman of you yet," he said. "Though I trust your prices will be more reasonable than your thieving brothers'."

He was already on his way out of the store, and James's temper snapped.

"My brothers are not thieves," he cried. "And nor am I."

Andrew stopped and turned back, and gave James his most dazzling smile.

The effect of that smile, impudent, confident, embracing, and reassuring, was remarkable. James thought he had survived a test of fire, and had triumphed and been included in the company of a god.

"Well, we shall see," Andrew said. He tipped his hat to the women who were still twittering about beans and swept out of the store. Alfred followed him, as closely as his shadow.

After he had gone, James looked at his hands, which were shaking slightly, but he was well satisfied with the meeting. He sold the women what they wanted, then, having no other customers, set to and swept the store.

At dinner that night he told Washington about Andrew, and, cautiously, suggested that they might soon own a slave. Washington raised his eyebrows in surprise, but listened to James's justifications.

"I'd rather the poor beggar was with us," Washington said, "than stuck in the fields like his brothers. I have seen terrible things done to them."

Washington, on his journeys of delivery, had seen much more of the actual workings of slave life than James. He had seen blacks flogged for minor misdemeanors, and it had shocked him at first, and repulsed him. But he was getting used to it.

"And it is the way of things," he said.

They agreed they would be kind to their slave, if he turned up, and never raise their hand to him in anger. They made a room ready in the basement, with a small bunk and some blankets, like getting a kennel ready for a new and costly dog, and wondered what he would eat. They took their own meals at the tavern across the road, and remembered there was provision for the feeding of slaves, in the kitchen.

Alfred came back the following morning, before Washington set off on his rounds. He had a small black boy with him, of eight or nine years old.

He tipped his hat to James and Washington.

"Massa," he said. "This here be Ephraim."

Ephraim was thin and scrawny, simply dressed and barefooted. He kept his eyes to the floor.

Alfred bent down and spoke to him.

"This yo' new Massas," he said. "Be a good boy, an' allus do what you tol'."

Ephraim nodded without looking up. Washington went to him.

"Well, now, Ephraim," he said. "I'm Massa Washington, and that's Massa James."

He waited a moment.

"Do you understand?"

Ephraim nodded.

"What is my name?" Washington asked him.

"Mass' Wash'n'ton," Ephraim murmured.

"Very good," Washington said. "And that man?"

91

'Mass' James," Ephraim whispered.

"Excellent," Washington said, and put his arm around the boy's shoulders. Ephraim stiffened.

"There's no need to be frightened of me," Washington told him. "I'm not going to beat you."

Ephraim nodded, but didn't seem convinced.

"Are you hungry?" Washington asked him.

"Chile bin fed," Alfred said, but Ephraim looked up at Washington with large and sorrowful eyes. He had been well fed that morning, but he was always hungry.

Washington smiled. The effect of his smile on Ephraim was similar to the effect of Andrew's smile on James the previous day. He looked at Washington adoringly and nodded his head.

"I's allus hungry," he said.

"Thought so," Washington said cheerily. "I am too. Why don't you and I find some bread and cheese and get to know each other."

He led Ephraim to the back of the store, found some fresh bread and a lump of hard cheese, and the two sat together, munching happily, while Washington told Ephraim what was expected of him.

Alfred came to James, and put some papers on the counter.

'Sign here, Massa," he instructed James.

James signed where he indicated. It was official. He owned a slave.

"Dat a hunerd dollar you owe Massa Andrew," he said. "But he take it in kind."

He tipped his hat, and left the store. James went to join Washington and Ephraim.

"He's a good lad," Washington told James. "His family should be proud of him."

"Where is your mother, Ephraim?" he asked the little slave, who looked at the floor again, because he didn't understand the question.

"Yo' mammy," Washington had already picked up a few words of the slaves' dialect. "Where is she?"

"Wi' Massa Jackson," Ephraim whispered. There was a tear in his eye. This big white man might be quite friendly, but he was his Massa, and Massas could turn on nigger boys at any moment. And he missed his mammy. Although he had only been parted from her that morning, he did not expect to see her again.

"Well, I'll take you with me sometimes, when I go to visit Massa Jackson's farm," Washington told him, for he missed his mother. "And you can see your mammy."

Ephraim looked at him again, as if he couldn't quite believe his ears, or his luck.

"Now, let's go and look at your room," Washington said, and led Ephraim away.

James stayed in the store, beset by two conflicting emotions. He was quite proud of the fact that he now owned a slave, of some value. He was becoming a man of property and substance.

But he was also ashamed. It had not occurred to him that Ephraim might miss his mammy. Or even that he had one.

10

After Ephraim it was easy, almost as easy as making money, which flowed to them in a steady stream at first, but then in a raging torrent.

They bought a house, and because they needed a cook and housekeeper, Alfred found them Tiara, a young, outspoken girl who cost four hundred dollars.

They decided to expand the small stable at the back of the store into a livery stable, and they needed hostlers, so Alfred found them Micah, a sturdy young man who was good with horses. Micah cost six hundred dollars.

When Tiara and Micah got much too close to each other and had a son, James discovered that he owned a healthy baby boy who hadn't cost him anything at all and was worth, on the day of his birth, fifty dollars, and who appreciated in value with each passing year. Tiara and Micah jumped over the broom, a slave custom, into the land of matrimony, and had several more children, all of whom belonged to James, who had never attended a slave auction.

The store did well, and they used that and the house they owned as collateral to buy some undeveloped lots on the outskirts of town. Within a year they sold three of them at a handsome profit. With that money they purchased lot #177, on which a cotton gin had been erected, and began processing much of the cotton from the district.

Washington, filled with wanderlust and the adventure of the frontier, explored farther south, to Natchez, which had been a Spanish town, and bought several lots near there. After the Purchase and Louisiana's later admission to the Union, settlement in the area flourished. Washington sold his land and tripled his money. He bought more land, cheaper land, farther from the town, and within a year sold that and bought more.

James and Washington had early on decided that, unlike most stores in Nashville, theirs would serve Indians. They were not to be allowed in while whites were shopping, but came in the evening, when the store was closed to others. If they wanted to make purchases during the day, they would come to the back, and Micah or Ephraim would relay their needs to James.

The Indians were keenly aware of local opinion and attitudes toward them, and just as aware of, and keenly grateful for, James's lack of that attitude. James was fascinated by them. He saw little to fear in them, and could not equate the countless stories of bloodthirsty savages with these reserved and downcast people who were struggling to survive in a world that was alien to them. They in turn respected his confidence, and he was befriended by Jimmy Doublehead, and his father, the Cherokee chief, Doublehead.

Chief Doublehead was old, and seldom smiled. In his youth he had been a fierce warrior, but after countless, fruitless battles against the whites, he had come to believe that his nation could not win against such overwhelming, constantly renewing, numbers of white men, who were better armed and better trained. He sought peace, as being in the best interest of his people.

He bent his efforts toward a harmonious accommodation between the races, and the whites came to regard him as the man who tried to civilize his people. He ceded and sold land to the whites. He opened a trading post, and supervised appreciable commerce. He adopted the white man's ways of agriculture, established a plantation, and owned several black slaves.

A scandal erupted when Doublehead ceded by treaty a large territory of land to the south, between Nashville and Huntsville. The Chickasaw claimed it was their land and outside of Doublehead's jurisdiction. A small war ensued, which both Indian tribes lost. Younger braves of his tribe rebelled, and accused Doublehead of surrendering to the white man. Chief Doublehead's reputation among the tribes was shattered.

He found it impossible to smile anymore, because there was nothing to smile about. Only his son, Jimmy, defended him.

Council was called, and one by one the young braves voiced their grievances against Doublehead, the U.S. Government, and all white men. Doublehead listened in silence, and hardly moved, except to restrain his angry son, Jimmy. It was council, and all were entitled to their say.

Bonepolisher, a sturdy Cherokee brave, made a long speech accusing Doublehead of infamy to his own tribe, and of making secret treaties with the white men, to benefit himself.

Doublehead heard him out, but his anger was rising.

95

"You have betrayed the people, your brothers!" Bone-polisher cried. It was the greatest sin an Indian could be accused of by his own people.

Doublehead got to his feet.

"You have said enough, Bonepolisher," Doublehead said, in a voice of thunder. "Stop, or I shall kill you."

In fury, Bonepolisher grabbed his tomahawk and raised it to strike Doublehead, who shot him through the heart.

The council adjourned in anger and confusion. Later that evening, Doublehead was sitting in a tavern with his son.

"It is a good day to die," Doublehead told Jimmy. And sent his son away from him.

Three men came in, Chief Ridge, a half-breed, Alex Saunders, and a white trader named Rogers. Doublehead stared at Rogers in contempt.

"You are not of our people," Doublehead said to the white man. "You live among us by our permission. I have never seen you in council or on the warpath. Go away, and do not bother me."

Rogers laughed.

Believing that his end was near, and perhaps wanting to hasten it, Doublehead struck the white trader. A fight developed, and others came to Doublehead's assistance, and shots were fired. The assailants fled into the night, but Doublehead's jaw was shattered by a bullet. A friend helped Doublehead down the street to seek help, but the assailants came out of hiding and attacked again. Doublehead fought like a panther, but was killed by a tomahawk blow to his skull.

In fear of his own life, Jimmy came to James, thinking he would be safe with a white man, and poured out his grief. James comforted him, and told him that if there was ever anything he could do for Jimmy and his family, in honor of the chief, he had only to ask.

The merchant James Jackson, who had been kind to the Indian people, was one of the few white men allowed to attend the funeral of the once great chief, who was buried according to the tribal ways.

James was fascinated by the intricate, exotic ceremonies, and found himself wondering about the relationship between man and the spirit world. These people did not believe in his God, but they believed in some powerful metaphysical force that caused awe in James. He thought that Chief Doublehead's personal dilemma exemplified the tragedy of all his people, of all the tribes. In order to live in peace with the white men, they had to surrender to them, because they could not win against them in war. Their land, pristine, primeval, was too valuable to be left to their stewardship, for it was unproductive. The march of progress could not be stopped, yet, surely, in this vast country, there was land enough for all? James approved of the concept behind the treaties, whereby the Indians gave land for white settlement in return for the right to live in peace on what was left, and he cursed those whites who coveted what the Indians still had. When he saw the wonderful, empty landscapes on which the Creek and Cherokee and Chickasaw still roamed, he envied them their freedom, and thought it was a sweet and simple life to live as they did, taking from the land only what could be replenished, living from the land that gave to them in abundance.

At the same time, in his darker moments, he knew how much money he could make if he could persuade them to part with some few acres of it. He cherished the idea that perhaps he could wrest a private treaty from Chief Doublehead, as others had done, and make that land available to settlers on a legal basis, and be rich beyond imagining.

When wealth did come to James, it was indeed from land, but not quite as he expected. Successful as James and Washington were in all their endeavors, the real money came to them when Thomas Jefferson, the president, put an embargo on all shipping from United States ports.

"Tom's gone mad!" Andrew cried, and railed and fumed, and swore it would bankrupt the country, which it very nearly did. James only vaguely understood why Jefferson had taken this action, but thrilled to be friends with a man who called the president Tom.

As James understood it, Britain, at war with France, had put an embargo on American ships sailing to European ports, and Napoleon retaliated by putting an embargo on American ships sailing to British ports. Jefferson put an embargo on all American shipping, to try to bring the two warring factions to reason with regard to neutral American commerce.

"Cutting off his nose to spite his face," Andrew cried again, stomping on the floor in rage.

The effect of the embargo was catastrophic. Some smart companies and ship's captains found their way around it by using ports in the Caribbean, but few goods came into America, and fewer left. The dormant secession movement in New England woke up sharply, because theirs were the ports most harshly affected, but Southern cotton growers, and those around Nashville, suffered as well. They could not get their cotton to British markets.

The farmers lived in hope that the embargo would be repealed, and tried to continue to pay their debts. Cash money was scarce and promissory notes abounded.

"Damned paper!" Andrew cried again. "It will be the ruin of us. Hard currency is the only honorable money!"

James and Washington obliged their customers to the limit of their financial ability, which was now considerable. When all else failed, they accepted land in payment of debts, and by the time the embargo was lifted they owned over fifty thousand acres. With the resumption of trade, the price of land rocketed to the sky. James and Washington sold half of what they owned at formidable profit, and bought yet more.

Washington was drawn more and more to the South, to Natchez. He loved the lazy, unhurried river life, and bought some barges to carry cargo between Natchez and New Orleans.

James's passion became a farm he had accumulated outside Nashville. It was the first estate he had ever owned, and he enjoyed the role of country squire. He gave soirees and picnics, and entertained the notables of the town. A frequent visitor to Andrew's house, he became involved in the politics of the South, and of the frontier, and met several of the rising young politicians of the day, Henry Clay and his son Henry junior from Kentucky, John McKinley from Tennessee, and John Coffee, a military man, and Andrew's aide. John Coffee and Andrew owned the Cloverbottom Horse Race Track, and James and Andrew, the two Jacksons as they were called, were always to be seen at the meetings. Both men loved the sport, and Andrew owned several blooded horses.

"You will never amount to anything."

His father's last words to him were the fuel to the engine of James's ambition, and yet he could never convince himself that he had achieved enough to prove his father wrong.

Thus James became one of the landholding gentry, though still in trade, the owner of a small cotton plantation, a cotton gin, a successful business, a breeder of racehorses, and Massa to more than forty slaves. He had never attended a slave auction, nor had he ever sent one of his slaves to the block.

Family gathered to him as rapidly as money. After his sister Martha died, Eleanor came from Ireland with her second husband, Thomas Kirkman, and their children, Mary Letitia, James, and little Tom, together with Martha's two girls, Mary and Anna. Thomas had an astute mind for commerce, and James put him in charge of the store. Sara and Jimmy came with their four children, Mary Ann, Jane, Robert, and Ellen. James employed Jimmy in his land office. Shortly after arriving in Nashville, Sara gave birth to a girl, who was called Letitia, in honor of Hugh's wife, in Baltimore.

Surrounded by loving family, rich and successful, still young enough and handsome enough, James had almost all his heart desired, except two things. He had no shadow, no personal manservant, as Andrew had Alfred, and he had never found a woman to love.

The first was easy. He discussed his need with Andrew, and Andrew sent Alfred looking. It took a year, but finally Alfred found a winner.

Cap'n Jack was in his early twenties when he came to James. His previous Massa, in Virginia, had seen the potential in him, and had taken the youthful slave, Jack, into the house, and trained him as a manservant. He also taught Cap'n Jack to read and write, which was unusual among slaves, and forbidden in some states. Cap'n Jack took full advantage of the benefits that had come to him, worked hard and well, and made himself indispensable to his Massa, who was old and infirm. He had a habit of calling everyone "Cap'n" because he could not bear to use the word "Massa," which accentuated his slave status, and eventually became known as Cap'n Jack himself. Andrew Jackson was a frequent visitor to the estate, on his many trips to Washington on government business, and Alfred and Cap'n Jack became friends. When Cap'n Jack's Massa became mortally ill, Alfred suggested to Andrew that he buy Cap'n Jack on James's behalf.

Despite the fact that this almost certainly saved Cap'n Jack from the auction block, he seethed with resentment about this change in his ownership. He wanted to stay and nurse his old Massa. He didn't want to be uprooted from the only home he had known, in pleasant Virginia, and be carted off to the frontier to a man he didn't know. Besides, he cherished the hope that his Massa would free him in his will. This was not to be. Although the old man was fond of Cap'n Jack, he did not believe in the practice of freeing niggers, no matter how loyal they had been.

"It the block, or the backblocks," Alfred told him with a wheezy chuckle.

Cap'n Jack was forced to admit that his dream of freedom had been false, and having no alternative, he accompanied Alfred and Andrew to his new Massa, but went with bad grace.

For the first few weeks it was a disaster. Cap'n Jack did as he was told by James, but with ill humor, and never extended himself. To reinforce his bitterness at his status, Cap'n Jack stopped calling white men "Cap'n," and called James "Massa," with scarcely concealed contempt. It made James angry. He had paid a thousand dollars for Cap'n Jack, and hoped for a servant as loyal and obliging and inventive as Alfred was to Andrew, not this surly, if competent man, who never questioned anything, and never took any initiative.

He lost his temper with Cap'n Jack, and threatened to sell him, but Cap'n Jack only shrugged.

"If'n that make you happy, Massa," he said. "To buy an' sell niggers."

That made James angrier, because Cap'n Jack had touched his conscience.

James was still ambivalent in his attitude to slavery. He had acquired slaves because it was the done thing, because it was expected of him, and because only slaves performed certain jobs. It was also true that he enjoyed the status that having so many slaves gave him. He believed himself to be a benevolent Massa, he never went to an auction or sold slaves away, and, for the most part, he treated his slaves well. His lenience had declined over time. He allowed his foreman on the plantation to use the lash mildly, or some of the children to be chastised with the switch, but he persuaded himself that his slaves were better looked after than any in the district. Ephraim, and Tiara and Micah's boys were almost like sons to him.

He lived in the South and slavery was the way of the South. He had not made his fortune on their sweat and labor, but by his own sharp brain and endeavors. He thought his slaves responded well to his treatment of them. They seemed loyal, and obedient, and none had ever run away. There were some dissenters, a couple of troublesome young men on the plantation, but James put this down to intemperate youth, and a few stinging lashes from the foreman's whip soon brought them to heel.

Still, the practice troubled him, although less and less as the numbers of those he owned grew larger, and he knew them less well, and was less involved in their lives. He calmed his conscience by telling himself that slavery was best for these people, who were illiterate and not able to survive in the white man's world, but most of the time he tried to avoid thinking about slavery, or freedom, as an issue.

Cap'n Jack was the living proof that he had compromised some of his ideals, and that made him angry. He discussed the problem with Washington, when his brother passed through Nashville on his way home to Ireland, for a visit to the old country.

Washington had no problem with slavery. He owned a number of slaves in Natchez, who operated his fleet of barges between that city and New Orleans. A natural leader of men, a natural authority figure, but with charm and good humor, Washington kept his slaves well disciplined, but although he tolerated harsh punishment, he enjoyed finding less extreme ways of solving problems.

"Don't get mad," he told James with a laugh. "Get Irish."

James got Irish. He called Cap'n Jack to his study one night, ordered him to sit, and produced a bottle of good whiskey. He poured drinks for both of them, and asked Cap'n Jack to explain his problem.

Cap'n Jack couldn't believe this was happening. Slaves were discouraged from drinking liquor—often it was forbidden to them—and no one, not even his first, much-loved Massa, had ever asked him what he felt. What he thought, yes, but never what he felt.

Sullen at first, he sipped on the whiskey, and felt the fire race through him. He didn't know how to say all the things that raged in his heart, but the liquor released his tongue.

"I ain't free," he blurted out.

"No, you're not," James agreed calmly. "You're my slave."

"An' what gives you the right to own me?" Cap'n Jack retorted. He was astonished at himself. Such audacity would surely get him flogged tomorrow, but it was done now. In for a penny, in for a pound. He was going to be punished anyway; he might as well make the most of his crime.

"I don't know," James replied, honestly. "But it is the way of it."

"Then the way is wrong," Cap'n Jack insisted. He gulped on his whiskey again, and suddenly all the distress and bitterness he had accumulated over the years came pouring out of him.

He was treated as an animal, or livestock, but he was not an animal; he could read and write, he could think, and he could feel.

"I think, therefore I am," James agreed. He poured more whiskey, and asked if Cap'n Jack's previous Massa had not treated him well.

"He was good to me," Cap'n Jack was forced to admit. "Like his pet dog, or his best stallion. But he never treated me human."

"I try to do that," James said. "But you resent me."

"Course I do," Cap'n Jack said. "Coz I ain't free. All

103

yo' niggers resent you. Coz you got the power over them."

It had never occurred to James, nor did he believe it. His people loved him. Even the troublesome few on the plantation were angry because of their work and their lowly conditions, he had thought, but not at him. He was sure, not at him. But he would investigate what Cap'n Jack told him.

Cap'n Jack fought for words to make him understand, but what words were there? What words could explain to someone who was free, and whose freedom was never in doubt, how precious freedom was? How could he explain what it felt like to be born in bondage, and know you would never be free of it?

Never be free to choose your own name, and your own life. Never be free to make decisions for yourself; never be free to travel where you wanted, to do what you wanted. Never be free of being sold. Never be free of the fear that your wife might be sold away from you, and your children. Never be free to create something of your own, to farm some small few acres, and give it to your son, saying I made this, yo' pappy made this. Never free to fight for yourself and yours, never free of the fear of unfair punishment, never free from the potential pain of the lash.

Never free to be a man.

"It don't matter if'n you don't never whump us," he said. "It is enough that you have the power to do it."

His mind exploded at the simple unfairness of it, the unbelievable injustice that had been done to him and his people, all because they were black. He fought back tears.

"You think we's proud to be slaves?" Cap'n Jack asked him, his anger nearly spent, and other emotions unsettling him.

James listened to the litany of grief, the sad song in praise of freedom, and thought of Fortan, the black sailmaker in Philadelphia, who made over a hundred

104

thousand dollars a year, and could look on his life with pride.

He thought of his peasant friends in Ireland, who toiled all their lives for some other man's benefit, and were prepared to die for a chance of freedom.

He thought of Sean, effectively slave to soil he did not own, and who did lay down his life to be free, and went triumphantly to his grave.

He remembered the shame he felt on the day he bought Ephraim, and did not even think of the boy's enforced separation from his family. He felt ashamed now, and when he saw that there were tears in his new slave's eyes, he was distressed.

"What can I do?" James asked.

"Make me free," Cap'n Jack said.

"Why should I do that?" James wondered. "I have paid a great deal of money for you, and you have given me no indication that you deserve your freedom."

"Did you earn yours?" Cap'n Jack responded. "Or was you born to it?"

He had gone too far, he was sure. He'd be sent to the block tomorrow, after a hundred lashes at least, but it was almost worth it.

"Yes, I was," James agreed. "You were not, for that is not the way of it here. But you could earn it."

Cap'n Jack brushed away the tear from his eye, and looked at him. Was this the bait they always dangled? His ol' Massa had said it to him so often.

"Work hard for me, Jack, and you could be free."

It had never been a promise, only a carrot, and in the end it had been a lie. A white man's lie, to keep the black man complaisant.

"If you work hard for me, willingly and well, then, when the time is right, I will give you your freedom."

Cap'n Jack didn't believe him. "When?" he asked.

"When you have earned it," James said, and believed it when it was said.

Cap'n Jack turned away. It was the old lie.

"I give you my word," James said quietly, for he had seen the disbelief in Cap'n Jack's eyes.

"I swear it."

What could Cap'n Jack do but believe him? It was his only hope.

11

The problem of finding a wife was not so easily solved. There had been several women in James's life, for he cut a dashing figure, and was considered quite a catch, but he had never felt more than passing affection for any of them.

It made Eleanor cross.

"For heaven's sake, Jamie," she chided him. She would never call him James. "You've had quite long enough to sow your wild oats."

James smiled ruefully. He had sown very few wild oats.

"You are a man of substance," Eleanor continued. "You must have sons. If anything should happen to you, God forbid, what would become of all this?"

James thought it was a cold-blooded reason for getting married and having a family, but he took her point. He looked at his estate. What would become of it all if something happened to him? He resolved to make a new will, in favor of Eleanor's boys, and Sara's.

"What are you waiting for?" Eleanor demanded, concerned for her brother.

"I don't know," James shrugged. "Love, I suppose."

Eleanor gave a small sigh of exasperation.

"Jamie," she cried. "Be your age."

James was tired of it. He knew what was expected of him. He wanted to marry; he wanted to raise a family. He loved having all his nieces and nephews around, and wanted his own sons and daughters. But he wanted to fall in love. He wanted to know what it was about love that moved people to do extraordinary things. He wanted to know what it was that the poets wrote about. He wanted to know what it was like to have a heart so full that the loss of the loved one might cause it to break.

"You found love," he said testily, to Eleanor. "You had Oliver."

"Yes, I did," Eleanor agreed. "And what a wild and wonderful time it was."

She lapsed into pretty memory for a moment, but then shook herself from the past and told James a tiny secret.

"But Thomas is the better husband," she said softly.

James was shocked. He had always imagined Eleanor and Oliver to be soul mates, a passionate couple whose lives intertwined in events of great moment. He could not imagine how the kind, balding, bespectacled Thomas Kirkman could be a better husband than the dashing, fiery Oliver. But he was grateful for the confidence Eleanor's confession gave him. He longed to be more like Oliver, Sean, or Washington, or especially Andrew, but doubted that he had that much bravado.

He wondered if he was scared of marriage because of his father. He could not countenance the idea that his children would not love him.

Mostly, he envied Andrew Jackson, who had found in his Rachel a marriage that James longed to emulate, and a woman that he adored.

Rachel Jackson was the most extraordinary woman he had ever met, and sometimes when he thought of his dead mother, whom he had never known, James thought of Rachel. She was dark-haired, pious and demure, dedicated to God and Andrew, although not necessarily in that order, and to her sons, who were not her sons.

The tenth of eleven children born to John Donelson, who had founded Nashville, Rachel had been her father's darling, a vivacious minx of a girl, forever getting into scrapes. When she was thirteen, she had accompanied her parents, her family, and others on an epic river journey from Virginia to Nashville. They traveled a thousand miles, mostly through hostile country. Several of their party were killed by Indians, and some others drowned. Rachel, brown as a berry, fleet as a deer, survived all the privations with unquenchable good spirits and a tomboy appetite for the adventure. She flourished on the frontier and grew into a stunning beauty, all dimples and laughter, cherry lips and lustrous eyes. She had her pick of suitors, married the handsome Lewis Robards when she was eighteen, and went to live with her new husband on his parents' estate in Kentucky.

The marriage was a disaster. Lewis was irrationally jealous, and violent toward Rachel when other men paid her attention. He ordered his wife out of the house. She returned to her family in Nashville, lived with her mother, and retired from the world. But not far enough. She took the eye of a dashing young attorney who had come to the district, Andrew Jackson.

A settlement was negotiated with the contrite Lewis Robards, and Rachel returned to her husband. He promptly forgot his contrition, and returned to his earlier, jealous violence. Rachel fled her husband a second time, and her family thought she would be safe from Robards in Natchez. Since she could not undertake the perilous journey through Indian country on her own, Andrew Jackson volunteered to accompany her.

In Natchez they heard that Robards had sued for divorce. They returned to Nashville and were married.

That was the story as they told it. From others, James heard a slightly different version. It was rumored that Andrew had seduced Rachel to elope with him, which James thought possible. That he had offered to fight a duel with Robards, which James thought likely, because Andrew fought more duels than any other man in the

108

country. That Andrew and Rachel had married biga-mously in Natchez, before the divorce was final, which James thought unlikely, Andrew was too smart a lawyer for that. Neither Andrew nor Rachel could ever be shaken from their simpler, more innocent version of the tale, but the rumor of bigamous marriage haunted them all their lives. Andrew challenged several men because of it, in defense of his wife's honor, and killed at least some of them.

The rumors had their strongest effect on Rachel. Because of them, and perhaps to counteract them, she withdrew from public life, and settled for simple hap-piness with the man she loved. It was hard to see any of the passionate creature she must once have been in the somberly clothed, deeply religious woman who was Rachel now, but sometimes when she talked with James about the early days in Nashville, she allowed a little of her old self to show. Her cheeks dimpled, and her eyes sparkled and flashed, and there was a hint of gentle mockery in her voice, as she teased him with hints as to her romantic past.

She adored Andrew, and he her, and their sadness was that they had no children of their own. Sons they had aplenty, orphaned boys of dead relatives, and later Andrew adopted a Creek Boy, Lincoyen, and he brought him up as his own. But their darling was Andrew junior, who was the only son they had from infancy.

Rachel's brother Severn and his wife, Elizabeth, had many children, and, after so many, when Elizabeth delivered twin boys, Severn sent for Rachel and Andrew. Elizabeth told her sister-in-law that they had been amply blessed, while she had not, and she gave Rachel the pick of the four-day-old twins. Rachel chose the littler of the two, and she and Andrew raised the boy with love and tenderness, and called him Andrew, in honor of the man who was his most doting father.

In the early days of their marriage they had lived on

109

Andrew's farm at Hunter's Hill, but with prosperity he bought a new estate, somewhat closer to Nashville, and built a lovely home for them, with landscaped gardens, that he called the Hermitage.

"Soon I shall retire from public life," he told James, "and live here, like a simple hermit, and contemplate the world."

James laughed out loud. Andrew was only fifteen years older than he, and James could not imagine that he would ever retire.

James was a constant and welcome visitor to the Hermitage, and when Andrew was away, as frequently happened, on military expeditions or affairs in Washington, James would pay particular attention to Rachel, to make sure she was not lonely.

They would sit together for hours in the lovely garden, and Rachel, who cared for James dearly, would talk to him of the past, and instruct him in the pioneer ways, and, like Eleanor, chide him for not being married.

"I can't get married," he told her, laughingly. "The woman I love is already spoken for."

She slapped his hand with her fan, and blushed, and hid behind dimples. These were among the sweetest days of James's life.

Cap'n Jack loved these visits too, for it gave him a chance to be with his old friend Alfred. The two slaves would sit together near the vegetable plot, telling yarns about their Massas, or gossiping about slave life, or simply sitting, in convivial silence, and dreaming, for a sunny moment, that they were free.

12

Cap'n Jack was determined to keep his side of the bargain with James. He assumed it was unlikely he would be given his freedom at any time in the foreseeable future, but he vowed to give James no reason to deny the promise.

He took charge of his Massa's life, and became the most diligent of slaves, as Alfred was to Andrew, constantly on guard for his Massa's welfare. He advised him, with information gathered on the remarkable slave grapevine, as to plots of land that might soon be on the market because of a death in someone's family, or what farmers might need to sell their cotton early, for need of money. He organized the house niggers, and kept a weather eye on the field hands. He made friends with Micah and Tiara and helped ease Ephraim through his adolescent years. Because his Massa loved racing he took a keen interest in the track, and learned about blooded horses.

Easy of manner, quick of mind, he made friends with the trainers and stable hands, and passed any tips he heard along to his Massa. Cap'n Jack was fascinated by the tiny jockeys, almost all black, a few free, most slaves, and became good friends with one in particular, Monkey Simon.

Monkey Simon came from Senegal, in Africa, where a form of horseracing was a traditional sport among the people. He had grown up with horses, and by the time he was twelve, despite his hunchback, he had ridden in several races. He was captured by slave traders, transported to America, and fetched a high price on the block, because good jockeys were highly prized. He was purchased by Archibald Simon, a friend of John

Coffee's, and brought to Nashville. He soon made a considerable name for himself, and the crowds adored him, and cheered when he won, which was often. His tiny size, his hunchback, and his riding style of clutching the horse's neck caused people to say that he rode like a monkey.

It was a tradition that newborn slaves, or those from Africa, took their Massa's surname. The jockey from Senegal became known as "Monkey" Simon, and the nickname stayed with him for the rest of his life.

It was Monkey Simon who taught Cap'n Jack about Africa.

For all his education, Cap'n Jack had no knowledge of Africa other than as a large continent in an atlas. His parents had been born in America, and two of his grandparents were white. Very few of the slaves ever talked about Africa, either because they couldn't remember it or, in the case of the newer arrivals, because they could not speak English, and by the time they had learned it, Africa was only a distant memory.

Monkey Simon was different. He was a quick study at languages, and remembered Senegal very clearly, and loved the country of his birth. On those days when he had run a race and was feeling pleased with himself, he would sit with his horse in the stable, chuckling about his success, and remember his earlier boyhood triumphs on the track, before he was captured. Cap'n Jack loved to be with him then, because sometimes Monkey Simon would chant the songs of his people, or tell stories of the tribe. Because of his racing success, many personal foibles were indulged by his Massa, and, a devout Muslim, Monkey Simon was never given pig meat to eat. He prayed to the east five times a day, was scrupulously clean in his personal habits, and could recite long sections from the holy book, which he called the Koran. The aspect of his slavery that distressed him the most was that he would never be able to make the pilgrimage to Mecca, as all good Muslims strove to do, at least once in their lifetime.

He tried to explain to Cap'n Jack what it was like to live in a place where the color of a person's skin didn't matter. Most of the Senegalese were dark, like himself, but not all were jet black. Some had married lighter-skinned traders from other countries, and some, when the big ships came with their sails like clouds, had children by the white men who sailed them. All these offspring were part of the greater community. No man was judged by the color of his skin.

Cap'n Jack could not imagine such a blessed country. He dreamed of seeing Africa, of living in such a society, and would beg his friend to tell him more. But the nostalgia for his homeland became too painful for Monkey Simon, and instead he took up his banjo and sang songs he had written about the Massas, and the strange ways of the white men and their Missys.

Although racing was a man's sport, it was acceptable for "Missys," white women, to attend the meetings as spectators, and so the Cloverbottom Race Track became the center of social activity in Nashville. It was here that Andrew introduced James to many of the leading citizens of the town, and the men who would become James's friends, it was here that James had his first encounter with dueling, some years before he bought Cap'n Jack, and it was here that he met a young widow called Sarah McCullough.

John Coffee, who owned the track, was a big, burly man, who was conservative in all things except his passion for horses and his devotion to Andrew. Something of a feud had developed between Andrew, with his horse Truxton, and Captain Joseph Erwin, with his horse Ploughboy. The horses had been matched in a forfeit race, but Ploughboy went lame, and Erwin paid the forfeit. At a later rematch, Truxton had been injured in training, and both James and John Coffee advised Andrew to withdraw the horse. Andrew would not, because the race had personal relevance for him. He had been told that Erwin's son-in-law, Charles Dickerson, had made disparaging remarks about Rachel's marital status, repeating the old rumors about bigamy. Having no proof of the slander, Andrew had let it go unchallenged, but he longed to get his revenge on the track.

He went alone into Truxton's stable, nuzzled the horse, looked him in the eye, and spoke to him as he spoke to soldiers. Truxton won the race by sixty yards.

Andrew thought it was the end of the feud, but heard that Dickerson had slandered Rachel again. Eyes bright with rage, he asked John Overton and James to represent him.

James had never been a second in a duel before—had never seen a duel—and it thrilled him to the core. Proud that his new friend had chosen him, but nervous about what to do, he accompanied Overton to call on Dickerson, and they presented Andrew's challenge. It was accepted.

On a warm May morning, James and Overton went by carriage to the Hermitage, and watched Andrew say a tender farewell to Rachel. He did not tell his wife the purpose of his absence, but James was sure that Rachel knew. It was not the first duel that Andrew had fought, nor the first in Rachel's honor.

It had been agreed that the duel would take place in Kentucky, because Tennessee had laws against the practice. They traveled to Harrison's Mills on the Red River. Alfred rode on the box with the coachman.

James marveled at Andrew's calmness. He spent the journey discussing politics, Jefferson, the president, and Aaron Burr, who was to be tried for treason and defended by Henry Clay. James knew a little of the strange story of Burr, and hints that Andrew was somehow involved in his plot to declare the Southwest

114

independent of the United States, but Andrew would not be drawn on the subject. He respected and admired Burr, as a brilliant but wayward politician and a crack shot in a duel, but otherwise he laughed the matter aside.

"Aaron can't be all bad; he killed Hamilton," Andrew said, and teased Overton, who was English. "Personally, I liked Hamilton, but he was a monarchist and all for England. He even tried to persuade George Washington to take a crown."

Andrew's commentaries on the history of the country, the founding of it, and the already legendary figures who had created it were eternally fascinating to James. Andrew had an ability to put everything in perspective, and made James feel as if he were a part of things greater than himself. He began to think he would like to become involved in politics, if only in some small way.

Andrew thought in grander concepts. He was more concerned that Jefferson should take some action against Britain. The British Navy was constantly harrying the American fleet at sea, and had introduced the first of many embargoes against American trade with Europe.

"We must fight England again," he insisted. "I was not old enough to do much good in the last war." He meant the Revolution. "I pray the next comes before I get too old to fight."

That Andrew should be looking to the long-term future at all was astonishing to James, whose mind was filled with thoughts of the coming morning.

They passed a pleasant evening across the Kentucky line. Andrew regaled those at dinner with his thoughts on the state of the world, and no one guessed the true purpose of these strangers.

James had shared a room with Overton, who fell asleep within moments of getting into bed. James stayed awake, almost until dawn, his mind racing with ideas and forebodings. He could not imagine what it must feel like to go to bed knowing that this might be your last night on earth, but memories of his nights at Gorey Hill, before a battle with the British, came to him. He remembered the fear he felt then, and prayed that he would never know such a feeling again in his life. He wondered what he would do if he was ever challenged to a duel, and did not dare to consider his response.

Alfred woke them and his Massa at five the following morning. James was completely uncertain about what was expected of him.

"Just be there," Overton told him. "I'll do all the rest."

Andrew joined them, and said he was looking forward to a good breakfast, after they had attended to business.

They met at the arranged location, on the bank of the river, just after dawn. It was a pleasant place, a small grove surrounded by poplars, and James saw deer on the opposite bank. Mist lay on the river.

Andrew got out of the carriage, stretched his arms and went for a quick stroll, to exercise his muscles. Throughout the short drive, he had talked only of the future.

Dickerson was already there, with his second, Dr. Catlett. They tossed for position and Dickerson won, but the sun was hardly up, so it made little difference.

James held the box containing the two pistols, and the duelists took their pick.

Andrew and Dickerson paced to position, and Overton gave the order to fire.

James thought that nature must have arrested time. Everything seemed to happen so slowly.

He saw Dickerson raise his gun, slowly, and point it at Andrew, slowly.

116

James was sweating. Dickerson was known to be a crack shot. Would the man never fire?

Alfred, standing near James, stared at the scene impassively, but was filled with emotion. There was more than one man's future at stake, if only one man's life.

Andrew stood stock-still.

Dickerson fired.

Andrew stood still.

James almost cried out in joy and relief, but only Dickerson spoke.

"My God! Have I missed him?" he cried, and stumbled away from his position.

"To your mark, sir," Overton ordered.

Slowly, so very slowly, Dickerson returned to his mark, like a condemned man approaching the gallows.

Slowly, so very slowly, Andrew raised his gun and fired.

There was a click. The gun had misfired.

Slowly, so very slowly, Andrew reset, aimed, and fired again.

Slowly, so very slowly, Dickerson swayed to the ground.

Dr. Catlett ran to attend him. He lived for the rest of that day in agony, and died that night.

James and Alfred moved quickly to Andrew, and saw with horror that there was a hole in Andrew's jacket, just below his heart, and blood all over his boots.

"I think he pinked me," Andrew said, his face contorted in pain.

They got him to a surgeon, who took out the bullet and patched him up. They got him home and put him to bed. Rachel nursed him, and when she could not, Alfred was always there. He did not leave his Massa's room for a month. When Andrew recovered, he gave orders that Alfred was to be moved from the slave quarters to a bedroom next to his own in the main house.

117

Rachel fell to her knees and gave thanks to God for her husband's deliverance, but she prayed for the dead man's wife as well.

"God have pity on her," Rachel begged. "And on her poor child."

Mrs. Dickerson had been six months pregnant when Andrew killed her husband.

13

James attended Andrew at three other duels after that, but none had the same impact on him as the first because none of the others was fatal. It was enough to satisfy the honor of both antagonists that they had accepted the challenge and presented themselves, and they simply fired their guns in the air. On two occasions, Andrew got drunk with his opponent afterward, and they would end the evening slapping each other on the back and laughing about their quarrel, but this never happened in the case of those who had slandered his wife.

Andrew got drunk often in the early days of his friendship with James, in the frustrating years of the embargo. Andrew could not bear inactivity or indecision. He longed for a chance to trounce the British, he longed to test his skill on a real battlefield, and the protracted negotiations among America, Britain, and France frustrated him.

"Let's hit 'em, and hit 'em hard," he cried, but James was never quite sure whom he wanted to hit, for Jefferson was included in his excoriation. James began to think there might be truth to the stories that Andrew had helped Aaron Burr in his wild plans to form a breakaway country centered in the west, if only to provoke a war. For Andrew longed for war.

Sometimes he would arrive at James's house or, if it

was early enough in the day, at the store, his speech slurred, and swaying on his feet. James would put him to bed to sleep it off, or send Ephraim with a message to the Hermitage. Then Alfred would come, hoist his inert Massa over his shoulders, as gently as a mother with a babe, and take him home in the gig.

Andrew was only a little drunk on the day he introduced James to his friends the Polks. They were at the racetrack, and Andrew's mare, Virginia, had won a splendid race and earned a handsome purse. Andrew was in an expansive mood, and kept introducing everybody to everyone, as though they had never met.

James already knew the Polks, who were a well-established family in the district, and did business with him at his store. He did not know the young woman who accompanied them that day, and who wore the black of mourning.

Sarah McCullough, born Sarah Moore, was from one of the country's oldest families. Her grandfather had founded the vast Moorfields estate, and her ancestry included Sir John Moore, who had been the Royal Governor of South Carolina in the early days of the colony. The family was of hardy, Scottish stock, and Sarah, born to wealth, was raised to be self-reliant and self-sufficient.

"Never ask anyone to do for you what you cannot do yourself," her father told her.

She could cook and clean and tend the vegetable garden. She was expert with horses, and a fair shot with a gun. She could plan elaborate menus with economy, and was a gracious hostess. She spoke French fluently, and her education had included the classics. She was a caring nurse, and on more than one occasion helped the slave women through difficult births.

She was also beautiful. An awkward gangly girl, and a considerable tomboy able to hold her own against her cheerful, pugnacious brothers, she lost her teenage

119

angularity, and blossomed into one of the most attractive women in the county, with silky, chestnut hair, and limpid amber eyes.

By the time she was seventeen, she had her choice of many suitors, and settled for a handsome, adventurous young man, Samuel McCullough, who came from good family and shared Sarah's appetite for adventure. His parents gave them a pretty house on good land, and several slaves, and Sarah's doting father provided her with a bountiful dowry. It was a good and happy marriage, and Sarah settled contentedly to her new life, though she and Samuel talked frequently of moving west, to the new territories, to lead the simple, rustic life of pioneers. When Sarah became pregnant, Samuel attended her with affection, and fussed over her, and bought her pretty gifts.

But a young slave girl on the property, Angel, who some said had the gift of second sight, told Sarah the news almost before she knew it herself.

"You's gwine have a baby, Missy," Angel said, and Sarah was astonished that Angel was right, and took it to be a good omen.

She became ill during her pregnancy, and the distraught Samuel rode to town, to find a physician. There had been heavy rain, and the rivers were swollen. Samuel urged his horse across a fast-flowing creek, but the animal lost its footing and master and horse were swept away.

Sarah's grief was profound, and for weeks she blamed herself for her husband's death. She took to her room and her Bible, and family friends worried for her mental state. Her father spoke to her, sharply but kindly.

"It is a tragedy," he said, "but it is not the end of the world. You must think of your own future, and the child."

Sarah, raised to an understanding that death is a fact of life, took her father's words to heart. To waste her life grieving for Samuel was an insult to his memory

120

and could prove to be a tragic misfortune for his baby, who would need a father. Her unborn child became her reason for living, proof of her husband's love and immortality. Through the child, Samuel would live forever. She delivered a healthy baby girl, and named her Elizabeth, after the mother of John the Baptist, who had been visited by angels, and who was friend to the mother of Jesus. Faced with the glory of procreation, Sarah's soul, like Elizabeth's and Mary's before her, magnified the Lord.

But she could not live where she was, for the house and everything about her was haunted by the ghost of Samuel. She moved in with her family, but was not happy. She began to think that she needed to move away from everything she had known, to cut all the links with Samuel and the past, and create a new life, for herself and for Elizabeth. Her father's good friend Thomas Polk offered Sarah and her child the hospitality of his home in Nashville. Sarah's father was against the idea, for he thought that Tennessee was still the wild and dangerous frontier, but Sarah was intrigued by the challenge. She spoke to the prescient Angel.

"Happen you gwine meet a new man dere, Missy," Angel said.

Sarah persuaded herself that Angel was right. The men of the settled states bored her—they were too conscious of her money and her position, and their own ambition—and, still young, she yearned for some of the adventures she and Samuel had planned.

She was nineteen when she accepted the Polks' kind offer, and taking only Angel with her as a friend and a mammy for Elizabeth, she set off for the frontier.

She settled to the life as if she had been born to it. She loved living so close to the edge of civilization, and endured its privations with grace and a sense of humor. She stayed in mourning for Samuel for the requisite twelve months, but toward the end of the year, she

121

began to venture out into society, anxious to enjoy herself to the full. Her first outing was on a Saturday. She went with the Polks to the Cloverbottom Race Track, enjoyed the fun of the meet, was amused by the slighly drunken owner of the horse that had won the biggest purse, and was introduced to a handsome and successful Irishman, who was some ten years older than herself.

James, conscious of her widow's weeds, tipped his hat to the lovely young woman and welcomed her to Nashville. He could hardly take his eyes off her. Her grace and composure reminded him of Rachel, and the twinkle in her eyes suggested, as with Rachel, that there was more, something wild and capricious, beneath her calm exterior.

He talked of her all the way home, to Cap'n Jack, and when he got home he talked of her to Eleanor and to Sara, and to anyone else who would listen. She was just like Rachel, he told them. His family breathed a collective sigh of relief. At last, they thought, Jamie had met his bride.

But James, conscious of her mourning period, did not press his interest.

It made Eleanor cross.

"For heaven's sake, Jamie," she snapped, "she is almost out of the mourning. And anyway, these things mean nothing here."

"It is not polite to call on her," James said, dreaming of Sarah.

"Well, if you don't someone else will," Eleanor said. "Or do you need lessons in the etiquette of the heart?"

Eleanor's barb had struck a bull's-eye. James, who could be the most dazzling and charming seducer of women with whom he did not envisage any long-standing relationship, was naive in the face of love. He dreamed of Sarah by night, and mooned about her by day, but he had no idea how to tell her of his feelings, and was nervous in case she might reject him.

Sarah was not nearly so coy. She made inquiries about James, and learned of his excellent character and obvious eligibility. She called at the store on small errands, and it amused her that he, although unfailingly charming to her, was always a little tongue-tied in her presence. She made it her business to befriend his sisters Eleanor and Sara, who thought her splendid. They invited her to a quilting party, and as they sat around the frame creating the colorful comforter, they told her of James's interest, and laughed at his shy reserve.

Sarah took matters into her own hands. If he would not come to her, she would go to him.

She talked to Cap'n Jack.

Cap'n Jack was eager to see his Massa married and with a family. The sooner James was settled, the sooner he might decide to fulfill his promise, and free his slave. He was completely sympathetic to Sarah's cause, because she was a sympathetic woman. Of the many that his Massa might choose, Cap'n Jack hoped it would be this one, for Sarah made him feel like an equal, despite the vast gulf between them, and he could not imagine her lying to him, or treating him, or any of the slaves, badly. Angel, Sarah's maid, agreed with this view of her Missy.

"If'n I's gotta be a wit' someone," she said, "druther be wit' her."

It was James's habit and pleasure to ride on Sunday mornings, after church, to inspect his property. Away from the cotton fields, it was lovely land, with several brooks and many shady trees. It pleased James's soul to ride through what was his, to breathe the softly scented air, and delight in nature.

"You will never amount to anything."

123

He had amounted to something, and would amount to much more yet. He had proved his father wrong, and if it was not yet enough, already it was considerable.

It was a warm and sunny day. Whippoorwills sang in the trees. Squirrels darted across the branches. Possums washed themselves at a spring, and flocks of tiny quail chased through the grass.

He saw the horse first, tethered to a sapling. Nearby there was a gig, and a picnic basket on the seat. He heard a small cry of alarm, and a tiny black woman ran to her mistress and snatched a baby from her breast.

He saw Sarah, who looked at him and stood, as if surprised. But she ignored, for a moment, Angel's pleas to make herself decent.

Without any sense of urgency, Sarah adjusted her bodice and blouse to cover her breast, but not before she was sure James had seen her fullness, the rounded, alabaster flesh and the rosy nipple. James, who prided himself on being a gentleman, hesitated quite a long time before politely averting his eyes.

He did not see Cap'n Jack crouched in a nearby bush, grinning happily at the success of his plot with Sarah. Nor did Cap'n Jack feel the need to look away from the seminakedness of the woman he hardly knew.

"Why, sir, you startled me," Sarah said, a provocative smile dancing at the corners of her lips.

"My most humble apologies," James responded, as politely. "I shall withdraw."

"There is no need," Sarah said, determined to detain him. "I think I have nothing to fear from you."

"Nothing at all," James agreed, not intending to go.

"It's such a pretty spot, and such a pretty day, we came for a picnic," Sarah said. "Should you care to join me?"

James nodded that he would, and as he dismounted, he thought he saw Cap'n Jack in the distance, walking

124

toward him. A tiny trace of suspicion tickled at his sense of humor.

"How did you know about this place?" He came to Sarah and made himself comfortable on the grass beside her. "It is private land."

Sarah's eyes were sparkling, teasing him.

"Should I leave?" she wondered.

"Oh, no," James said. "We have my permission to be here. It is my land."

Cap'n Jack came down the path and went to the gig. He organized lunch from the picnic hamper and set it before them. No one made any reference to his being there, or expressed any surprise at his presence. James leaned back against the tree, at peace with the world. He knew he had been most exquisitely conned, and didn't mind at all.

They passed a pleasant lunch, and found conversation easy between them. Cap'n Jack chatted with Angel, a small distance away, and Sarah nursed Elizabeth. James could not help but think of his afternoons with Rachel, and the better he got to know Sarah, the more she reminded him of Rachel.

The time came when Sarah needed to go into the bushes, and Angel was dozing, so James took Elizabeth, and held the child while her mother was absent. Elizabeth gurgled and chuckled and reached up to grab James's whiskers, and was perfectly happy in his arms. Later, when Sarah changed Elizabeth's linen, James watched the simple domesticity, and yearned for it in his life.

Toward sunset, when the mosquitoes came out, they realized they had talked too long, and made a hasty departure. It was five miles to the Polk residence, and Sarah should be home before dark. Cap'n Jack went back to the house, and James drove the gig, his horse hitched to it, pointing out the parameters of his land to Sarah, as if assuring her of his financial eligibility. They

125

arranged to attend church together the following Sunday, and to picnic again, at the same spot.

They saw each other every Sunday of the summer after that, and when her period of mourning was over, James began calling on her at her home. His suit received the full approval of the Polks, who wrote to Sarah's father, informing him of their hopes for a union between his daughter and this splendid bachelor.

Mr. Moore came to visit his daughter, and his heart was touched by what he found. The dull grief that had enshrouded Sarah was cast aside with the black dress and veil. Now his daughter was herself again, as she had been in the happier days of her life. She still thought fondly of her late husband, but looked forward eagerly to her next.

All of James's many friends indicated their approval of the union, and voiced their confidence in James. Mr. Moore questioned James most carefully, and if he found a certain lack of flamboyance in his prospective son-in-law, that only added luster to him, for Mr. Moore was concerned that Sarah should make a solid and reliable marriage rather than a spectacular one. There was enough flamboyance, enough cavalier behavior, in the other men of the frontier, with Andrew Jackson as the most grandiose of all, and while Mr. Moore was delighted by Andrew's company, he was pleased that Sarah had chosen a quieter man.

Before Mr. Moore left Nashville, he had given his blessing to James, who then formally proposed to Sarah, and she, as gravely, accepted. They had a party at the new Nashville Inn, and danced until dawn, and were happy. Perhaps because Samuel had been the first love of Sarah's life, she had spent her youthful romance in that love, and what she felt for James was deeper, more secure, and less intense. Sarah was the first true reciprocated love of James's life, but he found her when he was older, and had lost the foolishness of youth.

126

They approached each other and their marriage as adults, delighting in each other, but with a deep concern to lay the foundations for a lifelong partnership. Their great gift was laughter. James's Irish sense of humor touched some Celtic chord in Sarah, and others regarded them enviously, for their heads were always together, and their eyes were always smiling. They didn't seem to need anybody but each other, although they never excluded anyone else from their company.

Because of the confusion between Sarah, his fiancée, and Sara, his sister, the family began calling their new relation Sally, and it pleased her, because it made her feel young.

Sally, who had been Sarah, returned to South Carolina to visit her many relations, to put her affairs in order, and to show Elizabeth to her aunts and uncles and grandparents. She went to Baltimore and Philadelphia to buy her trousseau, and she met James's relatives there, who welcomed her into the family. She returned to Nashville the following spring, and in October, James Jackson married Sally Moore McCullough in a simple ceremony attended by two hundred friends and relations.

Andrew Jackson was James's best man.

Friends loaned them a small house not far from town so that they might be alone, apart from several slaves, for the first few days of their marriage. They drove there late on their wedding night, Cap'n Jack and other slaves riding beside them with lanterns. At the house, Angel had made ready for her Missy and new Massa. A supper was laid on the table, and candles lighted the scene. James carried Sally over the threshold, and once the couple were comfortable the slaves drifted away to the kitchen, and made their own party.

Sally went to the bedroom first, and made herself ready. James undressed in another room, and came to her after a decent interval. He was oddly nervous. He

127

had no doubt of his ability in the marriage bed, but he did not want to disappoint his bride, who had been married before. She had talked to him of Samuel, and he understood her passion for him, but he was anxious to prove himself the better man.

Sally was standing by the window staring out at the room. She looked ravishing in oyster silk, with her hair loose. James came to her, put his hands gently on her shoulders, kissed her elegant neck, and swore that he would do everything in his power to make her happy. She turned and her eyes told him that she believed him, and she swore a similar vow.

He bent to her and they kissed, and her mouth seemed to melt around his tongue. He picked her up and carried her to the bed, laid her down and lay beside her, stroking her, running his hands through her hair, and did not want his mouth ever to be separated from hers. He freed her breasts, and could not resist a whispered joke, that these were the reason that he had fallen in love with her. To his relief, Sally laughed, and told him that was why she had shown herself so boldly. The laughter was the key that unlocked James's passion. He buried his face in her breasts and explored her body with his hands and his tongue. With gentle hints and subtle persuasion, all modified by smiles and giggles, Sally guided him to those places that pleased her, and was expert enough in the ways of men to know what he needed.

When James entered her, she locked him to her as if she would never let him go, and called out his power and her surrender. James was filled with a sense of his own masculinity, and her soft and yielding capitulation to him made him feel, at his climax, the most sublime pleasure of his life.

They slept very little that night, because he could not get his fill of her. He no longer cared if he was a better lover than Samuel; he felt no sense of competition with the dead, because he, James, was living, and her master, and she had no alternative but him, now. When she whispered her need for his baby, he shared the longing, and told her that the seed he gave her was the seed of life.

The fact that he did not have to compete with anyone, anymore, for anything, freed him from restraint, freed him from inhibition, and while his conscious mind believed that she was giving herself, his soul knew better. He was engulfed by her.

They spent their honeymoon in idyllic circumstances. The house was a charming, well-appointed log cabin, set among tall trees. The crisp chill weather and the riotous colors of autumn filled their senses in the day, and the warmth and companionship of the marriage bed, and their lack of coy reserve, made the nights endlessly delightful. There were very few problems between them, and any that arose were solved with laughter, which remained the constant fixture of their marriage. Still they each kept a part of themselves closed from the other, believing that they had a lifetime to discover those things, and did not want to become overly familiar too soon.

After two weeks they returned to Nashville, and began the business of building their family.

A year later, Sally gave birth to a daughter, who was named Mary, as the biblical Mary had been the friend of Elizabeth. James was cock-a-hoop on the day Mary came into the world, and bought endless rounds of drinks for his friends at the inn, who ribbed him gently. Making a baby wasn't so difficult, they told him. Most men could do it. Even niggers could do that.

When he came in to see Mary for the first time, his heart filled with love for her. He could not believe that he had made this tiny, perfect thing. He held her in his arms, and sat in a chair by the window, and told her stories of how she was blessed by the fairies and leprechauns. Mary seemed to believe him, and snuggled contentedly into her father's arms.

James looked at Sally, and smiled, and thanked her.

"Are you disappointed she isn't a boy?" Sally asked him, for she had been worried. Like all the women of the frontier, she knew sons were critical to the family's survival, and James was obsessed by family.

James laughed and said no, but examined his conscience. In truth, he had felt a mild twinge of disappointment, but had shrugged it aside. When he held Mary in his arms, not even the memory of that disappointment remained, but Sally's question had revived it.

"No," he said again, wanting to convince her that he wasn't lying. "She is beautiful."

Then he gave Sally his most impish smile.

"And anyway, she's just the first," he grinned. "We can always keep trying."

They tried very hard, but were not successful in their efforts at first. Martha was born the following year, and Mary Ellen two years after that.

Everyone was kind, friends and relations, but they all longed for a boy, and James began to understand Andrew's obsessive need for sons. He consoled himself with the thought that at least he and Sally could produce children, while Andrew and Rachel could not.

This time James's prayers were answered. Sally delivered a son, a strapping, chubby boy, who was as healthy as anyone could wish.

The arrival of his son had an extraordinary effect on James. He held the boy, and stared at him, and, against the strong advice of Eleanor and Sara, took him outside into the warm night. He sat with his son for an hour and dreamed of the future.

He had ensured the succession of his family. His son would have everything that he did not. He would grow up surrounded by love, as James had not, and flourish and be a fine man, and inherit his father's estate, as James had not.

They would be friends, James swore to it, and while he would give his son the discipline a man needed to survive in the world, and to prosper, he would always know that he occupied first place in his father's heart. He would be honest and reliable and adventurous. He would be well provided for, he would want for nothing, but he would be given an appreciation of the value of money and the glory of labor. He would own slaves, but would be taught respect for the dignity of man. He would be given a sense of independence, and the will to expand and develop what James had created. He could be anything he wanted to be, a farmer or a general, or both, like Andrew, but he would be a son any man could be proud of, and always, he would be loved.

James felt the salt sting of tears in his eyes. He returned his son to his women, and went and got drunk with his friends at the inn.

The son came to be known as A.J., to avoid confusion with his illustrious godfather, but that was not his name. As if to give him a sense of the majesty of which he was capable, of the heroism that was his patrimony, through his father's dearest friend, as if to remind the boy always of the man James wanted him to emulate, he was christened Andrew Jackson Jackson.

Because always, there was Andrew.

14

Andrew Jackson, orphaned himself as a youth, gathered young men unto him, just as he gathered sons who were not his own. He awoke the limitless horizons of the boy in all of them. He put his great, embracing arms around them and swept them off to realms of extraordinary adventure.

An extravagant Pied Piper, his embrace was extensive and undiscriminating. Those who were prepared to follow his path were given spectacular rewards of excitement; the others simply fell by the wayside, unmourned and unnoticed by Andrew. Those who were in his way, he tried to eliminate, honorably, through duel or the courts, or by the stinging whiplash of his eloquent invective. He demanded discipline, obedience, and loyalty from his apostles, but encouraged them to explore the outer limits of their own individuality.

"He rides a streak of lightning."

James could never remember which of Andrew's entourage said that, but, oh, it was true.

So Andrew Jackson, the restless, roving visionary, had gathered James the merchant to him, and had shown him the places of legends, of chivalry and honor and breathless daring. To the misty shores of Avalon, where dedicated knights created the noble vision of Camelot, and quested the Holy Grail, and to the plains of Olympus, where fearless warriors challenged the gods. And standing in unquestioning support of the man who would be king was the flawless Rachel, the loving woman and wife, who represented all that was good on earth.

What James could not know was that he did not stand as high in his mentor's firmament as Andrew did in his.

When John Coffee and Andrew purchased the prizewinning horse Pacolet, they decided to offer shares in the animal to their loyal friends, those who could afford it, as tokens of their esteem. The first five shares were easily allotted, but they debated the sixth.

"Why not James?" John Coffee said. "He can afford it."

"Which James?" Andrew asked. His mind was elsewhere, and he knew several men called James.

"James Jackson," John Coffee laughed. "The merchant."

"Oh, yes," Andrew agreed. "Let's give the book-keeper a share."

Andrew's parents had migrated from Ireland, and made an arduous trek from Pennsylvania to North Carolina. They settled on an adequate piece of land, and began clearing their property. It was a hard life, and Andrew's father strained himself grubbing tree stumps, and died in agony. A few days later, his mother gave birth to her third son, and he was called Andrew in memory of his dead father.

The widowed mother raised her son according to the creed of Sparta.

"My door is always open to brave men, and perpetually closed to cowards."

Young Andrew adored his mother and took her lessons to heart. Gifted with a fearless bravery, a passion for the use of language, and a reckless disregard for his own physical well-being, he had a hot temper and an unshakable conviction of his own destiny. He was born to be a leader of men.

His Irish blood gave him a hatred of the British, and at the onset of the American Revolution he offered his services to his uncle, who had formed a small band of militia. At the age of thirteen, he was made a messenger, given a horse and a pistol, and conducted himself with complete disregard for his own safety. After an unsuccessful foray against British dragoons, Andrew and some others took refuge in a house, but were found by the enemy. Andrew resisted his arrest and received a blow to his head from an officer's sword, a bloody gash that cut to the bone, and he carried the scar of it for the rest of his days.

The death of his mother when he was fifteen devastated Andrew, but impelled him to live up to the remarkable standards of masculine behavior that she had set. At the end of the war he received a small inheritance from an uncle in Ireland, and he promptly squandered the money in a year of high living in Charleston, gambling, wenching, and cockfighting. He was broke and alone in the world, his only talents his quick mind, his gift of oratory, and an expert knowledge of horses. Relatives took him in and sent him to school, where he studied law. At the age of twenty he was made an attorney, attached to a traveling court. He found his way to Tennessee, and the reckless frontier living suited his temperament exactly. He settled in Nashville, practiced law, involved himself in politics, fought Indian marauders, and fell in love with Rachel Robards.

He also made the first of several fortunes. He accepted land, valued at ten cents an acre, in payment of fees, and with the rush of settlers to the district, within three years the price of that same land had risen to five dollars an acre.

The frontier adored him, a rollicking, roistering, gambling, dueling, mischievous fellow, who argued successfully for Tennessee's admission to the Union, and became, by popular vote, the state's first member of the House of Representatives. In Philadelphia, which was then the capital, he criticized George Washington, was the bane of the financial committees, and became fast friends with Aaron Burr. At the end of his term he was elected to the Senate, but he was a man of action, not negotiation, and he quit the upper house to return to Nashville and his beloved Rachel. His grateful state appointed him to the Superior Court.

He was a tough and respected judge, dedicated to rights of the individual against the state. He despised bureaucracy, he despised the banks who could hold an honest man in bondage, and he believed implicitly in the manifest destiny of the white man to inherit the land of America, for it was divinely ordained. His attitude toward the original inhabitants of the country was disparaging.

"They are fickle, and will claim any and everything," he told James. "The treachery in their character justifies our never having faith in them. A few gifts, a few bribes, to the chiefs and to the interpreters, will gain anything that should be ours."

Yet he was ambivalent about them. He saw them as the sons of Cain, who had forfeited their right to God's grace, but he admired them as mighty warriors, worthy foes to his superior skill.

There was another contradiction that puzzled James. For all Andrew's disregard for the rights of the Indians to their land, he was kind and generous to individuals.

"They are children," he said. "They need the strong, guiding hand of a father who knows what is best for them."

Later, when the war that Andrew longed for came, when John Coffee's men had destroyed the village of Talluhatchee and killed two hundred braves, they brought Andrew a little Creek boy, whose parents were dead. The women would not look after him. Andrew took the boy to his heart, called him Lincoyen, sent him to Rachel, his new mother, and made him part of the family. He had found another son.

Andrew's real wrath was directed toward weak white men, especially those who tried to achieve by politics what they were afraid to achieve in honest battle. Most of all, he despised the increasing encroachment of government into the lives of the pioneers, the true sons of the soil.

He loved Nashville and was bored by it. He found quarrels where he could, and defended his, and his wife's, honor against the merest slight. He ignored weak men, and challenged those strong men who were at variance with him.

He longed to prove himself in war, and despised the

135

tyranny of peace. His dearest ambition was to avenge his mother's death. Elizabeth Jackson had died of the plague, but Andrew blamed the British, and the intolerable circumstances brought about by the Revolutionary War.

When his old friend Aaron Burr proposed a wild scheme to persuade the British to aid him in a rebellion that would free the Mississippi Valley, or Florida, or anywhere, from the governance of, or alliance with, the United States, and to make himself ruler of that new country, Andrew was ready to listen.

But he gave a cautious reponse. He encouraged Burr, but kept his options open. Perhaps he believed that if Burr succeeded, there would be war, and he would fight valiantly for his country against his old friend. Perhaps he believed in Burr's vision, but detested Burr's readiness to parlay with Britain. Perhaps he was simply humoring his old friend to explore the limits of himself.

Burr failed. He was tried for treason and eventually acquitted, against the strong influence of Thomas Jefferson, but was forced into exile. Although Andrew was never directly implicated in Burr's plot, the taint of it stayed with him for some years, and turned many in Washington against him.

Andrew languished in Nashville, gathered about him like-minded fellows, befriended James Jackson, and waited impatiently for his day, which he believed must come, for it was his destiny.

15

"There is to be war," James told Sally.

Sally nodded.

"I suppose it was inevitable," she said. "And will you fight?"

James shook his head.

136

"Andrew has other plans for me."

Sally closed her eyes, and said a silent prayer of thanks. She had lost one husband already, and did not want to lose another. For the first time since she had known him, she blessed Andrew Jackson.

Jefferson was gone. Madison, the last of the Founding Fathers, was president. The economies of the northern and eastern states were in tatters. As predicted by Andrew, Jefferson's foreign policies toward the British and the French had brought the country to its knees. The protracted negotiations with the British had produced nothing. Still the country expanded. The Spanish, and several Spanish colonies, had revolted against Napoleon, and Florida had declared itself independent. Madison, unsure and uncertain of himself in other matters, annexed the territory as part of the district of New Orleans, and admitted Louisiana to the Union. The New England states, already staring at bankruptcy, threatened to rebel. More slave states would reduce their influence, and would dilute the original Union and its constitution. At loggerheads with Madison, they wanted peace with Britain and the chance to restore their trade. Foolishly advised as to Britain's position, encouraged by the Spanish revolt against the French, and to placate New England, Madison lifted the embargo on trade with France.

The British blockaded the American ports, an American naval vessel opened fire on a British ship, and the southern war hawks in the government, led by Henry Clay and William Crawford, and many throughout the land, pressed Madison to declare war on Britain. The immediate and long-desired prize was the British territory of Canada, the other America, which many, like Andrew, believed was part of the God-given whole.

Andrew was in a quandary. He despised Madison as a weak man, but approved of the war. Immediately, he volunteered himself and a militia division of two thou-

137

sand five hundred men, vowing to take Quebec. His offer was noted and ignored.

"It is because of my friendship with Aaron Burr," he told James bitterly. "They will make me pay for it."

Andrew had other reasons for despising Madison. The president had recently rechartered the national bank of the United States, and Andrew was livid with rage. The bank was a monster, the tool of government, whose octopus tentacles spread throughout the land, discouraging competition and issuing the false god of paper.

"Specie, cash money, is the one true currency," he roared. "All else is fraudulent paper."

He had reasons for his bitterness. He had frequently been the victim of promissory notes whose issuers failed to deliver what the paper promised, and he had lost more than one fortune because of it. Moreover, he was a resolute champion of the sovereignty of the individual states and believed that a central bank, the lapdog of the federal government, would eventually destroy their financial independence, and make the states entirely reliant on Washington.

Now, with the country at war, Andrew, like a champion stallion ready for the race, chafed at the bit. The Hermitage became his war room, and he called in all the young men he had trained and encouraged to be ready for this moment: Davy Crockett, the frontiersman, John Coffee, the loyal and fearless lieutenant, and young Sam Houston, an odd and eccentric youth who had abandoned his white family and lived tribally, with the Creek. Sam could speak three Indian languages fluently, knew all the ways and customs, was a frequent drunk, and was a daring, unconventional warrior. Andrew adored him.

James was there too. They sat around the table for hours on end, debating the news, railing against the disastrous conduct of the war, drowning in liquor their fury at the loss of Detroit without a single shot, and venting in impotent anger their frustration that they were not part of it.

Unknown to any of them, they had an unlikely ally to their cause, the Shawnee chief Tecumseh, which meant Crouching Panther.

The American expeditions into Canada were abject failures. The New Englanders, who had never wanted war, were ready to sue for peace. The tiny American army and smaller navy were overextended, facing three battlefronts—the north, the south in Florida, and the Gulf Coast, centered on New Orleans, which was vulnerable to attack from the British possessions in the Caribbean.

In the West, the charismatic Tecumseh was able to do what few other Indians had done, and gathered the tribes into a common cause against the white man. He had a vision of a great confederation of the Indian people which would extend from the northern lakes to the southern gulf, and would annihilate the whites. Encouraged by British agents to believe they would side with him against the Americans, Tecumseh and his devoted followers waged a war of attrition on the settlements of Ohio and the Mississippi.

Faced with disaster on all sides, the War Office finally accepted Andrew's offer, if he, in turn, would accept a subordinate command under General Wilkinson, in New Orleans. Andrew ranted and raved, but any action was better than no action, so he agreed. Perhaps as a sop, he was given the rank of major general.

Jubilation swept the Hermitage war room. Within two days they had raised the full complement of twenty-five hundred men, and made preparations to leave for New Orleans.

"But what can I do?" James said, rather plaintively, because he was feeling left out. He had thought of offering to enlist, but considered it better he stay with Sally, who was pregnant.

139

Andrew looked at him as if he had forgotten who he was, and then assumed his most benign and confidential manner.

"You have a marvelously important job to do here," he told James. "You must look after Rachel, who will be bathed in tears at my departure."

It was a job that suited James exactly, but Andrew had something else for him. Generous to a fault, he was perpetually short of money. He asked for a loan from James, to equip and uniform his men, and feed them, until funds arrived from Washington.

He needed five thousand dollars. James was only too happy to agree, thinking that he was making a magnificent contribution to the war effort, if only by proxy.

Besides, all Andrew had to do was ask. All he ever had to do was ask, and James would have given him the moon.

Andrew's division set off for New Orleans in the middle of the worst winter anyone could remember.

General Wilkinson wanted Andrew's men, but not Andrew. He ordered them to make camp at Natchez, to await developments. This made sense to Andrew for it would position his unit to respond to any British invasion along the coast, not just at New Orleans. Then an order arrived from the War Office ordering Andrew to disband his men and return to Nashville.

Andrew understood the ploy immediately. Without funds to feed his men, they would be easy recruits for Wilkinson. He wrote accepting the dismissal of his services, but insisted that he would return his men to their homes at his own expense.

The bad weather got worse, but Andrew triumphed. He led his men on an impossible journey through the snow and bitter cold, cajoling, urging, encouraging, careless of his own comfort, and he became the stuff of legend. His soldiers revered him for it, called him tougher than hickory, and because he was their father, he became known to them, and to the country, as Old Hickory.

On their return to Nashville, tattered and torn, cold and weary, reduced to eating horseflesh, never having fired a shot in anger, they were feted as heroes and showered with honors.

James glowed with pride and patriotism. Under the circumstances he could not possibly ask for the return of his loan, for it was his money that had sustained the gallant soldiers through their arduous trek.

Nor could he refuse Andrew another loan, for another expedition, this time against the Creek, in Alabama.

Tecumseh—Crouching Panther—had inspired many of the younger braves throughout the country, and if many rejected his calls for violence, several listened. A half-breed, William Weatherford, whose father laid claim to being the principal Creek chief, organized a war party, and attacked and destroyed the settlement at Fort Mims in southern Alabama. Encouraged by this success, other Creek had joined him, and now much of Alabama was under threat.

The news came to Andrew on his sickbed. He had been wounded by Thomas Benton and his brother Jesse, after a silly misunderstanding that had led to a duel between Jesse and Billy Carroll, Andrew's brigade inspector. Andrew had no part in it, and, wanting to keep his nose clean with Washington, had discouraged the antagonists, but to no avail. The duel was fought with Jesse winning the toss. He fired first but missed, and panicked, and turned his back on Billy Carroll, who promptly shot him in the rump.

Tennessee thought Jesse's discomfort was a grand joke, but Tom Benton, who had been a favorite of Andrew's, took his brother's side. He accused Andrew of inciting the duel, and Andrew had threatened to horsewhip him. It all came to a head at the Nashville

141

Inn when Thomas and Jesse, with some others, attacked Andrew. John Coffee, guns blazing, put them to flight, but Andrew was severely wounded, shot twice in the arm, and the doctors recommended amputation.

"I will keep my arm," Andrew said.

Rachel and Alfred nursed him, but none of their ministrations succeeded as well as the news that two hundred and fifty whites had been massacred at Fort Mims, and Weatherford was marching north, to other white settlements.

"By the eternal, these people must be saved," he announced, and Tennessee agreed.

Andrew got up from his bed and made ready for war. The governor of Tennessee commissioned a punitive expedition, and John Coffee formed the cavalry.

The day had come. This was Andrew's time.

He borrowed more money from James, against the promise of repayment as soon as he had Treasury funds, and again, James gave it willingly.

All Andrew had to do was ask.

James didn't tell anyone but Sally about the loan, because when he told her, she was angry. Andrew had often borrowed small sums from James and never repaid them. He still owed five thousand from the Natchez adventure. Now there was more.

It was the first sustained argument of their marriage, for James could not make her see his position, nor could he tell her with any truth what his position was. The loans made him feel part of the war, part of the adventure, but obviated any risk, except the financial one which he could well afford. Until this time, he had shared all his money dealings with Sally, but now he began to close this part of his life to her, and kept his business to himself.

The Creek War, as it came to be called, was a triumph for Andrew, and all who served him loyally. Sam Houston used his formidable knowledge of the Creek and their customs to send spies to the Indians, and encouraged those who had not fought to join with Old Hickory, who was undefeatable. Cherokee and Chickasaw, Choctaw and some Creek joined with Andrew. The spies reported Weatherford's numbers and intentions. Davy Crockett led a small band of men in forays of lightning speed and ferocity, aided by the shock of surprise, which all reinforced the concept of Andrew's invincibility. It was winter again, and the Creek were poorly supplied. Armed only with bows and arrows, a few muskets, and a desperate faith in their cause, they soon fell to the greater numbers and artillery of the army that they faced.

Andrew's obstacles were not all of Indian invention, but all added to his reputation. Four times, his poorly fed, poorly uniformed, and poorly supplied troops rebelled, and each time Andrew suppressed the mutiny by the sheer force of his personality and his iron determination. Still weak from loss of blood, wracked with dysentery, and living on acorns and horseflesh, he would not ask men to endure anything he would not suffer himself.

He thought of the men as his children, and called them such. In the case of Private John Woods, he sacrificed one of his children. Woods was condemned to death for refusing to obey a disciplinary order. Andrew believed he was part of a previous mutiny, but Woods, who was seventeen, had only recently taken his brother's place in the ranks. Militiamen, irregular volunteers, were seldom put to death, no matter how grave their offense, and Andrew had the power to reduce the sentence, but, like Abraham sacrificing Isaac, he chose not to do so, and no divine power stayed his hand.

Woods was duly executed by firing squad.

There was little talk of mutiny after that, and his men came to respect Andrew as never before.

Still he stared at disaster. After Andrew had won two

small victories, some Creek sued for peace, and Governor Blount of Tennessee was prepared to parlay. The increasing disaster that was the war against the British had soured him on military conquest, but Andrew would not accept his orders to abandon his base and return to Nashville. In a passionate letter to Blount he insisted that the frontier would never be peaceful until this insurrection was put down, and demanded more men. His obstinacy, and the War Office, which was desperate for any success, no matter how small, persuaded Blount, and Andrew marched on with five thousand extra troops.

After several minor battles he surrounded the Creek stronghold at Horseshoe Bend. Believing that the Great Spirit had promised them victory, the Creek fought almost to the last man, and by the end of the day the battlefield was a scene of carnage. Weatherford himself had not been at Horseshoe Bend, and Andrew went in search of him. At Fort Toulouse, which was renamed Fort Jackson, Weatherford surrendered.

The Creek war was over, and the victorious troops and their general went home.

To glory.

To a population utterly depressed by a failed war with Britain, Andrew was the hero they needed. His fame spread throughout the land, and cheering crowds lined the streets on his approach to Nashville. A state dinner was organized, and a victory parade.

All the buildings were draped in flags and bunting, and people came from all over Tennessee to see the triumph. Andrew sat on the official stand with Rachel, and because all his lieutenants and men were marching, James and Sally were invited to sit with them. Sally had baby Mary with her, and Rachel looked after Andrew junior, while Andrew dandled Lincoyen on his knee.

Bands played, people cheered, and the soldiers were resplendent. James felt himself in the company of heroes. He never asked Andrew for the return of his money, nor was it ever offered. As the troops marched past the reviewing stand to the salutes of their general, someone called out three cheers for Old Hickory. The crowd took it up, and the air resounded with the calls of Andrew's name. James, standing beside him, was moved to tears.

But Andrew had a surprise for them all. After the soldiers came a dozen Indian braves, prisoners, whom Andrew had brought back as hostages, or as evidence of the battles he had fought.

They were the finest of the fine—on horseback, nearly naked, bedecked in war paint and feathers. The crowd hushed in awe at sight of them, for these were the warriors as they were seen only in battle, in dead of night or heat of day, when very few white men lived to describe them, and no white woman had survived the encounter.

Their squaws walked behind them, and half-breeds with drums. Priests of the Cherokee and Chickasaw chanted ancient hymns in praise of the victor.

To James, it was the most exotic and extraordinary experience of his life, and it caught at his soul.

Before him was man in his purest, simplest form. Man of the wilderness, at one with the wild, lord of a lawless world, where survival required a consummate union with the earth and the heavens. Man the hunter, living from the land, and taking from it only what could be given back.

Andrew had no need to guess what James was thinking, for he felt it, and assumed that every man would when confronted with the challenge of these splendid creatures. Yet he owed a debt to his friend, and tried to communicate to him what his money had bought.

"It is to do battle on the plains of Mount Olympus," he said softly, so only James could hear, and perhaps Lincoyen.

"The landscape itself could be the domain of the gods, for it is the very best of America, pristine and pure. The unsullied handiwork of God."

He didn't speak for a moment, but stared at the Indians.

"These are not ordinary men," he said. "These are the most noble animals, bred by Hermes and blessed by Apollo. To do battle with them is to challenge the authority of Zeus."

Suddenly, some strange and mysterious anger exploded in him, and he turned to James in fury.

"And I choose to do it! I am not chosen by some panel or drafted by some committee! It is not my fate, for I am master of my own destiny. I choose to challenge these colossi, and I win!"

Andrew had James completely in his thrall, and turned back to look at his prisoners again.

"They are magnificent," he said softly.

At that moment, James would have given everything he possessed, everything in the world—he would have sold his soul to the devil—to know, if only for a moment, the heroic, surpassing majesty it must be to kill an Indian.

16

Andrew had other spoils of war. Sent to negotiate a peace treaty with the Creek, he gave them an ultimatum, and would not concede one single point of it.

Under threat of war and destruction, and in return for some small annuities to the chiefs, the elders of the tribes of the Creek, in council, ceded to Andrew Jackson, representative of the United States government, twenty-three million acres of land.

It was half of the ancient realm of the Creek and

covered most of Alabama and part of Georgia. Tennessee was no longer the frontier.

For the restless, journeying settlers, a new paradise had been found.

But before they could take possession of it, Andrew had to win another battle.

In order to teach the Americans a lesson, a small British expeditionary force had attacked the capital, Washington, and had set fire to the president's home. They withdrew and attacked Baltimore, but were repelled by gunfire. It didn't matter. The point had been made.

Tired of the war, the British amassed an army of ten thousand veterans, who had served under Wellington against Napoleon, and prepared an invasion of America on two fronts. One army, under Sir Alexander Cochrane, took Maine and declared it part of New Brunswick. He seized Nantucket and made a foray into Long Island Sound. New England demanded Washington make peace and threatened secession from the Union.

Another British army, with Jamaica as its base, was to attack New Orleans.

Andrew had a spy in Florida, where some British units were inciting the Seminole to revolt, and got wind of the invasion plans. He implored the government to send him south, but Madison, perhaps because the peace negotiators in Belgium were close to an agreement, delayed his response. So Andrew acted on his own accord, with only the blessing of Governor Blount of Tennessee. He was now the military commander for the Southwest, so he took his troops to New Orleans, declared martial law, engaged every able-bodied man he could find, and waited for the British.

He needed money for the venture, and James, once again, was only too happy to oblige. This time he would be repaid, not in cash out of Andrew's pocket or the federal treasury, but in something far more valuable than money.

147

Andrew had succeeded in having John Coffee appointed as a surveyor to map the new territories acquired from the Creek, and Coffee's boundaries erred on the other side of caution. Once the survey was complete and Andrew had returned from New Orleans, a company was to be formed, the Cypress Development Company, with Coffee and other friends as its principals, and James as secretary, to promote and develop vast acreages of this new land. To the surprise of everyone except James, Andrew, who was a prime mover of the enterprise, took only a few modest shares in the company. James guessed that it was because of his political ambitions. Andrew did not want his reputation to be sullied with the taint of speculation.

The British landed near New Orleans, but Andrew did not wait to be attacked. He sent a small army into the British lines, under cover of night, and produced chaos and confusion. When the British reorganized themselves to attack, Andrew had completed his defenses. The British forces, unused to the swampy land and unprepared for Andrew's unconventional tactics, were routed.

The battle of New Orleans was fought and won by Andrew at the beginning of January. Unknown to him, or to any of the participants, the negotiators in Ghent had signed a peace treaty between Britain and the United States the previous Christmas Eve, two weeks earlier, but the news had not yet reached America.

Nor did the Americans care. Andrew was hailed as the greatest general since Washington, the one true, unsullied victor in a useless war, even if the war was officially over when the battle was won. The country went wild for him, and he was proclaimed a hero. At a convention in Hartford, the New Englanders had agreed on an ultimatum that unless there was peace they would secede, but tore up the paper on the news of the victory and the subsequent news of the peace.

There was nothing his country would not grant him. All Andrew had to do was ask.

James, jubilant, assumed Andrew would run for president, and undoubtedly be elected. He had visions of himself as a powerful figure behind Andrew's throne, but the hero disappointed him. He was not ready for elective office yet; he enjoyed being a general far more, and there was work to be done.

Because Andrew wanted Florida.

It had been Andrew's ambition from the beginning. Florida had been held by the Spanish until Napoleon defeated them, and then the western section of it, which bordered the Gulf of Mexico, was annexed as a territory by the United States. The peninsula itself, still governed by Spain, was a wild and lawless land, peopled by pirates and hardy settlers, runaway slaves from Georgia and South Carolina, buccaneers, mercenaries, and criminals of all classes. During the war, the British had successfully incited some of the locals to revolt, and now the native Seminole Indians, together with some Creek who had fled Alabama, took up arms. Andrew believed that the South was not safe until Florida had been brought to heel. He offered his services to the new president, James Monroe, and marched to Pensacola, leaving his affairs in the good hands of his friend James Jackson.

Who didn't know what to do with the rest of his life.

James had settled into a comfortable routine. Partly because of his financial success and his industrious relatives, and partly because of his friendship with Andrew, he was one of the most prominent citizens in Nashville. He and some others had founded the first Academy for Females, he was on several boards and committees, and he had political ambitions, but he was bored. His personal life was full and happy, although there was a small tragedy when Jimmy Hanna, Sara's

149

husband, died of a fever, and Uncle Henry had passed away, but otherwise Sally and the children, Eleanor and Tom and their family, and Sara and hers flourished.

He had achieved so much, and yet none of it was original, none of it was unique to him. Even his plantation had been created by someone else; James had simply acquired it in one of his land deals.

He had outgrown Nashville, which once had seemed so perfect to him.

He wanted to do something grand and extravagant, like Andrew, but he knew he was not suited for military endeavors. At the urging of John Coffee, he went to inspect the land in northern Alabama that had been acquired in the Creek war, and fell in love with the wonderful, empty country.

A vision came to him, of a great estate that he would create, a vast cotton plantation that would be one of the finest in the country, and he would be a pioneer in this new territory, one of the first white settlers on the land so newly acquired, and one of its leading citizens.

He took Sally on a trip to inspect the new territory, and she shared his enthusiasm. She knew he was bored, knew he needed some new challenge, and the prospect of building a home to their exact requirements intrigued her. She also remembered her early dreams with her first husband, of moving to the wilderness, and creating a sylvan idyll, and there was enough of the girl in her and enough of the pioneer to want that still.

Acquiring the land was easy. The Cypress Development Company struck a deal with the government to exploit the area. Prior to Andrew's departure for Florida, the dining room at the Hermitage became a new boardroom, of peace not of war, and one in which James was a welcome participant. In long and cheerful sessions that went on till well past midnight, often fueled by liquor, they envisioned the development of northern Alabama. The lots would be decided according to John Coffee's survey. County boundaries were established. A new town would be laid out. It was to be called Florence, after the city in Tuscany, and architects and town planners were to be brought from Europe. It would be the finest city in the South, a cultural center and capital of a new Eden that would be peopled by those most honest and industrious of souls, the simple farmers, backbone of America.

These were heady and exciting days for James, who, as secretary of the development company and Andrew's associate, was at the very center of the activity. He threw all his energy into the enterprise, and yet did not forget himself.

He had a surprising visit from someone he had not seen in several years. Jimmy Doublehead, son of the chief, was living on a Chickasaw reservation to the south of Nashville, near Huntsville, and heard that James was involved in the new company. He came to see James to ask a favor. He wanted him to buy a particular piece of land.

They rode together to the place Jimmy had in mind, and when James saw it, his heart skipped a beat. A few miles south of where the new town of Florence would be, at a confluence of two rivers whose banks were lined with untidy cypresses, the land was rolling and gentle, ideal for cotton. Some small distance from the river there was a hill, and it was this hill that interested Jimmy.

"It is a holy place, sacred to my people," he told James. "It is a place of the old ones."

In the Indian mythology, the spirit of a warrior did not die with his body, but simply moved to a higher plane, and was available to the living for advice and counsel. Once a year, old Chief Doublehead had called the other Cherokee chiefs to this place, and they had listened to the guidance of the old ones.

James was deeply moved by the land and its significance, and felt humble.

151

"Why have you come to me, Jimmy?" he asked the young man.

"Because you were his friend, and you were kind to our people," Jimmy said. "You will preserve his memory."

James spent the afternoon exploring the land, and told Jimmy he would buy it, no matter what the cost. Already he could see a mansion rising on the sacred hill, but he was determined to do as Jimmy asked, and preserve Doublehead's memory.

"I will put a wigwam here," he said, pointing to an open space at the edge of the little hill. "And it will be available to a family of your tribe for all time, so that they may be near the old ones."

Jimmy said nothing, but bowed his head, in what James thought was gratitude. He could not know the despair that Jimmy, and all the Indians, were experiencing at this loss of their land. What Jimmy had done was pragmatic, but not his most desired solution.

The deal for the land was simple. The Cypress Development Company guaranteed to develop a minimum number of acres, and the government would receive two dollars an acre regardless of whether the land was sold or not. Whatever else was bid would be profit to the developers.

The auction was a circus. The first five hundred acres sold at an average of forty-five dollars an acre. The end of the war and the resolution of the old arguments with Britain, the swarming tide of immigrants from Ireland and Europe, and the availability of the new land opened the floodgates to settlements, and buyers flocked to the sales. The past president, James Madison, came with President Monroe. A potential presidential candidate came when Andrew Jackson made a special trip from Florida to bid for a lot. Out of respect for his service to the country, no one bid against him. The only land that was sold at the government minimum was sold to Andrew.

The gentry from five states came. Farmers from major, medium, and small land holdings came. Newcomers bought their first lots. Poor whites bid for a few scrubby acres to get a start in life. River frontage and the town sites fetched the highest prices, eighty-five dollars an acre. Church sites were purchased by Methodists, Baptists, Presbyterians, and Roman Catholics.

The directors of the Cypress Development Company bought land for personal use or for private resale. Apart from the site of his plantation, James bought twelve lots for himself, and another three in partnership with John Coffee.

By the end of the four-day sale, James was rich beyond his wildest imaginings.

On the afternoon of the last day, he drove Sally to the place that was to be their new home, and she loved it as much as he. Together they chose a name. It would be called The Forks of Cypress, for it lay where the two rivers, the Big Cypress and the Little Cypress, joined. He told her of its holy significance, and that he believed the land was blessed.

It was a magic time, a cool, crisp day, and the winter sun lay low on the horizon. Sally wandered away to inspect the property, and James was on his own for a few minutes.

He stared at the land. His land.

"You will never amount to anything."

His father's final words to him rang in his ears, and he laughed out loud, for he had proved them so wrong. He shivered at the awesome achievement, and thought it was the cold, but then he saw a small group of Indians standing on the path at the bottom of the hill, staring at him.

They did nothing and said nothing. They simply

stared at him, or at the hill that was the home of the old ones, as if they were looking at what they had lost.

James shivered again, and turned and called for Sally. She came to him, and when he looked back, the Indians had gone. He could not swear that they had been there.

"What is it, what's wrong?" Sally asked him. James laughed and threw aside his odd feeling of melancholy, or failure, or betrayal.

"Nothing," he said. "I'm a sentimental old fool, that's all."

She laughed, and took his hand. James pulled her to him and kissed her, lightly at first, but then with passion.

Sally looked at him in surprise, for his need was urgent.

"I want you," he whispered. "Here. Now."

He kissed her again, as violently as he had ever kissed her. He laid her on the ground, and took her there, in the open, like a peasant boy, as once, when young, he had taken a peasant girl under a hayrick in a flawless Irish summer that he had spent with Sean.

At the moment of his climax, he pulled himself from her and spilled his seed upon the ground, as if to consummate his union with the land.

The following day, both James and Sally caught chills and laughed together that it was because of their open-air frolicking in the winter weather. Sally's cold took a natural course and was gone in a few days, but James got steadily worse. By the time they were back in Nashville, he had congestive fever. He took to his bed, but the sickness did not diminish his passion for his new project. He engaged an architect to draw plans for a magnificent mansion, but the effort exhausted him. He fretted that he was losing time.

Sally took command. She asked their good friends John McKinley and Henry Clay, Jr., to scour the South, to locate and hire, or buy, the best available slave artisans and craftsmen, masons, carpenters, ironworkers, and plasterers to build The Forks of Cypress.

James, from his sickbed, anxious to move to his new home, gave orders that a log cabin should be built for his family at the edge of the site, and a small schoolhouse for the children.

He began disposing of his assets in Nashville. He called Washington and Thomas Kirkman to him, and offered them his interest in the store. Washington laughed that he didn't want it, he was well set up in New Orleans and loved the life, so the store was formally deeded to Thomas Kirkman for the sum of one dollar, in the name of Irish friendship.

Thomas was flabbergasted. Eleanor wept, and blessed her generous brother.

James did not want to move his precious blooded horses to Alabama until proper stables and a racetrack had been built, and so he arranged that his trainer, Colonel Elliot, should run the stables in Nashville, and be responsible for the horses. He made Elliot a partner in the enterprise.

He sold his plantation and most of his land. In the new year, he cast aside his illness as he cast aside his old life, and moved his family to the hastily constructed log cabin, to supervise the building of his mansion.

Now he had everything he had ever wanted. Now he was everything he had ever wanted to be.

In Florida, fortune briefly deserted her darling. Andrew's military victories were impressive, but the ruthlessness with which he inflicted his will on the Seminole was causing agitated controversy in Washington. When he executed two Christian missionaries, claiming they had incited the Indians to revolt, the controversy became uproar. When he invaded Pensacola for a second time and imprisoned the governor for sheltering Indians, the uproar became deafening. The loudest voices against him were William Crawford, the secretary of war, and his onetime friend Henry Clay. The House of Representatives threatened censure.

The furious Andrew traveled to Washington to defend himself, and prevailed. All the motions against him were defeated. Because of his military success, the Spanish formally sold Florida to the United States for five million dollars.

Andrew was given a hero's welcome in New York, Baltimore, and Philadelphia, and then returned to Nashville, to the Hermitage, and to his beloved Rachel. His feathers were ruffled, but his honor was satisfied.

The following summer, Andrew was appointed governor of Florida, but he came to see James, because he had some other business to attend to first.

He admired the mansion, which was now nearing completion, a simple elegant building in the temple style, with three enormous chimneys and twenty-one white columns surrounding the veranda at even intervals. A wide entrance hall ran through the middle of the house, with a cross hall at the rear. The kitchen and laundry were outhouses, attached to the main building by covered walkways.

Andrew helped James plant a magnolia sapling at the edge of the hill on what would be the lawn, and played with the new baby, Sarah.

"A sassy little thing," he laughed. "But there are too many Sarahs."

So he called her Sassy, which suited her.

Andrew junior and Lincoyen were with their father and played with A.J., while Cap'n Jack yarned with Alfred, and inspected the racecourse that had been laid out to one side of the drive.

"There is the matter of the Chickasaw land," Andrew said.

James waited, knowing what the outcome of the conversation would be.

But he would make Andrew ask, first.

*

Andrew had been commissioned by the government, with Isaac Shelby, to treat for some Chickasaw land, to the north, where Jimmy Doublehead lived. Andrew estimated that three hundred thousand dollars would be a sufficient outlay, and the sum was approved in principle. Privately, Andrew met with a chief, George Colbert, who was known as "the soul of the Chickasaw," and laid out his policy. Colbert's cooperation could enrich him personally, but if the land was not sold to the government there would be war, and many Chickasaw would die.

George Colbert was pragmatic. He agreed to persuade his people in return for a permanent annuity for himself and his brother, Levi, of the right to reserve some good land for himself, and the purchase of a piece of land he owned for twenty thousand dollars. Andrew agreed.

A formal public council of the Chickasaw was called. Andrew made a speech that was now familiar to him. If the Chickasaw did not agree to his terms, there would be war, and he would annihilate them as he had the Creek. If they did agree, the purchase price would be paid over ten years, after which they would move to new land, given freely by the government, in the west, beyond the Mississippi.

He shouted an offer. "One hundred and fifty thousand."

The Chickasaw conferred among themselves, and shouted back their collective response.

"No!"

"Two hundred thousand," Andrew shouted.

"No!"

Andrew offered two hundred and fifty thousand, and the response was still no.

Andrew appeared to confer with Isaac Shelby, and came back with what he said was his final offer.

"Three hundred thousand."

Shelby called that they were not authorized to go that

high, and Andrew responded that in order to be fair to the people, he would pay the difference out of his own pocket.

The Chickasaw were confused and George Colbert saw his moment. He made a speech in which he accepted Andrew's terms on his own behalf. His brother, Levi, made a speech in which he agreed to the terms, and one by one the chiefs accepted.

They demanded the first payment, and the Colberts wanted their bribes immediately. Andrew, perpetually short of ready money or reluctant to use his own, doubted that he could persuade the government to part with the cash quickly enough to satisfy the Chickasaw. He came to James.

"How much?" James wondered, after Andrew had asked him.

"Fifty thousand," Andrew said.

James stared at Andrew junior, A.J., and Lincoyen, who were playing settlers and braves on the land that would be the lawn. He could afford the money and could not deny Andrew, who had helped to make him rich. But he was planning on a political career himself, and he was concerned that some of his money would be used to pay the bribes. Still he agreed. He had never been able to deny Andrew anything.

Andrew nodded, but did not thank him. They chatted for a while about the prospect of Alabama being admitted into the Union, and Andrew urged James to stand for election to the new state's senate. Soon after, he said tender farewells to James, Sally, and the children, greeted Cap'n Jack affably, and left with his sons and Alfred.

James watched him go, and pondered what he had done. He remembered a small group of Indians, Creek probably, who had watched him on this same hill the day he bought the property, and he shivered a little, as he had shivered then.

Sally knew something was wrong, and worried that he might be ailing again. James shook his head, and walked into the shell of the house with her. They wandered through the spaces that soon would be rooms, planning how they would furnish them. Sally did not ask him about Andrew's visit. She guessed it was to do with money, and Andrew, but James didn't usually discuss these things with her anymore. To her surprise, this time he did. Sally listened in silence, and realized something extraordinary. Ever since she had complained that Andrew never repaid his loans, James had closed off a part of his life, his business dealings, from her. Now she thought she understood why. James would worry away at a problem until he either found a solution or, as in this case, needed her advice. It pleased her that he asked. It healed the only rift, no matter how tiny, that had ever existed between them.

"The money is nothing," she said. "There is the matter of your good name."

James nodded, for she had come straight to the heart.

"But I can't refuse him," he said. "I owe him too much."

Sally didn't entirely agree, but kept her counsel. On the matter of his friendship with Andrew, James could be extraordinarily touchy.

"The government will not pay?" she asked, looking for a solution.

"Eventually, but not in time," James said. "It has to go through all the requisite departments."

"So the land will be lost?"

"Not forever, because Andrew will not allow it to be lost," James told her. "He will make war, and he will win."

"Andrew always wins," Sally said with a smile.

She thought for a moment.

"What if you bought the land?"

James was astonished.

"Don't you think we have enough?"

159

That was not Sally's point. If the government were to give, through Andrew, deeds to some of the land, it would always appear that James's money had been used for a purchase. Then, at some later date, when the funds were freed by Washington and his money repaid, James would return the title deeds.

James assimilated what she said, and then laughed out loud. It was so simple, so beautifully simple. He hugged his wife to him.

"Oh, I love you," he said.

Getting Andrew to agree was a protracted business, conducted through correspondence. James wrote, expressing his concern at the size of the loan, and requesting some title deeds as collateral. Andrew replied, rather sharply, that he was surprised that James had reneged on his original unconditional offer of the money, and assumed that the bribes were worrying James, that the government would not reimburse them. There was no need for concern. Andrew had simply told the government that he had been forced to pay somewhat more for the land than he had expected.

Still James insisted on the collateral, and eventually Andrew give in. Title deeds to several lots of the Chickasaw land were made out in James's name, and he sent Andrew the money in return. Later, when Washington had completed its paperwork, James got his money back, and returned the deeds to the government.

James felt good. He had obliged his friend, and covered his own position. For once in his life he had outsmarted Andrew, who might be a better man on the battleground or in a duel, but in matters of business, James was the champion. He was also one of the richest and most influential men in the state.

Then came the news that his father had died, in Ireland. James was not sure what he felt, and guilty that he did not feel any special sense of loss. He thought that he should mourn his father as the man who had given him life, but that was all his father had done. How could he love a father who had disinherited him? True to his word, his father had left James nothing in his will.

Of one thing James was certain. His sons would never feel toward him the way he felt to his dead father. He called A.J. to him, and sat his son on his knee. He told him stories of Ireland, of shanachies and leprechauns and rainbows. He promised the lad that he loved him, and that he would create the finest estate in the South for A.J. to inherit.

A.J. nodded his head gravely, and thanked his father, but then begged for more stories about leprechauns. James laughed, and remembered some.

But when A.J. had gone to bed, James had several glasses of port, and got drunk, and tried to remember a father who never told him tales of leprechauns.

"You will never amount to anything."

"You will see, Father," James said to his empty glass. "You will see."

When Alabama was admitted into the Union, James allowed himself to be persuaded to stand as a state senator in the next election. He received petitioners gladly, and dispensed patronage. He was sought out by politicians from Washington and Montgomery, the new state capital, and his mansion was admired as one of the finest houses in the South. He bought racehorses for his stable, and Monkey Simon, from Nashville, as his master jockey, to train the younger men.

Determined that his staff, his slaves, would be of the first quality, he traveled with Cap'n Jack through Georgia and South Carolina, attending, for the first time in his life, slave auctions.

Cap'n Jack could hardly bear to watch as James inspected the slaves as carefully as he examined his pedigree horses, checking their bones, teeth, and physiques, and inquiring, as far as was possible, into their

161

bloodlines. Then Cap'n Jack steeled himself. He had sworn that he would never give James cause to back out of his promise of freedom, and so, however unwillingly, he helped his Massa choose the slaves. James purchased several excellent field hands, and then found a splendid, superbly trained butler, who came with the highest credentials and who had the odd name of Parson Dick.

It was Cap'n Jack who found Annie.

When he saw the beautiful woman with skin the color of coffee, who was said to have expert talent as a weaver, James's vanity was tickled. He would acquire her and build a weaving house, and all the cloth that was needed at The Forks of Cypress, for the slaves' clothing and blankets, would be woven on his estate. Only the very rich could afford to do that.

It thus happened that he bought the woman called Annie, whose previous Massa had sold her away because he believed she was cursed with ill fortune.

Perhaps he was right, for Annie had bewitched Cap'n Jack already.

17

Annie was a child of rape. Her mammy never told her this, but Annie knew it was true. Every time she asked about her pappy, Mammy's eyes got angry, and she would smack her, and tell her never to ask about him again. Then her mammy would cry, and tell her that her pappy was a white man who didn't want anything to do with her, but Mammy would look after her always.

Annie loved her mammy. Mammy had been born to an African mother and a Cherokee father, back in the old days when some white Massas had Indians as slaves, and not just black folk. Mammy's father could not bear his enslavement, and had simply curled up and died. Mammy's mother, from Africa, knew all sorts of things about magic, and taught them to her daughter, so Mammy knew lots of ways to heal people who were sick, to put a blessing on those who wanted a baby, or put a curse on bad people. Mammy taught all this to Annie, and some other things as well, learned from her Cherokee father. Mystical things that were also about the spirit people, and the power that existed in simple things, the trees and the animals and the birds, and the sky, and the very land itself.

Their Massa made Mammy work very hard, and she got sick. Annie tried to cure her with charms and spells and herbs, but she was very young, and didn't have the proper power yet. Massa came to see Mammy one day, and threatened to sell her away if she didn't get better. Then he saw Annie, whom he had never really noticed before; she'd always been just one of the pickaninnies. Now she was a beautiful young girl in her early teens, with a developing figure. The Massa told her to take off her clothes.

Mammy cried out and tried to stop him, but she was too weak. The Massa beat Annie when she didn't strip fast enough for him, and when she was naked he used his whip to prod her small breasts, and pushed it between her legs.

Annie was crying, but Massa didn't care. He told her to lie down on the floor, then he unbuckled his belt and pushed down his pants. He got on top of Annie and pushed himself inside her, suddenly, violently. Annie screamed in pain, but he wouldn't stop. He kept pumping into her, and the more she cried, the more he pushed and pumped. When he was finished, he got up and saw that there was a little blood on his thing. He laughed, and said now he was sure that Annie had been a virgin. He hit her again, to remind her that he was the Massa, and told Mammy to fix it so she didn't have a baby.

Annie lay on the floor after he was gone, until the

163

pain went away, and then she got up and went to Mammy, who was crying.

"Don't cry, Mammy," she said. "It don't make no never mind."

But she was lying, and Mammy knew it.

Mammy never got better and seemed to lose the will to live. She died soon after that, and Annie cried bitterly, because now she was all alone. That night she lay in her bunk; and tried to remember all the spells that Mammy had taught her to put a curse on the Massa.

Perhaps they worked, because Massa didn't seem very interested in her after that. He came to her a few times and did what he wanted, but he said it wasn't the same because she wasn't a virgin anymore, and he hit her, because she wasn't a virgin.

A lot of very unlucky things happened to Massa, and Annie believed they were because of her curse. He broke his leg when his horse reared at a snake. His favorite hunting dog was gored by a wild pig. His best fighting cock was killed in the pit. His newborn baby died. He had two bad seasons with his cotton and had to sell some of his slaves. Annie was one of them.

She was bought by an old man who had a big building with some looms in it, where other slave women made cloth that was sold at the market. Annie only helped them at first, but one of the women taught her the craft, and she became an excellent weaver. She liked the other women, and they were kind to her, but she was always sad, because she missed her mammy.

She'd been there about six months when her new Massa called her into his office one day. He told her to take off her dress, and he took off his pants and he did what her first Massa had done, only he wasn't so rough and it was all over very quickly. He made her swear never to tell anyone else about it, and he called her to his office every few days after that, and did it to her again.

164

The other women knew because he'd done it to all of them as well, and they told the ways to get rid of a baby if one came along. But Annie didn't listen to them, because she wasn't going to have a baby by a white Massa. She hated them all too much, and she knew what herbs and grasses to eat that would keep a baby away.

She also put a curse on her new Massa, but it didn't seem to work at first. Then one night there was a fire in the warehouse and most of the cloth was burned, and some of the looms. She was sold away again, this time to a big plantation where they needed someone to do the weaving. This Massa was quite good to her, and the overseer, because she was good at her job, and kept herself to herself, and didn't make trouble. She never became friends with any of the other slave women because they were a little scared of her. They knew she could make magic because she cured a baby boy who was sick with a cough. She built a special fire of strange-smelling herbs in his shack and made him smell the smoke, and he got better.

After that the young girls came to her when they needed cures, or a potion or a spell to make someone love them, but she would never put a curse on anyone for them, because that was her special gift, and she reserved it for herself.

She was indescribably lonely. She longed for some company, some contact with another human being, and for a while she had an affair with a field hand, but he was suspicious of her power, and married someone else. Her reputation for being gifted spread throughout the plantation, until eventually even the overseer and the Massa heard about it, and they made jokes about her, and teased her to do magic for them.

The Massa's wife, the Missy, didn't tease her though. When her daughter was sick with the whooping cough, she came to Annie, and begged her to make the child well. Annie built her fire of special herbs and sticks,

165

and made the child smell the smoke, and slowly, over the next two weeks, she got better. After that the Missy came to Annie whenever any of her children were sick. Sometimes Annie could help and sometimes she couldn't, but she was always honest with the Missy, because she knew the limit of her own knowledge and power.

She might have been happy at that plantation, except that people, white or black, came to her only when they wanted some healing. Otherwise, they seemed frightened of her, and left her alone.

The young Massa, the Massa's son, was a boy when Annie first came to the plantation, but he had grown up, and was a young man now. He started spending time with Annie, and even though he laughed about her skills, she thought him kind. Then one night he came to her and ordered her to get undressed, and he raped her. She knew she was his first woman, and so she was inclined to forgive him, but then he started laughing at her, and telling everyone how he had been broken in with the witch.

So she put a curse on him. Two months later, he was bitten by a cottonmouth when he was swimming naked in the river. Everyone knew he died from the snakebite, but no one believed it was natural, because she was a witch. Young Massa had said so. Ol' Massa got very angry, and ordered the overseer to beat her, but not to mark her skin. He stripped her naked and hit her with a wooden bat. She had livid bruises for weeks afterward, but he was clever and did not break the skin. When she was healed, ol' Massa called for the auctioneer and sent her to the block.

They took her by cart to a big city, and to some long, low brick buildings, where a hundred other slaves were locked in iron cages. They put her in a cage and gave her bread and cornmeal to eat. Some of the other slaves tried to be friendly to her, but she didn't talk to them because she was scared of other people. She heard that there was to be an auction soon, and over the next few days lots of Massas came to inspect what was being offered. A lot of the Massas were interested in her, because she was very beautiful, but she made a chant, to stop anyone buying her.

On the day before the sale, a black man came in, very fashionably dressed, a house nigger, she guessed. He looked at all the slaves, and then he came to her pen, and looked at her for a very long time, without saying anything, and she felt an odd feeling, for the first time in her life, that this man would never hurt her. He tried to talk to her, and she didn't say very much in case she was wrong, but she didn't make her chant.

The man went away and came back a little while later with his Massa. They talked about her and asked her some questions, and she gave them honest answers. They asked about her weaving, and she pointed to her simple skirt, which was of her own cloth. They felt the texture of the material and inspected the weave. They made her turn round and take off her bodice, and inspected her skin for scars of a lashing, but there were none. As they were taking their leave, the house nigger turned back to her and smiled.

She went to the block the next day, and a few Massas bid for her, but then suddenly the Massa with the house nigger made a bid that was much higher than anyone else's and everyone gasped in astonishment. She was sold to him. The Massa came to her, and told her he was sorry that she would have to stay here for a few days until transport could be set up, but he made arrangements to have her moved to the auctioneer's own slave quarters, which were a little more comfortable, and she wasn't barred in.

She guessed that her new Massa must be very rich, because when the slave cart came for her, there were four other black men, field hands, in it, and a lighter-skinned man who was immaculately dressed. He said his name was Parson Dick, and he spoke differently from the others, almost like a Massa. Four slave catchers had been employed to take them to their new plantation, and they traveled for four days, staying in the slave quarters of cheap inns at night. To her surprise, they weren't chained at any time.

"New Massa said not," Parson Dick told her.

Not that she, or anyone, could have escaped. One of the slave catchers was always on guard, and they had guns.

Besides, where would she escape to?

At the end of the fourth day they came to a fine plantation, with fields ready, although no cotton had been planted. There was a big mansion on a hill at the end of the drive, but it wasn't finished yet. Workmen were putting glass in the windows, and slate on the roof, and the grounds around it were still wild, and not yet a garden.

They were delivered to the overseer, a middle-aged man called Evans, and he warned them that he would not tolerate troublemakers or runaways. For all his bluster, Annie didn't think he was a very strong man, and the field hands sniggered softly when he turned his back to greet the Massa.

The Massa welcomed them, and told them he expected them to work hard, but that if they did he would treat them well. The house nigger was with him, smiling, Annie thought, at her.

The overseer took them to the slave quarters, a collection of newly built huts around a clearing, and assigned them their places. As they walked there, the house nigger walked with them, and pointed out the Massa's log cabin, in a field behind the big house, and said he'd be moving into the big house next month.

Annie's room was as good as any she had ever had, small and bare, with a small window, a chair and a bunk, but it had the smell of new timber, and that pleased her.

The house nigger came with the Missy, and she was very kind, and said she would organize some new clothes for Annie, who had only the dress she wore. She admired the weave of that dress, and said she hoped that Annie would be happy making lovely cloth for them.

The Missy left, but the house nigger stayed.

"I's Cap'n Jack," he said. "I's the Massa man."

Annie shrugged.

"Ain't nuttin' to be afeared of here," he said. "Ain't no one to hurt you here."

Annie shrugged again. She always got hurt, eventually.

Cap'n Jack stared at her for a few moments, then told her he'd come by to see her again soon and left.

Annie sat down on the bunk and stared at the place that was to be her new home.

Some people at her old plantation said she had the gift of second sight, but although she could see the future, it wasn't true. It was simply that Annie knew that nothing good was ever going to happen to her.

18

Cap'n Jack was fascinated by Annie from the first moment he saw her. A sad, silent woman in a pen at the slave market, she seemed filled with dark secrets, and some inner pain that Cap'n Jack guessed came from beating or rape, or from being sold away from her family. She bore her grief with such quiet dignity that Cap'n Jack wanted to take her into his arms and hold her, and never let anyone hurt her again.

He told James about her, and that she was a weaver, and James's eyes glinted with a spark of an idea that he wouldn't reveal to Cap'n Jack. They went to Annie and inspected her, and James was impressed. Cap'n Jack was pleased to see that she bore no scars from the lash on her back, but knew that some Massas had subtler ways of inflicting punishment. The following day, at the auction, there was some bidding for Annie, but then James surprised everyone by offering a price well above the highest bid. Cap'n Jack looked at him in surprise, but James only shrugged.

"She can do the weaving," he said.

When they got back to The Forks, James told his builders he wanted a weaving house, and put Cap'n Jack in charge of it. Cap'n Jack went to the slave quarters to pick out a site, but it was for Annie, and he wanted to keep her apart from the others.

There was a small grove of oaks halfway between the big house and the slave quarters, with a clearing in the middle, just large enough for a small house. This was the spot that Cap'n Jack chose. Here, Annie would be half hidden from the world. James approved of his choice and ordered a loom from Atlanta.

The new slaves were delivered a few days later, and were greeted by Evans, the foreman. Evans had been with James in Nashville, and was really an overseer, but James didn't like the title. Evans was gruff and shouted a lot, but was not really a strong man. Cap'n Jack doubted that he was the right man for the new job. In Nashville they'd had only forty slaves on the plantation, including the house niggers, and here there would be nearly a hundred working in the fields, and several more in the house. Evans organized the field hands, and Cap'n Jack was left in charge of Annie and the new butler, Parson Dick.

He took Annie to a hut, and tried to talk to her, but she only shrugged. Whatever her hurt was, Cap'n Jack knew it would take time to heal. He went outside and Parson Dick made himself comfortable on a log, waiting to be told where to go. They were pressed for space. The big house wasn't ready, the Massa and his family

170

were crowded into the log cabin, and not all the new slave quarters had been finished. In the end Cap'n Jack suggested that Parson Dick bunk in with him. The butler made a bit of a fuss, saying that things had been different at his old plantation, but it was either Cap'n Jack's hut or the shed with the field hands, so Parson Dick saw reason.

Parson Dick settled in and washed at the well. He was finicky about his personal cleanliness, and had not been able to wash properly at the slave market, nor on the road. He asked to be taken on a tour of the new house and to meet his staff, so Cap'n Jack conducted him through the nearly finished mansion, and introduced him to old Crosspatch, the cook who had come with them from Nashville, and her new young assistant, Julie. Parson Dick thanked Cap'n Jack and dismissed him, saying he would like to talk to the Missy next. Cap'n Jack was not used to being given orders by other slaves, but saw the sense of it and went to find Sally. Parson Dick settled at the kitchen table with Crosspatch and Julie and told them how he intended to run the house. Crosspatch, who had a short temper, flared, but Parson Dick told her he was in charge and if she didn't like it she could complain to the Massa. Julie giggled.

Cap'n Jack found Sally but she had some other jobs for him, for the furniture was starting to arrive from Charleston, and the new drapes and rugs. It was all in crates, for it had come from Europe, and so they stored it all in one of the back rooms in the house until they took possession. It was nearly midnight when Cap'n Jack finished his work, but that was not unusual these days. Ever since the Massa had bought the land and then got sick, Cap'n Jack had been in charge of many of the preparations for the new house.

He went past Annie's hut on the way to his own, but the candle was out, and he guessed she was asleep. He hoped the angels would guard her, and went to his own hut, where Parson Dick pumped him for two hours about the Jackson family, until Cap'n Jack fell asleep, fully clothed, on his bunk.

He woke at cockcrow, washed at the well, and saw Annie in line for her food. He greeted her, and told her she had no work to do until the loom arrived, but could make herself useful cleaning up in the house. She nodded and was pleasant, but otherwise ignored his existence. Cap'n Jack had his meals in the kitchen of the big house, which was the first part of the building to be completed, and ate his breakfast listening to Crosspatch's complaints about the new butler. She was particularly aggrieved this day because Missy Sally had sided with Parson Dick on some matter of the menus, but Cap'n Jack ignored her. Crosspatch was always complaining.

It was another chaotic day. The builders were scrambling to finish the house, Sally was trying to move furniture into rooms that weren't ready, Micah and Tiara were looking after the children, Ephraim was running round the stables getting ready for the horses which were soon to arrive, and everyone wanted something from Cap'n Jack.

As he walked back from the stables, Cap'n Jack saw Evans charging around on his horse organizing work gangs to plant the new season's cotton.

The new field hands were a crew of fine and able-bodied men, but, strangers to the Jackson household, had no special loyalty to their new Massa, and were testing the limits of the foreman's temper and ability to control.

"There gwine be trouble," Cap'n Jack said to himself, but it was not his business, and Miss Sally was calling him to help talk sense to the gardeners.

He hardly saw Annie that day, but after his evening meal he filched a couple of pieces of fried chicken from the plate and took them to her.

172

She was sitting in her hut staring at nothing, and humming some odd chant to herself.

"Got some chicken," Cap'n Jack said.

She took the chicken without thanks, and ate it with a surprising daintiness.

Cap'n Jack squatted on his haunches and waited till she had done. There was silence for a while.

"It was a purty song you was humming," Cap'n Jack said.

"African," Annie shrugged. "It from Africa."

"That where you from?"

"No," Annie said.

He asked a few more questions, but she only responded with a yes or a no, or a shrug, and then he heard Parson Dick calling him, so he bade her good night, and went to find out what the matter was.

He saw her every evening after that, and always took her some nice scraps of food from the main kitchen. She took the food but never thanked him, and responded to his questions simply. He told her of his life, but she didn't seem interested. He told her of how he had come to Massa Jackson, but she didn't seem to care. He told her of the promise of freedom the Massa had given him, and then she spoke.

"Ain't never gwine happen," she said.

Cap'n Jack told her she was wrong, that Massa James was different from other Massas, but she only shrugged.

"All Massas the same," she said.

Cap'n Jack felt cheered. At least she had started to take part in the conversations, even if it was on a negative note.

A few days later the new loom was delivered, and Cap'n Jack had it set up in Annie's hut. It was enormous and almost filled the little room, but they had no other place to put it until the weaving house was ready.

Now, for the first time, Annie showed interest in something. She traced her fingers along the wooden frame of the loom, and sat in front of it, and tested its span with her arms. It was an excellent piece of equipment, the finest that could be had, for James was not stinting on anything for The Forks of Cypress.

Annie began setting up the lines for the warps, and seemed to have forgotten Cap'n Jack was there.

"I's need yarn," she said after a while.

"Tell me what yo' want, I get it for yo'," Cap'n Jack replied.

She asked what cloth she was to make first, and then gave him her list and he went to organize it. When he came back, she was sitting at her empty loom, as if it was her natural home.

The yarn came, and she started weaving. Cap'n Jack loved to watch her. She worked gracefully, elegantly, shuttling the bobbin to and fro with a natural rhythm, patient in her labors, and as she worked, she hummed odd and lilting melodies that seemed to be from another place and time, and lovely cloth began to reveal itself, out of the complexity of wood and string and bundles of yarn.

Mostly, she worked during the day, but Cap'n Jack could come to her only in the evenings, and she took to weaving when he was there. She seldom spoke, but listened to everything he had to say, while she chanted and made cloth.

After a while he would fall silent and just watch her, enchanted by her easy grace, and lulled by the sweet songs she sang. Cap'n Jack was happy in her company, and slowly it dawned on him that she was as happy with him. In the winter he got sick and she nursed him, with herbs and strange potions. He got better. He began bringing his food from the kitchen, to eat with her, and always had enough for both of them. When the weaving house was ready, he supervised the moving of the loom, and found her some simple furniture, a bed and

174

a table and a couple of old rocking chairs that the builders had used and didn't need anymore.

He helped furnish the big house, too. At last it was ready, six months late, and they unpacked the crates and for the first time he saw what James and Sally had bought. The drapes were velvet and the rugs were intricately patterned and came from a place called Persia. The chandeliers were crystal, and some held over a hundred candles. The furniture was beautiful, mahogany and teak and cedar, hand-carved in Europe. The new cutlery was silver, and the crockery was of fine china from England with a pattern especially designed for James Jackson. The beds were magnificent four-posters, heavy and solid, with flowers and birds and small animals carved on the wooden posts, and canopies of brocade and damask.

The floors were polished until they shone like mirrors, and the rugs looked even more beautiful against them. Parson Dick, who knew a very great deal about a lot of things, told him that the weavers deliberately made a flaw in every carpet, because only the God they believed in could create something perfect. The dining table was long and gleamed with beeswax, and could accommodate twenty people without seeming crowded. The dining chairs were high-backed, and had tapestry covers. The paintings that adorned the walls were old and in heavy gilt frames, but then James commissioned a traveling artist to make portraits of all his family.

When the house was finished, relations and visitors came from all over the South to see the wonder of it. James was a state senator now, and politicians and businessmen and their wives, and the governor of the state, and even some politicians from Washington, the capital, all came to see the wonder that was The Forks of Cypress.

Shortly afterward they had a party, a housewarming and a christening, because Sally had given birth to another son, and he was called James Jackson III in honor of his father. Everyone agreed that the name was right and proper, but laughed at the confusion it would cause. If they called the father's name, would the boy come running, or if they spoke to the boy, would the father respond?

James and Sally toyed with nicknames for him. Sara and Eleanor were keen on Jamie, which had been James's pet name in Ireland, but the parents thought he should have his own identity. For a few days they tried Jimmy, because of Sara's late husband, but it didn't suit him.

The registrar of births solved the problem. He was a punctilious clerk from England, neat and fastidious, and trained in the old ways. When he wrote the new boy's name in the book, in the most elegant copper plate hand, he did not write "James," but rather the formal English abbreviation, "Jas."

It amused James, and he began calling his son "Jas." After a while everyone adopted it, but because it looked a little odd when it was written down, they added another letter to it, and so James Jackson, the son of James Jackson who was the son of James Jackson, became known simply as Jass.

The christening was a splendid affair, held on the new lawn in front of the house, near the magnolia tree, which had grown several feet since James and Andrew first planted it. Nearby there was a wigwam, which James had provided for an Indian family, but none wanted to live there, and so the children used it for play. A.J. pretended he was a great chief, and tormented his older sisters, and the slave children.

Eleanor and Thomas Kirkman from Nashville came with their son Tom, who was a young man now, and was engaged to Sally's first daughter, Elizabeth. Sara came with her boys, and John Coffee, who had a fine plantation near Florence, with his family.

Politicians and influential men were there in abundance, and while they enjoyed the celebration, their conversations, which they kept from the women, were all about the recent sensational case of Denmark Vesey.

A free black who lived in Charleston, Vesey had plotted with other blacks, slaves, to rebel against the whites, and had somehow amassed guns for the purpose. A nervous maid had discovered the guns, and the plot was revealed. Vesey and thirty-seven of his followers were executed.

It was not the first example of insurrection by blacks. Many of the men present could remember the bloody revolution on the Caribbean island of Santo Domingo, when the armies of the black general Toussaint L'Ouverture massacred the French and took control of the island. Or the Gabriel rebellion, much closer to home, in Richmond, Virginia. In each instance, the rebellions had eventually been bloodily suppressed, and new and even more stringent laws were introduced against the blacks.

It was happening now, in Charleston. A law had been passed that any free blacks arriving as crew on ships were not permitted to land, but had to be kept on board as long as the ship was in harbor, at the captain's expense. The law was taking its toll of sea traffic into Charleston, but the Southerners considered this a small price to pay for their security. Throughout the slave-holding states discipline had increased and punishment for any infringement been made more severe. Armed patrols to discourage runaways had been introduced, in addition to the regular slave catchers.

James had his own problems with this matter. Many of his new field hands were troublesome, and there had been a few instances of slaves running away. It angered James. He thought he was a benevolent Massa, and regarded the slaves as ungrateful, and their actions

177

threatening to his wealth and position. It was clear to him that Evans, the foreman, could not control such large numbers, and, regretfully, had to be replaced.

He spoke with John Coffee, who was pleased. Coffee had always regarded James as overly lenient with his slaves, and thought that perhaps with his new wealth and position to protect, and his outstanding plantation, James had found some backbone.

"Someone with a strong sense of discipline?" John Coffee asked.

"Whatever is necessary," James agreed.

Coffee thought he knew just the man. Egbert Harris had served under him against the Creek, and at New Orleans. He was working as an overseer on a small plantation in Georgia, but was anxious to find a situation closer to his home, in Nashville. John Coffee promised to investigate the matter for James.

By tacit agreement among the men, there was no discussion of slaves, slavery, or the Vesey plot with the women, and James spent a pleasant afternoon circulating among the guests and receiving their congratulations for his new son and his new house, and his new political career.

He was introduced to William Perkins, who was looking to buy land in the district. William Perkins was small, studious, and almost permanently worried. He was married to an ambitious woman whose given name was Pocahontas, but who preferred to be called Becky. It was the Perkinses' personal tragedy that neither of their two babies had lived, and they blamed the fierce coastal humidity of South Carolina. Becky was pregnant again, and William, having caught the Florence fever, hoped that the move inland would benefit his wife and coming child.

James was flattered by his attention and amused by his constant anxiety. He had recently bought two more small plantations, in Florida and Mississippi, and gave

178

William some basic advice. William hung on every word, jotted down notes, and would not leave his side. James spied his nephew, Tom Kirkman, who was moving to Florence when he married Elizabeth, to work for James. He introduced the two men, and told Tom to look after William.

That evening there was a fine family dinner. James, at the head of the table, and Sally, opposite to him, were surrounded by loving relatives. They started to tell tales of the old days in Ireland, and then sang songs and toasted the martyrs, Oliver Bond and Lord Edward, the Sheares brothers and Wolfe Tone.

"Erin go bragh!" they shouted, although they were a long way from Erin.

"And Sean," James said, raising his glass. He was already a little drunk.

No one else knew whom he meant, but toasted Sean anyway, and drank the health of the new baby, Jass, and welcomed A.J., who was attending his first formal dinner, to the clan.

It was midnight when they went to bed. Cap'n Jack, who had been on his feet since dawn, was dozing in his Massa's dressing room when James came in. He woke with a start, helped James undress, and was genially dismissed for the evening.

Cap'n Jack didn't go to his own hut, for that was not his routine. He went to the weaving house, as he did every evening, to be with Annie for a few minutes. Her candle was still burning, and she was sitting at the loom, weaving and humming one of her strange songs. She didn't speak or acknowledge his presence, but he knew she was pleased he was there, and that she had been waiting for him.

He sat in a rocking chair and did not speak.

"What's wrong?" she said softly.

He didn't reply, and when she turned around to look at him, she saw he was dozing. She woke him gently and told him to lie on the bed. He was too tired to argue, and did as he was bidden. Annie went back to the loom, to her cloth and her humming, and Cap'n Jack drifted to sleep listening to the lovely lullaby.

When he awoke a few hours later he was puzzled, because he wasn't sure where he was, and knew he was not alone. He realized that Annie had crawled onto the bed beside him, fully clothed, and was curled in the crook of his arm, fast asleep.

It felt right and natural to him that she was there, and wonderful, and his heart was golden. He didn't stir, but turned his head gently so he could see her better.

The moonlight traced in through the window, and a wayward moonbeam shimmered over Annie's face. She slept peacefully, with no hint on her face of the pain that she would not discuss with Cap'n Jack.

The soft light of dawn replaced the moon, and Cap'n Jack lay motionless beside Annie, wide awake, staring at his love, and caressed by her gentle breathing.

19

When Cap'n Jack and Annie got married, James gave them a splendid wedding party, because Andrew was running for president.

Annie had been reluctant to accept Cap'n Jack's proposal. After his first night with her, when nothing had happened between them, Cap'n Jack slept in the weaving house regularly, with Annie. As they got to know each other better, and felt secure with each other, a physical relationship developed. It was something that they both wanted and needed, just as they wanted each other in all aspects of their lives. They made no plans for a future, but accepted what they had now, and it was precious to them. For the first time in her life, Annie started to trust a man and she even stopped taking her special herbs and grasses to prevent a child, because she began to want a baby by Cap'n Jack. She still doubted the future, but lived, as she had always done, for the day.

She became pregnant. For a while she thought of doing something to herself to change her condition, but then she realized that the innocent thing inside her had become all of her hope. If it was a boy child, he could be raised in his father's image, as a man who was caring to women. If it was a girl child, she would have the life that Annie had never had, a life without fear of men, secure in the love of both her parents. Even if anything were to happen to Annie, and she fully expected her happiness not to last, Cap'n Jack would love and nurture the child.

She told Cap'n Jack of her condition, and he immediately proposed marriage, as she had known he would. She was puzzled that she had told him of the pregnancy, because she had no ready answer for his question. Marriage seemed very permanent to her, and Annie did not believe in permanence. Cap'n Jack wooed her beautifully, and did not press her, but presented all his arguments patiently. He courted her, and made her feel as if he were asking her to give herself, unlike other men, who simply took her.

Eventually, because she could think of no good argument against him, and because in her heart she wanted to be married to him, she accepted him, and the look on his face, of simple, unalloyed joy, made her glad.

Cap'n Jack told James, who immediately gave his consent. The slave then asked his Massa for a privilege. He wanted a proper wedding, and he wanted his old friend Alfred to be his best man. James said that he would write to Andrew and request permission for Alfred to come. Cap'n Jack asked him one more favor.

"Annie ain't got no pappy," he said. "You her Massa, you her pappy. Will you give her away?"

James was moved. The whole question of slavery had

been exercising his mind recently. The South was still quivering with righteous indignation and latent fear from the Vesey plot, and several states had sharpened their laws against blacks. Many in the north were complaining of the treatment of the slaves, and the South was closing ranks against their outrage. At the same time, James was having continuing problems with his own field hands. They were truculent and trouble-some; three more had run away, and one had never been found. Evans was worse than useless, and had indicated his readiness to step down, but John Coffee had not yet heard from Egbert Harris.

Cap'n Jack's request began to put the whole issue into perspective for him. He was father to his black children. They were an extension of his family, and he treated them well, if sternly, as he would his own family. There could be no better example of his relation-ship with the best of his slaves, in these troubled times, than the public admission of his role. He would be delighted to give Annie away.

He wrote to Andrew requesting that Alfred be Cap'n Jack's best man, and to his surprise, Andrew replied in person, rather than by letter.

He came to The Forks, unannounced, to see James. He brought Alfred with him, and immediately gave his consent to Alfred's role in the coming wedding. Andrew greeted Sally warmly, and the children, and insisted they call him Uncle Andrew. He brought greet-ings from Rachel, who was ailing and not able to travel, and told them the news of his sons. He met Jass for the first time, and played happily with the infant for a while, and then told A.J. war stories, and acted out the battle of New Orleans for the wide-eyed boy.

James and Sally watched from the veranda, as Gen-eral Andrew chased around the garden after A.J., who had been cast as the British Army.

"I wonder what he wants," Sally said softly, and James laughed.

"I'm sure you can guess," he said.

Andrew had a pleasant dinner with James and Sally, and was at his most charming. He described the new house he was building for Rachel to replace the older, smaller Hermitage. He told them all the gossip of the political world, and some of the intrigues that had caused him to resign as governor of Florida.

"It was for the best," he said. "Rachel found the climate abominable."

He kept his temper under control and joked about his political opponents.

"Shook them all when I retired," he laughed. "No one believed me."

"I'm not surprised," Sally said with a charming smile. "You're much too young to retire."

"I fully intended it," Andrew said. "I was tired. I was sick. I was not fit to be president."

There was a soft silence.

"You have changed your mind?" James asked him.

There was another silence.

"Yes," Andrew said. "I have changed my mind."

Sally excused herself, and Parson Dick brought port to the table. Andrew helped himself to a liberal measure.

"The country needs me," Andrew said. "We go to rack and ruin. The bureaucracy gets larger and fouler and more corrupt by the day, and the tentacles of government are reaching farther and farther into our lives, until they will strangle us."

It was the old cry, not only of Andrew, but of Thomas Jefferson.

"We are in debt," Andrew said, warming to his theme. James began to feel as if he were a crowd of a thousand, and Andrew was on a soapbox.

"How can a country as rich as ours be in debt?" Andrew demanded.

"The war?" James offered mildly, but Andrew snorted in derision.

"The war is an excuse," he said, close to shouting now. "It is the departments and committees and sub-committees that keep us broke—us, the poor simple farmers who pay for Washington's excess."

James tried hard not to smile. Andrew was certainly a farmer, but he was not poor, and very far from simple.

"And that bank!" Andrew sighed heavily. The central government bank was his special black beast. "They lend money freely when we don't need it, and foreclose on our mortgages when times are bad."

James thought that this was the practice of all banks, but it was true that the central bank favored the rich, and especially the industrializing North.

Andrew poured more port, and then smiled.

"But you know all this; we have discussed it so often," he said.

"So the time has come?" James asked.

"The time has come," Andrew agreed. "Not that I want it, no, by the eternal, I had as lief stay where I am, with my lovely Rachel and darling boys. But what can I do?"

James understood it was a rhetorical question, and had no need of a reply. Andrew would do what he had intended to do all along. In any case, it was all non-sense. Andrew's "retirement" was a fiction. He had been elected to the Senate in Washington, and spent more than half of each year there.

"The state legislature in Tennessee will formally nom-inate me for the presidency," Andrew said.

He paused for a moment.

"I want your help in Alabama."

I want your help. These were the sweetest words that Andrew had ever said to James. I want your help. The old lion, the hero of New Orleans, the greatest general since Washington, needed James's help. Through all the years that he had walked in Andrew's shadow,

184

James had waited for this moment. His political power seemed almost tangible to him.

"Anything I can do," James responded graciously. "You know you have only to ask."

Andrew nodded his head as graciously, and they got down to business.

He wanted James to use all his political influence to persuade the government of Alabama to nominate him for the presidency.

"I will propose the motion myself," James agreed.

Andrew was sure he would get a good popular vote, but in case there was a doubt, and the matter had to be resolved in the House of Representatives, he wanted James to start drumming up support for him.

"You know far more people in Washington than I," James said truthfully, but Andrew knew how to flatter his man.

"Your influence is more substantial than you imagine," he said. "Your opinion is well respected."

And he wanted money for his campaign.

"I thought we'd never get to it," James said, and laughed, to soften it. Andrew had the grace to smile, but was not altogether pleased by James's levity.

They talked until late, about Andrew's aspirations for himself and the country, and they talked of the old days. The drunker Andrew got, the longer his speeches about his glorious military career became.

Alfred sat in the kitchen with Cap'n Jack, while Parson Dick dozed in a corner, in case his Massa should ring. Alfred was enchanted by Annie.

He was unmarried, and longed to find a bride.

"Dump this ol' buzzard, an' take me instead," he said with a chuckle, and Annie smiled, and shook her head.

Alfred wished them both well, and told Annie stories of the old days in Nashville, and of the fun they'd had, and of their rowdy Massas.

It was a new world for Annie. She was with men

185

whom she liked and trusted, and they talked about their Massas with affection, but with a sense that they saw all the foibles and weaknesses of the men who owned them. They hated their slavery but had no alternative to it.

"Them niggers runnin' away," Cap'n Jack said, talking of the several runaways from The Forks. "Where they gwine go."

"Henry got away," Annie said, of the slave who had run away and never been found.

"He didn't come back," Cap'n Jack corrected her gently. "We don't know he got away. As like the catchers got him and killed him."

Alfred nodded. "Any case, I bin up South," he said. Many of the slaves referred to the North as up South. "An' it ain't a whole lot differen' there. Niggers is still niggers."

He changed the subject to happier things, and told them of some of the extravagant personalities he had met, with Andrew in Washington, and made them laugh. Then the bell rang, and Alfred and Cap'n Jack went to put their Massas to bed.

Sally stirred when James got into bed, but drifted back to sleep. James lay awake for a while, thinking of his conversation with Andrew. He had no doubt that Andrew would win the election—he was still immensely popular with the people—and it would not hurt James to support him or loan him money. It gave him some leverage over Andrew, and, once again, it amused him to think that he would have influence with the president of the United States. What pleased him most was that Andrew thought he needed his help, and had asked for it. The world turns, James thought.

Then he had several ideas, which coalesced into one, which he thought brilliant.

He would host a fine party, here at The Forks, and would invite every person of consequence whom he

186

knew. At this party he would announce his intention to support Andrew's nomination. He remembered Cap'n Jack's coming wedding, and decided to give his guests some real fun. Cap'n Jack and Annie would be married at this enormous party, and the world, and his slaves, would see the benign face of slavery. They would see that it was not all beatings and lashings and rape and exploitation, but rather a unique and unrivaled management of the land and people. The South was always on the moral defensive about slavery, and James would change that. He would take the initiative, and show everyone how the system could be used in the best interests of all the people, white and black.

The more he thought about it the more extravagant the party became, and the more successful his position, and he went to sleep with a big smile on his face that was only partly caused by the amount of port he had drunk.

Annie hated the idea when Cap'n Jack told her. She didn't want all that fuss. She didn't want all those people staring at her. She wanted a quiet ceremony, in which she and Cap'n Jack jumped over the broom into the land of matrimony, as her mammy's mammy had done. As all slaves did. But she had no choice in the matter. Her Massa had decreed it.

Of all the many fine functions given at The Forks of Cypress, the wedding of Cap'n Jack and Annie was one of the finest. Three hundred guests attended, and the Southerners brought their slaves, so that nearly five hundred people saw the couple wed. Andrew was in Washington, but he sent Alfred with Richard Coll, his aide from Florida, who was said to be sweet on Eleanor's daughter, Mary.

Annie was nervous, but looked lovely, in a dress that Sally had helped her choose, and they giggled about her full belly. Cap'n Jack looked splendid in new clothes provided by James. James's daughters Mary, Martha,

187

and Mary Ellen attended Annie, and little Sassy was a flower girl. A.J., looking very smart, stayed with Sally, and Tiara nursed Jass. At the end of the ceremony, the couple jumped over the broom into the land of matrimony, and everyone cheered. Even Annie smiled then.

A vast buffet was laid out on the lawn, and tables of food for the slaves at the side of the house. Slave catchers were employed to make sure that none of the visiting slaves ran away, and the field hands were given half a day off and allowed to watch from a distance. In any case it was fall, and the harvest had been picked.

After everyone had eaten, they gathered to hear James make a speech. He praised Cap'n Jack and Annie, and said how proud he was of them, and that this day represented proof positive to the Northerners that slavery was ultimately a benevolent institution. He talked about his dear friend Andrew Jackson, and his slave Alfred, who was best man at this very wedding, and went on to announce his support for the candidacy of Andrew Jackson for the presidency. He was wildly applauded.

The fiddlers struck up the tune, and there was dancing. James and Sally mingled with their guests, renewing old friendships, greeting acquaintances. James's nephew Tom Kirkman was there with Elizabeth, Sally's daughter by her first husband, and they were planning their own wedding.

"Not another," James laughed. "I can't afford it!"

William Perkins was there, whom James hardly remembered until Tom reminded him. Perkins had bought a property in Florence, and was full of gratitude to James and Tom.

John Coffee was there, with his family, and a man James didn't know. He was introduced as Egbert Harris.

"Told you I'd find you an overseer," John Coffee said to James. "This man's one of the best."

They shook hands, and talked briefly, and agreed to meet again later, when the guests had gone.

At the side of the house, the slaves had their own party, and made their own music, and had a high old time.

But James did not.

Full of good cheer toward the world, he talked with some of his political friends, and was surprised to discover the amount of antagonism that existed toward the idea of Andrew as president.

Andrew was uncouth, hot-tempered, and unpredictable. James could only agree.

Andrew was a dueler and a street brawler. James could only agree.

He had antagonized the Spanish in Florida. James could only agree.

He had antagonized Britain, which was the South's major trading partner. James could only agree.

He would destroy the central bank and allow state banks to flourish without control. James could only agree.

He had no experience in administration. James could only agree.

He was ruthless in his dealings with the Indians. James could only agree. He had obtained his Indian treaties illegally, sometimes, perhaps often, with bribes.

James's blood ran cold.

How did anyone know?

He left the party in a foul mood, and went to his study. He heard a tiny voice of doubt, like the whisper of wind in the trees before a storm.

Had he backed the wrong man?

He shook the doubts aside. Of course Andrew would win; the public adored him.

But did they?

They admired him—as a hero, a general, a soldier— but would they vote for him as president?

In the South, almost certainly, but in the North he was known to be rabidly against industry, which was the life blood of the New England states. He venerated the simple farmer, but believed in untrammeled capitalism, which sometimes destroyed the farmers whose cause he espoused. He was also a slaveholder, and dedicated to the expansion of the number of slave states, which the New Englanders fiercely resented.

Even if the public did vote for him, they might not vote in sufficient numbers, and if the election had to be decided in the House of Representatives, James could not swear to the outcome. For the first time, he understood why Andrew had come to him for help.

He cursed himself for a fool, for not thinking things over before he had so rashly allied himself to Andrew's cause. The damage was done; he was committed, but he would tread very carefully from now on. And he would ask Sally's opinion.

There was a tap on the door, and Egbert Harris came in.

"Sorry to bother you," he said. "But there's been trouble, with your slaves."

James was astonished.

"A couple of 'em got hold of some liquor and started a fight," Harris explained. "I guess it was a setup, because in the fuss another two tried to run away."

James was furious. On this day, of all days, after all he had done for them.

"Damned niggers!" he cried. "After all I've done for them."

Evans, he knew, would be useless. "Get the slave catchers," he shouted. "Get the bloodhounds."

Egbert Harris smiled.

"No need," he said. "I took the liberty. They didn't get far. One of 'em's a bit of a bloody mess. He won't try running away again for a while."

James wasn't sure what to say, but thanked Harris, and asked him his terms.

The money was quickly settled. The conditions took a little longer. Harris wanted total authority over the slaves, the permission to enforce discipline the way he saw it, and no questions asked. In return he guaranteed productivity.

"Though it'll take me a while," he said, "to bring 'em into line. Things have been lax around here."

James nodded. If the slaves had chosen this day, of all days, to run away, then things were in a worse state than he had suspected. He was filled with disappointment, and agreed to Harris's conditions.

"And the house niggers," Harris said.

James thought for a moment.

"Those who work in the house are valued and trusted, and have been with me many years," he said.

Harris shrugged. "Have it your way. Don't blame me if things go wrong."

He was rough and forthright, and James wasn't sure that he liked him, but he had no alternative. If the slaves needed discipline, then discipline there would be. It was agreed that Harris would commence with James in three months, after he had squared things with his present employer and gone home to Nashville to see his family.

They shook hands, and Harris excused himself. James sat at his desk, furious with himself about Andrew, and the wretched ingratitude of his slaves. Then he remembered who he was. One of the richest men in the state, of enormous influence, and a state senator. He was a powerful man. He would start to use his power. Even Andrew Jackson had come to him for help.

Egbert Harris started work as overseer at The Forks of Cypress three months later, as agreed.

Shortly before his arrival, Annie delivered a girl child to the doting Cap'n Jack, and they called her Easter, because she was born on the day of resurrection.

191

20

Sally tried to block her ears to the screams. She hated it when the slaves were whipped. She hated Harris for doing it, and hated the fact that it was necessary. In the first few weeks of his tenure, Harris had a whipping block made at the slave quarters, and instituted a regime of ruthless punishment for the slightest offenses. Every few days, it seemed, Harris would find reason to have one of the slaves flogged, and for the first time Sally heard, on a regular basis, the primal sounds that are made by a human being in unendurable agony, and she couldn't bear the screams.

She demanded that the block be moved to some location farther from the house because it was giving the children nightmares, and Harris had reluctantly acceded. It didn't make any difference. The pitiful cries of the victims still reached the house, and Sally began taking the children out, on picnics to the river, or into town, when she knew a flogging had been ordered.

She could not understand why it had all gone so wrong. As a girl she had been brought up with slavery, and believed in its necessity. On her father's estate, some slaves had been flogged occasionally, for serious offenses, and she hated it then but accepted it as a fact of life. In Nashville, when she married James, there had been very little trouble with the slaves, and Evans had maintained an easy discipline, by use of the switch or the rod or, on one occasion, selling away a young troublemaker, but otherwise she had thought the people happy.

When the mansion was being built, the workers had not caused any trouble. They seemed to take pride in their craft, and their foremen kept them in line.

But from the moment they had bought the new field

hands and started planting the new fields, everything had changed. In her own mind, Sally blamed it on the Denmark Vesey plot, which had caused considerable discussion in the slave ranks, and the runaways had begun then. She believed, as James did, that Evans did not have the necessary authority to enforce discipline in these difficult times, and while she disliked Harris, and bitterly regretted the necessity of employing him, she saw no alternative.

Her heart bled for James, who had worked so hard to achieve his ambitions; she blessed those slaves who were loyal to them, and she pitied and despised those slaves who were the troublemakers. She examined her attitude to slavery, and believed at the core of her being that it was the best possible institution for the welfare of the black people, who, like children, were not fitted to survive in the jungle of the white world. She allowed that there were several intelligent and literate blacks, and several who had done well for themselves as free men, mostly in the North, but they were the exceptions that proved the rule. She worried if she was simply rationalizing what was finally unjustifiable because she understood that the South could not survive economically without slavery, but she also rejected the argument that slavery was cheaper than paid labor. She knew how much their slaves cost them, both in purchase price and upkeep, and the sums were astounding. Mostly, she believed in the institution because of the benefits if brought to both races.

The validity of slavery, to Sally, was that it was so simple. If only the troublemakers could understand those benefits, as so many of their house niggers did. If only the screaming would stop.

She worried about James. He was making himself physically ill with worry, and could scarcely keep control of his temper these days. She understood that it was not only because of the slaves. For some reason, James was obsessed with the matter of Andrew's election, and she guessed that something had happened to make him doubt his support of his mentor. She knew this must cost her husband dear, for Andrew was his greatest friend. He adored the man, as a son might adore a father, and believed Andrew was partly responsible for their considerable wealth. She knew James had doubts about some of Andrew's beliefs and convictions, but she did not understand why the election was of such consuming interest to him.

Sally loved Rachel, but she didn't like Andrew. She thought him arrogant, overbearing, and selfish to a degree she had seldom encountered. He was condescending to Rachel, and she believed that he probably blamed his wife for their inability to have children of their own. She had watched Rachel change over the years, from a bright and vibrant woman to a dour and ailing recluse who seldom left the house and lived only through her vainglorious husband, and had devoted herself to his welfare and her sons, who were not her sons.

She disliked the influence that Andrew had once had over James, she was appalled by Andrew's cavalier attitude to money, and horrified by his hanging of the missionaries in Florida, and the execution of the boy, Woods, during the Creek War.

If James had finally realized that Andrew was not his best friend, if he had come to understand that Andrew was simply using James for his own purposes, if James was able to break Andrew's spell over him, then perhaps some good would come out of this terrible time.

If only the screams would stop.

As a mother, Sally had other worries. A.J., her darling, her beloved, her firstborn son, was going away to school. A.J. had been taught by tutors, as the girls were, but now James and Sally had decided he needed to be educated in the company of other boys. There was no suitable school yet in Florence, and so he was being sent to the Stevens Academy in Nashville. He would live with Eleanor and Thomas, and Sally was sure he would be well looked after, but her mother's heart ached for her son; she would miss him dreadfully, and worry about his safety. He was only eight and far too young to be going out into the world on his own, but she was a strong woman, and boarding school was in her son's best interests. She tried to devote herself to making his last few weeks at home memorable, but the unpleasant atmosphere that began at the slave quarters pervaded the house and their lives, and she found herself constantly distracted from what she perceived as her maternal role.

If only the screams would stop.

The new overseer, Egbert Harris, loved his job, because he loved war, and he believed that keeping the niggers under control was a continuing war of attrition that he was determined to win.

He had been born to a poor farming family, pioneers, in the Great Smokies, and Harris's early years were unrelentingly arduous. His father scratched a living as best he could from their humble acres, and made illegal whiskey in a still in the forest to supplement their meager income. His mother's life had been one of ceaseless child raising in impossible circumstances, and half her brood had not survived infancy or their early years. Immigrants from Wales, they had trekked to the frontier in the early days, and bought their acres on the best land they could afford, putting their faith in the bounty of America. But their farm was near the Cherokee land that straddled the Georgia border, and they were subject to constant harassment by raiding parties. One of their daughters died from a Cherokee arrow.

Egbert, their third surviving son, was a tough and resourceful boy, for whom the frontier was home. He shot his first deer at seven, at nine he caught a bear in a trap, and when he was twelve he killed and scalped his first Indian. Hoping to make his way in the world, he

195

left home when he was fifteen, and went to Knoxville, where he worked in a stable and developed his skill with horses. When he heard that Brigadier John Coffee of Nashville was looking for volunteers for the militia, to fight the British, he rode to Nashville in a day, offered his services, and was accepted.

The army became a second home to him, and he loved the life. Adept at living from the land and sleeping rough, he survived the rigors of the winter march to and from Natchez, and was promoted to sergeant. He fought in the Creek War, and revered his direct commander, Coffee, and his general, Andrew Jackson. He believed implicitly in the hierarchy of the army; he obeyed his officers and his men obeyed him, without question or demur. When a firing squad was needed to execute the mutinous boy, James Woods, Harris volunteered. The possibility of dying himself in any of the battles was of minimal concern to him. He did not believe he was going to be killed, but if he was, he would put up a heck of a fight first.

Most of all, he loved the challenge and the sense of camaraderie, and the adventure. His survival, like his fellows', depended on each individual's grit and skill and courage, and their collective commitment to each other. The possibility of not being strong enough, of being killed, was a direct sexual challenge to him, and he would pit himself against the most formidable foe to prove that he could win. After the battle he would be in a state of high sexual arousal, flooded by the life-force, and then he would force himself on whatever woman was available to him—white trash, Indian, or nigra, it made no difference to him. If no women were available, he would relieve himself with his hand.

Like his commanders, he had an unshakable faith in the divinely ordained destiny of the white man to rule this land. He respected Indians as fierce warriors, and loathed their despoiling presence on what should be

196

his. He could not understand why his father had to make do with a few scrubby acres, when these naked heathens had limitless vistas. It was his personal quest to wrest the land from the natives and give it to his family.

He saved his pay and kept his vow. Because of the land sales around Florence, the price of land near Nashville dropped to an affordable price, and he bought five fair acres. He built a log cabin with own hands, and moved his parents down from the mountains. They managed a good life for themselves, but the farm could not support him as well, so John Coffee found him a job as assistant overseer on a small plantation in Georgia. Before long he had the top job.

He ran the plantation as a military command, with military discipline, and while the slaves hated him, they dared not disobey him. To add some spice to what might have become tedious, he took to baiting the strongest and angriest of the hands, to try to provoke them to run away, or to rebel against him. He respected strong niggers for their strength, while he despised them for the color of their skin. Keeping weaklings and women in line was no challenge to him; testing himself against strong men was the true measure of his masculinity.

Still, he missed his family, and when John Coffee contacted him with a possible job closer to home, he took the first opportunity he could to call on his old brigadier. He came with Coffee to Cap'n Jack's wedding at The Forks of Cypress, and was appalled by what he saw. He believed what his parents had taught him, that the blacks were an inferior race of animals, who had been put on earth by God to serve the whites. He had no patience toward those Massas who were lenient with their slaves, and would cheerfully have murdered an abolitionist if he ever met one. The fact that James was treating niggers benevolently was abhorrent to him, and he agreed with Coffee that James needed some spine. He saw it as his good Christian duty to bring order to the chaos that was The Forks of Cypress.

He employed an assistant, his brother Albert, who shared his views on slavery, and the two of them instituted a rigorous discipline at The Forks. The lash was used as and when Harris or his brother saw fit, which was often, troublesome slaves were chained up at night, and slave catchers roamed the boundaries with guns and bloodhounds.

James protested at Harris's severity and the cost of the manpower, but Harris assured him he needed six months to bring the niggers to heel, and then his iron grip would relax. James, distracted by political affairs, agreed.

Yet Harris was clever. He understood James's passion for his blooded horses, and that the men who ran the stables were handpicked. He put a slave catcher near them, just in case of trouble, but otherwise he left them alone. He was a keen gambling man himself, and actually admired those stable slaves, such as Monkey Simon, or Micah or Ephraim, who knew their job and were content with the world of horses. The field hands were Harris's prime concern, and while he resented the ascendancy of the house niggers, he left them, for the most part, alone.

Except for Annie.

Black women, nigra women, had a powerful effect on Egbert Harris. He fantasized about them, and in his erotic dreams saw himself as a prize stallion subduing bucking black mares. He hated them for the sexual hold they had over him, but he could hardly restrain himself from taking them, by force preferably, for rape proved him to be the ultimate victor.

He controlled his urges most of the time, and most of the women did not interest him—the old, or the fat, or the young girls—but Annie was none of these things. Annie was a challenge. Annie, beautiful and with a full, rounded body, became the object of Harris's most urgent desires. It didn't matter to him that she was the mother of a young child; it didn't matter to him that she was married; he wanted her, and hated her for making him want her.

Annie was completely aware of Harris's sexual interest in her, for she had seen it too often, in too many other men, and was just as aware of his hostility to her. Harris frightened Annie. She doubted he would attempt anything because of her marriage to Cap'n Jack, but she did not trust him, and made some special chants to protect her house and her family from him.

Her greatest concern was not for herself, or even for her husband, because he lay under the wing of the Massa's protection, but for her baby, Easter.

Easter was gorgeous, a chubby, happy infant with a constant, gurgling laugh. Everyone loved her, but, apart from her parents, none more so than Jass.

The toddler Jass lived in an odd world. He was adored by his family, and Tiara, his mammy, but he was the second son, and A.J. had pride of place in everyone's affections. His mother tried to spend as much time with Jass as she could, but she was a busy woman, with a household to run and a family to raise. His father was usually closeted in his study and Jass seldom saw him. So Jass, who had the run of the plantation, attached himself to Cap'n Jack, and, through him, Easter.

Jass loved the baby Easter. When she was very little, Annie would put her outside on a blanket and Jass would sit near her, playing in the dirt and burbling to Easter as if she understood every word he said, when few people yet understood him. As they grew, he would point things out to her, or brush flies from her, and give her pieces of his apple, which Easter was too young to eat. Sometimes Tiara would put him down for his nap in the same cot as Easter, and then Jass

199

snuggled up to the baby girl, and told her he loved her more than anything. If he was taken away from her to go back to the big house, he would cry his distress, and sometimes threw a temper tantrum. Since he seemed so happy with the girl, they left him with her often, or with Cap'n Jack, who would walk with Jass around the garden, and play with him, as fathers play with sons. It was Cap'n Jack who spanked him if he was naughty, and Cap'n Jack who gave candies when he was good. Jass knew that Easter was Cap'n Jack's little girl, and because he regarded Cap'n Jack as some sort of uncle, or even as a father, Easter became his sister.

In the ugly months of Harris's rule, Jass and Easter seemed to be the only ones who were oblivious to the general despondency.

Annie saw Harris watching them sometimes, and watching Easter when Jass was not there, and worried for her daughter. She knew, they all did, of children sold away from their slave mothers, and she distrusted Harris so violently she thought him capable of anything.

But Harris was not looking at Easter, or Jass. He was looking at Annie.

She was weaving at the loom one day, and was sure she saw someone outside. She went to the window, and then to the door, but could find no one.

It happened again, a few days later, and when she went to the door, she saw Harris loitering under one of the oaks, with an ugly smile on his face.

She saw him again when she went to bathe in the creek. It was fall, and soon the water would be too cold to swim. She stripped herself naked and dove into the clean, fresh, icy water, and swam for a while, but then she heard a movement in the bushes, and saw Harris standing on the bank, watching her.

She didn't tell Cap'n Jack because there was nothing

he could do. If he lost his temper, which he might, and accosted Harris, which he might, or complained to Massa, which he might, things could very well get worse.

She avoided Harris as much as she could, and kept Easter inside the house with her, and Jass when he was with them.

She heard an odd noise one day, a small rattle on the windowpane. She thought it must be the wind, or a bird, or something fallen on the roof, and ignored it. She heard the rattle again, louder now, and realized that someone was throwing small stones at the window, as if to attract her attention.

She went to the door and when she looked out she saw Harris standing underneath the trees, some distance away, staring at her. He was rubbing his hand over his groin.

She slammed the door and ran to her baby, and held her fast, and dared not let her mind think of what Harris was doing outside.

It happened again. She tried to ignore the tiny volley of pebbles, but crept to the window. Harris was there, under the tree where he always stood, so that no one from the slave quarters could see him. He had pushed down the front of his trousers, and was caressing his naked self, in her full view.

Annie felt a fear she had not known since she came to The Forks. She stared in horror at Harris, almost unable to move. At the moment of his self-induced climax, she turned away, and wept. She was terrified by what he might do the next time the urge came upon him.

She told Cap'n Jack that night, late at night, because she couldn't sleep, and he knew something was wrong. She wept her distress, and her fear. He was not to do anything rash, she insisted, and certainly not tell the Massa.

201

Cap'n Jack held her until her crying was done, and told her he would think of something. Eventually Annie, exhausted, fell asleep.

But Cap'n Jack did not sleep. He lay awake for much of the night, churning with rage at what Annie had told him. He felt as if his wife had been raped. His first instinct was to attack Harris, but he knew that was stupid. He would be beaten for it, and nothing would be solved. He then thought of telling James, but doubted he would be believed. James would ask Harris, and he would deny it, and things would go on as before. He cursed his slavery, and cursed himself for being black, and dreamed of what he might do if he were free. Toward dawn he realized what he could do. It was so simple, he was surprised he had not thought of it before. He had to get Annie and Easter away from here, and to do that he, and they, had to be free. He would ask James to fulfill the promise he had made all those years ago.

He would ask for his freedom.

Surely James must grant it. Cap'n Jack had worked hard and loyally for so long, and what could the Massa want from him? He would bide his time, and wait until James seemed to be in a good mood, which wasn't often these days, and ask for his freedom. He would take Annie and Easter away, to the North, and find a good job, and build a little home for them, and they would be happy.

He fell asleep in contentment, and woke an hour later to the sound of the morning call.

Harris, meanwhile, had come to another conclusion. Loathing the power that Annie had over him, detesting his weak body for its fascination with her, appalled that he had exposed his need for her, in daylight, in public, he knew there was only one way to save himself from a violent action toward Annie that might get him into trouble.

He had to be rid of her.

21

As it transpired, Cap'n Jack's timing could not possibly have been worse.

In the November elections, Andrew had won a slight majority of the popular vote, but not enough to give him victory in the electoral college. According to the Constitution, the matter would now be decided in the House of Representatives, state by state. The three contenders were Andrew, John Quincy Adams, and William Crawford, secretary of the treasury.

The kingmaker would be Henry Clay, who had also run for president but was not one of the final three. Clay's votes, and his influence on the states, would dramatically affect the outcome.

James was astonished that Andrew had not won. The people loved him, and his supporters had been the most strident and demonstrative. That he had not been swept into office was proof to James that many doubted Andrew's suitability. He knew he was staring at the weightiest decision of his life. James still expected that Andrew would win, but did not know if he would continue to support him. In the weeks before Christmas he had received several important visitors who shared his doubts, not the least being Henry Clay himself, who was on his way home to Kentucky.

The two men knew each other of old, for Henry had been a sometime visitor to the Hermitage in James's Nashville days, and Henry junior, his son, was a good friend of James's.

Henry Clay expressed his delight with The Forks of

Cypress. He had heard much of it from his son, who had helped find the artisans to build it. He listened sympathetically when James told him of his problem with his slaves, and agreed that a strong hand, and a strong overseer, were vital to the effective functioning of the system.

But he was not there to talk about slaves.

"A muddy result," he said, speaking of the election.

"Andrew?" James asked.

Henry was silent for a moment. He had bitterly opposed Andrew's actions in the Florida campaign, had denounced the hanging of the missionaries, and had been the prime mover of the ill-fated congressional reprimand.

"Perhaps," he said.

Quietly but eloquently, he listed his reasons for not wanting Andrew in the president's office. It was old ground, involving Andrew's personality and behavior, but Henry made it sound damning.

"These are difficult times," Henry concluded. "We need a temperate man, I say, not an uncaged lion."

"Who?" James was thrilled. He felt as if he were being included in the real election process, the other election, the secret election by powerful men who decided affairs of state behind closed doors.

Henry shrugged. "John Quincy Adams, perhaps."

Adams was the son of the second president, the successor to George Washington.

"He is from New England, and it would make those states happy not to have a Southerner for president. It has only happened once before."

Henry adopted his most honeyed voice.

"In the end, of course," he smiled, "it all depends on you."

James laughed. "Me?"

"You and others like you," Henry said. "For the states have the power now, which is as it should be."

They talked for some hours about the country and its welfare and the electoral process. Again Henry spoke of his dislike for Andrew, and gently, very gently, raised the matter of the Indian treaties.

"There are even rumors of bribes paid by Andrew, and if that is true, the treaties could be annulled."

He let it hang in the air for a moment.

"If bribery could be proven."

James stared at the floor.

"But these are only rumors," Henry said, changing his tone. "And but a small part of the larger portrait of Andrew."

He had made his point clearly and effectively, without needing to stress it. Word of the bribes to the Indians had leaked out, and James was panicking. He did not know how much anyone else suspected.

Henry declined James's hospitality for the night, as he had friends at the Nashville Inn, and left before sundown.

James did not know what to do. He knew Henry had flattered him, that his would be only one small voice in the outcome of his state's decision regarding the presidency, but every voice counted now.

Andrew in the president's office was dangerous, for many, many reasons, but Andrew was his friend, Andrew was responsible for much of his fortune. Just as Andrew could be responsible for his downfall. If evidence of the bribes was found, James's part in the affair would be exposed. If the treaties could be annulled, that left much of his land ownership open to question.

He shivered in fear, and slept badly for the next few nights.

On Christmas Day, the security was reduced to allow the guards time with their families. Six slaves took advantage of this and escaped. When James heard the news, he shouted his wrath at Harris, who accepted his displeasure, but defended his position.

"Things were too easy here for too long," he said.

"And it was special circumstances, being Christmas Day."

He promised the return of the slaves, and James approved the expenditure for the slave catchers. Harris left, and James sat at his desk in despair. The plantation could not function effectively if things continued like this, and that put his income at risk. The rumors of the bribes were even more distressing, for they put his holdings at risk.

He talked to Sally.

Sally was worried about the runaways, because she thought Harris had put an end to all that, but agreed the circumstances were special. Things had been better since Harris had become overseer. There had been less trouble, and, over the past month, fewer beatings and floggings.

"Perhaps that is the problem," James said bitterly.

Sally calmed him down, and tried to put his problems in perspective for him. She guessed that the situation with Andrew was vexing him most.

"Why not let Andrew decide?" she suggested.

They had to go to Nashville in the new year, to settle A.J. at his school. James could call on Andrew at the Hermitage, explain his doubts, and listen to Andrew's answer.

James smiled and shook his head in wonder.

"You always see things so clearly," he said. Hers was the best possible solution, because James would force Andrew to make the decision. All Andrew had to do was ask, and set James's mind at rest, and he would be given what he wanted.

Still, it troubled him to confront Andrew, and he puzzled how he would tell his friend that he had doubts about him. As the day of their departure approached his mood became more volatile again, and the absence of news about the runaway slaves kept him angry.

The slaves were caught, fifty miles away. They would be brought back to The Forks.

"Get rid of them!" James said. "I do not want them on my property."

"A couple of 'em are good workers," Harris protested, but James cut him short.

"Sell and buy as you see fit!" He was shouting, and reminded Harris that he had said he needed only six months to bring the slaves to order.

"By the time I come back from Nashville I want this plantation functioning efficiently and effectively."

"I'll need authority while you are away," Harris said, smarting at his employer's wrath.

James signed the necessary papers, and Harris left. James punched his chair in his frustration.

Sensibly, Cap'n Jack had not approached James while the slaves were missing, for he knew his Massa's temper. The news that the runaways had been caught emboldened him, and he wanted to resolve his personal dilemma before James left for Nashville.

"What is it?" James snapped. Cap'n Jack should have known then, at that moment, that this was not the time. But his desperation to be free made him unwise, and he had convinced himself that James would readily fulfill his promise.

"I want my freedom," Cap'n Jack said.

James could not believe his ears. At some other time he might have listened more sympathetically, but it was loyalty that he wanted from his slaves now, not disavowal.

"You made a promise," Cap'n Jack continued, but James cut him off.

"I said that if you served me loyally and well, I would consider it, but this is not the time."

It was incomprehensible to Cap'n Jack. It was impossible that he could have done more. The Massa had everything he could want, a fine house and plantation, a family, sons to succeed him, wealth and position. What more could he want from Cap'n Jack?

207

"The plantation is in uproar, the slaves rebellious," James insisted. "If ever I needed your loyalty, it is now!"

Cap'n Jack hardly heard him. His mind was awash with disappointment and bitterness.

"You breakin' yo' word," he said.

James almost hit him.

"How dare you say that to me? Remember your place, man!"

"You promised!" Cap'n Jack was desperate.

"Get out!" James shouted. "Get out of my sight!"

Cap'n Jack looked at him dumbfounded. Tears of rage filled his eyes, but he did as he was told. He left the room, left the house, and went to Annie.

He clung to her, choking with emotion. It had all been a pipe dream. The promise had been the old lie, the white man's lie, and he had been fool enough to believe him.

Annie held him, and stroked him, and whispered love in his ear. After a while he quieted, and sat in a chair and stared at the wall. At nothing.

James called Harris to him, in his study.

"Cap'n Jack has been insolent," he said. "Put him in the fields for a week." It was a euphemism they all used. Little work was done in the fields in winter, but the hands were kept busy in the barns, and fixing the outbuildings.

Harris was pleased by the turn of events. It was his chance to break a house nigger, and it had curious implications for his obsession with Annie.

"That won't break him," Harris said.

"Then do what you must," James snapped, scarcely able to control his anger.

Harris nodded and turned to leave.

"But do not sell him away," James said quietly.

Even at this pitch of rage, he remembered all Cap'n

Jack had done for him, and his affection for the man, and had to believe he would keep his promise to Cap'n Jack, one day. He was a man of his word.

James and Sally, with A.J. and Sassy, left the following morning for Nashville. They did not take the older girls, for it would make the carriage crowded, and they did not take Jass. He had a slight chill, and Sally worried that the long journey and the cold weather would not suit the boy.

James, after a night's sleep, was feeling less hostile to Cap'n Jack, but he could not countermand his order to Harris without looking weak.

"He is a good man," he said to Harris, "And has served me well. Do not be too hard on him. A few days in the fields, perhaps."

Harris nodded. He had his orders. He had acted on them the night before. He and his brother Albert had gone to the weaving house, put manacles on Cap'n Jack, and taken him to the shed. They left him there, chained to a post, for the night.

Before they left the weaving house, Harris stared at Annie, who was clutching Easter. He said nothing to her—the stare was enough—and then they took Cap'n Jack away.

Annie stayed where she was, holding Easter, incapable of speech or movement. She tried to remember her curse, but could not, because she was too frightened of what the night might bring. It might bring Harris. She lay awake in fear all night, and when he did not come to her, she was even more scared, for she knew it boded evil.

"Just a few days in the fields," James said to Harris again, before he got into the carriage.

Harris nodded agian.

James settled in the carriage. Ephraim, who was driving, flicked the reins and they clattered away.

James sat in the carriage staring out at the empty

209

cotton fields. He was dreading Nashville. He wasn't sure how he was going to tell Andrew, who was dearer than a father to him, that he didn't love him anymore.

22

The runaways came back the following day, chained together, and already beaten bloody by the slave catchers. One had been given a rough crutch, because he was almost unable to walk. His leg had been badly torn by the hounds.

They stumbled into the clearing and fell to their knees. Harris made them stand up, and left them there, while he and his brother assembled the other slaves.

Harris went to the shed and unchained Cap'n Jack, but left his manacles on. He threw a bucket of water over him to reduce the smell of his mess, and dragged him outside with the others. He chained Cap'n Jack to a tree.

All the field hands were assembled in the clearing, staring at the runaways, trying not to imagine what might happen to any of them next.

Harris separated the two he intended to keep and ordered his brother to give them twenty lashes apiece. He would not flog the ones he intended to sell, and was furious with the catchers for marking them. Slaves who were thought to be troublemakers did not fetch the best price.

The floggings began, and whose who watched wept for their brothers, but did not cry out as loudly as those being punished. Their screams reached the house, and the slaves there, and from the stables, crept out to see, but kept their distance.

Both men being flogged fainted, and water was thrown over them. When it was done they were dragged away to the shed, and chained up, and a woman sent to rub salt into their wounds, to stop the bleeding.

Everyone waited.

It was a cold day, and the runaways were shivering. Harris simply walked along the line, inspecting them, and trying to evaluate what the catchers' beatings had cost him.

They waited for an hour, and then the auctioneer arrived in his cart with his men. There was no official slave market in Florence, but an enterprising retired overseer had set up a lucrative business, providing and disposing of slaves, as an agent for the larger cities.

Fear danced through Cap'n Jack's heart and mind. He could not believe the Massa would let him be sold.

"These four?" the auctioneer asked, and Harris nodded.

"And him," he said, pointing to Willis, whose brother Henry had run away the previous year, and had never been found.

"I ain't done nuttin'!" Willis cried, and clung to his woman.

"You're a troublemaker like your brother," Harris said. The men dragged Willis away from his screaming wife. Willis fought and punched, but they knocked him senseless and put him in the cart with the runaways.

Harris watched impassively, and then turned and stared at Cap'n Jack.

"And him," he said, pointing to a young, rough giant, Abel, who knew no one at The Forks and went quietly. He didn't care where he went, or whom he served; slavery was slavery, no matter who the Massa was, and one day he would be free.

Harris did not take his eyes off Cap'n Jack. Despite the cold, Cap'n Jack was sweating, shivering, praying that his knees would not give way.

"Fetch the woman," Harris said softly to Albert, who nodded at two catchers, and they went to the weaving house.

211

Slowly it dawned on Cap'n Jack, and a rage greater than any rage he had ever known filled him, and a fear, and an overwhelming despair.

"No!" he cried, from the pit of his soul.

Harris stared at him.

To Harris it was simple. James had said he had failed at his job, and Harris agreed. He had not brought order in six months, and since he could not blame himself and his methods, he had to find a scapegoat.

Annie.

If Annie had such a powerful effect on him, a righteous white man, what effect did she have on the licentious blacks? She was a whore, like all nigra women, who had bewitched him. So she must be a troublemaker, causing dissension among the hands, causing them to fight each other for possession of her, just as he would have fought any man to take her as his own. Women were the root of all evil, foul temptresses, wanton harlots, and he could not maintain order and discipline as long as she was at The Forks. So he would tell the Massa.

In any case, it would be too late when James returned. She would be gone, gone with her strumpet, lascivious ways, gone from his mind, gone from his flesh, gone from his lust, forever.

They brought Annie from the weaving house. She held Easter in her arms, and was not struggling because she did not know what was going to happen to her. Even if she had known, she might not have struggled. She had never struggled against her fate before, and she had never believed that her happiness with Cap'n Jack would last.

Cap'n Jack saw her and began shouting at her, telling her to run, to get away, begging someone, anyone, for help. He pulled at his chains, but they held fast to the tree. He used all his strength to jerk on them, to break them, to get free, like a crazed puppet unable to be rid of his confining strings.

Women were crying now, not because they loved Annie, but because it might happen to any of them.

Annie accepted what they did to her, because there was nothing she could do. Tears were streaming down her face. Although she had known her happiness could not last, she couldn't bear that it was going to end, it had been so sweet to her, and she called out a curse on the world.

She struggled when they took Easter from her, but a man held the child while they put the chains on Annie, and then gave her back. They pushed Annie to the cart, and one of the runaways leaned down to help her up, because of Easter.

"No," Harris said. "Not the brat."

His cruelty was breathtaking to them. He could not separate the child from her mother, surely not.

"The brat has done nothing," Harris said. "The brat stays here."

Time seemed to stop for a moment, and there was an eon of silence. Then out of the silence came a sound that none of the slaves watching wanted to hear again in their lifetime.

Annie screamed.

She screamed and fought and kicked and bit and screamed and begged and punched, and screamed again, the primal cry of a mother's pain.

Cap'n Jack screamed with her, and their cries melded in the winter air, in a duet of agony, and those watching tried to block out the sound, for it came from hell.

The auctioneer had no time to waste and was merciful. Unable to get the frantic, demented woman into the cart, he hit her on the head with the butt of his gun, and she fell to the ground senseless. They snatched Easter from her, and a woman ran to take the child, to hold her and shield her from the awful vision of her mother's going.

Cap'n Jack fell to his knees, weeping and scrabbling through the dirt, trying to get to his love.

213

They bundled Annie into the cart, and she lay on the floor of it, unconscious. Harris signed the papers for the auctioneer, and the cart rumbled away.

Cap'n Jack could hardly see through his tears, but climbed to his feet trying to catch one last glimpse of Annie. All he saw was a slave cart rumbling down the hill, and all he heard was anguish.

Harris waited till the slave cart was gone, and then made a speech. He told them he had been lenient with them. He had eased up on the discipline and punishments, and he had been repaid with ingratitude. Today was just an example of what he would do if any more slaves attempted to run away, or if any more of them caused trouble. He would forcibly separate husbands from wives, mothers from sons, daughters from fathers, just as he had done this day.

He kept them standing in the cold for the rest of the afternoon, and would not let them go back to their quarters. Easter was crying, but she was only the loudest, for all the women and many of the men were in tears of grief and discomfort.

Toward sunset he let them go.

"What about him?" Albert asked.

Cap'n Jack had fallen to the ground and lay there, motionless.

"Let him go," Harris said. The slave cart was well away by now. "See if he can shut the brat up."

Easter was still crying, although the woman who had been holding her was trying to feed her some porridge.

Harris walked away. Albert unlocked Cap'n Jack's chains, and left him lying on the ground.

Slowly, sensibility returned to Cap'n Jack, and rage. He lay still for a moment, letting his anger boil, until it must, perforce, explode.

He scrambled to his feet and ran screaming at Harris. Albert cried a warning, and Harris turned as Cap'n Jack fell on him, punching him, kicking him, but no match

214

for the overseer, who jabbed hard, viciously hard, in Cap'n Jack's stomach.

It winded Cap'n Jack, and gave Harris the advantage. He grabbed the slave, and called for Alfred. They dragged him back to his tree, chained him again, and Harris lashed him without mercy.

Not even the physical pain of the lash could match the agony in Cap'n Jack's heart, and he screamed and cried and begged God for mercy, not because of the whip, but because of what he had lost.

23

James approached the Hermitage unwillingly. He had always loved coming to this place before, but now he was filled with foreboding and guilt. He hoped he would not see Rachel.

He had avoided coming here for three days, and found some consolation in the company of Eleanor, in whose house they were staying, and Sara, who came to visit. He had not told them of his conflicting emotions toward Andrew, of his divided loyalties, nor had they asked. They greeted him warmly, and Sally and the children, and gossiped about their lives as if James had never been away.

Eleanor was in high dudgeon, because Richard Coll, who had been Andrew's aide in Florida, was paying attention to her daughter, James's niece Mary. Eleanor had no time for Coll.

"A brigand," she sniffed. "Like that eccentric Houston boy, or any of those who follow Andrew so blindly. Pirates, the lot of them."

James smiled wryly at Sally.

"They're not so bad, Eleanor," he said, "just young men sowing their oats."

"Mr. Coll's oats will not be sown near my daughter," Eleanor snapped, wagging her finger at James to emphasize her point. "You do not know what it's like, Jamie; you do not live here anymore."

According to Eleanor, Nashville had become impossible. Andrew had collected an army of supporters around him in his bid for the presidency, mostly young men or army veterans, and they were riding, rampant and roughshod, over the town.

"Getting drunk at all hours of the day, picking fights with innocent bystanders because they did not vote for Andrew, and doing in broad daylight things that decent folk do only in the darkness, in the privacy of their own homes."

She was working herself into a considerable state.

"And Mr. Coll is one of the worst of them," she said, her voice quivering with indignation. "But will Andrew call them into line? No. He only laughs and encourages them to greater excess."

She rounded on James.

"Heaven help us if he does become president," she said, as if it were all James's fault. "For I have seen his government."

Sally tried to hide her giggles, and James got cross with her, but gently, for he saw the funny side of it.

They took A.J. to his new school, and were satisfied by it. Sally thought it was too spartan, but A.J. told her not to be silly, he could look after himself, and asked his father if Ephraim could stay as his personal slave. James didn't want to lose Ephraim from the stables at The Forks, but promised to find someone for his son.

They went to visit Colonel Elliot, and checked on the progress of the blooded horses. James was satisfied that all was in order, and pleased with the colonel's work.

Then he had no more excuses. Sally offered to come with him, but he declined. He had to do this on his own, whatever it was he was going to do.

He rode to the Hermitage and sat on his horse for a

while when he got there, enjoying the view and admiring the new house that Andrew had built. It was much simpler than The Forks, but suited its garden setting to perfection. He dismounted, and walked in, leading his mount. A slave came running to take the horse.

James looked around, and saw Rachel. He was shocked.

She was sitting in the garden, with Alfred, wrapped up in blankets and reading from her Bible. She had lost a lot of weight, and was pale and looked ill, and her hair was quite gray.

Alfred saw James, and whispered to Rachel. She looked up from her Bible, and did not seem to recognize him for a moment, but then a golden smile suffused her face, and she tried to stand, to greet him.

She stumbled against her chair, and Alfred reached out to steady her. James walked quickly to them, and kissed Rachel and bade her sit, which she did gladly.

She was so pleased to see him. She smiled and laughed, and held his hands. She begged him to forgive her appearance; she had been in bed most of the winter, but was feeling better now, and was taking advantage of the lovely day to get some fresh air.

She asked after Sally, and the children, and expressed her sorrow that she had never met Jass.

James talked about his own sons for a moment, and asked after hers, and her eyes regained something of their old sparkle. She listed their various achievements at school, but talked mostly of Andrew junior, who was her darling.

There was a little silence.

"And Andrew?" James asked.

Rachel turned the pages of her Bible.

"It's such a pity you had to move away," she said. "He misses you, most dreadfully."

James gave a small laugh.

"He has so many friends," he said.

"No," Rachel said. "He has so many sycophants, and

careless, thoughtless young men, who like him only because his glory reflects on them."

She checked herself, as if she had said more than she intended. She fought to find a smile, but when she looked at James, her eyes were dull.

"He will be so pleased to see you," she said. "He is relying on your support."

James looked away. She will love him to her grave, he thought, and beyond.

He talked about silly things with her until she was tired and had to go inside. Alfred went in with them. Rachel went to her room, and Alfred took James to the dining room.

It was full of men, many of them young, lounging around, drinking and smoking, chewing tobacco. Andrew sat at the head of the table, which was piled with papers, surrounded by advisers, all telling him what he needed to do to win the presidency.

But Andrew was hardly listening to the older men. He laughed and joked with the younger, and told ribald stories with them, and cursed and drank.

He finds his youth in them, James thought. Or they are an army of his sons.

Alfred moved to his Massa, and whispered in his ear. Andrew looked up and saw James, and he roared a welcome.

"Well, James," he said. "They are trying to steal this election from me, but I will best them yet!"

It was as much for the benefit of the young men as for James. They cheered their agreement.

"You have come to be one of our army? You have come to offer your influence on my behalf?" Andrew said, but not as if it was a question.

"I came to talk to you," James said quietly.

Perhaps no one else in the room heard him, but Andrew did. The soft sapphire eyes hardened to blue

218

diamond. He stood up and walked out of the room, beckoning James to follow.

They went to Andrew's study. Andrew sat at his desk, and nodded to a chair for James, who preferred to remain standing.

"My enemies are determined to stop me," he said in a voice of quiet, rolling thunder. "By lies and corruption, and vicious slanders of supposed past scandals."

The question of Andrew and Rachel's possibly bigamous marriage had been raised during the campaign.

"But I will use their own tricks against them, and, by the eternal, I will be president!"

The thunder broke, and Andrew was roaring.

"I will do whatever is necessary, by fair means or foul, but I will be president!"

Something about James's manner was disturbing him.

"And I am relying on all my friends to help," he said, more softly. "To argue my case, to put my cause—"

He laughed.

"—to line a few pockets, if necessary. Eh?"

"I couldn't do that," James said. There had been enough bribery already, and he had done too much of it.

Andrew studied him carefully.

"But you will vote for me, in the Alabama senate?"

It was now. This was the moment.

"I want you to tell me why I should," James said, diffidently.

Some spittle was dribbling from Andrew's mouth. It always did, when he was vexed. He considered James's question, and then gave his response.

"Because I made you what you are," he said.

The room reverberated with his anger, and James could feel it crushing him. He must give in to it, or break away from it forever. Then Andrew's words thrust a memory of his last argument with his father into his mind.

"You will never amount to anything."

"I made you what you are."

It was the same thing said differently. They were the same men, powerful, arrogant men, who would not allow their children to cross them. It gave James extraordinary strength. He had walked away from his father once and made something of his life. He could do it again now, and he would survive again.

"Nobody made me," James said, furiously. "I made myself."

He walked to the door. Andrew didn't try to stop him, just as his father had not tried to stop him all those years ago.

"I will be president," Andrew shouted. But James knew he was not shouting at him, only at himself.

When James got back to Eleanor's he told Sally that he had broken with Andrew, and was shifting his support to Henry Clay. Henry gave all his votes to John Quincy Adams, who became the new president.

But Andrew kept his word. Four years later he was elected by an overwhelming popular vote. Just before he left the Hermitage for his inaugural, Rachel, worn out by the world, slipped quietly away to meet her Maker.

24

Cap'n Jack struggled to waken. His eyelids were heavy and his brain was numb, and he was sure he had been drugged. He knew other people were with him. He tried to focus and saw Parson Dick, and Tiara.

Then he remembered his pain, and closed his eyes again.

After his whipping, field hands had carried him to the weaving house, and took Easter to Angel. Tiara came with some of the women, and rubbed salt into the cut flesh on his back to stop the bleeding. They used herbs from the old days on his wounds, to try to stop scars from forming, and gave him laudanum to ease the pain and help him sleep.

The opium kept him unconscious for half a day, and when he stirred they gave him more, and he slept again. He drifted between sleep and waking for two days after that, and there was always somebody with him, to try to soften his memory when he woke.

Angel brought his daughter to him sometimes, so she would not forget her pappy, and Parson Dick came with beef tea for him to drink, so that he might regain his strength.

He lay on his stomach, because of the livid, bloody, oozing welts on his back, and sometimes he knew his friends were there, and sometimes he did not.

He opened his eyes again, because he wanted to wake, and begin exacting whatever vengeance he could on those who had so cruelly wronged him.

"Annie?" he whispered.

Parson Dick shook his head.

"She gone," he said.

Cap'n Jack didn't respond. He knew Annie was gone because he remembered every detail of her going. It was branded on his mind, and he would never forget. He asked because he hoped that maybe somehow she had come back.

"Massa find her when he come back," Tiara said, but Cap'n Jack didn't believe her, and perhaps she didn't even believe herself. She sprinkled some more herbs and salt on his back, and Cap'n Jack winced at the sting of it.

"Easter?" he said.

"She doin' jus' fine," Tiara assured him. "Angel lookin' after her."

Cap'n Jack nodded, and closed his eyes.

Tiara whispered a few words to Parson Dick. She had to get back to the house, to tend to the Jackson children.

221

Parson Dick nodded that he would stay for a while, and Tiara left.

Parson Dick sat waiting patiently until Cap'n Jack opened his eyes again.

"The pain bad?" Parson Dick asked him, and Cap'n Jack nodded.

"Want some more laudanum?"

Cap'n Jack shrugged. Parson Dick took a little bottle from his pocket, and made Cap'n Jack swallow some of the clear liquid. He had stolen it from Sally's locked medicine chest. Locks were no barrier to Parson Dick.

"Not too much, you had plenty," he said.

He was immaculately clad, as always, in black velvet and a brocade vest. He looked incongruous sitting in this smoky room, in the candlelight, beside the bloodied slave.

"Don't ever forgive them for what they did," he said. "Not ever."

Cap'n Jack would never forgive.

"And one day you will have your vengeance."

Cap'n Jack almost smiled. It was as if Parson Dick were reading his mind. But he smiled too, at the cultured, English tones of the butler. His accent and clothes were at war with his sentiments.

Parson Dick took a small wooden carving from his pocket.

"Keep this with you always," he whispered fiercely. "It has power. It is from the old country."

Cap'n Jack, who had closed his eyes, opened them and looked at Parson Dick, who saw the question.

"Africa," he said, and started to chant, in a language Cap'n Jack didn't know.

"Africa. O, Africa. Why did you let us go? Were we not your children? Why did you let them snatch us from you? We were your children, Africa, why did you let us go? We were the beginning, Africa, we were the start of man. Our kingdoms were mighty and our people brave, but you let us go.

222

"You let them drag us from you, and bring us, like the children of Israel, to bondage in a new Egypt, and we suffer, as the children of Israel suffered, but we have not forgotten you, Africa, and we will come back to you, Africa, if only in our dreams. I am Africa.

"May your spirits guard us, Africa, and destroy our enemies. Protect your children, O Africa, and make them strong, so that they may suffer their bondage, and live, as the children of Israel lived, and fly from it when it is done. Always, I am Africa."

Cap'n Jack understood only the one word, Africa, but that word, and the curious chant, coming from this curious man, educated, literate, and completely secretive about his background, struck a responsive chord in Cap'n Jack. He did not remember Africa, although it had meaning for him, just as Ireland had meaning for James's children.

He stared at the wooden carving, and it gave him strength. He drifted to sleep again, and it was a good sleep, a deep sleep, because although he was shattered by loneliness, he knew he was not alone.

Parson Dick put the carving on a shelf, and tiptoed out into the evening, to serve the Massa's family.

Cap'n Jack woke up a little later, because someone was prodding his arm. He tried to shake the sleep and the drug from his eyes, and saw a small, worried face, inches from his, staring at him, and asking what was wrong.

It was Jass.

Jass was bored. He'd been kept in bed for two days because he was sick, and his mamma and papa were away. He hadn't seen Cap'n Jack or Annie or Easter for ages, and he missed them. He ate the dinner that Tiara gave him, and then toddled on his own, as he had often done, out of the kitchen, and made his way to his friends.

He came into the weaving house, and he couldn't

223

find Annie or Easter, but he saw Cap'n Jack lying on the bed, and his back was all covered in blood. He got scared, because somebody must have hurt his friend, who wouldn't wake up. He'd seen them do it to some of the other black people, and they'd screamed so loudly he got scared and ran away.

When Cap'n Jack opened his eyes, Jass was so relieved that he started to cry.

Cap'n Jack put his arm around the boy, and held him close, told him not to cry, everything would be all right.

"Have you been bad?" Jass asked.

"No," Cap'n Jack assured him.

"Then why did they hurt you, and make you bleed?"

Cap'n Jack struggled for words to explain the unexplainable, but couldn't find them. He tried to sit up, but he gasped at the pain of it, and Jass started crying again.

Cap'n Jack tried to hush him, and even hummed a little lullaby, and slowly Jass calmed down, and snuggled into his friend's arm.

Having calmed the boy, he tried to find a way to calm himself. He saw the African carving sitting on the shelf.

"You love me?" he asked Jass.

Jass assured him that he did.

"You ain't gwine ever hurt me, not in all yo' days?"

Jass said not.

"Promise?"

Jass nodded his head.

Cap'n Jack picked him up under his arms, and held the toddler up to the carving.

"Say promise," he told Jass.

Jass did.

Cap'n Jack wasn't quite sure what he was doing, but he had to find some way to ease his aching heart, and this odd ceremony, before a pagan god, had some meaning for him, for in it was an unbreakable vow.

"Promise you ain't gwine ever do what yo' pappy done?"

224

Jass didn't know what his pappy had done, but promised anyway. He would promise Cap'n Jack anything.

"Promise you ain't gwine ever be yo' father's son?" Jass laughed.

"Promise," Cap'n Jack said sharply.

So Jass promised that he would never be his father's son, and Cap'n Jack was satisfied. In some small, unexplainable way, his revenge had begun.

He heard the shouts in the distance, Tiara and Angel, Parson Dick and some others, all running through the night, calling for Jass. They thought him lost.

Cap'n Jack struggled from his bed, his back screaming in pain, and carried Jass to the door.

He called to Tiara.

"The chile," he said, "is found."

PART TWO

MERGING

The weariness of wholly forgotten nations
I cannot cast from my eyelids.
Nor keep from my frightened soul
The silent falling of distant stars.

Hugo von Hofmannstahl

25

"Nigger lover," they chanted, just as always. "Nigger lover! Nigger lover! Nigger lover!"

Jass stood there, fists up, waiting for the blow. He never threw the first punch because he had not picked the fight, but waited, heart racing, for what he knew would happen.

When it came, it hurt, just as always. Wesley, his opponent, was only a year older, but that year represented to Jass a seeming ton weight of muscle, and he sprawled back against some of his school friends. The slaves, watching impassively in a group near the fence, sighed a collective regret, for they had been hoping for another outcome they knew to be unlikely. Just as always.

Jass was not unpopular at school; many of the boys liked him, some were his friends, and all respected his father's position, but they all enjoyed a fight, and the high ethics of boxing demanded not just a victim but also a valid cause. Jass had a good and supple physique for his age and was always prepared, however unwillingly, to defend himself with his fists, so picking on him could never be called bullying. Wesley would start discussing the economics of the Southern states, Jass would suggest ideas of diversification away from slave-based agriculture, and before long the others would be calling him an abolitionist and a nigger lover, and the fight would begin.

It was sport as much as anything, but it also confirmed Wesley's physical preeminence and reinforced certain concepts that most of them preferred not to question. These beliefs were reflected in the education given at the Reverend Sloss Preparatory Academy for Young Gentlemen, outside Florence. The North, their teachers told them, was another country, however nominally part of the United States, whence the flowing tide of abolition might one day swamp the triumphant sand castle of the South.

The South, they were taught, was a unique, essentially pastoral, society of unlimited potential, whose survival depended on an endless supply of cheap labor. It didn't matter how closely the governance of the South was linked to that of the North, or how passionately devoted a few of their teachers might be to the federal cause. It didn't matter that the present president, Andrew Jackson, now into his second term, was one of their own, a slaveholder dedicated to limiting federal power over the sovereignty of the states. It didn't matter that the president frequently insisted that the Union must be preserved, because the very fact that he said it only confirmed what most of them already believed: The Union was under considerable strain, with states' rights as the separating issue, and slavery as the separating fact.

Only recently, South Carolina had come to the very brink of civil war. The industrial North had successfully demanded high tariffs on imported manufactured goods, cloth and clothing, to protect its own industries. South Carolina claimed this was destroying the slave-based cotton economy, and had threatened to nullify the tariffs. Secession had only been averted by the adroit actions of the great president.

In Southampton County, Virginia, an insurrection had occurred, led by Nat Turner, a black preacher, in which fifty-seven whites, including several women and children, were killed. It brought back vivid memories of the rebellious plot by the free black, Denmark Vesey, ten years earlier, and was the Southern nightmare come to bloody life. A sensational manhunt followed. Over a hundred of Turner's followers were slaughtered, and the ringleader himself was caught, tried, and executed, along with twenty of his henchmen. But at the subsequent Virginia Convention, several proposals for the emancipation of slaves were only narrowly defeated, and the recent foundation of the American Anti-Slavery Society only added to the fortress mentality of the South.

Jass was no revolutionary thinker; he had no great moral argument against slavery. He had been brought up with it, had lived with it all his life, and every element of his education, except one, contributed to his belief in its present necessity.

The exception to Jass's otherwise conventional upbringing as a young Southern gentleman was his considerable friendship with Cap'n Jack. Such friendships were not, in themselves, unusual. All white boys of his class had black nurses, several had been suckled by slave women when their own mother's milk went dry, and they had all grown up with varying degrees of contact between themselves and the black populations of their plantations, farms, or houses. A reasonably energetic white boy, growing up secure in his authority, might have a range of friendships that covered the complete social strata—until he crossed the limiting threshold of puberty.

A boy can go where a man cannot, and at puberty, several unseen doors were closed to him. He had been raised to the concept of the sanctity of white women, and now his education began to include, by subtle inference rather than outright lecture, the baseness of carnal desire, and the profound evils of miscegenation.

They all had some knowledge of procreation—they saw it in the rutting animals on their farms—and now they were taught the sinfulness of giving way to these base desires, with women of any class or station but most especially with black women, since the resulting offspring would eventually defile and dilute the sacred white blood.

What puzzled Jass was that Wesley's conscience never seemed to bother him. He swore he had had

231

intercourse with a slave girl, but no visitation was ever made upon him by a wrathful God, nor on any of the others who claimed to have followed his braggart path.

Jass regarded such talk as foul, but his blood ran hot when Wesley first announced his ability to bring himself to private climax. Jass felt that powerful urge, but tried to resist it. It was wrong, they were taught, it was sinful, it was a sign of weakness of personality and sickness of the mind, and led to physical deformity. If their need got too desperate, Mother Nature herself would provide any necessary release in sweet, nocturnal dreams, to which Wesley snickered that sometimes Nature needed a helping hand. But the prohibition only intensified the desire, and occasionally Jass had succumbed, to be racked with guilt afterward. He longed to confide his confusion to someone, but since the death of his brother A.J., whose neck had been broken in a riding accident at Princeton two years earlier, Jass's only confidants were his classmates, his cousins, whose knowledge was as limited as his own, and Cap'n Jack.

Jass had grown up in the carefree country of reduced expectation that is the province of second sons. A.J., heir to the family estate, had given him scraps of guidance on matters of the world, but now he was gone, and Jass sorely missed him. His cheerful younger brothers, William, Alexander, and George, an inseparable trio, were at school in Nashville, and even when they came home to The Forks, Jass found it difficult to break into their tight-knit group. Three of his older sisters, Mary, Martha, and Mary Ellen, were married. Sassy was still at home, but was more interested in potential husbands than familiar brothers, and baby Jane, whom Jass adored, was a sickly child, and no companion to a teenage boy.

So Jass's most constant company had been the slaves, with Cap'n Jack as his surrogate father, and his tutors in the mysteries of life had been those same slaves, his friends at the Academy, and his stern, unyielding

232

schoolmasters, who seemed almost to condone the hypocrisy of what they taught. While physical contact with black women, any women, was publicly condemned, the more secular teachers also hinted that real men, unable to restrain their natural urges, should take their relief with whatever slave women were at their disposal. Jass found this half world of puberty confounding, confused by what he felt, by what he was taught, and by what he was experiencing.

Nor was his father much help to him. James liked Jass but still mourned A.J., and found it difficult to communicate with his second son. Cap'n Jack wasn't interested in Jass's adolescent problems because he had other, unrealistic, ambitions for him. Jass would now inherit The Forks, he would own property and slaves, and, determined to raise the young man to be the Massa he wanted, Cap'n Jack relentlessly, if amiably, exploited the rational side of Jass's nature by divorcing the idea of slavery from race. Rather than protesting that the enslaving of blacks was wrong, Cap'n Jack cultivated in Jass instead the economic necessity of a move away from the reliance on labor-intensive cotton, and thus slavery, until slavery itself became unnecessary. This put Jass desperately at odds with his peers.

Which is why, just as always, young Jass was defending himself, or his ideas, when actually he was well aware of the basic flaw in his own—and Cap'n Jack's—position. Economic survival would always depend on manual labor, whether it be field hands picking cotton or weavers at the spinning jennies in the industrial North, and what did it matter if that labor was white, which was unthinkable, or black, which was the status quo?

Cap'n Jack, a dreamer, not a thinker, had no ready answer for this, and Jass found himself caught in another dilemma. He was obstinate rather than passionate. He fought hard and well, not to protect a strongly held ideal but to protect himself from too much physical

233

injury. Wesley, having a cause to defend, was able to inflict severe superficial damage on his only slightly smaller opponent. It was a short, sharp fight, which ended with Jass on the ground, hand to his bleeding nose, while Wesley towered in habitual triumph over him.

"Won't you ever learn, Jackson?" he crowed. "That's how it is for nigger lovers."

He walked away to the cheers and backslapping of his gang, their slaves following them.

Cap'n Jack sighed and went to comfort his man's wounded pride and tend his bloody nose.

"I nearly had him that time," Jass gasped.

"Sho' thing, Massa Jass, yo' nearly did," Cap'n Jack agreed with the lie.

He hauled the young man to his feet, sat him on a log, and held a cloth to the bloody nose. School friends cantered away on horses, calling greetings to Jass. No rancor was held; they had enjoyed the fight, and Jackson was always such a damned good sport about it. The reluctant worthy waved an aching arm in response, and called as cheery farewells. Then he turned away and looked at the river.

"Wesley bigger'n yo'," Cap'n Jack said, although he knew it to be scant comfort. "He be gone in a year or two, Up South, to college."

It didn't help. "It doesn't make any difference. There'll always be another Wesley, somewhere." Jass stared at the river. "I'd like to beat him once. Just once, that's all."

He brushed aside regret and took Cap'n Jack's arm for assistance. "Don't tell my parents," he ordered mildly, as they walked to the horses.

"I never do, Massa Jass," the slave replied.

The afternoon was flawless, warm and lovely, the last of the dogwood blossoms dappling the countryside like wayward snowflakes. Although the school was on the outskirts of town and they had no need to pass through

234

Florence on their way home, Jass always enjoyed the long detour, trotting on Morgan, his chestnut gelding, through the main street to catch a sense of its bustle and purpose. The construction of a new building or some improvement in the town's infrastructure gave him a tremendous sense of pride.

My father made this, he thought to himself. If it were not for him this would not be here.

It wasn't strictly true—he knew that his father was only a shareholder in the development company that had created the town—but it encouraged his sense of the frontier tamed, and of the enormous potential of the country. Sometimes he wondered what country he meant, for often he felt completely alien from the Northern states, could not conceive of himself as a citizen of these United States, and took refuge in the more romantic, and possibly then more truthful, America.

America seemed to him to be without borders or boundaries, except those of the mind and the great oceans, and somehow the appendage "United States" limited this. He wondered if a fellow from New York or Boston could understand the call of the enormous, empty continent that lay just at the edges of their known world, and of the adventure that unlimited horizon promised. He yearned to see the wild Mexican province of Texas, the almost uncrossable Rocky Mountains, and the distant, legendary land beyond that the Spanish called California.

Part of him, too, longed to visit the Northern cities, for however much they were disparaged as dens of Yankee liberalism, they were always spoken of with excitement. He tried to imagine Florence a hundred, two hundred, times bigger, but then he could not imagine how a world without slaves functioned in any practical sense, and itched to understand what it was about slavery that seemed to make so many Yankees so very cross.

Torn between the desire to build or to explore, to settle as eventual master of a successful plantation or travel thousands of miles to a distant place and create his own empire as his father had done, he would spur Morgan at the edge of town and gallop home, Cap'n Jack beside him, through the lovely, fertile country.

The wind laved his aching body and bruised spirit, and the sense of the power of his horse, which he was controlling, inspired his blossoming manhood. They rode down avenues of untidy cypresses, on roads that had been created only by the traffic of horses and carts. They passed lonely farming shacks, on land only partly and recently reclaimed from nature.

He could easily imagine how it was when the true native people still lived here, smoke from their fires curling through the lazy afternoon to the distant, vaulting heavens. He could see himself in their company, as his father had been not so very many years ago, learning of their values and beliefs and endless, unwritten, recited history.

He loved those stories at his father's knee. He could listen for hours to the tales his parents told, his mother too, for they were both pioneer people who had come to this extravagant wilderness, done battle with it, and won. They had collected a vast repository of folklore that was, to the impressionable, dreaming Jass, a living thing, because his parents had lived it.

And if they were capable of doing what they had done, not so very many years ago, almost within the span of his own lifetime, then what was he capable of? What adventures awaited him out there, just a few miles farther than his parents had gone? What stories would he be able to tell his children one day, of frontiers extended and mountains crossed and wilderness made productive? He knew that out there lay the possibility of experiences richer than all the treasure on earth, in this country called America.

They broke through the sheltering trees, and Jass

slowed his pace. There it was, on a little hill, dazzling him as it always did, the pristine, elegant mansion, surrounded by cotton fields of apple-pie order on land that had been a sacred place to the native peoples. He could see the stallions grazing in a paddock beside the immaculately maintained racecourse, and wished that Leviathan was kept here instead of in Nashville, for he was the most famous stud in America. He could see the trim acres of the cotton fields, with row upon orderly row of the budding plants that yielded such a bountiful harvest. He could hear the distant song of the weeding gang as they moved among the sprouting cotton under the careful eye of Mitchell, the overseer.

The splendid vision caught at his heart, just as always, and all sense of the roaming life deserted him. His only ambition, at this moment, was to cherish this place, to nurture it, to watch it grow and be a haven of happiness and tranquillity, as it was to him now.

Cap'n Jack's thoughts on staring at The Forks of Cypress were colored by other experiences, different memories. For Cap'n Jack hated this house, which represented to him all the things he despised in old Massa James, all the many promises sweetly made and bitterly broken. Even building the house on this hallowed land now seemed to him profane, and represented the precise moment from which he could date his many bitter disappointments in James Jackson, whom once he had held in such regard.

Jass knew nothing of this, and smiled at him, just as always.

"Race you," he called, and galloped away. Cap'n Jack knew the pattern of it; it happened every day. Jass would make for the house, but halfway along the drive he would spur Morgan over the fence and gallop once around the racetrack before heading home, to the amusement of Monkey Simon and the stable hands, and the ire of Murdoch, the trainer, who thought it disturbed the broodmares. Cap'n Jack kicked his horse too, and, better rider, he could easily have overtaken Jass, but held back, to let the young man win.

Jass rode hard and fast now, laughing, as if suddenly freed of care, in what seemed to be exhilaration but might as easily be a mask for the impending moment when he must face his parents, and they would know he had been fighting again.

26

Pocahontas Rebecca Meredith Bolling Perkins fanned herself vigorously. "A wedding!" she exclaimed. "It's nothing but a charade! A fiasco! Just so a couple of nigras can jump the broom. Why, I feel faint even thinking about it!"

Sally smiled. Mrs. Perkins had felt faint several times that afternoon already, although the day was not overly warm. "A little more tea, Mrs. Perkins?" she asked. The fanning worthy gave an aggrieved nod, and Polly, a slave maid, refilled her glass with cool sun tea.

"That the president's daughter-in-law could do such a thing!"

She was in full flood now and Sally knew from experience that little could stop the flow unless something of more pressing import occurred. Which was hardly likely, given the thunderous ramifications of Sarah York Jackson's correspondence, which had arrived at both the Perkins place and The Forks that day. Although it was apparently a simple invitation to a wedding, Sally was sure that matriarchs (and not a few patriarchs) throughout the South would be as agog about it as their present visitor. The mail had been delivered to the Perkins estate at midday, and when Mrs. Perkins read the letter, her first reaction was to go and lie down with a sick headache, but almost immediately her second reaction took charge, for she had to

238

share her feelings with someone, and her daughter was not audience enough. Ordering Elizabeth to dress for visiting, she had summoned the landau, taken some care over her toilette, and arrived at The Forks in time for afternoon tea and, she hoped, some comforting apoplexy. But the wretched Jacksons hardly seemed bothered by the outrageous correspondence, and seemed to think the whole thing rather amusing.

"Well, that's Yankees for you," snapped Mrs. Perkins, as if Yankees were the reason for the world's ills, and took a sip of tea.

James, distracted by other letters, had taken little interest in the conversation, or monologue with interruptions as Sally thought of it. Now he looked up. "Sarah's hardly a Yankee," he said.

"Might as well be," Mrs. Perkins snapped back. "Mixing nigras and white folk at a social event, can you imagine? Is that your boy?"

As it was uttered all in one breath, it took Sally a moment to realize that the tiny, hoped-for miracle had arrived. Something had happened to distract Mrs. Perkins from her obsession with the wedding. Jass was galloping across the racetrack toward the drive, Cap'n Jack only yards behind him. Sally watched him for a moment, maternally satisfied that he was home safe, and knew just by looking at him that he had been fighting again. She was also acutely aware that Mrs. Perkins was making urgent, silent eye contact with her daughter, known to them all, but not to her parents, as Lizzie, who was sitting with Sassy on the lawn, some little distance away. Sally sensed matchmaking in the air.

Although only fourteen, Lizzie completely understood her mother's unspoken signaling from the veranda, but saw little need for it. She knew she looked pretty, she always made sure she looked her very best when visiting the Jacksons, and she knew she had little, if any, competition in the district. The potential

239

of Jass as her eventual spouse had never been overtly discussed by her parents, but their constant hints at the suitability of such a union made their opinion clear.

Lizzie thought it was a fairly good idea, too. Old James Jackson was much richer than her own father, a reasonably successful businessman who had small interest in agriculture but had bought a plantation near Florence five years ago to give himself a sense of place, and because land was a secure investment. The day-to-day running of the farm bored him, and he had little aptitude for picking overseers who might make up for his own shortcomings, so the plantation jogged along, and the Perkinses were able to dwell comfortably in the fantasy that they were landholding gentry. Not that they were poor—Lizzie would bring a handsome dowry to her marriage—but they were not, by any means, rich.

Lizzie was an only surviving child, raised alone, taught by tutors, only now being allowed to go to school to finish her education. The overwhelming influence on her life was her mother, and from her mother she was learning all the attributes of a Southern belle, as if the mother were creating in the all too willing girl the woman she herself had never quite become. Lizzie could flirt and charm and tantalize, even faint if necessary, with the best of them, but somehow none of it came naturally to her. It was as if she were playing a role that was demanded of her, and she behaved as if everything she did would be graded and commented on by her mother afterward. Which it was.

In her private world, her fantasy world, Lizzie might dream of a more dashing husband than Jass, a sweeping cavalier, but Jass was the reality: certainly rich enough, potentially handsome enough, and undoubtedly gentleman enough. They got on well together, and Lizzie thought she could manage him well enough to create in him, if not her ideal husband, then at least a reasonable

240

facsimile. That they were both too young to contemplate marriage was hardly a factor. Young girls, and their parents, had to plan for the future.

She glanced at Sassy Jackson, as if to reassure herself that she was the prettiest present, and turned to watch Jass. Followed by a black who seemed to be his personal slave, Jass took the fence, and his horse cleared it with energy and graceful ease.

"Why"—Lizzie affected what she thought to be her most seductive drawl, and primped her hair—"your brother is positively gorgeous. Last time I saw him, he was all gangly and spotty."

Sassy, aware of the subtext that was being prepared, giggled. She couldn't stand Lizzie. She was so very—young.

On the veranda, Mrs. Perkins echoed her daughter's sentiments. "What a fine young man he's becoming," she cooed. "Best keep him out of Elizabeth's sight. She has an eye for a beau."

Driven by some internal, maternal clock, Sally dismissed the idea out of hand. "Nonsense," she snapped, "they're both far too young." The rebuff didn't bother Mrs. Perkins, who did elaborate things with her fan, said "Mmmmm" in a way that allowed, she hoped, considerable interpretation, and glanced at the boy's father, who glanced at her, and she knew she was in striking distance, at least, of the mother lode.

But Jass didn't stop and dismount, didn't join them on the veranda, didn't even attempt to fulfill the various expectations of him. Instead he slowed to a trot, waved cheerfully at his parents, and spurred his horse away, behind the house, Cap'n Jack following. To the weaving house, Sally knew. To Easter.

"He's been fighting again," Sally said, perhaps to give Mrs. Perkins some doubts about her son's potential suitability. "He likes to pretend that we don't know." She didn't disapprove of fighting; she took the view of many pioneer mothers, that her door was always open

241

to brave men and permanently closed to cowards, but since the death of A.J., she didn't want anything untoward to happen to Jass. She felt a sudden flurry of exasperation with the world and with the boy. "It's happening almost every week. You should talk to him."

James knew this, and saw it as a thing to be proud of in his son. "All young men fight," he said, and Mrs. Perkins concurred. "All men fight," she said. "It is part of being masculine."

So Sally had a fit of motherly pique instead. "He never brings me his shirts to mend," she complained, but James smiled. "You'd only give them to a slave."

"That's not the point," Sally insisted. "I'm his mother."

Lizzie had reasons for disappointment, too. She spent most of her life being desperately bored. She had been brought up to it and should have been used to it, but she wasn't. The only ripples in her life were school, which was quite fun, although, try as she might, she wasn't overly popular with the other girls and there were no young men around, and visiting, when she could persuade herself, if only because she had a perky personality, that she was popular, and there were likely to be young men. Such as Jass. She'd spent the last hour waiting for him to come home, was bored with Sassy, who seemed much more interested in discussing her own suitors and playing mother to the three-year-old Jane Jackson than discussing Lizzie's future, and now here was Jass, looking gorgeous—she hadn't lied—and then he was gone.

"Why doesn't he come talk to us?" she complained. Sassy shrugged. "He's probably been in a fight. Easter cleans him up and mends his clothes so that we won't know." She giggled again. "He's so silly."

"Easter?" Lizzie's antennae were out for potential rivals, and she knew of no young lady in the district called Easter.

"A slave girl," Sassy explained. "She does the weaving."

242

Lizzie was considerably relieved. "Oh," she said. "Is that all."

Had Lizzie known more of the weaving house, her relief might have been short-lived. It hadn't changed much over the years; it still wasn't much of a place, a little shack nestled in a peaceful grove. The roof leaked in heavy rain, and it sorely needed a coat of paint, but the atmosphere inside was warm and comfortable and loving. Home is the familiar, home is where you are loved, and Jass knew that he was loved here, loved by Cap'n Jack and loved, without knowing that it was love, by Easter. He knew that his parents loved him, in their fashion, and his brothers and sisters, and he them, but when he thought of home it was as much this shabby shack as the great mansion on the hill. For this place was different. This was the cottage where he was king.

He brought his horse to a halt and dismounted. He knew he should have stopped to greet Mrs. Perkins and her daughter, but he didn't want Lizzie to see him battered and torn from his fight. "See to Morgan," he called, unnecessarily, for both he and Cap'n Jack knew that the horse would be seen to, but an order was given because he was the young Massa, and that's what good Massas did to prove they were not insensible to the chores of routine. Cap'n Jack was content to oblige, beyond the fact that it was his job, because he was content that this young Massa, whom he, as much as anyone, he believed, had fashioned and shaped, would be, one day, his ol' Massa.

Easter had been at the loom, but on hearing the arrival of the horses, she glanced out of the window, saw the state Jass was in, and went to fetch water, iodine, and a cloth. Thirteen years old and still a little gangly, she held the promise of a beautiful woman, with all of her mother's gentle calm but a certain cheekiness as well—sparky, fiery quirks to her personality that might have been inherited from her father, or

243

perhaps came from being brought up in a somewhat privileged atmosphere. The sale of Annie was seldom referred to anymore, but it still had powerful resonance for those who could remember. For the blacks it signified the most blatant example of the white man's dominance that had ever occurred at The Forks. For the whites, particularly ol' Massa James, it represented the nadir of the treatment of slaves under his dominion, and he preferred to block the event from his mind. Easter had grown up in the shadow of that memory, and was consequently much indulged by the blacks to solace her for the outrage, by the whites to atone for their guilt. She had always lived in this house with Cap'n Jack, she had received some general schooling, although not, of course, reading and writing, in the big house with the Jackson daughters, and she had inherited the role of weaver without question or demur. Tiara had shown her the ways, and she seemed to have a natural talent for the skill, a rhythm and grace about her that made it a pleasure to watch her work and gave the resulting cloth a neatness and texture to be admired.

And she had grown up with Jass, who spent at least as much time here, with her, as anywhere, with anyone. As his constant companion, she found few doors closed to her, and although she had felt the sting of the switch, infrequently, as punishment for minor infringements of adult rules, she was a well-mannered girl who was mostly content with the confines of her existence. A small part of her, of course, longed to live in the big house, or go to grand parties and wear pretty frocks, and another part of her wanted to be free, but only a part, and not a very large one. The concept of freedom, of being able to do what she wanted with her life, was a desirable ideal, but she had heard many stories of slaves, freed, whose lives were very much less than hers now. But then almost every slave's life was less than hers now, and if she was free, she might not have the thing she most wanted.

Because what she wanted was Jass. The fact that it was he who had occasionally inflicted the mild stinging pain of the switch was not without pleasure to her. It meant, in her mind, that she mattered to him. And she knew how to get her own back.

He strode into the cottage like a husband coming home, and stripped to the waist. "Fix my shirt," he said, throwing the garment to her. He took an empty corncob pipe from the shelf and sat in an old rocking chair by the empty fireplace. Easter came to him to tend his wounds and knew that only his pride needed real attention. "You gwine have some mighty bruises."

Easter's recognition that he had fought hard and well mollified Jass a little. "It's always the same old rut," he complained. "They won't admit that we've got to expand the economy, and whenever I try to talk about it, they all say I'm advocating abolition—Owwwwww—for pity's sake!" He flinched at the sting of the iodine.

Easter ignored his yell, and carried on, as did Jass. "—and I'm not saying we should abolish slavery, I'm saying we have to think beyond it—"

Easter hated talk of slavery and abolition. Most of the time she was able to convince herself of the lie that she wasn't really a slave, and this mystical new word, *abolition*, had frightening connotations, such as the possibility of not living at The Forks, of living somewhere else, of being apart from Jass. "Them's five-dollar words," she complained, hoping to shut him up, knowing she was wasting her breath.

"You've had learning; you know what they mean." He puffed contentedly on the empty pipe, but she flared a little. "You scare me when you talk like that! Freein' slaves. Where would I go? What would I do?"

Jass looked at her. She seemed at that moment so vulnerable, so in need of protection, that all he wanted to do was take her in his arms and hold her safe from the world, for the rest of her life. She made the boy feel manly.

245

"It's never going to happen; it's just silly talk," he said gently. "This is your home and always will be."

Then he smiled. "Besides," he said, "whatever would I do without you?"—which is what she had wanted to hear from the moment he came in the door, but she would not let him off the hook too easily.

"That's all very well and fine, Massa," she sniffed, "but I still don't get to go to no wedding."

He looked at her in genuine surprise, for he had been at school when the invitations arrived and thought the visit of Mrs. Perkins and Lizzie to be purely social. "What wedding?"

Parson Dick needed no telling. News of it had reached the slaves days before the formal correspondence had reached the whites, but since it was to be a black wedding, between black folk, none of the slaves had felt any need to inform their masters, and although they heard rumors that some white folk were to be invited, none of them were sure if their Massa was on the list, although Parson Dick, who could speak three languages but couldn't read or write, was fairly convinced that the Jacksons were when he had taken the envelope to his Master's study earlier that day.

"We will be going to Nashville next month, Parson Dick, to a wedding—" was as far as James got.

"Yes, sir, I know," said the butler, to save time. And perhaps to score a point. James looked at him in amazement. The accuracy and speed of the slave grapevine was a constant and remarkable amusement to him.

Parson Dick was helpful. "Everybody talkin' about it, suh. Alfred is marrying Miss Gracie."

James laughed. "How is it that whenever anything happens in this country, the slaves all know about it before we do?"

"Jungle drums, perhaps, Massa," Parson Dick ventured, maintaining a poker face. James was never sure quite how to take Parson Dick, although Mrs. Perkins

246

had no such hesitation. "That's exactly right," she cried. "Voodoo! Sheer voodoo! White folk and nigras guests at the same wedding!"

Parson Dick looked at her. "Disgraceful, m'm, I agree," but Mrs. Perkins's skin was far too thick for such subtle sarcasm. "You see!" she crowed in triumph, reluctantly preparing to leave. "Even the nigras are agin it!"

Slaves had brought the Perkins landau to the house. Soon it would be sundown, and so it was time to go, but Mrs. Perkins was not anxious to depart without at least some discourse between Lizzie and Jass. Playing for time, she was also looking for ways to shake the Jacksons from their complaisancy.

"You don't suppose she'll actually allow nigras to dance with whites?" she gasped, but the wretched people wouldn't even take that idea seriously. They only laughed.

'It's a wedding, my dear, not a revolution," Sally tried to placate her. Mrs. Perkins sniffed, taking a long time to put on her gloves. "You never know. Sarah's obviously a freethinker."

It was Lizzie who saw him first, face iodined, shirt darned, hovering at the side of the house, staring, she was sure, at her. She made a hurried farewell to Sassy, and moved as quickly as feigned lack of interest would allow to be near him.

"Why, who's this mess of a boy?" she asked the world, thus drawing everyone's attention to their proximity. "It can't be young James?"

Mrs. Perkins beamed in satisfaction; Sally concerned herself with tea things and Parson Dick; Sassy giggled and gave unnecessary orders to the slave nurse to tend little Jane.

But James stared at his son and Lizzie as if the best idea in all the world had just occurred to him.

Jass smiled shyly at her attention. "Miss Lizzie, you're looking lovely," he said.

Generally, girls of his own age confused Jass, but he liked Lizzie. She was so pretty. Somehow, she always made him feel like a callow boy, but that didn't matter because he had an exquisite revenge. Alone in his bed at night, when that vile thing happened to his body that demanded attention but could not be spoken of to anyone, or even considered in waking hours, he would fight against it and sometimes win. But sometimes the urge for the pleasure was so intense that he would lose the battle, and when he did, it was often Lizzie's face that he imagined, and her golden hair, and lovely body. He had no clear idea of what the unclad white female form looked like, but he assumed, and was assured by his schoolmates, that it was simply a paler version of the black, and so he had an intimate familiarity with what he imagined Lizzie's nakedness to be. It was his constant triumph over her perpetual skittishness with him.

Having no idea of what was in his mind, Lizzie rejected the spoken compliment. "Tush," she drawled, "just thinking of these nigra nuptials makes me glow. Poor Mamma's in a terrible pother."

Jass was puzzled; he couldn't imagine Lizzie missing out on a party. "You won't be going then?" he assumed.

Really, he could be quite dense at times, Lizzie thought, just a country boy at heart. "Of course we're going!" she explained. "Everybody's going. If only to see Miss Sarah make a fool of herelf."

Jass thought it would be a lot of fun. "I don't expect I am," he said ruefully. "I'm probably too young."

Lizzie was slightly relieved. Now she'd be able to enjoy herself at the ball, without the bother of having to flirt with him. "Such a pity." She was deeply insincere. "I might have saved you a place on my dance card."

She decided she'd done quite enough work on him for one visit. She had years to achieve the union after

248

all, and she was anxious to be gone. They wouldn't be home till after sunset now, and Lizzie hated driving at night, even with the security of the attendant slaves. It was so scary, night. She looked for a slave, and saw a gangly girl watching them. "Bring me my shawl," she demanded casually.

Easter had followed Jass to the house on some errand but, on seeing Lizzie, had forgotten what that errand was. She couldn't believe Jass could like this girl, all pale and pouty, but was terrified that he might. For all her fantasies about Jass, she knew the reality was that he would eventually marry a white woman, a woman of his own kind, and Lizzie was the first indication that the once distant prospect was becoming a nearer reality. Hating Lizzie already, she picked up the shawl and, as she was about to put it on, let it fall to the ground.

Lizzie slapped her. "Fool girl! That's best French chiffon!"

It wasn't a hard slap, but for Easter it was worse than the sting of the switch, for it carried with it all of this woman's ascendancy over her and thus, eventually, Jass. It didn't help that she heard him saying, quite sharply, "Don't do that!"

Tears, not of pain, sprang to Easter's eyes, but she was too well trained, or too proud, to run away. She picked up the shawl.

"She's just a clumsy nigra," Lizzie insisted, flushing at the rebuke.

"We don't treat our slaves like that," Jass said, and with such authority that Lizzie wondered if he might be more of a match than she had bargained for. She snatched the shawl from Easter and flounced away to the landau.

"I declare, are you a nigra lover?" she said, loudly enough for them all to hear, wanting, in some way, to hurt him, and knowing, from the dinnertime conversation of her parents, that Jass had problems at school because of his supposed liberal attitudes to the slaves. "It's a wonder you ain't going to Nashville."

Sally knew the slight was intended to hurt, and sprang to her son's defense. "Of course he'll be there." She turned to her astonished son. "Your father and I were just discussing it. It's time you were introduced into society and met some young ladies."

She might as well have said "other" young ladies, Lizzie felt, for it was clear to her, in that moment, that the biggest obstacle to her future with Jass would be Sally. But Jass was beaming at her.

"We could have that dance," he said in transparent delight.

To Lizzie, the visit had been a disaster. She knew that she had a potential enemy in Sally, she knew she'd been told off for her natural treatment of a slave, and she saw a lifetime ahead of being trapped in marriage to a young man who was so wretchedly, perpetually nice. Didn't he have any idea of how society functioned? Were boys not taught these things at school? Did she have to do all the work? She longed to think of a witty retort that would astound them all with its sophistication, but none came to her.

"Unfortunately, I remember, my card is full!" she said as she huffed into the carriage, and even that embarrassed her because they'd all know it was a lie, since they had no idea yet of what other young men had even been invited, let alone who would ask Lizzie to dance. She wanted the carriage to go, now, but her mother took forever to climb in, and wouldn't stop saying good-bye, and to Lizzie it was all the most mortifying experience of her life.

Finally they were on the move, but she refused to turn and wave, as etiquette demanded, even though she knew it would mean a lecture from her mother as soon as they were off the property. Had she looked back, she would have been disappointed again, because her intended was not waving with the rest of his family. He'd gone racing off to tell Easter the good news that he was going to the wedding.

News that Easter took almost as badly as Lizzie. "That's nice" was her only response, and it burst Jass's bubble of excitement more effectively than any of Lizzie's barbs. "Just because that silly girl slapped you," he responded, thinking it would help. "I told her off."

"And couldn't take your eyes off her!"

Easter wouldn't relent, and Jass didn't know what to do; he was too young, too inexperienced in the ways of sparring women. "Don't sass me!" he snapped, and walked away. But he couldn't let it go at that. Easter was his best friend, and he'd wanted her to share his fun. He turned back. "Damn you, Easter," he yelled, "you're no fun!" and continued walking away.

Immediately, Easter regretted her anger.

'I'm sorry, Massa Jass I—" she called, but not loudly enough for him to hear, and as immediately, she regretted her regret.

"Oh, damn you, too," she cried, and this time he did hear. And smiled, as he walked away.

27

J ass cut himself shaving, adding another tiny gash to the several caused by Wesley's fists. He staunched the blood with a cotton cloth, stared at himself in the mirror, and wondered if he would ever master the cutthroat razor. Cap'n Jack had taught him the use of it, had made it look easy, and whenever Jass watched his father shave, he seemed to flourish the perilous instrument with a careless, harmless grace that Jass envied. He didn't shave often—he didn't need to—but he enjoyed it; it made him feel grown-up. The first time he had ever

251

done it, scraping away at the fuzzy down on his upper lip, it had given him a surging sense of masculinity that had thrilled him. Easter had shaved him once, for fun, under Cap'n Jack's tutelage, but a similar feeling had occurred then, provoking embarrassment and confusion in him, making Jass wonder if he was quite normal, if this thing happened to the other boys so often, and adding a new and disturbing, if unknown, dimension to his relationship with the slave girl.

He hoped the tiny nick would distract from the other wounds to his face, but staring in the mirror, he knew it was a forlorn wish. Those cuts and Easter's iodine stains ensured that his family would know that he had been fighting, if they didn't already, and his sister would giggle, his mother would make a disapproving speech, and his father would beam amiably at his son, and encourage Sassy's ragging.

His body, though firm and taut, had the definition of a man's but the weight of a boy's, and he flexed his biceps, wondering if he would ever have the bulging muscles of Wesley and his older classmates. No longer a boy, not yet a man, he longed to be older, or younger again, or something, for he couldn't stand this nether-world he was living in. He still wasn't treated as a full-grown man, and the ways of adult men were confusing to him.

He wondered if he would ever understand girls, and wished they were all more like his mother, who was at least predictable. Lizzie's butterfly mind, leaping from one thought to apparently unconnected others, confused him, but it seemed to be a factor in all young women. His sisters did it too. He would be having a sensible conversation with them, and suddenly they would say something that seemed utterly logical to them, but which confounded Jass, as happened in his Latin class when he was going along swimmingly, and a new verb conjugation, or the unexpected use of a case, caused him to flounder.

252

He wondered why he thought about girls nearly all the time, why the very smell of them drove him mad, and why the closeness of Easter, tending his cuts, provoked such overwhelming urges.

Sometimes, he thought, the only woman he really understood was his mother.

The gong sounded downstairs. He was late for dinner. Just as always. He splashed water on his face to try to repair some of the damage, then hurried to put on his shirt and jacket.

The dining room looked grand, for Sally took especial pride in it, trying to re-create here the dining room in Ireland that James so fondly remembered. The oil lamps, with their exquisite, hand-painted glass shades, seemed to make the burgundy velvet drapes glow and gave a rich sheen to the carved mahogany furniture. The diffusing lamplight softened the sometimes stern features of the family portraits hanging on the walls, for the painters liked to make their wealthy subjects look authoritative. The table linen was crisply starched, the silverware gleamed, and the smells wafting from the pantry were mouth-watering. There was always some formality about the evening meal at The Forks, and the family was expected to dress for dinner, whether or not they had visitors, which they often did.

Tonight it was only the family. They stared at Jass as he hurried to his chair on his father's left. James glanced at the grandfather clock. "Cut yourself shaving?" he wondered. Sassy giggled. Sally glared at her and Jass blushed, but before he could reply, his father coughed and bowed his head. They all followed suit, and James said grace. Sally rang a small bell, and Parson Dick marched in with the tureen, and Polly, with the plates.

There was a tiny silence while the soup, lentil with ham hocks, was served, no one knowing which way the conversation would jump.

Sally broke it, determined to let Jass know she was vexed.

"I don't know why you always have to be fighting!" she admonished. Jass mumbled something about not starting it, and James came to his aid.

"Schoolboys' Debating Club?" He smiled at his son. Jass felt a sudden rush of temper.

"If only they *would* debate," he flared. "But the minute you start talking sense, they seem to think you're attacking the honor of the South! It's stupid to be so entirely reliant on one industry, one workforce. What if cotton suddenly went out of fashion, or something—"

Everyone laughed. Cotton was, is, and always would be. Cotton would never go out of fashion. It couldn't; there was nothing to replace it. You couldn't wear wool in the summer heat, and what would you do for bed linen?

"No one would have any clothes," Sassy said, which riled Jass a little more. All girls ever seemed to think about was clothes.

"All right," he countered. "What if there was some bug or weevil that got into the cotton and destroyed it, something we couldn't control? We'd be bankrupt."

He had them there, he was sure of it, but hadn't reckoned on his father.

"Oh, I think we'd manage." James's voice was calm. "There are other crops, sugar and tobacco, after all."

"They aren't as profitable as cotton, and need as many slaves," Jass argued, but his father was benign.

"We do own rather a lot of land, and that never goes out of style." He turned to his son. "But that's why you keep getting into trouble, boy." Jass hated to be called a boy, but loved it when his father spoke to him seriously, man to man. "To question cotton is to question the economic validity of the South—"

"But what if the Feds abolish slavery?" Jass jumped in. "Or if the slaves revolted, like Nat Turner—"

The very name Nat Turner unsettled the women; it was the stuff of their worst nightmares. Sensing this,

254

James tried to be calm, and ignored the interruption. "And to question slavery is to attack the South, which only gets you into more trouble."

Sally intervened, as much for herself as for her daughter. "Why don't you discuss this after dinner, in the other room?"

Sassy had gone very quiet. "Quite right," said James, and looked for a happier subject. "Are you all excited about the wedding?"

Soup done, Polly cleared the plates, and Parson Dick brought the roast to James to carve.

The change of course and subject had the desired effect. Sassy cheered up immediately, and Polly glanced at Parson Dick. They all had varying degrees of knowledge about the wedding, the whites and the blacks, from the invitation, from the Perkinses, or from the grapevine, although Jass, whose only sources were Easter and Lizzie, knew less than most.

"What's it all about?" he asked, and his family all spoke at once, to fill him in, and in relief from the talk of Nat Turner. From the confusion of names, opinions, and gossip, Jass learned what he did not already know.

When President Jackson's son, Andrew Jackson, Jr., had recently married Sarah York, the president gave his new daughter-in-law a slave maid, Gracie, as a wedding gift. Alfred, never far from the president's side, had fallen in love with Gracie, and she accepted his offer of marriage. Sarah, wanting the wedding to be celebrated in style, was organizing a grand function at the Hermitage, and had invited the gentry of the South, together with their most valued slaves, to attend. It was the inclusion of the slaves in the invitations that was causing the fuss.

"Can you imagine?" Sassy giggled. "Slaves? As guests?"

Jass was tickled pink. "What a grand idea," he laughed. "And not so very unusual—we often go to their weddings."

"To watch, or because we own them." Sassy shared some of Lizzie's outrage. "Never all mixed up together. No one will go!"

"I think most everyone will," James corrected his daughter. "Sarah is so close to the president. Who will turn her down?"

"Will you go, Papa?" Sassy asked. They all knew of the cooling of their father's friendship with the man who was now president. "I thought you and Uncle Andrew had a quarrel."

James shrugged it aside. "We've had our differences from time to time. That's all over and done with."

"Andrew Jackson has been a good friend to this family," Sally said. "He helped us considerably in the early days."

She was only telling them what they all already knew, but felt she had to defend the days of their youth. Whatever her private opinion of Andrew, she knew that he was responsible for much of their considerable fortune.

"If it's going to be such a grand occasion, what am I going to wear?" Sassy wailed. "I can't go in these old rags!"

Everyone laughed again. The "old rags" were gorgeous, handmade in Charleston, and worn twice at most, but a party atmosphere prevailed, and the rest of the meal was spent in a discussion of new clothes for Sally and Sassy, and of who might be attending the wedding and who might not. Jass longed to be away. The talk of the dresses had interested him briefly, if only because they were soft, feminine things, but now he wanted to see Cap'n Jack, for he was still puzzled by Easter's recent attitude, and needed older, wiser, male help.

As soon as they had given thanks for their meal, he begged to be excused, and scooted out of the room, to James's disappointment, for he had been planning to talk to his son.

"Off to see Easter," Sassy giggled, and she hurried away to find Angel, Sally's personal maid, and plan new ball gowns.

Suddenly then, James and Sally were alone but for the slaves. James stared at his wife for a long moment. The years seemed to be making her more handsome, not less, and motherhood had given both a tranquillity and purpose that enhanced her personality. She was born to be what she is now, thought James, and hoped she loved him still, knowing that she did.

Parson Dick coughed gently. "No," said James, "I'll take it here."

Parson Dick poured a small glass of port, looked a question at Sally, who shook her head slightly, and the butler and the maid left the room.

James sipped his port, and they sat in companionable silence for a while, the dull ticking of the grandfather clock a metronome to their thoughts.

Sally knew something was worrying her husband, and she guessed it had to do with Andrew. Ever since John Coffee's visit last week, when the two men had spent the entire afternoon in the study supposedly discussing business matters, James had been distracted. Well, she thought, he will tell me in his good time, if it's important, knowing that it was. James always shared his most worrying concerns with her eventually, unlike some men who treated their wives as decorative imbeciles when it came to business affairs. She could not imagine a better husband, and thanked her Maker that she had found this gentle, reasonable man. She saw his graying hair, the wrinkles around his eyes, and the thickening waistline, and it made not one jot of difference to her feelings for him. For this is how it was meant to be, she thought. This is what love is: We are friends as much as lovers, we will grow old together, and I would trust him, I do trust him, with my life. She prayed with all her heart for a similar contentment for her children.

Especially Jass. Because he was not born to the role of first son, she knew life was not easy for the boy. A.J. had been blessed with a more forceful personality. No one ever worried about A.J., for he seemed to understand naturally what was expected of him, and even as a youth you could see in him the future head of the family, master of the estate, the slaves, and their fortunes. But Jass was different. Honest, caring, and studious, he was scrupulous in his attention to other people's feelings, and she knew that his eventual responsibilities as master would weigh heavily on him, for she saw in the blithe boy a wretched affliction for those in authority: Jass could always see both sides of every question.

Briefly, bitterly, she felt a sudden stab of almost inconsolable grief, and cursed God for taking A.J. from them, not just because she loved her firstborn—which she did with all her heart; his death had caused her untold pain—but also because his presence would have made Jass's future so much easier. It hadn't mattered so much two years ago, when A.J. had been killed in that awful accident, because Jass had still been a boy, basking in the careless, carefree days of innocence. But it mattered now, as she watched him daily becoming more of a man, with a man's cares, and she knew, if only from Mrs. Perkins's fan language, Lizzie's flirting, and James's too ready receptivity of their plot, that a man's future was being planned for him. Not Lizzie, she begged, anyone but Lizzie, wanting for her son a woman who might more easily comprehend his forgiving nature and make considerably fewer demands on his gentle morality.

And then there was Easter.

As if tracking her thoughts, James smiled at her. "Easter's good for him," he said. He took a sip of brandy, and his tone was cautionary. "He's nearly a man, after all."

Yes, thought Sally, he's nearly a man. She felt a

sudden flash of temper again. But he isn't a man yet, he's still a boy, and I want him to be that boy for as long as his heart desires. She yearned for the pioneer days of their youth, when building a life was more important than sustaining a fortune, for she knew that now they were rich, now they were people of consequence, what her son might want in a bride was secondary to the successional needs of a good marriage.

He's still a boy, her heart insisted. But she looked at her husband.

"Yes," she agreed. "He's nearly a man." She wasn't trying to avoid the inevitable, merely delay it. For as long as was humanly possible.

The young man in question was looking for advice about women, specifically Easter, from his mentor, Cap'n Jack.

"She's growing up," Cap'n Jack told Jass. "She wants woman things."

Jass grabbed at the only straw he felt confident with about girls. "You mean pretty dresses and things?"

Cap'n Jack smiled. He'd had a long talk with Easter and knew that her ambition ran to much more than a frock.

"And invitations to weddings an' things." Cap'n Jack dropped the tiny bombshell lightly.

Jass was astonished. "You mean, she wants to go? But that's ridiculous, she's too young, she's not even a lady's maid, she—"

"Don't stop her wanting it, all the same," Cap'n Jack responded.

Jass stared at the night. Fireflies sparkled in the long grass.

The slave quarters, a collection of shacks around a large clearing, were almost a second home away from home to Jass, for he spent almost as much time here as in the mansion or the weaving house. A bonfire, a large pot of food simmering over it, burned in the middle of

259

the clearing. Most of the slaves had already eaten and were relaxing as best they could, gathered in little groups outside their shacks. Somewhere Monkey Simon was strumming a banjo, and a mother was washing a child in an old bathtub. A sense of tranquillity prevailed, for whatever resentments any of the younger, more hotheaded men felt for their status, no slave had run away from The Forks for years. There was no point in it.

Old Tiara, who had been Jass's nurse and now cared for her young grandson, Isaac, sat on a broken-down rocker, the boy on her lap, discussing the coming wedding with anyone who cared to listen.

"Yo' gwine be Alfred's best man?" she called to Cap'n Jack, only a small distance away.

Cap'n Jack shook his head. "Ain't seen too much of him. Not since the Massa and Massa Presyden' fell out."

He sorely missed his old friend but was proud of his status as most loyal slave to the president, whom he never called Massa Andrew anymore, but always Massa Presyden'.

"Alfred gettin' awful old," Tiara cackled. "Same like you. Time you was hitched agen, Cap'n Jack."

Her husband, Micah, was whittling on the stoop of their little shack. "Hush, woman," he said, knowing the command was useless.

"Don't yo' shush me!" Tiara was indignant. "Cap'n Jack need a woman to look after him, cain't go on dreamin' 'bout Annie fo' evuh an' evuh."

Isaac, warm and secure against his grandmother's capacious bosom, stirred. "Who's Annie?" he asked.

"You hush too, boy," muttered Micah. "She ain't with us no more."

A slave child must learn early, at his mother's knee. Or his grandmother's, and Tiara was always ready to pick at an old sore, as much for the young Massa's

260

benefit as Isaac's. "Don't you tell Isaac hush. No reason he cain't know what Massa did."

She was looking at Jass, but talking to Isaac. "She wer' Easter's mammy. Massa sol' her away."

Jass, who had heard the story many times, but had no memory of it, was not listening. His mind was filled with images of Easter in a pretty dress rather than the simple homespun she usually wore.

"Weren't the Massa," Cap'n Jack said sharply. "Wer' the overseer, Harris."

Tiara laughed derisively. "Don't make no never mind. She got sol' away."

She hugged Isaac to her. "Things differen' now," she told the boy, "but in the ol' days, hit didn't make no never mind if'n a slave had family. Massas sell anyone away if'n they had a mind. Sons from pappies. Mammies from sons."

Micah stopped his whittling and stared at the fire. "Still happen, most places," he said. There was no bitterness in his voice; it was a simple statement of fact. The only thing permanent to a slave was slavery.

"Not here," Cap'n Jack insisted. "Massa wouldn't let it."

In Jass's mind, the vision of Easter in a pretty frock gave way to Lizzie in the same frock. It shocked him from his reverie, and he heard Tiara speaking.

"Him Massa. An' all Massas the same. Don't give a hoot 'bout black folk, other'n to work their selves to the grave for 'em."

"That's tosh, Tiara," Jass broke into the conversation, without rancor, for it happened all the time. "We look after you, don't we?"

"Jes' sayin'." Tiara rocked in the gentle night. There was no point in starting an argument with Jass about it, for she would never win.

It was also true. Despite the visceral resentment many of the slaves felt about their servitude, the Jacksons looked after them reasonably well. Furious with Harris for selling Annie, James, on his return to The Forks, had sacked the man instantly, and had spent many weeks searching for a suitable replacement. Edward Mitchell had come to him with good references that praised his work but complained of a certain leniency in his treatment of slaves, and James had hired him at once. A man who used the whip as punishment of last resort rather than weapon of first defense, he had made some improvements to conditions for the slaves, and they, in return, had given a somewhat better productivity. Slaves were never sold away now, and were only purchased when absolutely necessary, both the Massa and the overseer preferring to train their own people, born and bred on the plantation. It was a poor substitute for freedom, but it was generally agreed that if you had to be a slave, The Forks was one of the better places to be.

If you had to be a slave. They all had a dream of freedom and prayed for a miracle that would somehow deliver them from their bondage, but the dreams and the prayers were tempered by the reality of their existence. The known was preferable to the unknown, and although the younger men talked of running away, they had no clear idea of where they would run to, except the vague, distant North, Up South as the slaves called it, and between them and any viable sanctuary was a hostile, perilous environment that few believed they would survive.

In the chaos of gossip and hysteria that attended the Nat Turner rebellion, one of their number, Samuel, a rash young man, saw cause for hope and did run away. It was one of the few times when Mitchell had thought it necessary to display his authority, and they had been locked in their quarters, even Cap'n Jack and Easter, the men shackled, until Samuel was returned. Mitchell employed slave catchers, with instructions that the runaway was not to be unduly harmed, and after a week they brought him back, hungry and miserable, bruised and bleeding from the unnecessary beating the catchers had insisted was necessary for his recapture. Samuel had been chained to a tree for a week, the time of his absence, through the blazing days of August, until Mitchell believed his promises that he would never attempt to escape again.

Samuel kept his word. For months he would not even talk of his time away, but as his wounds of spirit and body healed, he started to brag of it, the extent and unlikeliness of his adventures expanding with every telling, until they all devoutly wished he would shut up.

Freedom, then, was a double-edged sword, a longed-for dream and a terrifying prospect, and to someone of Tiara's years, not something she could easily imagine in her lifetime. But she hugged Isaac to her again, and begged sweet Jesus in heaven to make it a reality for him.

A distraction arrived, in the form of Parson Dick.

Immaculately attired, as always, Parson Dick looked considerably out of place in this community of field hands. Although black, he was more of an outsider here than the white youth, Jass.

"Cap'n Jack, the Massa want to see you," he called. "You too, Massa Jass." Duty done, he sniffed the air. "My, Missus Tiara, that pot likker sure smell fine—"

Although his elocution was usually flawless, Parson Dick could fall into slave idiom whenever it suited him. He thrived on knowledge, on gossip, loved to keep his finger on the pulse of the field slaves' thinking, and Tiara, an old sparring partner, was the key to that world.

Tiara glared at him. "Yo' get yo' victuals up the big house, Parson Dick, where yo' belong. We ain't good enough fo' house niggers like yo'." But she nodded to her daughter, Minnie, who got up and went to the pot with a bowl.

263

"But you gettin' mighty thin, Parson Dick, on all that white livin'," Tiara chortled. "Have some real food, mebbe put a little color back in yo' cheeks."

Everyone laughed, although they were never quite sure of Parson Dick. He settled comfortably on a log and accepted the bowl of pot likker from Minnie. "The Massa waitin'," he told Jass and Cap'n Jack, who now got up to leave.

There was a small silence, which Parson Dick broke, knowing that nothing would be learned from Tiara without something in return. "Be a whole lot of stitchin' goin' on," he began. "Gettin' ready for the wedding."

Tiara nodded. It was the introduction to gossip from the big house, which she loved. It was also the last thing Jass heard as he walked away, and it reminded him of Easter.

"I could ask my father," he told Cap'n Jack. "But I don't think he'd agree."

"Mebbe," Cap'n Jack said, and his tone told Jass to say nothing to James. "Mebbe."

Easter, bored with brushing her hair, had not joined the other slaves for the evening, as was her habit, because she was still miffed with Jass, and the world, and she wanted him to come to her. She looked out of the window and saw her father walking to the big house with Jass. She prayed that Cap'n Jack was telling him about her desire to go to the wedding, about which she had poured out her distressed heart to her father for a solid hour, and that Jass, being the young Massa, would do something about it.

Just in case God wasn't in a listening mood, she crossed her fingers and allowed herself to dream.

28

J ass loved his father's study. All the other rooms at
The Forks reflected Sally's personality, and although
she had been responsible for decorating this room, his
father's untidiness prevailed. The floor-to-ceiling
shelves crammed with books, the clutter of heavy
furniture, and the imposing oak desk suggested a world
where women seldom came—and they seldom did,
except as occasional visitors, or as maids, to clean.

James busied himself with the copious papers on the
desk, for he was not looking forward to this interview
with his son. Cap'n Jack waited near the door.

James looked at Jass, and his spirit failed him slightly.
The boy simply looked too young to be a serious
participant in the conversation James had in mind, so
he delayed matters by turning his attention to Cap'n
Jack.

"Our old friend Alfred is getting married at last," he
announced, stating what was for everyone, by now, the
obvious.

Cap'n Jack was courteous. "Yes, suh, I hear, suh."

James found the letter he pretended to have been
looking for, which had never been lost.

"You'll be coming to Nashville, of course, to valet
master Jass and myself. But there's more—"

He held out the letter. Cap'n Jack looked reluctant.
Jass smiled to himself, for what was being played out
was a continuing charade.

"I cain't read, suh," Cap'n Jack lied reasonably.
"Tain't legal."

James was not in a mood to waste time. "For heaven's
sake, you can read as well as I—" he began, but knew
he was wasting his breath. Whatever the truth of the
matter, Cap'n Jack would never admit his education,

even in the confines of this room, where he had no enemies.

"Oh, very well." James gave in, and glanced at the letter. "The president says that Alfred has requested you as his best man. Of course, you have my permission."

Cap'n Jack smiled happily. "Why, that's wonderful news, suh. Will you write that I accept?"

"I already have," James said. "I thought you would like to know. Thank you, Cap'n Jack."

Jass guessed that his father was simply procrastinating, that he had something more serious he wanted to discuss, with Jass, but was playing for time with Cap'n Jack. Please don't let it be about girls, Jass sent up an urgent prayer to heaven. They'd had a brief aimless discussion of morality some months ago, which ended with his father's admonition, "You know about girls, I'm sure. Don't ever be discourteous, or unmannerly, or, damn it, base, toward them," and had left whatever other information his son might need to Cap'n Jack, the men of the slave quarters, and the other boys at school. Jass had been even more embarrassed than James by his father's inconsequential ramblings and he now hoped Cap'n Jack wouldn't leave.

That part of his prayer was answered, for Cap'n Jack didn't go. He hovered by the door, until James, who had returned his attention to the papers on his desk, looked up. "What is it?" he asked.

"My daughter, suh, Easter. Annie's girl. She want so much to go to the wedding. Would mean a lot to her."

"Well, of course she can go," James interrupted, completely aware of the not so subtle emotional blackmail that was being used. Any mention of Annie stirred his conscience, reminding him of things he would rather forget. Still, some role had to be found for Easter.

"She can maid Sassy. Angel can teach her." Angel was Sally's maid.

"Yes, suh, thank you very much, suh. I tell her

tomorrow, and she learn good." Cap'n Jack was duly grateful, but a slight twinkle of triumphant conspiracy passed between him and Jass. "Good night, Massa."

Jass could hardly conceal the grin of delight that sneaked to his face. Cap'n Jack gave the merest wink to Jass before bowing to his master and leaving, and somehow Jass understood that the secret was to be kept from Easter for a little while at least, and that he would be the one to tell her.

"Well," said James, when they were alone. "Would you care for some port?"

Jass found himself caught in an agony of ambivalence, not for the first time that day. His father had never offered him port before, and part of Jass was cock-a-hoop that he seemed to have crossed some line of demarcation between boyhood and manhood with his father. Another part of him groaned inwardly. Almost certainly, this meant they were going to talk about girls.

"Perhaps a small one, sir." He accepted the invitation, and James nodded at the decanter on his desk. Jass moved forward to pour himself a glass.

In the hall, Sally was fiddling, picking dead buds from flowers in a vase, when Cap'n Jack came out of the study. She looked at him and he at her. They were old conspirators, and he left the library door slightly open, so that Sally could hear the conversation within.

Then he looked for something equally trivial to do, and began trimming candles.

Jass sipped his port and thought it wonderful. He had seldom drunk any alcohol, except at celebrations, and then only watered wine. He loved the taste of this sweet, thick liquid, loved the gentle fire that traced through his body as the wine did its work, and loved the small sense of equality it gave him with his sometimes distant father.

"Do you like it?" James asked.

"Very much, sir," Jass responded, nodding his head and taking another, confirming, sip of port.

There was a tiny silence, and then James took the plunge.

"It's never been easy for me to discuss personal matters with you, Jass," he began, and, having begun, found it easier than he had expected. "There are things I thought I would not have to discuss with you, but because of your brother's untimely death—"

He stopped, momentarily. A.J.'s accident had caused him terrible grief. Like Sally, he simply didn't discuss it with anyone, and tried not to think about it. It had become easier, of course. Time had healed the worst of the pain, although the aching hurt still washed across him in unguarded moments, causing, if only for an instant, an overwhelming sense of loss and of the unfairness of it. He looked at Jass, and could not, in all honesty, see in his eager second son an adequate substitute for his first.

"With A.J. gone," he continued, "you will now inherit all this." The vague "all this" implied a considerable fortune. "We have never talked about it, and it's time we did."

"Yes, sir," Jass responded dutifully.

"It is not easy, Jass," James said, wondering if he should call him James, "to be master of such responsibilities as I will leave to you. I hope, of course, that I will be with you for many years, and the assumption of your eventual role will be gradual. I will ease you into it, and you will always be able to come to me for advice and consideration."

I sound so pompous, thought James. Like my own father. What must the boy think of me? Why can't I come to the heart of the matter?

"It is not easy being master," he said again, unnecessarily, and stopped again. We're getting nowhere, he thought.

"But," he said, and knew it had to be now, "I won't

268

always be here. And if anything should happen to me, I want you to be ready. Do you like the Perkins girl?"

It came as a small bolt from the blue, and Jass was thrown by it, although the connection was obvious to his father.

"Well, yes, I guess. Lizzie's charming," was the best Jass could manage.

"She is also a most eligible heiress." His father, having taken the plunge, waded on. "You're too young to even contemplate anything—serious—with her, and if circumstances were different we would not be having this conversation. But—"

Jass knew where they were going. In that "but" a whole future lay.

It was apparent to Sally, too, still fiddling with dead flowers in the hall, and to Cap'n Jack, still uselessly trimming a wick that could scarcely be trimmed any more.

"—you will have to marry eventually, and I hope it will be sooner rather than later. I was not a young man when I married your mother, and I sometimes regret that I did not find her earlier."

He had completely lost track of how to say what he wanted, he knew, although his goal still beckoned him, if only he could reach it. Why is it so difficult? he thought again, although he already knew the answer. He was trying to control something that, ultimately, he did not believe was his to control. He lost his temper with himself.

"You must have sons, Jass!" he announced angrily. "Sons to inherit what I have created here."

As soon as he said it, his anger at himself increased, for he knew he sounded even more pompous than before. Jass was puzzled by his father's vehemence, but a second glass of port was making him bold.

"Of course, Papa," he said. "I'm looking forward to being married one day. But I was wondering about—" He found the word difficult to say, for he was suddenly feeling a complex anger, too. Here he was with his father, drinking port and discussing his future as man and master, yet he was still being treated as an inadequate boy. He felt an intense, burning need to communicate to his father that he wasn't a boy anymore, he was a man, in charge of his own destiny. Suddenly he wanted answers from his father to some of the questions that had been puzzling him.

"I was wondering," he repeated, "about love."

James stared at his son, as if staggered by his impudence. Love, he thought, oh, love. That is the heart of it. That is what I should be discussing with him, and what I am trying to deny him. I am considering everything that matters—this house, this land, this estate, this family, this fortune—but not the thing that matters most. I have not considered his heart. Is that what my father did to me?

To his son he said: "Love?"

Jass began a confused apology. "Where that comes into it. I mean, I know all about girls and things, and getting married, and babies, all the fellows at school talk about that all the time, but no one's ever talked to me about love."

It was eminently fair and reasonable, thought James, and completely unanswerable. He struggled to describe the indescribable. "Love is—"

What? A young man's dream? An intangible, foolish, impractical something, dictated by the heart, not the head, which if undirected could sabotage everything he had worked for, all he had built, the tiny empire he had created. Yet it was a most basic right of any man—and, he knew, totally unpredictable, perhaps dangerously so. He had never questioned, would never have challenged, A.J.'s right to love whom he would, for A.J. would have loved the right woman, James was sure. A.J.'s sense of responsibility would have dictated to his heart, and he would have chosen a bride who would

270

have been worthy mistress of this mansion. Why was he not so sure that Jass would do the same?

"I hope you will find love," he assured his son, longing for Sally to help. "But marriage and love do not necessarily go hand in hand."

They do, his heart insisted, they do. Let the boy love. But let him love wisely, his mind responded.

"When I first met your mother, I thought she was the most beautiful creature I had ever seen, and I—wanted her—at that moment—"

The unguarded thought had slipped out. So anxious was he to impress duty on his son that he was not embarrassed by the admission of lust.

"—but I didn't love her then, I didn't know her, I'd never spoken to her. Love came with knowledge. The more I came to know her, the more I came to love her, until now I cannot bear to be apart from her."

Sally's heart sang a sweet duet. This is my husband, whom I love. And this is my son, who has dared my husband to speak of love.

"But we married for different reasons," she hardly heard James continue. "We married for mutual benefit; we married to have a family. Love came later."

Whatever motives she had for wanting to overhear the conversation in the study now seemed irrelevant to Sally, for she knew her son would love whom he would, marry whom he must. She hoped they would be one and the same woman, but if not, she hardly cared, for the boy would be his own man, and that, for Sally, was all that mattered. Only one tiny cloud troubled her otherwise flawless horizon. She moved to the study and softly she closed the door.

"Easter's turned into a fine girl," she said to Cap'n Jack.

"Yes, missus," the slave replied.

"Master James is very fond of her."

"Yes, missus."

271

Sally moved away, as if that were the end of the conversation, but, at the stairs, turned back.

"Let us hope he doesn't become—too fond—of her." Her meaning was precisely clear, and Cap'n Jack looked at her steadily.

"No, missus."

Why did she fear this so? Why, in this moment of otherwise complete certainty about Jass's character, did she have such profound misgivings about a simple slave girl?

Sally moved in what she often thought was a hypocritical hemisphere with regard to her son's libido. She knew, as did all Southern mothers, that most of their young men found their first sexual pleasures with slave girls, and that many of these young men continued to take that pleasure throughout their adult life. She knew—they all did—of older male friends who kept a black mistress, or several concubines, or of those who simply raped their slave women as and when the urge took them. It was seldom discussed by the women, and then only "behind the fan," but oh, how busy those fans could be, feeding the embers of gossip into lurid flames of speculation.

In the more sensational cases, such as that of Mr. Herrisvale, only three counties away, who had taken his black concubine into the main house, into the very nuptial bed, relegating his true and lovely white wife to the second-best guest room, the fans had worked overtime, for every white woman could only too easily imagine herself in a similar predicament. The dear, sweet Mrs. Herrisvale had absolutely no recourse of any kind. As wife she was chattel, to be done with as her husband wished—in many ways, Sally frequently thought, no better than a slave—and no matter how much her family might rail on her behalf, the husband was lord of the estate and king of the lives of those who dwelt therein, and if he was of a cantankerous nature, like Mr. Herrisvale, all the suffering Edna could do was

272

bear the indignity with as much fortitude as she could muster. Her outraged brothers had demanded her return to them, with or without her substantial dowry, but Mr. Herrisvale had kept them at bay with shotguns and the full force of the law. "We can only be grateful," swooned the fanning gossips, "that our dear husbands are reasonable, faithful, Christian men."

But were they? What woman could be sure that her husband was not finding some pleasure, at least, in the slave quarters, and if he was, what might this lead to? Surely Edna Herrisvale had put her complete faith and trust in her husband, and look at her now. Yet for many of the wives, the slave concubines were a considerable relief, for it meant fewer sexual demands on them. And a mightier relief too, on behalf of their daughters, for if the young beaux had no other outlet for their base desires, the virginity of every young Southern belle was potentially at risk, and for a girl to go to the altar already deflowered was a shame no mother could bear.

Still Sally worried about Jass's fondness for Easter. She guessed that any eventual physical relationship with Easter would keep him satisfied and happy, for the realist in her knew that her son must be developing carnal needs, and she prayed that he would eventually find a bride who would not be too obtuse in the bedroom. Yet that other, maternal, side of her dreamed that her boy might be temperate of desire, that he would remain a virgin until his marriage, and that he would be as sweet and undemanding of his spouse in bed as he was in life. That this hope somehow emasculated her son was a demon fear she worked very hard to keep at bay.

She wanted for Jass a simple life, she told herself, and Easter was an unnecessary complication.

"Good night, Cap'n Jack," she said, and went up the stairs. If anyone had influence over Easter and Jass it was Cap'n Jack, and she was relying on him to do his utmost to put restraints on their friendship.

273

"Good night, Missus Sally," Cap'n Jack replied, and started turning down lamps.

What Sally did not understand, for she had no knowledge of it, was the bitter complexity of Cap'n Jack's ambition. Unable to persuade Annie's new owner to part with his new slave, even for considerable sums of money, Sally had spent countless hours comforting Cap'n Jack, and believed that his pain had eventually healed.

She was wrong.

All the furious vows of vengeance Cap'n Jack had made the day Annie was sold away still raged beneath his compliant exterior. He had no clear idea of how to achieve his goal, or even what his goal might be, but he had the slave's gift of patience, and fortune seemed to be playing directly into his hands. The deep friendship of his daughter and Jass held promise of future fruition, and the death of A.J. would eventually elevate Jass to a position in which Cap'n Jack's primitive oath to subvert his father's expectation of him would have some real hope of success. The stories of Mr. Herrisvale and his black concubine had encouraged exaggerated ambitions in Cap'n Jack, and the thought of Easter as surrogate mistress of this mansion, however disparaged by the world at large, put him at direct variance with what Sally wanted. If this were not possible, if Easter's ascendancy, or his own, were less spectacular, something else would happen, Cap'n Jack was sure, for the actual focus of his triumph didn't matter. The revenge itself was all.

Leaving a few candles burning to light his Massas, young and old, to bed, he left the hall and went out into the night.

In the study, James thought things were going rather well. "A family is everything, Jass, in this world of ours. Without family we are nothing, and you must start thinking of your future. You will meet many young women, of course, at Nashville, and when you go to college—"

He felt the need to invite some comment from his son, since he was trying to exercise such control over the boy's future. "Are you content with New Jersey?" he asked.

"Oh, yes, very much," said Jass. "If they'll have me—"

"You won't have a problem there," James said. "Money talks, even to the old Yankee colleges." He could have bitten his tongue off; he was even denying his son's scholastic ability. So he looked for a compliment.

"Always remember that you are a highly desirable young man, if only because of your position and your wealth, and you will be much sought after. But you could do a lot worse than Lizzie Perkins. She's a fine girl, and would make a splendid wife, I'm sure. Talk to her, call on her, get to know her."

"Yes, sir." Jass was dutiful again.

"Good," said his father, anxious now for it to be over. "Well—that's about it. Best to bed, eh? It's getting late."

"Yes, sir." Jass, who had been hoping for another glass of port, went to the door.

James could not let it go at that. He'd botched the whole thing, had probably confused the boy more than clarified anything, and felt that nagging sense of guilt.

"I've been very proud of you, Jass," he said, with a sudden rush of affection. "You've never let me down."

"Thank you, Papa." Jass was astonished. This was the closest his father had ever come to an expression of love. A similar, sudden affection flooded him, and the boy in him wanted to run to his father, give him the biggest hug of his life, and tell him how much he loved him. The man in him knew that such an action would only embarrass both of them and probably destroy the moment, so he smiled and pretended to be a drunk instead.

"And thank you for the port." He grinned and left the room, staggering in mock inebriation.

James laughed. Jass was a good lad; he'd behaved beautifully in the face of a difficult interview. Now that it was over, James couldn't remember why he had thought it so urgent, why it couldn't have waited a day, a week, a month, a year, for pressuring the young man to accept the concept of an arranged marriage was something that could easily have been delayed until the boy had sown at least a few of his wild oats.

He stared at the silver horse's head, and it reminded him again, as it always did, of his own father, and of the bitter disappointment that James had seen in his father's face the last time they had spoken. How proud of me he should be now, he thought, with all that I have achieved.

Then he looked at the letter from Andrew lying on his desk, and it reminded him of what John Coffee had said to him a week ago, and he remembered why the necessity of the talk with Jass had seemed to have such a pressing urgency.

29

Upstairs in his room, Jass undressed and slipped on his nightshirt. All his senses were sparkling, and he decided he must be a little tipsy. Gee, it felt good. He wondered if he dared sneak downstairs for another glass, but he opened the windows, saw the light spilling onto the veranda, and knew that his father was still in his study. He gazed at the stars, and smelled the heady scent of jasmine. Crickets sang, frogs croaked, and somewhere an owl hooted.

He turned down the oil lamp, and the room was bathed in moonlight. He got into bed, loving the crisp linen sheets, and sank into the luxurious embrace of the feather mattress, which he blessed his mother for buying a year ago. Until then, all the children had slept on sturdy, unyielding horsehair, but after A.J. died it was as if his mother suddenly rejected the spartan upbringing they had previously endured; she went on a shopping spree, replacing all the bed furnishings in the children's rooms. She had even bought a new mattress for A.J.'s bed, although, of course, he would never sleep on it. Jass, lost in a fluffy cloud of eiderdown, looked at his brother's bed, next to his own. It was kept freshly made up, the linen changed each week, the sheets turned down by the maid each night, as if Sally believed that one day A.J. would come home to her, and rest again where he belonged.

It should be moved out, he thought, knowing he would never dare to suggest it to his mother. A.J. is gone. This is my room now.

That he had even had the thought astonished him. His mind was racing in unfamiliar territories he knew must be a result of the conversation with his father. He was James Jackson the Third. He was the young master now! It was the first time he fully appreciated the implications that everyone else had accepted the day A.J. died. He would inherit The Forks of Cypress, and its welfare and his family's welfare devolved onto him. He would marry and have sons and they would inherit it from him and their sons after them. A great dynasty flowered in his mind and suddenly he understood the full importance of what his father had so obscurely presented to him. Sweetened by the wine, the awesome responsibility did not daunt him, but aroused and excited him. He saw himself dispensing wisdom and justice at his father's desk, in his father's study, in his father's stead. He would stand for public office, as his father had done. He imagined himself as host at a great levee, his family around him, and his wife by his side.

But who would she be, he wondered, and how would he know who was the right woman for him? How would he know if he loved her, and how would he know if the woman he loved could fulfill the role that her position as his wife demanded? Would it be Lizzie? Did he love Lizzie?

The only answer he had was to the last question, and it was no. He didn't love Lizzie. At least, he didn't think so. Certainly, he could see Lizzie swanning around The Forks of Cypress, but he couldn't imagine Lizzie in his mother's role, and surely could not imagine her as mother to his children. Maybe his father was right, maybe love came when you got to know someone, and he determined he would do all in his power to get to know Lizzie better, and see if love developed.

Jass had only the haziest notion of what love might be. His sisters seemed sure of it, their noses always stuck in those awful romances, penny dreadfuls his mother called them, that were full of swooning heroines and knights in shining armor, and Jass couldn't imagine himself in that latter role. Mary Ellen had been so convinced of her love for Abram Hunt that she made plans to elope with him when she was only sixteen, hardly older than Jass was now. Abram was actually waiting at the gate for her when Sally heard about it, and stopped them. A lot of tears were shed by Mary Ellen before her parents relented and gave their permission. And his cousin Mary Kirkman, in Nashville, did elope, with Richard Coll, who was Uncle Andrew's ADC. Old Aunt Eleanor was furious, and vowed that she'd never speak to her daughter again, and when Uncle Andrew went to try to talk her round, she had fired a shotgun at him.

So what was it that girls knew about love and he didn't? How did you find out? Did you read books? Did you ask girls?

Then again, his father had said that he would be attractive to girls, if only because of his position and his wealth. He wondered how much his inheritance would

278

be, but had as little conception of the reality of money as he had about love. He knew a sum had been made over to him at his birth, as with his brothers and sisters, and was told he would never have to worry about money, but he had no idea what the original sum was, or what it was now, for his father handled all those things. Nor could he begin to estimate what his father must be worth. Leviathan had earned over $100,000 in stud fees he knew, because the newspapers said so, and horses were only a hobby for James, so what about his enormous holdings in land? He supposed that he would have to take care of the money one day, and he determined to make a closer study of financial matters in the future.

A new and much more interesting fantasy developed. If he was so rich, so eligible, so much sought after by potential brides, he would be able to have his choice of the prettiest women around.

Images of every young woman he'd ever met flooded into his mind and danced across his ceiling, led by Lizzie, in a dazzling array of seductive beauty, and he allowed himself to be flattered and cajoled, teased and flirted with by each and every one of them, the dashing eye at the center of their hurricane of gorgeous attentions. Other, darker-skinned, women appeared now, vying with the whites, and memories of all the pretty slave girls he had ever seen jostled with their young mistresses in his febrile imagination.

But the only one who made him smile was Easter.

If Jass's dreams were sweet with lust, his father's thoughts were filled with foreboding. It cannot all be a house of cards, he thought, but dreaded that it was.

He poured another glass of port. He shouldn't drink so much. He knew it, his doctor had proscribed it, but he needed the comfort of oblivion now. Surely he was unassailable? He had never done anything criminal or illegal, he was president of the Alabama Senate, he was rich, and the value of the land that he owned was enormous.

If he owned the land. There was the problem. He had never had a moment's doubt about his right of title to any of it: He had paid for it, it was all properly registered with the requisite authorities, it was signed, sealed, and delivered in his name.

"Damn you, Andrew!" he said out loud. "And damn me, too," he said a moment later, more softly. "I should never have had any part of it." But if he had never had any part of it, he would not be what he was now.

John Coffee had called a week ago, alone, without his family. The general was in an expansive mood, and he and James behaved as they always did, with considerable civility to each other, as if they were still friends. They shook hands, and spent a pleasant hour discussing the affairs of Alabama and the country, and gossiping about political enemies.

Then John was silent for a while, as if something was troubling him, and stared out of the window.

"Andrew is determined upon the removal of the Indians," he said softly.

Everyone knew of Andrew's determination to persuade—or force—the remaining Indians to migrate. Many had made the long journey to the promised sanctuaries in the West, but their stories of deprivation along the way made miserable hearing. Many others had simply refused to leave the land that was sacred to them, and were suffering for their obstinacy. In six months, the final payment was to be made to the Chickasaw, and they were obligated to leave their land. No one knew how peacefully they might go, for the Cherokee in Georgia were resisting every effort to make them leave.

"For God's sake, why doesn't he let them stay where they are?" James said. "They have suffered enough."

John turned to look at him. Really, the man is a fool, he thought, a weak, dangerous fool. But a gullible one.

"It is for their own good," he said reasonably. "They cannot live amongst us as equals; they don't understand our ways, and have no desire to learn. Their language is useless in a white society, and their superstitions incompatible with our Christian religion. Nor can they live amongst us in their tribal fashion. Their hunting grounds are lost to them, and they have no understanding of the proper use of the good land they occupy, and so they starve."

It was the usual justification for their removal. As more and more white encroachments were made, legally or otherwise, on Indian land, the condition of the native peoples was rapidly degenerating, James knew. The election of Andrew to the presidency had only accelerated this. Sensing a friend in Washington, Georgia extended its laws over the Cherokee in its state, abolishing the tribal units, denying them the right to vote, to seek legal redress in court, to prospect for the gold that had been discovered on their land, and Indian land on which there was no farm or village was appropriated for white settlement. It was an illegal move— Indian lands were actually under the protection of the federal government—but Andrew had completely supported the state's actions. Mississippi and Alabama had followed suit, and intertribal disputes, rampant bribery and corruption among the white Indian agents, alien diseases, the abuse of alcohol, and the Indians' failure to understand, and therefore compete, in the white marketplace were only adding to the Indian misery. Small bands of desperate Creek and Cherokee were attacking white farms in Georgia. People were calling it a war, but all they wanted was food.

"If they do not go, they will die," John continued. "If they do go, they can live, in peace and freedom, governing themselves, in the new lands in the West.

281

The many treaties we have made with the more reasonable Indians guarantee it."

It was a harsh position, James thought, but probably a realistic one. As to the treaties, there had been so many, warranting so much that had later been denied, they seemed irrelevant. His heart bled for the disadvantaged, dispossessed race.

"But a number of liberal hearts are bleeding for the savages," John now said. "The wretched Henry Clay is adamantly opposed to the removal, if only to spite Andrew, and he has much support. They want to have the treaties declared invalid." James knew this too; the newspapers were full of it.

With guilt as its wind, fear, like an approaching, unwelcome storm, appeared on James's untroubled horizon. Even if only one of Andrew's treaties with the Indians was renounced, any of them could be, including the one that governed this land. His land.

"Which treaties?" he wondered, with an outward calm he did not feel.

"Any of them," John echoed James's private thoughts. "All of them, perhaps."

It was an old business, which James thought long forgotten, but it had come back to haunt him.

"But we won the land in war! We paid them for it!" James almost shouted. "They took the money! It is a contract in law."

"Well, yes, we did," John remained calm. "But we didn't pay them very much, nothing like the true worth—"

"The land has no worth, it has no value, unless it is available for white settlement!" It was so simple to James, he couldn't understand that it could be questioned.

"Sometimes you sound exactly like Andrew." John smiled, as if to reassure his troubled host, but actually having the reverse effect, which was what he intended.

An awful realization hit James, somewhere in the pit

of his stomach. I am no better than the rest of them, he thought. Let the Indians have their land, but other land, not mine.

"It is being said in Washington that Andrew obtained the treaty corruptly, by paying massive bribes," John continued. "Particularly to the Colbert brothers."

He had used the singular "treaty," not the plural "treaties," and now he added a clarification that might have been an afterthought but was, in reality, well rehearsed.

"I mean the Chickasaw treaty."

James already knew that. "There were no bribes," he insisted, knowing he was lying.

John sighed. "Well, actually, there were," he said. "And you were at the heart of it. It would be a pity if evidence of them ever came to light, don't you think?" Suddenly he was bored with James, and wanted the business done.

James was visibly shaken, and John was satisfied. "I did nothing," James insisted. "I bought my land and paid for it, and that is all."

"You also lent a very great deal of money to Andrew at that time." John twisted the knife. "What do you think that money was for?"

James could only fall back on a lame excuse. "To pay for a war," he said.

John barely disguised his irritation. "Don't be naive," he snapped. "The war was over. It was to ensure the victory."

There wasn't much more to do. "It is said there are letters between Andrew and yourself that might shed more light on the matter. Andrew believes that any letters he wrote you should be returned to him, for his safekeeping." He was brisk now.

James knew exactly which letters he meant, and knew they were political dynamite. He kept them locked in a strongbox. They were safe there; he didn't want them in anyone else's hands. Especially not John's.

In that moment, he hated John. The man's always been a bully, he thought, and found some streak of stubbornness in himself, if not exactly courage.

"They are private correspondence," he said. "If Andrew personally requested the return of them, and if I believed it necesary, I would deliver them myself."

John saw the flash of temper in James, and knew it was a waste of time to argue.

"Very well. I have to go to Washington tomorrow, to answer questions about the treaties. May I tell Andrew that you will keep those letters private? I need hardly say that publication of them could cause very serious damage to your considerable reputation."

James nodded. He hardly heard the rest of their conversation, didn't remember John saying good-bye, although he responded by rote, but sat at his desk, trying to come to terms with what John had said.

Driving home in his carriage, John was well satisfied with his afternoon's work. He did not despise the Indians; he simply saw them as savage beasts, lions in a jungle, who stood in the way of progress. He resented their unproductive occupation of so much rich land, and believed the white man's right to that land was divinely ordained. He wished the Indians no especial, individual harm. Like Andrew, he could be kind and generous to those who were useful to him or allied themselves to him in the prosecution of his ideals. He particularly admired the warriors, the braves, worthy prey for his military skill.

He did despise weak men, especially those lily-livered dunces in Washington. How could he explain to them, here in the prosperous afternoon of his life, what it had been like, all those years ago, in the exultant morning? Andrew had led them in battle against the Creek and they had won, obtaining a cession of land in the victory spoils, but no one, not even he as subsequent surveyor appointed by Andrew, knew how much land the Creek could be said to own. Indian lands had no borders or boundaries as white men understood them. The Cherokee, who had aided them in the war against the Creek, laid claim to much of it, as did the Chickasaw. So Andrew and John, by force, persuasion, coercion, and—it was a fact of life—bribery, had simply appropriated as much of the land as they could.

And what did it matter if money had been paid to a couple of individual Chickasaw in the treaty for their land, rather than to the whole tribe? The government had what it wanted, which was the point, and the Chickasaw would soon be gone. Why make a fuss about it now?

He had also come to despise James.

James was only a tiny fragment in the elaborate jigsaw of Indian removal that Andrew was piecing together. So much gossip and misplaced indignation surrounded his dealings with the Indians that one more scandal could hardly matter. But the imminent removal of the Chickasaw, and the desperate plight of the Cherokee, was causing furious argument, especially from the hypocritical New Englanders, who had annihilated or banished their Indian populations long ago and now claimed piety. Positive information that a treaty had been obtained illegally, by bribes, could cause the whole thing to blow up in their faces. James had that proof because his money had paid the bribes, and despite the repair work that had been done to the rift between them, Andrew no longer completely trusted James, and thought he should be neutralized. Which John, very effectively, had done.

Put the fear of God in him, he thought. He sneezed, and wondered if he was catching a summer cold.

James didn't eat that night, didn't even leave his study, and the tray that was sent in to him remained untouched. He thought of burning the incriminating letters, destroying them and proof of his culpability

285

forever, but he also knew that as long as he possessed them they gave him powerful ascendancy over Andrew. Sally probed him gently later, in bed that night, but he could not discuss his troubles with her, or with anyone, until he had come to terms with them himself. In the week since John's visit, he had worried and fretted about what had been said, and it was only today that he had been able to come to any decisions.

It was unlikely, he was sure, that his titles to his land would be questioned. Sure, but not certain. The battle between the states and the federal government as to who had what authority over which land was a continuing and complex one. He remembered that, years ago, half the squatters in what was now Kentucky had lost title when Washington had denied North Carolina's assumed rights to the territory. He remembered that the most profitable business for any lawyer on the frontier was from the endless claims and counterclaims as to who owned land. He had thought all the dealings of the Cypress Land Company to have an unassailable basis in law, but he had come to understand over the years, when he admitted the truth to himself, that much of what the company had sold had been obtained by Andrew and John Coffee in an appalling, and probably illegal, land grab.

And it was certain that if anyone found out that his money had paid the bribes to the Colbert brothers, it would destroy his political career and the reputation he had worked so hard to achieve.

The darkest truth of all was one he could hardly bear to admit, for James had come to believe that what had been done, was being done, to the Indians was no different from what the British had done to his countrymen in Ireland. He now believed himself to be as corrupt as his sometime oppressors, a complaisant pawn in a dreadful colonization, subjugation, and degradation of a native people by a foreign power.

That he was not alone in feeling this didn't help.

Many of his associates, business and political, were now expressing concern over what had been wrought, but it was especially bitter for James, for he saw he had been so easily corrupted. Settled and affluent, away from Andrew's powerful influence, he had begun to believe that every acre he had purchased was contributing to the destruction of a race. Nor did he seriously believe Andrew's, or John's, or anyone's, assertions that the removal would be the end of it. The frantically expanding society that was America needed ever more space, and going west was the clarion call of the pioneers. James had heard it, like uncountable others, and it still beckoned him; he longed to go farther still, to the fabled land of California. Realistically, he knew that he would never see the distant Pacific, but others would, driving the Indians before them until the proud few who were left stood with their backs to the boundless ocean, and then where would they go?

The bitter fires of injustices he had seen in his youth, in Ireland, were kindled again in his heart. Enough, he thought, we have done enough. It must be stopped.

Andrew was the lock and the letters were the key. Andrew could make anything happen; the world seemed to jump to his command. If Andrew could be persuaded against the removal, if he could be made to see the necessity of an accommodation with the Indians, of learning how to live compatibly with them, side by side, perhaps something could be salvaged from the wreck.

The arrival of the wedding invitation that morning had fallen on his troubled soul like manna from heaven. Andrew's accompanying letter had been in a reasonable, placatory tone, making few references to the subject that was so vexing James. He would see Andrew in Nashville, at the wedding, and persuade him of the folly of the path on which he was so resolutely determined, or else he would threaten to publish the letters. That would make Andrew see sense. And at heart, he told himself, Andrew loved the Indians; they were his children, he their father.

Having come to a decision, or having decided on a course of action at least, James felt much better, and another concern presented itself for his attention.

Jass.

He was quite proud of his son—no one could deny Jass's sense of duty and honor—but part of him longed for another son, or different aspects to the one he had. Oh, for a son who would give his father a sense of exhilaration and danger, make him stand in awe of the giant that sprang from his loins, a son like the man James had always wanted to be.

A son who would ride a streak of lightning. Someone had said that once about Andrew, and it summed up James's longings exactly. Andrew rode lightning. So had Sean. A.J. might have. He wasn't so sure about Jass. He saw too much of himself in Jass, and just as a shepherd is a king to his flock, so a son is a monument to the man who created him.

For James lived in an agony of self-doubt. As with his present guilt about the Indians, the high moralist in him believed that slavery was an unbearable sin. He wanted to free them all, to set up this estate as a utopian ideal of what a prosperous, well-managed and slaveless plantation could be. The other part of him, the pragmatic, practical, materially ambitious part, had cast his lot with Andrew, and thus with the institutions the South espoused, and thus with slavery and with the appropriation of Indian land. And it had made him rich. And it had given him power. His father's final words to him were a distant whisper now, but they still had painful echoes:

"You will never amount to anything."

He had proved his father wrong. He had amounted to something, whatever the cost, and he took a resonating pride in the achievement. The Forks of Cypress and all it represented were his and would remain so, by right of title and right of tenure. But would Jass ever amount to anything? That was the constant, secret fear the father held for his son. The fear would never be voiced, for he had sworn that he would never say to his sons what his father had said to him, though when he had first made that vow, he had no conception that he might have a son who would even warrant the thought.

Jass would amount to something; he would see to it. If the boy could not do it for himself, it was up to the father to do it for him. So Jass must marry, and marry well, sooner rather than later, and have sons, and those sons would ensure the future prosperity of all he had striven so very hard to achieve.

He was drunk now, he knew it, and found himself staring at a dreadful truth. He hadn't worked so very hard for anything. It had all come to him from someone else's largess. A man more daring than he had given him everything he owned, crumbs from a giant's table. He hadn't ridden on any streak of lightning, merely on Andrew's coattails.

The absolute inadequacy he now felt, together with the drink, made him sentimental. His thoughts turned to A.J., and to the sons he might have had. Waves of loss washed over James, and he found himself crying, tears that might have been for his dead boy, but were as much for himself.

30

Early next morning, Easter was hanging newly dyed cloth on the line to dry when she became aware that Jass was nearby. She looked at him, wondering if he had news for her. Cap'n Jack had shrugged his shoulders when she asked him if he'd said anything to the Massa about the wedding, and ordered her not to fill her head with dreams. But she didn't want to believe him.

Jass was lounging against a tree with a silly grin on his face, watching her. He knew something, she was sure. Why didn't he tell her?

"Pretty color," he said. The cloth, still dripping wet, was dyed a deep reddish brown.

Easter lost her temper. "You got nuttin' better to do than stare at me?" she demanded. She jammed the clothes prop under the line, and stalked away to the weaving house.

"It's all right," he called after her, laughing. "You can go. You'll be Sassy's maid. And you can wear a pretty frock and everything."

Her reaction was not delayed for an instant. She squealed with delight, and ran toward him. He met her halfway and she jumped into his arms. Elated by her joy, he swirled her round and round in the air and knocked into the clothes prop, which dragged the line down on top of them, and now they were rolling together on the ground, covered in the wet cloth.

Laughing together, without a care in the world, until he was on top of her looking into her eyes, and seemed to be looking, she felt, into her very soul, and she could see inside him, almost to his heart, when suddenly something changed.

In that moment, all of Sally's fears had come true.

Jass pulled himself away from her, got up and turned his back, as if to hide himself from her.

"Look at my clothes," he said, angrily.

Easter wasn't sure what had happened. It had been so wonderful, locked in his laughing embrace, the warmest place in all the world, and then she'd felt this unaccustomed hardness pressing against her belly. She knew what it was—she was not a stupid girl—and it didn't bother her. It felt natural and right. Clearly, it bothered Jass.

She wanted to say something to calm him, to let him know that she loved that special closeness of him, that he could do anything he wanted with her, but she feared his rejection.

"Yo' mammy gwine be mad," she ventured. "That dye don't come out."

He muttered something about fixing his clothes, and walked away. She didn't know he was vowing that he would see less of her from now on.

She looked at her own clothes. They were covered in dye, too, and Easter let out a howl of disappointment. They were only her work clothes, but they were all she had. What would she wear to Nashville?

The summer passed in an orgy of preparation for the coming wedding, and a constant parade of visiting relations, so that the house seemed to be cluttered with Jacksons and Hannas and Kirkmans and seamstresses and drapers and tailors. The family would be in Nashville for a week, which meant ten complete new outfits for Sally and Sassy, for no woman of substance would consider wearing the same thing twice in such formidable society.

Merchants in Florence sent bolts upon bolts of cloth for their inspection. House slaves stitched and sewed and measured and fitted, and the house was filled with such an overwhelming urgency of female matters that Jass was happy to be out of it all. He had been measured for new clothes too, by the tailor from Florence, but it had taken only a few minutes of time, and he found it difficult to understand how the women's could take a whole summer.

Jass was trying to keep his vow not to see so much of Easter. The unspeakable thing that had happened in their embrace had shocked him. He knew what it meant, and he knew that he wanted her, but he wasn't ready for such an enormous adventure yet, such a complication to their relationship. Even on those few occasions when he did try to see her, it was mostly a waste of time. She was having only two new dresses for Nashville, simple linen for day, muslin for evening, but she fussed about them almost as much as any woman going to the wedding. In any case, she was in the big house most of the time, getting instruction from Angel in her new duties, and didn't want to be away from the center of dressmaking activity when she had nothing else to do.

Cap'n Jack was as busy as the rest of the staff, at the beck and call of the visitors and responsible for the welfare of the visitors' slaves.

Jass, left to his own devices, spent the time riding and swimming and visiting friends from school in the district. He even spent a cheery afternoon with Wesley, who enjoyed Jass's company when they had no quarrel, and delighted in titillating Jass with his most recent conquests of female slaves. They had sparred together for a while, and Wesley had given Jass several hints on the finer points of boxing, even though the information might very well be used against him in some future fight with Jass.

William, Alexander, and George had come home for the summer from school in Nashville. They were always pleased to be with Jass, but were completely content, possibly happier, with their own company. Cheeky, bustling, even more of a tight-knit group than before, they became known to everyone as the Trio, and several more distant relations, elderly or absentminded, began to forget their individual names.

They had arrived at the beginning of summer in a bustle of boxes and carts and schoolboy noise, in the care of their cousin John, who had come to look for a house in Florence, since several of the Kirkmans were moving to Florence. The Trio clutched at their mother, weeping, begging her never to send them away from her to that awful school again, but within minutes they were gone, causing havoc in the gaden, chaos in the kitchen, and endless tolerant vexation from Tiara in the slave quarter, for she had been nurse to them, as she had to all the boys, and still loved them and their boyish games.

The Trio left chaotic, frustrated joy in their wake wherever they went, and especially for Sally. She loved them all dearly, but it was a less fretful love than she had lavished on her older children when they were young. She guessed that she had become used to motherhood, and didn't worry so much whether she was doing the right thing. So she could shout at them, and cuff their ears, and laugh at their games, or simply tell them to get out from under her feet when she was too busy with other things. Whatever her other duties though, she tried to set an hour of each day aside, exclusively for them.

Running a household as large as theirs was never easy for Sally, least of all in the summer months when they had so many visitors. Although she could rely on Parson Dick, and Julie, the cook, several of the younger girls needed constant supervision, were frequently sick or forgetful of their duties. Sometimes, Sally thought, the more house slaves you had, the more work there was to do. She envied those few Northern hostesses she had met who, employing domestic staff, could sack them if they were incompetent or lazy, for it seemed excessive to Sally, but not to some others, to have a slave girl whipped or sold away for neglecting to empty a chamber pot or dust under a bed. Her various female relatives understood this—they shared the problem— but still they made demands on her time, for she was one of the reasons they had come.

Jass found it hard work trying to remember all the family connections. Elizabeth, his mother's daughter by her first marriage, had married his cousin Tom, which meant she was both his half sister and his first cousin once removed. But what about Sam, their young son? Was he first cousin twice removed, or second cousin once removed, or half nephew? These things seemed to matter in a family, especially to the women. Aunt Letitia Hanna was the family authority, and very sharp with Jass whenever he flunked a relationship. "You will have to find an intelligent bride," she had admonished once, clearly dismissing him as a dunderhead. "Someone has to remember all their birthdays."

The cotton ripened, the buds bursting with the white gold that was their fortune. It was going to be a good yield, over a bale an acre, and with the recent reduction of tariffs demanded by South Carolina, the profit would move from the good to the spectacular.

The work songs of the picking gangs could be heard everywhere on the plantation, drifting in to James through the open windows of his study, where he sat for hours on the sultry, sweaty summer days, counting his wealth, as if knowledge of the scale of it was insurance against its ever being taken away. When not in his study, he spent time at the stables inspecting his lucrative stallions and watching their training. He still fretted about John Coffee's visit, but the horses calmed him, or distracted him, and he put on a jolly, Irish face for his relatives, especially when they were Irish.

It pleased him, too, when rich landowners came with their wives and daughters to call, the girls doing their best to make an impression on young Jass. The aristocratic families of the South were always plotting their survival, and although Jass was too young to be in a serious race, it was never too early to start building alliances. It pleased James, and thrilled Jass, that he was the object of these welcome attentions, and it amused Sally that any visit by a family with a daughter to dispose of was quickly followed by a visit from Lizzie Perkins and her mother. Sally watched with approval as Jass grew better and better at conducting himself in the presence of young ladies, and toward the end of summer, Sally realized that Jass was going to be a considerable catch.

She had always thought him a good-looking boy, but the Jass who was measured for his new clothes at the beginning of summer was not the Jass who was fitted into them at the end, even though allowance had been made for growth. The cuffs of his trousers had to be let down a solid inch, and the sleeves of his jackets. His chest had filled out and his neck thickened, so that his new shirts were already tight, and Sally clucked in despair.

That clucking stopped when he tried on his new evening clothes, and presented himself for her inspection, grinning because he knew they suited him.

The elegant velvet coat, the pearly white jabot, flowing in elaborate ruffles from his neck, and the beautifully cut stovepipe pants changed him, before her very eyes, from a boy bursting out of his seams to a strikingly handsome young man.

"What on earth are you crying for?" he laughed. And Sally laughed too, and could not tell him why.

The end of summer also brought the last of their visitors and, for James, the most welcome.

Sara came from Baltimore with her family, and for a few days James tried to lose himself in an orgy of Irish reminiscence, and music, and stories of their youth.

Sara could see that something was troubling her brother but, like Sally, knew it was useless trying to provoke him to talk before he was ready. The two women discussed it at length, but Sally could shed little light on the matter.

It had begun with the visit of John Coffee, she said, and she was sure it was related to Andrew and, somehow, the Indians. James scanned the newspapers avidly when they arrived, but was interested only in that one subject. A few weeks before, some reporters from the Washington newspapers had come to interview James, but he had refused to discuss his private business dealings.

Then John Coffee died, of a chill he had caught

coming back from Washington. James had ambivalent feelings about the death. He tried to mourn the friendship they had once enjoyed, but had grieved enough for that long ago. He sent his condolences to the family, and attended the funeral, and said all the appropriate things, but there was a constant sense of relief in the back of his mind that John, at least, would no longer trouble him. He did feel a genuine sense of loss at this evidence of the passing years.

Toward sunset, on the day before she was due to leave, James asked Sara if she would like to visit the stables with him. They walked to the racecourse arm in arm, gossiping, and leaned on the fence to watch the horses being exercised. Lauderdale, grazing in a paddock, came trotting over to his owner.

"He's from Miss Shipton, and he's going to make me a fortune," James said, stroking the stallion's nose and feeding him the apple he had put in his pocket for the purpose.

Sara laughed. "All you've talked about this last hour, this last week, is how much money you've made. As if you were scared of losing it."

James smiled. She could read him like a book. That was why he had brought her here. If anyone could make sense of it, it was Sara.

The story came pouring out of him, in flooding relief. He told her everything, kept nothing back. Except his present feelings about the Indians.

Sara felt keenly her brother's distress, and was not surprised that Andrew was at the heart of it. She wanted to crow in triumph, "I told you so." She wanted to box her younger brother's ears for getting involved in the sordid mess, but knew that would get them nowhere.

"You lent Andrew money," she said. "What Andrew did with it is his business. You've been lending him money for years. Did he ever pay a penny of it back?"

James stared at her, trying to come to terms with the

296

simplicity of the statement. It was true. All he had done was lend Andrew a sum, admittedly a very large sum, of money. And that was all.

"Oh, James"—there was a trace of sadness in Sara's voice, but she couldn't resist the dig—"we've been trying to warn you about Andrew for years, Sally and I. Why didn't you listen?"

She knew the answer. James had wanted to be part of something grand, something magnificent, and ambition had clouded his mind. Men leave such a mess behind them wherever they go, Sara thought. 'Tis women have to do the cleaning up.

"The only evidence of anything is in those letters," she said. "As long as they remain under lock and key, your nose is clean."

Sara wasn't sure what he was thinking now, but pushed her case. Living in Baltimore, closer to the heart of things than James, tucked away on the other side of the Appalachians, she had heard the stories about Andrew coming out of Washington. He was already an old man when he first became president; now his years in office were said to be making him more and more cantankerous, more vindictive toward his enemies, less and less tolerant of opposition. She wanted James done with Andrew, and she feared his great, soft heart might lead him to actions he would regret.

"Don't give them to Andrew, I beg you. Who knows what the old devil would do with them?"

She knew it was useless to publish them. The resulting scandal would surely harm James, but Andrew, as usual, would find a way to wriggle out of it. And she didn't completely disagree with Andrew on the matter of the Indians.

"As for the Indians," she continued, as if guessing his moral dilemma, "there's nothing you can do. We can't give back every square inch of land to the bloodthirsty savages, go back where we came from and pretend we were never here."

297

She was smiling, he knew, teasing him with the absurdity of the idea.

Then she became serious again. "This isn't the British in Ireland, Jamie. This was wasted land before we came."

She hadn't used his pet name since he was a boy, and he almost laughed in relief. Sara's analysis of the settlement of America was so very realistic. He couldn't alter the past; he couldn't unmake history; he couldn't pretend the European migration to America had never happened and send everyone home again. That would create a new race of dispossessed, the children who were born here—they had no other home to go back to. His guilt at the piteous plight of the Indians had clouded his objectivity, and he now saw that he had been an easy victim to John Coffee's blackmail. John had simply been telling him to shut up, to keep quiet about what he knew. James would oblige.

Still, Sara was wrong. There *was* something he could do. He could still talk to Andrew, try to persuade him to end the removal of the native people. But he would do so with a considerably lighter heart.

Sally, on the veranda, could see them talking and guessed they were discussing whatever it was that had so been distracting James these last several weeks. She felt a mild twinge of jealousy that her husband should choose to discuss these things with his sister and not with his wife, but it quickly passed. When they walked toward her, Sally could tell, from James's laughter and the energy in his stride, that Sara had resolved whatever problem had been vexing him so. She blessed her sister-in-law for being a practical, pragmatic woman, and waved cheerily to them as they came up the hill.

298

31

In the first week of September the family traveled to Nashville. It took them a full day to cross the river at Muscle Shoals; their carriage had to be ferried across, and then the luggage wagon and the slave cart. Jass spent most of the day at the water's edge, fishing or, with Cap'n Jack, chatting with the black laborers, and from one of them he bought a few freshwater pearls. They were silly, small, irregular things, but the man hadn't wanted much money, and Jass thought they would be a nice gift to some young woman, even Lizzie perhaps, for he was intent on cultivating relationships with girls. Sally and Sassy sheltered from the sun at the inn on the northern shore, so he saw little of Easter. She was wide-eyed at this exotic new adventure of travel—she had never left The Forks before—but she was taking her new duties as Sassy's maid seriously, and hardly left Angel's side.

The Trio had stayed behind at The Forks. They were not invited to the wedding, and were not returning to their school in Nashville, much to Sally's relief. She hated sending these youngsters so far away from home to school, too young, she told herself, for such separation from a mother's watchful eye and warm embrace. A.J. had done it, and Jass, and she'd hated that as much, but they'd had little choice—the Stevens School in Nashville was the nearest suitable institution. Since then, Reverend Sloss had opened his Preparatory Academy in Florence, but that had no facilities for elementary education. James had murmured platitudes about character building, which left Sally entirely unimpressed, and the only consolation Sally could find was that the boys would be under the careful eye of Eleanor. Now, and not before time, thought Sally, the reverend gentleman had extended the age limits of boys he would accept, and the Trio were to go there, as did Jass, and could live at home.

The journey was slow, the pace dictated by the slave cart. The carriage was hot and uncomfortable, jarring their bones as it bounced over the rough roads. Sometimes Jass rode on Morgan, but he didn't want to tire the horse unnecessarily, and mostly kept him tethered to the slave cart. Then Jass preferred to ride on the box with Samuel, the coachman, who claimed to have covered all this territory before, in the few short days of his freedom, when actually he had never left the outskirts of Florence, and knew the road only because he had driven the coach to Nashville and back many times. Ephraim drove the luggage wagon, and Easter and Angel were with Cap'n Jack in the slave cart.

Each evening they would stop while it was still light at travelers' hotels, around which small settlements had grown, and Jass was allowed to join his father in after-dinner conversations with the older men or, in the hour before sunset, free to explore the surroundings.

Jass had made the journey many times, but as a boy, going to and coming from his school, and he now saw the adventure with a young man's eyes. This is still the frontier, he thought, and it thrilled him and horrified him. He saw a slave being mercilessly lashed in public for some hurt, real or imagined, to his master, and he had turned away, for it provoked subconscious memories of another lashing he had seen, as a boy, to a man who was now his friend and walked beside him. Once he saw a white man shoot another to death with a pistol, in full view outside the hotel, for what Cap'n Jack, talking to other slaves, discovered was a question of honor.

Conversely, he experienced hospitality from almost everyone he met, a sense of welcome to a stranger, which his father assured him was the nature of these people. He knew his family occupied a privileged position—because of his father's status, because they were guests traveling to an important occasion, and because they had made the journey so often that many of the innkeepers and their families remembered them—but even so, the generosity that was extended to them warmed his heart.

The later discussions with older men, in his father's company, both intrigued and bored him. Alfred and Gracie's wedding was on everyone's lips, a source of amusement to some, evidence of the increasing uppitiness of niggers to others, and this led to discussion of the man Jass called Uncle Andrew, who, however, was not related to him and whom he had never met.

Here in the West, Andrew's actions as president had only increased his already legendary status. He was seen as champion of the little man, the settler, the battling individual. People here believed him dedicated to enfeebling the bureaucracy in Washington, reducing the undue influence of the industrial Northeast over their lives, and by removing the federal deposits from it, curbing the outrageous power the centralized bank had previously enjoyed. Only a few speculators and businessmen dissented from this view, and then vehemently.

It had always been the same, his father explained. Andrew was an extraordinary man, capable of arousing violent passions in people, both toward him and against him.

Above all else, Andrew was seen as the salvation of the white settler from the bloodthirsty savages, the consensus being that the sooner the land was rid of all Indians, the better life would be. It puzzled Jass that his father would walk away every time this subject was raised, nor would he discuss it with Jass.

Easter had hoped to see more of Jass on this journey than she had done all summer, but she knew something had happened in their relationship, something he had

301

to come to terms with for himself. He didn't ignore her, he still visited the weaving house, but now he kept a distance between them, as if determined to avoid actual physical contact with her, and she missed the easy familiarity they used to enjoy. Here on the journey, when he was riding Morgan, he'd trot beside the slave cart for a while, pointing out new things to her, but Angel and Cap'n Jack were an obvious, inhibiting influence to any intimacy between them.

At night she'd be too busy to see him, for she and Angel had to unpack the trunk, prepare the clothes for the morning, and see to their mistress's comforts before they could even begin to think about their own. They ate and slept in the dingy slave accommodations attached to the hotels, and while she enjoyed listening to the slaves of other travelers, she was too shy to voice opinions of her own. Up from well before sunrise to long after dark, drowsy on some uncomfortable cot in a lousy communal shed, Easter decided that traveling was an overrated experience and longed for the comforts of the little shack that was home.

At a small village on the last night before reaching their destination, James took Jass to a revival meeting in a field nearby, the settlement being too small for a church. James, although he believed devoutly in God, was not a deeply religious man and adhered to no particular church, but the emotional ferocity that the frontier preachers could arouse fascinated him, and he thought the experience would be interesting for Jass.

The meeting was already in progress when they arrived. Some fifty people attended, country folk, poor whites, gathered in from outlying farms and settlements. Many of them had traveled many miles to find some relief from the abject hardships they daily endured, some promise of future glory. Simply clad as they were, with weathered faces and gnarled, knotty hands, Jass could not imagine that these austere people

302

would provide any of the exotic entertainment his father had promised. He had not reckoned on the Preacher man.

He heard the Preacher before he saw him, a voice thundering at heaven, but in a language that Jass had no knowledge of, and could not understand. He was silent as they reached the clearing, and all heads were bowed in prayer. The Preacher was standing on a cart, his Bible clenched in his fist. A couple of lanterns tied to sticks in the ground provided small illumination and ghostly shadows. Jass could see some spectators watching from the surrounding trees, a few black faces among them, but his father led him closer to the cart, the center of things.

Suddenly, the Preacher looked up. "You are all sinners," the Preacher yelled, and a murmur of agreement ran through his congregation. It unnerved Jass, for in the dim light he thought the Preacher was staring directly at him.

"Liars! Swindlers! Hypocrites!" the Preacher cried. The assenting murmur of response from the accused was louder now.

"Fornicators!"

Jass blushed. He knew what the word *fornicator* meant. Wesley used it all the time, and while Jass had never had actual physical contact with a woman, the private fantasies he sometimes enjoyed seemed just as reprehensible. He wondered if his father knew, or could guess, for his guilt must surely be branded on his brow.

"And as sinners you are damned," the Preacher shouted again.

"Yes! Yes!' a responsive voice yelled back.

"There is only one way to redemption," the Preacher continued, waving the Good Book of direction in the air. "God is your only salvation, and your only path to Him is the blood of the Lamb!"

Now the Preacher shouted again in that alien tongue, and another man in the crowd called something in

303

response, but it seemed to Jass to be in a different language. He wondered if the two understood each other.

It made no difference. It wouldn't have mattered if the entire sermon had been delivered in tongues—and much of it was—because even if the sounds were incomprehensible to others, Jass knew what they meant, and knew they were all directed exclusively at him.

The throbbing voice of the Preacher touched some deep well of unchanneled, teenage emotion in Jass, and he was gathered into the mounting ecstasy. He moved forward, away from his father, perhaps to hear the Preacher better, perhaps to be part of the now swaying throng. The Preacher warned fire and brimstone, and the crowd shivered from the heat. The Preacher cried hell and damnation, and the crowd simply cried. The Preacher held out the promise of salvation, and some-one fainted in relief.

The voice roared on. Jass was not an individual now but an engulfed fraction of a mounting collective frenzy. The Preacher jumped down from the cart, and came into the midst of it, ranting eye of a hysterical cyclone, laying his hands on swooning bodies, casting demons out of a babbling farmhand, and yet seeming to direct a torrential energy on Jass, as if demanding from him some ultimate submission. Jass was euphoric.

The unspeakable happened. Jass was incredulous. How could the vile monster assert itself here, in this exquisite company? The dreadful hardness was incontrovertible proof to Jass that he was guilty of sin beyond all reckoning, and he fell to his knees at the Preacher's feet, weeping for forgiveness of something he could not even name, and begging for salvation from his accursed path.

Then it all seemed to stop. The Preacher, having done his work, gave a few final, less extravagant admonitions; the congregation got up, dusted themselves down, resumed their earlier, self-contained composure, and departed, on carts, horseback, and foot, into the night.

Jass looked at James a little sheepishly, wondering what his father would think of it all. James didn't say very much. He walked his son back to the hotel, asking only a few mild questions about the evening, but Jass couldn't shake the conviction that his father was laughing. At him.

Sally was furious. A devout Presbyterian, she had an aversion to all extravagant forms of worship and had tried to stop James from taking Jass to the meeting. She rounded on her husband in fury and demanded to know why he hadn't stopped Jass from taking part.

"He was being saved for Jesus," James responded calmly. "I didn't think it was my place to interfere." Jass saw the twinkle in his father's eye, and knew for sure what he had guessed. James thought the whole evening was the best fun. Sally knew it too, because she also saw the twinkle, and ordered Jass to bed so she could have a few words with James alone.

She came to him a little later, before he fell asleep, sat on the edge of his bed and talked to him calmly, whispering, because Sassy was slumbering in the next bed.

"I am very angry with your father," she said softly. "I have no love for these evangelist religions. They bring comfort to a number of the poor country folk, I know, but for me God is to be found in quiet contemplation, not in public display."

She paused, not sure quite how to phrase what she wanted to say, for it didn't pertain only to God.

"If you have truly found Jesus, of course, I couldn't be happier for you, but I wasn't aware that you had ever lost him." She kissed his forehead.

"Always remember that emotions can be easily

305

manipulated, and that love is a thing of the mind as well as the heart." She wondered if he understood what she was trying to say, but decided to leave it at that.

"Good night, my darling," she said, and left the room. Jass mumbled a good night, and turned to face the wall.

James was awake, lying in bed reading, when she came into their room. She was still cross with him.

She began to undress in silence. James put down his book. "He'll get over it," he offered, to make the peace. "It was a good experience for him."

"I'm sure it was an experience," she said. "Whether it was good or not is a matter of opinion."

She sat at the dressing table to put on her nightcap. She didn't want to be near James, not yet. Not until he said he was sorry.

"I'm sorry," he said. The laughter in his eyes betrayed him. "I'm very angry with you," Sally replied, but she could never be very angry with him for very long. Besides, her initial temper was being replaced by curiosity.

"I can't imagine it happening to Jass," she said.

James, to whom the whole evening had been amusing but of little consequence, could think only of a platitude.

"Still waters run deep." He patted the space beside him. "Come to bed."

Sally finished her toilette, and did as she was bidden, snuggling into her husband's arms.

"Do you really think Lizzie will be suitable for him, one day?" It was the first time she had raised the subject of Lizzie with James.

He was careful, sensing Sally's dislike of the idea. "She's going to be very pretty," he offered.

"She's so very young, and so very brittle," Sally said. James nodded. "She'll grow up, grow out of it."

Sara's realistic appraisal of the situation with Andrew

306

had dulled James's eagerness to settle on the concept, at least, of an early union for Jass, but it was still there.

"I hope Jass enjoys his youth," he told his wife. "But if anything should happen to him, or to any of the other three, or to me—"

He didn't refer to the loss of A.J., but Sally knew what he meant. The succession to the inheritance was paramount to families like theirs.

She smiled at her husband. "Nothing's going to happen to you for a very long time," she said, lovingly.

James looked into her eyes. "I surely hope not," he said. He held her in his arms, kissed her full on the mouth, and she surrendered to his loving embrace.

"Hush," she murmured when her mouth was free. "Don't wake the children."

Jass stared at the bedroom wall. He couldn't believe it! He guessed from the rhythmic noise of the bedsprings in the next room that his parents were doing—that—right then and there. How could they, after what he'd been through?

He rolled over in his bunk, away from the wall, and tried to block out the sounds and come to terms with what it was he'd been through. Away from the Preacher's influence, he didn't feel very much more certain of what God might be than at the start of the evening. Had he found Jesus? He wasn't sure. He knew he'd found something, even if it was only a rock-solid determination that he was going to have greater discipline over his body in future. But was that all?

What was the love of Jesus? What was the love of God? What was God? He didn't know. Confusing questions about the relationship of God to man assailed him. If there was only one God, why were there so many religions? If God was love, why was there war? If killing was forbidden in the commandments, how could God forgive soldiers? How could you take an eye for an

307

eye and turn the other cheek at the same time? Even though his teachers had always given ready answers to these seeming contradictions, now Jass began to doubt their authority. If fornication was so wrong, why was the urge to do it so overwhelming? If it was wrong to do the unspeakable, why had He made it so pleasurable? Some of the younger slaves did it too, he knew, because he'd heard them giggling about it.

And what about the blacks? Where was the dividing line between animals, blacks—or come to that, redskins—and white people? Wesley had talked of a slave girl who was as white as his sister, and two of their own slaves were only a kind of pale yellow, so why were they black, and why didn't they have souls, as the Reverend Sloss insisted? If Ham was the first nigger, why didn't he have a soul like his brothers? If niggers didn't have souls, why did so many of them believe in God? And how did God choose? If Wesley, or anyone, did a slave girl and she had a baby, that baby wouldn't have a soul, but when he got married to a white girl and had a baby, that child would. Did souls descend only through the white maternal line? Were mothers that sacred?

In that case, if Jass had found Jesus, as the Preacher claimed, why was his mother so angry? Perhaps it was this that caused the greatest confusion of all, for Jass had loved Jesus all his life, and as his mother had pointed out, how could something be found if it had never been lost? And if his mother was right about that, then what about the other thing? If it was true, if the Preacher, whom he didn't know from Adam, had manipulated his emotions so easily, what happened when you fell in love with someone? If you loved someone with all your heart, how much control did the adored one have over you? Obviously quite a lot in my case, Jass thought. He would have to tread very carefully around girls from now on.

He was tired. The emotional outpouring of the evening had exhausted him, and he felt drained and vitalized all at the same time. He drifted to sleep in the reassuring knowledge that he had certainly experienced something, whatever it was, that was somehow part of growing up, for the questions that were concerning him now were not ones he had ever asked himself before.

32

On the afternoon of the fifth day they arrived at their destination, the slave cart having slowed their progress, and went straight to cousin John Kirkman's house, where they were lodging.

Town, Aunt Eleanor told them, was full; there was no room to be had at any inn, lodging house, farm, or private house in the district. Sarah had scandalized the South with her invitation, and consequently anyone who thought they were anybody and hadn't been invited had done everything in their power to ensure that they were. Plantation Massas who would have a black whipped to death without turning a hair had pulled every string they could, political and social, to watch two nigras jump the broom. Eleanor's eyes danced with glee, and she laughed until tears rolled down her cheeks.

Jass was fascinated by his aging aunt. She had been merely a daunting woman with a slight mustache when he first became aware of her as a child, but he had come to know her well in the years he spent at school in Nashville, for she had charge of him then. At first he had been unable to reconcile his father's funny stories of her when young. He couldn't imagine this forbidding woman in black bombazine as a redheaded revolutionary in Dublin married to a great Irish martyr, but because of that past, it was with her that he first raised some of the troubling questions that Cap'n Jack had put in his mind.

He contrived to be alone with her in her pretty garden and, somewhat diffidently, asked her about slavery.

Aunt Eleanor had snorted in derision. "Half this so-called Southern aristocracy is just jumped-up bog peasants who've made their pile on the backs of men they don't even pay a wage."

She was no freethinker, however. "I've no love for the nigras, Jass," she continued. "Dirty, shiftless, and lazy, most of 'em, who'd cut your throat for a shillin', and should have been left in the jungle where they belong. But if a man works, he should be paid for it."

Jass was confused. "We own slaves," he said.

Eleanor smiled ruefully. "And so do I," she said, with a wistfulness that Jass didn't understand. She owned some house slaves, one of whom, Joshua, was digging in the vegetable patch.

"When I first came here," Eleanor explained, "I wouldn't have a bar of it. I thought it was a disgrace against nature, and I was shocked that Jamie—your father—had taken to practicing it. But it was the custom, and life was hard then, awful hard—you young folk have it easy—and in the end it was simpler to swim with the tide than against it. And it didn't bother your poor, dear Uncle Thomas, God rest his soul."

A sadness had settled on her. "I often asked myself what Oliver—"

She looked at Jass and realized that probably he had no idea who Oliver was. "My first husband," she explained, and memory of him fluttered in her heart.

She looked at the gardener. The sadness vanished, and as if to complete her case against herself, she yelled to him.

"Joshua! Put your back into it, man!" The voice was stentorian. "I could have dug that whole patch by now."

Joshua muttered something inaudible and carried on

at his usual pace. Eleanor looked at Jass, and there was a smile of self-mockery twinkling in her eye.

"At least I know what I am," she said. "Which is more than can be said for most of these Southern kings in their cotton castles."

An old campaigner from a lost war, she still had advice for the young.

"Never give your nigras reason to hate you, Jass," she said. "Because one day they'll have their revenge. It is the nature of things."

So they became friends. She never had direct answers for Jass on moral or political questions he raised but would put the various sides of an argument, and encourage him to arrive at his own conclusions. The only subject on which she never equivocated was the British in Ireland, and she would lecture him for hours on the evil of their cause.

"Why didn't you stay and fight them?" Jass asked once, and Eleanor looked at him sharply, but her reply was surprisingly reasonable.

"It's terrible hard to be wed to a man who gives his life to a great cause," she said. "And realize that his dyin' made not one jot or tittle of difference to anything. The Irish were still starvin', and the British still lived off the fat of their land. So I came here. And look at me now."

She laughed again, a vulgar, raucous laugh. "All piss and wind, I suppose."

Jass blushed scarlet. He'd never heard a woman use that word before.

"And I met your Uncle Thomas," she said gently, "and I had a wonderful life with him."

Now she was old and frail, and could walk only with the help of canes or, preferably to her, the arms of a strong young man. She was pragmatic about her declining years and intended to move to Baltimore, with Sara to look after her. "To die," Eleanor said cheerfully, "looking at old Ireland."

311

"You'll live for years yet," James retorted.

"I may," Aunt Eleanor nodded. The smile faded from her face. "God forbid."

She would sell this house and cousin John would move to Florence. It is the end of the Nashville years, James thought. A chapter in our lives is closing. Florence is the future now. The South.

The wedding was not until the coming Sunday, with a welcoming barbecue the day before, but the week was to be a hectic social calendar of luncheons, levees, and soirees. The gathering of the clans, James explained to Jass.

Slaves had been heating water all day, and now the women bathed in the outhouse, while James and Jass used the creek on the edge of the property. After a week on the road, they felt filthy, and Sally longed to let down her hair and have Angel examine it for any lice picked up in the tawdry travelers' hostels. The visitors from Florence crammed the house. Jass was sleeping in the attic with his young second cousin, and they had a jolly time, the boy delighting in taunting Jass's authority by giving voice to all the new cuss words he had learned, and juvenile allusions to bodily functions. James and Sally were in the guest bedroom, Sally was sleeping with the Kirkman girls, Easter and Angel were sharing a cramped outhouse with the female slaves, while Cap'n Jack, Samuel, and Ephraim bunked in the barn.

The next morning, James took Jass to Colonel Elliot's stud farm, although really it belonged to James, and the colonel was in his employ. Jass was allowed to trot Leviathan around the ring, and thrilled to the beauty and power of the animal. He was even more pleased that his father included him in the business discussions, and he started to feel a sense of the scope of what would one day be his. Most of the talk was about improving the bloodlines of the horses, and Jass shared the general excitement when James agreed that the colonel could begin negotiations to purchase Glencoe, the most famous stallion in England.

That afternoon, the Donelsons gave a formal reception for those out-of-towners who had arrived, and Jass was exhilarated, treated for the first time as his father's heir. He was only slightly disappointed that Lizzie wasn't there, as the Perkinses were not arriving till Thursday. It was the first time that Jass understood the size and complexity of the network of Southern families, either blood- or business-related. His father's description of the clans being gathered seemed exact, for cousins who had only heard of each other had the chance to meet, daughters of great estates had to be introduced to potential suitors, new friendships were formed and old relationships elaborated on.

Births, marriages, and deaths had to be enumerated, the former congratulated, and the latter condoled. For the most part, this followed a rigorous recitation of accepted ritual, but Jass was enchanted by old Mr. Morissey, a distant friend of his mother's and wealthy associate of his father's. Morissey's brother, an acknowledged rogue, had disappeared to Texas after a shady financial scandal. Now news of his death in some settlers' battle with the Mexicans in Texas had reached the family, which somewhat redeemed his honor. But old Mr. Morissey, who was ancient of days, acutely deaf, and rode in a Bath chair pushed by a slave, would have none of it.

"I'm so sorry about Nicholas," Sally yelled into his ear trumpet. "Whatever for?" Mr. Morissey yelled back, assuming the rest of the world to be as hard of hearing as he. "The man was a scoundrel. I trust he met an unpleasant end and is dancing at the sharp end of Satan's pitchfork." Jass giggled, and turned away.

Easter, watching from the sidelines in the protective shadow of Cap'n Jack and Angel, was overawed by it all. She had never seen such a parade of obvious wealth or felt such blatant and innate power accumulated in the hands of a very small group of people. Receptions at The Forks of Cypress were grand, but paled to insignificance compared with this. Open landaus delivered streams of superbly attired men and their richly dressed wives. Beautiful young women in gorgeous gowns were everywhere, most of them dancing around Jass, Easter thought, and realized that this was his natural world. Hope of his being any kind of constant figure in her life was limited to one certainty: He was her Massa and she his slave.

Even the other slaves present inhibited her, for many of them looked and behaved as if they were far grander than those who owned them. Many were almost as well dressed as their Massas, and their manners were flawless. Parson Dick might have been confident in their company, but Easter felt like a field hand and saw her father as a country bumpkin. Easter looked at her simple linen frock and determined that she would wear only her muslin when she went out again.

Angel hardly left Sally's side, and Cap'n Jack had old friends to talk to, so Easter was left on her own. Standing under a tree, she was wishing the ground would open and swallow her up, when she heard a voice.

"Ain't you the prettiest thing?"

An extremely handsome young slave was staring at her. Tall and dignified, only a few years older than herself, he might have been the stuff of Easter's dreams if they had not been running in another direction.

Easter was mortified, and had no idea what to say.

"Cat got yo' tongue?" the young man asked, still smiling. "I's Reuben, I's with the Murphys of Virginia."

It was an invitation to introduce herself, she knew, but Easter, after another glance at the sophisticated company, was petrified. So she ran away and found a hiding place behind the big house, and didn't come out until she heard Angel and Cap'n Jack calling for her because it was time to leave. She never told them why she had disappeared so abruptly, but she determined she was not going to spend the rest of the week in such misery, and wondered if Jessica, the Kirkman maid, had a dress she could borrow.

Cap'n Jack had not yet seen Alfred, but James gave him permission to do so that evening, and, if necessary, to spend the night at the Hermitage.

The Kirkman house was only three miles from the Hermitage, but Cap'n Jack took a long detour through town. He thrilled to see how Nashville had grown. There were even stone buildings now, and streets he hardly recognized. Imposing houses with well-established gardens stood on blocks of land that had been farms not so many years ago. Well dressed, walking alone in what had become a place he didn't know and scarcely remembered, Cap'n Jack was able to pretend, for a while, that he was a free man, with his paper of manumission in his pocket instead of his Massa's travel pass.

Little had changed at the Hermitage, though. The gardens were still beautifully tended, and the weathering of the years had aged the house and given it a sense of permanence, as if it had always stood there, and always would. Still, Cap'n Jack felt a little unsure of himself. It was late, nearly twilight, and none of the gardeners was working, nor anyone who might have remembered him. If it were not for the few lamps burning inside the house, he would have thought it deserted. He wasn't sure where Alfred would be. In the old days, the slave lived in the big house with his Massa, but now that Washington was his home and he was only a visitor here, Cap'n Jack wondered if he should go to the slave quarters first.

A wheezy chuckle solved the problem for him.

"Why, yo' ol'—!" It was Alfred, coming out to greet him from the kitchen.

He hadn't changed much. Although his hair was

315

gray, his face was unwrinkled, and his eyes sparkled with welcome. Cap'n Jack felt an enormous sense of relief. Whatever else had changed in his world, Alfred was a constant.

"Yo' young buzzard!" he called as happily, though Alfred was several years his senior. The men shook hands warmly, and embraced, and Alfred led him to the kitchen to eat.

The family, young Massa Andrew and Missy Sarah, were out visiting, and had taken Gracie with them, so they had the place to themselves. They gossiped about old times and new, and of the cooling of the friendship between their two Massas.

"Ain't evuh gwine be like it was," Alfred said. "Massa Andrew old, an' he think yo' Massa done him wrong."

His mind was full of his Massa, and the gossip from Washington.

"Weren't right to come," he said. "Ol' Massa Andrew sick; he need me there. Ain't nobody else c'n look after him like me."

He turned away, as if worried about Andrew, but then chuckled.

"He tole me I had to git wed here," he said. "It yo' home, Alfred, he said. It's where yo' gwine die and be buried; it's fittin' yo' be wed there too."

He paused again.

"I don't like leavin' him there on his ownsome," he said. "He old."

The cook had fed them and ignored them, but now she roared that she was sick of the pair of them cluttering up her kitchen. Alfred roared back at her, but winked at Cap'n Jack, and they said their good nights to her, and made their way to the little room in the slave quarters where Alfred was staying.

"Still got my room in the big house," he said, "but all these folk in town, weren't nowhere's for Gracie, so she in it. I in here."

He winked. "Got summat else, too." He rummaged in his trunk and found a bottle of moonshine.

"Speshul occashun," he chuckled wheezily.

Cap'n Jack laughed in anticipation. Usually they were forbidden to drink liquor, but Alfred's special status made it unlikely they would be reprimanded if caught. They could get drunk, just the two of them, and for this night at least, it would be like the old days.

And it was, it was, for a while. Warmed by the liquor, they talked of times past, and of Gracie, Alfred's bride-to-be, who had astonished everyone when she accepted his offer of marriage, for she was twenty years younger than he.

"Glad I waited all these years," Alfred sighed happily.

They were drunk now. Alfred's smile faded, and he looked at Cap'n Jack.

"Time you got hitched agin," he said, "afore you're too ol'."

"Never found the right woman." Cap'n Jack didn't want to think about Annie, and had another swig of moonshine.

Alfred wasn't easily distracted. "Only time Massa James evuh did you wrong," he said, "sellin' Annie away."

"'T weren't the Massa, 't were the overseer," Cap'n Jack insisted. "An' I got Easter to remember her by."

Alfred shook his head and laughed at the lie.

"Massa's in charge," he said. "Give overseer the aut'ority. All white Massas the same, don't give a hoot 'bout niggers, 'cept to work theirselves to the grave for 'em. An' beyond."

Cap'n Jack was puzzled, but thought it was the liquor. Death was the end of their bondage. Not even white Massas had authority over death.

Alfred had another swig of moonshine. He struggled to his feet.

"Oops," he said. "I ain't 'zackly my nat'chrel self."

317

He giggled, but there was no humor in it. "C'm here." He beckoned Cap'n Jack outside.

They wended through the gardens, supporting each other, and giggling in whispers. Alfred stopped to relieve himself, and looked at the stars.

"'Tain't fair," he said, and although Cap'n Jack was not sure what he meant, he agreed with his friend.

Alfred led the way to the little cemetery. A pillared monument had been built in the center of it, and they stood near it.

"Ol' Missus," said Alfred, unnecessarily, for Cap'n Jack could read the inscription.

Alfred pointed to the ground beside it. "Ready fo' ol' Massa," he said. "The ol' devil gwine be buried here, next to her."

"But he won't go to heaven," Cap'n Jack chuckled.

Alfred was not in a laughing mood. "If'n he wants to he will, and he wants to, coz that where she is."

He pointed to a plot of ground only a few yards away.

"An I gwine be buried there!" he said in sudden fury. "Massa says! You ain't evuh gwine get away from me, Alfred, he says. You gwine be buried right near me, so's I can yell fo' yo' when I needs yo'."

He turned on his friend.

"'Tain't fair! I cain't get way from him in life and I cain't get away from him when I's dead."

His mood changed abruptly, and tears came to his eyes.

"'Tain't fair," he said again. "Massas say they own us niggers body and soul."

He looked at his future grave site, and shook his head.

"An' they do," he said. "They own us livin', an' they own us dead."

33

On Saturday evening, the great Southern families assembled in Nashville descended like royalty on the Hermitage.

Easter was astonished. She had thought the parties during the week were wonderful, but they were only rehearsals compared with this. Coachmen and footmen were wigged and liveried. The women had saved their finest evening gowns for this occasion, and were aglitter with jewels, the men all in formal evening wear. Slaves had been borrowed from surrounding plantations to line the driveway with flambeaux, although there was still light in the sky. A slave choir, assembled on the lawn outside the house, serenaded the guests as they arrived.

Despite many reservations as to the reason for Sarah Jackson's invitation, the tacit consensus was that this should be a glittering social occasion. The widowed President Jackson did much entertaining in Washington, but he was old, and even though Emily Donelson did her best as hostess, the affairs were boorish, redolent of the smoking room and the stag party. There was a social vacuum in the land, and who better than the glorious Sarah to fill it, and transfer it here? She wasn't a Yankee, and she lived in Nashville, and visions of that city becoming the cultural capital of the nation filled many matrons' hearts. Nashville was close to Memphis, Louisville and Lexington, and even New Orleans, close enough to all the new cities on the western side of the Appalachians, and Atlanta was not too far away. It was some distance to the coastal cities of Charleston and Savannah, of course, but it served them right, as many of the newly rich of Alabama and Mississippi found those cities to be insufferably elitist about position and money.

That it was even farther from the large Northern cities, and half a continent from Boston, delighted them. Too often, they'd had to make the arduous journey to Washington or New York or Philadelphia for politically important social occasions, and now the supper would be on another table. Sarah's wedding, for no white thought of it as Alfred and Gracie's, was a chance to show the world the triumph of elegant Southern sophistication, and how well the niggers were treated, and if any of those niggers got uppity and forgot their place they'd get a good thrashing.

There were two reception lines in the garden, one for the whites and one for the blacks. There were two of everything, one for the whites and one for the blacks, and woe betide any nigger who crossed the line, although any white could do so with impunity.

Sally laughed as the Alabama Jacksons descended from their carriage and went to the receiving line.

"I feel positively dowdy," she said, although she looked wonderful in the dark-blue taffeta gown, and probably knew it.

There was surprisingly little confusion, for all knew their places. The whites were greeted by Sarah and Andrew junior. The slaves who had been invited were greeted by Alfred and Gracie, and the slaves who had not been invited but were attending their Massas and Missys were directed to the kitchen, where they would be fed. Easter was attending, not invited, but Alfred had specifically asked to meet her, so now she stood in the black receiving line with her father and gawked at all about her.

Jass could see Lizzie already in the garden, for the Perkinses had been among the first to arrive, and she looked beautiful. He knew she'd seen him too, because she tossed her head and pretended she hadn't.

"James—Sally—oh, thank God you came." He heard Sarah's laughing, lilting voice, was surprised to find they were at the head of the line. He'd been wondering if he should give Lizzie the freshwater pearls or save them for someone else.

Sally was laughing too. "This is quite a hornet's nest you've stirred up," she said to Andrew junior, and Sarah giggled again.

"Don't blame me; this was all her idea," he said, and shook hands warmly with James.

"Well, Alfred's been with your father for longer than anyone can remember, we had to make a fuss," Sarah said to her husband, and turned to Sally again. "Isn't it fun?"

They knew Sassy, but not Jass. He was presented, and was fascinated by Sarah's bubbling personality and sense of humor, and suddenly Jass knew why she'd decided on such a celebration. She wanted fun; she wanted to make a little dent in a society that Jass already suspected could be smotheringly smug. For no reason, Jass laughed, and without knowing what he was laughing at, Sarah laughed with him. She is the most beautiful woman I've ever seen, Jass thought, and cursed his fortune. If she were not older and married, he would have immediately given her his pearls. Moving away with his family, Jass caught sight of Easter cowering in the black receiving line, and laughed again, and told himself he was going to have a good time.

Easter couldn't bear the idea that she was about to meet the famous Alfred, her father's dearest, perhaps his only, friend, and right-hand man to the president. She tried to hide behind Cap'n Jack, but to no avail.

"This be Easter, Annie's girl," she heard her father say, pulling her forward. Easter caught a glimpse of a stern face appraising her, and sank into a deep curtsy.

"Chile's pretty," she heard him say.

"Chile's scared!" Now it was a woman who spoke, a

warm, welcoming voice. Easter looked up and saw that the woman standing next to the stern man was glaring at him and smiling at her, all at once.

"An' no wonder, yo' starin' at her like yo' stare at me when I done summat' wrong. Here, girl, Easter, ain't it?"

The woman helped her up. "I's Gracie," she said. "An' I's the one done fixin' to marry this gristly ol' turkey."

Everyone laughed, and suddenly Easter wasn't shy anymore. "Yo' stan' by me," said Gracie, "and help me 'member the names a all these folk I ain't never met and ain't evuh gwine meet again."

Easter was happy. She had a job to do; she wouldn't be left on her own as she had been at most of the other parties. She stood beside Gracie, glowing. If she wasn't exactly mistress of the mansion, she was in a position of some eminence.

Alfred looked at her approvingly. "Chile's pretty," he said again to Cap'n Jack. "An' you stan' by me, Cap'n Jack, yo' my bes' man."

Having been received, the guests assembled on the lawn. There were long tables set out, groaning with food and punch, at one end, for the whites, and other long tables, complaining rather than groaning, and with lemonade not punch, at the other end, for the blacks.

There was one band, but two dancing areas. The fiddlers struck up a tune, and the whites danced with the whites, the blacks danced with the blacks. Jass looked for Lizzie, who seemed to dance with every young man but him. Easter kept her eyes on Jass. Sally sat with Mrs. Perkins and some other friends on the sidelines, while James mingled with his many business associates.

After an hour or so, the band took a break, and the slave choir assembled to sing spirituals for the guests while they ate.

Listening to the sweet music as he was helping himself to some food, something puzzled Jass. It was silly that niggers don't have souls, he thought, yet they're encouraged to sing about heaven. But he was hungry, and the smell of spit-roasted hog distracted him.

Easter was in line at the black table, piling her plate with food. Or rather, she was a fixture at the black table because she was bored again and the food tasted wonderful and eating helped pass the time. She was also enchanted by some of the conversations around her.

"Why, this sho' am beautiful," said an elegantly dressed slave. "Sweetest chicken I evuh et," said another. Easter giggled, and suddenly she longed to be at home, in her simple house with her simple friends. This world was too complicated for her.

"Ain't this the prettiest night?" she heard someone say, and knew who it was. Eyes wide, mouth full, she turned to Reuben.

"But not as pretty as you," he said, and winked at her. Easter was shocked, not because he winked but because he winked at her. Surely he didn't think she was pretty?

"Don't believe I evuh heard yo' name?" He really was very handsome, Easter decided.

"My name is Easter," she said, in fair imitation of Lizzie. "And I am with the Jacksons."

"My, my," Reuben said, suitably impressed. "The Nashville Jacksons, of course?"

"Why, no," she said, pleased with herself. "Massa James Jackson of Alabama is my Massa, and I think I hear my Missy callin' me now."

She walked away, feeling that she'd handled him a lot better this time, and went looking for Jass.

Who was looking at Lizzie. Sitting in a little arbor, surrounded by enthusiastic young men of Jass's age,

323

Lizzie looked wonderful. She seemed to have grown up a little over the summer, and had taken particular care with her dress for this occasion, palest blue, like her eyes, with elegant frills in flowing muslin. She was handling her beaux with great aplomb, and Jass decided he would not give her the pearls. They were not good enough. That lovely neck demanded emeralds or rubies at least, if not diamonds.

"I declare, Miss Lizzie, you grow more lovely every time I see you,' a pimply young man said to her.

"Why, thank you, Chester. You must be nearly old enough to shave by now." Lizzie simpered like lemon.

Chester blushed, and the others laughed. Another young man stepped up to her execution block.

"I've been shaving for years now, Miss Lizzie," he said in his deepest voice.

"Then you should try to grow a mustache, Anthony," Lizzie purred. "It might make you look a little older."

The others laughed at Anthony now, led by Chester. Lizzie looked around for another victim and saw Jass.

"Is that the Jackson boy I see over there?"

Jass sprang forward. "Yes, Miss Lizzie," he offered.

"Fetch me a little more chicken," Lizzie hardly looked at him, and waved her empty plate in the air. Jass grabbed it.

"I'd be delighted, Miss Lizzie, if you'll save a place for me on your dance card tomorrow." Jass had decided to bargain.

"Why, sir, I told you, my card is full." Lizzie was better at haggling, and sighed and looked helpless. "But I would die for a little more chicken."

Jass had no counteroffer, and capitulated. "Right away, Miss Lizzie," he said, and turned toward the food table.

"An uppity boy, but useful," Lizzie told her swains, and they all laughed at Jass now.

As Jass piled chicken on Lizzie's plate, Easter, who had overheard Lizzie's last remark, sidled up to him.

"Why yo' wastin' yo' time with her?" she demanded. 'She's jus' playin' with yo', laughing at yo'."

Jass looked at her, and, his vision blurred by the heady company, he saw only a bothersome slave girl in a cheap frock. She had no place in this world, his world. She had no idea of the complex forces that were driving him to a friendship, at least, with Lizzie, and perhaps something more. How could he make her understand? He didn't understand it all himself.

"Keep your place, Easter," he told her sharply. "You're too young, you wouldn't understand."

He walked away. If they'd been in the weaving house, Easter might have hit him, or at least put a double dose of iodine on his cuts, but they were here, in public, and anyway, things had changed between them. She had never seen that look in his eyes before, and it frightened her, because she saw she was irrelevant to him. She had been reminded, by him, of her true place in his life, and it hurt.

The band had started to play again, and couples were dancing. Easter wandered on the edge of it, longing for some young man, preferably Jass, to come along and sweep her onto the dance floor. A young man did, but it wasn't Jass.

"May I have the honor?" Reuben asked, offering his arm. Easter hesitated for only a moment.

"Why, suh, I believe yo' may," she said, and smiled her most dazzling smile. He led her onto the dance floor, and they danced and danced, and Easter put aside her cares and had a wonderful time, although she had on one occasion to tell Reuben very sharply to keep his hands where they belonged. But she could not rid her mind of Jass.

Almost everybody had a good time that night, except James. He had been in a party mood, looking forward to an evening of fun and laughter, a little too much to

325

drink, a few dances with Sally, and good talk with friends and associates.

He'd had fun at the beginning, and laughed a good deal. He'd danced with Sally and had drunk a little too much. Perhaps because of the drink, the talks with his male friends depressed him.

It was only natural, he supposed, that the most frequent topic of conversation was Andrew. It was Andrew's house, Andrew's slave who was getting married, and Andrew's party in absentia, but there was more. Andrew strode through all their lives like a colossus, and gave the younger men a sense of what it must have been like in the glory days of the Revolutionary War, which some of the older men present remembered, and the War of 1812, which younger men could recall. It was Andrew who had paid off the national debt incurred in those wars. It was Andrew who had broken the power of the central bank. It was Andrew who was the champion of their right to rule themselves, it was Andrew who understood the power and purpose of the original Constitution, because he personally knew many of the men who had framed it, and it was Andrew, single-handedly, many believed, who was ridding the country of the red-skinned savage, by whatever means necessary, fair or foul.

It was there that so many of the arguments began, old arguments that James had heard so many times before and wanted so desperately not to hear again. It was generally agreed that most of Andrew's methods for removing the Indians were foul, but whether this was admirable or reprehensible depended on your point of view. What shocked James was the general acceptance that he had some proof of the illegality of at least one of Andrew's treaties. How can so many people know what is in a private correspondence? he thought angrily, and walked off into the night, to be alone.

*

326

It was Becky Perkins who saw him leave and pointed it out to Sally, who was puzzled. James had been in a remarkably good humor when they had danced together earlier, but Becky thought he had left angrily. When he didn't return after twenty minutes or so, Sally went looking for him.

She found him at Rachel's tomb. She hadn't really looked anywhere else. She guessed that something someone had said about Andrew had made him angry, and whenever he had been angry with Andrew in the past, it was to Rachel he had gone. It was a pretty night, a cloudless, star-spangled sky, and she could hear the revelers in the distance, but it was peaceful here in this quiet cemetery.

Sally didn't speak; she was sure James knew she was there. It was the first time she had seen the completed monument. It had a terrible finality to it, and for a moment she missed Rachel dreadfully.

"She chose this spot herself," James said after a while. "I think she knew she would not make old bones."

He was silent again. He looked at the stars, and then at his wife.

"How can he bear to be without her?" he said suddenly. "I could not live without you."

Sally moved to him and he put his arm around her. Just for a moment, she felt a spark of anger with his procrastination, but it quickly passed, for his sensible caution in all things was one of the reasons why she loved him.

"You must finish it," she said. "Whatever it is between you and Andrew, you must resolve it, once and for all. It is Andrew, isn't it?"

James nodded.

"Put an end to it, my dear," she implored him. "For your own sake if not for mine."

James looked at her, and knew he had not treated her fairly.

"I promise," he said.

34

The revels lasted until almost dawn, and some of the young bloods didn't bother going home but bunked at the Hermitage, wherever they could find a bed. So there was a slightly faded air about the guests when they assembled at the Hermitage again the next day to witness the wedding; a little starch had gone from their clothes, and because of the success of the previous night, a little of the stiff formality from their behavior. No one took the wedding quite seriously, except perhaps the celebrants. For the whites it was only a couple of niggers jumping the broom, however well connected one of those niggers might be, and for most of the blacks, it was the only real party they had ever been invited to, no matter how restricted the celebration was.

They all assembled on the cleaned-up lawn and looked anxiously at the approaching rain clouds. Gracie, lovely in her white gown, was given away by Andrew junior, but Alfred, never nervous about anything, was in such a state of jitters he forgot her name in the ceremony and had to be prompted by Cap'n Jack. Everyone laughed, even the white minister conducting the service, and only Jass puzzled for a moment as to why two soulless niggers would have a church wedding. At the end of the formal service, Cap'n Jack and Sarah brought the broom, and Alfred and Gracie jumped over it into the land of matrimony. Married at last, he kissed her, the crowd cheered, and the rain started.

"Into the barn," Andrew junior yelled, and everyone made a dash for cover.

The huge barn had been made ready in case of this very eventuality, and everyone was in a jovial mood.

The week had been a howling success, and on this, the last day of the festivities, they were all prepared to let their hair down, have a good party, and then go home. Nature had helped.

Even amid all this benevolent goodwill, the rules of race absolutely prevailed; they were as natural as breathing to all these people, white and black. Some pretension had been abandoned though. When old Mr. Morissey's slave, pushing the Bath chair, tripped on his way to the barn, sending the old man sprawling into the mud, several young men, white and black, rushed out into the downpour to help, and together carried the complaining veteran into the barn.

When the band started to play the first tune, a lively reel, Alfred led Gracie into the center of the barn, and everyone oohed and aahed, as was proper, but no one was sure of the protocol, and it was the blacks who broke the impasse and followed the dancing couple's lead, never for one moment crossing the invisible line that had been drawn by some unseen white hand down the middle of the room.

"What the hell," cried Andrew junior. "Can't let the niggers have all the fun." He took Sarah's hand and they joined in the dance.

It was all reels and gavottes and polkas, and a furious determination to have a good time. Jass was in the thick of it, and asked half a dozen young ladies to dance, and to his surprise, they all accepted. Lizzie, who was bored with her callow partners, became rather jealous, and eventually she did the unthinkable. During a small break in the music, she went to Jass, who was chatting happily with his most recent partner, and informed him that she had managed to squeeze him into her dance card. The band struck up again, Jass grinned broadly, positively glowing with perspiration, Lizzie thought, and he grabbed Lizzie and whirled her onto the floor.

"I didn't say it was this dance," Lizzie protested, but

Jass only laughed. "I don't care," he said, and suddenly Lizzie didn't care, for his enthusiasm was infectious, and she danced as enthusiastically as he.

"My, but they make a handsome couple," Becky Perkins said, watching from the sidelines with Sally and some other older women. The fellow hens clucked approvingly.

"Nonsense," Sally snapped, "they're both far too young." She looked at Jass and Lizzie, dancing with teenage energy, and thought she had never seen her son so happy.

Easter was miserable. She'd spent most of the time hiding from Reuben, whose hands, she had discovered last night, were far too inquisitive. Every time she'd sneaked a look at the dance floor, she'd seen Jass with a different partner, and now he'd been with Lizzie three dances in a row. Jass was so clearly having a good time that Easter was now jealous not of Lizzie but of the good time. Something inside her snapped. She was young, here was a chance to enjoy herself, and even if Reuben did have wandering hands, they couldn't wander too far or else she'd yell for her father. She knew he was looking for her, and moved to a position where he could find her.

"Bin looking for you everywhere," he said.

Easter feigned indifference. "You ain't the only nigger I dances with."

He grinned happily. "You ain't dancin' now," he said, and offered her his arm.

Easter was about to accept, but she heard the music and saw that the dance was one she didn't know. She hadn't had much teaching, a few lessons with Sassy and the occasional improvised hop in the slave quarters, and while she could manage simple jigs, this was a dance she hadn't seen. It looked complicated: With lots of whooping and hollering, people would swirl about with one partner, and then at some signal Easter couldn't pick up, would change to another partner and swirl about with them.

Reuben saw the tiny doubt in her eye, and correctly guessed the reason.

"It's easy," he assured her. "I c'n teach you."

Easter, longing to dance, accepted his assurance. "I hopes yo' c'n teach yo' hands to mind their manners, too," she sniffed, and followed him to the floor.

He taught her quickly, or she learned fast, and oh, it was fun. The general mood infected her: This was the last day, tomorrow they'd be going back home to dull normality, and Easter was determined to make the most of these last few moments. She threw herself into the dance with an abandon that rivaled Jass's energy, only partly in the hope that if he caught sight of her, he would see she didn't need him to have a good time.

He did catch sight of her, and she him, and he waved happily, as if pleased to see her enjoying herself, and she waved back and swung toward her next partner, and into his arms, and into what seemed to be, for a few moments, the end of the world.

For she had crossed the invisible line. She stared at the incredulous white man in horror, and immediately all her training leaped to the fore.

'I so sorry, Massa," she said, and tried to get away, but he would not let her go. It was Easter's misfortune to have danced into the arms of Ralph Morissey, who had inherited all his father's intolerance and prejudices.

"Does anybody own this nigra?" he roared, and the party came to a stop.

Perhaps they had all been expecting it to happen, the whites anyway, and some of the blacks, or even wanting it. They had all been flirting on the very edge of the line, taunting it, daring it; it had added spice to the day, and it was as if they needed a sharp reminder, before going home, of the natural order of their lives.

Easter sank to the floor, still held in Morissey's grasp. The dancers stopped dancing. The band stopped playing. The room fell silent. A white man was asserting his dominance over a black, and there was nothing anyone in the barn could do. The only man who could help Easter was not there.

Cap'n Jack was in despair. His daughter was being humiliated there, and visions of Annie being torn away from the girl, screaming, to some unknown fate, flooded his mind. Shaking with shame and fury, he looked desperately for James and tried not to believe that he wasn't there to save Easter, just as he had not been there to save Annie.

"I say, who owns this nigra?" Ralph Morissey called again.

It took Jass a moment to realize what was happening, and when he did, he looked around for his father. He could not see James, and then remembered him leaving some time before with Henry Clay, who had arrived in Nashville unexpectedly that morning.

He looked at his mother, and she was looking at him. She nodded her head very slightly, and Jass understood that it was all up to him. His stomach lurched, but he could not shirk his duty—to himself, his family, his tribe, or to Easter. He was, at this moment, her Massa.

He started walking toward Morissey. People moved aside to let him pass. The silence was deafening. His own footsteps thundered in Jass's ears, and Easter's gentle weeping. He heard a voice mutter behind him, "Flog the bitch."

The walk lasted forever, but eventually he was there. He looked Morissey in the eye, and held out his hand to Easter.

"Come along, Easter," he said. "I'm sure you have work to do."

She took his hand, and Morissey, honor satisfied, let go his grasp. The niggers knew who was in charge again.

The silence continued as Jass led Easter away, he

332

didn't know where, anywhere, just to get her out of there. Now they walked through the black section of the room, and the slaves, eyes downcast, parted for them in embarrassed silence as surely as the triumphant whites had done. Easter kept her eyes to the floor, to hide her tears and her shame, and Jass stared straight ahead.

Cap'n Jack moved now. There was a small room attached to the barn, a shed or workplace, and he went to it and opened the door. Jass nodded to him gratefully, and took Easter inside.

Even after they had left the room, the silence continued, until Andrew junior broke it.

"What am I paying you for?" he called to the orchestra. "Play!" They began to play, sensibly, a slow waltz.

A few couples started to dance again, and gradually something of the old mood returned—to half of those present. The blacks had been put back in their place and did not immediately see the sense in provoking more of the white man's wrath. For the next three or four dances, it was a white man's party.

James was not in the barn because Henry Clay had come to talk to him. He had arrived at the Hermitage that morning from Ashland, his home in Kentucky, where he had been spending the summer. He had made his respects to Andrew junior, who was not thrilled to see him, and Sarah, who was enchanted by his easy elegance, and he had watched the wedding from the house. When the rain started, he sought out James, who was the reason for his visit. They had been given the use of Andrew's study, which amused them, for both knew it was Andrew they were going to discuss.

They circled the issue warily for a while, until James could not contain his curiosity.

"How are things in Washington?" he began.

"I've no idea," Henry laughed. "It's been a pleasant summer in Kentucky, away from it all. I do not relish going back."

He was lying, and they both knew it. The cut and thrust of politics was life and blood to Henry.

"And Andrew?" James asked, smiling in gentle provocation.

"Military men should be employed by governments, not in charge of them," Henry laughed in response. "This second term is Andrew's last campaign, and he is determined to win the war."

He took a pinch of snuff. His levity did not fool James. He knew Henry was vitally concerned about the welfare of the country.

"He rides roughshod over Congress, and has torn the Constitution to tatters. He claims a mandate from the people, but all they did was elect him to an office, not crown him king. He claims to be the champion of the states, but he gathers ever more power into his own office. John"—he was referring to John Quincy Adams, Andrew's predecessor—"never used the veto once. Andrew threatens it every day."

They were old enemies. Henry was particularly bitter about Andrew's veto of his bill to recharter the United States Bank. Andrew's bitter opposition to the central bank had led to its effective demise and to a rash of new state banks, operating under a patchwork quilt of legislation by the individual states.

"He won't be there much longer. Another eighteen months—" James said.

Henry laughed again. "Nothing will change. Van Buren will ride to the presidency on Andrew's coattails, and continue all his policies because he has none of his own."

"You could run against him," James suggested, but although Henry shook his head, his reply was enigmatic. "Perhaps," he said.

334

He took another pinch of snuff. "But Martin would be a formidable opponent, if only because he bathes in Andrew's aura," Henry continued. "We'll see.'

There was a small silence. James waited and wondered and guessed. Henry came to the point.

"If you had information, written documents, that would help discredit Andrew, would you release them?"

James felt a deep and churning anger rise. How did everybody know?

"What documents?" he asked, evenly.

"Bribes paid to certain compliant Chickasaws in return for a treaty." Henry did not mince matters.

James shook his head. "I have no such evidence," he said. "No such proof."

"A very large amount of Chickasaw land was deeded to you by the federal government immediately after that treaty was signed," Henry said. "Long before the land was generally made available."

He stared at James, as if willing him to renounce the lie. But Henry was not Andrew, and his steady gaze only caused James's anger to erupt.

"It was collateral for a loan," he exploded. "I've lent him fortunes over the years, going all the way back to New Orleans, and never seen a penny in return. This time I wanted insurance."

Henry sighed, knowing he was wasting his time. He had not expected to succeed, but he would not have forgiven himself if he had not tried.

"Did you get your money back?" He smiled. There was no point in antagonizing James any further.

"Yes," James said. "I got my money back."

Henry kept trying, but gently now, for he understood the truth. James did have proof of Andrew's culpability, but in releasing it he might destroy himself, and few men are willing to be their own executioners. Eventually they said their good-byes, and Henry made to leave.

335

"All I did was lend him money," James said again, as Henry left the room.

In a small side room of the barn, Cap'n Jack and Angel were trying to comfort the wretched Easter.

"Hush, chile," Cap'n Jack said. "'Twere an accident. No one gwine blame you."

"They all did," Easter cried. "'Tweren't my fault!"

Angel nodded because she saw the injustice of it. "I said no good would come of it, black folk mixin' with white," she said. "'Tain't fittin'."

Easter stared at the party through the open door. What hurt her most was that Jass had not stayed with her. He had brought her here, said a few sensible things while she cried, and then left her. She could see him dancing with Lizzie, as if nothing much had happened.

Reuben came to the door. "Feelin' better?" he asked, with genuine concern. Easter stared at him, and then at Jass dancing with Lizzie, and could not cope with any of it. She slammed the door in Reuben's face, and fell into Cap'n Jack's arms, weeping again.

If there had ever been a chance that Cap'n Jack would forget or abandon his vows of vengeance against James, it was gone now. Easter had been silly and forgetful, but no more than that, and surely did not deserve such a public humiliation. James was not directly responsible for what had happened, but he was a Massa of slaves, and that in itself was causing a blind fury in Cap'n Jack. Not even Jass's triumphant behavior was of any solace to him.

But Jass had impressed many of the white women present, and especially Lizzie. The boy had looked like a man, had behaved like a man, striding across the silent dance floor to protect his property. Several female hearts had fluttered, and Jass was not short of dancing partners, but Lizzie deflected any rivals by refusing to

336

let him out of her sight or her arms. At the same time, being sensible, she did not attempt to silence any of the flattering attention that was surrounding Jass.

Jass loved it. He had met his first challenge in the adult world, and had triumphed. Nor did he mind the fact that Lizzie was constantly beside him. She was pretty, she was his own age, and she was flirting with him outrageously. Jass knew he would have sweet dreams that night.

He even felt some charity toward Easter. At first, when he realized the enormity of what she had done, his only thought was to thrash her hide, but now, hero of the moment, he decided that she'd been silly, she was only young, and he looked forward to smacking her cute little tail.

He wondered how much more he could achieve. The barn was hot, the evening cool. He suggested to Lizzie that they take a turn outside, and she had flutteringly agreed.

The rain had stopped, leaving behind the pretty smell of a damp garden. They strolled together arm in arm for a while, and then Jass summoned up his courage.

"I wonder if—" he began, "—when we get back to Alabama—I might call on you."

Lizzie, knowing the future that her parents at least were mapping out for them, feigned surprise.

"Whatever for?" she asked innocently.

The question confused Jass; the answer was obvious to him. 'Well, you know, so we can—get to know each other better."

Lizzie waved her fan rapidly, as if she were having hot flushes.

"Why, Mr. Jackson," she drawled. "I do believe you're courting me."

Jass, to his surprise, didn't blush. "I guess I am," he laughed.

"My," Lizzie said. "I don't believe I'm quite ready for

337

that." She saw the disappointment on his face, and added her intended rider. "But I don't suppose there'd be any harm if you came to see me once in a while—"

Jass laughed again, feeling wonderful. Having got this far, he decided to push his luck.

"Oh, Lizzie," he said and hoped it conveyed some passion. He leaned close to her and kissed her on the lips, his as firmly closed as hers.

Lizzie allowed it to happen, and then broke away in apparent outrage.

"Sir!" she cried. "Just because I squeezed you into my dance card does not give you the right to violate my person! Don't you ever kiss me again!"

For a moment, Jass was confused, and believed that she meant it.

"Not until you have learned to do it properly," Lizzie laughed, and ran back to the barn.

Jass laughed too, but didn't follow her. He had accomplished enough for one night, and knew there was no more to be had. He had stared at the stars, and found it hard to believe that life, with its many daunting confusions, could offer such enormous rewards.

Only one tiny problem clouded his flawless horizon. He had kissed Lizzie chastely, lips closed, as he kissed all women—his mother, his aunts, his sisters and his cousins—but she had suggested it was not enough. Obviously, there was more to kissing than Jass had understood.

He wondered whom he could ask about it, and dismissed any of the older men he knew, because perhaps it was something he should already know. Wesley, he decided. On his return to Florence, he would seek the advice of his old nemesis, Wesley, because now they had something in common.

He didn't want to go back to the party, which was in its closing stages anyway. He wanted this night to last forever.

Jass sat on a log and savored the night and took joy in the company of his newfound friend, Jass.

35

Jass kept his promise to himself, but James broke his word to Sally. He wrote to Andrew soon after their return to Florence, but it was because they heard of a chimney fire that had destroyed the Hermitage. There had been no loss of life, but the letter was full of sympathy, for James knew how much the mansion he had so lovingly built meant to his old friend. He did not mention the removal, or the contentious letters, telling himself that this was not the time, that he wanted to restore a working relationship with Andrew again before raising such difficult matters. Andrew replied a few weeks later, and was courteous and wrote of his determination to rebuild the Hermitage exactly as it had been. It pleased James to have such a warm response and he was becoming less concerned about the removal. The Chickasaw were going west, and while he heard many stories about their privations along the way, James decided that Sara was right. It wasn't the same as the British in Ireland: The Indians were being given good land, to live in peace and prosperity in their tribal manner. It was young Doublehead who helped bring James to this conclusion, although he was hardly young anymore.

It was a cold November afternoon. James was alone in the house, but for several slaves. Sally and Sassy were staying with Mary, who was in confinement again, and Jass was spending the weekend with his new friend Wesley. The Trio were with Sally and Sassy.

The winter sun was low and without warmth. The dogs had been uneasy since midday, restless and whining. Several times, James had looked out the window and thought he saw people moving among the distant trees, but assumed it to be the normal business of the plantation. Toward sundown, the dogs started barking in earnest, incessantly, excitedly, as at prowlers, and James went outside to investigate, hoping a slave had not been foolish enough to run away.

Mitchell and Noah, a slave guard, were on the front lawn, both with dogs straining at their leashes, desperate to get to some quarry. Other slaves had gathered near the house, silently, curiously, looking to the horizon. Standing among the distant trees, in small groups of two and three, family groups, were some Indians, Cherokee or Chickasaw, James guessed, tribally dressed for winter. They had luggage with them, bundles and packs, as if they were going on a journey.

They did nothing but stare at the mansion, or the hill on which it stood. They seemed to have no purpose or intention, and their stillness maddened the dogs more than any movement.

James became aware of Cap'n Jack standing beside him.

"It's Doublehead," Cap'n Jack said.

Young Chief Jimmy Doublehead, now a man of forty, was standing at the gate, a woman beside him carrying a child, and a couple of elders. Like the others, they did nothing but stare at the house.

"Kennel the dogs," James said.

Mitchell was reluctant. You never knew, with Indians.

"Sir, them's Injuns—" he began, but James cut him short.

"Kennel the dogs!' he commanded.

Mitchell glanced at Noah, and at the Chickasaw, and having no choice, obeyed the order, pulling the dogs away, behind the house.

Once the dogs were gone, Doublehead and the elders began walking to the house. It was a cold evening. James shivered a little, and went back inside.

Shortly afterward, there was a tap on the door of his study, and Parson Dick came in, followed by Doublehead, his squaw, and the elders. James rose from his desk to greet his old friend.

"Jimmy, how good to see you," he said warmly, holding out his hand. But Doublehead did not accept the greeting, and spoke in Cherokee.

"You know I can't speak your language," James said, and laughed. "I know I should, the years I've lived here, but let's speak in English."

But Doublehead spoke again in his language. There was a small silence, and James was embarrassed. The gravity of the Cherokee's demeanor disturbed him.

"He says he will not speak the white man's tongue," a quiet voice said, and James realized that it was Parson Dick.

"Since he is forbidden by white man's law to live among you, he sees no need for your language," Parson Dick continued.

James was astonished that Parson Dick had any knowledge of Cherokee, but was more concerned at establishing some communication with Jimmy.

"What does he want?" James asked.

Parson Dick spoke in Cherokee, and Doublehead replied.

"You told us we could live amongst you as equals, but that is denied to us," Parson Dick said. "Now you tell us that we cannot even live amongst you."

He listened again.

"What will you tell us next? That we cannot live?"

James had no reply. He was excluded from Doublehead's world now, just as Doublehead was being excluded from his.

"They are going on a long journey, to new land in the West, away from the power of the white man, and they are very pleased."

Although a Cherokee, Jimmy had been living on the Chickasaw land since his father's death, had married a

Chickasaw woman, and was now going west with these people, but James was surprised. He had not thought that the enforced removal would be a source of comfort to any Indian.

"I wish them well," James said. "It will be a difficult journey."

Parson Dick translated and listened to the reply.

"Many have gone before and have not survived," he told James. "But they have no choice, for if they stay here they will surely perish."

He listened to Doublehead. James looked at the squaw. Cradling the child in her arms, she stared ahead, not seeing him, not seeing anything. She seemed to James to have no sense of future, no sense of hope.

"The chief wishes to thank you for the many kindnesses you have shown to him and to his father, and he asks that you grant one more."

Anything, James thought, I would give anything to be free of this guilt.

"Anything," he said.

Doublehead spoke, and Parson Dick translated.

"This land is sacred to the tribe, the spirits of their ancestors live here. The child, the chief's new son, has not heard their voices, and they wish to take the spirits with them, to the new land, in the West."

They were in territory that James did not understand. He looked to Parson Dick for help.

"It will be a short ceremony," he said, "and they will be gone by dawn."

"Of course," said James, surprised that it was so easy, and wishing they were gone now.

Parson Dick told Jimmy and the Chickasaw of the assent, and they moved to go.

"Tell him—" He stopped, not knowing what he wanted to say. "Tell him—that as long as I and my family own this land, they will always be welcome here."

342

Doublehead turned to James in amazement, and saw an unbridgeable gulf between his people and the white men who pretended to be their brothers. He spoke, for the first time, in English. The point he wanted to make was so basic to his thinking that he did not trust any translation.

"You do not own this land," he said. "You may have the use of it while you live, but you cannot own it."

He knew James didn't understand, but he had to try to make someone comprehend. He had so little time.

"You use the land while you live, a few short years, and pass it to your sons. But if they are killed in battle, or if they have no sons, who does the land belong to then?"

James could stand it no longer. "It is my land, forever!" he cried out.

Doublehead knew he had touched a deep chord in James, but suddenly felt inadequate to express the depth of his feelings.

"The land is eternal, and we are mortal," he said. "You cannot own land."

He saw, with astonishing clarity, that James was scared, and understood that he was scared of death, that the white men were scared of dying. Their afterlife, their spirit world, was in some other, unknown country, and they were afraid to go there. Suddenly, all the wars and the treaties and the bargains and the promises seemed a useless waste of time, because the Indians had never understood the basic fear that possessed the white men. Doublehead knew that he would never see the new land in the West because he had no heart for it. He knew that he would die on the journey, and his spirit would roam forever, free, in this country of his ancestors. All he cared about now was his son, whose life was not yet chanted. He couldn't bear to look at James anymore, and left the room. The squaw, who had never looked at James, followed, with the elders.

Parson Dick did not leave. James had slumped into his chair, and Parson Dick waited for some response or order that he was sure would come.

He coughed gently, and James looked at him, as if surprised he was still there.

"Yes, a brandy," James said, and was silent while Parson Dick poured the drink. Doublehead was wrong. James did understand.

"How do you know the language?" he asked eventually.

"My Massa before you was a Cherokee chief," Parson Dick replied.

He left the room. James's mind swirled with contradictory thoughts, his heart with conflicting emotions. He had seen, with a clarity that rivaled Doublehead's, the great chasm between the white world and that of the native peoples. For one small, glorious moment, he envied them. The idea that his spirit might dwell for all eternity on this land that he loved was precious to him, but he did not believe in such spirit life, and for one small, terrible moment he felt a visceral fear of the God of wrath and judgment.

He took a sip of brandy, and relaxed. It was easy now. Since the two peoples would never understand each other, it was better that the Indians go. Andrew had won, Andrew had been right all the time. Since they could not co-exist, they should not even try.

James felt better than he had done in years.

The ceremony was short and very simple, and James was charmed by it. The Chickasaw built a fire on the lawn, and sat around it, chanting, a few men beating small drums. Two elders danced around the fire, summoning the ancestors, James knew.

Slaves had gathered to watch. The drumming and chanting seemed to evoke some primal, distant memories in them, of other times and other countries that

344

most of them had no remembrance of, and they began swaying to the rhythm.

Doublehead, his son cradled in his arms, walked to the center of the circle of people, and as the beat quickened, he raised his son to the stars, to hear the voices of the old ones. Again, it struck that distant echo of memory in the slaves, and they sighed, or it might have been the gentle wind in the leafless trees, but for a moment James thought he heard the old ones answer.

A shiver ran down his spine. This simple ceremony had touched some mystic, primal chord in James, in a way that no Christian idea ever had, and it frightened him. If these people were truly in touch with the spirit world, if they could so easily evoke forces, passions, instincts that were inaccessible to whites, or at least discounted by them, then perhaps the wrong being done to them was greater than James had ever allowed himself to imagine. He looked at his slaves, who so obviously had some visceral understanding of the rituals being enacted; perhaps they too understood things that were alien to James. And if it was wrong to disinherit the Indians, was it as great a wrong to disinherit the blacks?

Already James knew the answer, but to proceed along that path was even more destructive to the world he had created than any of the previous terrors he had felt. He turned his head away to break the spell being woven on him, and tried to dismiss what he was hearing, what he was seeing, and what he was thinking, because he wanted to, as simple superstition. These are primitive peoples, he told himself, the red and the black, and it is incumbent on us to defend them and protect them. But without us they are nothing. Without us, the land is nothing. Without us, the world returns to pagan savagery, and has no meaning.

He went back into the house and poured himself another brandy. Tomorrow, the Indians would be gone,

345

and there would be no further questions about their land and how it was appropriated.

The Chickasaw were as good as their word, and were gone by dawn, on their long journey west, to Texas. Apart from the ashes of a fire, there was no evidence that they had ever been there.

And it is proper that they go, James thought. We have done our best for them.

It is the duty of the strong to look after the weak.

Jass was not weak, but he enjoyed the protective arm of Wesley around him. To his surprise, it had been easy to embellish their small acquaintance, and it had flowered into a curious friendship. The unlikely foundation to it was the cause of their previous quarrels. Jass was interested in black people in a general sense, but Wesley was developing a passion for black women.

"Oh, I love them, man," he said almost every day. "Especially in a proper bed, that black skin on a white sheet."

Jass blushed the first time Wesley said this, because he could imagine it only too well. He tried to think of Lizzie on crisp linen sheets, and while it was exciting, it didn't arouse him nearly as much as an image of Easter in the same situation. Wesley, sensing the weakness, played on it, giving laughing, voluptuous descriptions of his encounters with slave women, which aroused fierce urges in Jass. Then he would tease Jass about his sensitivity on the subject of slavery, and Jass, still basking in the warm memory of white female congratulation in Nashville, began to think that perhaps slavery was the best solution for the blacks.

It surprised Jass too that Wesley, school champion, constantly surrounded by admiring cohorts, had very few close friends. He was welcomed and immediately liked wherever he went, perceived at first, Jass could tell, as the quintessential young Southern man. Wesley reveled in the adulation, but delighted in shocking

346

people because he knew he would be forgiven much. Emboldened by this very charity, Wesley's challenges to revered institutions were becoming sharper and more caustic, and attitudes to him were changing. He would skate, wildly, dangerously across the thinnest ice of decency in conversation, especially with young ladies, and initially this sauciness had provoked a few raised eyebrows and the comment from older men that he was a young ram. Often now, however, he would go too far, the ice would crack beneath him, and the words "Young scoundrel" were frequently whispered, not always behind his back.

Like Jass, Wesley was a second son, born to money, but his older brother was healthy and not adventurous, and so, barring accidents, it was unlikely that Wesley would ever inherit the family name or position, and he felt no sense of impending responsibility. "Life is for living," he would tell Jass, and was directing all his burning, golden energy to that end. His attitude to slavery was simple: It always had been and always would be, it was essential to their survival, and it was right, and if the Feds ever tried to abolish it there'd be a war. Wesley loved the South and all it stood for, believed it was one of the greatest civilizations the world had ever known, and longed for a chance to thrash the Yankees in battle.

Or to thrash anybody, because it wasn't the cause, Jass learned, it was the fight. It was the danger. It was the adventure. Wesley was bored. Reckless with a young man's energy, Wesley hated school, hated the idea of college, and hated even more the idea of a life as indolent second son, indulged and pampered, waiting in the wings for a role that, once his older brother had sons, would never be his.

"And then what do I do?" he despaired.

"Get lost in New Orleans, I imagine," Jass had laughingly responded, for everyone knew of that city's free and easy reputation.

Wesley shook his head. "No, whores are fine, but why pay for something when you can get it free?" The most compelling argument for slavery in Wesley's mind was that it provided him with an endless supply of women who could not say no to him.

"And anyway, that's for after the battle," he continued. "It's the fight that gets your blood up."

Jass was staying with him for the weekend, and they were in his room, in separate beds to sleep. Suddenly Wesley jumped up, and began shadow-boxing with the wall.

"It's all this bloody civilization," he said. "Everything's so neat and ordered now. There aren't any good battles left."

"Texas," Jass said, smiling because he knew the effect the word would have, and because Wesley looked funny, feinting at the wall in his nightshirt.

"Yes, Texas," Wesley almost groaned. "That's where I should be."

Texas was his dream. Texas was the new frontier. There was going to be a war in Texas, no doubt about it, for the white settlers there were chafing under Mexican rule, and the Mexican general, Santa Ana, was determined to bring them to colonial heel. Scores of young men were heading for Texas.

"That's the place for me," said Wesley, his eyes bright with longing. "Kick the Dons' cods in daytime, and javer their women at night."

He fell back on the bed, and grinned at Jass. "There's this little mulatta down in the slave quarters," he teased. "Hotter than the sun in August. Shall you go down there with me?"

Jass laughed, and shook his head. It happened all the time. Wesley was determined that Jass should lose his virginity in his presence, but delighted in Jass's persistent refusal.

"I know, saving it for someone special," he mimicked Jass's response. He punched his pillow, and was silent

348

for a moment. Then he took a little bottle from a drawer in the table beside his bed. He held it out to Jass.

Jass was inclined to shake his head again. He'd had laudanum a few times when he was sick, and once, recently, with Wesley, who stole it occasionally from his mother's medicine chest. Jass had loved it, loved the sensation of floating on a fluffy pink cloud, all time and care and guilt removed. It was so wonderful, it frightened him too, and he worried that Wesley was falling prey to its powerful addiction. He didn't want to offend his friend, nor appear childish, so he took the bottle, put it to his lips and pretended to swallow. Wesley laughed, took the bottle back and swigged the drug.

"Better than being bored to death," he said, and lay back on his pillow, to prepare for the dreams.

Jass relaxed too. He'd taken only a tiny drop of the opiate, but it was enough. He began to feel warm and slow, and his heart swelled with affection for his restless friend. He laughed at the very idea that he could call Wesley his friend, but was thrilled with it, for he often felt that Wesley was taking him to places he would never have gone by himself, if only in his mind. Like riding an eagle, he thought.

He chuckled again at the things they had done together. Now when he puffed on his corncob pipe, there was tobacco in it, because Wesley had taught him to smoke. Once they had tried hemp, and Jass had loved that at first, but fought against it, and had become ill. And once he had gone with Wesley to that mulatta in the slave quarters. He'd stayed outside, but had listened in excitement and embarrassment while Wesley took her.

He wondered why he was so reluctant to do it himself. There were endless opportunities in Wesley's company, and part of him wanted to take that step, to cross that threshold of experience, but a greater part of him said not yet. And try as he might, he couldn't keep his mind off Easter.

He chuckled once more at an image of Wesley as Emperor of Texas, surrounded by a harem of Indian and black women who were dressing him for battle, and then the image changed and altered, and Wesley was on his horse now, galloping off to battle some thousands of the enemy, and single-handedly gaining bloody victory over them all.

He chuckled again, out of sheer, disbelieving astonishment when, the following August, Wesley came to him and said good-bye.

He was not going to New Jersey, to the College at Princeton Village, as his family and friends believed.

"It's not for me, old man," he said. "Too bloody boring. Will you tell my family in a couple of weeks, when I'm safely away?"

He had money in his pocket, given him by his father, and a gun, and he rode a fine horse.

He was going west, to Texas.

36

That summer was bittersweet for James. The departure to the west of Doublehead and the Chickasaw had closed a large and unpleasant chapter in the book of his life, and he found himself less and less interested in the affairs of his state and his nation, more and more devoted to his personal affairs and his family. Sassy's marriage to her beau, Bob Andrews, gave him joy, but then his darling daughter Jane had died of diphtheria, and Mary's newborn child had not survived birth. Mary herself never recovered from the ordeal and the loss, and passed away in March. It had hit James hard—he loved his firstborn daughter—but it was not the acid grief he had felt for the loss of his firstborn son. He found comfort in the living, and took particular pleasure in Sam Kirkman, Elizabeth and Tom's grave and serious son, who, at five, was discovering the joy of a doting grandfather.

Spring eased his sense of loss with its promise of the renewal of life, and summer, with its abundant stream of visiting friends and relations, healed his pain and gave him a new purpose and vigor. He was alive and master of a fine estate, and that was what mattered most to him.

And then there was Jass. James thoroughly approved of his son's friendship with Wesley, who seemed to have kindled bright new flames of confidence in Jass, if not adventure. Perhaps they were always there, James thought, and it was I who wanted too bright a fire too soon. He encouraged the friendship, for he saw in the increasingly wayward Wesley something of the larrikin he missed in his son, and through that friendship he saw his son becoming more like the boisterous Wesley.

He was not prepared for the news Jass gave him on a hot day in August. He had not seen Wesley at the house for a few days, nor had Jass gone to visit him. One night after dinner, when Sally had withdrawn to leave them to talk, James asked if they had quarreled.

Jass was silent for a moment, and it was clear some serious problem was vexing him.

"Wesley's gone to Texas," he said.

James was surprised, but no more than that, for the moment. "I thought he was going to Princeton."

Jass shook his head. "He's taken the money his father gave him for college and he's gone to Texas. He's sure there's going to be a war with the Mexicans, and he wants to be part of it."

James laughed lightly, but it was double-edged. For just a moment, he dreamed that Jass might have gone off on such an adventure, but as immediately dismissed the thought. Jass's proper place was here, and his son had behaved properly. But, oh—

"Well, he's right. There will be a war." James wasn't

quite sure what to say. Some battle for the future status of Texas seemed inevitable. Men from all over the country were headed there, to resist the colonial bondage of Mexico. But Wesley seemed very young.

"He's very young," James said.

Jass was more concerned with something else.

"The thing is"—he blurted it out—"I am to tell his father."

James laughed again. He began to see the problem.

"And he'll know I've known for two weeks, and he'll be furious I haven't told him before, and there'll be the dickens of a row."

James was amused, but adopted a serious manner, knowing that was what Jass wanted. "I assume you gave your word to Wesley?"

Jass nodded, but it was no great comfort.

"Then you must keep your word. We all have to face rows at some time in our lives," he said. "And I'll go with you."

He went with Jass, as moral support, but let Jass do all the talking. James saw it as a small rite of passage for his son, for Wesley's father, he knew, was a stern old martinet, who would not be pleased by his son's disobedience.

To the surprise of both of them, Wesley's father took the news well.

"The boy's a troublemaker, destined for a scoundrel, I fear," he said calmly. "If he wants to go and kill a few Indians, sow his oats, get it out of his system, it could be the making of him."

Jass was surprised. "I think it's Mexicans he's planning to kill, sir," he said.

Wesley's father looked at him as if he were a fool. "Mexicans? They are not our enemy in Texas."

"But, sir, it is a Mexican colony," Jass insisted.

"And we will take it from them," Wesley's father said. "We will take it or buy it or annex it, depending

352

on the whim of the president. It will be a slave state, as it is now and properly should be, and help diminish the undue influence of those wretched New Englanders."

It made sense, except for one thing. The thesis had to be completed: "But then what will we do with all those Indians?"

James stared at the man, hating him, hating his clarity of vision, for as soon as it was said, James saw an awful result.

"What will the native Comanche and Apache feel about all those Creek and Choctaw and Chickasaw that we have sent there?" Wesley's father chuckled. "There will be bloody war, and we will have to sort it out, and the Indian problem will be resolved in this land finally, and for all time."

James could not bear to believe it, and knew it was true. He had known it all along, and had denied it to himself for so long. The Indian question was not resolved by the removal. We would take Texas, and then California, and the wars against the Indians would go on, until the remaining few would stand with their backs to the great ocean, and then where would they go? It was an old nightmare for James.

Wesley's father chuckled again. "Even those damned Cherokee, for they will go west and will meet their destruction."

The Cherokee in Georgia were resisting every considerable effort to persuade them to go west. But they would go, James knew, if not by treaty, then by force. Andrew would make them go. Apart from the Cherokee, only some Seminole in Florida were violently resisting removal, under their chief, Osceola.

Some new thought had disturbed Wesley's father, but it had nothing to do with white dominion. "Whatever shall I tell his mother?" he wondered aloud. "She dotes on him so."

Jass was volubly relieved that the interview had gone so well, but James was silent as they rode home, possessed by dark foreboding. Why did the Indians haunt him so? Would this nightmare never end?

It got worse in October when James received an unwelcome visitor. Dr. David Evans was a missionary to the Indians who had traveled west with some of the Creek and was now returning to Georgia to plead for an end to the removal. He was trying to enlist whatever political support he could find, and had letters of introduction to James from Henry Clay.

"You are an old friend of the president, I believe." The minister wasted no time. "I beg you, sir, to do everything in your power to persuade him to end this merciless extinction of a people."

He knows about the letters, James thought immediately. "Andrew will not be president for much longer."

"He is president now." Dr. Evans was relentless. "And architect of this most foul thing."

James wanted to scream at him to go away, but he listened politely. The good minister's description of the journey west was horrifying.

"They have no real understanding of what is happening to them, and no will to make it succeed. They are uprooted from their natural home, and are on a journey that has no point or meaning to them, for where they arrive will mean nothing to them. Since they are not afraid of death, and because they see no real point in living, they die. There is not sufficient food to nourish them, or blankets to keep them warm. What food is provided is usually rotten, and their hunting grounds are lost to them. And so they die. There is cholera amongst them, and because they do not have hope, they have no will to fight it, and so they die."

He told his tale just as it was, without elaboration, and the factual simplicity of it made it more shocking to James.

"If it is summer they perish from heat; if it is winter

they die from cold. Of the four hundred that I journeyed with, one hundred and twenty reached the great river.

"Only pitiful provision has been made for them, and so they spend the money they were given for their comfort on arrival to survive the journey there. Some of their Army escort rob them. Many merchants along the way deceive them. All of us destroy them.

"A few federal officers who travel with them are often so distressed by what they see that they dig deep into their own pockets to try to buy some few creature comforts, but it is a task that would defeat Hercules.

"And when they reach the so-called promised land, what is there for them there? They stand like Ruth on alien soil and know not which way to turn. They cannot hunt, for they do not know what to hunt. Or where. They cannot read this land for they have no voices of the old ones to guide them. The whites who are there do not want them. The Mexicans do not want them. The Indians who are there do not want them. And so they are destroyed in this New Jerusalem."

"Not all of them, surely," James said.

"Not all of them, no," the minister replied. "But too many of them. And after the coming war with Mexico— for there will be a war—what will happen to them then? Will the so-called Republic of Texas tolerate these savages? I think not. They can hardly tolerate the Indians already there."

"It is over. There is nothing I can do," James said. "Nothing we can do."

"No, for them it is over," the minister agreed. "But I am come to save those who have not gone. The Cherokee, in Georgia."

He understood that it was probably a waste of time to try to persuade the government of Georgia to alter its policy toward the Cherokee, but did not understand it was a waste of time to try to persuade the federal government—Andrew—to change its mind. He begged for James's assistance.

355

"There is a story told," he said, "of rose trees that the first Indians planted along the way to guide those who came after them. And as more came, they took cuttings from those bushes and planted them farther along, until the way from here to Texas was a path of roses."

He stopped for a moment, for his emotions were getting the better of him.

"It is only a story, a sweet, romantic one, told to ease our guilt. There is no path of roses. Only a trail of heartrending tears."

Alone at night, James wept. He knew that young Doublehead was dead, for he had seen that lack of hope in the chief's eyes that evening in his study, and without hope, what point was there in life? He prayed, fervently, that Doublehead's son was alive, but then wondered why? If his future was death, what point was there in life?

"I will do what I can," he had told the minister. "But it is not much."

It could not be much, he knew. Even if he published the letters, they would make almost no difference to the plight of the Indians; the removal would continue, the destruction of them would go on. Only one person could ease the pain.

Colonel Elliot was in Lexington making arrangements with Tom Flintoff to travel to England and finalize the purchase of the stallion Glencoe. There was no real need for James to go to Kentucky, but he wanted to be part of the excitement. It also put him closer to Washington.

He didn't tell anyone, even Sally, of his intention; he was not even sure what he intended. He spent several pleasant days discussing horses in Kentucky, and was guest of honor at several parties given by horse-racing men, for James was one of their most prominent number. Cap'n Jack attended him, and Ephraim had driven them there in a gig, since Sally was worried he might catch a chill if he rode horseback. When the day of departure came, Ephraim naturally headed for the Knoxville road.

"No," said James. "We are going to Washington."

Cap'n Jack looked at him in surprise, but James would not explain. He had written a letter to Sally the previous night, telling of his plan to resolve, finally, his differences with Andrew. He wondered why he hadn't told her before, because when he left The Forks he had taken the correspondence with Andrew from its safe place and put the letters in his pocket.

They journeyed in silence. James did not know what he was going to do. He knew he was going to do something.

Cap'n Jack asked no questions. The Massa's business was the Massa's business, and he guessed, correctly, that James wanted to see Andrew. For himself, he was delighted that he might have the opportunity to see Alfred again.

At dinners in the hostelries where they spent the nights, the talk of Andrew's achievements as president diminished as they got closer to Washington. Ordinary folk, the working people, revered him, but the Virginians of James's class disparaged the hick frontiersman and his arrogant ways. James put it down to simple jealousy. Virginians were used to being part of the ruling elite, and were Andrew's avowed enemies. Still, it lightened his heart. Andrew became less and less of a legend, more and more of a man, and it was the man James had to persuade, not the giant.

He checked into a hotel in Alexandria, having been warned that accommodation in the village that was the capital was almost impossible to obtain, and sent a note to Andrew asking to be received. The reply was immediate and a generous affirmative.

They traveled by ferry across the river, hired horses on the other side, and rode through the farmland to the White House. James was fascinated by the few extravagant buildings that stood among cow paddocks, beacons to a great future amid a sea of mud.

The president's mansion was impressive enough from the outside, though smaller than James or Cap'n Jack had imagined, and looked a bit silly stuck here in this swampy wilderness. The inside was also shabbier than they had expected, dusty, giving a feeling of not being finished and lacking any sense of home, although Andrew had lived here for seven years. Rachel would have made the difference, James knew.

Cap'n Jack was disappointed. There was no sign of Alfred. He guessed, again correctly, that Alfred would be with his Massa, and was again disappointed when James, on being ushered upstairs, told him to wait. Cap'n Jack settled on a broken chair that had been badly repaired, and waited.

Andrew had been ill, and was sitting at a desk in his bedroom, Alfred never far from his side. There was a small bowl of food on the desk, mashed potato and milk, and some rice.

He looked so old, gaunt, and wasted, James thought, but of course he *was* old, twenty years James's senior. He seemed to be sleeping, and a tiny dribble of spittle was running down his chin. The unruly hair was thin and white now, where once it had been a golden mane. James looked at Alfred, who shook his Massa lightly, and Andrew woke.

The limpid blue eyes looked around, searching for a target, and settled on James.

This is it, James thought, the end of everything between us.

This is it, Andrew thought, the end of a small, irrelevant business that should have been finished years ago.

He greeted James warmly, and they mutually inquired after family, and then there was silence, and

358

Andrew seemed to drift away somewhere—to a tomb in Nashville, James suspected.

Then Andrew rallied. "Well?"

James put his case, and Andrew listened politely, attentively. Occasionally Alfred came to him and with a handkerchief wiped the dribble from his Massa's chin.

When James had finished, Andrew was silent again and stared at the papers on his desk. When he spoke, he looked helpless.

"What would you have me do?" he said. "The Cherokee are under Georgia law. I cannot interfere with the workings of a sovereign state."

You are the president, James wanted to shout at him. You have done so much, you can do anything. They call you king!

"You have in Florida," James insisted.

"That is different. Osceola declared war on us. I had no choice but to act."

James knew logic would have no effect. "Do not make them go," he said softly. "Do not send them to their deaths."

"I cannot make them go or stay," Andrew said. "It is not for me to choose. They have elected to stay, and therefore they must abide by Georgia law. All I can do is offer them a possible alternative."

"It is an alternative that will lead to their destruction!" James tried hard, tried his best.

"It is the only hope they have." Andrew hardly appeared to have heard him.

"It is in your power to ensure that the treaties are enforced," James insisted.

Andrew smiled.

"In the West, on federal land, I can protect them. In Georgia, I cannot. We are not at war with Georgia. I cannot send in the army," he said. "I cannot protect them from what they have chosen to be."

"I beg you to end this thing," James said. "You know

359

what must happen to them if they stay, and what will happen to them if they go."

Andrew nodded gently, and James thought he saw a tear in the old man's eye. It is just age, he thought, like the spittle on his chin.

"I do what I can to save them," Andrew said. "And will always do what I can to protect them, but only what I can, under the law."

James knew he was wasting his time, had always known he would be, but wanted it over.

"I could publish the letters," he said.

Andrew nodded again.

"Yes, you could. But I don't see the point of it. An old correspondence about an issue that died long ago. It will change nothing, except to cast a small slur on my character—"

He laughed and coughed at the same time.

"Which character is already so vilely slandered, in so many ways, by things so much more vile."

He looked at James, and didn't appear to be so old.

"And cast a very large slur on your character, which is not used to infamy."

He was changing, before James's eyes. He wasn't slouching anymore, and the eyes were no longer soft, like the sea, but bright and hard, like sapphires.

"In a year I will be gone from here, and soon forgotten," he said. "I am already much too old. But you are still a young man. Why needlessly besmirch what you have so valiantly achieved?"

A palpable energy began to fill the room.

"Do you have them with you?" Andrew asked.

James nodded. They were in his pocket. He wondered why. Why did I bring them with me? Why didn't I leave them at the hotel, or locked in the box at home?

"Give them to me," was all Andrew said.

James took the letters from his pocket and handed them over without demur. Perhaps this is what I have wanted all along, he thought. The burden of responsibility is not mine anymore. I am free, at last, of this terrible guilt.

And all Andrew had to do was ask. All he had ever had to do was ask.

Andrew didn't even look at the letters, knowing they would all be there. He put them in a drawer and locked it.

Neither of them spoke for a while, and when Andrew did, it was softly, sadly, with no trace of anger but an aching sense of loss.

"Have you so misunderstood me all these years?" he said, and James knew it was not a question.

"Do you think it nourishes me to see my children so piteously downcast? Do you think I do not weep for them? Do you think I have not fallen on my knees and begged almighty God to take this burden from me?"

He fell silent. He turned away from James, and when he spoke again, he seemed to be struggling to control his feelings.

"The earth was not made for savage beasts to roam upon at will." His voice trembled with emotion. "Those who stand in the way of honest industry must be swept aside. It is the order of Divine Providence, and I accept it with humility."

Perhaps he was crying. He put one hand to his eyes as if to shield his grief from sight and waved the other at the man who had once been his friend, dismissing him. James looked at Alfred, who was still attending his Massa, and left the room.

As they walked away from the White House, Cap'n Jack glanced back and thought he saw Alfred at an upstairs window, but it was only a shadow of approaching night.

James hardly spoke for several days, but the farther they traveled from Washington and the closer they got to home, his spirits obviously lightened. Cap'n Jack thought he had cast aside some terrible burden. As they drove into Florence, on a crisp bright winter day, James

361

looked out of the window at the bustling town, and chuckled.

"Massa?" was all Cap'n Jack said, leaving open the possibility of response.

"I think we will bring Glencoe here," James said, eyes bright with some new purpose. "I think we will bring all the horses here and make The Forks of Cypress the finest stable in America."

37

There was one thing left to do, one small piece of unfinished business to attend to before the new life could begin.

On Christmas Day, James summoned Cap'n Jack to his study.

James was at his desk, filling out a paper. He continued to write while Cap'n Jack waited, and then looked at his slave.

"I thank you for your many years of loyalty," he said. "No one could have served me better."

A curious anticipation tingled in Cap'n Jack. "Thank you, Massa," he said calmly.

James had a little speech prepared. "When you first came to me, I did not hold with slavery, but it was the custom of the land. I promised you then that if you worked for me, willingly and well, I would give you your freedom one day."

Anticipation gave way to excitement. Cap'n Jack knew his hand was shaking, his stomach churning.

James held out the paper.

"Here is that freedom now," he said. "A little later than it should have been, but not too late, I trust."

Desperate emotions punched at Cap'n Jack's heart. Here it was at last, the dearest gift anyone could give him, the thing he had longed for all of his days, the thing any slave might easily have sold his soul for.

"No, thank you, Massa," he said.

James closed his eyes. Not this, he pleaded, not now, the sin is too old, it has been atoned for a million times.

"Don't do this to me," he said.

Cap'n Jack could not do anything else. The vengeance he had nurtured for so long had become part of him, like the blood in his veins. He could hear Annie's screams in his ears as she was being dragged away that day. He could feel the uncontrollable anger, the inconsolable grief, the terrible fury he had known that day. He wanted to hurt the man he held responsible, and knew that he could. He was not his own man now. The demon had him.

"You broke your promise. You let Annie be sold away," he said.

"I wasn't here, it wasn't me," James's voice was a whisper.

"You the Massa," Cap'n Jack said.

"I needed you!"

Cap'n Jack could hardly hear. "What good freedom to me now? I's too old. Where c'n I go? What c'n I do? My life's here, Easter's here, all that's left of Annie."

"But you can stay here!" James lost his temper and yelled at the impassive man. "Free!"

Cap'n Jack stared at him. "Yes, Massa, I will stay," he said. "And every time you see me, every time you look at me, you will remember what you did to Annie, and the promise that you broke to me."

He left the room without being given leave. He left the house and walked to some quiet place under the trees. His hands were shivering, but it was not because of the fierce cold.

He had won. After all these years, he had his vengeance. But it gave him no joy. He couldn't understand why the taste in his mouth was so foul.

James was slumped at his desk, staring at nothing. The paper of manumission had fallen from his hand and fluttered to the floor.

38

In the spring, the stallion Glencoe arrived in New York. Glencoe stood slightly over fifteen hands, his color a rich, warm chestnut, with an elongated diamond star. His head was fine, his neck swan-like, and his muzzle pointed. He was the most famous horse in England, the pride of Ascot, and James had paid handsomely for him. When the ship that brought him across the Atlantic docked, hundreds of onlookers gathered, applauding in admiration as the magnificent animal was led down the gangplank, onto the pier and American soil. The press was fulsome in its praise of James, calling him the most successful importer of thoroughbreds in American history. Glencoe, it was believed, would eclipse even Leviathan's performance. It was hoped that the arrival of the horse at his new home in Alabama would help speed his owner to a recovery of his good health.

For James was not well. He'd caught a chill in the spring and had not been able to shake it off. He had planned to be in New York to greet Glencoe, but after only two days on the journey had turned back, and taken to his bed. He had seemed to be recovering, when little Jamie, Tom and Elizabeth's new boy, died at only eight months from diphtheria. They had all grieved for the child, but the death of small children was a fact of their lives, and already Elizabeth was pregnant again. But James had taken it especially hard, and it had caused a physical relapse in him.

The fever got worse; the congestion moved to his lungs. Sally was worried, but Dr. Hargreaves, who lived with the Simpson family in Florence, could find no especial cause for alarm.

"It is the process of growing old," he told Sally as they walked to his gig after a visit in July. "And he has never been hale."

Sally didn't agree. When she had first known James, all those years ago in Nashville, he had been as healthy a man as you could wish to meet. His frequent chills and bouts of minor illness had started around the time they moved to Florence, and Sally blamed the climate here, languid even in winter after the spikier weather of the Cumberland River. But none of her husband's chills and minor ailments had lasted as long as this. Perhaps the doctor was right; perhaps they were simply growing old, although Sally did not feel it. Rheumatism bothered her in winter, and arthritis occasionally, but otherwise she was as fit as any woman in her forties could wish. James was eight years older. She felt a flash of resentment at the passing of time. He is not old, she wanted to shout at the doctor, but could not. James had already lived longer than many of his contemporaries.

"You should discourage him from strong drink," the doctor was saying, as he had said so many times, on so many visits, knowing James's fondness for port. "And make sure he gets plenty of rest and relaxation."

He left laudanum, in case the cough that bothered James got too troublesome, and promised to maintain his weekly visits, for he was doctor to the whole family, and advised on the health of the slaves.

Sally decided to take a stronger command of her husband's welfare. It wasn't just the chill that worried her. Sally had no immediate fear that he would die—he seemed to have a whole new zest for living since his return from Washington—but again, she had to face the prospect of his mortality, and she dreaded being left alone, without him. So many wives of her acquaintance had became widows, many much younger than she.

She knew that trying to stop James from keeping his

finger on the pulse of his many business affairs would be an unwinnable war, but at least she could limit the attention he gave these matters, for their practical world was functioning smoothly, she knew. Cooper, the overseer of the new plantation at Panola in Mississippi, was a splendid fellow, who ran the estate as if it was his own, and Mitchell, the overseer here at The Forks, was thoroughly reliable, maintaining a clockwork efficiency, and if not actually liked by the slaves, he was not too bitterly resented by them, Sally thought. Tom Kirkman was managing their business in land, and under James's direction was doing remarkably well.

So Sally decided that James could afford to be interrupted from the cares of the material world. Previously, she and the rest of the family had treated his study as a private world, to be entered only if invited, but now, after he had spent a couple of hours in there, she would sweep in unannounced, without even knocking, and demand that he spend a little time with her. What surprised her was that he didn't seem to mind, and would smile and put aside his papers, and join her on the veranda or in the garden or, on cooler evenings, in the warmth of the sitting room. On the hottest days, he would sit with her in the little sitting area of their bedroom upstairs, the windows open to catch a breeze.

Actively, she discouraged strangers or acquaintances from making too many visits, for she knew that most were simply calling on James for letters of introduction, or advice on local matters that others could have easily provided, or for loans. As actively, she would ask close associates to be sensible of his physical condition, to limit their demands on his attention, and to spend as much time discussing frivolous news as affairs of the nation. And as actively, she encouraged relations to call, especially any who had young children, for James, she knew, loved those distractions. In particular he adored the company of young Sam Kirkman, Elizabeth's surviving son, a studious boy with an intriguing ability to alleviate his own gravity by laughing at the seriousness with which he regarded life. Elizabeth's new pregnancy also delighted James, and he fussed over her, petted her, and would look longingly at Jass, wanting a grandson by him, Sally knew, for Elizabeth was not of his blood, and Thomas, her husband, only his nephew.

Still, it surprised her that James never seemed to mind these unprofitable claims on his attention, but welcomed them, whereas previously any intrusions into the hallowed world of his business dealings had been prohibited. What Sally could not know, for James never told her, was that he was weary of the empire he had created.

There were no challenges left. He had done everything, even more than he had ever dreamed of; he was everything he had ever wanted to be. And he felt empty.

He could buy more land easily, he had the resources to create more plantations, but where was the challenge in that? He had more land already than several princes in Europe, and the acquisition of more held no delight for him. He saw the fevered speculation of the land boom that was flourishing around him and wished them all joy of it, but he wanted no part, for he had done that when young, and there were no frontiers to be tamed now, no wilderness to be put to the plow, only farms to be run, and farming bored him. There were no great political battles to be fought: The business of his state and of the United States was functioning smoothly, apart from its dealings with the remaining holdout Cherokee in Georgia, and James had abdicated any involvement in that. Andrew had left the presidency and was an invalid at the Hermitage, in the care of Alfred, While Martin Van Buren was leading the country on the exact path Andrew had defined, but without the zeal. The Mexican massacre of whites at the Alamo hardly seemed to touch him, nor did Sam

Houston's surprising victory over Santa Ana at San Jacinto.

It was only a matter of time before the new Republic of Texas was admitted into the Union, for otherwise it would fall under the influence of Britain, and Washington would not allow that. With the inevitable shadow of civilization falling over Texas, the last great frontier of excitement was gone. Even the uncrossable Rockies had been conquered, and then there was only pastoral California, which James still dreamed of seeing but knew he never would.

There was nothing to do anymore, he had decided, which was another way of saying that he had ceased to be of any real importance to anyone but himself and his family. Whatever influence he might once have had over the affairs of his state, if not his nation, was now limited to his prestige and his signature, and even they were not necessary to anyone else's dreams.

There are no great battles left, he thought, or none that have any use or need of me. I have become irrelevant.

Perhaps he was even irrelevant to his family, although not his wife. His daughters were all gone now, married with families of their own, and even though they were sweet to him and dutiful, he exercised no real authority over their lives. The Trio, he knew, were good sons, but even though they loved him and obviously respected him, and though he loved them and could provide a father's advice and guidance, the future pattern of their lives was starting to emerge, and since The Forks would not be their future, they were already talking of lives beyond it.

Which left Jass. Jass the dutiful, Jass the caring, Jass the obedient second son who strove so valiantly to fill the empty shoes of the first, and who failed constantly, not because of any shortcomings on his own part but because his father's expectations of him were impossible to fulfill. Jass saw lightning as a wonder of nature,

James thought, not as an immortal stallion to tame and ride.

It was the mortal stallion, Glencoe, who thrilled James now, the horse who would outdistance Leviathan and secure James's place in the racing annals of his country, but it was a poor substitute, not even second best he knew, for the history books that might have recorded his achievements as they would Andrew's. And so he allowed himself to be distracted from the emptiness of his material world by the woman without whom he knew he could not, would not want to, live, and the darling grandson, the grave Sam, who seemed so determined to write his own future, and had some inkling, at least, of what lightning might be.

But where is there left for him to play? James wondered in his darker moments. The plains of Olympus are gone, neatly furrowed by some giant plow, and all a boy can aspire to now is more of civilization.

Now, more than ever, he came to rely on Cap'n Jack. When the congestive fever was at its worst, it was Cap'n Jack who held a little bowl to his Massa's mouth to receive the phlegm. It was Cap'n Jack who changed the sheets on his bed when, as happened once, James soiled them, and Cap'n Jack who washed his Massa clean. It was Cap'n Jack who wiped the sweat from his fevered Massa's brow, Cap'n Jack who fed him soup when he was too weak to feed himself. It was Cap'n Jack who carried his Massa downstairs and up to bed when he could not manage the staircase on his own. It was Cap'n Jack who sat with him, Alfred to his Andrew, for endless hours, always there to see an order carried out or a wish fulfilled.

With the awful abscess of vengeance lanced and healed, Cap'n Jack now felt only a total emptiness. The thing that had so obsessed him, that had given him the will to live, was replaced by the surprising realization he found in a tiny corner of his heart: James was Cap'n Jack's best friend.

It was Cap'n Jack who took his Massa to the stables, when he was feeling better, to see the arrival of the new stallion. They sat with Murdoch and Monkey Simon, too old to race now, too valuable to sell, and dreamed of the winners Glencoe would sire, and of the old races they had won in the days of their youth. They would sit together on the veranda, the ol' Massa and the slave, and talk endlessly of the days in Nashville, and of the fun it had been. They seldom mentioned the move to Alabama, they never talked about Annie, but James delighted in news of Easter, and would have the girl brought to him, and would spoil her with silly treats of candy, and once a new frock.

It was Cap'n Jack who sang lullabies as James drifted to sleep, and slept himself on a palliasse at the foot of his Massa's bed, in case he should be needed in the night.

Frequently, at night or when he dozed in the afternoons, James dreamed of Ireland, an Ireland of his memory, that gave him no desire to return to the country of his birth, for what he dreamed of was gone, he knew, scythed by the passing years. He dreamed instead of playing in the fields of his youth.

Of Carrickmacross and Ballybay, not as they might be now but as he remembered them. Of Jugs and old Quinn. Of poteen and soda bread, and peat fires on misty mornings. Of rain-washed fields and white-walled cottages. Of lowering skies and breaking sunlight. Of croppies, hare hunts, and hurley. Of swirling fogs and shrouded legends. Of superstitious priests, storytelling shanachies, and pole-vaulting messengers.

And of Sean. Blessedly, kind, unvengeful death had not added a moment to Sean's years and he was now, in James's dreams, what he had always been, laughing, golden, riding rainbows.

Sometimes, too, he would dream of leprechauns, and if one of them looked exactly like Andrew, it was the generous Andrew of his youth, and he would take a little dust from the pouch at his side and sprinkle it on James, and James would be riding the rainbow too, sparkling with the magic powder, riding through iridescent, prismatic light, the primary colors of life, down toward the crock of gold that nestled, as the leprechaun told him, at the foot of the rainbow, faster and faster, falling toward the glittering prize that shone before him, falling, falling, until he knew that in a moment he would have it, the pot of fairy gold, the fabulous treasure that was beyond all reckoning. Falling, falling to a greater light whose source was only inches from his touch. But always before he reached it, he would wake up, and when he woke he was filled with a sense of loss, of something sought and not achieved, and the lack of it made him yearn to dream again.

Sometimes he would not find the leprechaun in his dreams, and he would be astride Glencoe, galloping across the dew-soft emerald grass toward a great city he knew was Dublin. Others would ride beside him for a while, on animals not as fine as his, and just as he recognized them and waved to them in cheery greeting, Lord Fitzgerald and Pamela, or Oliver Bond or Uncle Henry, Eleanor or Sara or Jugs, their horses would fail them, and they would fall behind. Then Sean would appear, galloping, laughing, always laughing, until he too could no longer keep pace with the reckless James, and would fall behind.

He would ride into Dublin, through shouting crowds, and all his friends would be there again, cheering with the mob, and James knew that he had just won a tremendous race. As suddenly, everyone disappeared, and he would be alone in the empty streets of the city, searching for them, and riding down a tiny, dark alley that led, he was sure, to the Liberties, the decrepit slums where all his friends were hiding. The houses would slowly give way to leafless trees and bushes ablaze with flowers, and he would find himself riding down avenues of endless, fragrant roses.

371

Those roses stayed with him in his waking hours; he could not rid his mind of the image that the missionary had conjured up. He could not bear to hear stories of the Indians trekking west, for all the news that reached him was of nothing but deprivation and starvation and death. He did not want to know about the new treaty made with the holdout Cherokee at New Echota, for however magnanimous it seemed to be on paper, he knew it could lead only to the same awful fate, and while he blocked from his mind the picture of another nation walking west to its doom, the image that replaced it was one of endless rows, here to the horizon, of withering, lifeless rosebushes.

Not even the recruitment of local young men for a small army out to drive the few remaining Lower Creek out of southern Alabama stirred James to any protest.

There is nothing I can do for them, he told himself. I did everything I could. Yet even as he said it, he knew how great was the lie.

39

William Perkins caught a more contagious disease than the congestive fever that was afflicting James. Eventually it would prove fatal to his financial well-being and his wife's physical health, but there was no preventive medicine for it. It was called Land Fever, and an epidemic of it had swept the frontier states. As ever more Indians were removed, more Indian land became available for white settlement, and more white settlers flooded in.

Perkins, a naturally cautious man, thought he was immune, but his wife's temperature soared as she heard the stories of the easy fortunes that were being made, and she communicated the virus to him. Perkins thought long and hard about a course of action, and finally made an eminently sensible decision. He asked the advice of Thomas Kirkman, who took him to see his father-in-law, his Uncle James.

James had several reasons for offering generous help. It is always flattering when a successful student asks his teacher for advice, and Perkins had sought out and listened to James when he first came to Florence, and had done well. Now he had money to invest, not a lot but enough, and wanted to make more, if only to make Lizzie's financial future, already secure, impregnable. James guessed that the redoubtable Becky Perkins had already made plans to spend a good portion of whatever profit was made, but she amused him, and he loved to hear the gently told tales of marital woe from the henpecked husband. And then there was Lizzie.

For whatever reason, James still cherished the notion that Jass and Lizzie would wed, and the constancy of their friendship gave him continuing hope. He gave Perkins some good advice, told Thomas to keep an eye on him, and wrote a couple of letters to influential friends.

It worked like a charm. Perkins was offered and bought shares in a new development company, and within three months had doubled his money. Under Thomas's direction he also bought four lots in Tennessee, and within the same period sold them at four times their original cost.

There was no stopping him now. Caution to the winds, and, increasingly against Thomas's advice, he bought land wherever he could find it for sale, only to sell it again, almost always at some profit. It was as if he had suddenly discovered the secret of Midas, and as his reputation for canniness increased, so did his profit, for it was generally reckoned that if he bought land, it was going to double in value overnight, which, in many cases, it did. Speculators, bankers, and simple settlers all rushed to the developments with which Perkins was associated, and it made him, for a time at least, something of a celebrity, and gave him a formidably increased bank account.

The new money provided Mrs. Perkins with the fuel for her most extravagant dreams, which she indulged with increasing ostentation. They owned over eighty slaves on a plantation that needed fewer than half that number. Where she had once been Becky to her friends, she now preferred her given name, Pocahontas, and she began to dress in the Oriental style made popular by Dolley Madison years before, turbaned and overly bejeweled. The dinners she gave were famous for the sumptuous table she served and the troops of attendants she provided, a footman to every chair. She traveled, if only to visit near friends, with a considerable retinue of footmen and lackeys and page boys. This vulgar display of wealth made her unwelcome to some of her less fortunate friends, and an object of derision to the more successful, and so the tolerant Jacksons were called upon at least once a week. William Perkins would sit in the study with James, supposedly seeking more counsel, but actually unburdening himself about his wife's demanding excesses. James, amused and astonished by his protégé's success, gave frequent warnings of prudence, which Perkins accepted miserably, for his success terrified him.

"There is nothing I can do," he said sadly. "They throw the money at me." James knew it was true, for he remembered the panic buying that had attended the sales of the Cypress Land Company, and while Perkins's profits were not quite in that league, they were still very handsome.

Meanwhile, Mrs. Perkins was perpetual shadow to Sally, wallowing in self-pity, weeping of the fool that Fortune had made her with this newfound fortune, and pouring out her grievances with the world. She understood that the new unfriendliness of so many of her neighbors was caused by "the green-eyed god," but it still hurt, and she couldn't pretend she didn't have money. Not when every coup of William's was broadcast in the newspapers, journals, and taverns as they happened. Nor was it her fault that William had been so astute in business, and they so obtuse. No one, it seemed, understood the problems that fame and fortune brought with them, and she had only dear Sally to turn to for advice. Not the least of her difficulties was disciplining the army of nigras she commanded.

Lizzie called at The Forks more frequently than even her parents, and came because she wanted to see Jass.

Her parents' newly increased wealth, and perhaps time, had calmed Lizzie. Still an exemplary Southern belle, she had started to develop a morbid fear that she was going to be left on the shelf. At any social gathering, at any picnic, ball, or levee, Lizzie was, at the beginning of the occasion, the center of attention, but she had begun to see that it was not because anybody actually liked her, but because she wasn't dull. All the most eligible young men would flirt with her, flatter her, and laugh at her jokes at the beginning of the evening, but as if they were passing the time with her until they were able to ascertain which young lady it was that they really wanted to be with or, in the case of the less bold, had summoned up enough Southern courage from Lizzie to approach the actual object of their affections. Even worse, Lizzie could not avoid the conviction that people were laughing at her behind her back—once they had done laughing about her mother.

She dared not voice these fears to her mother, from whom she had learned her patterns of behavior, and anyway, how could you tell your mother what the world thought of her? She could not talk to her father because he would have been hurt, and she had seldom received sensible advice from her father on anything that really mattered, only the dictum "Talk to your mother." If she had friends she trusted, she might have confided in them, but Lizzie looked at her long list of acquaintances and realized that she didn't have any friends she would trust with such confidences.

Instead she took a long, hard look in the mirror, and tried to work out what it was she was doing wrong.

She was pretty, she could see, but so strong was her new fear, she could also see that she wasn't actually much more than pretty, as were most girls of her age. Certainly she was not flowering into any great beauty. Her nose was longer than it should be, her lips were thin, and there was a kind of bland ordinariness to her features. She tried to laugh flippantly at the image in the mirror, but in a moment of remarkable self-appraisal for one who was still quite young, she saw that most of her elaborately cultivated mannerisms simply made her look silly.

Then the most awful truth of all appeared in the mirror. She had always understood, or been taught by her mother, that boredom was a maiden's lot, and so Lizzie had endured her boredom, thinking everyone else was doing the same. Her reflection told her she wasn't bored at all. She was lonely.

A lifetime of that loneliness suddenly yawned in front of her. She considered the potential young men who might alleviate the terrifying prospect, and it dawned on her that her card was seldom filled in after the first three dances, and then only by older men, married men or relatives, who might have been taking pity on her. Toward the end of the evening Lizzie would always find herself sitting on the sidelines with the older women and, heaven forfend, the spinsters.

Perhaps it was this knowledge that she was not the most desirable catch around that made her more determined than ever to catch Jass, but there was something deeper to it. As she became less brittle, she found herself liking Jass more. She no longer bothered about her parents' obvious desire for her to make a good union; she was motivated by something more intensely personal. She wanted to be with Jass because when she was with him, she wasn't lonely.

There was another reason why Lizzie enjoyed going to The Forks of Cypress, and that was James. Lizzie was acutely aware of how ridiculous her mother looked, with her stupid entourage, and couldn't understand why her father didn't put some curb on the extravagance. The mirror told her why. Lizzie had not only subjected herself to the scrutiny of honesty, she had done the same for her parents. Her mother's vanity and desperate need to prove her worth and social standing now struck Lizzie as silly, and her father's subservient acquiescence to whatever her mother demanded seemed pathetic. This created a void in Lizzie's life, for she had a strong need of paternal guidance, and what was lacking for her in her own father she found in James. She would sit with him for hours, reading to him, or chatting, delighting him with scurrilous gossip of the small town that was their world, entertaining him, pampering him, and even gently flirting with him. Free of the constraints of family behavior, she dazzled him, for with him she could be what she had been trained to be all her life, the perfect Southern rose.

James came to adore her, and looked forward to her visits with a special sparkle of excitement that almost no one else could arouse. He became jealous of her time, and especially of any time she spent with Jass, as if the father were rival to the son. At the same time, unaware of the contradiction, he encouraged Jass to see more of Lizzie, convinced of their suitability for one another. Lizzie, James thought, could give Jass the edge that he needed, for beneath her magnolia exterior was a determination of iron.

Sally was suspicious of this new Lizzie at first, believing she was cultivating James in order to cement the idea of a union with Jass, but she could not easily ignore the evident affection that the two developed for each other. Sally was sure her first impressions of Lizzie had not been wrong, but obviously she was making a conscious effort to improve herself, which Sally applauded. She doubted that she and Lizzie would ever be close friends, but she was pleasant company now and, given the wretched excesses of her mother's behavior, deserved ten out of ten for effort, at least. Sally disliked cattiness in other women, and controlled any small tendency to it in herself, but occasionally she would give vent to a tinge of what she called "womanly smugness."

Perhaps Lizzie has realized she isn't such a catch after all, Sally thought, and has decided the rest of us are tolerable company.

Jass, on the other hand, was becoming more and more of a catch, "a strapping young man" was the way Aunt Letitia described him, and no one was more aware of this than Easter.

She adored him. She wanted to be with him for ever and ever, and it distressed her that she was seeing him less and less. He still came to the weaving house almost every day, but she thought it was from habit rather than from any real desire to be with her, because the familiarity that had once come naturally to both of them they now had to strive for. It wasn't easy anymore. He still sat in the old rocking chair at the end of the day, and puffed on the cob pipe, and talked about the world, but he avoided any physical closeness, and because there was this unspoken barrier between them, a limitation had developed in the way they talked to each other. Often he was silent for long periods of time, while Easter worked, and if she asked him what was wrong, he'd shrug and say nothing was wrong, or that she would not understand. Easter was convinced she understood only too well. In the old days he would have talked about anything with her, but now he had secrets, if only in one area. He would never talk about his feelings toward Lizzie, and the less he said, the more Easter wanted to know.

That Lizzie was becoming more and more of a fixture in Jass's life was evident to everyone on the plantation. They rode together two or three times a week, laughed and joked together, and Jass delighted in showing her every aspect of the estate. If ever Lizzie expressed boredom with the details of farm life, Jass would laugh and say, quite loudly, that since she would be mistress of a plantation one day, she should learn how they were run. He never said that she would be mistress of *this* plantation, but the current view among the slaves was that it was only a matter of time. Parson Dick confirmed this to Tiara when he told her that at meals she took in the big house, Lizzie sat on ol' Massa's right, and behaved as if she were already mistress.

"They gwine be married one day," Tiara said to Easter when they were sitting outside Tiara's shack one evening. Easter lost her temper, called Tiara an ol' bitch, burst into tears, and ran away to the weaving house. Tiara took it in her stride, nodded sagely, and looked at Cap'n Jack.

"That gal bustin' her heart for summat she cain't ever have," she opined, and from then on all the younger slave girls would giggle and whisper amongst themselves whenever Jass went to the weaving house.

Easter tried to talk about it with Cap'n Jack, but she'd seen little of him that summer; he was always in the big house nursing the ol' Massa. He spent what few hours he could with her, and she asked him about Jass and Lizzie.

Cap'n Jack shrugged. "Ol' Massa want it to be," he said, "but young Massa ain't made his mind up."

He laughed. "Wait till young Massa go Up South to college," he wheezed. "He gonna find girls there put Miss Lizzie in the shade of the ol' oak tree."

Which made Easter more miserable than ever. Cap'n Jack knew this, but didn't try to soften the blow.

"Young Massas gotta try all the food on the table afore they decide what they wants for dinner," he said. "An' mos' times they gwine pick white meat, not dark."

Any dreams Cap'n Jack once had that Jass might sweep Easter up to the big house as his true beloved were now forgotten. It wasn't going to happen. It was still possible that Jass would want to have Easter one day—for a night, or a week, or a while—but that would be all, and given the increasing separation he saw between them, he doubted even that. Nor did he care. There had been too many wasted years of pain and bitterness in his life, and now he just wanted everyone to be happy, or as happy as the circumstances of their lives would permit. That his daughter clearly was not happy distressed him, but there wasn't much he could do about it.

Even the sweet dream of freedom for himself and his people that had once flourished so strongly in his heart now seemed to Cap'n Jack impossible, and certainly not something he would ever see in his lifetime.

"Don't waste yo' life dreamin' on things yo' cain't ever have," he said, stroking his daughter's hair.

40

One sultry morning in August, James felt remark-ably better. The fever had left him, his lungs were clear, and the promise of the sweltering day invigorated him instead of bringing its usual enervation.

He dressed with Cap'n Jack's help, thanked the slave for his loyal attention, and dismissed him for the day. Cap'n Jack was reluctant to leave, but James insisted. "Have some time to yourself; you've seen enough of me," he said with a smile, "and surely I have seen enough of you." Cap'n Jack accepted the joke in good part, and went down to the kitchen, where Julie made him a large plate of sausage, gravy, and grits.

James breakfasted with Sally and Jass in a buoyant mood that thrilled Sally and cheered Jass. The Trio were staying with friends near Charleston for a seaside summer, which Jass might have enjoyed, but he had chosen to study instead. Fewer relations were visiting this year, if only because the older relations were becoming fewer, or older, and less inclined to travel, and the younger had other, newer relatives to nurture. Father and son talked with a lack of reserve that Jass found unusual but welcome, and joked about Mrs. Perkins's latest extravagance, a little slave boy, jet black and exotically costumed, whose only duty in life was to follow Pocahontas wherever she went with a large ostrich-feather fan.

Breakfast done, Sally and Jass went their separate ways, Sally to spend the day indoors, sorting out last summer's preserves and bottled fruit with Parson Dick, for the cellar was the coolest room in the house, and Jass to a day of riding and swimming.

James sat at the head of the empty table, and nodded to Parson Dick that Polly could clear things away.

James seemed lost in thought, and Parson Dick lingered, in case he was not fully recovered from his illness, or to see if anything was needed.

After a few moments, Parson Dick coughed gently, to let his Massa know he was still there. James looked at him, as if surprised he was not alone. "Thank you, Parson Dick," he said. Now Parson Dick was surprised. It was not a dismissal.

"Sir?" he said.

"Thank you," James said again, and left the room.

Parson Dick was puzzled, convinced that something was amiss. He told himself it was not his place to interfere and went off to a day of inventory with Sally.

*

James went upstairs and changed into his riding clothes. It was so nice to be alone. Much as he loved Sally, much as he depended on Cap'n Jack, much as he needed someone when he was ill, the lack of any moments of solitude irritated him. He couldn't even fart in private, he told himself, and dressed in his riding clothes, he went downstairs and out of the house.

"Saddle Glencoe," he told Murdoch.

Murdoch was surprised and reluctant. The horse had only recently arrived, was still settling in; it was unwise to disturb such a fine specimen. He presented the list of excuses, and James listened abstractedly. What Murdoch did not say was that he didn't trust James to ride Glencoe. He wasn't a good enough rider.

Suddenly James, bored with procrastination, turned on Murdoch.

"I am the Master here!" he roared in what seemed like fury but was actually only an urgent communication of a desperate need.

Murdoch saw no point in arguing if the man was in such a foul mood. He was the Master. He paid Murdoch's wages. He'd paid a small fortune for the horse. He had a right to ride it if he wanted to. He could do anything with it if he wanted to. He could kill it if he wanted to.

Any damage done to the horse would only be small and would mend, Murdoch prayed fervently, saddling Glencoe himself.

It felt wonderful to be astride this, his most famous possession. James trotted Glencoe around the yard, knowing that every man present was watching him, even Monkey Jack, who had once been one of the greatest jockeys in America and the first to put Glencoe through his paces. James was riding him now.

I am the Master, he thought again. This is my horse. He will do as I bid.

He spurred the horse to a canter and headed for the

track. Murdoch watched in aggravation, but kept his silence.

James could feel the gathering power of his mount and urged him to a gallop. Hard and fast he rode, and it should have been wonderful, but James felt only an increasing frustration. It was not enough. He had to know more. He had to know what it was like to take the animal to its fullest potential. He had to know what it felt like to be true master of the most famous horse in the world.

He saw the low fence ahead that separated the track from the drive, and he remembered Jass taking that fence every day on his return from school. He told himself that if his son could do it, he could to it.

He headed straight for the fence. Murdoch closed his eyes. Monkey Jack watched in silence, not sure if he wanted his Massa to fail, which might hurt the horse, or succeed, because then he might not stop and the horse might be hurt more.

James and Glencoe cleared the fence easily, exquisitely, elegantly, the horse landing surefooted on the other side.

They had momentum now. Their blood was up, and they could not stop there, nor did either of them, man or beast, have any desire to do so.

Murdoch was furious. "Tell Miss Sally," he ordered Ephraim. "And Cap'n Jack."

Ephraim took off running for the big house. Murdoch went to saddle another horse, to go looking for his endangered charge.

Sally, in the cellar with Parson Dick, had no idea of the commotion at the stables.

Pattie, changing sheets in Jass's room, glanced out of the window and saw them, and was surprised, for she knew the ol' Massa was only up from his sickbed today.

"Wouldn't let my pappy do it," she said to no one, and went about her duties.

James knew it was wrong, knew he was breaking every rule in regard to the treatment of his precious horses—he'd written most of them himself—and he didn't care; it only added to the rollicking joy he felt. Free from the constraints of caution and prudence, they were racing now not against any mortal competitor but against the relentless passage of time. The weight of responsibility had fallen from James's shoulders and taken years from him, so that he felt like a boy again, errant and naughty and young.

"I can do anything," he called to no one as they galloped down the lane, and knew there was one more thing he needed. Before, he had simply wanted to do something wild, something that would give him a joy in living again, but now he had a purpose.

He slowed the horse to a canter, looked about, then directed the horse off the lane and into the fields of the plantation.

It was not a fence, although it fenced in a large paddock that was being allowed to lie fallow; it was a hedgerow, unattended over the years, and now rambling and unruly and more than a tall man high.

James kept his distance from it, looking at it, considering it, and Glencoe snorted and stamped and pawed the ground, as if in anticipation of some real adventure.

James knew the jump was too high, and he didn't care. He knew he could harm the animal, and he didn't care. He knew he could hurt, or even kill, himself, and he didn't care, for he was not of this time and place. He was on an Olympian plain with only this Promethean creature and a formidable challenge, and the bridge between the horse and the challenge was himself.

"We can do it," he said to the horse, knowing the horse already knew, sweating, steaming, nostrils flaring, urgently restless, as if after a lifetime of controlled and perfect discipline this moment of triumphant freedom was unbearably precious to him.

"I can do it," said James. He kicked the horse on. The

sound of thunder rang in his ears, as the horse pounded to the challenge.

"I can do it!" James cried as the horse left the ground and soared over the hedge. Flying now, flying on a great streak of lightning, riding now, riding on any rainbow and arching to the ground.

"I can do anything!" James yelled at heaven, as the horse landed flawlessly on the other side.

They looked a dejected pair as they walked up the great drive home, but it was only exhaustion. They were partners, James and Glencoe, in a conspiracy of freedom. Stable hands came running to them to take charge, but James stayed mounted and walked the animal up the little hill to the house.

They were all there, as he knew they would be, Sally and Cap'n Jack, the house slaves and Parson Dick. Even Mitchell the overseer. What did he have to do with it all? And Murdoch, who had lost the trail and had returned here.

"Time to face the music," he whispered to Glencoe as he slid to the ground and allowed Ephraim to lead the animal away.

He was tired, he wanted to go to bed, and he wondered why there had to be a fuss. Murdoch spoke first, as was proper.

"That was very wrong, sir," he said. "Happily the animal is not harmed, but I could not continue to serve you if it happened again."

James took the lecture in good part. "It's all right, Murdoch. It was very wrong, and it will not happen again," he promised. "I am sorry. Perhaps you should see to Glencoe."

Murdoch accepted the apology, but with bad grace, and stomped away. James determined to go to him later and try to make him understand, but he couldn't do it now, he was so very, very tired.

Sally started to speak, but James interrupted her,

385

because suddenly something of desperate urgency needed to be done.

"Fetch my son," he said.

He fell to the ground. Sally cried out and ran to him, but Cap'n Jack got to him first, gathered him up in his arms, and took him into the house.

Sally led them into the sitting room, and Cap'n Jack laid his Massa on a sofa, loosened his collar, and told Parson Dick, who had followed them, to bring water.

James was ashen gray, his breathing shallow. Sally was terrified, for she had seen death often enough to know the shadow was passing over her husband. "Send someone for Hargreaves," she ordered Cap'n Jack, praying that help might arrive in time. Mitchell, hovering in the door-way, unsure of his place, hurried away to fetch the doctor.

Cap'n Jack felt James clutching at his hand. "Jass," James whispered. "Get Jass."

Sally nodded to Cap'n Jack, but James would not let go of his hand, for perhaps Jass would not come in time. He had to make them see, he had to make them understand, there was something Jass had to know, and it mattered to him more than anything in all the world, even more, at that moment, than his life.

"Jass," he said again. "Tell him—"

He couldn't finish. Why was it so hard to say? It was so simple, he'd known it for years. Why was it so difficult for him now?

"There is God," he gasped, but Sally stroked his brow.

"Hush, my dear," she said. "We all believe in God. Rest—"

"No!" James managed to cry, for that wasn't it. "There is God—"

How could he make them understand? He saw Cap'n Jack's hand clasped in his own, the black on white, and thought that might be a way. There was so little time. He held the slave's hand close to his wife's face.

386

"There is God," he managed to whisper, and fell back against the headrest. Cap'n Jack leaned in close. James whispered something more. Cap'n Jack thought he heard the word "everyone," but wasn't sure. He leaned closer again.

James was smiling at him. The smile never left his face, but Cap'n Jack knew that his soul had left his body. He was there and then he was not there, and Cap'n Jack would never be able to pinpoint the moment of departure with any accuracy.

He looked at Sally, and told her what she already knew.

"He gone, Missus," he said.

Sally closed her eyes. She wanted to grab hold of her husband and drag him back from wherever it was that he had gone, but she knew he wouldn't come. She wanted to cry out, to make him hear her, wherever he was, and come back to her from that awful place, but she knew he would not hear her.

She didn't cry out; she whispered an order to the slave instead:

"Fetch the Master."

41

Jass swam easily in the flowing stream. Although it had been a warm summer, the creek water was still cool and refreshing, caressing his naked body as ice calms a burn, the gentle pressure of the current soothing his muscles, tense from a hard ride on Morgan.

The unspeakable happened, not from any immediate sexual need but the continuous pressure of the surrounding element. Jass was aware of it and indulged the sensation, swimming harder now, and recognizing the need that was being signaled that had to be filled.

For Jass was determined to lose his virginity before

he went to college, which left him a year to achieve his ambition. All his classmates had told him, truthfully or otherwise, that they had taken the final step into the world of manhood, and laughed at Jass for his lack of initiative. Then he had received a vibrant letter from Wesley in Texas. The western adventure had proved to be everything that Wesley had wanted. He had joined Sam Houston's army, had fought in battles for the new republic, and was living the life of a young man's dreams. Following the model of his hero, Houston, he had abandoned European comforts and had taken two Comanche women in polygamous marriage. He had been made blood brother into their tribe, was learning the skills of a warrior, and had even scalped a man, a Mexican, in some small skirmish. But reading between the lines, Jass could tell that Wesley had no sense of permanent obligation to either woman but would abandon them if he was bored, or if some new horizon beckoned. Home was the prairie, their house a teepee, and he sang the glory of wild Texas. He had adopted the Lone Star Republic as his new country, and almost seemed to regret the political bartering that would eventually incorporate his new nation into his old. Now it is a challenge to any true man, he wrote. If it becomes part of the United States, those petty fellows from Washington will turn it into something as dull as the rest of the world.

The letter made Jass envious. Compared to the swashbuckling Wesley, he felt himself to be a callow, inexperienced boy who had not yet even been brave enough to take a woman, while Wesley had already savored all the delights that virile masculinity had to offer. He stopped swimming, climbed onto a flat rock, and stretched out to bask in the warmth of the sun and consider the possibilities.

Lizzie was not any part of the solution. He liked Lizzie very much, he wanted her in his life, and what he felt for her was something he wanted in his life, too.

He didn't think it was love—he still didn't know what love was, or thought he didn't—but it was something positive, and he imagined that he and Lizzie would always be friends. He didn't have a lot of carnal thoughts about Lizzie, a few but not many, and when he did it was only to get his own back on her for a silly tiff they'd had, or because she would sometimes edge her way into his nocturnal dreams and there were few other white women he wanted to dream about.

Lizzie was a white woman of a certain class, a possible, potential bride, and, Jass imagined, a virgin, and he would no more have attempted to seduce any such woman than fly to the moon.

He had heard stories of a few white women of easy virtue who lived in Decatur, but they expected payment for their services, and Jass didn't want his first experience to be with someone like that.

This narrowed the field to nigras, which expanded the potential co-celebrants of his initiation to a remarkable number. Almost any black woman he chose to have was available to him, any of his own slave women, any of his friends' slave women, or any slave women owned by strangers. In the two latter cases, the actual owner might cause a fuss, but if he asked that owner first, it was probable the permission would be granted. As to his own slaves, his power over them was such that he had only to snap his fingers and they had no choice but to lie down and open their legs to him. They could holler and protest for all they were worth, and it would do no good. He was their Massa, and as such had the right to dispose of them as he wished, and no court in the land would say otherwise.

Wesley had done it like that, although the girl had neither hollered nor protested, but had giggled along with it. Or so Wesley had said. Most of the others in his class claimed a similar experience, with varying degrees of willingness and submission among their conquests, and only Adam, two months Jass's senior, boasted, with considerable relish, of whipping and raping a slave girl to achieve his end.

Jass didn't want it to be like that either. Jass wanted his first time to be an event of some moment in his life, not a quick shaft in a barn with an illiterate field girl, giggling or otherwise. He wanted a girl he could talk to, easily, seriously, intimately, or laugh with, and already he knew who she was. His problem was that he didn't know how to extend their relationship beyond simple friendship.

Because Jass wanted Easter. Perhaps he'd always wanted her, even before he knew what wanting her was, and he certainly wanted her that day he told her she could go to the wedding. God, he could have done it to her right then and there, rolling on the ground covered in those stupid wet sheets, and she wanted him, he knew it, he could tell from the look of her, the feel of her, the way her legs parted slightly as she felt his hardness pressing against her—

He rolled off the rock into the stream, in case anyone was watching him, although he guessed he was alone at this tranquil bend in the river, his secret spot.

It was always the same when he thought of Easter— he got hard in a second—and when he was near her it was worse—the sight of her, the touch of her, the very musk of her excited him to a point of inner turmoil that he had no idea how to express, and so it was easier not to be near her.

They knew each other too well, he decided. They'd shared a lifetime of growing up together, but their relationship did not include the intimacy and importance he gave to the act of copulation, and he was concerned that any suggestion of it by him would make her think he was taking advantage of his authority over her. So he avoided Easter and found excuses for not being with her, when actually she was the person he wanted to be with all the time, more than anyone else in the world.

Nor could he discuss it with Cap'n Jack, because he couldn't imagine going to a man, even a slave, and saying, excuse me, but I want to do your daughter, which is what it boiled down to, no matter how nicely expressed. It wasn't the same as asking a father for his daughter's hand in marriage—he couldn't marry Easter, there was no future in any kind of relationship with her, even a physical one, but, oh, how he wanted her.

Lolling in the shallow water, he had no answer to the problem, which had been tormenting him for months, and he pushed himself toward the deeper water, to swim to the shore, in the hope that the exercise would clear his mind.

And he saw Easter sitting on the bank he was heading for, watching him. His clothes were beside her, in a neat pile, where he had left them.

He stopped swimming and stood waist deep in the water. With any other slave, male or female, he would have had no embarrassment. It didn't matter if a slave saw the Massa naked; he was still the Massa, clothed or unclothed, and inhibitions of prudery were reserved for people who did matter, people of one's own kind. Easter was different. Easter mattered to Jass.

"What are you doing?" he demanded.

Easter shrugged. "Watchin' you," she said. "Ain't no law agin it."

"There is because I say so. Now clear off," he ordered, more sharply than usual because she had been on his mind.

Easter had decided on her own course of action. She sorely missed Jass's company and had come to see him now if only to be near him for a while, to tease him, to pretend it was still like it once was between them.

"Coz you nekkid? Bet you'd let Miss Lizzie see you nekkid," she giggled.

Jass was slightly shocked. "Don't talk about Miss Perkins that way," he began, and Easter interrupted him.

"It's Miss Perkins this an' Miss Perkins that all the time these days," Easter said. "What happened to plain ol' Miss Lizzie?"

Jass was trying hard not to smile, for he had realized something obvious, something he should have understood before. Easter was jealous of Lizzie. "You wouldn't understand—"

Easter interrupted him again. "Oh, I unnerstan'," she said. "You got the fever fo' Miss Lizzie, an' never come se yo' po' Easter no mo'."

Jass wanted to giggle. It was going to be all right. This mild expression of both jealousy and lust by Easter had made it all right. It would be easy between them now.

Still, he had to play the game, to see where it would lead. "That's foul talk," he said, not meaning it, for it excited him to talk this way with Easter.

Easter knew it was all right too, that they could be friends again now; she knew it from the tone of his voice, and the look in his eye. She loved playing games with Jass.

She grabbed his clothes, and threw them farther up the bank.

"Yo' c'n just cool off in that water a l'il whiles longer," she giggled.

"You bring my clothes back this minute," he demanded, but the sense of fun in his voice gave him away, and Easter only laughed with him.

Jass began advancing, very slowly, out of the water, inch by inch revealing slightly more and more of his nakedness.

"I'll whip your hide," he called, grinning at her. "Wouldn't be the first time," Easter grinned back, making it clear she was ready to enjoy the experience.

It was now or never, Jass thought. One more step would reveal to Easter what Wesley called the family jewels, and Jass was ready to take that step when he heard a horse galloping toward them.

392

Easter heard it too, and turned in surprise. She saw the rider first, and turned back to Jass.

"It my Pappy," she said.

Cap'n Jack rode up to them and dismounted. He spoke sharply to his daugher, and she thought he was angry, but it was only because of the urgency and privacy of his business.

"Git yo' tail outa here," he ordered Easter.

She hesitated, a fraction too long, wondering why he was cross. She couldn't imagine he was bothered that she was here with the naked Jass. Her delay annoyed Cap'n Jack, and he smacked her, hard, on the rear.

"Do as I tell," he roared. It shocked Easter—he hadn't raised his hand to her in years—and she ran away quickly, slightly scared of him.

"What's the matter, Cap'n Jack?" Jass asked with as much surprise. Cap'n Jack did not immediately reply. He looked around, saw Jass's clothes and picked them up, brought them to the water's edge.

"Get dressed, Massa," he said.

In that single, simple word, Jass knew what the matter was. Cap'n Jack always called him "Massa Jass" or, to other people, "young Massa." The use of the word "Massa" could mean only one thing.

Cold and lonely emotions that he had never experienced flooded Jass, of which the most stringent was fear—for himself and of his new responsibilities. He hardly remembered getting dressed, but did remember that his clothes felt as if they belonged to some other, younger man. Cap'n Jack had turned his back while Jass dressed. He'd seen the boy naked many times, but Jass was not a boy anymore. He was in a position of ultimate and absolute authority over Cap'n Jack now, and his new role deserved this much respect. He sensed the cessation of movement from Jass and turned to him.

"Yo' Pappy dead, suh," he said. "Yo' the Massa now."

Jass stood stock-still, almost at attention, drawing on

resources he didn't know he had. There was so much to do, and he was the authority for it all to be done.

"I sorry to be the one to tell yo'," Cap'n Jack said.

Jass blinked, and looked away to the river. What should he do first? he wondered.

"Thank you, Cap'n Jack," he said. "I'm glad it was you."

Still he stared at the river. The sense of an awful loss and a found burden was starting inside him.

Cap'n Jack watched him carefully, sure that Jass would behave well but still careful, in case his estimation was wrong.

For just a moment, that surging sense of loss absolutely overwhelmed Jass. He wanted to cry, and knew he could not. He clenched his fists till the nails broke the skin of his palms, and bit his lip, hard, and fought the tears furiously.

Somewhere deep inside Cap'n Jack another emotion raged just as furiously, for just as small a time. This boy owns me, he thought. I am a man, and this child owns me. For that brief moment, the bitter nail of bondage pierced clean through Cap'n Jack's heart. As immediately, the wound was healed by other considerations. I could have been free, his mind said. I chose this path, and I will see it to its end.

As immediately, he knew that Jass had regained control of himself.

"Best see to yo' mammy now, Massa," he said.

Jass turned to him, not a boy anymore, nodded, and moved to his horse.

Slaves had carried the body of James to the Massa's bedroom. Sally sat beside the bed, her eyes closed, rocking gently, keening silently, waiting to give full vent to her grief until she had done what she had to do.

She was lost in a sea of silent grief and only a few specific sounds gave her any sense of direction, of finding a way toward tomorrow. She could hear Angel weeping softly just outside the door, and wondered why a slave should weep the death of a man who owned her. Through the open window, she could hear the sound of slaves in their quarters singing a spiritual, and that she understood. It was not an expression of their grief, but a calming of their fear, for they were in new and frightening territories, they had a new Massa, and things might be different now, and not necessarily for the better.

She heard the sound of horses in the drive, and then footsteps on the gravel, then the veranda and then the hall, and she knew what they meant. She let go of her husband's hand, moved to the window, and stared out at nothing.

When Jass came into the room, he knew what he would see, but wanted to delay it for just one more tiny moment. He looked at his mother, and she looked at the bed. Do it, her eyes pleaded, get it done, and then I can be alone.

Jass went and sat beside his father. Sally had no desire to know what he was thinking, or what kind of good-bye he was saying to the man who had given him life. It was a private thing, between them, just as whatever good-bye she would say to the man she loved was a private thing to her, and need never be known by anyone else. It was not their business.

Jass knew he wanted to say something to his father, but couldn't think what, because this wasn't his father lying there. It wasn't anyone, it was simply a thing. Whatever his father was or had been was somewhere else now, or at least not here. He felt guilty that he didn't feel more involved in some way, and said a little prayer, in the hope that God would forgive him, and that wherever his real father was, he would be at peace.

After a little while, Sally knew that it was time to speak.

"He wanted to tell you something," she said. "I don't know what it was, but it was important to him. I think it was about God."

"I wish I'd been here," Jass said. He got up from the bed and went to his mother.

"I am so very sorry," he whispered.

Sally nodded. A single tear spurted out of her eye, just one, and fell to her cheek, like a little arrow failing to find an unknown target. She shook her head, almost angry with herself, and turned to Jass.

All the myriad things, the fears and hopes and dreams and worries and pride and care that a mother feels for any of her children starting on a bold new journey flooded Sally's heart. He was too young for such an adventure.

The king is dead, long live the king.

"You are the Massa now," she said.

Jass turned away, and then looked back at her, but she had turned away from him. Whatever else they needed to say, whatever else they wanted to discuss, would have to wait. She had done what had to be done; now he had to do what he must. She had anointed him with her tears and ceded her life to him. To his care. To his responsibility. To his whim. Or to his caprice.

"Yes," he said, and left the room.

It was done; she had nothing else to do. She could be alone with her grief. She went and sat besides James, lonelier than she had ever been in all her life, and wept.

They were all there, waiting in the hall for him to come downstairs. They had been there, waiting for this moment, when he arrived at the house, but duty demanded he do his business with his dead father and his living mother first, and they had pretended they were not there, had turned their backs as he strode into the house and walked up the stairs.

Now he was theirs, and they had assembled in a line in perfect pecking order. Mitchell, the overseer, was first. Murdoch, the trainer, was second—not because his was the second-best job, but because he was the second-ranking white. Parson Dick came next, followed by Julie, Angel, who was still crying, and then all the various house slaves. Cap'n Jack, because of his privileged and undefined position, and because he had already done his business, was not in the line but was outside, getting ready to greet the swarms of arrivals—the doctor first, and relatives and undertakers and associates and friends come to pay their respects—who would descend on the house.

They heard the door shut, and all eyes turned to Jass as he came down the stairs, and all approved what they saw. The natural transfer of power that attends to any son when his father dies had already happened. Jass was years older than he had been a few minutes ago.

He came to the head of the line. Mitchell, hat in his hands, spoke first, for all of them.

"We are all very sad by your great loss," he said, and then spoke for himself. "Hit was my pleasure to serve your father, sir, and hit'ld be my pleasure to serve you."

"Thank you, Mitchell," Jass said. He shook the overseer's hand, and moved to Murdoch.

"I am truly sorry, sir, he was a fine man." Murdoch was not lying. He held James in great regard. The events of the morning were all part of the job. "I look forward to serving you, sir."

Jass shook his hand, and moved to Parson Dick. Slaves did not ask to be allowed to continue in their jobs, but the Massa had to be shown the proper respect.

"My sincere condolences, sir." Parson Dick bowed his head slightly, to hide a flash of angry resentment. Like Cap'n Jack, he had known Jass all his life, from puling infant to toddling boy to spotty youth and now this colt had complete ascendancy over him, owned him, lock, stock, and barrel, and could do whatever he wished with him. Because he was white. Jass shook his hand too, which surprised the usually imperturbable

397

Parson Dick, but Massas are Massas, and all are different, and all have their own idiosyncrasies, and Parson Dick knew it was kindly meant.

Jass moved down the line, doing what had to be done, what was expected of him, and inside he was screaming, let me get out of here! Last in the line, a kitchen skivvy, a scrawny girl—he didn't even know her name, Trixie perhaps—was overawed by the solemnity and ceremony, and as Jass moved to her, she screamed, threw her apron over her head, and ran away to hide in the pantry.

It broke the strained formality of the occasion, and made Jass want to giggle. Polly and Pattie ran after Trixie, Julie mumbled apologies, and Angel, listening on the stairs, had another bout of tears. Jass, suffocating, took the opportunity to escape. He turned away and walked quickly out of the house.

He strode across the lawn with no sense of direction; he had to be away from here, away from them all, away, somewhere, anywhere, where he could be alone. And not alone, because what he wanted, what he needed, was the opportunity to be completely himself, without considerations of what he had to do for other people, only the unconfining freedom to do what he knew he must do, for himself.

He knew where he was going, and he started to run. Field slaves, who had come close to the big house to be near the center of an important event in their lives, didn't try to speak to him, to stop him, for somehow they understood the urgency of his need, if not the need itself. A few doffed their hats, but otherwise they left him alone.

He ran with lung-bursting energy to the place where he had to be.

He burst in the door, slammed it behind him, and stood, panting not only from exhaustion, staring at her. Easter had been sitting at the loom, not to weave, but because she was comfortable sitting there, trying to work out what a future might be, if Jass might be different now that he was someone else, now that he had this new dominion over her. As soon as he came in, she knew why he was there, what he wanted, but it was uncharted sea for her, and she wasn't sure what she should say, or if she should say anything.

His eyes told her not to speak. He looks so lonely, Easter thought, so old and young all at once, and she knew, without question or hesitation, where she had to be.

She moved to him and took him into her arms, and he folded into her engulfing embrace, like a child coming home. His mouth found hers, and her lips weren't enough. As if there was no other place it could be, his tongue touched hers and filled her yielding mouth and could find no barrier of resistance. She pushed her groin against his, and could feel that hardness she had felt once before, long ago, and had wanted with all her heart to feel again. Other new and wonderful emotions, sensations, longings, surged through Jass as his mouth moved down to her neck, his hands opened her bodice and her breasts were free to him, his at last that he had only dreamed of, and the reality was sweeter than he could have possibly imagined. He wanted the moment to peak now and to last forever.

He looked down at her breasts and then up into her eyes, and seemed to drown in them, but he knew the sea was deeper yet, and he had no desire to escape his fate. He put his hand to her face, and the contrast in colors shocked him, spurred him, inflamed him. It was what Wesley had promised, the white and the black, all sensual texture and lustrous desire.

He laid her down on the little cot, and lay astride her, kissing her still. His hands caressed her thighs and found their way under her skirt and petticoat by their own volition, it seemed, reaching upward, until suddenly he found the hot, wet warmth of his goal. She had unbuttoned his pants, and now he was free and it felt wonderful, flesh upon flesh, the colors of it dazzling him, flawless white on exquisite black and he wanted to lose himself forever in her sheening body.

Easter bit her lip in pain as he pushed inside her, pain upon pain, and ever more pain, until she might have screamed for him to stop, and then suddenly she exploded and there wasn't any more pain and she felt him hard inside her and she cried out at the wonder of it, rocking with him, meeting the thrust of his hips, until he cried out, and she could feel him pulsing into her and she knew he had given her the sweetest gift it was in his power to give.

When it was done, he stayed inside her for a long time, moving only a little, to make them both more comfortable, side by side, still keeping her in his embrace. Easter was not sure what to do; she didn't want to move, but didn't know if he did, didn't know if it was her place, now that it was done, to give him some indication that he was not under any obligation to stay. She stirred a little, as if to move away, but he increased the pressure of his embrace slightly, and she knew that she had no need to go, and that he had need of her to stay.

Moonlight bathed them, filtering in through the little window. They did not speak, for there was nothing that had to be said. Their faces were so close together she could feel his steady breathing, and she wondered if he was asleep. Then she felt a tiny trickle of moisture on her cheek, and she knew it was from him. She held him still, letting him cry, letting him mourn his dead father and could not know that he wept as much from joy at what he had found as grief for what he had lost.

When she knew he was not crying, she felt an urgent desire to express an emotion, but it was one she had never experienced before, a tender, dulcet emotion that began somewhere in the pit of her heart and drifted out of her as a moaning hum that became a lullaby. It never formed into a song, or any that she knew; there were no words to it, or none that seemed necessary, it was only a sound, the gentle primal sound of a mother lulling the fear of the dark from her child.

His breathing, already even, steadied some more, and he drifted to sleep. Easter stayed awake for a while, lulling him still with the soft song. The tears were still damp on his cheek, and she leaned to him, and kissed them away with her mouth. She settled back, her head resting on his shoulder, and stared at the vague outline of his face that the moonlight gave her, and then dozed for a while. He moved in his sleep, rolled toward her, and she, only half conscious, moved with him, until her back was pressed against him and she was gathered into his slumbering embrace.

Toward dawn he stirred, and caressed her gently, and she woke to the hardness of him against her. She turned to him, and he stroked her and kissed her, sweetly, gently, softly, for a while; then he moved astride her and, without any urgency, went inside her again, to the place that both of them wanted him to be.

42

They became lovers in the purest sense, in that all they had was their love. Their past was both a foundation and an irrelevance, and they had no possibility of a future. All they had was now.

They lived according to the manners and mores of their place and time—he was Massa of a great estate and she his slave. Separately, they went about their separate business. Except by chance, Jass never saw her in his other life, but lived in the bosom of his white family, adjusting to his new status, counseled by friends, besought by his father's associates.

Easter spent her life without him as though nothing had changed between them, although the greatest change was in her. Secure in the knowledge of his love, she lost all sense of jealousy or ambition. She had everything she wanted; now was everything she wanted to be, except for the one thing he could give that might make her life complete. Brought up to a clear knowledge of the reality of her situation, she harbored no ambitions to be mistress of the big house, for it scared her, had no yearning for elaborate gowns or grand functions, or visits to other places, for since her journey to Nashville, these frightened her too. Alone among the slaves at The Forks of Cypress, and any others of her acquaintance, she had no wish to be free—that was the most terrifying prospect of all, because the gain of it might mean the loss of something infinitely more precious to her. Already she knew she could not have some of him, that other him, but that was no more than she had always known. She knew he must be married one day, to a white woman, but so strong was her love that this caused her no concern. She had no desire to keep house for him, or care for him, except in those few hours when he was hers, and then she was content with as much as he was able to give. The only little gift she wanted from him now was the simplest, cheapest, most dear thing it was in his power to bestow: a child, not to bind him to her but to have a part of him, the best of him, so that wherever he might go, even if he should, which she did not for one moment consider, leave her.

They moved in parallel but separate directions, without the desire or ability to acknowledge each other, to each other or to the world. But late in the afternoon, he would come to her, and they would sit for a time, often not talking, he in his old rocking chair, puffing on his pipe, she at her loom, her senses reveling in the nearness of him, the security of him, content with what she had, and when he did talk, listening to his opinions or his problems or, to make her laugh, his gossip, and she would offer advice if she felt able, and smile at his jokes, and nurse his body or his heart if either needed attention. The most precious time of all was the night, when their other worlds were sleeping, and he came to the weaving house. It might have been the smallest hovel of his kingdom, but it was the one place where he could be free of newfound responsibility, the one place where the burden of decision that sometimes he felt inadequate to bear was taken from him, and he could simply be Jass again. So to him it was a castle, and she his triumphant queen.

They told no one, but everyone knew. Cap'n Jack had not slept at the weaving house the night old Massa died, for he knew Jass was there, but had found a disused cabin at the slave quarters and had made it his new home. Easter cleaned and sometimes cooked for him, or Tiara would, but the new domestic arrangements were only occasionally discussed. At night, when the slaves were gathered round the campfire enjoying the few moments when they were their own masters, some of them would rib Cap'n Jack about his daughter and the Massa, but Cap'n Jack only smiled, for everything was coming to pass as it should. Some of the younger men thought it was an insult, the Massa taking advantage of a slave, but their elders shrugged. It was, to most of them, inevitable. Jass and Easter had been inseparable as children, and now, it seemed, would be inseparable as adults, and as Tiara insisted, "it was nat'chrel."

Sally thought it inevitable too, and said nothing. Despite any reservations she had once had about the possibility of this relationship, now she was glad of it. She had seen Jass take a premature leap from heir to Massa, and saw that he was faltering, awed by the immensity of what was now his, and the fact that he was finding some brief hours of careless happiness each day, that he had a friend who expected nothing from him, was sweet to her.

*

403

It was Sally who raised the question of college. They were at dinner, Jass sitting at the head of the table, and the Trio were in a gleeful mood.

"But it isn't possible," Jass said. "There's too much to do here."

Sally, watching him assume a role he was not quite ready for, didn't agree.

"Nonsense," she said. "The plantation is running very smoothly. Mitchell has things well in hand here, and Tom and I can make any major decisions. With your authority, of course."

The Trio were all in favor, and dreamed of the devilment they could get into if Jass were away.

"Of course, it's your decision," said Sally. "But I think it might be good for you. It would give you"—she chose her words carefully—"breathing space."

Jass was silent for a while, and toyed with his food. After the death of James, he had abandoned the idea of college, believing it was his duty to run The Forks of Cypress. But too often he felt overwhelmed by his role. The holdings were so extensive, and so complex, he relied completely on the advice of his mother, and his cousin (brother-in-law?) Tom Kirkman, or the overseer, and he wondered how his father had been able to keep track of it all. Tom seemed to understand all the nooks and crannies, and had suggested that when the prices were right, they reduce some of the unwieldly estate. The plantation in Missouri was up for sale, and Colonel Elliot had offered to buy the stud farm in Nashville. Tom took charge of these negotiations, and often Jass felt as if he were in the way, or unnecessary, but the responsibility for the many lives under his dominion, and the ultimate right of decision, caused him sleepless nights. Sally knew this, and believed that he had the right to the days of youth. A.J. would have been well into his twenties when James died, but Jass was only in his teens. She hoped that college would give him the respite that he needed, allow him time to grow.

404

Jass was thrilled by the idea. He still had a young man's wanderlust, and while New Jersey wasn't quite the same as California, at least it was a journey. He knew a degree was completely unnecessary to his future, but it might give him a sense of achievement. More than everything else, he thought it would be fun.

"And you can take a slave," William said. "To look after you. I'm going to take Ephraim when I go, to look after my horse."

Then he remembered himself. "If that's all right with you, of course." Jass smiled his assent.

"You could take Easter," George giggled. "She'd really look after you."

"Don't be foul." Jass was stern, but amused by them. "Of course I'd take Cap'n Jack."

"But what will Easter do for four years?" asked Alexander. "She'll get awfully lonely."

"I could look after that," said William cheekily, and winked at his brothers, who fell into fits of laughter.

His mother was furious. The relationship between Jass and Easter was never discussed, or even mentioned, in the house. "If you can't control your tongue, you'd better go to your room," she said.

"Sorry, Mamma." William didn't look remotely sorry, and George had the devil in him.

"More to the point," he said, "what will you do about Lizzie?"

Jass looked at Sally. He had no idea what he was going to do about Lizzie, whether he went to college or not.

Lizzie was a major part of Jass's problems, for she had taken James's death hard. He had come to represent the father figure she so sorely needed, and she transferred many of her emotional requirements to Jass, making demands of him that he was incapable of fulfilling. She wanted paternal authority and youthful suitor all in one. She deferred to him in all aspects, but constantly tried to exact decisions of him about her life, which, Jass thought, were not his to make. She was forever offering him unwanted advice about the plantation, and his affairs, and most of all, his perceived position, until Jass could hardly bear to be with her. Then she would change, or her idea of him would, and she would become the coquette, the silly, flirtatious Lizzie of old. And this, compared with the tranquil calm of Easter, was even more infuriating to Jass. Then she might weep, and insist he didn't love her, which confused Jass since love had never been mentioned between them. But long ago he had asked permission to call on her, which was, within their world, something of a commitment, which Jass felt honor-bound to fulfill. He had to consider marriage, for he had to have children. Much as he loved his brothers, The Forks of Cypress was his, and he wanted it to pass to his son, and his son's sons, and if nothing else, he wanted to prove his manhood. To provide a new heir of direct lineage was the simplest thing that he could do, and the most profound, even if he floundered in all other aspects of his authority.

Nor could he think of another white woman who interested him more than Lizzie, for he was most eligible, and he had no shortage of applicants for his hand.

The simple truth was that Jass had very little interest in white women on a sexual basis. The coffee skin of Easter so entranced him, so beguiled him, so excited him that, like Wesley, paler beauty hardly stirred him.

Once you go black, you never go back. Midnight velvet. All the schoolboy jokes about black women danced in his mind. It's true, he thought, it's true. Even now, sitting at dinner with his family, he wanted to be away, to be with Easter, to lose himself in that wondrous body.

He told her afterward. They made love, and lay together in the little shack, and he told her he would be

406

away for four years. The vacation breaks would be too short, and the journey too long, to allow him to travel such a distance home.

"You'll be all right," he said. "You'll be looked after. If there's anything you need, you only have to ask."

She was silent for a long time, and he knew she was crying, although no sound or movement betrayed her. He held her close.

"And then I'll come home," he said later, when he knew she was calm. "And I'll never go away again."

Still she didn't speak.

"It won't be for another few months," he whispered, "but if there's anything you want, anything I can do for you before I go—"

She said something then, but so softly he could hardly hear. But he knew what it was, for she said it often, gently when they caressed, or crying it out when they made love.

She said it again, now.

"I want yo' baby."

Lizzie didn't take the news as well. Expecting an argument, Jass delayed telling her until he had little choice. She stared at him in utter bewilderment.

"Whatever for?"

Jass shrugged. "So I can get my degree."

"What good is that to you?" Lizzie was on the verge of temper. "Do you intend to enter a profession?"

Jass tried laughter, but it didn't work. "Don't be silly," he said. "It's just—"

He wondered why it had become so important to him.

"I need to do something, something of my own. I don't want to ride through my life on my father's coattails."

Lizzie had one of those odd moments of clarity that came to her occasionally, when her world was falling apart and she looked in the mirror.

"That's all very well for you," she said. "But what about me? Four years without you."

Jass laughed again. "You'll be fine. You can go to all your balls and parties and picnics and not have to worry about dragging dull old me along."

Lizzie stared at him in amazement. He doesn't know who he is, she thought, doesn't appreciate his position. He never has. He needs me.

"I'm not interested in parties," she said, and let the tears trickle down her cheeks. "I need you."

Which was the real truth of the matter. Lizzie needed Jass—someone—desperately. And unlike Jass, she didn't have many choices. She played her ace.

"I think it's very unfair," she said. "I had thought your intentions to me were more immediate."

"Oh, Lizzie, I'm still too young to get married," Jass lied. Some of his peers had already announced their engagements.

"Married, perhaps, but if you want me to wait for you for four years, I think you should give me some indication that I wouldn't be wasting my time."

Jass didn't know if he wanted her to wait but saw no harm in it. At this moment his future seemed limitlessly happy. Young and rich, strong and mated, sought by a fairly beautiful woman who would make a fine mistress of the manor, soon he would be free of his pressing responsibilities and was looking forward to four years of carelessness. Already he was becoming a carefree freshman at college, and he saw no harm in making a promise to Lizzie that, in four years' time, he might not necessarily have to keep. Anything could happen in four years, and knowing Lizzie's low threshold of boredom, he imagined she would eventually find another beau, which prospect didn't disturb him, although at this moment, about to set off on his great adventure, he felt as close to Lizzie as he ever had. Or perhaps ever would.

408

Every young man going to college should have a sweetheart waiting for him at home.

He smiled at her, and put his arm around her.

"Hush, now," he said gently. "Don't cry. I promise that if you are true to me while I am gone, you will not be wasting your time."

It sounded pretty good to him, and he believed it at the moment that he said it.

Lizzie believed it too. "Oh, Jass," she said, and closed her eyes.

Her lips were only inches from his, and Jass knew what she wanted, what he should do next, and found himself wanting it too. He kissed her. She yielded to him, but did not open her mouth.

It made Jass angry. She had chided him at Nashville for his chaste, youthful kiss, had told him to learn to do it properly. Well, he had learned. He'd had an extraordinary teacher. For one fierce moment, he pretended it was Easter in his arms, and forced his tongue into Lizzie's mouth. It was good, because she was so surprised, but it wasn't great. There seemed to be limits on how far his tongue could go, certain hard edges. When he kissed Easter, it was completely different, soft and endless, without any sense that there was bone within this flesh, just warm, wet flesh, soft, sweet flesh, forever, without end.

Still, Lizzie was amazed. She had allowed young men to kiss her, and one had poked his tongue, as a sort of dare, quickly between her lips, but she had almost bitten it off and made a considerable fuss. The circumstances were not right to make a fuss with Jass now, nor did she want to, for now he was everything she wanted him to be, her lover and her father and her master.

She was puzzled because she expected to feel some hardness in his groin, pressing against her. All the other girls told her this happened, giggling about the pleasure it could give, and swooning at the prospect of the pain it was supposed to cause. She certainly felt something pressing against her, but it was soft and squashy, and she quite enjoyed it. She was also considerably relieved. She'd heard that once the beast was unleashed, she would have no power to stop it, and it frightened her, for while Lizzie was interested in the potential pleasure, she was terrified of any possible pain.

She backed her hips away from his, and then broke from the kiss.

"Did I do something wrong?" Jass wondered.

"Oh, no," she said, and had to make him understand. "You do know that I love you, don't you?"

It was important that he did. She could not give herself to him, even at some distant date at least four years away, without love.

Even more importantly, she had to know that she was loved in return. So she asked him.

"Do you love me?"

"Yes, of course," Jass said.

And because it didn't sound entirely convincing, even to him, he added something else.

"With all my heart."

And wondered why Easter never asked him that question, and knew it was because she had no need to ask.

His family gathered on the veranda to wave good-bye to him, and Cap'n Jack, although Easter stood in the trees some distance away. He had spent the night with her, but now he had to ignore her, except for a simple wave.

She had not told him she was pregnant.

410

43

Jass did well at college. A serious and capable student, he had no difficulty achieving adequate grades, but since his eventual degree was of little moment to him, and of less value to his station, he studied only as much as was necessary, and spent the rest of his time enjoying the respite that this sojourn away from Alabama allowed him.

The adventure began with the journey. Accompanied by Cap'n Jack, he had traveled through Knoxville and Charleston to Alexandria, so that Jass might visit the nation's capital across the river, and on to Baltimore and Wilmington, before arriving at his destination, the College of New Jersey, situated by a lovely lake, near Princeton Village. Virginia was his first surprise, his first sense of the age and history of his country, the first time he had seen buildings more than fifty years old. Cap'n Jack was his guide as far as Washington, having been there before with his old Massa, but when they ventured farther north it was virgin territory for both of them.

It was in Washington that Jass saw free blacks for the first time in any numbers, and he was puzzled that the sight was not more momentous for him. They were like blacks anywhere, going about their business, ignored for the most part but, it seemed to Jass as they journeyed on, as much reviled and despised as anywhere in the South. Raised to the concept that all Yankees were nigger lovers, he was astonished at the way blacks were treated throughout the North. Mostly they seemed to live in enclaves of their own, worked as domestic servants to wealthy whites or as field hands on farms or as unskilled labor in the few factories he saw. Their poverty was dire, and many were beggars, which would

411

not have been tolerated in the South and certainly was not necessary there, and Jass wondered when they would arrive in the Negro haven that the North was supposed to be. He never found it. Intolerance abounded, there were many taverns and inns that Cap'n Jack could not enter, and when they stayed at travelers' hostels or hotels, Cap'n Jack had to sleep in the nigger quarters out back. Just as it was at home.

Even in New Jersey, which Jass had thought to be a true Yankee state, he discovered that there were still slaves. Under pressure from New York and Pennsylvania, New Jersey had reluctantly legislated for abolition at the turn of the century, but significant concessions had been made to slaveholders, which meant that there would be some slavery in the state for several years to come. At college, Cap'n Jack was domiciled in the scarcely adequate quarters provided for the blacks who attended the wealthy students, and Jass was appalled to discover that the Northerners often dealt with their "free" servants far more wretchedly than the Southerners treated their valuable slaves.

"Boston," George Pritchard, his roommate from Delaware, told him. "They love their blacks in Boston. Only there aren't many there to love. It's the bog Irish who are the problem in Boston."

"I'm Irish," Jass laughed in response, and George, a studious young man, looked at him seriously.

"No," said George, "you are a gentleman. The rest of us are in waiting."

It was true. His father's death and his inheritance had given Jass an authority that set him slightly apart from his fellows, who still lived in expectation of their patrimony. Jass had access to his own money, and, generous as ever, he could be counted on for small loans when other students' finances were tight. Although the day-to-day business of The Forks was handled by Tom Kirkman and Mitchell, Jass was still informed of major decisions that had to be made, and his advice was waited on, and while Jass appreciated the responsibility, from time to time it gave him the feeling that, again in his life, he did not quite fit in. Richer than any of his fraternity, and most of their fathers, he was still a freshman, battling Livy and Xenophon, fogged in by algebra, with Horace and Demosthenes and trigonometry to look forward to. Not yet twenty-one, he wanted the carelessness that his peers enjoyed, and yet a letter written by him could result in fortunes lost or made from the sale or purchase of land, or affect the lives of the many slaves he owned, and he was continually concerned with the price of cotton. He took his duties and responsibilities seriously, and sometimes felt old before his time, and often, oh, he longed to be silly.

But he was also different because he was mature in another area. His relationship with Easter, and the emotional security it provided, took the frivolous edges from him. He missed her, but without any sharp sense of loss because he knew she would be there for him when he returned. He never wrote to her because she couldn't read, but sent occasional bland messages to her in correspondence with his mother.

He wrote to Lizzie, inconsequential letters with formal endearments, and received volumes of gossipy pages in response, filled with trivia about Florence, and The Forks, and the extravagances of her mother. And it was a letter from Lizzie that informed him that some slave, the weaving woman, had miscarried, shortly after Jass's departure. The father, Lizzie insisted, was unknown.

Jass stared out at the night, concerned more for Easter than for himself, for he knew how important the child was to her. He neither knew nor cared if Lizzie was aware of the truth, but correctly guessed that she was not. She made no great issue of the matter; it was two sentences in a page devoted to happenings at The Forks, and she moved immediately to other news. Jass guessed that Cap'n Jack had not known of the preg-

413

nancy—at least he had never mentioned it—and decided not to tell his slave of the miscarriage, but he wrote to his mother, asking her to buy a small present and give it to Easter.

The young men from the Song Club were practicing some little distance away under ivy-covered arches, and the sweet melody lulled Jass, and caused him to think of the power his seed contained, the ability to create life, and the prospect of a child by Easter became dearer to him, perhaps because of the loss.

To compensate for this, he threw himself into student activities, but again, because of his position, the others would often defer to him when decisions had to be made.

He fenced, and rowed on the lake, and joined the Debating Club, where the increasing division between the North and the South was a frequent topic. More than half his fellow students were from the South—the college had a reputation for providing a classical education to young Southern gentlemen—but there were sufficient Northerners, and some of those avowed abolitionists, to provoke lusty arguments. Jass listened attentively to the calls for emancipation, and agreed with many of them, but in his heart he could not reconcile the appalling conditions in which so many blacks lived in the North with the comparatively comfortable conditions that his slaves enjoyed. Someone told him this was an excuse, a way to justify their subjugation, and Jass wondered if this was true, and allowed that it might be. George Pritchard, in particular, both in formal debate and casual conversation, urged Jass to free his slaves, to strike a blow for liberty, to establish the first plantation in the South that paid its labor, but while it was an ideal that Jass had long ago espoused, he would only smile at George, and tell him the time was not yet right.

"The time is now," George insisted. "For I tell you, old man, you cannot survive with slavery."

414

Jass never responded to this, but inside he heard a small voice telling him that they could not survive without slavery.

He wondered why his mind had changed, and knew that he was, to an extent at least, scared of his own position. To try such a bold experiment would bring the wrath of the South on his head, might destroy the plantation that was under his stewardship, might bring about his family's financial and social destruction, and Jass was not brave enough for that.

And tucked away in a tiny corner of his heart was something else. Jass did not really believe that The Forks of Cypress was "his". His father had thought that—the successful maintenance and expansion of the estate had been lifeblood to James—but Jass felt himself more of a caretaker, looking after something that already existed for the benefit of someone yet to come.

His son.

As the months passed, the idea of having a son, a child, an heir, became increasingly important to Jass, who, often, wanted to be rid of the burden that had come to him. Sometimes he yearned to be with Wesley, out there, in the nowhere, with Easter beside him, living in a simple log cabin along a crystal stream, farming a few manageable acres, and letting the rest of the world do what it would. The rest of the world was too complicated.

This new world was fascinating to Cap'n Jack. He did not enjoy most of the aspects of college life. His privileged position at The Forks was taken from him; here he was just a slave, treated by everyone but Jass as inconsequentially as the other slaves and servants. The bunkhouse in which he slept was cramped and uncomfortable, the food provided was barely adequate, and his companion blacks were either servile, in the case of the slaves, or trouble stirrers in the case of the servants. The nights were spent in endless argument,

415

the servants urging the slaves to rebel, to escape, or fight their bondage, and the slaves begging the servants to leave them be or complaining or making plans to run away, which none of them would ever do.

But, oh, the days! The days of Cap'n Jack were magnificent. Since it was believed that none of the slaves could read or write, they were allowed to squat on the floor at the back of the classrooms in case their masters should have need of them. Thus Cap'n Jack, who could read and write, was introduced to worlds he had never known existed.

Helen launched a thousand ships, and made men immortal with a kiss. Achilles killed and died for love of Patroclus. Romulus founded Rome and Cleopatra destroyed Antony for love. Charlemagne conquered Europe and William invaded Britain. Columbus discovered America and Byron found Greece. France deposed a monarch and instituted a terror, while England created an empire and lost America. A multitude of inquiring minds and provocative artists were paraded before him: Homer, Socrates, Plato, Horace, and Cicero; da Vinci, Michelangelo, Rubens, Rembrandt, and Titian; Erasmus, Copernicus, and Galileo.

No one told him of the slaves who populated Greece and Rome and added to their glory. No one told him of the great, lost kingdoms of Africa, except that of Sheba and its queen who beguiled a biblical king.

It was George Pritchard who led the way. "But if Sheba came from Africa," he said to the professor, "was she black?"

The room fell silent. None of the students had ever considered this. The professor had.

"We do not know that the realm of Sheba was actually on the African continent," he said. "More probably, the southern Arabian peninsula—"

George smiled. "Then she was"—he trod carefully "—swarthy at least?"

Cap'n Jack listened intently.

"Swarthy, yes, undoubtedly swarthy, I think that's an admirable word," the professor agreed.

"Brown, that is?" George pushed his point.

"Well, brown, perhaps light brown, like many Semitic peoples. I can't see that it matters." The professor was not happy with the direction.

"No, I don't suppose it matters at all." George was all innocence. "It had simply never occurred to me that Solomon loved a mulatta."

Jass turned slightly pink, and grinned, and there were some sharp hisses of disapproval from other students.

"That's a very abrupt way of putting it," the professor said, "but I think there is a lesson here. The beauty of the Bible is that it exposes us to the complete range of human experience. It tells us how to worship, how to live, how to behave, even, in Leviticus, what to eat. It also tells us, very clearly, what we should not do."

He'd dealt with precocious students before.

"Solomon may very well, as you so coarsely put it, Mr. Pritchard, have loved a mulatta. It is a not uncommon syndrome even today, in certain iniquitous places. The city of New Orleans, I believe, is awash with it. But Solomon broke his covenant with God, and fell from grace."

He looked sternly at his class. "So I urge you young gentlemen to think very carefully before giving way to the lusts of the flesh. Only in Christian marriage with Christian white women will you attain your true potential."

Suddenly he shouted at them.

"All else is base fornication!" he thundered. It had exactly the effect he knew it would. Some cheered, some tittered, and some blushed.

Except Jass, who was, for an instant, transported back years in time, to another place, where a wild Tennessee Preacher had accused him of the same thing.

417

And except Cap'n Jack, who had experienced what he thought was a revelation.

He stayed on the shore that evening while Jass rowed on the lake. He stared at the setting sun, and thought of the mulatta Queen of Sheba, who came from Africa, or someplace very close to it, as his people had come from Africa, and he allowed himself to dream, for a moment, that his ancestors might have served as attendants to the queen who had stolen a great king's heart and worshiped in the temple of Solomon. For the first time in his life, he had a sense of personal history.

His mind raced on, entranced by what he had learned, and fascinated by how much more there could be to learn. He had heard the debates about slavery and believed in his heart that it must end one day. What concerned him was what happened then. He shared Jass's fear that his people of the South might be reduced from slavery to live in circumstances similar to so many in the North, and he knew now that the only possible way to avoid this lay in education. He had to be ready, his people had to be ready, for the glory days of freedom that must surely come.

Unknown to anyone else, Cap'n Jack became the most avid student at the college. He squatted at the back of every class, his books on his knee, partly covered by a little rug, listening intently to every word that was said. He soaked up knowledge. There was much he didn't understand, Greek was beyond him, but he picked up a few words of Latin and French. This actual book learning was of little importance to him; what mattered was the discussion that the books provoked, and he understood that simple reading, in itself, was not enough. It was where the knowledge took your mind that was paramount. Because he had no formal basis of learning, it was not, in any sense, a rounded education, but he became a jackdaw of knowledge, piecing together scraps of informaton until they formed, in his mind at least, a representative whole.

During the breaks, Jass and Cap'n Jack would travel together, to New York once, which frightened both of them a little with its pure, hectic energy, and to Connecticut, where the dazzling colors of fall made both of them gasp in wonder. They went to Delaware and stayed with George's family, where Cap'n Jack was allowed to sleep in the main house, albeit in a little attic room with one of the family's white staff, and was treated as an equal servant. It disturbed Jass, for the Pritchards were a caring family, committed abolitionists, who employed blacks and whites on an equal basis. They did not force their beliefs on Jass, except by example, and the excellent example they set made him feel guilty, for this was the world that Cap'n Jack had envisioned, in the days of Jass's youth, and then Jass had believed it was eventually possible. Since the death of his father, he had come to believe that this utopian ideal was not possible, not in the South at least, perhaps because he thought it might be destructive to what he was supposed to maintain.

To Cap'n Jack it was another revelation. This was the way things should be and could be, the way he had envisioned them without any evidence that they actually existed somewhere, except in that vague, dreaming Up South of freedom that the slaves imagined the North to be. Freedom itself was not enough, he knew that already: Without some basis for advancement, which was contained in that simple word *educashun*, freedom was only a beginning. But, oh, what a glorious start. Now Cap'n Jack fiercely regretted his rashness in refusing his papers of manumission when James had offered them. He understood he had been motivated by his need for revenge on James, but the vengeance had been foul to him, and what he had lost was precious beyond his dreams.

He thought that he might ask Jass for his freedom. No one knew what had happened between the two of them on that fateful day in James's study, except perhaps Sally, but he had refused the offer, and he was sure Sally knew that too. And part of him was wary of raising the matter, because without Easter life was meaningless to him. He could easily tell Jass that the ol' Massa had promised him his freedom, which was true, and Sally would confirm it, but even if Jass accepted it, he would never free Easter—she meant too much to him, and he would be scared of losing her. And he knew Jass had changed. He knew that the responsibilities of his new role had subverted Jass from the Massa Cap'n Jack had tried to train him to be. It was never spoken between them—they seldom spoke of important things anymore—but it was evident in Jass's manner and actions. And in his relationship with George.

Journeying back from Delaware, in George's company, Cap'n Jack allowed a little of his new knowledge to show, by quoting Shakespeare to them. George was intrigued, but Jass, to Cap'n Jack's surprise, was angry.

"For God's sake, where did you learn this?"

"In class, with you, Massa," Cap'n Jack replied.

"Don't ever let anyone know. Forget what you have learned," Jass demanded.

"Where's the harm in it?" George asked, as surprised as Cap'n Jack at Jass's reaction.

"There are those in Alabama who would lynch him for it," Jass replied, and inwardly cursed Cap'n Jack for not keeping whatever it was he knew to himself.

They rode in silence for a while, and then George looked at Jass.

"How can you bear to live with such a system?" he said. And Jass exploded.

"Because it is our system," Jass cried. "You know nothing about us; you have never come to us to see how we manage things. You hear some ghastly stories about wrongs that are done by some to a few slaves, and you indict us all. It isn't like that; it isn't what you think it to be."

He struggled to control his temper, because he liked George.

"Put your own states in order, find jobs for your own blacks, feed your own niggers first, before you tell us what to do."

George was proud of his family and the way they lived. "Some of us have, I think," he said, gently.

It marked the beginning of the end of their friendship. They stayed roommates to the end, and were polite to each other, often more than that, but they avoided serious discussion of the division both knew existed between them.

Both graduated well, and said fond good-byes, and knew they would not see each other again.

The eager youth who had gone to college came back as a man, and the despondent slave who had gone to the North came back as a literate, educated teacher.

Coming home was wonderful. Nothing much seemed to have changed, though a great deal had. Florence was bigger now, although Jass smiled and thought of it as a village compared to the great cities he had seen. The hotel had been destroyed in a fire, and a new and grander one was replacing it. A few folk remembered and waved a greeting as they trotted through the main street. They galloped the final miles home, along a path they had ridden so often, and just as always, Jass brought his horse to a halt when they were in sight of the mansion.

He stared at it for a few moments. The racecourse had fallen into disrepair, since it was no longer used. Jass had no strong interest in racing or breeding, and Tom had realized good money by the sale of the pedigree stock. Murdoch had gone with Glencoe to Colonel Elliot, and Monkey Jack with them. Otherwise everything was as it always had been, the fields white with cotton, the gangs working. The house stood on the hill, the twenty-one graceful columns sparkling white in the afternoon sun. For all Jass appreciated his years away, for all he had grown and matured, he felt like a boy again, looking at home as he always did on his way back from school, knowing he was safe again, knowing he would be loved.

Cap'n Jack was beside him. Things had not been easy between them for the past year. Knowing of Jass's displeasure, Cap'n Jack had become ever more secretive about his learning, and guarded his tongue in conversations with Jass, in case he should offend.

Jass had tried to apologize to Cap'n Jack, but only for his anger, not for what he had said. He knew the slave had continued to learn, and disapproved of it strongly, for the danger it represented to the man who had brought him up, and also to himself, as that slave's Massa. Above all, Jass did not want change.

But now it was different; now they were at the end of their long journey. He turned and smiled at Cap'n Jack.

"Race you," he said. Cap'n Jack was ready.

Both men spurred their horses and galloped home.

44

Sally was pleased with him. His years away had given him the authority she had hoped for, the time to mature, and there was a bonus too. Jass's liberal ideas about slavery had been of considerable concern to her. Sally took the simple view. She had always seen slavery as a necessary institution, and while she cared quite deeply for many of her blacks, it was as illiterate, incapable children who needed the firm guidance that the whites could provide. As with a child, or a pet dog, she could not bear the idea of sending them out, free, into a white man's world, for she believed that few of them had the skills to survive in that world, and she had heard the horror stories from the Northern states, magnified and gaudily colored in the Southern retelling, of poverty and destitution.

"Freedom" seemed ridiculous to her, if it brought with it such deprivation. She had no patience with whites who treated their blacks badly, for she believed, as a devout Christian, that it was the responsibility of the strong to protect the weak. She believed, as devoutly, that since blacks could not be sent back to Africa, the institutions of the South, benevolently discharged, were their best alternative. Abolitionist literature was proscribed in the South, but Sally was an educated woman, and she was able to glean, from discussion and discourse with travelers, and the few Southern sympathizers to the cause whom she met, and with Cap'n Jack, her dear friend, what the arguments for emancipation were, and thought them sentimental.

She talked a great deal with Cap'n Jack, about the North, about abolition, and wondered if she was simply rationalizing, finding justifications for an abhorrent condition, but had found some simple beliefs in her heart. The basic creed of abolition was that all human beings had the right to be free, but were blacks human beings? She did not regard them as animals, but she did not believe they had souls. They were, in her mind, special creatures who, like Lucifer, had fallen from God's grace and were without the sense of personal discipline that might restore them to His favor. Left to their own devices, they were idle and shiftless, children of the jungle, induging animal passions and instincts. Without a firm guiding hand, they could easily destroy the order, the industry, the civilization, that Providence had destined good Christian whites to bring to an unruly world.

The economic arguments against slavery seemed to

her to be the most ridiculous. Abolitionists, Cap'n Jack told her, believed that the South wanted to maintain slavery because it provided an endless supply of cheap labor.

Sally was astonished. Cheap? Slavery was not cheap, at least not at The Forks of Cypress. Parson Dick was easily worth a thousand dollars, if not more, and a good field hand might be five hundred. Then there was the cost of feeding and housing them, of providing medical care, of tending the young and nursing the old. She did some rough calculations in her head and decided that to run the plantation with paid labor might be more economical than with slaves, certainly as far as the household staff was concerned. But then all those slaves would be free, and would bring chaos where there had been order, and the whites would have abandoned their covenant with God. —

She thought she might like to visit the North one day to see for herself. Certainly, the effect on Jass had been salutary. He no longer talked about the possibility of an eventual move away from slavery but seemed instead to have espoused the status quo. Which was all to the good in Sally's mind. For better or worse, they had cast their lot with the South and it had been good to them; they were Southerners, and to question slavery, or any aspect of their glorious civilization, was tantamount to treason from an economic point of view, and heresy from a religious one.

She no longer worried herself unduly about Jass's undiminished fondness for Easter. If he needed an outlet for his passions, for he was a young man in his prime, she was relieved that he had settled on the reliable Easter and had not become a rake, or libertine, indulging himself with any slave woman who was at hand. The relationship was settled and discreet, and while there had been some mild, amused gossip about it "behind the fans" before Jass went away, for it indicated his loss of virginity, now it was no longer of any scandalous value and was seldom if ever referred to, even by the inquisitive chatterbox Becky Perkins. Indeed, it was Sally herself who had raised the matter with Mrs. Perkins one afternoon when they sat on the veranda taking tea, for she wondered how much Lizzie knew.

"Lizzie is an innocent gel," Mrs. Perkins replied, fanning herself vigorously and unnecessarily, for her black boy was waving a larger fan over her head, and in any case it was fall, and there was a chill in the air.

"An innocent gel who understands little of the baser desires that men are prey to," Mrs. Perkins continued, her vowels Anglicized these days in imitation of a visiting English duchess she had met. "And it is better for all concerned that she remain innocent, don't you think?"

Sally thought so and said so. Mrs. Perkins nodded agreement. "We women understand."

She paused for a moment, then raised her fan and spoke behind it.

"And so much better," she whispered, "for their eventual union."

There it was, in a nutshell. Now, above everything, Sally's ambition for Jass was to see him married and with children. She would prefer his bride were someone other than Lizzie, but Lizzie seemed to be the only contender. Jass was charming to the many other young ladies who came to call on him in increasing numbers, but he seemed to have no interest in them as potential partners. If Sally had not known about Easter, she might have worried that Jass had no libido at all or, horror of horrors, that he might end up like young Antony Beaumont, who had disgraced his family when caught by his father in an abomination with a black field hand. Mr. Beaumont had taken a whip to his son and left a pistol in the young man's room, in order for him to do the decent thing, but Antony had behaved like a cad and had run away with the field hand to that

Sodom of the south, New Orleans. The breathless gossip about this had made Sally even more grateful for Easter.

So there was only Lizzie, but even in her case, Jass showed no real desire to extend their relationship beyond the rather complex friendship they enjoyed.

"There's plenty of time," Jass had said, when Sally raised the matter at dinner one evening. "I've only been back a few months."

Neither Sally nor Mrs. Perkins thought there was plenty of time—it had already dragged on quite long enough—and so Sally found herself in the unlikely position of being in alliance with Lizzie's mother to bring about a union that Sally did not entirely relish.

"Time is getting on," Mrs. Perkins said, and she was not referring to the day. "Lizzie has many suitors. If Jass is not careful, some other young man will snap her up."

It wasn't true. Sally knew that. Lizzie had very few gentleman callers and spent as much time as she could with Jass.

"Snap her up!" Mrs. Perkins said again, snapping her fingers and causing several of her attendant slaves to rush to her, to see what she needed.

Lizzie was riding with Jass, but had she been with her mother she would have agreed, for she was pining for Jass to snap her up. The young man whom she was quite fond of had gone away to college and had come back four years later as the husband of her dreams. Partly this was because there was no one else, but mostly it was because he was now a very handsome and mature young man who was still gentle and caring but with an edge to him that Lizzie adored. He never forced his opinions on her, or on anyone, but had a sure authority about him, so that if he disagreed with something, or thought it wrong or improper, she knew immediately what he felt, and wild horses would not

426

drag him from that opinion. Lizzie loved this, for it gave her the freedom to do whatever she wanted, and if she stepped over the line, which she seldom did for she was careful with him, he would firmly, if gently, put her in her place. The only thing he could not be drawn on was the possibility of their marriage.

"There's plenty of time for that," he said, whenever she raised the subject, which, when he first came back from college, was quite often. She had pushed him quite hard at first.

"Why, Jass," she said. "I had thought your intentions toward me to be honorable."

"Oh, they are," he told her. "Entirely honorable."

"Well, surely, you do not expect me to wait for you forever?" Lizzie primped herself a little. "I have so many suitors, and I do not intend to be left on the shelf."

She certainly did not intend to be left on the shelf, but that was where she was heading, she thought. Most of the other young men she might have wed were married now, and the few who weren't showed little interest in her except as a jolly friend (for Lizzie, secure in the hope that Jass would eventually ask for her hand, could be very jolly at parties, when the pressure of snaring Jass was off), but she could not understand why Jass didn't do what she yearned for him to do.

Nor did Jass entirely understand. He wanted to be married and, more important, he wanted to be a father, and if he was going to marry anyone, he guessed it would be Lizzie. In many ways, he thought, his relationship with her paralleled his relationship with Easter. He had grown up with Easter, known her all his life, and the progression from friends to lovers seemed natural to him, without any dividing line, so that somehow they had always been lovers, whether bedding or not, and more important, they had remained tremendous friends. He had not known Lizzie as long, but he had known her as long as he had known any white woman outside his family, and they were friends, even if their friendship was of a different nature from his with Easter. Lizzie made constant demands on him, while Easter made none. He put this down to the differences in their respective stations and personalities, and assumed that one day he would cross a similar line with Lizzie and take her to bed as his wife.

The difference was that he had an urgent desire for Easter and he didn't desire Lizzie.

She is more beautiful than ever, he thought, when he first saw Easter on his return home.

Which she was. Then a girl, now a woman, she had an extraordinary grace and elegance about her, which dazzled Jass.

The girl he had known had been his friend, and when he had taken her, or she had given herself to him, on the night his father died, it had not felt as if he were seducing an acquaintance. He'd had a need, and he went to his friend and she had fulfilled it. Her body had been no secret to him, for he had bathed with her when they were little, and his no secret to her, for there are no secrets between such friends as they. That he had found new depths to their friendship, inside her body, was simply an extension of what they had always had, and what they were always destined to discover. Even the small separation that had existed between them when he had first been dazzled by Lizzie seemed proper, for it had made him appreciate Easter even more. He had no sense of her as "lover," for that had a sense of the temporary to it, and he knew that his love for her was, as with his mother, the most permanent aspect of his universe. She was, to him, home.

This recent separation, of four years, was the great test of this love, and when he had been with her in the weaving house on the first night of his return, he had been a little scared, for he did not know if her feelings to him had changed. And while he could take her as his right, he didn't want that, he wanted it to be as it always had been.

She had been scared of him, too. She had no way of knowing if he had found some other woman while he was away, or if his taste for her had changed, and the loss of her baby had caused a sadness to her soul, which she carried with her as if light had faded from her heart, and made Jass ache to comfort her.

He came into the weaving house and smiled that silly grin, and sat in the rocking chair and puffed on his old cob pipe, and suddenly he wasn't scared of her, or of anything, anymore, for this is how it had always been and always would be and if she had changed a little physically, it was only in the way that he knew he had grown. She was still Easter, only more beautiful now, and he wanted her as much as he had ever wanted anything.

They had sat until dawn, talking some times, silent others, neither wanting the security of the moment to end, and then, without speaking, they had undressed and climbed into the rickety cot. He put his arms around her, looked into her eyes, and those eyes told her what she knew he would never, could never, say. She gave her mouth to him and it was as soft and yielding as ever, limitless as ever, and he mounted her and filled her with his seed, and prayed with all his heart that the seed would take hold, and nourish and grow, and give her the priceless gift that both of them so sorely wanted, even as he knew it was not now, this was not the moment, for no matter how deeply he went into her, she still seemed infinite to him, and there was something just beyond his reach, which he longed, with all his heart, from the very core of his soul, to grasp.

429

45

The slaves were staring at the night sky in awe. Some cried out in fear. Others fell to their knees and prayed.

Tiara began to sing a spiritual, believing that her love of the Lord would save her from the destruction of the world that was so imminent.

Sally stood with the Trio on the veranda and watched in wonder. Sally's rational mind told her there was nothing to worry about, but the superstitious Sally, the religious Sally, was disturbed by this evidence of the majesty of nature. A star shower had fallen on them some years ago, and the river had flooded, devastatingly, soon after. What new catastrophe might this be an omen for? The Trio whooped and hollered and played on Sally's fears. Polly and Pattie hid downstairs, their heads covered by their aprons, weeping. Other house slaves peeped out from windows.

Cap'n Jack was moved in profound ways that related to the knowledge he had acquired at college. He thought this must be how Galileo felt, as he contemplated the heavens. His mind ranged and roamed over centuries of learning, and he felt at one with the classical scholars, as his learning had provoked him to be. He walked with Claudius Ptolemy through the library at Alexandria, imagining the world from God's point of view.

Parson Dick was in his room, gibbering a prayer to a little African totem, eyes wide with terror. He had known it was coming. A few years ago, the stars had fallen from the heavens, thousands of them, scattering over Alabama, but Parson Dick had not been frightened then, for they were only a harbinger of the fateful day that was to come.

It was now.

Jass and Easter stood together in the clearing outside the weaving house, looking at the black heaven.

Some others had joined Tiara in the spiritual, and the lovely choir filled the air around them, counterpointed by the sobs of fear they heard.

A comet blazed through the sky, a bright sliver of light dazzling toward earth.

They had known it was coming, the newspapers had been full of it for days, but no one knew what it presaged. Clergymen thundered the doom it would bring, the vengeance of a wrathful God upon an iniquitous world. Others believed it heralded the second coming of the Lord. Scientists denigrated all this—it was only an astral phenomenon—but few were inclined to believe them.

They stood in awe of it.

"Some people say it means the end of the world," Jass said, and moved closer to Easter.

She knew he didn't believe it, he had told her so, but she knew he was fascinated by the reaction it caused in others, and knew he was entranced by its beauty.

For Easter, it had another meaning.

"An' some folk say it is the star that guided the wise men to Bethlehem," she whispered softly.

Something in her voice made Jass turn to look at her. She looked wonderful in the moonlight, the starlight, her face enthralled, without that mysterious sadness that she had carried with her. He could almost see the comet reflected in her eyes.

"I's gwine have a baby," Easter said.

As soon as Jass heard her, he knew that he had known before she told him, for he had known without knowing the night that it had happened, one night not so very long ago, when he knew that he had reached inside her and touched the outer edges of her soul. He felt a vault of exultation that pitched him to some other place, riding on a comet in the sky perhaps, through the celestial heavens.

431

His silence bothered Easter. "Ain't you got nuttin' to say?" she whispered angrily.

How could he tell her of his bursting heart? The only possible way to express his feelings was in simple, teasing domesticity, as if she had just taken in a stray dog.

"Oh, plenty," he said, and didn't smile. "Another damn mouth to feed."

For an instant, Easter was furious with him, the salt sting of tears in her eyes. She had expected so much more of him, and yet this is how he always was in moments of deep emotion. She longed for the words of love he would never say. She turned away.

"They say it hurts like the devil, you know," she heard him say, and heard the laughter of happiness in his voice. "And you never could stand a lick of pain."

She knew now that it was all right. His love was almost tangible to her.

She turned to him, and he had a grin on his face as wide as any cotton field, and his arms were open in the most welcome invitation she had ever received in her life.

She moved to him, into his strong embrace, and he held her against him and hugged her hard, so hard she thought the tiny thing nestled inside must feel the strength of his arms, and his love, and she wanted to cry out with happiness, and let the sweet tears flow.

Locked in each other's arms, they were one being, the three of them, oblivious of the night and the world, oblivious of some slaves watching them curiously from nearby, and oblivious even of a comet, glistening in the sky.

46

If Jass rode a comet when he heard Easter's news, Cap'n Jack was over the moon. He had only learned of Easter's previous pregnancy and subsequent miscarriage when he returned to The Forks of Cypress, and was devastated for his daughter. And for himself, for he was lonely. He had devoted his life to Easter and had lost a great part of her to Jass, and he missed what he had once had. He was furious with Jass for not telling him; he was sure the Massa had known, and if he hadn't known, he wasn't a good Massa.

"She's my chile," he said to Tiara. "He should a tole me. I had a right to know."

"Massas is Massas," Tiara shrugged.

The new pregnancy gave Cap'n Jack a purpose again, in a life that was otherwise empty. New knowledge blazed inside him, but he had no one to share it with. He could not teach any of the other slaves what he now knew, or even tell them of it, for learning was a dangerous thing to them, and they were scared of it. Few things seemed to infuriate a Massa more than knowledge that a slave could read and write. There were some exceptions to this, such as Cap'n Jack, who had acquired his original ability secretly, before he was bought by Massa James, and a very few Massas actually taught their preferred house niggers some basic skills of arithmetic, the better to keep the household accounts, and the alphabet, to make lists. Generally though slaves could expect a whipping if they mouthed words from a book, or had ability with a pencil.

Despite this, Cap'n Jack decided that the new child would have learning, in preparation for that better day that Cap'n Jack was sure would come. He no longer believed that he, or his generation, would ever be free;

he was not even sure that he wanted it for himself, and Easter was slave to something, and someone, that manumission could never release her from, but the child was different. Cap'n Jack had seen the future at the Pritchard home in Delaware, and he had heard the strident voices of the Northern abolitionists and knew they were prepared to go to extraordinary lengths to achieve their purpose. He believed that freedom must come, someday, somehow, though when and how were unfathomable to him. When it did come, though, he was determined the child would be ready for it.

Sweet Lord, let the chile be free!

Sally was less pleased. That Jass had a slave mistress was one thing. That he would now have a slave child was something else. It happened everywhere; they were called "children of the plantation," a euphemism for bastards got by their white Massa, and you saw them running around, coffee-colored replicas of their sires, who had no real place in either world. Sometimes paternally shunned and despised or, more often, ignored, sometimes taken in by their white families, they still had no expectation of a future other than slavery. Often they were as despised by the black communities. Slaves and black, they were also something else, something apart, something separate and different. Their parentage was also the source of much malicious gossip behind the fan, and Sally did not want her son to be the butt of scurrilous jokes from idle, ill-intentioned busybodies, at least not until Jass was married and had heirs.

Essentially, Sally did not want her first grandchild by Jass to be black.

No one had officially told her of Easter's first pregnancy, but she guessed quickly enough, for she was attuned to the slave grapevine, as far as domestic matters were concerned, and Easter's condition quickly became apparent. Sally had sighed in relief when Easter

434

miscarried, and found herself praying, and hating herself for doing so, that a similar misadventure would occur again.

If it should not, something else had to happen, but she bided her time until the moment seemed right.

On a warm spring day, Sally and Jass went to Florence, and spent several hours with Tom Kirkman in his office. They were doing well. Tom had divested them of most of their holdings in other states, at good prices, and the fortune James had left them was intact. She could tell that Jass was relieved and knew that he had been worried. The relief came from his sense of duty to the estate, and the worry from the fact that now almost everything they owned was invested in cotton. Long ago, Jass had insisted that it was dangerous to be completely reliant on one crop, and he raised that same fear now. Tom handled it beautifully. In many ways, Sally thought, Tom was more like James than ever Jass would be. Yes, the price of cotton was down, but not to a point of any serious concern, and it would rise again. They still owned enormous amounts of land and had considerable sums of money on deposit in several banks. The risk is spread, Tom comforted Jass, when he wondered if banks were safe.

Elizabeth came by at the end of the afternoon, with young Sam and her new boy, John, and Jass happily dandled the little fellow on his knee, while Tom and Sally wrapped up the business matters. Fatherhood is what he needs now, Sally thought, although she was not considering Easter's child as part of that paternity.

They drove home in the open landau, enjoying the pleasant ride. Jass was in exactly the mood that Sally had been waiting for. He had been worried about the meeting with Tom because he fretted about the estate, but had been reassured by the figures he had seen. He had still the smell of infant, the baby boy John, about him, and he seemed abstracted, and talked about John when Sally asked him what he thought of Tom.

Sally let his mind drift for a while and then asked about Lizzie.

"She's fine," he said. "I was with her two days ago."

Having planted the seed, Sally gave it time to take hold, and then moved closer to the heart of it.

"You've known her for a very long time," she said, casually.

"Years," Jass agreed.

"Don't you think it would be fair to her to come to a decision? You can't leave her dangling like this forever."

Jass did not look at his mother. "I know," he said.

"Of course, if you'd rather it was someone else—?" Sally doubted this would be the case. Jass had no interest in any potential bride other than Lizzie.

The landau had turned into the drive of The Forks. Jass stared at the house on the hill, hopefully, Sally thought, imaging Lizzie as mistress of it. She was not exactly thrilled by the idea herself, but mistress there had to be, and if it was to be Lizzie, she would make the best of it. But it had to happen soon.

"It would be such a pity to lose all this." She waved a hand at the estate as she spoke. "And if anything were to happen to you—"

Jass knew she was right, and that he had to take some action, soon.

"Yes, it would," he agreed again. "And Lizzie's the one. It's just—"

"Then what are you waiting for?" Sally saw little point in procrastinating now.

It was a good question. Jass did not know what he was waiting for. He wasn't sure he was waiting for anything. Except, perhaps, some spark of the fire that Easter kindled in him.

"I don't know," he muttered, and found a vague and inadequate response. "Love, I suppose."

"Love can come later, dear," she said, and took his hand, without looking at him. "Duty must come first."

It was what his father had said to him, years ago, on

436

a warm night when they had drunk port together and first discussed the concept of matrimony for Jass. With Lizzie. Perhaps it is destiny, he thought, with no real enthusiasm for his fate.

He got out of the carriage and helped his mother down.

"You go on in," he told her. "I need some exercise."

Sally kissed him lightly on the cheek, and went into the house. Jass strolled to the edge of the lawn and looked out at the newly planted cotton fields. The sun was setting, and the gangs wending home, the work song drifting to him across the balmy evening. He imagined Lizzie walking beside him, her arm in his, a slave nurse following them, toting a baby wrapped in a shawl. To his surprise, the image came easily, and was not disagreeable to him. He turned and saw Easter, some distance away, walking with Tiara.

Easter was full and fat now, and for a moment, and for the first time in his life, the image of her was imperfect. That she was big-bellied with his child was precious to him; he had fussed over her through the early days of her pregnancy, determined she should not miscarry again. As the child had grown and the danger receded, he had worried less but loved the experience more. He had spent hours in the weaving house, sitting close to Easter, his hand on her stomach, a huge grin suffusing his face when he felt the baby move. At night he would lie with her, caressing her fullness, and he had learned how to make love to her with greatest convenience and satisfaction despite her swelling body. He longed to know if it would be a boy or a girl, but as much as he wanted a son, he was realistic enough to appreciate that a girl would present fewer problems. He wanted a son he could present to the world, while any child of Easter's must be hidden from view. It was this thought, coupled with the image of Easter, that brought home to him, with unshakable clarity, the truth of his situation.

437

Waddling along with Tiara, Easter looked to be exactly what she was, a slave who could never be more than his paramour. Much as he loved Easter, much as he desired her, even in this condition, as intensely as he ever had, she could never be mistress of his household, she could never walk beside him, arm in arm on the lawn, in the cool of the evening. Nor could she ever give him what he so dearly needed in a child. He might love the baby of the union, with all his heart, but he could never admit that love to anyone, except perhaps Easter. Ultimately, he realized, he could not admit the love to the child, for then the child might expect more from him than Jass could give.

The proof of his fecundity, in Easter, and the understanding that he had signally failed to do his duty, which was to provide an heir, spurred him in a way that little had done since his father died.

Easter was his to love and cherish for as long as they both should live, and the child was his gift of love. But the days of his youth were over; he had sown his wild oats. Duty must be attended to now.

He went into the house and found his mother.

"I thought we might have a dinner next week," he said, with a briskness that surprised her.

"For the Perkinses."

Lizzie arrived looking lovely. Since it was too far, and too unsafe, to drive home again at night, they would stay over. They came in the afternoon and were shown to the rooms, and met Sally and Jass later, on the veranda, to take tea.

Becky Perkins was agog with anticipation. A formal invitation from Jass could mean only one thing. She had lectured her daughter for days on her proper behavior, had vetted every item in Lizzie's wardrobe, had supervised the packing of the chosen garments, and had lost her temper several times every day with each and every one of her slave retinue, which caused them all to shout at each other. And then her dear, long-suffering husband had actually raised his voice to her. She had taken to bed with a sick headache but got up again an hour later because she realized she had not organized her own wardrobe for the occasion.

Mr. Perkins was used to domestic chaos, but his wife's present hysteria caused his ulcer to go wild. His adventures in the land trade had leveled off, he had made his fortune and now stood in awe of it, and his abiding obsession at present was the maintenance of that fortune, which, to his consternation, proved far more difficult than the making of it. An ill-timed sale of a few acres, resulting in a small loss, sent his stomach haywire, and he lived in the constant fear that he might completely lose his sense of timing, and with it everything he had acquired. He was not particularly excited about the visit to the Jacksons. While he wanted to see his little girl married, young Jackson had kept her on a string for so long that he hardly believed this invitation signified what his wife insisted it did, and he was concerned at the cost to him of a suitable wedding for Lizzie if she did marry into such a station. On top of all this, he would be away from his study, from his ledgers, for two whole days; the price of land could collapse around him, and he would be unable to salvage anything from the wreck. He was so distracted, he shouted at several of his wife's slaves, for the first time, although their very presence infuriated him. The cost of buying them had been a huge outlay, and the cost of maintaining them was the stuff of his nightmares.

"How many damn niggers do you need?" he had yelled at his wife, who had stared at him in astonishment, burst into tears, and gone upstairs to her room.

Throughout it all, Lizzie had been an island of calm in the hurricane of her mother's chaos. The arrival of the invitation had caused her heart to flutter, for she guessed precisely what it implied, and a later note from Sally had effectively confirmed this. Suddenly, all Lizzie's fears and anxieties about being left on the shelf flooded out of her; the years of chase were to yield their prize, and it was a considerable one. She bore her mother's panic with grace and humor, and massaged her father's temper when he despaired of Becky's improvidence. When she was alone in her room, she looked in the mirror for hours at a time, critically examining every fault she could see, ruthlessly demanding much of herself, and sedulously schooling herself not to simper, for she knew it drove Jass mad.

Still, she was not immune to a sense of excitement, but it was a private one, detached from her parents'. She lived through the days tingling with joy, and as their carriage drove up the long drive to the house that would soon be hers, Lizzie experienced a sense of hope for a happy life that she had seldom known before.

Upstairs in her room at The Forks, she took great care about her toilette, and came down to the veranda in a demure dress of palest yellow, offset with little bows of apple green. Sally, she could tell, was pleased, and Jass, when he turned to her, seemed to see her with new eyes.

"Why, Lizzie," he said, "you look absolutely lovely." In a sense, he was seeing Lizzie for the first time, at least in her new role. They had not met since he had written the invitation, and his attitude toward her had changed. Whereas before he had looked on her as a friend, to go riding with, to escort to balls when he had no other young lady on his arm (even though it was a friend with whom he had a curiously intimate relationship), now he had accepted that she was to be his wife and his expectations of her had radically changed. She understood these expectations exactly, was determined to fulfill them, and, if first impressions were anything to go by, succeeded with honors.

They decided not to go riding—the day was too warm and Lizzie's dress unsuitable. They took a turn about the lawn instead, and when Lizzie casually slipped her arm through Jass's, for his protection, he chuckled. It was exactly the picture that had come to his mind ten days ago, and it seemed right and natural. All that was missing was the slave nurse carrying their infant son. Perhaps she was his destiny, after all.

It was about this time that Easter's waters broke, and she yelled to Cap'n Jack to fetch Tiara.

Jass looked at Lizzie. "I have something very important to say to you," he began, but didn't finish.

Lizzie was so excited she almost simpered, but took stern control of herself.

"Yes," she said breathlessly, looking into his eyes.

"Ask you, I mean," Jass continued. "But I should speak to your father first."

"Oh, poor Papa is so distracted by business affairs." Lizzie was anxious for it to be done. "I'm sure there's no need to bother him. He will be content with whatever I decide."

Jass grinned. They both knew, and each knew that the other knew.

"And your mother?"

"Will surely have an attack of the vapors if you don't ask me soon," Lizzie giggled. Suddenly she found she was enjoying herself. And enjoying Jass's company. And even enjoying being Lizzie, which was a novel experience to her these days.

Jass looked about him. The setting was pretty, but not quite what he wanted. If he was going to do this thing, and he was, then he might as well do it properly.

"Not now," he said. "This evening. Before dinner. In the moonlight."

Lizzie laughed again, and pretended, and made sure he knew she was pretending, to the vapors, in imitation of her mother.

"Why, sir," she said. "I hope your intentions are entirely honorable."

Jass was enjoying it as much as she. "Oh, they are," he laughed. "Entirely honorable."

441

In a sense it was done already, and they both relaxed and spent a pleasant hour chatting about inconsequentials, for they could not yet, of course, discuss the future.

Then they parted and went upstairs to dress for dinner.

Jass was angry. His bath had not been poured, nor his clothes set out. He rang for Cap'n Jack, but it was Parson Dick who came to explain and apologize. Cap'n Jack was at the weaving house with Easter, and Oliver, who should have taken over, was sick. Parson Dick had been on his way up to attend to things himself when Jass rang the bell. Jass climbed into his bath, while Parson Dick laid out his clothes.

"You'll be one slave richer tomorrer, Massa," Parson Dick chuckled. "I'm afraid Missy Easter's yelling fit to bring the roof down."

He was puzzled by Jass's response. At first there was silence, while Jass soaped himself and assimilated the news.

It was an extraordinary world, he thought, soaping himself luxuriantly. He was proposing to one woman in a hour or so, while another gave birth to his baby. Easter's timing was, as always, flawless. He started to laugh, and ducked his head under the water.

All Parson Dick heard, in the bedroom, was the laughter, and then a curious gurgling sound.

Easter screamed in pain. "Lordy, Lordy," she cried. "I cain't stand it!"

Tiara was calm, mistress of the weaving house for this little while, a couple of other slave women helping her.

"Yo' gwine yell a whole lot more afore you're done," she said. "It like shittin' a watermelon. It big and it gotta come out. It'd help if you breathed steady."

442

She breathed, long and slow, with Easter, to help her along. "Steady now, steady," she said.

Cap'n Jack had been barred from their presence, but was outside, peering anxiously in through a window. Would the child never come?

Jass was waiting on the veranda when Lizzie came to him. The night was still and fragrant with the scent of wisteria. He looked very handsome in his formal evening clothes, and happy, for his sense of humor had stayed with him.

Lizzie had changed into an evening gown of gentle, rustling blue satin, with a simple rope of freshwater pearls around her neck. It was a clever piece of jewelry, for Jass had given her the pearls a few years ago, casually, for they were of no value, as if he didn't know what else to do with them. They were pretty little things, and Jass was charmed that she wore them now. She stood looking at Jass for a moment, and he at her. If anyone had been watching, they looked to be a perfect couple. And several people were. A couple of guard slaves had stationed themselves under the magnolia tree, to see, at least, and, they hoped, to hear some of the conversation, for all the slaves knew what was going to happen, and someone had to report back to them what the Massa said.

Mrs. Perkins was trying to watch, but was having difficulty finding a suitable vantage point without appearing too obvious. She'd come into the hall with Lizzie, feeding her daughter instructions as they made their way downstairs, but had stayed at the door, trying to get a glimpse of Jass. He was in the wrong position for her to get a good view of him, so she went into the sitting room, and could just see him from that window, but then Sally came in and wanted to talk. She managed to keep a weather eye on the happenings outside for a few seconds, but then Jass and Lizzie walked along the veranda, away from her and out of her sight.

"I guess you know what I'm going to say," Jass began, after some trivial talk of the weather.

Lizzie saw no need to speak, but smiled, demurely.

"We've known each other for so long, you must think I'm an awful slow coach," Jass continued. "But everyone's always said we make such a splendid couple, so why don't we prove them right?"

With exquisite formality and regard for the romance of the situation, he dropped to one knee.

"Will you marry me, Lizzie?" he said.

Lizzie smiled down at him. "I thought you'd never ask—"

And then something odd happened to her. It was so perfect, and such a relief, and held such tremendous promise of future happiness for Lizzie that she started to cry.

She looked away, to regain her composure. Jass had done everything perfectly, and she wanted to let him know how very much she appreciated him, and what he was offering her. Even his delay of the proposal from the adequate afternoon to the romantic evening was in impeccable taste. The only thing that puzzled her was the constant screaming she could hear from some distant place on the property, but no one else seemed to be aware of it. She imagined it was a slave being flogged, but even so she was surprised because she didn't think Jass whipped his female slaves, and certainly it was a woman's pain.

She turned back to Jass, and spoke as seriously as she had ever done in her life until then.

"I'll try to be a good wife, Jass," she said. "And give you fine sons."

He stood up, took her into his arms, and kissed her tenderly. Lizzie gave herself to him, and wanted the moment to last forever, but then there was a discreet cough.

Parson Dick was standing in the main doorway. Of

all the listening ears, he had managed to hear the most, and had goodly gossip for Tiara.

"I'm sorry to intrude, sir," he said. "But dinner is served."

Jass laughed. "Thank you, Parson Dick," he said, and offered Lizzie his arm. She laughed, took the proffered arm, and they walked into the house.

And she heard that screaming again, louder than before, and could not imagine what it was, but hoped that she never experienced a pain that would cause her to scream like that.

47

"One mo' push, a big un," Tiara urged.

Easter had lost all sense of place and time. She was lost in a sea of pain and pushing, and coaxing from the women, as the monstrous giant inside her refused to leave its lair.

"It's nearly there," Tiara insisted again. "Push, c'mon, push!"

Easter pushed with all her might, and felt a slithering between her legs, and the baby plopped out onto the bed. Tiara snatched it up.

"My lordy, it's a sweet l'il girl," she told them all.

Easter sighed, and lay back on the pillow, in relief and exhaustion, glad it was over. She was happier still it was a female baby. Like Jass, she knew a boy child would have had a more difficult life on the plantation. A girl could be more easily hidden from view.

The other women tied and cut the cord, and Tiara cleaned the gunk from the baby's mouth and eyes, and smacked her hard on the bottom.

There was a great, indignant cry from the ugly, scrunched-up moppet who had just been born, but, like

Oliver Twist, if she had known what life had in store for her, she might have yelled even louder.

The women washed the baby, and when her skin was clean, they stared at her in consternation, and then at Tiara, who took command. She wrapped the child in swaddling clothes, and gave her to her mother.

"Purty l'il thing," she said. She looked carefully at Easter.

"An' white as cotton," she added, unwillingly.

At that moment, Easter didn't care; she hardly heard what Tiara had said but wanted the baby in her arms, safe, where she was meant to be. The infant sought her mother's breast, and snuggled there, content. Easter stared at her, and Tiara's words formed meaning in her mind.

It could not be denied. Although it was still impossible to tell what the eventual color of her skin would be, she was the palest child any of them had ever seen delivered from a slave.

A tiny fear shimmered through Easter's heart, not for herself but for the baby. Life was especially hard for those of light skin. She hugged the baby to her, to protect her from life's storms.

"Mebbe she darken up," Tiara comforted, but neither she nor Easter believed it.

"It don't make no never mind," Easter said, a little defiantly. "She beautiful."

"Ain't she jus'," Tiara smiled.

Outside, Cap'n Jack was doing a little hop of glee. He wanted to tell the world, shout at the moon, that he was a gran'pappy. This was his life now, this was his hope for the future, this would be his reason for living. Most of all, he wanted to tell Jass.

Julie, the cook, had done the family proud. They'd had a soup of crawfish, caught in the dam by Ephraim, and a leg of mutton, attended by two roast capons, with

446

new potatoes and sweet potatoes, fresh string beans and baby carrots, all with a thick, delicious gravy.

The table looked elegant, the room warm and imposing. The men wore formal evening clothes, and the ladies were beautifully gowned, although Mrs. Perkins was ostentatiously caparisoned with too much opulent jewelry. Every time Mr. Perkins looked at his wife, he remembered the cost of the gems, and he wondered if Becky would ever stop spending money. He ate little, even though he was not paying for the meal, because of his stomach problems, and because he always ate frugally, as if to counteract the expense of his wife's gargantuan appetite. William and Alexander were away at college in New Jersey, but George still had another year at Reverend Sloss's Academy in Florence, and he had joined them for dinner.

The triumph of the evening was the dessert, which Parson Dick and Polly were serving, an elaborate confection of cake and pink, strawberry-flavored icing, dotted with cherries preserved in brandy. Jass had opened a bottle of French champagne to drink with it.

"To the happy couple," Mr. Perkins said.

Sally and Mrs. Perkins raised their glasses in the toast. Lizzie smiled, and looked radiant.

"It will be the wedding of the year. Of the decade!" Mrs. Perkins gushed. "And not a nigra to be seen!"

Sally laughed. Alfred and Gracie's wedding in Nashville was remembered occasionally, and it still rankled with Becky Perkins.

"Are you still smarting about that?" Sally asked. "It was such fun."

"It was a disgrace to put blacks in such proximity to white women," Mrs. Perkins retorted. "I said no good would come of it. And no good did. Why, wasn't it one of your slaves, that gel who danced with a white man?"

Jass tried to defend Easter.

447

"That was all a silly mistake," he said. "And she didn't actually dance with him."

Lizzie had clear memories of the wedding and its attendant parties, but she only vaguely remembered the incident they were talking about, and the fuss it caused. A blurry image came into her mind of Jass leading some nigra out of the barn. She had a funny name, a very Christian one. Christmas? Easter?

Mr. Perkins was inclined to make a speech.

"Nevertheless," he droned, "we must be constantly on our guard. Miscegenation will be the downfall of the South."

Jass looked at him steadily.

"I've seen plantation children you would swear were white," Mr. Perkins continued. "We all have. How can we know what they really are? And if their blood mixes with ours, we'll all have a touch of the tarbrush soon. Why, in that cesspool, New Orleans—"

Sally thought it was time to change the subject.

"Perhaps we ladies should retire—?" she hinted, and Becky Perkins stood in relief. The subject was hardly a fit one to be discussed in front of ladies.

Lizzie was about to rise when a slave came bursting into the room unannounced. Lizzie was shocked. Really, discipline in this house was very lax. Something would be done about it when she was in charge. She glanced at Sally, who seemed oddly anxious about the arrival, or perhaps it was just the rudeness of it.

Cap'n Jack was breathless and beaming.

"'Scuse me, Massa," he said, "fo' comin' in like this, but a slave chile jus' been born, a sweet l'il girl."

None of the Perkinses could understand the fuss. Slave children were born all the time, and no one rushed into dining rooms to announce it.

None of the Jacksons knew quite what to say, and for a moment there was a thunderous silence. Then George did a terrible thing.

He giggled.

He blushed with embarrassment and stuffed his napkin into his mouth to hide his laughter, and Jass and Sally tried to cover for him.

"That's wonderful news, Cap'n Jack," Jass said. "Give the mother our congratulations," Sally said at the same time.

Cap'n Jack responded to Sally. "I surely will, m'm," he said. "Easter's doin' jus' fine. I so sorry to disturb you." He left the room.

Mrs. Perkins humphed and sat down. Now she understood. Everyone knew that Easter was Jass's *folie d'amour*. Well, most people knew. One person in the room didn't know. She looked at Lizzie.

Everyone looked at Lizzie. And Lizzie stared at Jass.

It was not that the truth came to her in a blinding flash. It was as if small pieces of a puzzle, gathered together over the years, slowly began to form and fit with each other, and make a complete picture.

"Easter?" she said, and Jass held her look.

"She does the weaving," he replied, knowing that Lizzie had to know eventually. Lizzie looked at the assembled party, at her mother, who was doing elaborate things with her dessert, and at her father, who was caressing his complaining stomach and staring at the ceiling. She looked at George, who was trying hard to be serious, but she knew that a grin was twitching at the corner of his mouth. At Sally, who was staring at her plate. None of them would look her in the eye except Jass. Suddenly Lizzie realized that she was the only one who hadn't known.

She couldn't absorb it, but knew it was true. Easter. The name had flitted around the edges of her mind over the years, and she could only just put a face to that name, but when she did, the face allied itself to Jass's. She knew Jass must have been getting "relief", as some women called it, from someone—all men did, apparently—although what he was being relieved of was not exactly clear to her. Mrs. Perkins had instructed her

449

daughter zealously in all matters of society except those pertaining to cohabitation. The little knowledge that Lizzie did have had been garnered from more sophisticated girlfriends. But she knew enough.

Now it was all crystal clear to her. She stared at Jass in horror, and despised him. What hurt her most was that she had found out now, when only a few seconds ago she had been so very happy.

She felt like an abject fool. She almost fainted, and it was a genuine swoon, not the affectation that she used as a social accoutrement. She clutched the table for support.

"Suddenly, I do not feel very well," she said. "The wine—the heat—"

She ran from the room. Mrs. Perkins saw all her plans for a brilliant marriage and a secure future for Lizzie fade to nothing. She hurried after her daughter.

"She gets sick headaches," she told them in unnecessary explanation, and was gone.

Jass and Sally both stood, not knowing quite what to do. George remained sitting, shamefaced.

Mr. Perkins was babbling on about the cost of slaves.

". . . so much cheaper when they are born to the plantation, an endless supply of free labor," he said. "We should give thanks to God. Although the cost of maintaining my wife's entourage—"

Sally nodded to Jass, and left the room. Jass sat down, and offered Mr. Perkins more champagne.

Mr. Perkins declined. "My stomach, y'know. Do you have any port?"

In the weaving house, the lamp was low. Easter was asleep in the bed, and Cap'n Jack was sitting in Jass's rocking chair, by the embers of the fire, rocking the tiny baby on his knee, and singing her a soft lullaby.

Sally came in. Cap'n Jack was pleased to see her, although he regretted it was not Jass.

"Here she is, m'm," he whispered. "A little princess."

450

Sally took the child and held her close. She was incredulous. The babe couldn't be this white. It wasn't possible. What on earth would her life be like?

As the child snuggled into her bosom, Sally's heart was touched by her, and she felt the first stirrings of something she always felt when she held her new grandchildren for the first time, something very close to love.

Lizzie had run to her bedroom and thrown herself on the bed, weeping. She heard her mother come in and sit beside her, but ignored her until the pain was less intense.

"I won't marry him!" she cried, but her words were muffled, her face buried in the pillow. She meant it, though. Lizzie had a very strict morality, and despite a superficial sophistication, a very limited knowledge of the world. Jass was hers; she had no intention of sharing him with another woman, and especially not a nigra.

"I won't, I swear I won't," she cried again.

Mrs. Perkins, who had been waiting for the worst of the storm to pass, was ready for her.

"Oh, yes, you will," she said. Her tone was gentle and crooning, but there was steel behind it.

"You will have a long engagement," Mrs. Perkins continued. "And in time you will become used to the idea—"

"Never!" Lizzie protested into the pillow.

"—and you will be grateful for it!" Mrs. Perkins commanded. She had to make her daughter understand. Perhaps she had been very wrong to shelter Lizzie from certain facts of life, but she had always assumed her daughter would learn these things from other girls. She'd been so determined that Lizzie would become a "lady" that she had even been unable to tell her about a woman's times of the month, but had her slave housekeeper do it. Lizzie had learned things from her peers,

451

but she was so wrapped up in becoming the belle her mother wanted her to be, she paid little attention to it. So the knowledge was piecemeal, like Cap'n Jack's learning, and never formed a consistent whole.

"A woman's lot is not a happy one, and the slave girls are our salvation," she told Lizzie. "If it were not for them, we would have to submit to our husband's brutish desires whenever they felt—healthy—"

It got through to Lizzie. The idea of the monster unleashed appalled her. But not Jass, surely? He was such a gentleman to her. She had not expected that he would be inexperienced on their wedding night, but she had not thought he would have a permanent mistress, and how could he allow the fact of his infidelity to be thrown in her face tonight, of all nights? It was this sense of hurt to herself that was provoking such bitter disappointment. She had a truly terrible thought. She looked up from the pillow.

"Not Papa, surely?" she said in wonder. Not her dear, sweet, tubby, balding Papa?

Melancholy settled on Mrs. Perkins, and she nodded her head.

"All men are the same," she said. "Lecherous brutes."

"Not Papa?" Lizzie said again, and Mrs. Perkins nodded again.

"If it were not for our slave girls, I don't know what I would do," she said sadly. "Your father is a demon when he's aroused."

It wasn't true. Mr. Perkins made very few sexual demands on his wife, far too few in her book, but Lizzie was going through a dangerous crisis, and had to be brought safe to a haven.

"Next summer, you will go to Paris, France, for your trousseau. That will take at least a year." Mrs. Perkins believed that time was the great healer. "And then you will have to visit all your relations—"

Lizzie stared at the ceiling.

*

452

Jass stared at his glass of brandy. Mr. Perkins had retired to bed, and Jass had admonished George, and then laughed with him about the incident, and accepted his brother's congratulations. George had a keen sense of the irony of the situation, and had accepted Jass's invitation to some brandy. George expressed his surprise that Jass was not more worried about Lizzie.

"Oh, she'll come round," Jass said casually. "Her mother will talk sense into her."

"What if she decides she won't marry you?"

Jass had not seriously considered this possibility. He was sorry that Lizzie had found out the way she had, but at least it was out in the open. Jass had no intention of ending his relationship with Easter after his marriage, and so the sooner Lizzie got used to the idea, the better.

"She'll marry me," Jass told George. "I'm too good a catch for her."

George raised his eyebrows. Jass was not normally so cocky.

"Bit full of yourself, aren't you, brother?" he said in surprise.

Jass grinned and winked, and suddenly he was good old Jass again. "Don't you think I have reason to be? I'm a pappy!"

He jumped on his brother, laughing, and the two of them wrestled together on the floor of the study.

Now Jass was alone, in his father's study. My study, he corrected himself. He felt on top of the world, and did something he had never done before. He put his legs on the desk and stretched out, relaxing in the comfortable old chair and staring at his glass of brandy.

He wanted for nothing. He was Massa. He was rich and strong and free and mated. He was about to make an excellent marriage, and he was a father, and would father a dozen sons, and his virility would be envied throughout the South.

Sally came in a little later, and found him still

stretched out, still staring at his brandy, dreaming of the future, a grin on his face.

Jass guessed where she had been.

"Her life will not be easy," Sally said. "She looks as white as you or I."

Jass assimilated this, but did not really understand his mother's concerns. There were pale nigras everywhere, high yellas, mulattas, whatever you called them, and they lived their lives happily or unhappily, according to their circumstances and personalities. He could see no particular problems for his light daughter. She would have an especial place in the slave hierarchy, and live a life of relative comfort, as her mother did. Nor was he disappointed that Easter had given birth to a girl; he was relieved. He thought that he could love a girl-child slave. He doubted he would have the same affection for a nigger boy.

"Does she have a name?" he asked Sally.

"Cap'n Jack calls her Princess."

Jass nodded, and mouthed the word "Princess" a few times. He knew his mother was angry, although he wasn't quite sure why, and was determined to provoke her.

He held up his glass. "Aren't you going to congratulate me?"

Sally glared at him, furious with him. He didn't seem to understand the problems he had created, for the child as much as for the family, didn't appreciate the gossip there would be about it, a cotton-white child running around the plantation with only one likely father. Was he so careless of his position? What was it about men? Why could they not control themselves?

"Oh, you men!" she said angrily. "The havoc that you cause."

She left the room.

Nothing could shake Jass's boundless good humor; indeed, his mother's inexplicable wrath only added to it. She had been stern with him since his father died, all with the best intentions, Jass knew, to help him fit into his new position. But he also felt that she was trying to organize his life, and the idea that he had done something that annoyed her, but something that most Massas did, most men did, was pleasing to him.

Energy filled him. He got up, went to the bookshelves, and took down the leather-bound book that was the Slave Register.

He found a new, clean page, inked his quill pen, and filled in the date of the birth, and the mother's name. Under "Father—If Known" he just put a dash.

The next column was the value of the slave. Jass thought about this. Properly, he should have written $50, if the child was well and healthy, but he didn't want to make her too valuable, because he didn't want anyone else to appreciate her value.

He wrote $5 instead.

He had not filled in her name. He scratched with the quill, and mouthed "Princess" again a few times, but he didn't like it, hadn't liked it when he first heard it, and it got no better with repetition. If not "Princess," then what?

He toyed with some other names, but none of them pleased him. Suddenly he had an idea. He laughed aloud, and wrote something down.

All the world was sleeping, apart from a newborn baby, tucked up snugly in the wooden cradle that Cap'n Jack had carved for her.

And Jass, who had crept softly into the weaving house, and was now staring down at his daughter. Already happy, now he thought his cup brimming over. In the dim light he could hardly see the color of her skin, and if there was a paleness about her, it was only natural to him. She was his daughter. He had made this thing, this tiny, fragile, exquisite thing. He had created it, given it life; it was the seed of his loins.

"Hello, Queen," he said softly.

He picked her up out of the cradle and sat with her in his chair, rocking her gently. The child seemed content in her father's arms.

They sat together for an hour or so, and then Queen decided she was hungry and started to whimper. Easter stirred immediately. The crying of the child caused her milk to move down in her breasts. She saw Jass nursing Queen, and for a moment wished that this was how it might always be, but knew it could not. She knew that Lizzie was visiting, and from the chattering slaves, she knew why.

She moved on the bed, so that Jass would realize she was awake. He looked at her, tenderly.

"Was it bad?" he asked her.

Easter shook her head. "Popped out easy."

"Liar," Jass grinned. "I could hear you all the way up at the big house."

It seemed cruel to tell her now, but she had to know, and surely, at this moment, she must know that he loved her.

"While I was proposing to Lizzie."

He hoped for some indication of her feelings, but she gave none. Queen cried again, and Jass tickled her under the chin, to quiet her.

"She's hungry," Easter said.

Jass brought Queen to Easter, put the child in her mother's arms, and sat on the bed beside them.

"Her name is Queen," he told Easter.

Easter made no comment, but opened her nightgown and put her breast to Queen's mouth. She watched the girl sucking contentedly for a moment, and then said to Jass: "You should have a wife. You need a son."

She had never harbored foolish dreams of any elevation of her status. She knew that she would never be more to Jass than what she was, his slave mistress, while another, white woman ruled in the big house, and she had been slightly surprised at Jass's constancy to her. Still, she loved him, and wanted as much of him

456

as she could have, and tonight had been special to her. She had not wanted to hear of his proposal to Lizzie tonight, and now she wanted to hurt him in some way. Or if not him, then Lizzie, by default. An extraordinary burst of anger and pride and possession swelled through her. She had something that Lizzie could never have. She glared at Jass.

"But I have the best of you," she said, fiercely.

48

She was three years old, and small for her age, a tiny sparrow of a girl, prettily dressed in white muslin, scattering rose petals before her Massa and his bride, Miss Lizzie, as they walked away from the altar. She looked enchanting, and many of the female guests gathered on the lawn at The Forks of Cypress to watch the ceremony wished for a child as demure.

She was shy, and she seldom smiled, but when she did her dark-brown eyes danced with happiness. She didn't smile very often because she didn't have a great deal to smile about. Other slave children teased her about her snow-white skin, and she never saw her pappy, who was away somewhere, miles away, and she was told that he would never come back to her. She loved her mammy very much, and her gran'pappy, who was called Cap'n Jack by everyone else. She loved the house in which she lived, a little shack tucked under some trees, away from the quarters where the other slaves lived. Her mammy worked very hard, weaving cloth for all the slaves on the plantation. Her gran'pappy didn't seem to work very much at all, but spent a lot of time with her, teaching her things about the world, and some funny lines on paper that he called the A B C. She liked it when her Massa came to visit Mammy, because he'd sit her on his knee and tell her funny stories, and a few times he'd given her little presents, and she hugged him and told him she loved him, and would have liked him to visit more often. She wished she could lie in the bed with him, like Mammy did sometimes, and go to sleep in his arms, because she always felt safe and happy when he cuddled her.

She didn't speak to him when she saw him outside the weaving house because he was the Massa and didn't want to be bothered with a little slave girl like her, Mammy said, and told her he would have her whipped if she was a naughty girl, so she kept her distance from him because she didn't want to be beaten.

She would have liked to live in the big house. Her mammy took her to the kitchen of it sometimes, and that one room was bigger than the entire shack she called home. She liked it best there when she saw Miss Sally, who was quite old, and who always gave her candies or little presents, and told her stories. She didn't like it when there were other white people staying there—visitors, Mammy called them—because then she wasn't allowed to go near the big house, not even if there were little boy and girl visitors. She wasn't allowed to play with them because they were white and she was a nigra, but she thought she didn't look like a nigra, she looked just like the white children.

Her name was Queen, and she was very proud of it—she thought it made her special—but her gran'pappy always called her Princess, which puzzled her. She'd never been to a party before, and this one was very special, her mammy had told her, and she had a very important job to do. She was scared when she saw how many people were there, and they were all very grandly dressed, but her gran'pappy said her dress was the prettiest. She'd rather have worn a dress like Miss Lizzie's, which was all frills and flounces in purest white, and she had a little crown on her head, and a long white train, made of the same material, or

458

nearly, as Queen's dress. She'd seen some of the slaves sewing little glittery things on the train, and out here in the garden those glittery things caught the sun and sparkled, and made Miss Lizzie look just like a princess. She didn't like Miss Lizzie very much—she'd only seen her a few times, and she always looked very stern—but today she was smiling a lot, and Queen thought she must be happy.

Queen was happy that day. As she walked along the red carpet, throwing out her rose petals, she heard lots of fine ladies say oooh and aaah, and laugh, and say how lovely she looked, and some of the men even clapped their hands, and no one had ever done that to her before.

She got to the end of the carpet, and didn't know what to do. She saw Miss Sally standing there, dressed in black, looking very frightening; only she wasn't frightening at all, Queen knew that, and she ran to Miss Sally, and threw her arms about her, and asked her if she'd been a good girl.

"You were a very good girl," Sally told her. "Everyone loved you."

Queen laughed. It had been easy really. She waved to her mammy, who was standing with Gran'pappy and some of the other slaves a long way away, watching. She wished her mammy had a nice dress, but she always wore that simple gray linen, and a shawl, and a scarf around her head. She was very beautiful, but you couldn't always tell, because of that ugly dress. Queen had to wear ugly clothes most of the time, but she loved pretty dresses, like the one she was wearing now.

Miss Sally took her hand and asked her if she was hungry, because it was time to eat. Queen nodded, because she was very hungry. She'd been really excited that morning, and had been sick and cried a lot, until her mammy told her she wouldn't be able to go to the wedding if she didn't stop. So she stopped, and went to the wedding, and now she was hungry.

Miss Sally took her to the long tables set out in the garden, where all the food was. There was another woman with them, Miss Lizzie's mammy, who wore a lot of fussy clothes and jewels, and always had a couple of young men slaves near her. Her mammy told her this was Miss Becky, and although Queen had seen her lots of times—she came here often with her daughter—she'd never spoken to her. She was a little bit scared of her. Not really truly scared, just a little bit, and sometimes she thought Miss Becky was funny.

When she saw the long tables covered with food she nearly cried again because she'd never seen so much food in all her life, and it all looked wonderful, and she couldn't decide what she wanted. But Miss Sally fixed a special plate, just for her, and they all went to sit on garden chairs under the shade trees. Parties, Queen decided, were things she wanted a whole lot more of.

Mrs. Perkins thought it was a wonderful party too. More than anything, she was relieved that it had finally happened. Lizzie had held her to her promise, and it had been a long engagement. The trips to London and Paris had been fun, although Becky hadn't enjoyed Charleston very much, a hoity-toity place, she thought, and no one was very impressed with her fabulous new gowns and her entourage of slaves. "The green-eyed god," she said to Lizzie, but Lizzie had only smiled, and sometimes Becky couldn't resist the feeling that her daughter was laughing at her.

She hadn't enjoyed their visits to their relations in Virginia and North Carolina at all. They'd made such a lot of fuss and bother about her retinue, which was so pretty—how did they expect two traveling women to manage without six nigras? Obviously none of them understood the importance of Lizzie's impending union, though she had told them about it incessantly, and she decided that most of her relatives were hicks at heart. Their touring had taken two years, and Becky

460

was glad to come home to Alabama and plan the wedding in earnest. It took them a year to work out all the details, partly because Lizzie was still a little funny about that weaving gel Jass was so fond of, but that seemed to be calming down.

She'd taken charge of every detail of the wedding ceremony and subsequent breakfast herself, and had a devil of a job persuading Mr. Perkins to open up the moneybags to pay for everything she'd ordered. Really, he could be such a tightwad at times, and she never understood why, because they were loaded. She'd expected at least a little moral support from him, but no one, not even William, seemed to appreciate how hard she'd worked to bring this whole thing together. She'd been physically ill the whole of last week and had to drag herself from her sickbed for fittings for the green grosgrain frock she was having made, and even the wretched dressmaker had argued with her, and told her off for putting on weight, and it all got so much she burst into tears, standing there in her bodice and camiknickers, which was very embarrassing.

At last, it was all over. Her work, her life's work perhaps, was done. Lizzie was formally, officially wed, and was mistress of one of the richer estates in the South. Not quite as rich as it once was, Becky surmised, when old James was alive, but still rich enough. Jass seemed to have very little head for business matters, and left most things to Tom Kirkman, who was dear and hardworking but rather dull, with no great flair about him. And William had been a pig about Lizzie's dowry. Finally, it had all come together with scarcely a hitch, and when she saw Lizzie walking down the aisle toward Jass, and the minister joined them in indissoluble union, she felt as if a ton weight had been taken from her shoulders, and wept copiously. From sheer relief.

She sat on a chair near Sally and that dear little girl, and tucked into a plate of fried chicken. She was very

461

tired. Her shoulders sagged, she had a splitting head-ache, and she promised herself a week in bed to recuperate. Sally had been a dear friend throughout it all, and Becky felt she could be herself in her company. Not too much of herself, of course, because so many people were there, and obviously watching them, and envying her. She pulled herself together, and looked about for something to say.

The little girl was eating her food quite daintily. Surprising, for a nigra child; obviously she'd been brought up well. Not surprising, when you considered who her father was.

"I must say, the child has lovely manners," she said to Sally.

Sally was intrigued. Becky seemed to be going flump. She looked old and tired, and some steel seemed to be missing from her spine. Even her vowels were less extended than usual. And it was the first time she had ever mentioned Queen.

"She's a darling," she said, hugging Queen to her. Often, Sally had to stop herself from becoming too fond of Queen. It would be different, she was sure, when Jass and Lizzie had children.

"She'll make a splendid companion for any daughters Lizzie might have," Mrs. Perkins continued, speaking behind her fan. "It's such a sensible arrangement, tho' it's taken Lizzie awhile to get used to the idea."

She looked at Lizzie and Jass, who were surrounded by well-wishers. She's almost human today, Sally thought, as if she were falling apart now that it's all over, coming back down to earth.

Mrs. Perkins sighed. "I don't know what I'd do without our nigra girls. Mr. Perkins—"

She snapped her fan shut, pointed it at her meek, tubby husband, who was worrying about business matters with some associates, then opened the fan and spoke behind it again.

462

"—can be a regular demon, you know." She rolled her eyes a very great deal, to indicate that her husband was a positive Casanova. Sally tried to hide her smile.

The enormous, three-tiered cake was cut, and everyone cheered, and Queen ate three pieces; then she walked hand in hand with Sally as they wandered through the crowd talking to people.

Lizzie had gone to the house to dress for going away, and Mr. Perkins collared Jass for a few words of advice, as was befitting.

"I must say the place is looking splendid, Jass," he said, a little pompously, Jass thought. "Your father would be proud."

Jass was in a good humor, and indulged his new father-in-law.

"We're doing well, I think," said Jass politely. "Not as well as we were, but the price of cotton will pick up."

Mr. Perkins shook his head doubtfully. He didn't trust anything to do with money.

"Putting something away for a rainy day, I hope?" He mopped his brow with his handkerchief. It was a sultry day. There was a storm coming. "There are a few storm clouds out there."

Jass knew he didn't mean the weather. He tried to be casual.

"Nothing serious, surely?"

Everything was serious to Mr. Perkins. He'd lost quite a lot of money on a foolish transaction a few weeks ago, and with the cost of the wedding and Lizzie's dowry, he thought his world was collapsing. Although he was still rich, he was not as rich as he had been.

"The abolitionists are getting quite strident," he fretted. "And this new Republican party may take up their cause."

463

"Well, that's the North." Jass shrugged it aside. "And in any case, the end of slavery wouldn't be the end of the world."

"It would be the end of the South." Mr. Perkins was shocked by the heresy.

"Not if we diversify," Jass said blithely.

Mr. Perkins smiled. He loved winning arguments, and he remembered that Jass used to make a lot of speeches about diversification when he was a young man. Hadn't put one of those ideas into effect, of course.

"I don't see you doing that," he said slyly.

In that instant, Jass could have killed him, because he too remembered his own ideas. And he had tried, but perhaps not hard enough. He often talked to Tom about planting something other than cotton, but neither of them could think what. Cotton was not as profitable as it had once been, but nothing was more profitable than cotton. And the price would surely rise.

Luckily, Tom and Elizabeth joined them at that moment, with Hugh and Sam, who was an owlish and serious young man. Sam was going to Harvard next week, to study medicine, and had come to congratulate Jass and say good-bye. Jass knew Sam was going to college, but was surprised. Was he really old enough? Had so many years gone by?

When the time came for Jass and Lizzie to leave, they climbed into the carriage, and all the guests gathered round to say good-bye. They cheered and waved and threw confetti and sang songs as the happy couple rode down the drive.

Then a man Queen didn't know grabbed her and lifted her high in the air.

"My," he said. "Aren't you the prettiest little thing."

He looked at some people he seemed to know, and called out to them, very loudly.

"Whose little girl are you?"

Everyone around Queen suddenly seemed to be very

angry, but Queen didn't think she'd done anything wrong. Miss Sally moved quickly to her and sounded cross.

"You must be very tired, Queen; you need a nap," she said sharply. Her mammy came rushing up and grabbed her, and her gran'pappy.

"I'll see to her, Miss Sally," she said, and carried Queen away. Queen could see that the man who had picked her up was talking to someone else, and then he shouted something out, and he sounded cross too.

"How could I tell?" she heard him say. "She looks white as cotton. How was I supposed to know she's a nigra?"

Her mammy started walking faster when she heard that, pushing her way through the crowd, and there was a crack of thunder. It frightened Queen, and she began to cry.

It rained for days. The river flooded, and the roads were impassable. Lizzie and Jass had to spend the first few nights of their honeymoon at the hotel in Florence rather than traveling to Charleston to get the ship to Europe.

Usually, the slaves didn't mind heavy rain. It meant that no work could be done in the fields, and the lenient overseer, Mitchell, gave them the days off. This time it was different.

Mitchell gathered them together inside the barn on the second day of the rain. A young white man was standing beside him.

"You can't go into the fields today," Mitchell told them. "So we'll use the time to fix things up around here."

He turned to the young man standing beside him.

"An' this here's Mr. Henderson," he told the slaves. "He's gonna be helpin' me from now on. You mind him, y'hear? Same as you mind me."

The slaves eyed Henderson warily. They were all

used to Mitchell, had the measure of him, but they knew he was getting old, and they weren't sure about this new assistant overseer. They didn't like change because usually it wasn't for the better. They stood in the leaky barn until someone told them what to do.

Henderson was anxious to please.

"The barns need work," he said to Mitchell, who looked at the leaking roof and nodded. His arthritis was bothering him badly, and he was content to leave the day to Henderson, who wouldn't be able to do too much damage.

"If'n you like," he said. "Hit ain't the weather for it."

He limped away. "Damn rain," he said, to no one in particular. "Plays merry hell with the harvest."

Henderson waited till Mitchell was out of the barn; then he turned to the slaves.

"I want a work gang up on the roof to fix the leaks, a dozen men," he ordered sharply.

The slaves waited. No one wanted to be up on the roof in this weather.

They hesitated a fraction too long, for suddenly Henderson barked a military command at them.

"Jump to it! I ain't afraid of using the lash!"

The slaves groaned inwardly, but shuffled about, trying to look busy. Clearly there were going to be changes, and none of them for the better.

Mitchell had lingered outside and had heard Henderson use his authority. He wasn't too worried about it. All young men were overeager in a new job, and the slaves could stand a little shaking up.

The arthritis in his leg was troubling him badly, and he limped away to somewhere warm and dry. He hoped that Henderson would work out, because then he could retire. Not for a year or two, of course. But soon.

Henderson knew he was on trial, and knew that if he made a good impression, one of the plum jobs in the district was his for the taking.

Youngest of five sons of a dirt-poor tobacco share-cropper, Henderson had been raised to the land and was a good and muscular worker, determined to better himself in life. He had no expectations from his father, a drunkard with whom the boy had been constantly at war, and he had upped and left six months ago, with a couple of dollars his mother, old before her time and ailing from a life of unrelenting hardship, had given him. Living by his wits and his strength, which he offered for hire wherever he could find work, he had been searching for a position with potential. He had heard of The Forks of Cypress and its aging overseer, and that there was no white assistant to succeed to the job. He did his homework well. He found out all he could about Mitchell, discovered the man was considered lenient in his treatment of blacks, spent hours thinking up proper responses to possible questions, and, in speech at least, tempered his own ruthless, lifelong dislike and distrust of niggers. His timing and responses were perfect. He presented his most reasonable face to Mitchell, who liked the boy and decided to give him a chance.

The roof of the weaving house was leaking, too, seeping in through the cracks, dripping into buckets set out by Easter. She'd complained about it several times to Mitchell, but nothing ever got done. Mitchell forgot a lot of things these days.

She sat at the loom trying to weave, but a persistent drip was making the new cloth damp. It aggravated her, and she was not in a good mood.

Cap'n Jack was sitting on the floor with Queen, holding up some brightly painted cards that he'd made for her.

It was a game that Queen loved. Cap'n Jack held up a C, and Queen knew that, it was for Cat, and D was for Dog. But she always had trouble with the next one—it was a big word.

467

"Effalump," she tried.

"No, chile, that's 'el-e-phant.'" Cap'n Jack laughed.

"Filling her head with useless nonsense," Easter grumbled, ignored by both of them.

"What's an elly phan?" Queen asked her gran'pappy. Although she already knew, she loved the story.

"A elephant is a great big animal, with a long nose that's called a trunk," Cap'n Jack told her. "He live in Africa, where yo' mammy and yo' gran'mammy and me, and all yo' family come from."

"I ain't from Africa, I's from Alabama," Easter grumbled her counterpoint.

Cap'n Jack ignored her. "Africa is a beautiful country, long, long ways from here, where everybody free and happy," he told the child.

"Is that where my pappy is?" Queen longed to meet her pappy.

Cap'n Jack didn't look at Easter. Queen's paternity was a bone of contention between them. Cap'n Jack thought Queen should know who her real father was, but Easter, ever more practical, forbade it. It would seriously offend the Jackson family and would be of no advantage to Queen, for even though everyone knew it was true, it could not be admitted. She had seen the other slave children taunting Queen about the color of her skin, and to claim the Massa as her father would make her the object of even greater derision. Children of the plantation were simply that, and she wished her father would forget his silly, and even dangerous, ideas about some eventual equality of whites and blacks.

Aware of Easter's feelings and, in his more realistic moments, forced to agree with them, Cap'n Jack still harbored unrealistic dreams for Queen, much as he had once done for his daughter. He longed to see Queen taken into the big house, as some Massas did with their half-caste offspring, even though the paternity was never admitted. These chosen few children had a better life, Cap'n Jack thought, than those who were relegated to a life with the field hands, and Cap'n Jack prayed it would happen to Queen one day. He hugged her to him.

"No, chile, yo' pappy's a very important man," he whispered in her ear. "An' if'n yo' learn good an' work hard, one day yo'll live in a fine house with yo' pappy, an' wear pretty dresses, an' be happy, like a Princess."

Easter was furious with him. "You stop that, Cap'n Jack, yo' hear?" Why couldn't he understand it would never be, and that Easter didn't want it to be? Queen was hers; she made Easter's world whole and complete. She didn't want to lose her, and didn't want to expose her to the less than tender mercies of Lizzie. "She a slave chile, and she allus will be! Jus' like I'll allus be a slave, and yo'll allus be a slave!"

Cap'n Jack ignored her anger. "We gonna be free one day, yo' hear the talk, the day is comin'," he whispered, as much to Queen as to Easter.

The edge of Easter's fury had gone. At least they'd changed the subject. "We won't be here to see it," she said.

Cap'n Jack didn't argue, for there was no point. But in his heart he believed the day was coming. Every time he heard white folk talking these days, it was about the Yankees, and the North, and abolition. He remembered his own years in the North, and what he had seen and learned there, the good and the bad. He believed that when freedom came, the blacks had to be ready for it. There was no use in having freedom if they didn't have learning, if they couldn't better themselves. He dreamed of that better day for Queen.

Easter was still speaking. "She be better off learnin' weavin', or sewin', or summat useful."

She glared at the rain dripping in.

"Or fixin' roofs."

Cap'n Jack had been promising to fix the roof since last winter. "I'll git roun' to it one day," he said.

469

Easter laughed. "Chile die of newmonya 'fore that day happen."

She busied herself at the loom. Cap'n Jack rocked Queen on his knee. She was tired, and was drifting to sleep. He hummed a gentle lullaby to her, softly, so that Easter would not hear.

"The day will come, chile," he sang. "The day will come."

The rain was relentless, and Easter took matters into her own hands. Since Jass was not there, she knew the person who would help was Sally, but knew she had to be careful. She was called to the laundry one day, to help iron sheets that had not dried properly in the rain, and Sally was there, sorting through the linen with Pattie and Jessica. Sally never acknowledged Easter's presence in the big house.

Easter began to mumble to herself as she ironed. Slaves often mumbled to themselves, and a good mistress listened to the mumbling, for much could be discovered from it.

"I suppose we could turn these sheets sides to the middle," Sally said to Pattie, intent on household affairs. "It seems a waste to throw them out."

She left gaps in her comments so that Easter's mumbling might take form and meaning.

"But we seem to have enough pillowcases to get us through the winter."

"Rotten, no-account, leaky house me an' the chile lives in," Sally deciphered Easter.

"I'm certainly not taking another trip to Charleston until spring," Sally said in counterpoint.

"Roof's useless, e'vry drop a rain comes in."

"But we do need some towels." Sally was listening intently now.

" Po' l'il Queen could catch her death of cole." So that was it, and of course, something had to be done, for Queen's sake. Easter could stop mumbling now, but

470

Sally had to let her know the message had been received. She turned on Pattie and Jessica.

"I've never known a household to get through towels the way we do," she said, as if it was the slave maids' fault. "This is good sturdy cotton, too. You'd think it would last a little longer."

Pattie and Jessica, who was young and learning the skills of a chambermaid, started mumbling that it was nothing to do with them, Massa George was to blame.

Sally spoke to Mitchell, and Mitchell gave the job to Henderson. With a cautious warning.

Henderson was intrigued. He'd heard of Easter, the Massa's whore, and her bastard child, had seen them from a distance, but until now had no reason to go to the weaving house. What he knew of them surprised him. If the Massa wanted some nigra on the side, that was all right by Henderson, although he'd never had a taste for black flesh himself—it revolted him, and he hated to see the high-yella brats they fathered. But this bitch seemed permanent to the Massa; they had an ongoing connection, and he could not understand that, especially when the new mistress was such a gorgeous creature. Henderson would have gladly given his right arm for a woman like Lizzie.

He took a couple of men to the weaving house, threatened a whipping unless they did a good job, and went inside.

How could the Massa bear it, how could any white man? This grubby little shack, and this drably clothed slut. He could smell her from the doorway, at least in his mind, and it disgusted him. Not that she was ugly; she was quite a piece of woman, and if that's the way your fancy went you could do worse. If that's the way your fancy went. He stared at the child playing on the floor, and his gorge rose. She'd fool anyone. Could be white, sitting there, staring at him with those big, round, scared eyes. But she wasn't white. She was a

471

nigra. The chaos she'll cause when she's grown, he thought. Some unsuspecting white boy'll do her, and get a bastard, and they'll take over the world one day, and we'll all end up like them. Lazy, shiftless, and good-for-nothing. He thought of his own mother, who'd worked so hard all her life and had nothing, and it infuriated him that this pickaninny and her mammy could have pretty much what they wanted, all because the mulatta was good in bed.

The child was scared of him, he could see. And fear, in others of him, had a powerful effect on this young man who had never had dominion over anyone except a few no-account darkies.

"It'll be fixed by nightfall," he said to Easter, looking at Queen. "Hope it'll be to your satisfaction, Miss High and Mighty."

Easter was unsure of Henderson. "Thank you, Massa," she said.

He turned to her, and knew that she wasn't scared of him, and wanted to make her fear him, for it was sweet to him.

"And in future, if you've got any complaints, you bring 'em to me," he told her. "Don't go running to the big house."

Easter said nothing. That angered Henderson even more. He walked close to her, so that she might sense his power.

"I know your game," he said. 'You may be the Massa's fancy woman, but you're still a slave. And I'm in charge of slaves."

"Massa Mitchell the overseer," Easter said calmly. But she was scared, just a little bit; Henderson knew that. He could smell fear. He didn't have to push too hard.

"He wouldn't know what time of day it is." Henderson was not afraid to be honest with her. "Couple of years, he'll retire, and his job's for me. Then things'll be different round here."

472

He didn't want to push too hard, not yet, and might not have under different circumstances. She could go running to the Massa and pour poison in his ear, and if she had enough power, she could even get him sacked. But the Massa was away for at least a year, and by the time he came back, Henderson was determined his position would be unassailable.

"And I've got a long memory." He turned his attention to the sniveling child. "So you keep a civil tongue in your head, and that brat of yours. Or you'll be sorry."

Queen started to cry. It pleased Henderson, who looked at Easter again, and then left.

He thought that Easter would be no trouble to him because he could always scare the child, and the child wouldn't tell. He felt satisfied with his morning's work, and yelled some abuse at the niggers on the roof.

Easter ran to Queen, picked her up, and hugged her hard. She sat on the bed with her daughter and hummed a little lullaby.

The world was changing too fast for her. Lizzie, even though absent, was mistress now, and no one could guess what changes she might introduce on her return to The Forks, or how she might affect her new husband's attitudes and behavior.

And Henderson was right. Mitchell must retire soon, and clearly the slaves could expect a different order when he was gone.

If only Jass were here. Jass would make everything all right.

49

The honeymoon had begun disastrously. Jass and Lizzie had planned to spend the first night at the Florence Hotel and then make a leisurely journey to

Charleston, but the rain made the roads impassable, and they were forced to stay at Florence for four days. It seemed so silly. They should have gone home, but even the road to The Forks had turned into a quagmire, and anyway, Lizzie showed no particular desire to spend the early days of her marriage under her mother-in-law's eye.

The first evening had been pleasant enough. They had dined in a private room, and the staff had done their best to give the dinner some sense of romantic occasion. Lizzie had retired early, to prepare herself for her wedding night, and Jass had stayed talking with the proprietor, who was a close acquaintance, and had drunk several glasses of port.

Jass felt at peace with most of the world as he climbed the stairs and made his way to their room, but a little part of his brain was worried about what must happen next with Lizzie. The port had not dulled his concerns.

She was in bed when he came in, wearing a pretty nightdress, with the blankets pulled up, demurely, under her chin. Jass had chatted about the weather; then he sat beside her and kissed her gently, and he knew that Lizzie was scared. What was of more concern to him was that he felt no sense of anticipation or arousal. She was not unattractive to him, but it was in a general way, as a pretty friend, lacking that sense of desire and passion he felt when he was close to Easter. After a while he excused himself, went into their sitting room, and changed into his nightclothes. When he came back to the bedroom, Lizzie had turned down the lamps, and because of the rain there was no moon. Jass felt his way to the bed, lay down beside Lizzie, and she curled into the crook of his arm and chattered nervously about their coming year in Europe. Jass understood that she was trying to delay the inevitable, but it had to happen and he was tired, and the port was making him drowsy.

He kissed her again, and forced his tongue into her

474

mouth. Lizzie did not protest, but she did not relax. He fondled her breasts and lay astride, and she submitted to him, as she had been told to do, and as she knew she must, but she didn't appear to be enjoying herself in any way.

Jass was lost. His only experience of a woman was with Easter, who yielded to him readily, willingly, and with a sense of abandon. He wondered what on earth he could do to calm the fears of his shivering bride, and what he might do to excite himself, for her fear was unmanning him.

Lizzie was in a turmoil. She wanted Jass, desperately. She wanted to prove to him that she would be a good wife, but the prospect of the thing that had to happen was terrifying to her. She had no sense of titillation, for there was an edge of impending violence to his kisses, and the one honest thing her mother had told her about her first time was that it would hurt. When he thrust his tongue into her mouth, Lizzie almost screamed in horror, for she realized that she had no possible route of escape, and when he lay astride her and she felt, for the first time, that hard thing pressing on her abdomen, she almost fainted in fear of it. Now something odd had happened. The hard monster wasn't hard anymore; it was soft again, and all sense of urgency had deserted Jass. She couldn't believe it was over—it couldn't be this short, this easy, and there had been no pain—but some crisis had passed and Lizzie relaxed and started to enjoy herself.

She loved lying in his arms as he gently caressed her shoulders, and she allowed her own hands to explore his chest, and his biceps, and his neck, and she even let her fingers trace their way to his lips, and he kissed them gently. If it was always going to be like this, then Lizzie wasn't scared anymore; in fact she quite liked it, and found herself liking it more and more as the minutes ticked by, and nothing was going to hurt her now. She felt sensations she had never experienced, of

475

warmth and security, and she felt a curious tingle somewhere in the pit of her stomach, and moistness in that place she didn't like to think about.

It changed again, without any evidence that anything had changed. Jass took her hand and dragged it down to his stomach and put it onto the monster that was hard and hot. It felt enormous to Lizzie and malevolent, for it stopped that warm feeling inside her, stopped the tingling, and brought back all her old fears instead. Suddenly, he seemed to get angry, and moved on top of her and pushed her nightgown up, exposing parts of her that had not been exposed to a man, or to anyone, before. He pushed up his own nightshirt, and she felt the thing, hard and hot and throbbing, pushing against her stomach, trying to find some other place, and she struggled against it with all her might.

To no avail. Jass had been dreaming of Easter. Now he wanted Easter, wanted her with every fiber of his being, and he was intolerant of Lizzie's procrastinations. The more she struggled against him, the more he had to find release, and suddenly he pushed inside her. He met some resistance and pushed again, hard again, and Lizzie cried out in pain, but Jass didn't stop. It had to be, and even though he didn't want to hurt Lizzie, she had to know that he was her husband and her Massa, and his rights were inviolable. To an extent, her resistance to him made him only more determined to prove his authority to her; it excited him, because of that very dominance that was rightfully his.

Lizzie could not believe the pain he caused, could not believe that he would willingly cause her such harm, and she knew that some little part of her had been ruptured and broken. He lay on her now, humping and heaving, while she wept, and even though the pain eventually receded and was replaced by a degree of pleasant feeling, she could not imagine a lifetime of having to submit to this awful thing whenever Jass desired it.

He cried out and, mercifully, stopped moving. Lizzie

476

lay wondering what more could possibly happen to her, and then, to her relief and surprise, he moved off and lay beside her. He said some sweet things, and drifted to sleep.

Lizzie could not sleep. She lay awake until dawn, reliving every moment of the nightmare in her head, and weeping sometimes, for she felt as if he had made a great, open wound in her body that would never heal.

It got better between them, as everyone had told her it would. It never hurt again as badly as the first time, and sometimes, when Jass was patient with her, and caressed her, Lizzie felt those nice tinglings, and sometimes almost felt as if she would enjoy the act itself, but it never lasted long enough, and Jass was always so aggressive when he was on top of her. What Lizzie never knew, but sometimes guessed, was that he was always thinking of Easter.

They were cooped up in the hotel room for four days, and had their first rows, because Lizzie was sure she hadn't pleased him in bed and was determined to make up for it in other ways. She fussed over him too much, and tried to make decisions for him, and he got irritated. Then she got bored with the hotel room, and her temper flared, and they had a row about some silly thing. Jass stormed out, and Lizzie cried her distress, and when he came back was ready to beg his forgiveness. But when he came back he had a smile on his face, and apologized to her, as a gentleman should. The rain was easing, the roads were still impassable, but he had found a paddle steamer that was going upriver to Decatur and had booked them on it. The accommodations were fairly primitive, but at least they were on their journey.

They traveled for a year, and both loved Europe, although they never came closer to loving each other. They settled into a pattern that suited both of them, which began on the Atlantic crossing. Alone of the female passengers, Lizzie did not succumb to seasickness and, as the only woman presenting herself at meals in the cramped dining room, took advantage of her situation, and put all of her considerable social skills on display. Jass would watch her at lunch or dinner, a splendid hostess in an unlikely environment, charming them all with her wit and sense of humor. He was sure they could find a balance in this. She would be mistress of The Forks, impeccably fulfilling all their public duties, efficiently running their private lives. He would make love to her as their situation required, and she would be mother to his children, and probably a good mother too, Jass thought. For the side of him that needed another kind of love, he had his mistress, Easter.

The conditions of their new relationship were never voiced between them, but Lizzie knew they existed and was not unhappy with them. Jass indulged her every mood and whim; in Paris she shopped until she needed several more cabin trunks to get her new wardrobe home, and he seldom said no to her. He required her presence in his bed two or three times a week, and Lizzie was prepared for it, and found ways to make the experience less arduous. In the better hotels, they would have separate bedrooms, and Lizzie appreciated his generosity, for she knew why it had been done. To show her gratitude, she made sure his life was as full and interesting as was within her ability to arrange, and she indulged the romantic in both of them by taking him to the most romantic places she could find. It was she who organized the dinner parties, and made them glittering affairs, she who organized his wardrobe and his requirements, she who took him for picnics to pretty riverbanks and picturesque villages. She made no more demands on his time than he was prepared to give, and did not complain if he went exploring on his own. So they arrived at an understanding that made life pleasurable to both of them, that was based on the friendship they had before their marriage, but that now was deeper and more fulfilling because their lives were so inextricably intertwined. Each was essentially happy, and if there were missing elements that might have made that happiness more complete, both thought them a small sacrifice to make for their general sense of contentment.

Sometimes Lizzie longed for children, but her fear of the pain of childbirth was so great she was glad she had not become pregnant. Sometimes Jass longed for Easter, but she was there, waiting for him, and his absence from her only made his heart fonder of her and, by extension, of Queen.

They were away for fifteen months. It was longer than they had planned, but they were having such a good time they saw no need to return. The estate was in the capable hands of Tom Kirkman, the mansion was Sally's domain, and the price of cotton was high. In London, Jass met enough people who were sympathetic to the Southern cause to persuade him that the South would always have a formidable ally, and this allayed his concerns about the increasing friction with the North. Lizzie, for her part, was not overly anxious to assume her new role at The Forks, for it meant that she would be displacing Sally, and Lizzie still had certain nervous fears about her mother-in-law.

But eventually they got homesick, and bored with the wandering life, and they came home and were glad of it. They had laid the foundations of an excellent marriage, and were anxious to put their new domestic life into effect.

Lizzie knew he would go to Easter, and she tried to block the idea from her mind, tried not to think about it, and mostly succeeded. There was nothing in the mansion to remind her of Easter's presence. The weaving house was discreetly tucked away, and Jass was discreet about venturing there. From time to time, she would see that little white pickaninny wandering about the plantation, and when she did, it stabbed at her heart, for she had not yet provided Jass with an heir

479

and had no little baby of her own to love, and she was jealous of Easter, because of Queen. Sally seemed to understand this, and fond as she was of Queen, she would try to see her away from the house, or at least away from Lizzie's sight. Sally also behaved beautifully in the matter of the succession, handing over the reins of running the household to Lizzie without demur, but always there for help and advice.

In truth, Sally was pleased to be relieved of much of her responsibility. Since James died, Sally had found her role arduous, for it had lost its meaning for her. She had worked hard and capably all her days, and now she was looking forward to a rest. She made a decision that once Lizzie was comfortably settled in, she would travel herself for a while, not to Europe, that was too strenuous for her, but to friends and relatives throughout the South. She also intended to go North for a while, to see for herself what all the fuss was about. And she was pleased with Lizzie, for she seemed to be making Jass happy.

Jass was happy, his life divided into compartments that made one entity. Always daunted by the myriad details of running the estate, he had Tom and Lizzie, with Sally standing by, to run the house, the plantation, and all the intricacies of their lives, leaving him free to concentrate on the overview. And he had Easter. He had gone to her on the first night of his return, and nothing had changed between them, and now he believed that nothing ever would. He had coped with all the great changes life had thrown at him, and survived, and there wouldn't be any more great changes to cope with. He was free to enjoy life.

The only thing missing was a son, by Lizzie, and he was puzzled that she had shown no signs of pregnancy. He did not connect this to the fact that Easter had never become pregnant again, because he didn't want her to have another child.

480

Because there was Queen, and Queen was enough for him.

He loved her. She had grown while he was away, but was still small for her age, and serious and demure. She seemed to carry the weight of the world around with her and seldom smiled, but when she did it dazzled him and broke his heart. All the pent-up love he had for a child of his own was directed toward Queen, and if that love could never be expressed, it did not in any way diminish its value.

She was so pretty, too. He was out for a walk one day and saw her playing ring-around-the-rosy with some other slave children. He hid behind a tree and watched them for a while, delighting in his lovely daughter.

The smile faded from his face as he heard what the other children were singing:

"Queen, Queen, say she white, but she nigger like us!"

Queen was standing in the center of the ring of children, tears in her eyes.

"I am white," she cried. "Look at me!"

"Queen, Queen," they chanted. "Ain't got no pappy, don't know who he is."

"He love me," Queen called at them, in despair. "He ain't ever gonna let anyone hurt me!"

The more she protested, the more they jeered, until she broke, and stood amongst them weeping her distress.

Jass could not stand it. He moved quickly from behind the tree, and called out to them.

"Get out of here, you little brats!"

The sight of the Massa, angry, scared them, and they ran away. Queen was on her knees, still crying. Jass came close to her, and put an arm around her, told her not to cry, he wouldn't let anyone hurt her.

"They call me names." Queen was wretched.

Jass remembered his days at school when they used to call him "nigger lover" and beat him up. He smiled.

"People used to call me names, too, when I was little," he told her, drying her eyes with his handkerchief. "I wonder why people do that?"

Queen had no illusions. "Coz I different. Coz I look white. Coz I can read."

Jass had no idea of this, and was shocked.

"Don't ever tell anyone you can read, Queen," he commanded her gently. "Some people wouldn't like it. They might hurt you."

She looked at him with innocent eyes. "My pappy would stop them," she said. "You could stop them."

At that moment, he would have stopped the world for her. He longed, with all his heart to take her into his arms, and hold her close to him, and never let anyone hurt her, ever again. He might have done it, for her face was inches from his, trusting him, and he thought they were alone, but salvation arrived, in the form of Cap'n Jack.

"The chile botherin' yo', Massa?" If Cap'n Jack had known what was in Jass's heart, he might have stolen away, and left his granddaughter to her father's love. But he did not know. How could he know?

Jass stood up and told Cap'n Jack to take her to the kitchen and find her some candy. Something in his tone told Cap'n Jack what he could not have known before. Queen ran to her gran'pappy's arms.

"She been trouble, Massa?" Cap'n Jack asked.

"No trouble at all," Jass replied.

He knew who was teaching her to read and did not mind. He would have stopped it with any other slave, but his daughter was different. He went to his study, and then to the weaving house, which was empty.

Easter came back with provisions and found Jass hunting through the few drawers and cupboards. She was surprised. He seldom came to her in daylight anymore. He ignored her.

"What you looking for?" she asked, dumping her vegetables on the table.

"Nothing," he said, casually. Then he found Cap'n Jack's homemade alphabet cards, and showed them to her. In that moment, Easter was fearful, even of him.

"What are these?" His voice was even, and Easter looked him in the eye. Her fear passed.

"Nuttin'," she said.

Jass grunted, and put the cards back where he had found them. He took a couple of small books from his pocket and put them with the cards.

"What that?" Easter was puzzled.

"Nuttin'," he said, with a poker face, and a grin twitching at the corners of his mouth. He moved into her arms and kissed her, and they made love in the warm afternoon.

When he had gone, Easter looked at the books he had left. She could not read the books, but she understood the pictures. They were children's books, of fairy stories.

Another book, recently published and not available at The Forks of Cypress, was causing uproar throughout the country. Called *Uncle Tom's Cabin*, its presentation of plantation life, and the way whites treated niggers, was causing astonishing and renewed debate in the North about slavery. Those Southerners who had read it had originally dismissed it as a fiction, but the intensity of the Northern passions it had aroused caused fury to replace apathy in the South. Lizzie was terrified of it, not for itself, for she had never read it, but of the storm it had created. The new Republican party had always espoused the cause of abolition, but now one of its younger politicians, Abraham Lincoln, had made a passionate speech in Peoria, denouncing slavery. He appeared to have tremendous support in the North, and there was even talk that eventually the issue would be decided by violence. Certainly all of Lizzie's male friends claimed they were ready to make the ultimate sacrifice to defend the slaveholding states and their life-style. Lizzie found herself weeping at the slightest provocation these days.

She was pregnant. She was appalled at the prospect of bringing a child into such an unstable world, and she did not understand that much of the emotional tight-rope she was walking was because of her condition. She was sick every morning, which she hated, her ankles seemed to be swelling already, although she had months to go, she was getting headaches, and she was dreading the prospect of the pain of giving birth. She came into the dining room one evening, saw that the silverware had not been polished to her liking, and burst into tears again. Sally, who had followed her in, was calm and kindly, and sat her down, and Lizzie couldn't contain herself any longer, and told Sally the awful truth.

Sally didn't laugh. She saw that Lizzie was genuinely scared of what was happening to her body and had not been educated to understand the natural processes. She calmed Lizzie, and told her things that Becky should have told her long ago, and by the time Jass, who had been delayed in Florence, came in, Lizzie had ceased crying but was not in the brightest mood.

"Why's everyone so glum?" He was in a splendid mood himself. The tension between the North and the South had caused the price of cotton to go sky-high in London.

Knowing he didn't know, Sally tried to cover for Lizzie.

"We've been discussing politics," she said.

"Something ladies shouldn't bother their pretty little heads about," Jass laughed, and rang the bell for soup.

He was hungry. To his surprise, both women snapped at him.

"Don't be patronizing, Jass!" Sally barked.

"Of course it bothers us!" Lizzie was all fire. "All this fuss with the Yankees, we could all be murdered in our beds—"

Parson Dick and Polly came in with the soup.

"—like that dreadful business with Nat Turner killing white women and children—"

Jass, surprised at what he had unleashed, tried to calm her. "That was years ago," he began, but Lizzie was unstoppable.

"And everyone's saying there could even be a war, and then we'd all be killed and what am I going to do about my poor little baby?"

That stopped everyone. Parson Dick glanced at Polly.

Jass broke the silence. "What baby?"

Now that it was out in the open, Lizzie wondered why she had been afraid to tell him, and felt an enormous sense of triumph. She became impossibly coy.

"A little flower is growing under my heart," she simpered, and hoped she looked suitably maternal.

Jass was thrilled.

"Oh, Lizzie, that's wonderful!" He hardly knew how to express his joy.

"Of course, I'm hoping for a boy," Lizzie said, delighted by his obvious glee.

Jass chuckled happily. "A baby! Thank you, Lizzie."

She smiled sweetly. "Well, you did have something to do with it, Jass," she said, and felt grown-up, for the first time in her life.

The soup was spent with plans of fixing up the nursery, and possible names for boys, and finding a good slave to be nanny, and when the main course was served, Jass decided they needed champagne. Parson Dick offered to fetch it, but Jass loved choosing the right

485

bottle of wine for the right occasion. The two men went to the cellar together, where Parson Dick offered his congratulations, and Jass had an idea.

They all drank the new baby's health in sparkling wine, and Jass told them of his plan.

"We could bring Queen here to live," he said. "As a companion for him. Or her. They'd grow up as friends and she'd scare away the black bogeyman."

He was surprised at the silence that greeted him. Sally could guess Lizzie's feelings.

"Do you think it's quite wise, Jass?" she said. Jass was a little put out.

"I think it's an excellent idea, Mother," he retorted.

He did not hear Lizzie's still, small voice saying, "No."

50

Queen woke up because she heard voices. They were not loud, but they sounded cross. It surprised her, because she knew it was her mammy and the Massa, and they didn't get angry with each other usually. They were in the only other room, where her gran'pappy used to sleep before she was born, and she lay in her cot near the loom and tried to work out what was wrong. She hoped the Massa wasn't angry with her mammy, because she didn't want her mammy to be whipped, like Isaac had been the other day by the new white man who had come to work here. As she listened, she began to realize they were talking about her, and she got very scared because she didn't want to be whipped, either. She tried to think of things she'd done wrong, but she didn't think she'd done anything bad recently, and then she realized that her mammy sounded sad as well as cross. She heard mammy say, "No," quite loudly, but she could not make out what

486

the Massa was saying, so she sneaked out of bed and walked on tippy-toe to their door to listen.

"It's for the best," she heard the Massa say. There was a little silence, and she knew her mammy was crying, not real tears, but crying inside, where it really hurts.

"She all I got," Mammy said, very softly.

When the Massa spoke again, he sounded kind again. "She'll still be yours," he said, and Queen thought he must have kissed Mammy. "But she'll live in the big house, that's the only difference, and be companion to my little boy."

Queen was puzzled. She liked the idea of living in the big house; they had a lot of parties there, and it wasn't very far away. But she didn't know who the Massa's boy was; he didn't have a little boy as far as Queen knew. Perhaps that was why he was always so nice to her.

Mammy said something else, which Queen couldn't hear properly, about Miss Lizzie, and then the Massa sounded angry again.

"Lizzie won't harm a hair of her head," Massa said. "I'll see to that."

They must mean her, and Mammy must think Miss Lizzie was going to do something nasty to Queen. Queen crept back to her bed. The idea of living in the big house was fun, but not if Miss Lizzie was going to be nasty to her, and even though the weaving house wasn't very far away, it was far enough. But the Massa would save her, he'd said so.

She snuggled into bed and lay dreaming of parties at the big house and pretty dresses. Perhaps she might even get to sleep in one of those big beds with a post at each corner and some material over the top like a tent. Mammy had shown her one when they went visiting the big house once, and Queen loved those beds. You could crawl inside, into the nice soft sheets they had there, much softer than the blanket Queen slept under, and you could close the curtains at the sides of the bed, and no one in the world could find you. Then she thought of living away from Mammy, and she got scared again. She wondered if Miss Lizzie would let her see Mammy when she wanted to, and Gran'pappy and Tiara, who was very old and very kind, and all the people she loved. She didn't like Miss Lizzie, who always seemed cross, and she had seen Miss Lizzie hit one of the slave girls once when the Massa was away. Queen didn't want Miss Lizzie to hit her, and if the Massa was away, and Miss Sally was old and resting, like she sometimes did, what would she do? She wished she could close some curtains around her own little bed now, because she didn't want anyone in all the world to find her.

Jass was angry. He couldn't understand why everybody was so against his splendid idea. Lizzie had been pouting ever since dinner, and then Sally had spoken to him quietly when Lizzie had gone upstairs to bed with a headache. Sally was in a quandary. She loved the idea of Queen living with them, but she understood Lizzie's feelings, for to bring Easter's daughter into the house was a considerable slap in the face. Sally tried to present Lizzie's point of view, but the more she argued, the more stubborn Jass became. It wasn't as if the child was to be brought up as one of their own—she would still be a slave—but it would be good for her, good for the new baby, good for all of them to have that dear little creature running round. He didn't tell Sally of his real affection for Queen, nor of his true reason for wanting her in the big house—to protect her from the other slaves. Perhaps he didn't understand those reasons himself. He did understand that he wanted some influence over Queen's education, for even as he rejected his paternity on any official basis, he loved her and wanted her to have the best life he could give her.

He and Sally had something of a row, but, as he said, he was the Massa, and his wishes prevailed.

He came to see Easter, to give her the good news, and she was still as against it as Sally and Lizzie. She seemed to feel that she would lose Queen somehow, and he got angry with her. She'd still see the girl every day, and he had thought she would be proud to have her daughter brought up in such comfort and luxury, with such advantages. Part of Easter agreed with him. She knew the child would now be exposed to a life that Easter could never give her, and she wanted that for her daughter, although she had no idea what eventual use it might be to her. Mostly, she knew she would miss Queen, no matter how often she saw her. She would no longer affect the girl's upbringing, no longer have her to cherish on the cold nights when Jass was not with her, no longer be responsible for the flesh of her flesh. She also dreaded Lizzie's reaction, and what Lizzie might do to Queen. She thought that this was how her own mother must have felt when she learned that she was to be sold away from her only child, and she wept for herself, and the mother she could scarcely remember.

Jass saw the tears, and tried to kiss them away, and put a positive face on the prospects for Queen. In the end, Easter had to agree. She had no choice. He was the Massa.

And he was her love. His comforting caresses changed to intimate endearments, and she gave herself to him, as she always would, and gave him the most dear thing that was hers to give.

She put a brave face on it, and told her daughter the good news, and was surprised by Queen's reaction. It seemed to come as no surprise to the girl. She listened gravely to her mother, and was silent for a little while afterward, and then asked if Miss Lizzie would beat her.

She looked so lost and frightened, and so very tiny at that moment, far too small to be setting off on so great an adventure, that all Easter wanted to do was hold her close and run away somewhere with her, and keep her safe from Miss Lizzie and all the nasty things that might happen to her in life, run away even from Jass.

She didn't run away. She couldn't: She had nowhere to go, nor the genuine desire to leave. She held her daughter close and whispered to her that the Massa and Miss Sally wouldn't let anyone hurt her. Queen stared into her eyes, as if looking to see if she was telling the truth, and seemed convinced, and almost smiled. Easter knew that something else was troubling her, and asked what it was.

A tear moistened Queen's eye. "I don't have any nice dresses to wear," she said, miserably.

Easter's heart almost broke, and she spent the next few days making a couple of pretty dresses for Queen, and a smart little pinafore to wear over them, to keep them clean.

Cap'n Jack was all in favor of the idea. To him, it was not similar to the situation with Annie, because Queen would still be with them. What was paramount in his mind was that Queen would now have the advantage of real learning, for undoubtedly she would go to school with Lizzie's children, and she would learn to dance, and how to conduct herself in social situations. She would learn how to become a lady, which was Cap'n Jack's immediate dream for her, and she would be raised in her father's household, which, to him, was her true station. Tempered by the reality of a slave's existence, he saw Queen taking her first steps on the path to her true ascendancy, to her true place as her father's daughter.

So it was that on a warm summer day, Easter took Queen to the main entrance of the big house. She knew she should have used the back door, but if her daughter was to be taken in by this family, then it would be done properly. Queen was neatly dressed and was wearing her new pinafore. Easter carried a small bag with the girl's other few belongings. She rang the bell.

Still, Easter had a heavy heart, and she wondered what Queen was thinking. Queen had been excited all morning, and very nervous, but hadn't said much. As they waited for a response to the bell, Queen seemed to be mulling something over in her mind, and then she looked at her mother.

"Why the Massa come see you all the time?" she asked. "Like he was my pappy."

Easter knew that Queen must learn the truth of her parentage one day, that the other slaves would make sure of it, if they hadn't hinted at it already. Even so, it was difficult territory. For both of them.

"Hush up 'bout yo' pappy, yo' hear, or I take a switch to you," she said, and the words were fiercer than her tone. "Yo' pappy ain't here, an' that's all there is about it!"

Then she relented, for at that moment she didn't want Queen to have a pappy, not even Jass. She wanted her all for herself. She hugged her daughter.

"Jus' remember yo' got a mammy that love yo," she said tenderly. But she had to prepare her for the future.

"And a Massa that love yo'. Jus' like he was yo' pappy."

Parson Dick opened the door and was surprised to see them, but understood why Easter had not gone round the back. He almost smiled in sympathy, and led them into the hall, telling them to wait while he fetched the Missy.

They were an odd couple, the two of them, and looked shabby, the half-caste, dowdily dressed woman and her tiny daughter, standing nervously in the grand hall with its chandeliers and sweeping staircase and somber portraits of all the Jackson family. The sheer magnificence frightened Queen and brought home the truth of her situation to her. She would never be able to

491

imagine this as her "new home" as Mammy had told her it would be. She'd never be able to run laughing down those stairs, or pad across that polished floor in bare, muddy feet, as she did at her old home. She clutched her mammy's hand tightly.

Lizzie came down the stairs, almost as nervous as they. She was especially irritated that Easter had used the front door, but had few ways of venting her displeasure, for who knew what the woman would tell Jass, and Jass was so adamant about this whole wretched business that Lizzie was not prepared to cross him. Nor was she about to lose the confrontation.

"You should have used the back door," she said sharply.

She stared at her rival, never having studied her before. Easter had always been a vague shadowy figure to her before she learned the truth of Jass's affections, and since then Lizzie had scarcely been able to look at her.

Now she did, because she had to, and because she could. She could not imagine what Jass saw in her. The woman had a certain thick-lipped prettiness about her but almost went out of her way to make the worst of herself, in that plain dress and dreadful scarf. "Mammy," Lizzie though, "a regular nigra mammy," and wondered what it was that made her so desirable to her husband. Easter's disregard of her own beauty was almost painful to Lizzie, who took such care about her appearance, and her careless physical grace made even Lizzie understand something of the process of physical desire. To save herself, she mentally dismissed Easter as an immoral slut who had some secret, sexual hold over Jass that Lizzie would never understand.

Then there was the child. A scrawny midget of a thing, with no personality, staring at the floor and trying to hide in the folds of her mammy's dress.

And white as cotton.

"You may go," Lizzie said to Easter.

Easter didn't go. She put her arm around Queen.

"I still see her, Missy?" she begged in a plaintive voice that gave Lizzie, for a moment at least, all the power over this woman for which she longed.

"Of course you will. This is another house, not another country," Lizzie said, without any trace of kindness. "But you should know—"

She could not resist. She had to turn the situation to her advantage.

"—this is the Massa's decision. I do not approve of it." She would show this woman who was Mistress. "But since it is to be, the child will be given every advantage. She will be trained as a lady's maid, with all the necessary etiquette. So be careful when you see her. I do not want her learning your nigra ways."

It had a different effect from that which Lizzie intended. The slave seemed to draw comfort from Lizzie's words. It was the Massa's decision, about the Massa's child, and it was Easter who had power over the Massa. Obviously, Lizzie did not want it to happen, but there was nothing she could do to stop it.

"I only wants the best for her," she said, and Lizzie, to her horror, thought Easter was smiling.

"What you want has nothing to do with it," she snapped. "We own her!"

She let that sink in for a moment, and was then tired of it all. "Say good-bye to her and go."

Easter knelt, hugged Queen to her, and whispered in the child's ear.

"Yo' be a good girl, like I teach'd yo', and do what you tole, allus. Jus' like yo' had a new mammy—"

Lizzie turned on her in fury. "I am her Mistress," she said. "Not her mammy!"

It frightened Queen, who clung close to Easter.

"Come along, Queen."

Queen didn't want to go, she didn't like Miss Lizzie, but her mammy kissed her, gave her the little bag, and pushed her forward.

"Queen!" Lizzie commanded again.

"Go with her," Easter whispered.

Reluctantly, Queen moved forward. Lizzie was already climbing the enormous staircase. Head down, Queen followed her up, her tiny legs only able to take one step at a time. She looked up a couple of times to see where she was going, and all those grim people in all the pictures on the wall stared down at her, ready, Queen was sure, to have her whipped if she did anything wrong.

Once, she looked back. Her mammy was still standing in the hall, and Queen knew she was crying. She wanted with all her heart to run back down and hug her mammy, tell her not to cry, and go home with her to the weaving house, and wake up from this nightmare.

But she had to do what her mammy and the Massa and her gran'pappy and everyone she knew told her she must.

"Queen!" she heard Miss Lizzie shout, angrily.

"Queen," she heard her mammy whisper.

Queen was determined not to cry.

PART THREE

QUEEN

Not they who soar, but they who plod
Their rugged way, unhelped, to God
Are heroes; they who higher fare,
And, flying, fan the upper air,
Miss all the toil that hugs the sod.
'Tis they whose backs have felt the rod,
Whose feet have pressed the path unshod,
May smile upon defeated care,
Not they who soar.

Paul Laurence Dunbar

51

"Queen!"

She heard William calling her again, but didn't respond, because he'd called several times, and she couldn't decide which bonnet to wear. She had only two, her dark-gray one for best and Sundays, and a blue one for other times. Today was not Sunday, but she was wearing her Sunday best dress and should have worn her gray bonnet, but she wanted to wear her blue one because it looked nicer. It was a little shabby, however, from constant use, and she hemmed and hawed and changed her mind, and her bonnet, a dozen times, while William, who had been ready half an hour earlier, had gone on ahead. Queen knew they were all waiting for her, but today was a big day. They were going to visit Missy Becky at The Sinks, which was a frequent event, and then they were going into town, which was not, and she wanted to look really pretty.

She settled on the blue bonnet, grabbed her gloves and almost empty reticule, and rushed from the room.

William was at the bottom of the stairs.

"I thought you'd never be ready," he called, as Queen came clattering down the stairs, a pretty sixteen and vibrant with youth.

"Sorry, Massa Bill," she cried. "I couldn't decide which bonnet to wear."

William was never very cross with her, and was laughing. "You've only got two, and Papa's going wild!"

Queen reached the bottom of the stairs and she and William were moving quickly outside when Parson Dick appeared in the hallway.

"Massa William! Miss Queen!" He was always telling

them off. A tubby, gray-haired grizzly bear, William called him. "Young ladies and gentlemen do not run."

They only laughed, and continued running. Parson Dick was used to being ignored by them, and went to the kitchen. The family would be away for the afternoon, and Missy Sally was having a nap, so he could relax until Massa Henderson came to tea with his new bride.

Jass saw them first.

"There you are at last," he cried. It was a crisp winter day, and they'd been waiting twenty minutes. Lizzie, pregnant, rugged up and impatient, was in the landau with Mary, William's younger sister, and Poppy, a slave nurse who was tending the babies, Little Sally, who was five, and Eleanor, who was two.

"Sorry, Papa," William said happily, to cover for Queen, as they climbed into the carriage. "I couldn't decide which cap to wear."

"But you only have one," said Lizzie, who was feeling the cold.

"I know!" William laughed again, smiled sweetly at his mother, and grinned at Queen. Everyone knew he was protecting his slave. He was only eleven, but he adored Queen and always took her side in any argument.

"Well, you both look very splendid, all 'forked up,' " Jass said, anxious to be away. He nodded at Isaac, the coachman, spurred his horse, and led the way down the drive. Isaac flicked the horses, and the carriage followed.

Queen saw her gran'pappy, Cap'n Jack, sitting on a log some distance away, whittling, and waved at him. He didn't do very much except whittle anymore, he was quite old, like Missy Sally, and Massa had told him to take things easy.

Cap'n Jack guessed it was Queen who was waving at him, although his eyesight troubled him—anything a distance away was unclear—and he waved back. He guessed she looked pretty, because she always looked pretty when she went out with all the family, and he watched the carriage until it was a blur to his sight. He sighed, and went back to his whittling, cursing his weak eyes. He was getting old, he knew. It had been a bitter blow when Jass relieved him of his duties, although it was kindly meant, and replaced him as valet with a younger slave, Alphis. Cap'n Jack knew he had earned some rest, but he didn't want to feel old because he didn't want to die.

It was his dream that he would see freedom, at least for some of the slaves, if only for Queen, before he died, but that happy day seemed as much a dream as ever. A lot of angry words were being said about the North, he knew, but Southerners had been saying angry words about the North for as long as he could remember, and nothing ever changed. A year ago, ol' white Massa John Brown had tried to free some slaves and had been hanged for it. The gentlemen of the South, and a lot of the Missys, had been frightened into a frenzy, but after the hanging it had all calmed down again, just like it had with Nat Turner. Now everyone was in a turmoil because of the presidential election, but Cap'n Jack didn't think it made much difference who won, and if it was Linkun, they'd probably hang him too.

He bitterly regretted turning down his own freedom once, and wondered if it would have made a difference to Queen's status if he had responded differently. But Queen had not been born then, and the ol' Massa, James, had said nothing about freedom for Easter.

He spent his days whittling now, or gabbing with some of the older slaves—the young men had little time for him—and avoiding Massa Henderson's eye, and dreaming of foolish, forgotten yesterdays that are an old man's memories.

*

499

Queen loved going out, going driving, going to town. It didn't happen very often. They called on Miss Becky every week, but she was very old now, and although she was always pleased to see them, she talked about things they didn't understand, and she didn't seem to mind very much when they left. William said she was funny in the head because of something that had happened before Gran'pa Perkins died. Once every three months Massa Jass would take them into town shopping, but he didn't like taking the children because he said there were a lot of undesirable people there. Today was a complete surprise. All the grown-ups had been very depressed and very excited all at once for weeks now, because of the election and what the Yankees were doing and saying, and a lot of very important, very angry gentlemen had visited The Forks, and kept talking about war, which frightened Queen. Massa didn't say anything about it all for a long time, and then this morning he told them they were going on an outing.

They were thrilled, because they loved these outings. William thought the excitement of the past few weeks was a lot of fuss and bother about nothing, anyway. He couldn't believe that anyone would go to war because of slaves and freedom—it wasn't important enough— and while Queen wanted to believe that there wouldn't be a war, she couldn't think of anything more important than being free.

Except, perhaps, to clarify her relationship with her pappy and the Massa, who might be one and the same person. Everyone else seemed to think they were, and Queen had come to believe it too but she didn't under- stand why she was still a slave and a nigra, and he her Massa, if she was white and he was her pappy.

Polly was the first to say it, years ago, soon after she'd come to live in the big house. Polly was fat and middle-aged, and thought she was something much more important than a serving maid. She resented

Queen and was always yelling at her for things she'd done wrong. One day, Queen was in the kitchen, where she ate her meals, and a cup had somehow slipped from her hand and broken on the hard stone floor. Polly shouted at her, and told her she didn't care if the Massa *was* her pappy, she'd spank Queen if she didn't learn to be more careful. Everyone had gone very quiet for a moment, and then Parson Dick told Polly off, and Julie, who was old and fat and always smelled of food, had pulled Queen onto her knee and rocked her and told her not to take any notice of a Miss Flibbertigibbet like Polly.

Queen didn't understand what all the fuss was about, but every so often one of the slaves would make a comment about the Massa and her pappy, and Queen had grown up understanding that in some mysterious way they were one and the same person, and that was why Queen looked white. She asked her mammy about it when she was ten, but Mammy said the same as Julie, that she shouldn't pay no nevermind to such things, and that didn't help very much. Other things confused her. If the Massa was her pappy, she didn't understand why Miss Lizzie was always stern and cross with her, and she was never cross with William or Mary. She didn't understand why she had to eat her meals in the kitchen when the others ate in the big dining room, and she didn't understand why she had to sleep on a hard pallet at the foot of William's bed, while her brother slept in a big, comfortable four-poster.

Mostly, she didn't understand why she was a slave. Mammy told her it was because she was a nigra and all nigras were slaves, but Queen knew she didn't look like a nigra—she was at least as white as Miss Lizzie or Miss Mary—and she didn't like a lot of the nigras very much. Parson Dick and Julie were nice, and Poppy and Pattie, and even Polly these days, and she liked the coachmen, who were always kind to her. She didn't like the field hands, who were really black, and they said funny

501

things about her, or they ignored her, and so Queen returned the insults, and never went to the slave quarters unless she was sent on an errand, or to see her gran'pappy, Cap'n Jack.

She developed a rationale for her position, which, once she came to an understanding of the mysteries of the body, she passionately believed. She was a secret child, born of a great love between her pappy and her mammy, who was really a queen of somewhere, in hiding from people who were trying to harm her. Her pappy looked after her, but couldn't admit she was really his daughter because she was the eldest, and then she'd be more important than all his other children, even William. She believed in her heart that one day everything would be all right, and that her Massa would finally embrace her as his true daughter and find her a prince to marry, and she'd live happily ever after at The Forks with her pappy and her mammy, and Miss Lizzie would be sent to live with the field slaves.

Queen hated Lizzie. Miss Lizzie. Ma'am. It didn't matter what Queen did, Miss Lizzie would find fault with her, and scold her, or, sometimes, take the switch to her, although she only did that when the Massa was away. At first, Queen had wanted to run away, back to the weaving house, back to her real mammy, and would cry herself to sleep every night in the little attic room she lived in when she first moved to the big house. Slowly it got better, or easier to bear. After William was born, Lizzie had been sick for a long time, and Julie had taken charge of Queen, which was much nicer. When Lizzie got well, things got worse, and then she got sick again when she had another little baby, Jane, and things got better. Jane died when she was very young, and Miss Lizzie had stayed in her room for weeks, but when she came out she was crosser with Queen than ever. Things got better again after Mary was born, and for quite a long time afterward, because Miss Lizzie had been really ill.

When William was about five he moved into his own bedroom, the same one Massa used to sleep in when he was little, and it became Queen's room as well, for she had to look after him. The two grew up together as brother and sister who were not brother and sister, but young Massa and slave. They became good friends, but sometimes William laughed at Queen, and reminded her that she was a slave, and sometimes he said unkind things, especially about nigras, which hurt Queen, even when she agreed with him. Next year Queen was to move out of William's room, because he was growing up, and look after Mary. Mary was nice, but always poorly, and Miss Lizzie's favorite. Queen knew she would miss William.

She saw her mammy sometimes, walking around the plantation, but she wasn't allowed to speak to her then. In the early days, when she first moved to the big house, Queen thought her mammy walked by on purpose, just to see her, and she ran to her once, and hugged her and cried, but Miss Lizzie had been really angry and Mammy hadn't walked by as often. Once a week, on Saturday afternoons, she was sent to visit her mammy for a few hours, and Queen loved those visits. They'd sit and talk for hours, and Easter wanted to know everything that was happening at the big house, and how Queen was being treated. Queen used to tell her of the times when Miss Lizzie was nasty to her, and begged Mammy to tell the Massa when he came to visit, so that he would stop Miss Lizzie, but Mammy said she had to put up with it because of the other advantages she was getting. Still, it did seem to Queen that Miss Lizzie had been a little bit less cross after that, and she was sure someone had said something to somebody, and that someone was her mammy and that somebody was her pappy, the Massa.

Queen adored Jass. He was always kind to her, and gave her little presents at Christmas and on her birthday. She loved him so much she called him her pappy

503

once, but Miss Lizzie had been really angry then and had insisted that Parson Dick cane her on her bare bottom. Parson Dick didn't want to do it, Queen knew that, but he was a slave like Queen, and had to do what he was told. He caned her hard and told her never to say it again, and Queen was a good girl and did what she was told, and never called her Massa her pappy again.

She attended the dancing classes and music lessons that the tutors who came to The Forks gave William and, later, Mary. She learned to sew and to set and wait at table, and Julie taught her to cook. She wasn't allowed to take real school lessons, because she wasn't allowed to learn to read and write, but that didn't matter because Cap'n Jack taught her those things, although he made her swear on a Bible she would never tell anyone, but she knew Massa knew because he gave her a book for her birthday once. She became supremely skilled at self-protection, she seldom said the wrong thing to anyone anymore, she bit her tongue when Miss Lizzie was sharp with her, she ignored the other slaves when they made fun of her, and she learned to put on one face for Lizzie and another for Missy Sally, who always treated her nicely. She didn't inquire too much about the outside world because the world she lived in was complicated enough, and because she had no ambition to live anywhere else but at The Forks of Cypress with her true pappy and her real mammy.

She loved going out though, if only to escape for a while from her sometimes suffocating circumstances, and town was a real adventure. But first they had to visit Miss Becky.

The Sinks was a pretty house, in a glade about three miles from The Forks. The Massa had built it about five years ago, when Massa Perkins died. Miss Becky had made a lot of fuss about it, and was furious when Massa told her the name of the house, because she said it was very unromantic. She preferred to call it "Chez Pocahontas," which Queen and William thought was funny. They giggled about the name now, as the carriage pulled into the drive, until Lizzie told them off sharply, and told Queen to remember her place.

Tragic circumstances had attended the Perkinses a few years ago. Convinced that his fortune was being frittered away by his wife's extravagances, William Perkins had plunged, once again, into land speculation, this time with disastrous results. If he had consulted wiser, more cautious minds, catastrophe might have been avoided, but he was convinced he was a better businessman than any of his associates, and especially Tom Kirkman, who had been his original adviser. After all, Tom had not been doing all that well recently. The Jackson fortune was still considerable, but no one could deny that it had not thriven under Tom's stewardship. He had ignored all his father-in-law's precepts, divested them of much of their land and invested everything in cotton and the banks. Which was fine, thought William, when the price of cotton was high, but cotton was a commodity subject to market forces, and banks frequently failed.

Willing prey to his fears and unscrupulous developers, William invested far too much money in new territories in the West, and bought thousands of acres in California, sight unseen. When this land proved to be unusable, unsellable desert, the Perkins fortune collapsed, and William with it. He panicked, and sold everything he had at giveaway prices. He also sold his wife's slaves. Becky was away in Atlanta attending some function, and, knowing he didn't have much time, he called the auctioneer in one morning, and by evening all the slaves but three were gone: the cook, the housekeeper, and the gardener.

Becky was speechless with rage when she found out, and wept for her darling darkies, and for herself. How could she live? How could she visit anyone of quality now, bereft of attendants? How could she hold her head up in public? She took to her room with a sick headache, and swore she would never speak to her husband again. She never did. The money resulting from the sale of the slaves was a useless, tiny flame quickly extinguished in the ocean of William's disasters. Blinded by panic, he could see no alternative but bankruptcy, and died of a bleeding ulcer the day after Becky withdrew to her bedroom.

All this affected Becky's mind. Increasingly unstable since Lizzie's marriage, she dwelt near the border of the insane, but the loss of money, slaves, position, and husband in such quick succession persuaded her to cross the dividing line and take up residence in the comforting country of the deranged. Lizzie was distraught, but Jass had been good to Becky, and built her a house so that she might be in close proximity to her daughter, and had given Becky a couple of slaves to look after her. She spent her days in a sweetly remembered but illogically recalled past. Above everything, she realized how very much she had always adored her husband, and her loveliest memories were of William, who was waiting for her patiently, in another house he was building somewhere not far away, and of her former slaves, who were mysteriously visiting her husband, and would come for her one day, carriage ready, to take her to him. In her more lucid moments, she understood that William was dead, and she saw no reason for living, but Fate was cruel to her, and would not remove her from her vale of grief.

She loved her daughter, but Lizzie had her own life as mistress of a great mansion, and The Sinks was not Becky's idea of the house that suited the woman she had once been. She loved Jass, but he did not provide her with enough slaves to regain her foothold in society. She loved her grandson, young William, who had been named in honor of her late husband, but he was not the William she wanted. She loved her other grandchildren:

506

the little ones were just gorgeous and she wanted to run and tell her William all about them, but he was never there. She wished they wouldn't bring that half-caste girl with them all the time. She reminded Becky of things she would rather forget, but young William was very fond of her and it was proper that he have a personal slave, although it was high time the girl moved out of his room. If only she weren't so very white. Queen, as the mostly white nigra slave child of her son-in-law, perplexed Becky. Indeed, the whole issue of black and white, slave and free, was confusing to her, as was much of the rest of the modern world, and she no longer collected gossip or trivia or scandal, because without William she had no one to tell it to, and without darkies she could not go visiting. Everything she had ever been was what people perceived her to be, and she could not bear to be thought of as a lonely widow, eking out a solitary existence on someone else's charity.

She greeted them now, pleased to see them but frantically worried about events in the world, and filled with questions. The few visitors who still came to see her—Sally, and the minister's wife, and some others who, distressed by her present circumstances, had forgiven her past affectations—had kept her informed of the developing crisis between North and South, and Becky was agog to know the outcome of the presidential election. Jass had little positive news for her. The results had not reached them yet, which was why he was going into town, but the general feeling was that Abraham Lincoln would win on a platform dedicated to limiting the extension and expansion of the slaveholding states, and that if he did, South Carolina would almost certainly secede from the Union. It had threatened it before, effectively done it before, thirty years ago, and over the last couple of years the Southern dealings with Washington had been increasingly, dangerously, fractious.

Becky said nothing, but held Little Sally to her, and tears dribbled from her eyes. Any fool could tell that this Lincoln was an abolitionist at heart, however cunningly disguised. The slaves believed it, they talked of nothing else, and Becky trusted their gossip. Thus a Republican victory would put an abolitionist in the White House, with inconceivable consequences for the South, but it hardly seemed to bother her family. They took tea, and chatted about inconsequential things, without seeming to understand that they were standing on the very brink of a precipice. When they said their good-byes, Becky begged Jass to send news of the election as soon as he knew the outcome, and he promised that he would.

Jass kept his word, but tardily. He did not send old Ephraim to tell Becky the result until the next day, and by then it was too late.

Nathan, one of Jass's slaves who attended Becky, heard the news from Joshua, the gardener, who heard it from some men who had been rafting downriver. Nathan told Mary, the cook, who told Becky.

"Massa Linkun Presyden," she said.

Becky said nothing, but puzzled as always about the phenomenon that was the slave grapevine. How had news of his victory, for Becky had no doubt that it was true, reached them before it reached her? Unable to read or write, or at least forbidden to, what could they know of Abraham Lincoln, how did they have news of him, and how had he become their hero? Becky didn't know very much about him herself, but what she did know frightened her.

"Us gwine be free," Mary said, as a statement of fact, without any excitement or rancor.

Becky finished her supper in silence, and went to her room. She spent a long time preparing for bed, tying her hair in cotton curlers and putting on her best nightown. She tried to avoid thinking about the future,

508

although the future as envisioned by Mary kept impinging of her mind.

She was troubled by the nightmare of John Brown. Denmark Vesey had been one thing, and Nat Turner another—they were nigras—but a white man freeing slaves! Killing white folk! Becky could not imagine what the world was coming to. Or rather, she could, for she knew that the election of Lincoln almost certainly presaged a war between the states—no one had talked about anything else for weeks—and while she believed passionately that the dear Southern boys would fight to the very last drop of their blood, and would whip those Yankee curs in a matter of weeks, she dreaded the possibility of their failure. If the South lost, the ramifications were too appalling to consider, for how could they live without slaves? What would happen to her, and to Lizzie, and to all of Lizzie's dear children, who would never know the fabulous society that was their birthright? She had an awful vision of Lizzie trying to run The Forks of Cypress without any slaves, and the very idea of it made her weep in horror.

Free nigras! It wasn't fair to them; they were children, the house ones, who needed a firm, guiding white hand. And the field hands, the bucks, would be running around raping and pillaging at will; no woman would be safe in her bed. It was all very well for the Yankees to claim the blacks were equal, but they were not, any fool knew that, the Bible said so, and in any case, there were not so many blacks in the North for the Yankees to be scared of. Thinking about a violent, impoverished South gave her a sick headache, and she climbed into bed, determined not to leave that bed until she felt better. She picked up her Bible and it fell open at Revelation. It was an omen to Becky. The last days were upon them.

Rather than contemplate the absymal future or think of her impoverished present, she let her mind frolic through the groves of her favorite realm, the past. She dreamed that her retinue attended her still, as they did in her glory days, when she was young, when the world was her oyster and she its most precious pearl, and when William was there, to shield her and provide for her and protect her.

She called out his name, and a miracle happened! A man came in the door, although it was locked, she was sure—she always locked it in case the darkies should forget themselves and come bursting in to ravish her, or some white abolitionists to murder her. For a moment she was convinced it was an avenging John Brown, come to destroy her, sword in one hand, Bible in the other, and her heart skipped a beat. And another. And another. And as her heart went haywire, she realized it was William; she could see him clearly, and the door was open, and there was light in the hallway beyond.

He stood by the bed and smiled at her, and she felt a flooding sense of relief. He had come back to her, as she had always known he would, and now she could pour out her heart to him, and tell him of her many problems, and he would make it all right again, and she could hold her head up high.

Now was not the time to talk, she knew that. He held out his hand to her, and to her surprise, her sick headache had completely disappeared. She felt better than she had done for years. She knew he wanted to take her to show her the lovely new mansion he had been building for her, so she took his hand. He helped her out of bed, and they walked together toward the door, toward the light, which was getting stronger and stronger and held no fears for her, even though she was improperly dressed for daylight, and her hair was a mess.

But this was a welcoming light which told her that nothing mattered anymore. She knew with absolute conviction that when she walked with William into that dazzling light, she would, at last, be happy.

510

52

With defiant shouts of bravado, the South had lived in expectation of the possibility of the election of a Republican president for months. It would surely lead to secession by at least some of the states, and no one could chart those unpredictable, stormy waters. Jass had tried to shield his wife and children from the rumors and the passions kindled, but today was a momentous day, perhaps a historic one, and he felt they should have some understanding of the forces at work, for their lives might never be the same again.

They said their farewells to Becky at The Sinks, and headed for Florence. William and Mary were chattering excitedly, in a party mood, for visits to town were rare, and even Queen, usually so shy in front of Lizzie, was joining in the fun. Until Lizzie reminded her of her manners. Queen fell silent then, her eyes down, fiddling with her handkerchief. Jass forgave Lizzie in his mind, as he always did, for he knew she was on edge about the day, and worried about her unborn child. He rode beside the carriage and talked happily to the children, and occasionally to Queen, who looked up at him with adoring, grateful eyes.

As they neared Florence, Jass began to regret his decision, for half the county seemed to have had the same idea. Carriages packed with countryfolk were descending on the town from all directions, and rough men on horseback calling and hallooing to each other as if in boisterous anticipation of a wild party. Yet this is what it is, thought Jass, and I cannot shield them from the experience forever.

Isaac guided the horses carefully through the packed streets, and brought the carriage to a halt outside the bank, where Jass was to meet Tom Kirkman. The greatest crowd was gathered around the telegraph office, but throughout the town the festive, volatile air prevailed. People were milling around, aimlessly, excitedly, waiting for the news that might change their lives. Young men roamed the streets publicly announcing the glory of an independent South and the fate of the Yankees if Lincoln won, while older men on the hustings urged those same young men to join militia units, in preparation for the coming Armageddon, and other, more sober souls bewailed the catastrophe of secession, and the glory of the Union.

Queen found it all very frightening, and Lizzie was appalled. She hadn't wanted to come, certainly hadn't wanted to bring the little ones, but Jass had business to do, and she hadn't wanted to stay alone at The Forks without his protection, on this day of days. She refused to leave the carriage, and resisted her older children's pleas to be allowed to walk for a while, until Jass interceded on their behalf.

Mary looked at the paramilitary activity in wonder and a little fear.

"Is there going to be a war, Papa?" she asked her father.

"Of course not!" Jass was reassuring. "Why would Americans want to fight Americans?"

No one had an answer for that. Except Queen.

"Perhaps because of slavery," Queen said, and made Lizzie angry.

"Hush, girl," Lizzie snapped. "Speak when you're spoken to."

Queen looked down, and William jumped in. "It looks like war," he said.

"It's all a lot of fuss and bother about nothing," Jass told them, with more conviction than he felt. Nor did he tell them why he was going to the bank. "Don't you worry your little heads about it."

He gave them a little money and told them they could look in the shops for half an hour, but they must be careful, must never lose sight of Isaac and the carriage, and should not, under any circumstances, speak to strange men.

"Oh, Papa," William groaned. "Everyone knows us here."

"Times have changed, and there are a lot of strange men in town," Lizzie told him. "Queen, you may keep them company and look after them."

They set off in high spirits, the three of them, William, Mary, and Queen, and excitedly nervous. Jass watched them for a moment, reassured Lizzie as to their welfare, and went into the bank. Lizzie stayed in the carriage with Poppy and the babies, and told Isaac to keep his whip ready.

It was the best fun. Queen was a pretty girl, and even the roughest boys made way for her as they passed by. Some whistled, which made William giggle. They stopped to listen to a very loud man on a soapbox, exhorting the brave to join his militia unit. He wore an old uniform that had seen action against the Indians in the West, and he was attended by a couple of younger men, in newer versions of the same uniform.

They didn't really understand what he was shouting—it all seemed to be about blood and death and honor—and Queen thought the uniforms were ugly, but it aroused the older people listening, and they cheered and clapped everything he said.

It was a chilly afternoon, and they were quickly bored, and moved away to find other amusements. Farther down the street, a minister was on another soapbox, proclaiming the glory of the indissoluble Union that was the United States, but only a small group was listening to him, a few cheering, most booing, and a fight broke out between some young men and one of the minister's supporters. Queen tried to shepherd her charges away, but William made a fuss because he wanted to see the fight. Queen told him she

513

couldn't stand the sight of blood, and reluctantly William agreed. They moved away, but fifty yards down the street they heard a wolf whistle. They turned to see that the three young hooligans from the fight were following them. They were poor whites, crackers, but dressed in their Sunday best.

"Those rude boys!" Mary was angry. "How dare they!"

William winked at Queen, stopped walking, and pretended to look into a shop window. "I think they like you, Queen," he said, for the fun of it all appealed to him. Queen wanted to be away, out of here, home where it was safe, as quickly as possible, but she had to attend William, and he seemed to be enjoying himself.

They stared in a shop window, and within moments, they saw the reflections of the young men behind them. They turned from the window and the young men tipped their hats.

"Afternoon, sweetheart, pretty day," the biggest and handsomest said to Queen.

"We don't speak to strange men," Mary told them tartly, while William pretended to be doing nothing.

"Oh, we're not strange," another laughed. "Just strangers."

"And we'd like to be friends," his pal agreed.

Mary could do a fair imitation of her mother as Southern belle when she wanted to. "Pay no attention to them," she told Queen.

"Oh, don't be so heartless." The first young man played this game. He had no interest in Mary, who was too young, but if she was companion to that older, dark-haired, violet-eyed darling, that was fine by him. "We've come to enlist for the war, and you might be the last young ladies we talk to in years."

"We might even die," another chimed in. "Defending your honor."

Although they included Mary in the fun, they were

staring at Queen. It made her nervous, and she tried to hide behind Mary.

"My papa says there isn't going to be a war," Mary insisted, and the boys laughed.

"Then your papa doesn't know much," the third one, who was very spotty, said, and moved closer to Queen. "So how about it? One little kiss for a soldier on his way to defend your honor?"

He grabbed the terrified Queen and gave a peck on the lips before she really knew what was happening.

The boy grinned in triumph and his friends cheered. "There, that didn't hurt, did it?"

It repelled Queen. She felt his hot breath on her face, stale with the smell of beer and unwashed teeth, saw spots of blood on his shirt, and knew it was the blood of the man the hooligans had beaten up. She felt the power in his arms when he grabbed her, knew she would be helpless if he wanted any more from her. She knew he was white and she was a nigra. She turned to William for help, and he had enjoyed the sport, but now took command.

"I'm surprised at you," he told them. "How dare you kiss my slave girl!"

The effect was startling and immediate, and was what William intended and Queen wanted. All sense of flirting deserted the young men, to be replaced by surly anger. For a moment, Queen thought they might hit her. The one who had kissed her spat violently, and wiped his mouth. Queen saw hatred in his eyes, hatred for her.

"How was I to know?" He shouted his grievance to the world. "The bitch looks white."

His friends were as angry. "Keep her off the streets; send her back to the cotton fields where she belongs," the first said, as they moved away.

"Damned high yallas," the third called back. "Ought to be put down at birth."

They were gone, still shouting abuse, and Queen shivered in relief. She was used to slights about her color and her blood, but she had no experience of men, and had never encountered anything like this before. She had seen for the first time what the other slaves talked of sometimes, this irrational urge of violence by white to black.

"Thank you, Massa Bill. I was scared," she said.

William had been scared for a moment, too, but was proud of the way he had coped, and continued his role as Massa.

"Pay no attention, they're just poor white trash," he told Queen.

But someone else was crying.

"I don't want a war," Mary sobbed, for the anger of the young men, and the violence behind it, were something she, like Queen, had never seen before. She longed to be back in the security of The Forks. "I hate soldiers."

At The Forks, all was calm and peaceful. Angel, who was almost as old as Sally, climbed breathlessly up the stairs to wake her mistress from her nap, for visitors were expected. Sally was asleep on top of her covers, and woke to Angel's nudging. She drank her tea while Angel fixed her hair, and prepared herself to receive. She heard the gig in the driveway, and sighed, for she was not looking forward to her afternoon.

Henderson was wearing his best suit and had polished his boots to a military shine, for he was seldom invited to the big house for social purposes, and wanted to impress. His new wife, Letitia, wearing one of the fine dresses she had brought with her from Charleston, stood beside him, agog with anticipation at this sudden and unexpected leap in her standing, and determined not to be overawed by her surroundings or her husband's employers.

But she could hardly restrain a squeak of amazement

516

as Parson Dick opened the door and they swept into the hall, grander than anything she had ever seen.

"The Mistress is in the sitting room," Parson Dick said. He led the way, opened the double doors, and announced them. Sally, dressed in stern black, rose to greet them, and Letitia Henderson moved forward, took Sally's offered hand, and bobbed a tiny curtsy, which she immediately regretted.

Alec Henderson had not been immune to the talk of war. He had taken stock of his life and had decided to put his domestic house in order. He had advanced beyond his wildest imaginings. As he had predicted and intended, he had assumed the function of overseer when Mitchell retired, and worked hard and well in his new capacity. His was a tougher regime for the slaves than the previous overseer's had been, but something of Mitchell's attitude to the slaves had rubbed off on Henderson. He had been raised to believe blacks were scum and less than animals, but Mitchell had persuaded his able student that they were simply animals, valuable ones at that, and responded better to reasonable treatment than to ruthlessness. The abuse of his power, Mitchell told him, would simply lead to runaways and less productivity. At first, Henderson had dismissed the arguments. Seething with resentment toward his martinet father and the way he had been treated as a boy, he tended to vent his frustrations with his own life on those less fortunate than he, the niggers. Mitchell had seen this and had spent long hours with the young man, and become something of a surrogate father to him. By example and patient instruction, Mitchell had calmed Henderson's rash temper and persuaded him that the proof of true power was in how little you needed to prove it. Whites were the natural masters of niggers, and they knew that and accepted it. Any brute fool could have a nigger whipped for any small justification, but what did you do if the justification became

517

greater? Have them whipped some more? Flog them till they were dead? Dead they were useless, and alive they were valuable livestock.

Henderson had never appreciated that slaves had actual and considerable monetary value before, and while Mitchell never changed the young man's basic attitude to blacks, his financial arguments had a profound effect.

For Henderson worshiped money, and was determined to have his share. He knew he would never be rich in the way Massa Jackson was rich, but if he did his job well, and saved carefully, he could look forward to the day when he would have a small farm of his own, and several slaves, and live in comfort and security for the rest of his life. It was all coming to pass as he had hoped. For ten years he had been overseer, living in the cottage provided for him, cooked for by a Jackson slave with provisions acquired from the big house kitchen, and had been able to save most of his wages. Once a year he gave himself a treat, a week's holiday by the sea at Charleston, and during that week he allowed himself a couple of visits to whores, but otherwise he lived a spartan existence and now had a reasonable stash of gold, which he kept in a strongbox under the floorboards of his cottage. He was not wealthy by any means, but he was better off than many of his unlanded peers. He was tough and aggressive with the niggers, and demanded hard work from them, but although he used the whip occasionally, he controlled his urge to flog them on any provocation, and things at The Forks were running smoothly, if not as moderately as once they had.

Success and security had mellowed him, and for a couple of years he had been thinking it was time to find himself a bride, but he couldn't work out where he might meet one. His position gave him occasional access to women of his new class, but he had no social skills with them, and was happiest in the company of other

518

men. He wouldn't touch mulattas and despised white trash, for he had grown up in their company and they reminded him too much of his disadvantaged youth.

Talk of war had given an urgency to his intentions for matrimony. If there was a war he would fight, for the idea of free niggers was viscerally repugnant to him. He had come to respect the skills of many of the slaves under his command, and guessed that some few of them would cope with the unthinkable, with freedom; some might even be good farmers, and that made a mockery of his dear dead mother, and of the way she had worked herself to the grave, and died poorer when she left this world than when she came into it. But if there was a war and he had to fight, he would be away from The Forks. He doubted he would lose his job—the Massa could hardly dismiss him for defending the Massa's existence—but his cottage would be empty or, worse, occupied by some temporary overseer, and his store of gold left to the mercy of looters. He could not carry the precious metal with him, and he had no faith in banks.

A dutiful wife would solve the problem by remaining in residence and protecting his interests while he was away. The right wife would increase his standing in the local community. A good wife would look after him, provide him with a bed partner, and give him a son, whom he could teach to be as good a man as himself, and who would inherit all that Henderson was single-mindedly working for. Without an heir, his good fortune was meaningless, since he had no intention of leaving anything to his wretched brothers and sisters.

But where to find such a wife? Happily, the same possibility of war that had accentuated his problem also solved it for him. After harvest he had gone to Charleston for his annual leave and, bored with taverns and whores, had attended a meeting of militant Southern loyalists in a church hall. South Carolina was already threatening secession from the Union if Lincoln won

519

the election, and the debate was firebrand stuff of white supremacy and Yankee knavery, and of the joy and prosperity that must dwell in every Southern heart if the slave states were forced to break away from the North. In Henderson's case, as with most of those present, it was preaching to the converted, but it stirred his blood anew, and he decided on a visit to the whorehouse afterward. He never got there. When the speeches were done, refreshments were served by the women of the Church Ladies' Union, and Henderson's eye had been taken by the lovely Letitia.

Beauty is in the eye of the beholder, but perhaps only Alec Henderson could have thought Letitia Palmer lovely. Most would have called her plain, but she was everything he was looking for in a wife. Moderately educated and obviously able, Letitia had a commanding personality and was always on the lookout for a spouse, for she was terrified that her prospects of a husband were close to nothing. Oldest daughter of a drunken father who held on to his job as manager of a lumber store by his fingernails and the fact that he was white, and of a hardworking mother who ran a moderately successful millinery shop, Letitia had nursed and raised her siblings, cooked and cleaned for all the family, coped with her sottish father when her mother could not, and spent her free time stitching in the hat shop. Now her younger brothers and sisters were old enough to fend for themselves, and she, with time for herself at last, found that she had missed the carefree boat of youth, and was in sharp danger of being left stranded on the lonely island of spinsterhood.

Because of her mother's hat-making business, she had learned to conduct herself properly on the shopgirl rung of society, but no one had ever taught her how to enjoy herself. She had no idea where to find a husband and put her trust in God to provide a solution. A devout woman, she joined the Social Club of her local church, but she was so used to organizing her wayward family she overzealously organized everyone else, and was not popular. To compensate for this, she made herself indispensable, and now any social function connected with the church saw Letitia in command.

Thus she met a clean and sober young man from Alabama, and on discovering that he was unmarried, had prospects, and was looking for a wife, Letitia almost wept her thanks to the good Lord for showing her the way out of her valley of despair.

"Some more tea, Mrs. Henderson?" Sally asked politely.

The grace and elegance of the Jackson mansion, and the simple unforced authority that Sally possessed by right of rank, breeding, and money, had made the new Mrs. Henderson speechless with awe and envy for the first few moments of their visit, but she had quickly recovered, determined not to let her husband down, and equally determined not to let this rich old biddy get the better of her.

"I think not, Mrs. Jackson," she responded in her plummiest tones, learned in the millinery shop. "I believe I have had an elegant sufficiency."

There was a tiny pause while Sally prayed that Jass and Lizzie would come home soon and save her from this dreadful creature, but she was gracious.

"Cake?" she inquired, when she could think of nothing else to say.

There was a commotion outside, and the sound of horses, and Sally could hardly hide her relief.

"I think that's the Massa now," she said.

Jass, carrying two small boxes with him, was in curiously high spirits, given the momentous news that they had learned in Florence. Lizzie was weeping at that same news, Mary was weeping because she'd told her mother of the incident with the three boys, and William and Queen had been severely scolded, and were pretending to sulk.

Isaac and Polly helped Lizzie and Mary from the

coach, and Poppy with the youngsters, while Queen and William scampered after Jass.

"Mr. and Mrs. Henderson are waiting, sir," Parson Dick told him.

"Oh, damn," Jass responded. "I'd forgotten—"

Lizzie was already on her way upstairs with Mary, giving orders to Poppy about baths for the youngsters, and telling William and Queen it was time for their supper. Jass knew he was on his own.

He went to his study, locked the small boxes in his safe, and strode into the sitting room.

"Sorry, the time slipped away," he announced, kissed his mother, and looked at the overdressed, over made-up, overeager woman sitting expectantly on the edge of the sofa.

"Is this your bride, Alec?" He shook hands with Henderson. "You're a sly one, keeping such a pretty woman secret."

Mrs. Henderson was his loyal servant from that moment, and simpered, while Sally did her best to hide her amusement.

"Happened so fast, sir, on my leave," Henderson began, but his wife was way ahead of him.

"Took one look at him and I said to myself, Letitia, I said, that's the man for you," she gushed.

Queen and William had hung back from Lizzie's commands and had their ears to the keyhole of the sitting-room doors. Parson Dick saw a perfect target, two round little rumps stuck in the air, smacked them both lightly and ordered them upstairs, where their supper was waiting.

"Young ladies and gentlemen do not listen at closed doors," he commanded. They yelled at his gentle smacks, and giggled their way upstairs.

When they were gone, satisfied that the coast was clear, Parson Dick leaned down toward the same keyhole.

522

"My dear mother's heart is broken, of course, that I'm living so far away from home, and my poor father"—Mrs. Henderson took out a handkerchief and dabbed her eyes—"all this talk of war, and me getting wed, his only comfort is the gin."

Jass did not dare look at Sally, but knew he had to give them the news.

"Then I'm afraid he's going to need rather a lot of comfort," he said with a poker face. "Abraham Lincoln has been elected president."

He remember his promise to tell Becky, but saw no sense in disturbing her evening. He would send Ephraim first thing in the morning.

53

"I said to myself, Letitia, I said, that's the man for you!" William giggled, in fair imitation of Mrs. Henderson's affected tones. "Isn't she awful? Why did he marry her?"

He was already in his nightshirt, and Queen was folding his clothes, as she always did.

"I think he's worse than she is," Queen said. She didn't have much to do with the overseer, but whenever they met he was sarcastic to her, and to her mother.

"Perhaps they were made for each other." William was bored with the subject and sat on the window seat. He was in a curious mood. The events of the afternoon had excited him. He'd seen plenty of fights at school, had taken part in several, but had never seen adults beating anyone up before, apart from when one of the slaves got whipped, and that didn't count. The short, sharp, ruffian violence of it had exhilarated him and he had felt like cock of the walk, a few minutes later, at his ability to cope with the hooligans. The talk of war, the pounding hysteria when news of Lincoln's election spread like wildfire from the telegraph office, and the fun of Alec Henderson's matrimony had invoked some new, exciting emotions in him, which somehow all had to do with girls. They were on the brink of stirring times just as he was edging into manhood, and he longed to be older and part of it all.

He wondered if he was old enough to have a proper girlfriend, not like Harriet Peters whom he escorted to Sunday school. Ten years old, she sometimes allowed him to hold her hand, and once, sweating with embarrassment, he had pecked her on the lips, but she screamed, and slapped his face, and told him never to touch her again. Of course, she hadn't meant it, and sat next to him at Sunday school the next week, and shyly held his hand.

"I hope there is a war," he said, staring out at the moonlit, winter landscape. "It would be such fun." He had an adventurous soul, and found much of his life at The Forks boring. Lizzie was trying to mold him to be a Southern gentleman in the way that Becky had molded Lizzie to be a Southern belle, and William resisted it strongly. He was his father's son, and, like Jass when he was young, he wanted adventure, he wanted to be a pioneer, like Gran'ma Sally, only there weren't many frontiers left. The South Seas, perhaps, or Australia.

Queen was also thinking of the afternoon, but had a different view. "I don't think I'd like war," she said. "It might be dangerous."

"Oh, pooh," William laughed. "You wouldn't know very much about it. The men would all go off somewhere a long way away, and have a big fight, that's all. We'd beat the Yankees, they'd beg for mercy, and then it would be over."

"What if the Yankees won?" Queen wasn't convinced it would be so simple.

"That isn't possible," William said seriously, "because they'd try to free the slaves and God doesn't want that. God's on our side."

Queen didn't say anything, because there was no point in arguing with Massas about slaves, but turned down William's comforter, and made the bed cozy with the warming pan.

William's thoughts turned from war to love again, to Letitia Henderson and Harriet Peters.

"I wonder what it's like to be in love?" That surprised Queen, because her mind was still with a possible war. She allowed herself to dream.

"I'm going to marry a prince on a white horse one day," she said, but William laughed.

"Oh, Queen, don't be silly. You're just an itty-bitty slave girl," William told her, kneeling beside the bed. "Who'd marry you?"

Queen knelt beside him and said something privately, to God: "Someone will, one day."

William had begun the formal prayers, of lying down to sleep, and souls being kept. His soul, and his family's, and even the soul of Harriet Peters. Not Queen's soul, of course, because nigras didn't have souls. His papa had told him that, years ago.

"And please let's have a jolly fine war that lasts a long time," he ended up, but wondered if God would approve of his prayer, so he added a little charity. "But only let Yankees get killed."

In case that wasn't enough, he added a little more. "And send someone nice for Queen."

"Amen," both prayed, and laughed.

William climbed into the big four-poster with its warmed sheets and cozy blankets, while Queen snuggled into the uncomfortable pallet at the foot of the bed.

"Good night, Queen," William said affectionately, for they were friends.

"Good night, Massa Bill," Queen said to her brother. They lay in silence, thinking their separate thoughts. Queen seldom voiced hers, because it was not her place, but told her feelings to her good friend God.

"If the war doesn't last very long, I won't be old

enough to fight," William lamented softly. "So where shall I find adventure? I suppose I could become a missionary or something—"

He was lulled to sleep by the balmy breezes of tropical islands, and the image of himself saving Harriet from some niggers who were cooking her in a big pot.

Queen could not go to sleep so easily that night. She didn't mind William's jibes about her matrimonial prospects, she was used to being called "an itty-bitty slave girl" because she was tiny and a slave, but she knew a handsome prince was waiting for her somewhere in the world, and not very far away. This night, she had other things to think about. Like many of the slaves, she knew that events of some importance to her life were in train, but she could not fully appreciate what they were, because she heard only one side of them.

The slaves in the kitchen talked about war, and even though they had no experience of it—what they knew was learned from other, older, field slaves who might have served with their Massa in the Mexican War—the stories didn't seem to fit with William's idea of one big battle a long way away. Mexico was a long way away— Queen wasn't exactly sure where it was—but she knew there'd been more than one big battle. Her gran'pappy had stories of war, too, and someone called Massa Andrew fighting the Injuns and the British, and those wars seemed to last a long time, and lots of people got hurt. She had heard Miss Sally and Julie making all sorts of plans for extra provisions to be put in the cellar, "just in case," but if William was right, then just in case of what? If the fight happened a long way away, why were they stocking up with food here at The Forks? Was the fight going to be near here? The idea of war and battles close to the big house really scared her, especially if the soldiers were like the boys who had accosted her that afternoon.

God's role in a possible war confused her most of all.

She loved God as the Massa and Miss Lizzie and her mammy and gran'pappy and Miss Sally and everyone told her she should, but if God was on the side of the South, did that mean He wanted Queen to be a slave for all her life? Whenever she asked anyone questions about God and some of the confusing things He did, they all told her He moved in mysterious ways, and obviously that was true. She tried to imagine what God looked like, and saw an image of a big, cross old man with a long white beard, and thunderbolts in his hand, but that wasn't very comforting, and she was taught that God was love. The greatest love she could think of was for her pappy, and so she drifted to sleep dreaming she was lying in the Massa's arms, safe in the love of God.

Sally could not sleep. The news of Lincoln's election to the presidency had come as something of an anticlimax to her. Like a gathering storm, it had been on the horizon for months, sweeping toward them with increasing and inexorable certainty, but now that it had happened and had not plunged them immediately into war, it was something of a relief. Not that the danger was past, but Buchanan was still in the White House, it would be four months until Lincoln actually took office, and perhaps, in that time, sanity could prevail. She guessed that some states, at least, would go through the initial processes of secession. South Carolina had called a state convention to begin the process even before the election results were known, but South Carolina had threatened withdrawal from the Union before, and had always backed down. And no one, surely, wanted war, no one wanted the dismemberment of the country. Sally knew very few people who actually advocated disunion, but all those same people believed that if push came to shove, the Southern states could go it alone. The problem was that they might not be allowed to, for Lincoln seemed to care less about the freeing of slaves than he did for the maintenance of the federation.

And what was so important about emancipation? Why were the wretched abolitionists so strident in their views? Why had the Yankees been foolish enough to elect Lincoln? Confusion set in, for she knew in her heart that it was not just the Yankees who had voted for Lincoln; many Southerners must have done so, if only out of fear of the consequences of secession. Briefly she cursed all men, vain creatures who insisted on imposing their views on others. Finally, she realized that what she wanted was for the South to be left alone, to go about its business, and if that meant a confederation of Southern states, then perhaps it was the best solution. There was no need for war. Please, God, don't let there be war. Yet she wept, for she had loved her nation all her life; she had been proud to be a citizen of the United States. For eighty years that blessed country had thriven and prospered, and that it should all end now, over an issue that was irrelevant to the general welfare of the majority of the people, was untenable to her. Why should slavery bother the North when they did not have it?

It would be a bleak Christmas, she thought, and practicality salvaged her from despair. There was so much to do, so many presents still to buy—they hadn't even begun to plan the menus yet—and she took refuge from the depressing affairs of the day in lists of provisions and gifts. Realistically, she knew that her lists would have to be longer than those usual for Christmas, since they had to be prepared for the worst. Already, with Parson Dick and Julie, she had made sure the cellar was well stocked, but she would have to lay in more blankets and sheets, and check with Jass that the barns were full. Like sheep jumping fences, the lists lulled her, and she drifted into an uneasy sleep.

*

528

Lizzie had been feeling chills of fear since that afternoon, when the wild atmosphere in town had disturbed her, and the chaos that surrounded the announcement of the election results had terrified her. Lizzie had never seen such violent emotions on display before, and if this was what the prospect of war could unleash, she dreaded to imagine the unknown horrors that the face of war must bring.

Lizzie was essentially secure and happy in her life, and, like Jass, she loathed change. Jass had proved to be a good and undemanding husband. Lizzie's more dominant personality amused him, perhaps because he had a refuge from it, and he indulged most of her foibles. He asserted his conjugal rights from time to time, but because he was temperate in his demands, Lizzie was happy to accommodate him. She hated the pain of childbirth and its attendant illnesses, and wondered if the illnesses were not brought on by fear of the pain, but it was her duty to provide Jass with children, and so she bore them with fortitude. She had been desolate when tiny Jane died, so soon after childbirth, and she prayed that her new baby would be strong and healthy, a boy, she hoped, in case anything awful should happen to William. Like war.

Sally looked after most of the domestic issues, leaving Lizzie free to socialize and entertain, and while the two would never be close, they had become friends. Lizzie could shop and party, and never have to worry about the dinner menus unless she chose to, and then Sally always deferred to her. She could fret and fuss over the children, or Becky, and Sally would always be there to offer advice and a grandmotherly shoulder for the children, or Becky, to cry on. Lizzie could pamper and spoil Jass, when he allowed her to, or ride around the estate in the company of the politicians and business associates who called with increasing frequency because of the political crisis, or because of their genuine fondness for Jass and his increasing interest in the affairs of their state, and some of them, perhaps, because Lizzie was such good fun.

She had learned to tolerate Queen, who was meek and demure to her, which flattered Lizzie, and she enjoyed the sense of power it gave her over Easter's brat. She had even learned to tolerate Jass's continuing relationship with Easter, because it was discreetly conducted, and relieved Lizzie of at least some of her duties in the bedroom.

Now she believed this almost flawless life was under threat, and she was frightened. It was no use looking to Jass for comfort; he only laughed and said they might all be better off if Alabama did secede. He was almost enjoying himself, Lizzie thought, and had spent much of dinner gossiping about the new overseer's wife, whom Lizzie was sorry she hadn't met, because she sounded dreadful. Whenever she or Sally had tried to talk about the ramifications of Lincoln's election, Jass had been patronizing, and told them not to bother their pretty little heads about it. That had made them cross, but he was so dear and jolly, the meal had passed pleasantly enough.

The evening had been different. Sally had retired early as she often did. She had a little sitting area in her room, and she liked to go there and be alone, and write her diary. Jass and Lizzie had sat together, as they always did, but he had his head stuck in a book. Lizzie did some petit point, and all her fears for the future had simmered through her again, but Jass had been no comfort.

She wanted to be alone with him, not alone as they were here, but upstairs, in bed, drifting to sleep in his safe embrace. She put down her needlework.

"I think I'll go to bed," she said, and kissed him, hoping he'd get the hint.

He looked up from his book. "Sleep well, my love," he said.

So that was it. He was going to her. She didn't want him to go, not tonight. How could he be so thoughtless?

"Will you be long?" She could hardly express her need more plainly.

"Oh—a while," he responded. "I have some things to do."

For an instant, she hated him. She could well imagine what it was he planned to do. But she needed him, or his reassurance.

"Is there going to be a war?" Her voice had a tiny quaver in it, like a lost little girl.

Jass heard the cry for help, and closed his book.

"I'm sure not, my dear," he said calmly, kindly. "I'm sure it's just talk."

She almost believed him, and felt foolish for being scared. He was always so reasonable, and knew so much more about what was going on than she, who waited on the vagaries of any fashionable wind.

"It's so scary, war," she said. She looked at him longingly, hoping he would change his mind, and left the room.

Jass put down his book, and sat in silence. Lizzie was right, it was so scary, war. Yet exciting, too, for the talk of it, the rumor of it, the prospect of it, made Jass feel as if he had just wakened from a deep and lengthy sleep.

For fifteen years, he felt, he had done nothing except live a prosperous, pleasant, unambitious life. For fifteen years, he had been Massa of this plantation, yet he had allowed others the control of it. Tom Kirkman and Sally between them managed most of the business affairs, largely because Jass did not really understand the complexities, and had no real urge to learn. He knew that his patrimony had decreased in that time, because while Tom was a conscientious and able bookkeeper, both of them erred on the side of caution, as if neither was prepared to put the great inheritance at risk. Yet by not

531

taking risks, by swimming with the tide, by having no vision, he had wound up with an estate worth today perhaps half what it had been when James died. Jass had always believed himself to be a simple caretaker of the family fortune, but now he saw that he hadn't taken care of it very well. There had never seemed much point. He'd never be able to do what his father had done, create an empire, and to grasp at something when you didn't believe you could achieve it was a waste of time. He had no real interest in politics, as his father had had, no interest in the wheeling and dealing and political chicanery that were necessary to an illustrious public career, no real interest in anything other than trying to be a good husband and father.

He wondered where his dreams of youth had gone. He no longer felt the urge to settle on the frontier, or cross the Rockies, or see California. It might have been different if he'd gone with Wesley to Texas, all those years ago, and left the inheritance to one of his brothers, but his sense of honor and responsibility would not have allowed him to do that. He wondered what it would have been like if A.J. had lived and become Massa, and Jass had been free to follow his own star, but he wasn't sure what his star was.

Even in the trivia of life he had failed to be his father's son. James had been one of the most renowned breeders of thoroughbred horses in the country. Jass had a few fighting cocks, which didn't do very well in the pit.

For fifteen years, then, he had jogged along with no sense of direction, and the estate had dwindled around him. Now Fortune had matched him to his time, and he stood on the brink of his adventure.

Secession by at least some of the Southern states would happen. Jass was sure of that. And since those states couldn't survive on their own, they would band together in some way, and a new golden age of prosperity lay before them. Free of the constraints of Wash-

532

ington, of federal regulations and tariffs, free of the debilitating need to defend and fight for their right to own slaves, this new confederation of Southern states could form its own alliances and trading patterns and partners, and the resulting wealth would no longer have to subsidize the impecunious Northern industries and the increasing bureaucracy of the federal government. The many visitors to The Forks over the last few months had persuaded Jass, if only because of the residual influence of his father's name, that he could be a voice in this New Jerusalem, and Jass had been flattered and motivated, and had agreed. The Southern states would be free at last to become masters of their own destiny, and he would be part of it.

If the North let them. Few of Jass's friends wanted war; they wanted to be left alone, to get on with their own business, and if that meant leaving the Union, so be it. But the North, that is the federal government, that is, Lincoln, had sworn they would not, could not, leave. The Union would be preserved, no matter what.

Well, some of them were going to leave—it was as certain as night follows day—and then Lincoln could either back down or go to war. From all he had heard, Jass did not believe that Lincoln would back down, and the idea of war between Americans was not new. Bloody war, civil war, had existed in Kansas for almost all of the decade. Settlers from the North were determined the territory should be admitted to the Union as a Free State, and others from the South had been as determined on an opposite outcome.

Jass no longer cared if slavery was right or wrong for others; it was right for them, for the South. He had seen the figures for the plantation and knew that the Jackson fortune would dwindle even further, might diminish entirely, without slaves, and this was true for most of his peers. It didn't matter to him that slaveholders were a minority of the Southern population: Slave owning was the Southern way, the basis of the Southern economy; it kept the few wealthy, so that prosperity would trickle down to the many. Without slavery, the South could not exist.

Nor could he bear the thought that his own niggers, whom he believed he cared for and protected, should end up as homeless beggars in city slums, as he had seen in the North. He had no desire to increase the realm of the South; if the new states and territories wanted to be free of slavery, then let them join a free-state Union, which is what he believed Washington now represented.

For there was no real union between the North and South, and never had been. Eighty years ago, a group of sovereign territories had joined together in a common cause, and once the British were defeated they had little in common. All the arguments and treaties for union were a waste of time, because disunion was inevitable. The Missouri Compromise, Henry Clay's Compromise of 1850, the Fugitive Slave Act, and so many others were all attempts to paper over an essential gulf.

"A house divided against itself cannot stand," Lincoln had said, and Jass agreed with him. And since the house was divided, then let it fall into its separate parts. His fervent prayer now was that the North would not interfere with the Southern ambitions, but if they did, if there was war, the South would fight to protect its own, and Jass would fight to protect what was right-fully, morally, his. And they would win.

Lizzie had been wrong about his plans for this evening. He would go to see Easter, but later. First he had other, more important things to do.

He went to his study, opened the safe, and took out the two small boxes Tom had given him at the bank. Each was filled with a thousand gold coins, British sovereigns. Jass went down to the cellar and buried one of the boxes in a small hole that he had prepared the previous day, under the duckboards, so that it would be unseen.

He took the other box, a lamp, and a small shovel, and went out into the wintry night.

Not far from the weaving house, in a small grove of trees, was an old, spreading oak. The ground around it was hard, but Jass was full of vigor, and he quickly dug a hole, laid the box in it, and covered it over. He tramped on the freshly dug earth, covered the small scar with dried leaves, and hoped for rain to disguise his handiwork, but in any case he had chosen his spot carefully. Few people had any reason to come here.

The physical labor had tired him and energized him, and now he went to Easter.

She was in bed, asleep, but stirred when he came in. She lay silent for a while, watching him wash his hands in the basin.

"What you bin doin'?" she asked.

He turned and smiled at her. "Nuttin'," he said. She knew better than to question him further.

He stripped off his clothes, and climbed into bed with her, snuggling hard against her, letting her body warm him.

She stroked his hair, and bided her time. She always knew when he needed to talk to her.

"There's going to be a war, Easter," he said at last.

She did not really understand the implications, very few people did, for wars didn't happen in Alabama, except once, long ago, against Indians, but no one could remember that, and Indians didn't count.

She understood one thing, though. She knew the war would be about slavery, and that if the North won, she might be free. It frightened her, for she didn't want her life to change.

"Because of slavery?" She knew it, but wanted to hear him confirm it.

"Yes," he said.

They lay in silence again, while another, as frightening, thought crept up on her.

535

"Will you fight?" Her voice was a tiny whisper.

He didn't speak, but she felt his head nod.

"Because of slavery?"

Now he moved astride, and looked into her eyes.

"Because of you," he said. "Because I couldn't bear to lose you."

Love of him swept through her, and she gave herself to him, and when he kissed her, he ignored the taste of salt tears on her cheeks.

Afterward, they drifted to sleep, but woke as they always did, just before dawn. He dressed and went back to the big house, and remembered to tell Ephraim, who was already at the stables, to ride to The Sinks and tell Miss Becky that Lincoln had won the election.

Ephraim stared at him for a long moment.

"We gwine be free, Massa?" he asked.

"Hope not," Jass replied blithely. "I couldn't afford to pay you wages."

He went upstairs, took a bath, dressed for breakfast, and came downstairs again. Which is when Ephraim came back with the awful news that Miss Becky had died in the night.

Jass told Lizzie himself, and William and Mary, while Lizzie wept. The rest of that day was spent in coping with the bereavement.

It was not until two days later that he had the time to take Sally for a walk to an old oak tree behind the weaving house.

Already there was scant evidence of the hole he had dug. He showed it to her, in case anything should happen to him, and told her of the small provision it contained for their uncertain future.

536

54

Pocahontas Rebecca Meredith Bolling Perkins was buried two days later in a simple grave next to that of her dear departed husband, William. Her death cast a further pall of despondency over the Jackson family, and no one except Jass looked forward to Christmas with much enthusiasm. Lizzie took to her bed for a week, partly out of grief for her mother, partly out of concern for the general political situation, and partly out of care for her unborn child. Sally took over as surrogate mother, and tried to brighten everyone's spirits, but she was concerned at what the coming year would bring, and had no real heart for frivolity. William and Mary had never experienced the death of a loved one in any real sense—they had been too young to fully understand the passing of Gran'pa Perkins—and Becky's death disturbed them greatly. Christmas became more of a religious holiday than a festive one to them, for death and the dangerous times had turned all their thoughts to God.

Except for Jass, who mourned for Becky but gloried in the preparations for the coming Southern triumph. He spent little time with his family, but journeyed each day to Florence, to plot and plan with like-minded friends, and to be near the telegraph office. Hope of a bright, independent future, and the excitement of possible action, overrode their genuine fear of war. All of them believed that the critical arguments between the North and the South, as old as the country, had to be resolved, but there were many who were dedicated to the Union, and the arguments for and against breaking away raged between lifelong friends.

In the middle of December Jass received a letter from his old college chum, George Pritchard. The letter was friendly and informative, describing the Northern attitude to the election, and the present public mood. Although a few thought that if any Southern states wanted to secede they should be allowed to go in peace, for it was not worth blood to keep them, most of his friends believed that the Union must be preserved at no matter what cost, and the truculent Southern states be brought to heel. George reiterated his strident opposition to the institution of slavery, and asked Jass to cast his lot with those Southerners, and there were many, George thought, who believed in emancipation. Most of all, he begged Jass to use whatever influence he had to persuade his political friends in Alabama not to take the dangerous path of disunion.

"We are the future," George wrote, "it is molded by us, and perhaps the die is already cast. But we cannot go lightly into this unknown territory, for it may bring the end of that which we both hold dear and for which we would gladly have given our lives, our country. We are one nation, under God, indivisible. It is my most fervent belief that the new President will act most forcibly against any attempt to wreck that covenant, and that will set friend against friend, cousin against cousin, brother against brother. Surely there must be a way to bring about a peaceful resolution to this crisis, for I cannot believe that, in your heart, you wish to kill me, just as I have no desire to destroy you. Yet if the extreme voices on both sides have their way, that will surely be the outcome, and all of us will lose."

The letter ended warmly and affectionately with the compliments of the season to all the Jacksons from all the Pritchard family, and George wished especially to be remembered to Cap'n Jack.

Jass was touched by the letter. He read it twice and then put it away in a drawer. It was too late; the die was already cast. Alabama would not be the first to secede, and if no other state did, Alabama would not, he knew from discussions with his political friends. But if another state took the giant leap first, Alabama would not be the last to follow.

On the twentieth of December South Carolina adopted the ordinance of secession from the Union. Throughout the state the announcement was greeted with bands, church bells, and cannon fire, and joyously received by the populace. Whatever their attitude to South Carolina's actions, the rest of the South held its breath, but nothing happened.

Outgoing President Buchanan chose to do nothing. The president-elect could do nothing. So nothing was done.

Euphoria swept the South. Sanity had prevailed. South Carolina was now a sovereign country, and no wrathful Yankee army challenged her independence. Christmas Eve in Florence was as splendid and exultant as anyone could remember. The churches were full. The shops stayed open late; the taverns didn't close their doors. The streets were thronged with people, all wishing each other, from the bottom of their hearts, the merriest Christmas and the happiest of New Years.

There were dissenting voices, those who, like George Pritchard, took their pledge of allegiance to the Union as a most solemn vow, but they were lost in the extravagant excitement and the general relief that there wasn't going to be a war. Jass was euphoric, and galloped home from Florence, shouting the news to anyone who might listen. He gathered his family into his joyous embrace, and Christmas became, after all, a splendid celebration, with Jass the most genial Santa Claus.

The slaves at The Forks had no cause to celebrate or the means to do so. South Carolina's action was fatal to their dreams, and the lack of retaliation by the North proved the promises of Linkun to be empty. They knew little of him except what they had heard through the grapevine, but they had allowed themselves to believe, because they wanted to, because they needed to, that he represented a possible end to their bondage. Now all they saw was a future as hopeless as their past.

Cap'n Jack shut himself in his cabin, and swore he would not come out until he was carried out, in his coffin. Queen was allowed to spend part of Christmas Day with her mammy, and she and Easter went to Cap'n Jack's cabin and banged on the door, begging him to join them at the weaving house, but he would not. The last best chance of seeing freedom in his lifetime was gone and now he wanted to die, he shouted at them.

The women shrugged and left him to his tantrum. They spent a happy day together, with no special celebration, content to be in each other's company, and content with the way the world was going, for neither of them wanted war, neither of them particularly wanted the slave dream of freedom to become reality without the condition both women attached to it, which was that they be allowed to stay at The Forks, in circumstances they both understood. For each woman, in her separate way, loved the same man, and that man was their Massa.

Parson Dick was as depressed as Cap'n Jack, but had a happier solution. He stole a bottle of brandy from the cellar and decided to get drunk. Not wanting to be alone, he tucked the bottle under his jacket and went to Cap'n Jack's cabin.

"Go away," the recluse shouted.

"I got liquor," Parson Dick called softly.

After a few moments of silence, Cap'n Jack opened the door. Parson Dick went inside, and the two old friends drowned their sorrows in Jass's good cognac.

Like the other slaves, Parson Dick had heard the rumors that this new president was their champion against slavery, but he had more immediate reasons than most to hope that the rumors were true.

540

For Parson Dick had fallen in love.

A few months ago, the Coffee family had requested that Jass loan them Parson Dick for a week. Their own butler was ill, they had two important functions to host, and it seemed silly to buy a new slave, but they would happily pay for the temporary butler. Jass, genial as ever and having no particular need of Parson Dick that week, had agreed. Slaves were frequently hired out to others, and their Massa paid for their services, so Parson Dick made the short journey to the Coffee plantation on the other side of Florence with his warrant of travel in his pocket, and quickly took charge of the household. As he was serving port one evening, a guest commented on the excellence of his manners. Massa Coffee laughed, and said he hoped so, the damned nigger was costing enough. Then Parson Dick found out that Jass was receiving forty dollars for his hire, with not one cent of it going to the slave.

Expert at simple arithmetic, Parson Dick multiplied forty dollars a week by fifty-two, and realized that if the money had come to him he would be earning over two thousand dollars a year. Parson Dick was stunned. He knew he had value as a slave—on the block he would have fetched a splendid sum, perhaps as much as three thousand—but that was a once only figure, and this new sum represented a regular income. Like every slave, he longed to be free, longed to be paid for his labor, but because the dream of freedom was so elusive, he had never bothered to work out what he might earn when that glorious day came.

Two thousand dollars a year! It was a phenomenal sum, and it infuriated him that Jass was receiving that money and not he. Later that night he sat in the kitchen with Ruby, the Coffee housekeeper, with whom he had struck up an immediate friendship, and poured out his grievances to her. Ruby was completely sympathetic, completely understanding, completely supportive, and even more bitter about her circumstances than Parson Dick. She had been owned for many years by a Massa in Georgia, had nursed him through his ailing final days, and on his deathbed, he had promised her freedom. Once the old man had gone, his surviving relatives saw no need or reason to honor the pledge, and had sold Ruby to her present owners.

Fueled by Parson Dick's indignation, she worked out what her weekly value might be, and the pair realized that, jointly, they would bring in over three thousand a year. If they were free. The figures shocked them.

They also realized that they wanted to be together, to be a pair, to be married, but they had no way of achieving it or, if they did marry, of living under a common roof, for they had separate Massas and lived on different plantations. It was remotely possible that if they told their Massas of their love, then the Coffees might trade their butler for Parson Dick, or the Jacksons swop their housekeeper, Pattie, for Ruby, but it was unlikely. It was too complicated. Slaves chose their partners from other slaves on their own plantation, not from the world at large. And neither Parson Dick nor Ruby wanted to be wed in slavery. The life they envisioned together in the Coffee kitchen was as a working pair, living in freedom, earning their joint income. Much as they adored each other's company for the short week they were together, the driving force for both of them was their innate fury at their status. Desperate overachievers, they lived in the ill-founded hope that excellence at their jobs would earn them their freedom. They preferred to maintain that fury, and that hope, by being forced to live apart when they were so blatantly intended for each other.

If they were free, they promised each other, it would be different. And they would be free, one day.

They sustained a curious relationship by sending occasional messages to each other by way of other slaves. When the seed merchant made his rounds of the plantations, his boy would bring messages of affection from Ruby to Parson Dick, and the draper's assistant would return the sweet nothings when he journeyed, by a rambling route, from The Forks to the Coffees.

The excitement surrounding the election of Lincoln had persuaded Parson Dick that freedom for the slaves might become a reality, and so the lack of any action by the Yankees against the state of South Carolina was an especially bitter blow for him.

"Never going to happen," he told Cap'n Jack, slurring his words through a small pond of brandy. "We ain't never going to be free."

Cap'n Jack agreed with him, and they both got even drunker, and swore eternal friendship. Then both were sick, and passed out, and had foul heads the next morning.

In the big house, New Year's Eve was an even happier celebration than Christmas. Jass and Lizzie gave a party for friends and family, and even though Lizzie was still distressed by her mother's death, she had come to terms with it, and was, again, a splendid hostess. William, George, and Alexander came with their wives and new families, and Elizabeth and Tom, with their hordes of children. Sam Kirkman, their eldest son, was with them, and Elizabeth his wife, and Elizabeth his baby daughter. Sam had graduated Phi Beta Kappa from Harvard, and was now practicing medicine. Jass joked that if there was a war, Sawbones Sam would be in his element, but everyone laughed, because nobody believed anymore that there was going to be a war.

Queen was allowed to watch the dancing from the hallway, but when the clock struck midnight she was alone.

They sang "Auld Lang Syne," and then Jass raised

543

his glass in a toast. "To the South," he cried, and most of them raised their glasses.

"To the Union," Sam Kirkman said softly in the silence while they drank.

No one cheered, no one drank with him, and it soured the party atmosphere for a while. But Lizzie was too good a hostess to let a little thing like politics, and an argument between close relations, ruin everyone else's fun. She organized music and dancing and distracted the children with silly games.

Sam's quiet affirmation of loyalty to his country depressed Jass. He watched the games with Lizzie for a while, and kissed away the few tears she shed because Becky was not with them to celebrate. Becky had always loved parties, as did Jass, but now he was a different man, and Sam had killed his appetite for celebration. He wandered away from the group, and tried to avoid his nephew.

He saw Queen sitting alone on the stairs watching the fun. Since it was such a special occasion, he took a glass of champagne to her, and sat on the stairs with her for a while, chatting about the evening, and wished her Happy New Year.

Queen had never tasted champagne before, nor any alcohol, and even though it was only a small glass, just two or three sips, she loved the sweet, sparkling drink, and the bubbly effect it had on her. It made her want to dance, and her body swayed in time to the party music. Jass saw what was happening and smiled. He stood and offered her his hand, asked her if she would like to dance.

Queen could not believe her ears. This must be what Jane called being drunk, for it was unreal to her and wonderful. She sat staring at her adored father until he smiled again, and repeated his request. Believing him now, Queen accepted his offered hand. Jass led her to the center of the hallway, and to the distant music they could hear from the ballroom, he danced with her. They were alone, the two of them, in the vast, empty hall, the portraits of their ancestors staring down at them.

It was the happiest night of Queen's life.

55

The Southern celebrations continued well into the New Year. Not even the seizing of United States arsenals provoked a reaction from Washington. There was a small hiccup in early January when someone burst into the tavern in Florence, where Jass was drinking with friends, to tell them that President Buchanan was sending a warship to reinforce the federal garrison at Fort Sumter, a small island in the middle of Charleston Harbor. They all raced from the tavern to the telegraph office, where the news was confirmed. There was general astonishment that it was the passive, lame-duck Buchanan who had taken this aggressive action, and a general, sobering realization that there were many federal army forts throughout the South. If there was to be a war, the North had a natural advantage. A few men immediately enlisted in militia units, for there was no Southern army yet, while the others champed at the bit for news, and insisted that Alabama should show her solidarity with the sister state.

Jass, wanting to be close to the source of news, the telegraph office, slept at the hotel for the next few nights, to the distress of both Lizzie and Sally, who felt he should be at home with them. For the following week, the South held its breath. Six days later, they heard that the ship carrying the reinforcements, the *Star of the West*, had turned about under fire from Charleston shore batteries, and jubilation returned. The independence of South Carolina had been challenged, the rebellious state had won, and on the same day Mississippi withdrew from the Union.

"The Yankees," Alec Henderson told Letitia, "are all piss and wind." Mrs. Henderson clucked at the language, but forgave her husband because these were stirring times, and she agreed with him. Still, she determined to try to curb his potty mouth when order was restored to the land.

Momentous news now reached them with dizzying speed. Almost every day, it seemed, another state seceded. Florida, and then, to considerable rejoicing in the streets of Florence, Alabama, Georgia, Lousiana, and Texas were the next to leave.

When the telegraph officer rushed out to tell the assembled multitude that Kansas had been admitted into the Union as a slave-free state, he was jeered and pelted with mud and small rocks. He got a cut over his eye, but took it in good part. It was only sport, the boys were in high spirits, and who needed Kansas?

Delegates from the seceding states were to meet in Montgomery, Alabama, to form a new provisional government. Jass had no official role, but was set upon a political career and had many friends of influence, so he decided to attend, if only as a spectator. Lizzie and Sally were inclined to argue with him, but Jass lost his temper. They were all perfectly safe at The Forks, he assured his women; no harm would come to them. The North was not going to do anything to hinder the rebellion; they were having a peace convention in Washington, for heaven's sake. And even if some retaliation did eventuate, at some later time, Florence was a very long way from the center of any possible action.

"What if the baby comes?" Lizzie asked him, crying softly, but even the prospect of a new child, another son perhaps, did not deter Jass.

"You've had babies before, and it isn't quite due yet," he whispered to Lizzie. "I'll only be gone for a couple of weeks."

*

Thus Jass went to Montgomery, and was present at the creation of a new country. The name chosen for that new country was the Confederate States of America, and Jass was profoundly moved. This was how it should be, he thought; this was how it should have been all along, for the very name itself represented what he believed America to be. A confederation, a group of sovereign states banded together in a common cause, not a federation, which implied surrender of power to a central authority. When Jefferson Davis was presented to them as president, the bands played what was to become their anthem, and Jass sang "Dixie" as loudly and lustily as anyone there.

He rode back to The Forks with a full heart. Now that the deed was done, it was as if a festering boil had been lanced. He was filled with a sense of peace and purpose. He attended his family with care and affection, and went about his business with an unaccustomed vigor, for now the new country had to be made to prosper.

It didn't matter that the new country had no treasury, Jass, like many others, invested heavily in Confederate bonds, believing them to be gilt-edged. They had cotton and powerful allies, for Great Britain had to protect the supply of that cotton to its mills in Manchester. Even if the North was initially belligerent to the South, it was unlikely to take on John Bull, and must eventually accept the fact of the new Confederacy. The two nations in America would live in harmony and prosperity, and the Jackson fortune would become greater than ever before.

But what was a country without a king? Sally was less sanguine about their prospects. Although she believed in the idea of confederation, she had no faith in Jefferson Davis as their leader. She had met him several times when James was alive and active in politics, and was astonished when he was chosen as their president. The Confederacy needed a visionary general, not a pedantic schoolmaster. An intelligent and erudite man, Davis had an unpredictable temper, and was given to prolonged bouts of melancholy. Sally had known many powerful men, with Andrew Jackson, whatever his faults, as the greatest, and could not see in Jefferson Davis the dynamic aura of natural leadership. Whatever his political skills, he had no charisma, and in a moment of absolute panic, Sally saw the unraveling of the complex tapestry that had so recently been woven. Unlike Lincoln, Jefferson had no popular mandate and few skills of oratory, and she could not imagine anyone following him to death or glory. The South was bound together by a single idea and a single issue, slavery, and for that moment of panic she could not imagine that the idea itself was strong enough to bind them through the prospective crisis. The Union had been based on a single idea and a single issue, but that idea was freedom. Was slavery as powerful an ideal?

Still, she had no choice but patriotism and cast aside her doubts. Provided Lincoln did nothing rash, and the South nothing to provoke him beyond its simple existence, they might prevail.

In March, Abraham Lincoln was inaugurated as president of the United States of America.

And still there was no war.

In April, Lizzie gave birth to a son, who was christened James, after his father, grandfather, and great-grandfather.

Transcendent emotions flooded Jass as he held his new son for the first time. A new boy for a new country. It seemed so fit and proper, and Jass, who had never been unusually religious, was moved to an extraordinary awe of God, his creator. He fell to his knees, prayed for a peaceful life for his new son, and made a most sacred, solemn oath to defend the boy's patrimony with every drop of blood in his body.

*

On the same day, the Confederate States demanded the surrender of Fort Sumter, and when the Federal commanding officer, Major Anderson, declined, Southern bombardment of the island began. Anderson surrendered two days later, and two days after that, Lincoln declared a blockade of Southern ports and called for seventy-five thousand volunteers for three months. The immediate Southern reaction was simple indignation. If Lincoln thought he could whip the South in only three months, he had better think again, they told each other.

Virginia, Arkansas, North Carolina, and Tennessee seceded from the Union, a rampaging mob attacked Union troops in Baltimore, there was a stirring parade by the Alabama Dragoons through the streets of Florence, and Jass enlisted as a private in the 4th Alabama Regiment.

He looked very fine in his uniform of simple gray, uncluttered by decoration. He had not discussed his intention to enlist with any of his family, but had gone with Henderson to a meeting at the Wesleyan Hall in Florence. He heard the speeches and watched the fellows enlist, and the ladies present gave them little Confederate flags as they did so. Jass knew he had no choice. He could easily have avoided military service, for he owned more than twenty slaves and was, by decree, exempt. He could as easily have formed his own regiment—he had the financial means to do so—and ridden off to glory as their colonel. He could easily have deferred any decision until the course of the war was known.

But not to fight was the coward's way. Jass believed in his cause, and his sons, William and James, gave quickening momentum to his ideals. He had heard the cries that it was a rich man's war and a poor man's fight, for the slave-owning rich were a small minority in the South, and to give the lie to that, he resisted a commission. He enlisted as the common man enlisted,

549

and would fight beside the common man, for the common cause.

Lizzie fainted when he told her, and on recovering, screamed her distress, but Sally's heart filled with love for her son, and pride that he had so stalwartly heard the call.

Her heart was overflowing again now as he stood before them to say his good-byes.

It was a perfect April, a day he would dream of in the dark nights to come. The family was gathered on the veranda, slaves watching from a distance.

Henderson was near the magnolia tree saying good-bye to his wife. They had debated his enlistment several days before it happened, but briefly, because Letitia was in favor of it. She was proud of the man she had married, a good honest laborer, and believed it was his God-given duty to fight for his country. She didn't love him as Jass loved Easter, or even as Lizzie loved Jass, but she was fond of him, cared for him, and while she would miss him, she doubted that any real harm would come to him. The war would not last long, a few months at most, and it would be almost two months before he came within sight of a Yankee army. And even if he was hurt, or killed, she would have reason for pride in him. She had been happy with him for the few short months of their marriage, but it was the fact of her marriage that was most dear to her. Life as a widow was infinitely preferable to life as a spinster, which had seemed to be her fate but a few months before.

Henderson, on the other hand, was excited at the prospect of a few battles, and bloodying some Yankee noses, for he was bored with his life as an overseer. It was the same thing, day in, day out; the only challenge was the weather, which no one could predict, and keeping the niggers in line, which wasn't hard when he held the whip. Married life had been interesting for a few weeks, but Letitia was a stern taskmaster, always on his back about something or other. She had less patience with niggers than he did, and was forever urging him to flog them more, which made life difficult because he remembered and respected Mitchell's advice to him—it had served him well. Letitia kept a good house, and was obliging in the cot, but he had started to miss his freedom.

He went to see Mitchell, who agreed he should enlist, and agreed to visit The Forks from time to time to check that things were running smoothly. They found a young man, Tom Parsons, to fill in as temporary overseer, and when Henderson went with Jass to the Wesleyan Hall, he had already decided to join up. He waited till Jass took the plunge first, for Henderson thought it was sensible that the two of them be in the same regiment. Jass Jackson was his bread and butter, and he'd be able to keep his eye on the Massa, who wasn't, in Henderson's opinion, cut out to be a soldier. He was surprised, and a little disappointed, that Jass went in as a private. If he'd been an officer, Henderson could have been his sergeant, but there was never any point in telling Jass when he had his mind made up, so Henderson had accepted his fate and followed his Massa.

Now, standing under the vast magnolia, he kissed Letitia politely, said all the right things, he hoped, mounted his horse, and waited to follow the Massa again.

Jass shook William's hand. The boy had been excited at seeing his father in a soldier's uniform, but now fear assailed him and he was close to tears. His training stood him in good stead, and he didn't cry, but hugged his father hard. Jass kissed Mary, and said good-bye to the little ones, then moved to his mother.

Neither said anything for a moment, and both smiled a little, but without joy.

"I hate to see you go," Sally said.

"I hate to have to go," Jass told her, although it was not entirely true.

Sally embraced him. "Be brave," she whispered. "Do your duty." She didn't want him to go and she didn't want him to die, but he had to go, and she put her faith in God that he would not die. She knew that she would have to say good-bye to all her sons, for all had enlisted, and it was probable that one of them, at least, would be wounded, or worse. But a man was either brave or he was a coward, and it had comforted her during the last dark days before Jass's departure to know that all her sons were brave.

Jass held her close for a moment, and the truth of his circumstances hit him hard. He longed for war, he longed to prove himself in battle, he felt he had wasted too many years of his life, an idle, rich man's son, and now he had the opportunity to be the man he had always promised himself he would be. But he had to face the truth of it. It was war, and he might die. The smell of his mother caressed him, the smell he had known all his life, from before his memory of it. This is what he wanted to take with him; this is what he wanted to remember of home, the loving embrace of his mother.

He had another memory to take with him, but it was not of home. It was of the woman he cherished and to whom he had never been a failure. It was the memory of Easter, plump and full now but as exciting to him as she had always been. He had spent some of the previous night with her, after Lizzie was asleep, and when dawn came he told her something that was important to him.

"If anything should happen to me," he whispered, "always know that I will have loved you until the moment of my dying."

He knew that she understood, because she hadn't wept, as Lizzie had been weeping for days, but had held him to her, and had hummed a lullaby from some place deep inside her soul, just as she had on their very first night together, and he had drifted to sleep in her arms, knowing that he was loved.

Easter was standing with Queen, at the end of the veranda, watching him say good-bye. Jass moved reluctantly from his mother to Lizzie, whose face was blotchy with tears.

"This is it, my dear," he said, for want of anything better to say. He wished he could think of some intimate truth to give her in farewell, but he could not say to her what he had said to Easter, because it was not true.

Lizzie was distraught. "I can't bear it," she cried.

"I'll come home safe, I promise," he said. Suddenly, he grabbed her, held her to him, kissed her hard, and forced his tongue into her mouth. For suddenly he hated himself. The memory of his farewell to Easter rang in his ears, but she was a nigger, and Lizzie was his wife, mother of his children. It was Lizzie he was ready to die for, to protect.

"I love you," he whispered harshly, when his mouth was free. But Lizzie would not let him go. She hung on to him for dear life.

"Don't go," she screamed. "You don't have to go!"

Letitia Henderson clucked in disapproval, and glanced slyly at her husband. She thought Mrs. Jackson would have had a greater sense of proper behavior.

Jass tried to pull himself away from Lizzie, but she clutched at him, tried to drag him back, screaming at him.

Sally moved to help, but Lizzie was a frantic woman, and Sally too frail. None of the other slaves dared touch their hysterical mistress, and so Jass had to do the unthinkable.

He called to Easter and Queen.

They did what had to be done, and pulled Lizzie from him.

"Go now, Massa, quick," Queen said, when he was free. Lizzie was sobbing desperately, in Easter's arms, but still Jass couldn't go. There was one more thing to do.

They looked so frail, so helpless: his old mother, his weeping wife, and his little children. Even William, trying so hard to act like a man, was obviously only a boy. Someone had to take care of them.

"Look after them, Queen," Jass begged. "They need you."

It was a sublime moment for Queen. The Massa, her father, had given her charge of his family. It was a sacred trust.

"Yes, Massa," she promised. "Good luck."

Family matters done, he was anxious to be away. He walked quickly to his horse and mounted, and together he and Henderson galloped away down the drive.

Queen ran to the edge of the lawn, to wave farewell. Easter had given Lizzie to Sally's care and now walked slowly to join her daughter. They stood together and watched Jass go.

Queen looked at Easter, with the question that was always in her eyes. She had asked her mother outright, only a few days ago, when Jass first enlisted. Seeing him dressed like a soldier had frightened Queen; she didn't want him to go to war, she didn't want him to die. She ran to her mother in the weaving house and poured out her distress. Easter, as always, had comforted her and stroked her hair.

"There, now, chile, he'll come home safe, I promise," she crooned.

"You cain't know that," Queen muttered.

"I ain't never tole you a lie," Easter said.

It was true, Queen thought, her mother had never lied to her. But perhaps she had never told her the complete truth, either.

"Then tell me true now," she said. "They say the Massa's my pappy. Is it true?"

Even now, after all these years, Easter resisted it. She

554

didn't believe it could do any good for Queen to know, yet she knew Queen did know.

"It don't matter," she said, and turned away, but that was not enough for Queen.

"It matters to me," she cried, "coz half of me is missing!"

She had to make her mother understand why it was so important. "I's black but I look white. You're my mammy, the black side of me, and I love you."

She turned her mother's face to her. "But who's the other side of me?" she begged. "The white me. Where'd she come from?"

Easter was crying. She understood her daughter's need. "From love, my chile, I swear to you," she said. "From love."

They stood together now, in front of a grand house on a little hill, and watched him ride away to war.

It could not matter now, Easter persuaded herself. And told Queen the truth.

"Pray for yo' pappy," she said.

It was as if a great weight was taken from Queen's shoulders. In a practical sense it made no difference to her life—she was still a slave—but things that had never made sense to her now became clear. She knew she'd always known—her father's constant visits to her mother, the way he had protected her and taken her into the big house, the way he had treated her with some slight special attention, the things that other slaves had told her—but it had been knowledge without knowing. To know the truth for a fact was different from guessing it by rumor.

She waved to her pappy until she could no longer see him.

They rode for days, Jass and Henderson. At every village and town they passed through, others joined them, and others again as they rode on, until, by the time they reached the North, they were a great army.

But why that army fought, the purposes of its war, had never been explained to those who were the ultimate cause of it, the slaves.

Sally believed that if the slaves did not understand the reasons for the war, they could become the enemy. With so many white men away, discipline would become increasingly difficult, the number of runaways would increase, the work force would slowly disappear, and the problems of running the new country would be insurmountable.

Someone had to make them understand why white men were ready to shed their blood to defend the institution of slavery. It was not, in Sally's mind, just for the benefit of whites. It was for the good of the slaves as well.

She had Tom Parsons gather them together one evening, shortly after Jass had left.

She stood in the middle of the clearing, surrounded by all her family, for she had insisted on their presence, and Mrs. Henderson. The house slaves stood to her right, the field slaves in front of her. Queen and Easter stood together, but apart from the others, for they belonged to neither group.

Tom Parsons cracked his whip and yelled at the slaves to be quiet, which was unnecessary because no one was talking, and Sally stepped forward.

"We are at the beginning of a great adventure," she told them, her voice crisp and clear in the warm night air. "And only the good Lord in heaven knows how and when it will end."

She paused for a moment. She had practiced the speech several times, but it was important to her that they understood how passionately she believed in what she was telling them.

"Some of you will have heard that this war is being fought for and against slavery, but that is not true. The South is fighting to protect its own way of life."

Tom Parsons had his eye out for troublemakers, but

found himself paying more and more attention to Sally's speech. He was young and impressionable, and had never really understood what the war was about. He'd been excited by the founding of the Confederacy, and had caught the general fever of war, but his God-fearing parents had told him that it was the beginning of the Millennium and heralded the Second Coming of Christ, which dashed his exuberance. Sally seemed to have a more pragmatic view.

"The alternative is too dreadful to imagine," Sally continued, "especially for you nigras. You have all heard the stories of your people in the North. Of hunger, and sickness, and poverty. Of homeless nigras forced to beg for crumbs of bread, of sleeping in gutters, dying friendless and alone."

Very few of the slaves had heard those stories. It was not what they knew of the North, of freedom. And even if the stories were true, they did not matter.

"That is not our way," Sally told them. "When you are born, we nurse you. When you are hungry, we feed you. When you are sick we nurse you, when you are old, we care for you, and when you die, we bury you. That is our Christian duty."

She was completely unaware of an unspoken dialogue going on among some of the slaves. Jeremiah, the blacksmith, simmered with anger. He was a skilled and able tradesman, and he believed he could make a good living for himself and his family, if given the chance. The chance was all. If it was his destiny, which he did not for one moment believe, to die alone in a Northern gutter, then so be it. He wanted the choice, he wanted to be free, to succeed or fail, and no one, for all Missy Sally's fine speeches, had the right to deny him that. He looked at some of the other slaves, and knew he was not alone in his anger.

The slaves had discussed the war as avidly as any whites. Many believed that it heralded the glory day of deliverance. John Brown had been the harbinger, and

Linkun was the new Messiah. Fervently believed rumors told the slaves that Ol' Linkun was amassing a righteous army that would sweep through the South, gather the dispossessed black peoples into its bosom, and lead them to the mountain. A few, the old and less able, those without family, were scared, for they had never known any other life than that of a slave, and despite the tantalizing hope that freedom promised, it was new, unknown, and frightening territory.

For some, mostly the able-bodied younger men, it could not come quickly enough, and a few, like Jeremiah, were realistic enough to comprehend that the South would not yield easily. The war would be bloody, and it was possible the Yankees might lose, although it would be a cruel God who gave victory to the South. All Jeremiah wanted was his chance, which might, he thought, be now.

"I cannot believe, in my heart, that God, in His infinite wisdom, could allow us to lose this war," Sally said. "But He helps those who help themselves, and so it is our bounden duty to strive together, to keep our houses and our fields in good order, until the blessed day of peace comes, and brings our men safe home. I ask you to kneel and pray with me."

Tom Parsons closed his eyes and prayed most fervently. The others knelt, obediently.

"O Heavenly Father," Sally led them in prayer, "our Creator and Provider, we pray to You now in this our hour of need. We beg You for peace, O Lord. We beg that in Your infinite wisdom You spare lives that would be needlessly lost in battle, but, if war it must be, that You grant victory to our glorious Southern cause."

Queen and Easter were not praying for the war, or for the South, but for Jass. As Sally did now.

"And we ask You to bless and protect our beloved son Jass, to keep him from harm, and bring him safe home to the bosom of his family. But if his time on earth is done, we pray that You receive him in Paradise, and attend him with angels."

"Amen," Queen whispered.

"Amen," Easter whispered.

"Amen," chorused the slaves. Those that were left.

When Tom Parsons opened his eyes, he had a bit of a shock. He was sure that a few of the slaves were absent. He said nothing to Sally, but when she had gone back to the big house, he did a head count.

Jeremiah and three field hands had gone missing during Sally's prayer, as well as Alphis, Jass's new valet from the big house. Taking advantage of the chaos that war must bring, and believing that the Massas had better things to do than go chasing after a few niggers, they had taken their chance. Away, away down Freedom Road.

Tom Parsons, who had been responsible for them, was too young, too callow, and too scared to face the wrath of his employers, and ran away himself.

He spent the night in a friend's barn in Florence, crept into town before dawn, and enlisted in the army.

56

When the bullet burst into Jass's chest, he felt as if he had been hit by an invisible steam train. The brute force of it knocked him to the ground, senseless.

He came to a little later, and had no idea where he was. It was still daylight, and there was this awful pain in his chest. Around him, he could hear a few whimpers for help and shouts of pain, and somewhere a long way away, a distant cheering, but otherwise all was quiet. He moved his hands, to see if he could, and then felt his chest. It was wet and sticky, and Jass knew it was his own blood.

"I am dying," he thought, without any sense of fear. He prayed that death would end the pain which was becoming unbearable. Just when he thought he could not stand it anymore, when he must scream to the very heavens to make it stop, his body was kind to him, and he passed out again.

He drifted to the surface sometime later, and the pain was still there. It was dark now, or nearly so, and he could still hear the cries of wounded and dying men all around him. He tried to sit up, but that made the pain worse. Mosquitoes buzzed in his ears, and their bites added to his misery. He fell back on the ground, waited for something to happen, and commended his soul to the mercy of sweet Jesus.

Jass and Henderson had journeyed to the North, to Richmond, Virginia. They were given some peremptory basic training, their horses were requisitioned for other purposes, and their regiment was assigned to Manassas. It was a road and rail junction on a stream, Bull Run, which ran into the Potomac River. The commanding officer, General Beauregard, was a splendid veteran, who kept his soldiers from boredom by long hours of training. At first, the green troops responded well, and a sense of camaraderie developed among them. They lived in tents, ate simple food in almost ample portions, and spent the long, oppressive summer nights singing songs of their youth, or telling tall tales, or writing to loved ones. Those who were illiterate found educated friends to write their letters for them, and Jass, who longed for action, was a popular scribe.

So the nights passed pleasantly enough, but oh, the days! The days were hot and unbearably humid, and the steamy weather enervated them, sapping their resolution as surely as it drained their energy. Their thick woolen uniforms chaffed at their perspiring bodies, and the endless hours of drill and instruction rubbed at their spirits. Chiggers burrowed into their flesh, mosquitoes sucked on their blood, and lice nested in their hair and clothes. They cursed their officers, cursed their wretched lot, and, above all, cursed those wretched Yankees, who had brought them to this hellhole, and were too chicken to fight.

The day will come, their officers told them. The day will come. Toward the middle of July, rumors reached them that a vast Yankee army was amassing a few miles away. They were put on alert, but no attack came, and scouts reported that the Yankees seemed more interested in setting up camp than waging war.

"All piss and wind," a disgruntled Henderson told his fellows, for he was anxious to fight, to get it done, and get out of this accursed place. But not to home. To some other, more congenial site of battle, and he prayed that the war would not be short. Despite the miserable conditions and his constant discomfort Henderson was actually enjoying himself. Secure with himself, for he was, by his lights, a very successful man, his years as an overseer, as an organizer, stood him in good stead. Older than many of the volunteers, he found that the other men respected him and looked to him to interpret their officers' commands. He became a sergeant by natural process, long before he was promoted to the rank, and he relished the rough and ready masculinity of a soldier's life. It was as if he had spent the rest of his life in training for this time. He'd never had much fun, he'd worked hard to advance himself, he'd settled to a comfortable married life, and now, suddenly, he was free of social ambitions and could be the youth he had never been. He thought fondly of Letitia, and wrote to her regularly, in simple terms for he was not well educated, but he looked forward to some leave as a soldier because women of a certain class loved soldiers and would do anything for them. Anything. He had a good supply of wild oats that he had never sown when young, and when the chance came he did not intend to be mean with them.

They lived on rumor and wild speculation, and when the news that the Yankees had attacked spread through the camp like a grass fire, every man stood to. And stood down again. It was only some small skirmish on the other side of that deep stream. Still, something had happened. Southern reinforcements were on the march to them, they heard, and, not quite as green as they had been a few weeks ago, they knew a battle was looming.

When Sunday came, they knew this must be the day, for groups of civilians were gathering on a nearby hill to watch the coming fray. Many came in carriages, were elegantly dressed and had picnic hampers, as if to watch soldiers die were a charming Sunday diversion. Southern spectators might have done the same if the situation had been reversed, but the sight of all these Northerners come to watch the bloodshed caused a deep and abiding anger in many a Rebel soldier's heart.

Jass simply waited to be told what to do. His company was assembled, and stood in ranks in the blazing sun, weapons primed and loaded. On a small hill across the stream, cannon were being assembled by blue-coated soldiers, aimed directly, Jass thought, at him. They heard distant cries and gunfire, and then silence again, and then a rumor swept the ranks that the Southerners were retreating. Fear snaked through the men, and a few boys began to whimper, convinced that this was their last hour on earth. Then other rumors were whispered along the ranks. There had been a retreat, but General Jackson and his men stood like a stone wall against the advancing Yankees. The tide of battle had turned.

Jass was puzzled. He hadn't expected war to be like this. It was possible, if the day went on like this, that he would not see any action at all. He did not know what he had expected war to be, but he had not thought it would be boring.

They were assembled about a mile from a stone bridge, hot and sweating under the blazing sun. Still they could hear distant cries and gunfire, but now the shouts seemed to be coming nearer, and hope started to blaze in their hearts, for these shouts were not of anger, but of fear. The sound of panic ran toward them at the speed of men in retreat, and suddenly it burst upon them. Hundreds, perhaps thousands, a great mass at last, of Union soldiers were running toward the bridge, to cross to the North, to safety. Now the cannon on the opposite hill started firing, as if to protect the fleeing men.

Jass's troop was given the order to charge, and hearts surging with glee at the sight of the retreating Yankees, blood pounding with expectation of a fight, fear of dying the adrenaline that made them brave, they charged toward the bridge.

Jass had no sense of place or time. He was an animal now, intent on his prey, in the middle of chaos and confusion. Sounds thundered about him, of guns and screaming and, loudest of all, his own blood throbbing in his ears. The very ground under him seemed to shudder as cannon balls landed among them. He looked once toward the distant hill, where the cannon were, and saw lines of soldiers dressed in blue and tiny puffs of smoke coming from their guns, but he did not hear the sound of those guns until some moments after the smoke had appeared.

Then something hit him with the force of an invisible steam train. He felt a searing pain in his chest, and fell to the ground, senseless.

He was found later that night, unconscious and bleeding, lying in a field of dead and wounded men, by a friend who did not recognize him.

Wesley was a veteran of killing, an able and eccentric fighter, who had spent the past twenty-five years in a wild and lawless life. He was a gun for hire, an Indian

563

fighter mostly, who spent his days slaying braves, and his nights in sweet domestic comfort with his Comanche squaw. They lived in a little shack by a pleasant river in the foothills of the Rocky Mountains, and Wesley had a fine collection of Indian artifacts, and several Redskin scalps. But already the frontier was not what it had been; settlers were slowly occupying the pristine territories of Wesley's youth. Federal soldiers were building forts and governments were whining about law and order. Although there was land enough to spare, and adventure enough for any man, the wilderness was slowly being tamed. Wesley wondered if he was simply getting old, for the chase had lost its thrill, his squaw and half-breed children bored him, and he was disgusted by the ambitions of so many of the settlers, who lived in fear of the hunting grounds and were determined to bring a bourgeois civilization to what had been primeval. The Indians were not his enemy anymore; the white man was.

When he heard of the possibility of war between the North and the South, he knew where he wanted to be. He made provision for his family, saddled his horse, and rode to Richmond, where he offered his services, by old family connection, to General Beauregard, as a scout.

He cut an unlikely figure. His hair was long and held back in a ponytail; his face was weathered and gnarled. He scorned a traditional uniform, but wore fringed leather decorated with several small Indian totems to ward off the evil ones, and a tanned human scalp hung from his belt. He lived rough and alone, in a small teepee he had made for himself, and men laughed at him behind his back, but feared what he represented.

He was an excellent scout, and it was he who had warned of the first Union reconnaissance of the day, which had been routed. He was furious at the initial Southern retreat, for a man stood and fought, and he won or he died, but he did not run. He had approved of General Jackson's exhortations to his men to stand firm like a stone wall before the Yankees, and he had nodded in satisfaction at the subsequent Yankee withdrawal, which turned into a panicked rout.

Now he wandered the battlefields alone. He was not averse to scavenging from dead men, but his true purpose was as an angel of mercy. If he found a man alive but mortally wounded, Wesley used his hunting knife to help that man into the dark night. If he found a man alive but simply wounded, he would call the medical orderlies, for they, as green as the soldiers, had no experience of the carnage of war, were overwhelmed by the numbers of the injured, and could not always differentiate between those who would live and those who would die.

So it was that he found a man who seemed familiar to him, and carried the wounded Jass, fireman-fashion, to a medical tent, for this one, Wesley knew, would live.

Duty done, he slipped out into the night again, back to the killing grounds, and went about his business.

Sam, Sawbones Sam, bright medical star of the Kirkman family, had traveled with his mother, Elizabeth, to Richmond to stay with friends, for he knew his services would be needed. When news of the battle reached him, he went to Manassas and offered his services. It was Sam's first experience of war, and when the bodies, hundreds upon hundreds, were brought to the medical tents, he had initially been appalled at the useless carnage. But his training served him well, and he patched and sewed and cut and amputated, and comforted those who were beyond his help.

Like the young soldier, who could not have been more than eighteen, who had fallen under some horses and had been fatally trampled.

"Am I done for, sir?" the boy had asked, and Sam had told him the truth.

The boy was silent, and then admitted his most private fear.

"I'm scared, sir," he said.

Sam was used to death, although never in such quantity.

"It's easy," he told the dying boy. "You will see a great light, and all you have to do is follow it."

The boy was silent again, but had another awful fear. He had not joined the army for any great cause, although Dixie, glorious to him, was cause enough. Bored with his life on a small farm, he had enlisted for excitement, for adventure. In other times, he might as easily have escaped the monotony of his life by seeking his fortune in a big city, and he had left home with a solemn promise to his mother, which both of them knew was useless, to avoid harm's way.

"What will my mother say?" he said so quietly that Sam could hardly hear him.

He closed his eyes, and Sam knew he would never open them again. He sat with him for a little while, for his own benefit as much as the dying boy's. It was nearly dawn, and he was exhausted by blood and pain and death.

It happened quietly, peacefully, and no one but Sam marked the boy's passing. Sam sighed, and turned to the man lying on the next blanket, who would live. His awful chest wound had been bound with bandages, and he had been sleeping from the effects of the laudanum that Sam had given him from his small, private stock, but now he was drifting to the surface. He opened his eyes.

"How is it, Jass?" Sam asked.

"Bloody dreadful," Jass replied, for the effects of the opium were wearing off, the pain was filtering through his lungs again.

He tried to focus on the face smiling down at him, and a fragment of memory came to him.

"Sam?" Jass almost smiled.

Sam nodded, and Jass closed his eyes, for Sam would protect him. If he could be protected. He looked at Sam again.

"Am I dying?" he asked his nephew.

"No, Jass, you'll live," Sam told him. "I worked my guts out to save you."

Relief flooded through Jass, but then he winced in pain. Sam gave him a little more laudanum. The army did not approve of lulling drugs for enlisted men. They were too costly, and might lead to addiction, but Jass was not a soldier anymore, only Sam's uncle.

"You had a bullet through your lung," he said softly, as if it was good news. "And you'll be no more use to the army."

Jass could not begin to assimilate the implications of that, for something else had a greater importance.

"Did we win?" he asked.

"Yes, we won," Sam said.

Jass almost smiled. "Then God be thanked," he whispered. "I wouldn't have wanted to die for nothing."

Two days later they moved him to an army hospital at Richmond, where Elizabeth, his half sister, took charge of his nursing.

He was released from the hospital and honorably discharged from the army, but he was still unfit to travel and spent the early fall recuperating from his wounds at the home of friends in the lovely Virginia countryside.

"It is the end of the war for me," he began a letter to his mother, but then put down his pen in bitter disgust.

He had not expected it would end like this.

57

Queen didn't know what to do. Her father was coming home. Much as she longed to see him, she felt she had not lived up to his expectations of her. She had been charged by him with a most sacred, solemn duty, the protection of his family while he was away, and she had failed. It might have been easier with a full complement of fellow slaves to share the burden, but they were reduced to half their number. Julie, the cook, was dead. There had been a brief epidemic of typhoid in the summer, and Julie and some others had succumbed to it. Polly was gone, fled with a field hand. Since Tom Parsons, the replacement overseer, had mysteriously disappeared, discipline among the field slaves had fallen apart, and several had run away. There were slave catchers, but they were mostly old men and young boys, and the number of runaways in the district so large that there was little hope of any but a few being recaptured. Mitchell had tried to help, but he was old, his arthritis troubled him badly, and he had simply stopped coming to The Forks. Pattie was still there, but she was not young, and was always sick. She was shamming, Queen was sure, but had no way of proving it. Poppy had taken over the cleaning, but the big house was too much for her; she grumbled and complained, and shirked her duty, and spent most of her days loafing in the laundry room.

Mrs. Henderson was worse than useless, constantly demanding help from the slaves, and as constantly telling Sally and Lizzie to use the whip to maintain discipline. Queen was the most common target of her waspishness, for Mrs. Henderson thought the girl was uppity and should be kept in her place. Queen was scared of Mrs. Henderson, for she still had authority as the overseer's wife, even though he was away. She could tell terrible lies to the Massa and Henderson when they returned, and possibly have Queen whipped, which she had threatened to do herself.

The house had to be run and the cotton had to be picked, and there weren't enough able-bodied people left to achieve either. Parson Dick divided his time between the house and the fields, picking like a veteran, Cap'n Jack struggled to keep up with him, and Easter helped Queen with the cooking for the family. They had managed tolerably until Mary and Little Sally got sick, and then Easter had to spend her days nursing them.

Miss Lizzie was worse than useless, imaging herself as mistress of what had once been, and now frantic with worry for her babies. Miss Sally tried to help, but she was old and walked with a cane, and her eyesight wasn't the best anymore, and William had his school-work to worry about. It fell to Queen to look after Eleanor and baby James, who, mercifully, hadn't caught the diphtheria, and it was Queen who went out into the fields and yelled at the slaves to pick cotton. Sally had called on Massa Tom Kirkman for help with the harvest, but he couldn't find any extra hands. Every plantation had a similar problem, and most of Tom's family were gone, his older sons enlisted, his daughters married and caring for their own families, his wife, Elizabeth, nursing in Richmond, and his younger children trying to run their own house. He had organized a picnic at The Forks one Sunday, and brought with him several friends and relations. They made a party and picked cotton, the whites out there in the field with the blacks; it had been tremendous fun, and they'd gathered a good crop, but it was a drop in the ocean of what had to be done, for the harvest was bountiful that year.

And it all had to be picked because they needed the money. The Confederate dollar was worth only sixty-seven cents of a Yankee dollar, and was dropping like a stone every day. The price of cotton had fallen because of the blockade of Southern ports, and so they needed every boll they could get.

The fields spread white to the horizon, and the gold that cotton once had been became a curse to Queen. If it was not picked soon, it would rot and be useless.

She sighed, and bent her aching back to the task. Because she was so tired she didn't get enough sleep, and because she didn't get enough sleep she was always grumpy, and because there was so much to do, she didn't know what task to attend to first. Except to pick cotton.

Today she had baby James and Eleanor with her, because Easter was tending the invalids. They were no trouble, James slept happily in the little wooden cot that Queen had once used, and Eleanor played at the side of the field, and watched over James, but they were an added responsibility, and she had to go to them every hour at least, and see to their needs.

If only Jass would come. The letter said it would be at least a month before he returned, and Queen didn't know how to cope for another four weeks. Or even one.

As she picked, she grumbled, enumerating her woes to God. Parson Dick laughed at her, and told her it was a waste of time—God was white and didn't listen to niggers—but Queen told him to mind his business. Parson Dick laughed again, and stretched his back. He looked at the acres of cotton that still had to be picked, and wondered why he bothered. Who would whip him now, if he did less than he had to? He could run away, flee with his darling Ruby, and probably avoid the slave catchers, but where would they go, who would employ them, how would they live? Nothing had changed. Between them and any safe haven was the whole hostile territory of the Confederacy, and sympathy for runaway slaves was nonexistent. Those that had gone were fools,

Parson Dick thought; a few might make it to the North, but most would be recaptured and imprisoned or pressed into further labor by unscrupulous whites.

So Parson Dick stayed, and because he had formidable resources of pride in himself, he put his hand to any task that came his way, and did it with a will. The other slaves were grumbling at their increased work load, and slowing down when they needed to speed up, for cotton was their bread and jam in these uncertain times.

What they needed was a Massa, and since no Massa was there and Queen had too much else to worry about, Parson Dick took on the role of leader. He started to sing, softly at first, a work song, and soon it caught on and lifted everyone's spirits, for this much, at least, was as it had always been. They were picking cotton.

The calming sound of the work song drifted to the house. Sally heard it and it cheered her soul. It was the first positive thing, no matter how tiny, that had happened since Jass went away. The absence of the Massa had created a void in all their lives, which no one could fill, but now he was coming home and everything was going to be all right again. That he was wounded distressed her; that he was out of the army did not. He had done his duty, and was needed here, for home was the battlefront now.

The letter from Jass had arrived the previous evening. Tom had brought it, and Sally had struggled to read it in bed, but her eyesight was too bad. She had forced Queen to read it to her that morning, when they were alone in the kitchen after breakfast. Queen still denied she could read, although everyone knew it was a lie, and, as Sally had said to her, who would whip her for it now?

She wondered if Queen had told the other slaves that Jass was coming home, and that was why they were singing the work song, but she guessed not. The return of the Massa had little meaning for the slaves.

Upstairs in the nursery, Lizzie heard the distant song, but it brought her no solace.

It wasn't fair of God to let her babies die. He couldn't be so cruel!

Yet they were dying, Lizzie knew. Mary and Little Sally had diphtheria, and there was nothing anyone could do. She'd nursed them for days, wiping their fevered brows, praying for their return to health, sleeping in a chair beside them, so they would know their mother was always near.

She was so tired. All she wanted to do was sleep, but she couldn't sleep until her little ones were better. Or gone. But they couldn't go, not yet; she had to make them hold on, just for a little while longer, another few weeks, because Jass was coming home, and when he came back they'd get better, because when he came back everything was going to be all right again.

Easter was with her, bathing the sweat from Little Sally's face. The child's breathing was labored, and Lizzie was in despair.

"She's slipping away, I know she is! Do something, Easter," she begged the slave.

"Nuttin' we can do, Miss Lizzie," Easter said softly. "'Cept pray."

Anger at her own inadequacy to help her children swept over Lizzie, in mounting hysteria. She got to her feet, moaning, and paced around the room, looking frantically for something to do.

"We can't just sit here! My poor babies—" she cried.

"Hush, now, Miss Lizzie," Easter said. She got up from the bed, and took Lizzie by the shoulders to calm her.

But Lizzie's fury exploded. Her frustrated passions finally found a focus. She hit Easter's comforting arms from her.

572

"Don't you touch me, you nigra slut," she screamed. "You want my babies to die. You don't care about them; all you care about is your brat, Queen! Haven't you had enough from me? You stole my man! Now you want my babies dead, too!"

There was no consistency in her thinking; all of her hurt over the years and all of her present impotence came flooding out. She ranted and whimpered by turns, her arms flailing uselessly.

Easter, not knowing what else to do with the hysterical woman, slapped her hard across the face.

Lizzie was stunned. She could not believe a slave, this slave, had touched her, struck her.

"How dare you," she whispered vehemently. "I'll have you whipped, I'll have you sold away. Get the overseer!"

Easter remained calm.

"Ain't no overseer here, Miss Lizzie," she said. "There's only us, now. We got to help each other."

The simple, calming truth of it forced its way to Lizzie's fractured mind, and for the first time she genuinely understood the fact of their appalling circumstances. Her passion spent, she slowly dissolved into tears, and folded into Easter's arms.

Easter led her to the chair and sat her down.

"There now," she said. "You sit here with your babies. I get you some broth."

Lizzie nodded, still crying, and took Little Sally's hand, held it to her cheek, while Easter caressed her the while, and then left the room.

Through all the days of her children's illness, it had never occurred to Lizzie that Easter was almost as sick as they.

Halfway down the stairs, Easter felt faint, and leaned against the wall for support. It was only a fever, she told herself; it would pass. She was flushed and sweating, and a wave of nausea passed through her. She had to sit down on the stairs.

She didn't know how long she sat there, but after a little while she felt better, and hauled herself to her feet. As she did so, there was a scream of distress from the nursery. Easter clutched the banisters and started to make her way back up.

Sally came into the hall and tried to climb the stairs, but stumbled a little. Easter saw her and went to help.

"Don't worry about me," Sally cried. "The babies!"

But Lizzie appeared at the top of the stairs, carrying the dead Mary in her arms.

"She's gone," she said simply, and stood there, not knowing what else to do.

Easter ran up the stairs to the nursery. Sally struggled to follow, but before she was halfway up, Easter came back out to them.

She shook her head. Lizzie sank to the floor, keening for her dead children.

All the life-force seemed to drain from Sally, and she let out a great animal howl.

How could God be so cruel?

They buried the two little girls in the family cemetery. It was a pretty spot, and peaceful, in a grove of trees, sheltered from the world. The slaves' graveyard was on a hill a few hundred yards away.

Cap'n Jack and Isaac had dug the graves the previous day, and the preacher came from town to bury the children. Lizzie was very brave and didn't cry. Dressed in her mourning black, she seemed to have found some unexpected reserves of strength in her grief, and held William's hand throughout the service. Mrs. Henderson cared for Eleanor and James, because Easter was sick in the weaving house, and Queen was picking cotton. William was distressed, but Lizzie was good with him, and told him that the babies were in a far happier place.

When the service was finished, Sally stayed behind and watched Cap'n Jack fill in the graves. The sound of earth falling on the tiny coffins distressed her, and she wandered away to the grave of James, and wondered if he knew what straits they were in.

"Why did you leave us so soon?" she whispered, and for a moment she understood all of Becky Perkins's longings to cast aside this mortal coil and lie in eternal bliss with the man she loved.

It was a warm, gentle evening, and peaceful here, away from the tribulations of the world. The presence of her old friend comforted Sally's bleakness of soul. Cap'n Jack seemed to understand her mood. His work didn't take long, for the graves were small. He laid aside his shovel and sat near his old mistress.

For a while, neither felt the need to speak, and then Sally voiced a little of what was in her mind.

"So many dead," she said, looking about the grave-yard. "So many that we loved."

"We all got to die, Missy," Cap'n Jack said softly.

Sally nodded. How long would she live, and what new tribulations were in store? But Jass was coming home, everything would be all right again, and her thoughts turned to happier times.

Moved by the reliable presence of the man who was her friend, Sally took Cap'n Jack's hand. He was surprised, for whites very seldom touched their slaves, but understood her need.

"We been together a long time," he said. "We seen some things."

Sally nodded, and smiled. "You knew old Massa before I did," she remembered.

They both thought of the past, when they were young. Cap'n Jack gave a wheezy chuckle.

"'R'member how we set him up? I tole you where he went ridin', an' you was there, nursing yo' chile, Miss Elizabeth, by yo' first late husband?"

How could Sally forget? She remembered it as if it were yesterday. She saw the river, and the tree she sat under with her tiny daughter. She could hear the horse's hooves again, as the handsome young Irishman galloped toward her. She saw herself opening her dress, ostensibly to feed little Elizabeth, but actually so that when James rode by he would see things men were not supposed to see, in those days.

"Showing much more of myself than I should have," she laughed.

"One look at yo' lovely bosom, an' he was gone, hook, line, and sinker!" Cap'n Jack was lost in the same memory.

"And you saw the same thing because you were hiding behind a bush to make sure everything went well." Sally laughed again, and slapped Cap'n Jack lightly on the hand. "Oh, we had some times."

"We surely did," the slave agreed. They sat together in the graveyard until it was dusk, and then Cap'n Jack helped Miss Sally home.

When Lizzie got back to the house, she made sure the children were fed, sent William out to play, and put the young ones to bed. She did all this herself, with only occasional grumbling assistance and instruction from Poppy, because Queen and Easter were not there. The children's food wasn't very good because Lizzie had never cooked so much as a pan of water before, but the children didn't seem to mind. When Mrs. Henderson, who had accompanied her, protested that slaves should be doing the cooking, Lizzie told her, rather sharply, to mind her place. They were her children, and if Lizzie wanted to feed them herself, that was her business. Mrs. Henderson sniffed, said she knew where she wasn't wanted, and left with rather ruffled feathers. Lizzie was pleased with herself. She couldn't stand Mrs. Henderson, and this was the first time she'd voiced her true feelings.

Later, alone in her room, Lizzie did something she hadn't done in years. The death of the two children had been a cathartic experience for her. She had been

576

distressed when tiny Jane had died, but she was only a few months old. These two had been different, because Lizzie loved them as little people, not as helpless babies.

She knew she wasn't going to like what the mirror would tell her, but she had never shrunk from it before, and she was brave enough, and honest enough about herself, to face the consequences. In any case, she already knew what it would say.

She had behaved badly since Jass left. She hated his going, and the war, and she had taken refuge from it by playing her accustomed role as helpless mistress to the hilt. But having to cope, alone, with the death of the children had made her understand that their world had been turned upside down. She realized that, for the duration of the war at least, she might have to respond differently to things, because she now understood that even when Jass came home, the war was not going to be over, and it might all get worse before it got better.

What surprised Lizzie was that she saw something to be proud of in the mirror. She saw that she could cope.

"I shall pick cotton," she told Sally at dinner. Parson Dick, whose hands were raw and blistered, almost dropped the soup tureen. Sally stared at her daughter-in-law in astonishment, and William giggled.

"Well, the cotton has to be picked, and we don't have enough hands," Lizzie said defensively, although the only reaction, apart from William's, had been silence. "If it rains, the crop will be ruined."

Parson Dick moved as quickly as good manners would allow to the kitchen, and told Queen, who was banging pots on the stove, to come and listen to this at the pantry door.

"Do you think you're up to it?" Sally couldn't imagine Lizzie as a cotton picker.

"I've no idea," Lizzie replied honestly. "I've never

done it, I didn't think I would ever have to do it, and once this war is sorted out and things are back to normal, I don't intend to have to do it again."

No one said anything, because no one realized she had finished.

"But the harvest is in danger, and I am the mistress of this plantation." Lizzie couldn't bear silence. "If the men are ready to sacrifice their lives for our survival, the least I can do is risk a few blisters."

"Bravo, Mamma," William applauded. "I'll pick cotton, too."

Queen and Parson Dick, huddled together at the pantry door, looked at one another in amazement.

"Wonders ain't never going to cease," Queen said, and hurried away to prepare the main course, because Sally was ringing the bell.

"I wish I could help," Sally said. "I feel so useless." She was impressed by Lizzie's resolution, and wondered what had wrought this change in her. "You're too old to pick cotton, Gran'ma," William laughed, and Sally gave him her best "old-fashioned" look.

"I used to be good at it," she said, knowing it would shock the boy. "We had to turn our hands to all sorts of things, back in the early days."

She looked at her openmouthed grandson, pleased with the effect, for truthfully, she had never picked cotton in her life. But she had done many things, and would have picked cotton if the need had arisen.

"The days when I was young," she added, tartly.

What she couldn't tell them, because she didn't know, was that it was backbreaking labor. Out there all day, in the baking sun, bent over those miserable damn bushes, the prickers tearing your hands. Lizzie had dressed for the occasion in her oldest clothes and had a sunbonnet on, and at the beginning she had quite enjoyed herself, but she was not prepared for the

578

searing pain that arced through her back every time she stood.

Queen thoroughly approved of Lizzie's decision—they needed all the help they could get—but some of the field hands were not so sure.

"Tain't fittin', the Missy pickin' cotton," Isaac grumbled. He had a strong sense of order.

The day was sultry and overcast, with storm clouds billowing toward them. They labored on, a small band of convicts in a prison of white.

No matter how much she picked, it seemed to Lizzie that there was still as much as before. Finally, she couldn't stand it.

"I can't! I can't do it anymore," she cried, and sat on the ground. William ran to his mother.

"We got to, Miss Lizzie," Queen called to her. "We got to pick this field 'fore it rains."

"I'll help you, Mamma," William said, though his hands were bleeding and raw.

Lizzie looked about at the endless cotton, and groaned. It wasn't fair; she wasn't born to this, brought up to this. For the first time in her life, she blessed the existence of nigras.

She looked at her eager son, and accepted his offer of help. She would complete the day because she had said she would, but that was enough, she would have done her bit, and she would never go near a cotton bush again. Leaning on William, she climbed to her feet, and bent her back to her hated task.

Within the hour, Mrs. Henderson arrived, in high dudgeon. She had been enjoying a pleasant morning shouting at Jasmine, who cooked and cleaned for her, but the girl had eventually lost her temper. She told Mrs. Henderson that she should be out picking cotton, like the Missy, and then she'd know what it was like to be a slave.

Mrs. Henderson had hardly believed her ears, and had boxed Jasmine's for telling lies, but the girl stuck to her story. So Mrs. Henderson put on her best bonnet, and came to see what it was all about.

"What is this? Mrs. Jackson, what are you doing?" she cried in outraged distress, every fiber of her bourgeois, white Southern upbringing and aspirations insulted to the core.

"Queen needed help," Lizzie said lamely, glad of the interruption.

Mrs. Henderson was appalled. "So Queen is in charge now? Queen can order the mistress of the house into the fields, like some common nigger?"

"It was Mamma's idea," William defended Queen, while she, worried about her mother, lost her temper and shouted at Mrs. Henderson.

"Someone got to do it," she yelled. "Ain't enough of us niggers left!"

Mrs. Henderson turned to Queen, hating the uppity, bastard girl. Queen the adored, Queen the darling, Queen the treasure of the big house, whose very white-skinned existence flaunted her father's carnal baseness to the world, and was an affront to good Christian morality.

"Don't you sass me!" She began calmly enough, but reason failed her. She exploded in fury, her pent-up animosity to Queen flooding to the surface.

"Don't you ever sass me, or you will regret it to the end of your days."

The sheer violence of it shocked Lizzie and William, although the slaves had heard worse, and had felt worse, for the lash of the whip was more painful than the lash of the tongue.

Lizzie felt duty bound to excuse Queen, whom she didn't like, because it had been her idea.

"I do need a break," she said, and Mrs. Henderson took charge. "You come with me, Mrs. Jackson; there's water over here." She led Lizzie to the water bag.

"Five minutes," Queen yelled, defiantly.

Lizzie was already gulping water like a dying man in a desert. William came running to her for his share, and it was he who saw the cart first.

"Who's that?" he asked.

Lizzie put down the water bag and stood panting at the fence. She squinted in the direction of William's pointing, to the main gate, and saw a cart, with some men in it, stopped there.

Someone in the cart helped another man down, and that man now came trudging up the drive.

Mrs. Henderson saw the man, too.

"Please God, let it be—" she whispered.

But Lizzie knew who it was, and was running for all she was worth. Mrs. Henderson realized who it was too, and walked away, quietly, to be by herself and pray for her husband's welfare.

"We ain't done yet—" Queen called to Lizzie, but Cap'n Jack stopped her.

"It the Massa," he said quietly.

It was Jass, home from the war. Lizzie, screaming at him, ran to him, pell-mell into his arms, and clung to him as if she would never let him go.

Sally had spent the day with Easter, in the weaving house. Easter was very ill, and when she had not come to the big house in the morning, Sally had gone to her. Sally could only guess at the problem, and feared it might be typhoid. It might as easily be diphtheria, caught from the children, or exhaustion, or measles, or any of a dozen fevers. Queen, who had less experience with illness, was worried, but relieved by Sally's presence, and, reluctantly, had gone to her place as mistress of the cotton fields.

It was serious, Sally knew, for she was used to death, and could guess it was hovering by. She had made Easter as comfortable as her condition would allow, and wiped the sweat from her with cold compresses. For a while, Easter slept, but uneasily, and when she woke, Sally knew the end was near. Easter's eyes were yellow, her skin dull, and she was having difficulty breathing.

Sally went to the door to call for help, and saw a little slave girl playing not far away.

"You girl," she called, and remembered the child's name. "Tilly! You run fetch Queen, you hear? Her Mammy's sick. You run as fast as you can."

Tilly was wide-eyed with fear. She knew the old lady with the white hair was the old Missy, but had never been spoken to by her before. But she was a well-mannered girl and did as she was told.

"Run!" Sally cried.

And Tilly ran.

Queen stood in the cotton field, Cap'n Jack beside her, and watched the distant figure of Jass put his arm around his wife and son, and walk with them to the big house.

He was home at last, and everything was going to be all right. He'd solve all their problems: She wouldn't have to work in the fields anymore and could spend her time nursing her sick mother, and Easter would get better, because Jass was home.

She looked at the field. All the slaves had stopped work to watch the return of the Massa.

"Still got to be picked," she called to them. They bent to their task, and a few of them started the work song again, for it was a sad homecoming, with the Massa's two little daughters buried.

Queen worked hard and with a will. In an hour she could take a break and go see to her mother. Perhaps she wouldn't have to come back to the fields this afternoon; she'd ask Jass when he talked to her. He'd speak to her soon, she was sure, but it was only right and proper he should talk to his wife first.

She was surprised to hear someone calling her name.

She looked up and saw that sweet child, Tilly, running to her. Perhaps the Massa had sent for her.

"Queen," Tilly called. "Come quick! Yo' mammy's sick!"

There was nothing in Queen's mind now but her mammy. She had seen her that morning and knew she was not well, but Easter's true crisis had not developed until later, when Missy Sally had come to look after her so that Queen could work. If Missy Sally was saying she was sick, and no one else could have sent the message, then it was serious.

She dropped her bag and ran, with lung-bursting energy, through the field. Flecks of cotton danced in the air, sparkling in the sunlight, like pure white gold, as she ran.

Cap'n Jack ran too. But to the big house, to tell Jass.

Grief flowed on grief for Jass, until he thought he must drown in an ocean of sorrow. Despite his bitterness at the brevity of his military career, he had come home with such high, bright hopes, to be loved and to be in a world he understood.

As he got down from the cart, he stared at his property with a mounting sense of unease. He'd been away only six months, but there was an atmosphere of disrepair and neglect about the place. He saw the distant figures picking cotton, but only half the number there should have been, and there were still acres to be picked before the rain came.

Then Lizzie, dressed as a field hand, ran screaming into his arms, and clutched him, and wept, and blurted out the news of the death of his daughters. He hardly knew how to respond, for it was too shocking and unexpected and the enormity of what had happened was too great for him to assimilate.

He took his wife and son to the big house, sat with them in the kitchen, and said very little while he heard

583

the stories of their deprivation in his absence. He wished they'd stop, because he wanted to be alone, but could not be yet, because he was husband and father.

Then Cap'n Jack burst in, and told him that Easter was dying.

Without saying a word, Jass got up from the table, left the room, left the house, and walked, faster and faster, to the one place in the world that was constant to him, and was not constant anymore.

He heard Lizzie call after him. "This is your family!" She sounded angry, but he didn't care.

He shivered with fear as he walked. He could see it now, nestling in the trees as it always had, the cottage of his dreams, and he began to run, as he ran to it once, so many years ago, on the night his father died. She had been there then, waiting for him, as she always waited for him, and she had to be there now, because she was always there.

But just as he started to run, he heard an awful scream from inside the house, and he stopped running, for he understood what the dreadful sound meant, and his blood ran cold.

He came into the weaving house and saw what he had known he would see. Easter was lying on the bed, her eyes closed in death.

Queen was beside her, sobbing, and clinging to her mother, as if to drag her back from her new dominion, and Sally was comforting Queen.

He hadn't spoken, had hardly made a sound when he came in, but somehow Queen knew he was there. She ran to him, threw herself at his feet and clutched at his legs, begging him to bring her mammy back, to make everything all right again.

He saw what she did and heard what she said, but without seeing and without hearing. The only thing he could see was the awful image of Easter, and then his mind exploded, and refused to accept what his eyes saw. He turned his head away, so that he wouldn't have to look at her.

Sally came to Queen and pulled her from her father, the Massa.

"Come, girl, come," she said. "Save your grief till later. We must get a winding sheet."

Just once, Jass looked at Queen, and that once was almost enough, for she saw the unbearable grief in his eyes, and a pain, and a loneliness, more intense than her own. She allowed Sally to pull her away, and left her father alone with her mother.

He didn't look at her, and he didn't go to her, because there was no point. She was not there.

He sat in his old rocking chair, and stared at nothing. Waiting. If he did what he had always done, sat and waited for her, then she would come back from the well, and sit at her loom, and they'd be together again, nothing could keep them apart, and everything would be as it had always been.

He sat for hours, seeing her dance in his mind, a living and beautiful thing, who had taken possession of his heart at some time before he could remember, and had nursed and cherished him through all his life.

He didn't move or speak. Night came, and still he sat there. Then, without understanding how it happened, he knew she wasn't going to come back from the well, ever again. He knew he would never see her, living, again, and prayed that her soul was in some sweet and gentle resting place.

For a great and simple truth had overwhelmed him. He had known it for so long, all his thinking life; perhaps he had put it out of his mind because it made the world too complicated. The implications of it now were so frightening, he could not, at this moment, bear to consider them.

Black people did have souls.

He turned and looked at the body.

"Oh, my love," he said.

And he wept.

58

It was as if someone had turned out a lamp in Queen's heart, or God had snatched the sun away. Although the awful truth of Easter's death had burst into her soul at the moment of her mammy's going, Queen understood that it was to a place she could not follow, and disbelief fought with knowledge. A tiny part of her nursed, cherished, the idea that her mammy was only resting somewhere, and would come to her again, but the greater part knew Easter's loving embrace was gone forever, and she was filled with an unassuageable sense of loss. Anger battled with despair, and loneliness was the champion. Under Sally's careful instruction, she had gone about the necessary business, and had sat outside the weaving house for hours waiting till Jass had finished whatever it was he still had to do with her mother, clutching the winding sheet to her, and keening softly. When Jass left the weaving house late that night, Queen went in, and kissed and caressed her dead mother, and wept her distress. Then, refusing Cap'n Jack or Sally's help, she had washed Easter's body, gently as a daughter should, and made her hair pretty, and wrapped her in the winding sheet.

As she tended the body, unanswerable questions assailed her, of which the greatest concerned Jass, for now he was her nearest living relative, apart from Cap'n Jack, and the living link of love with her mother. For she knew it must have been love, and knew it was a love that fell outside the parameters of conventional domesticity. As a slave, it was not strange to her that Easter so willingly accepted the limits that their society imposed on their relationship, and to have had the small proofs she did of the Massa's love was a treasure sweeter to Queen than any she could imagine. It was what she wanted now, some word, some look, and, most wondrous of all, an embrace, from her father, but it never came. Apart from that one, tiny, anguished look that Jass had given Queen, when she had thought she had seen into his soul, Jass ignored her, and this added to Queen's sense of bereavement. She had thought that he loved her, but now, in her time of greatest need, his reassurance did not come. Cap'n Jack was kind to her, and Sally, but they could not fill the void in her heart. On the night that Easter was buried, Queen could not sleep. Comfortable and warm in her tiny cot, she could not bear to think of Easter lying in the wet, cold earth, eaten by worms. It was Sally who was able to persuade her that the ground would be kind to her mother, and cherish her mortal remains while her spirit found a greater comfort.

Jass was not thoughtless of Queen, nor did he intend to hurt. It was simply that he was trying to find a way to cope with his own grief, his own loneliness, and to avoid considerations of his world turned upside down. He longed to fight for his country, but he no longer believed in the cause his country fought for. Jass now believed that slavery must end one day, for the forces of the world and his own heart were against it, but he could not let his country be vanquished by his brothers. Queen was the physical embodiment of the contradictions that raged within him. Restless and dispirited, he spent most of his days in Florence, anxious for news of the war, and getting drunk with men who were too old to fight, and boys who were too young. He was bitter because he had been forced back into idleness, while good men, friends, were dying.

Neither side appeared to be winning, and the list of the dead was growing daily. Almost everyone who

587

came to The Forks had a friend or cousin or brother or son who had paid the ultimate sacrifice.

It was winter. Barren, inanimate winter. The trees were lifeless and bare. The slave graveyard, so prettily situated in the other seasons, was desolate now. It suited Queen's mood, for the weeks had not eased her sense of loss. A simple wooden cross marked Easter's grave, among so many dead. Next to her lay Julie, who had gone so very recently, and Ephraim who had also died of the fever. Not far away was Solomon, who had escaped from The Forks of Cypress once, and been recaptured and brought back, and never ceased to bore them with the tall tales of his freedom. Over yonder was Tiara, who had helped Queen to be born, and had been kind to her when she was little. She was gone soon after Queen moved into the big house, and lay beside her husband, Micah, in perfect peace.

Queen came here almost every day, to tend the grave and keep it neat and clean. And to talk to her mammy, who was, to her, still a living creature, safe, in God's comforting arms. Jass's return had not made everything all right again; if anything, their physical circumstances were worse. The war, which everyone had thought would be over in a few short months, dragged on. Food was scarce; all they had was what the farm could provide. It would soon be Christmas, but no one could find any reason for cheer.

Queen, wrapped in a blanket to keep her warm, sat by her mother's grave and told her these things. She was cold and lonely, she worked too hard, and no one ever seemed grateful for all the things she did; they accepted them as if it were her place to care for them, and demanded as much from her as she could give, and then demanded more. To them she was a slave, she knew, and it was her duty to slave for them, but Queen could not accept that she was only a slave. No one understood that Queen looked after them all because they were her family.

If only she weren't so tired all the time. If only her mammy were here, with her, to help.

"I miss you, Mammy," she whispered, too exhausted even to cry.

She sat for a while and pulled a few old weeds from the grave. Not many, because it was winter, and not even weeds grew in winter.

She became aware that she was not alone. Someone else was standing in the trees near her, watching her.

It was Jass.

Wearily, Queen dragged herself to her feet.

"I sorry, Massa," she said, knowing her place.

He shrugged his shoulders. Place didn't matter very much, here. Neither of them said anything because they couldn't think of anything to say. Gossip was irrelevant, sacrilegious here, and all the news was bad.

But the silence was awkward. More than Massa and slave, they were not as much as father and daughter. Yet he had to speak to her. If her loss was as keen as his own, could they not find some little comfort from each other?

"Do you come here often?" Jass asked, and Queen nodded.

"You work very hard," Jass said. "Thank you."

Queen closed her eyes, and felt warm again. At least the Massa understood how hard she worked. At least her father had said thank you.

"I'm sorry we're not more help to you," Jass said, and it was Queen's turn to shrug.

"Not your place, Massa," she told him. She did not understand his mood. He was here with them, safe from the war.

"Sometimes I wonder where my place is," he said, and his bitterness confused her.

Why did he hate himself so? Queen wanted to go to

him, hold him, tell him they loved him. Tell him that she loved him. She didn't, because she didn't know how. No one had ever taught her. She wondered if her mammy had ever told him how much she had loved him. Or he her.

She turned away, unable to cope with his bleak, winter mood, but her need for him was too strong. She turned back, but he was gone.

Jass walked down the hill from the slave graveyard. He had wanted to be there alone, to sit and talk with Easter for a while, but Queen was there, and he felt guilty at disturbing her. The child had so little; he could not take away what little she had. He had found no comfort from her; rather her evident sense of pain had increased his own. Thoughts of death and dying filled him. The family cemetery was at the bottom of the hill, and he went to it, and stood at the graves of his daughters. Cap'n Jack had said they died easy, but that wasn't true. No one died easy.

He yearned to be away at the war. He wasn't sure what the cause was anymore, except the protection of his place and his family, and they had to be protected. He tried to block his mind to the matter of slavery, because to deny the rightness of it was to deny the South, and everything Jass understood himself to be. What was important was the South, not for the maintenance of slavery but for its sheer survival. Militarily, the South seemed to have a small advantage; at any rate, they had not lost. Perhaps the North had originally understimated the skill and ferociousness of their enemy. Perhaps they had misunderstood the whole rationale of the war. The South was fighting for its very existence; the North was fighting only to win. But the North had the resources to assemble a vast war machine, Jass knew, and when that was in place the possibility of a Southern victory required every possible man.

One of those men was Jass. Discharged from the

army but determined to fight, he had talked with his brother William, who had presented a solution. William, a Confederate state senator, knew all the ins and outs of political intrigue. He intended to raise a company, the Franklin Rifles, and would pay for their uniforms. He would present his company to the army command; it would be accepted into service and William given a commission considered appropriate.

There was no reason why Jass could not do the same. He could afford to do so, and the army would infinitely prefer to have his troops under its command than roaming renegade free.

He told them at dinner, and Lizzie was predictably angry. As usual, Parson Dick was listening in the pantry, and relayed the news to Queen in the kitchen.

"Miss Lizzie don't like it," he said.

"Miss Lissie don't like nothing," Queen sniffed, busy with the meal. "Set them taters out for me, Poppy," she called to her unwilling assistant. "And you get that meat out to them, Parson Dick, you hear?"

"Not much point. Nobody's eatin', 'cept young Massa William." Parson Dick was enjoying the row in the dining room.

Queen didn't want her father to go, and was as angry as Lizzie. She banged a pot on the stove. "Ain't none of our business," she snapped. "We cook it an' serve it. If'n they eat it or not's up to them."

Parson Dick took the stewed rabbit into the dining room. When he was gone, Queen's energy deserted her. Why did he have to go? He was wounded, he had no reason to fight. Why did he want to leave them alone again, when they needed him here?

Lizzie tried so hard to be reasonable, but could not see Jass's point. He couldn't protect them if he was hundreds of miles away.

"What if the Yankees come?" she said for the umpteenth time. "A handful of raggedy slaves can't protect us."

Parson Dick bridled at the word "raggedy" but presented the rabbit to Sally.

"They'll never get this far South," Jass insisted.

"They might," Lizzie countered.

"Then it's up to me to try to stop them!" Jass was angry, and Lizzie and Sally both knew it was pointless trying to change his mind when he was this determined.

There was a small silence while Jass fumed and Lizzie sulked. Sally tried to restore order.

"Well, now, rabbit," she said. "We haven't had meat for a while."

"A scraggy ol' thing Massa William shot this morning," Parson Dick told her, and winked at William, who, alone of those at the table, was pleased that his father was going back to war. The fathers of most of his school friends had gone, and even though William understood that Jass had been wounded, he wanted a soldier father, especially an officer. He hadn't understood why Jass enlisted as a private the first time.

Jass assembled and paid for his company, the 27th Alabama Infantry, offered it to the Confederate Army High Command, and was appointed lieutenant-colonel. They marched out in January to Fort Donelson, where they were assigned.

Sally was pleased. Fort Donelson was named after the family of her dear departed friend, Rachel Jackson, Andrew's wife, and was situated on the banks of the Cumberland River, near Nashville. Jass would be safe there, hundreds of miles from the Northern battlefields.

She was wrong.

A vast, unstoppable, blue-clad army appeared, it seemed from nowhere, from the west, conquering all in its path. Fort Donelson fell to the forces of General Grant, and Nashville soon after. Jass was taken prisoner of war.

592

"Perhaps it is God's will that I do not fight," he told his mother in a rare letter during his incarceration. "At least, He seems to be doing His level best to keep me from this war."

He prayed for a similar blessing for his family and cursed it for himself.

59

Young Davy brought them the news first. For days they had expected it, but when it came it was shocking.

"The Yankees done took Florence," he yelled as he ran up the hill. "Ol' Linkun's in there killin' everybody!"

He'd taken the buckets down to the cesspit that morning, wide-eyed with fear, because the rumors said there were Yankees everywhere, and while they were supposed to be friendly to black people, Davy wasn't so sure. He'd heard Miss Lizzie talking about them the other day, and the terrible things they did to women and babies, and if they were that mean, obviously you couldn't trust them. He emptied the buckets and was about to go back when he heard a horse galloping toward him. There weren't any trees or bushes nearby, and he surely wasn't going to jump into the muck-filled pit, so he stood his ground, and was filled with relief to see that the man riding toward him wasn't a soldier.

The man didn't stop. "Run tell your Massa, boy," he cried, galloping past Davy. "The Yankees have taken Florence!"

Davy needed no second bidding, but ran for all he was worth, Miss Lizzie's stories of the misdeeds of Yankees pounding through his brain.

The few slaves in the field, tilling the soil in readiness for the new planting, stopped work and tried to assimilate what they heard. If the Yankees really had taken Florence, it wouldn't be long before they got here. It was coming, it was coming, hallelujah, it was coming. Freedom was at hand. They laughed among themselves, but instead of taking the day off, or the rest of their lives, they went back to work with renewed vigor, and took up a joyous song.

Sally, organizing the beating of rugs with Poppy, heard the song and was pleased. An odd thing had happened over the past few months. She had always believed that the plantation was an island unto itself, and all who lived there, white and black, were interdependent on each other. In a sense it was true. Miles from their nearest neighbors, the travails of their daily lives, the births and deaths, arguments and marriages, parties for the whites, beatings for the blacks, were the basis of their conversation, with occasional snatches of misunderstood gossip about the outside world reaching them through visitors or the grapevine. The well-being of the plantation was critical to all of them, because if it was a good harvest they all ate well, and, for the slaves, their Massas might be in better tempers, and if it was a bad harvest, everyone suffered. Yet one group had privilege and the other did not, and if Sally thought of it as a community, the slaves regarded it as a prison. They made the best of that prison, and while a few, especially among the house slaves, had considerable affection for some of the whites, there was always a barrier.

In the last few months, that barrier had, to a considerable degree, been removed. With no Massa and fewer slaves, they had all got to know each other better. Now everyone was dedicated to the common cause of immediate survival. If there was food, everyone ate; if there was none, no one ate. If jobs had to be done, they all pitched in to do them. They maintained the charade that things were as they had been because that was the

594

ordered world they all understood, and in these frightening times, order was all they had to cling to. Isaac, solid, reliable Isaac, had been put in charge of discipline, and even given, to Lizzie's howls of protest, a gun. He used it to shoot rabbits, because very few of the slaves left wanted to run away. There was nowhere to go. Jeremiah and two other runaway field hands had been recaptured and returned, bloodily beaten, and while they still talked of escape, they did nothing about it. The runaways told awful stories of the outside world—they'd lived in the woods bordering small farms, they'd eaten nothing but turnips and potatoes for days, and when one of them ventured to a house to beg, he'd been shot at. They all understood that if they could get away, and get to Union lines, they would be free, or hoped so, but no one was very sure where the Union lines were. So they preferred to wait, and see what the war would bring. They had no Massa and no overseer, except Isaac, so life was tolerable, and they ate regularly. Happily, the barns at The Forks were still relatively full, and the first spring vegetables ready for picking.

The most obvious evidence of this new communality to Sally was that she now knew the names of all the slaves. Such as the boy Davy, who was running toward her, yelling at the top of his lungs. She'd been expecting his news for days; everyone in Florence had been prepared for an invasion. There was no army nearby to protect them, only some local militia units, and Sally, like everyone else, had been living in dread. But she put her faith in her fellowman, and gave no credence to Lizzie's lurid imaginings.

They were here, at last. It would not be long before they came to The Forks, Sally was sure, because she could guess what they needed.

And two days later they came.

*

595

"They look so fearsome," Lizzie said. "Brutal."

"Pull yourself together," Sally urged. "They're only men."

Lizzie corrected her with a fierce, defiant whisper. "They're Yankees!"

But she stood beside her mother-in-law and tried to maintain her composure as a small troop of Union soldiers made their way up the drive. They were a foraging detail, requisitioning food. Once the first shock of occupation had settled down, Tom Kirkman had come out to The Forks, to assure them that the soldiers were reasonably well-behaved and looking for provisions. He'd volunteered to stay, to protect them, but Sally had laughed.

"You against so many, Tom? You said we had nothing to be afraid of. Go home to your family."

Tom had gone, and the following morning Davy, who had been stationed near the road to town as lookout, gave the news of the arriving Yankees.

The captain, on horseback, led his men up the drive. He was impressed by the grace and elegance of the house, which was as fine as any he'd seen, and he looked with pity at the bunch of ragged slaves cowering near the trees. These were the blacks that made the fortunes that built the mansions such as this.

He stopped his horse on the lawn in front of the veranda and looked at the small group assembled there. An old woman, and a frightened, defiant younger one. A couple of children, and some few house slaves.

And a beautiful young white woman, dressed as a servant. Mulatta, probably, but hard to tell. The sergeant called the men to a halt.

"Ma'am," the captain said to the old woman, and touched his cap, out of respect for her sex and her age, not her station.

Sally squinted and wished she could see his insignia of rank better.

"Good morning, Lieutenant," she said, and he did

596

not correct her demotion of him. "We are, as you see, a depleted family. There are no men here."

She did not see his eyes stray to the male slaves, but corrected herself anyway.

"Apart from these few slaves. I trust you mean us no harm?"

They were all the same, these tough Southern matriarchs, he thought, the backbone of the whole society.

"We mean no harm to anyone who is loyal to the United States," he said, by rote. He'd done it a thousand times before.

"I cannot swear allegiance to your flag, sir," Sally responded as he knew she would, as they all did. "I believe in a different cause."

"Believe in whatever cause you like," he told her. "As long as you do not intend to fight. I do not think that you would win."

He looked at the slaves and women, and then at his own rough-and-ready soldiers, his point well made. Sally was surprised at his civility.

The captain was a very civil man, and loved his country. Second of three brothers who had enlisted in the army, he was a college graduate, and a teacher at a good school until the war came, this wretched, Rebel, war.

He went through the details, formally, officially, as he always did. He told of the food they needed, and of the chits they would be given in return for that food. He told them of the cotton seed that he intended to seize.

"That is our only source of income!" Sally cried, and the captain smiled, for that was why he was taking it.

Business done, he accepted her offer of refreshment, and listened to her protests about the cotton seed.

"You will not harm us, but you will bankrupt us?" Sally reasoned.

"Orders, ma'am," the captain said, although it was

597

not true. It was his own idea, born of his own bitterness. If it had been in his power to drive every Southern family to bankruptcy, he would willingly have done so. It was with some pleasure that he added to her distress. Units of the local militia had destroyed bridges to try to delay the Yankee advance, and the cotton gins were to be blown up in retaliation.

To his surprise, Sally was there the following day, sitting in a carriage on the riverbank, the cotton-white, pretty mulatta sitting beside her, watching as the gins were destroyed. Sally went because she had a complaint to make to the captain, and because she wanted to see the destruction. Half the town was there for the spectacle. The buildings were blown to smithereens. The riverbank shook with gunpowder.

"How would you have us live now?" Sally asked him, quietly.

He didn't look at her, and his face betrayed nothing of the vengeful emotions he felt.

"I've lost two brothers in this war, ma'am, killed by Johnny Reb," he said quietly. "I don't care how you live. Or if you live."

He tipped his hat to her and rode away.

"I hate him," Queen said softly, and took Sally's hand.

Sally shook her head. "He's only doing his duty." She could not find hate in her heart now, only an overwhelming sense of sorrow, and of loss.

But Queen had no alternative to hate. On the previous day, some of the captain's men had beaten her gran'pappy, Cap'n Jack, viciously. Queen had not wanted to come, but Sally insisted she be present for her complaint to the captain about the behavior of his men.

They had been taking supplies from the barn, loading them onto a Jackson cart, and Queen had protested they were taking too much. The soldiers had made sport with her.

"Leave us something!" she demanded.

"I'll leave a little bun in your oven, lady," the sergeant laughed. They surrounded her, teasing her, taunting her, thinking her white and a serving girl. They smelt of sweat and stale beer; their faces were rough with stubble and their eyes bright with lust.

Queen was terrified. She didn't understand men; she had no experience of them. The house slaves were no threat to her, the field hands were either kind or ignored her, and although a few visiting white men, her father's friends, had winked at her and called her pretty, she had been secure from their advances because of the family. No one had ever taught her how to handle men, for no white woman would bother with instruction, and a slave woman had nothing to teach her, except submission to what the men wanted. The incident of two years ago, in Florence, when the three hooligans accosted her flared in her mind, but they had been boys, and these were soldiers.

She hit their hands away when they touched her, and spat in their faces, but her anger only seemed to excite them more.

"She wants to play," one said, laughing to his companions.

"I know a game she'd like," another grinned. He grabbed at Queen and pulled her to him. He held her face with one hand, her body with the other, and kissed her. She tried to break her mouth away, but he was strong and his grip like a vise. His stubble grazed her face, his rough uniform chafed her body, and she could feel the hardness of him, at his groin, shoving against her. He pushed his tongue into her mouth. She tried to scream, tried to bite, but he was ready for that, and clutched his hand on her jaw, so she could not move it.

She heard a voice. "Don't touch her!"

It was Cap'n Jack. He held a hefty stick in his hands, raised in the air, ready to strike.

The soldier who was kissing Queen looked at him in surprise.

"Who's this?" he laughed. "Your fancy man?"

Cap'n Jack hit him across the shoulders with the stick, and they all turned on him. Desire for a pretty girl became lust for blood, and, methodically and efficiently, they beat him senseless, while Queen screamed her distress.

When they were done, Queen ran to him, weeping, screaming for aid.

"Help him, please," she begged Cap'n Jack's assailants. "He my gran'pappy."

The beating had sated them, and when they heard of the family relationship, perhaps they were shamed, the sergeant at least. He called his men to order, and led them away.

Queen ran to the slave quarters for help, and Isaac and Jeremiah had taken Cap'n Jack to his bunk, where Queen nursed him, and bathed his wounds. When Sally was told, she came to see him, and ordered that he be moved to a comfortable bed, in the big house. She complained to the captain, who apologized, reprimanded the men, and ordered the return of the Jackson cart. No further action was taken because Cap'n Jack had hit first.

No one thought he would live.

He did live, after a fashion, for a while. The worst of his external wounds healed, but there was some internal damage. He was almost always in pain, and was incontinent. His mind wandered, and he seldom knew where he was. There was no physician to attend him; the local doctor had volunteered for the war, and the medical student who was running the practice said nothing could be done and prescribed laudanum.

Queen took charge of him, washed him and bathed

him, fed him and changed the sheets on his bed when they were soiled. Sally stayed with him when Queen could not. To everyone's surprise, Lizzie volunteered as well when Queen or Sally needed a break, although mostly she was busy tending the children, for Poppy had to run the household.

For a time Cap'n Jack didn't seem to recognize Queen or Sally, and he seldom spoke, except for a few muttered words—"Annie" and "broke his promise." Toward April, he seemed to get a little better, as if the spring were renewing him. He recognized people and things, and managed to speak, but the effort of it obviously distressed him. He lay for hours holding Queen's hand, gently caressing it with his thumb, and saying nothing. When Sally was with him, he talked a little more, of the old days in Nashville, and of the ol' Massa, and he always asked about Jass, who was a prisoner of war and of whom there was little news. Talk of Jass's incarceration depressed Cap'n Jack, and he would fall silent, and then mutter a few words of friendship and happiness and youth.

Sally understood his difficulty in speaking, and so she talked instead. She chattered endlessly about the old days in Nashville, when they were happy, of parties and picnics and pedigree horses, and of mutual friends, of Alfred, who lay in a tomb near his Massa now, loyal slave in life and death, of Chief Doublehead and Monkey Simon.

"Gone. All gone," Cap'n Jack said. But he would not go himself. It was as if he were waiting for something, some signal that he could leave secure in the knowledge that the better day was coming for those he left behind, as he had always promised.

In early April, they began to hear gunfire. It was distant and muffled, but incessant, continuous. It lasted for two days.

It was the sound of a battle at Shiloh, over twenty

601

miles away. Sometimes the relentless, dull noise caused the glass in the windows to rattle, and the crockery in the cupboards to shimmer. Lizzie heard it, and clutched her children to her. Mrs. Henderson heard it, and moved to the big house. Sally heard it, and prayed for the dead.

Parson Dick heard it when he was washing dishes. A little tremor caused a cup to rattle on the table. It dropped to the floor and smashed. Parson Dick looked at the plate in his hand. He smiled. And when the cannon fired again, so many miles away, he threw the plate over his shoulder, and let it break where it landed. And another. And another. Parson Dick was laughing now.

The slaves heard the noise when they were gathered around the campfire on that warm spring night, eating their evening meal.

"Awful close," said Davy.

"The closer it come, the closer my freedom," Jeremiah told him. Davy idolized Jeremiah. But not enough to run away with him.

"Oh, man, I's gwine get me some of that," Davy dreamed.

Isaac dreamed of it, too, but was more practical. "An' what you gwine do with it, boy?" he asked Davy.

"Get me a job," Davy said, surprised by the question. "Earn money."

"You cain't do nuttin' 'cept pick cotton an' empty shit pans, an' yo' ain't too good at that," Isaac said, and the others laughed.

Davy was angry; everyone was always laughing at him, when he tried so hard to please.

"Go North," he sulked, knowing Isaac couldn't have an answer for that. Everybody talked about going North. The old people called it "Up South" which Davy thought was stupid.

"An' beg fo' food, an' sleep in ditches?" Isaac burst Davy's bubble.

"Hear tell the Feds is takin' on niggers to fight, payin' 'em, too," Jeremiah said, to relieve the pressure on Davy. "Damn, I'd fight for freedom."

"Let's do it, eh?" said Davy, who had a young man's energy.

"Yeh, but yo' better get a good night sleep first, an' make sho' yo' belly's full," Isaac said. "Ask Jeremiah, he know about freedom."

"It's a'comin', Isaac," Jeremiah replied, still embarrassed from his previous, failed attempt. "Yo' c'n laugh, but it's a'comin'."

"Yeh," Isaac agreed, dreamily, for he wanted it as much as any of them. "It's a'comin'."

They drifted to sleep that night to the sound of the guns at Shiloh.

Queen heard the guns, and shivered in fear. Cap'n Jack heard them, and almost smiled.

"What is it, Gran'pappy?" Queen whispered. He mumbled something she couldn't quite catch, and leaned close to him.

He tried to tell her, but it hurt to talk. He whispered words that he knew she did not hear, but leaned back on his pillow and smiled. For even if she could not hear him, he knew she could hear that other sound, and that was all that mattered, for it was the most glorious sound of all. It was the sound he had waited for all his life.

It was the herald of freedom.

60

Still Cap'n Jack did not die. He seemed to be waiting for something more than the sound of distant gunfire, and clung tenaciously to a tiny thread of life. Whenever Sally went to see him, he asked about Jass, and she began to understand that he could not bear the idea of his young Massa being a prisoner. His mind had regressed to a happily remembered past. Often delirious, he would mutter about the days when Jass was a boy, and Cap'n Jack was closer to him than his own father. Confused and irrational, he could not remember that Easter was dead, and talked of the joyous day when Jass came home from the war to Easter. At other times, Jass became confused in his mind with James when he was young, a golden, brawny, Irish youth, who had engulfed Cap'n Jack in friendship and promised him his freedom one day. Eventually, his memories always turned to Annie, and when they did he became bitter, and fell silent.

Queen spent as much time with him as she could. It was a relief to be with him, to escape from her many and increasing duties, for life was becoming, daily, it seemed, tougher for them, and the news from the war bleaker. Queen had schooled herself to understand that her gran'pappy was dying, and while it distressed her, she was no novice to death now. Besides, too many other new emotions were claiming attention from her heart.

None of them had experience of war, or of this strange new world without Massas. The duties of life, of the house and plantation, fell increasingly upon the women, but it was not a life any of them understood. The white women had been brought up to plenty, and scarcity was an alien burden. The slaves had been used to discipline all their lives, and the present disorder of their existence confused most, frightened some. They had existed without hope for tomorrow for all of their lives, and while there was a hope now, of this intangible freedom, it was as elusive as ever and as close as whispered rumors. It was generally believed that it was only a matter of time, but how much time, how long, O Lord, how long? The Yankees had come, but had not brought freedom with them. The Rebels had retaken Florence, and the Union troops had retreated to the

northern side of the river. The slaves had no understanding of the confusions of war, and lived on rumors
of it, but each rumor was contradicted by its successor,
and so they clung to the old ways and what they
understood their lives to be, but again, without a Massa
and an overseer, the old order was gone, and no one
celebrated its temporary replacement. Some slaves, the
younger men, had been pressed into service by the
Confederacy, not to fight but to dig for the sappers.

Law and order, as such, had almost ceased to exist.
Pillage and robbery were commonplace and rape was
not rare. Bands of men, some in uniform, some not, but
all armed, roamed the countryside, taking what they
could, at will. To protect themselves against lawless-
ness, the entire community at The Forks of Cypress was
united against the world, although that unity was as
temporary as the weather, and would disintegrate at
the first positive sign of what the future might be.

They all held their breaths and went about their
business, waiting for something to happen, even Cap'n
Jack, and when it happened, it was double-edged.

It came to Jass first. Tom Kirkman brought the news to
Sally on a warm October day. Jass's imprisoned regiment had been exchanged with a Northern unit. Jass
was a free man again. Sally whispered a tiny prayer of
thanks for his deliverance, and waited for Tom to tell
her the sweet news of her son's return. It was not to be.
Jass had been promoted to colonel of his regiment, and
was being sent south to Fort Hudson, near Vicksburg,
in Mississippi.

Tom had other news of freedom. Lincoln had
announced his intention to sign a proclamation eman-
cipating the slaves, in all the states, as if the Confederation did not exist.

"He can't do that," Sally said, knowing that Lincoln
could do anything he wanted.

Tom smiled, and agreed with her statement and her

605

thought. If it happened, it seemed likely that those slaves in Southern territories under Union control would be freed. He almost didn't care. He was tired, perpetually tired, and he could not shake off a chill he had caught.

"Here?" Sally wondered, and Tom shrugged. Much of the area around Florence was held by the Federal Army, but battles raged for control of the river, both sides determined to hold what they had, and take what they had not.

"Everywhere," Tom said. "I don't know how he intends to enforce it, but it will bring chaos to us, if it is true." Sally could not imagine how it would directly affect them, as part of the Confederacy, and she put aside concerns for what might happen in the future, and gloried in what had happened now. For Jass was free.

She told Lizzie, who let out a shriek of joy, and went racing to tell the children, but then came running back to find out when Jass was coming home. On being told that he was not, much of her joy deserted her briefly, and she sulked alone in the sitting room. But still it was good news, or better news than they had heard in a very long time, and, calmer now, she found the children, and hugged them to her, as hard as she had hoped to hug her husband.

There was someone else to tell. Sally climbed the stairs slowly and paused to catch her breath on the landing. Then she went up the little attic stairs to Cap'n Jack.

Queen was with him, bathing his chest. The room smelled awful, of waste and illness, and that other rich and heady aroma that Sally knew betokened the presence of death.

Queen covered Cap'n Jack with a blanket when Sally came in.

"He say he dyin'," she blurted, grumpily. "I can't talk him out of it."

"The Massa has been freed," Sally said softly, so that Cap'n Jack would not hear. She saw a light sparkle in Queen's eyes, one she had not seen for months.

Queen stared at Sally, hardly daring to believe that it was true.

"When he coming home?" she asked.

"Not for a little while," Sally told her, guessing that Queen wanted to be somewhere else. To be alone, perhaps.

"I'll stay with him," she said. Queen nodded, trying to contain her joy. She made Cap'n Jack as comfortable as she could as quickly as she could, and then went to the door.

"Thank you, Missy," Queen said. "I got to tell Mammy."

She hurried from the room. Sally smiled. She understood the girl's need to be at her mother's grave, to tell her news she could not hear, and wondered why she felt no need to tell James. Or be with him, beside him, alone in the silent cemetery with the man whom she had loved.

When Queen had gone, Sally settled in the chair beside the bed, and took Cap'n Jack's hand, to let him know that she was there.

He seemed lost to her, in some other world, and for a moment Sally thought he might be gone already, but then he opened his eyes and stared at her.

"I dyin', Missy," he said.

"Now why on earth would you want to do that?" Sally said gently. "When the Massa's coming home."

She knew he understood, because a duller version of the same sparkle that had brightened Queen's eyes glittered into his. His lips moved in what she knew to be a silent prayer.

"Massa Jass free," he said. "Now I can die happy. The good Lord's a'callin' me, Missy."

"I'm sure he would wait a while," Sally said, knowing He would not.

"Massa Jass free," Cap'n Jack said again. "Oh, blessed freedom."

Suddenly, Sally understood what he had been waiting for, why he would not leave, and she wanted to fulfill his dream.

"And you are free," she said.

Cap'n Jack stared at her.

"You've been free for a very long time," she continued. "I have the paper downstairs in the safe. Massa James gave it to me years ago, believing you would ask for it one day."

It wasn't true. James had told her, years ago, of his offer of freedom to Cap'n Jack, and of his subsequent refusal. Furious with his slave, he had burned the paper.

"If he ever wants it, he'll damn well have to ask for it," James had said. But what did it matter now, if he asked or it was given? Sickness, weariness, pain, seemed to vanish from Cap'n Jack's eyes. If I have done nothing else good in my life, Sally thought, I have done this.

"Free." Was it a question or a statement? Sally couldn't tell, and it didn't matter. The lies were nothing. The result was all.

"And soon all the slaves will be free," she said. Perhaps they would, if Lincoln had his way.

Cap'n Jack smiled, then frowned. "Queen?"

"Queen and all the slaves," Sally reassured him. "Very soon."

"Oh, Lordy," Cap'n Jack whispered. He closed his eyes, and squeezed her hand. Then he turned away from her, turned to the wall.

Sally sat holding his hand, and felt his grip slowly loosen until there was nothing of it left.

She looked about the empty room, and tears stung her eyes.

"What on earth am I going to do without him?" she

cried out to no one, and was unable to control her choking voice.

They buried him in the slaves' graveyard, next to Easter. No one cried, because no one had any more tears to shed. The war had left them bereft, not of grief but of the means to express it. They moved through life now in an emotional vacuum, accepting whatever was given them, and little of it was good.

Sally stood next to Queen at the grave and read her favorite passage from the Book of Common Prayer, which spoke of loss in terms of hope.

"We seem to give him back to Thee, O Lord, who gavest him to us. But as Thou didst not lose him in the giving, we shall not lose him by his return."

When the service was done, Queen helped Sally down the hill. They did not speak to each other because they had no need to speak. They simply shielded each other against loss.

Soon after, rumors began to fly among the slaves, and life and vigor returned to them, and the mounting optimism of the slaves was matched by the increasing pessimism of the whites.

And Queen was petrified.

She heard the rumors, but no joy came to her with them. She snapped angrily at those who told her the news, and said it hadn't happened yet, and it didn't affect her. What worried her was that it might. She threw herself into preparations for Christmas with febrile energy, and when the blessed feast came, she tried to make herself indispensable to the family, as if she belonged to them, was part of them. They had no idea of the fear besieging her, and treated her no differently than usual. Or perhaps they did, a little, for her unspoken but incessant demand for proof of their affection, for some recognition of her place with them, wearied them and caused them to snap at her. So Queen's fears magnified. She didn't dare ask Sally if the rumor was true, for fear that it was. She wouldn't ask Lizzie, and, with Cap'n Jack gone, there was only one person she trusted.

She went to Parson Dick's room one night, and tapped on his door. She heard fear in his voice when he asked who it was, and when she told him, there was silence. She went in. Parson Dick was packing, stuffing his clothes into a big old bag made of carpet.

"What you doin'?" she asked.

"Getting out of here," he told her.

She panicked. "But you can't!" she cried. "We belong here."

"I don't 'belong' here, I don't belong to no one," he said. "An' now Abe Lincoln's made that legal."

"We still slaves!" she insisted. "This ain't the North. Abe Lincoln can't do nuttin' down here."

The rumor was that Abraham Lincoln had issued a proclamation freeing all the slaves, in any state, as of the first day of the coming New Year.

"We can get away is what we can do," Parson Dick said. "Over the river, to Union lines."

"They catch you, they bring you back, whip you good!" Queen tried to sound casual, but failed, and Parson Dick laughed at her.

"They ain't going to waste time catching slaves now; there'll be too many on the run!"

He looked at the miserable Queen and felt a sweep of pity for her.

"You come with me and Ruby," he said. "We look after you."

Queen shook her head, defiantly.

"This here is my home," she said. "This here is my family."

"You ain't nothin' to them, 'cept some skivvy slave," he replied. But she did not hear him, or did not want to.

610

"Colonel Jass is my pappy," she said.

Parson Dick understood her fear, and the foolishness of her dream.

"Oh, girl," he said gently. "What you think your pappy's going to do? You think he's going to raise you into the bosom of his family, and say to all the world you is his true-born daughter?"

Queen looked at him uncertainly. That was what she wanted to happen, what she wanted to believe would happen, but faced with the actuality of it, it seemed unreal.

"Slavery's finished, thank the good Lord in heaven," Parson Dick pressed his point. "But it going to bring hard times for the Massas, and they going to stick to each other like glue. They never going to admit that all those mulattos and quadroons and octoroons and Lord knows how many 'roons is begat out of white blood!"

Queen was trembling, and shaking her head. She didn't want to hear any more.

"You stay here, you nothing, you worse than nothing, coz they won't even admit that you exist," he said softly, sadly, accurately predicting her future.

"It ain't true!" she cried. "You don't know! My Pappy loves me!"

Crying, she ran from the room. She stumbled down the back stairs and into the kitchen. She stood in the middle of the room, gasping, panting, not knowing what to do. A ferocious energy invaded her, and she began to clean what was already clean, scrub what was already scrubbed, tidy what was already neat, as if the faultless management of the house proved her indispensability to it.

A few hours later, when everyone was asleep, Parson Dick crept from the house to the stables. He took an old nag, fair wages, he thought, for his years of service, and rode into the night. He met Ruby at a bend in the river near Florence, a spot they had arranged in whispered assignations conveyed by the seed merchant's assistant. They spent the day in the woods, and the following evening they stole an old rowboat they found on the riverbank, and made their way across the river. By morning, they were behind Union lines and threw themselves on the mercy of some soldiers. Although they were treated roughly, as runaways, they were fed, given the use of a tent, and no serious attempt was made to return them to their owners. With the tolling of the church bells on New Year's Day, they were free.

Those same church bells proclaiming the New Year sounded ominous to Sally, tolling for a way of life that was dying. The Emancipation Proclamation had no direct effect on them—they were beyond its jurisdiction—but already it was working indirectly. It hurt her deeply that Parson Dick, most reliable, she had thought, of their slaves, had been the first to take advantage of this new situation, for she had little doubt as to what he had done, and others, she was convinced, would follow. The Union Army, Northern law, was too tantalizingly close to them. Yet she had to do everything in her power to stop them from going, even if that meant the unthinkable. Hands were needed to run the farm, for without the farm the whites could not live, and Sally was aware of the paradox. The white South depended on the enslaved blacks for their very survival. They did not have the means to keep the slaves against their will if they chose to go, and Sally determined that she must make them choose to stay.

Once again, she had them gathered into the clearing, although Isaac was in charge of them now, and she came to them as supplicant, not as mistress. She told no one else of her plan. Lizzie would not understand, Tom would disapprove, and Mrs. Henderson would resist it fiercely. It was possible that if it was generally known, Sally would be accused of treachery to the cause.

"Abe Lincoln has issued an order making all slaves in

612

United States territory free," she began, and stopped again for a moment. It was not easy for her. She heard the muttered prayers of some of the slaves. If the Missy was telling them, then the rumors were true. Free at last, free at last.

"That order does not apply to this plantation, or any in the Confederacy," Sally continued, and heard the sharp intakes of breath, the audible disappointment. "But the army of the United States is only twenty miles away, freedom is only twenty miles away, and I do not have the means to make you stay."

She knew that they didn't understand why she was telling them what they already knew.

"And so you are free," she said. "Free to do what you want, go where you will."

The reaction surprised her, for there was none. She could hear the wind rustling in the leafless branches of the trees, but she could not even hear the slaves breathe. Then she became aware of another sound, close to her. Queen standing two feet behind her, as if to reinforce her own position, was crying.

"There is nowhere you can go, except to the enemy, for in the South, if you go and you are caught, you will be treated as runaways. And if you go to the North, you will be enlisted into the army, to fight against us. Possibly to die."

She was surrounded by bewilderment. Freedom had come, but somehow it seemed empty. Jeremiah spoke for the many.

"What c'n we do, Missy?" he asked Sally.

"You can stay," she said. "I need you to work the land. I cannot pay you anything, but I will share with you what we have. You will eat as we eat, and live as we live. When the war is over and the Massa returns, when the future is clearer, we may make other arrangements. For the moment, all I can offer you is a safe place to be, a roof for your heads, and a bed to sleep in."

She stopped. It was too hard; she couldn't do it. All her formidable resources suddenly deserted her, and she wanted to break down and weep. It had come to this: It was she who had to bring the whole house of cards tumbling down. And it had been so easy. And yet it was too hard. Tears filled her eyes. She could not bear that they might go, she feared too genuinely for their welfare, and her own and her family's, but she could not believe that they might stay.

"What you gwine do if'n we go?" Jeremiah asked her.

"I don't know," Sally told him honestly. "Pray for you. Pray for all of us."

There was silence again, and the sound of shuffling feet. Jeremiah was the spokesman, the leader. It rested on him. The weight of the decision frustrated him. It had all seemed so easy. They would be free and they would go and make new lives for themselves. But they were free, and where could they go? Very few of them actually wanted to go North now. It was alien land to them, enemy country, and filled with war and danger. Most of them had been born and grown up on this plantation; very few of them had any concept of the world beyond it, and those who did, like Jeremiah, had no affection for it. In the short days of his escape, he had never been so hungry in his life. He could go, and make it to Union lines, and even join the army, fight for freedom, but he had freedom, Missy Sally had given it to him, so what was there to fight for? Here was food, here was shelter, here was what he knew. This was his place. It was so easy. Everything else was too hard.

"An' if'n we stay, we free?" he asked, trying to establish his options.

"If you stay, you are free," Sally assured him.

Jeremiah shrugged.

"I reckon I gwine stay, fo' a l'il while, anyways," he told the others. "This here the only home I got."

He walked away, and slowly the others followed. They talked about it later, when Sally was gone, and most of them agreed with Jeremiah. They would stay, for a little while anyway, because they had no other place to go. What astonished them was that they felt no different, now that they were free. It took some little while for them to comprehend the majesty of what they had. And when they did, they had a party.

Sally stood in the clearing, watching the slaves shuffle away. She had won; she had achieved what had to be done; she had ensured, for the moment at least, the survival of her family, in some form or other. Later decisions were for later. If, as the truth of their new situation dawned on them, some few ran away, she would cope with that then. If, by some miracle, the South won the war, which Sally didn't believe was going to happen, the institution of slavery would have to change, and they would face those complications then. If, when Jass came home, he wanted to rescind her order, that was his business and would be coped with then, but he could only do it if there was a Southern victory. All Sally had done, she told herself, was to accept the inevitable. At this moment, the whites needed the nigras to survive, and, at this moment, survival was all she cared about.

She turned to Queen. Drained of all energy, she needed the girl's help to walk back to the big house.

But Queen was not there.

Terrified by the prospects Sally had offered the slaves, for Queen had no doubt she was included, she ran to her mother's grave, and knelt beside it.

"I's free, Mammy, I's free," she whispered.

And wondered why she was so very scared.

61

Tthe war ground on, each day bringing them closer
to a conclusion that even the most sanguine Southerner began to accept as inevitable. They hardly understood why they fought anymore. For every inch of
ground they gained, they seemed to lose two. But not
to fight was unthinkable. A stand had been taken and
must be upheld. They no longer fought to win, they
fought not to lose, but every battle seemed to bring
retreat, or, if it was won, news of another loss
elsewhere.

Jass could justifiably have applied for leave on many
occasions, to go home and spend some days with his
family, but he chose not to. His life had become war,
and unfamiliar country places its battlegrounds.
Edwards Depot and Big Black Bridge. Fort Hudson and
Champion Hills. Vicksburg. They abandoned Mississippi, harried every inch of the way by the avenging
General Grant, and his regiment, or what was left of it,
was sent to Georgia. Every skirmish lost, every yard of
ground surrendered, brought Jass closer to home, until
he thought he must stand and fight alone on the very
steps of The Forks of Cypress. Wounds had hardly
healed before new injuries claimed his attention, but he
was impervious to them now, inured to pain. He was
as indifferent to the recognitions of his valor that were
bestowed upon him; his medals had no more meaning
to him than his scars. Honor was his only armor, and
this he wore with immeasurable pride. He had no fear
of death, for it was a proper alternative to defeat, but it
eluded him and condemned him to face the greater
loss, of country, and of cause.

When they told him that he must lose an arm,

smashed up in a battle for an indefensible mountain pass at Kennesaw, he had only two questions.

"Will I be discharged?" was the first.

The doctor shook his head. "Colonels don't need two arms," he said, preparing for the operation. "But we need every man we can get."

Jass could face the rest of his life without an arm, for the odds were that his life would not be long. He could not live with failure.

"Will it hurt?" he asked, as the doctor picked up a saw.

"Like thunder," the doctor told him, nodding at two orderlies to hold Jass down. "And I have nothing to ease the pain."

Jass nodded and closed his eyes. He felt the firm grip of the orderlies, and then a searing, screaming pain as the doctor began his work.

Florence fell again to the Yankees, and the citizens lived in fear of the destruction that must come. Atlanta was gone, burned, burned to the ground, not one brick of the proud and noble city left. Sweet Atlanta, capital of Southern dreams, gone to ashes. Sherman was marching from there to the sea, his army leaving a swath of desolation and destruction, of barren land, in its wake. Any southern victory, no matter how small, was followed by a Yankee retribution many times greater than the provocation. But Florence was not destroyed. Colonel William Hamilton of the U.S. Army was a gracious soldier, who sought victory, not vengeance. His established his headquarters at the Coffee plantation, and concerned himself for the welfare of his unwilling hosts. He gave orders that the citizens were not to be molested, and came to be known as "the good Yankee" for his charity.

He attended the funeral of Tom Kirkman, who had died, worn out from worry and overwork and loss of faith in the future, and was gracious to Elizabeth, the widow, and to Sally and Lizzie, who no longer cared if solace wore blue or gray. Death was a constant in their lives. Tom, and his son James, killed in battle, and his little granddaughter, Ellen, Sam's child. Every woman in Florence wore black, not just to the funeral, for every woman had reason to, and the most fervent prayer of all of them was that the nightmare end soon.

Yet it was not to be. Already a Confederate force under General Forrest was moving upriver toward the town, which must become a battleground again, and while they longed to be ruled by their own, they wanted the war to be over.

Sally dared to ask Colonel Hamilton when he thought the end would come, and he was kind but not gentle to her.

"When you give in," he smiled. "Or when we conquer you, for that will be the inevitable result of your failure to surrender. Apart from those already under arms, we are amassing an army of half a million men, and you cannot withstand that."

Sally turned away, appalled by the immensity of it, and by the bleakness of their prospects. Hamilton was a reasonable man in victory. She could not imagine every Yankee would be the same.

"The South cannot win, and the North will not lose," he continued. "What should be of greater concern to all of us is what happens afterward."

That, at least, Sally could agree with, and thoughts of a postwar South troubled her mind as they rode home. They would have no slaves, and while she doubted that there would be a mass migration of blacks from South to North, she understood that the relationship between the races would be radically changed. It was already. Perhaps half her freed slaves had stayed; the others had drifted away as opportunity presented itself, or dreaming provoked. Some younger men had enlisted in the Union Army, and two girls had become whores, camp followers of Northern troops. Those that were left at The Forks were different people now, truculent if given orders, lazy if they did not understand why something had to be done. They worked for themselves rather than the general good, as if preparing for the time when they would leave.

As the blacks became more self-reliant, less dependent on their former Massas and Missys, so the whites withdrew into themselves, isolating themselves, and the previous free discourse between the two races was at a minimum. Sally had not been alone in her precipitate action of freeing the slaves, and awful stories reached them of blacks taking vengeance on their erstwhile Massas. Some houses had been burned to the ground before the blacks escaped to the North, and, in one scandalous case, some bucks had whipped their aging Massa. It foreshadowed the chaos that every white believed would accompany black freedom, and even at The Forks the women did not feel safe.

Jeremiah, who, to Sally's surprise, had stayed, was hardly with them anymore, making himself invaluable to the Union troops, shoeing their horses, hammering their iron, and receiving payment for his services. It was only a matter of time before they lost him, Sally was sure.

Queen had stayed. Inevitably, Sally thought, and it was Queen who concerned her now. In the coming postwar society of whites, there would be no room for Queen, who was trying to insinuate herself more and more into the family's embrace. There had been an altercation that morning, when Lizzie had refused to allow Queen to attend Tom's funeral.

"But he family," Queen grumbled.

"Not your family," Lizzie snapped, thinking that was the end of it.

But it was not the end of it. Sally knew there was more to be done. It would be hard and it would be cruel, but it was unavoidable.

Queen herself provided the opportunity. There was no tea or real coffee because of the Northern blockade of Southern ports, but they had developed a curious substitute out of ground-up hickory acorns. Queen brought a cup of the brew to Sally in the sitting room. Lizzie was upstairs, supervising William's schoolwork. Little James and Eleanor were napping.

Sally sipped her drink, and Queen did not leave. She asked a few questions about the funeral, still obviously irked that she had been barred from attending, and then announced her news.

"Jeremiah gone," she said. "Jus' upped an' left. Didn't even say to tell you good-bye."

Sally nodded, for it came as no surprise to her. She also knew that Queen was reminding her of her own loyalty.

"Do we know where he has gone?" she asked Queen.

"Workin' for the Yankee army, I guess," Queen shrugged. "He jus' a no-account nigger."

She went to the door, but Sally spoke before she left the room.

"And where will you go, Queen?" she said.

Queen stopped. Perhaps it was the moment she had been dreading.

"Now you are free, you must think about where you will go, and what you will do," Sally continued.

Queen did not turn to look at her.

"I ain't going nowhere," she muttered. "I stay here and serve you."

The tiny silence that followed was filled with volumes of unspoken emotion. The inevitable confrontation had come, and Queen prayed with all her heart that Sally would give her the answer she longed to hear, and refused to consider that she would not.

620

"We have no place for you here," Sally said softly, and the words formed ice in Queen's heart.

Still Queen did not look at her.

"But this is my home," she whispered.

She should have turned to Sally, for then she would have seen the tiny tears that Sally now brusquely brushed away. There was another silence, while Sally composed herself to the task at hand. It was not easy for her, because she loved Queen. But nothing was easy for her these days, and it had to be done. For both their sakes.

"The world as we know it has gone," Sally said, more calmly than she felt. "And it can only get worse. We cannot feed the family even now, and after the war I don't know what we will do."

Now Queen turned to her, ran to her, knelt at her feet. But it was too late.

"I help you, Missy," she cried. "I cook and clean and garden. I do everything!"

Sally took her sweet face in her hands. Oh, she loved Queen and did not want her to go. But she could not let her stay.

"Child, we love you and have tried to do right by you," she said. "But you are a nigra, and the times will be hard. Your best place will be with your own people."

Queen was shaking her head, fighting Sally's grip, wanting her embrace.

"I ain't a nigra, I's white!" she screamed. "My pappy won't let you turn me away!"

Sally used all her strength to hold the girl's face firm, and looked hard into her eyes. She spoke with absolute resolve.

"You must never think of Colonel Jackson as your pappy," she commanded. "You are a child of the plantation, like thousands upon thousands of others. And that is all."

Queen could not believe the firmness of Sally's voice,

621

or the coldness of her eyes, or the truth of what she was hearing.

"No!" she screamed again. "I'll never leave. You are my people!"

She scrabbled to her feet, and ran to the door.

"You are my family!" she shouted angrily at Sally. She left the room, slamming the door.

Alone, Sally found that her distress was battling a deep and rising anger. They had been so stupid. There should never have been union. After an alliance with the North to drive out the British, the Southern states should have gone their own way, formed their confederacy then, all those years ago, and none of these present disasters would have happened. Some few, romantic, idealistic men had rammed through a pan-American concept with scant regard for the people it might affect the most. Like the Indians, the nigras had never been seriously considered by the founding fathers, in their rush to white independence, the Northerners because they had so few of them, the South because they had no problem. But it was not possible, and never had been, for slave states to imagine they could share government with slave-free states. And like the Indians in the grab for land, who was paying the price of this lack of foresight now but those same nigras that everyone claimed they were fighting to protect? If the South had gone its own way, become its own country eighty years ago, then Queen's predicament would never have arisen. Oh, they had been so happy. Why could not those damn Yankees leave them alone?

Queen had no such thoughts. Filled with an anger far more complex than Sally's, and a hurt and a loneliness far deeper, she ran from the house, without any sense of purpose or direction. She might have run to the graveyard and called her distress to her mammy, but it was not her mammy she needed now, and not self-pity that possessed her, but rather a raging anger at her dispossession. She ran to the deserted weaving house instead, and fell on the bed where she had been conceived, weeping, and called out her love for her pappy.

62

When peace came, in a gentle spring, it was not as a benediction but as an anticlimax, coupled with relief and an absolute sense of desolation. They hardly dared look at the ravaged country, for there was nothing. What had once been another Eden was a wasteland, barren and bankrupt.

The men straggling back from the war had no choice but to see the devastation, and to comprehend its vastness. After the surrender of the South, the soldiers of the Confederate Army laid down their weapons and began their long walk home. Penniless, dispirited, hopeless, they trod through fields that had once been fertile, along roads that had once resounded with bustling business. As they marched, they were joined by a new army, a fulsome, extravagant, free-spending army. An army of Northern opportunists, who saw in the ravaged South a feeding ground of opportunity for fortunes as yet unmade. The generals of this army had noble ambitions for the reconstruction of the South but the foot soldiers wore florid suits, carried carpetbags stuffed with the most precious ammunition, Federal banknotes, and their training manual was a bible of chicanery. Marching with them came other battalions of high-minded missionaries, devoted to the capture of the newly freed black souls, while many of the mortal targets they sought passed them by, walking North to promised riches.

"All them niggers let loose on the world," Henderson

said to a weary companion. The bitterness of the veterans was intense. Everyone, it seemed, had food in their bellies but them. Even the poorest of the carpetbagging businessmen was rich compared to those who had fought for the South. The missionaries came with the blessing of their Northern churches, or their own life savings, and fed any hungry black they saw. But for the whites, for the soldiers, there was nothing but further abasement.

Henderson had walked for days. He had been stationed at Richmond in Virginia since his promotion to sergeant three years ago, and had seen the vagaries of the war from its front lines. His regiment had laid down its arms the day before the general surrender at Appomattox, and after ten days of indecision and enforced idleness, and infinite frustration, bright news had come to them. Lincoln, wretched Lincoln, architect of their destruction, had been killed, shot to death by some righteous, avenging angel. The men of the South had cheered and hollered at the news, and picked fights with their Northern captors. Order had been restored with rifle butts and broken bones, and the following day they had been told to go home, by whatever means they could. Which meant walking. There was not a horse or cart to be had, even for ready money, which was in shorter supply.

Footsore and weary, nursing new blisters and old grievances, Henderson was resting with a hundred other veterans outside a barn. A sympathetic farmer had given the veterans use of his outbuildings, and scores of men were resting there. Blacks, walking North, used the fields opposite as their resting place. No Confederate soldier would have shared his sanctuary with them, even though there was no Confederacy left. And carpetbaggers were practicing their craft. One of them stood under a tree near the returning soldiers, hawking his dollars.

"Any man who wants to sell his land, I'll give him a fair price for it!" he barked at the broken men. "Cash money! Greenbacks! No questions asked."

"I got five fair acres in Georgia," a man responded. Five fair acres was all he had. Confederate troops had not been paid in weeks, or months, and anyway, the Confederate dollar was worthless paper. He sold his five acres for five dollars, which was a fortune to him.

"A man could buy the whole South for a good honest meal," Henderson said to the veterans near him. No one replied, although they all agreed with him. At that moment, they would have sold their souls for a good honest meal.

But not Henderson. All he had to do was get back to The Forks of Cypress, where a comparative treasure awaited him, God willing, tucked away in a little box under some floorboards in his cottage. He had told no one, not even Letitia, of its existence, and while he knew her life had been hard while he was away, he guessed that the Jacksons would have provided basic necessities for her. Besides, a little suffering, a little hunger, a little deprivation, would be good for her. It was nothing compared with what he had been through, and might knock some of the edges off her. So, barring some terrible accident, fire or flood, which were both unlikely, or marauding Yankees, which was possible, he expected to find his store of gold intact when he returned. And he would be, comparatively, rich. Yet all the gold on earth could only partially alleviate his bitterness. Everything that he had striven so hard to achieve was meaningless, for the slaves were ascendant, and the white man trash. Often his thoughts turned to his dead mother, and he could not bear to think that her lifelong struggle for existence had been without sense or meaning, and that her place in the scheme of things had been reduced to less than that of the humblest nigger.

Like the poor black who stood before him now,

begging for food. There were no missionaries nearby, and the black, who had been called Washington by his hopeful mother, had accepted in good faith the promise of Abraham Lincoln. All men, whatever their color, were equal now. On his way to the city that bore his name, whose streets, he was told, were paved with gold, he hadn't eaten for two days, and doubted that the returning soldiers camped in the barn had much to share, but might have something.

"Get away from me, you nigger bastard," Henderson drawled lazily at the man. "Or you'll wish you'd never been born."

Washington bridled inside, but stood his ground. Perhaps this veteran hadn't heard the news.

"Yo' cain't do nuttin' to me," he said. "I's free now."

Henderson stared at him, secure in his recent rank, his expected wealth, and the authority given to the whites, he believed, by God.

"Can't I?" he said, and his tone was the more ominous for its powerful understatement. "Listen to me, boy, and you listen good. You get your ass out of here, get to your Yankee friends as fast as you know how."

The other white soldiers said nothing, but their hearts were with him, Henderson knew. All they needed was a leader. All they needed was someone to voice what they all felt.

"We might have lost the war," Henderson continued, seizing the moment. "But we're men, and we can still fight, and we will. You ever get in my way, you or any of your jungle kin, and we will come to you in the dead of night, with flames of retribution, and roast you so good, hell will seem like a better idea."

He had not prepared the words—they came to him from some deep, dark place in his soul—but as he said them he saw what he described, and it made him feel better. It also made his companions feel better. Listlessness about their condition gave way to unspoken hostility, directed generally to all niggers, and, at this moment, to just one, whose name was Washington.

"I warn you, boy, it's acoming," Henderson said.

No one doubted him, certainly not Washington, who was scared by what had been said, and by the palpable atmosphere of violence the words had evoked.

"Yes, suh, Massa," Washington said, already moving away. "I sorry, Massa."

Henderson watched the retreat of Washington with a small sense of triumph. It had been so easy. It would be as easy, in the future.

He turned to his enraptured audience of disadvantaged whites, and felt the heady taste of power.

"Giving 'em freedom, giving 'em the vote, it don't make a lick of difference," he said. "They're still niggers."

Some men nodded, and a couple moved closer to him, younger men, who longed for action, and for whom the defeat had been especially bitter, as if reassured by his easy, commanding presence. They talked into the night, of the future, of the protection of their families, and of the sweet smell of burning nigger flesh.

Henderson slept well that night, for the first time in weeks. He hadn't felt so good since he heard of Lincoln's assassination, which he saw as divine and proper retribution. The future was looking good after all. The war was not over; it would simply be conducted differently now, covertly, by small groups of like-minded, true Southern men. And women, for he had no doubt that Letitia would share his purpose, and even less doubt that Letitia would be alone.

"Let the niggers have their day," he said to his newfound friends before he bunked down. "A long, dark night is coming."

63

Queen had solved the problem of leaving The Forks of Cypress by the simple expedient of not going. Sally had not put a time on her departure; she had simply indicated that Queen should go at some time after the war, but when the war ended, the Massa would come home, and everything would be all right again. The Massa wouldn't make her leave; her pappy wouldn't make her go. So she stayed, and did all that she had promised she would. She cooked and cleaned and scrubbed and gardened, and tended to the household as if they were her own dear family, which, in her mind, they were.

She could not run the fields—that was beyond her—for as the Southern defeat became more and more obvious, more and more slaves decided to take their chances on another life, and left The Forks in search of a new bright day. Gradually, the mansion fell into disrepair, and the land became useless, the fields untended, the cotton unplanted, the fences unfixed. By the time the war ended, only old Isaac and young Davy were left to struggle against Nature's reclamation of its own, and even they had their hopes set on somewhere else. There was so much to do, they chose to do none of it, and spent their days whittling and dreaming.

"What we gonna do, then?" Davy asked Isaac, as he did every day. "Go, I guess," Isaac replied, as he did every day.

Davy nodded. He wanted to go; he wanted some adventure, some high life, some fun. He thought Isaac would go too, and didn't want to leave without him, but their choices of destination were so many they could never make a decision, and they had a residual loyalty to this place. Or to Missy Sally, who was kind to them, which amounted to the same thing.

"Ev'ry nigger goin' North," Davy said, hoping they could decide on a direction, if not a haven. Really, he wanted to go somewhere else. "Be full up with black folk soon."

Isaac looked at the empty, wasting fields. "We could stay," he said. "We ain't got nowhere else."

But Davy was young, and, like a bird who has no alternative but to fly from the nest, whatever the danger of falling, he wanted to stretch his newly freed wings.

"No, man!" he cried. "I wants me some freedom!" He knew Isaac wanted it too, just to try the taste of it. After all, if they didn't like it, they could always come back. "Hear tell y'c'n have a high ol' time in N'Orleens."

He had heard wonderful stories, of music and dancing and beautiful women who were only too ready to cosset an energetic young man, and Davy had energy to spare, when there was something he wanted to do.

Isaac didn't seem all that keen on New Orleans, and they lapsed into silence, Davy contemplating unfulfilled lust, and Isaac wondering why he felt no real urge to go anywhere.

Queen banged her way out of the kitchen door, in a grumpy mood. She was always grumpy these days. She saw Isaac and Davy sitting whittling by the well, and wanted to bang their lazy heads together.

"Cut me some firewood, Davy," she yelled. She came to the well with her bucket, and stood waiting for Isaac to draw water. Isaac clambered to his feet, but Davy still wasn't too sure of this freedom thing, and wondered how far it could be pushed.

"Don't feel like it, Missy Queen," he drawled, sticking a straw in his mouth and lazing back on the grass. "I's free now."

Queen could, when she wanted to, turn it on. "Well, you better start feelin' like it, and get yo' free nigger ass choppin' wood, or you don't get fed!" she exploded.

Davy, who had taken orders all his life, and knew nothing else, looked uncertainly at Isaac, who chuckled.

"Ain't no one else gwine feed yo'," he told the reluctant boy. "An' yo' cain't cook."

That surely was the truth and persuaded Davy to action, although he still thought that freedom meant more than it seemed to. But it was not sensible to argue with Queen, who was in charge of the kitchen, in charge of everything, and had a very short temper. He got to his feet and wandered off to the woodpile.

"I's a-choppin', Missy Queen," he assured her reluctantly. "I's a-choppin'."

Queen sniffed, and waited for Isaac to fill her bucket. She didn't speak to him, because he was only an ol' nigger, and she was family.

"Pretty day," Isaac said, to break the silence.

"An' you better get fixin' the plow, or you don't get fed either," Queen snapped, and toted her bucket of water back to the house.

Isaac watched her go. There was no point in fixing the plow, because even if the fields were tilled, there was no seed to plant, and he was bored with taking orders from that grumpy half-caste girl. Davy was right, they should go. Even if they ended up living on the land, like a few other ex-slaves from the Forks, camped in the forest only a few miles from their former home, they would be their own men, in charge of their own existence. While they stayed, though, it was better to keep out of Queen's sight. He wandered off to the barn as if to repair the plow, but once inside he settled on some straw and took a little nap. It was a warm day.

In the kitchen, Queen banged a pot on the stove and filled it with well water, to boil. The weight of the bucket had strained her arms, and she was tired, always tired.

"Workin' my po' fingers to the bone, for folks as

don't appreciate it," she told the empty room. Or God, to Whom she voiced her many grievances these days.

She slumped in a chair at the table while she waited for the water to boil. If only the Massa would come home, he would appreciate how very hard she worked, he would be kind to her, and make her feel as if she mattered. Miss Sally and Miss Lizzie couldn't manage without her, but they never said thank you or please, never spoke to her, pretended she wasn't there, that she didn't even exist. She did everything for them, and for the children when they were here—cleaned their clothes, cooked their food, emptied their bedpans—and they accepted it all, as if it happened by magic. She couldn't go on, she was exhausted, she hadn't even had time to visit her mother's grave in weeks, there was so much else to do. But she had to go on, somehow; it could only be a few more days, at the very most, and then he would be home again.

Ol' Massa Henderson had come home last week; he'd been in fine spirits even though he'd walked a thousand miles, cheery and jolly, although not to Queen, and had whisked his wife away for a holiday in Charleston, to see her family. He seemed to have money, she didn't know how—perhaps soldiers were paid a lot. He talked of buying a general store, of setting up in business for himself. If soldiers were well paid, the Massa would have money when he came home, and that would be such a relief; she wouldn't have to scrimp and save every penny that Miss Sally gave her, and wonder how on earth she could feed the family that night. But Massa Henderson had no word of Jass, nor had Miss Sally heard anything from him.

She knew he'd lost an arm. A letter had come last year, and Miss Sally couldn't read well anymore. She'd left the letter lying on her table and when Queen came in to clean the room had wondered aloud, of no one, what news it might bring. So Queen had read the letter, and Jass said he couldn't imagine why the good Lord had given him two arms because he was doing just fine with one. Miss Sally had cried, but still wouldn't admit that Queen was there. It was as if she were listening to a ghost, someone who had been there once, and wasn't anymore.

Queen had cried that night, and hoped that losing the arm hadn't hurt too much, and tried to imagine what he looked like. It didn't make any difference, he was her pappy, and she'd look after him and take care of him, nurse his body if he needed it and his soul if he would let her. One of the dogs had lost a leg once, caught in a trap, and rather than put him down, old Solomon had nursed the animal back to health, and kept him as his own. The dog managed fine with only three legs, and was a sweet, dear thing. Queen's heart had gone out to him, and she had always tried to save a few tidbits from the table for him. It wouldn't worry her that her pappy's body was incomplete. It would make him need her more.

The water boiled, and she made the fake coffee, reminding herself that she had to roast and grind some more acorns, poured two cups of the drink, put them on a tray, and left the kitchen. Deliberately, she went the long way to the sitting room, through the hall, because she was taking stock of what had to be done before the Massa came home. Paper was peeling from the walls. The drapes needed to be washed. She couldn't possibly do it all.

Sally and Lizzie were in the sitting room, enjoying the spring day. It was a mercy that warm weather had come because they couldn't spare wood for a fire. Lizzie was doing tapestry work, to make some cushions. Sally, her eyes failing, was struggling to sew a patch on young James's pants. William and Eleanor lived in Florence these days, with their aunt Elizabeth. It made it easier for them to go to school, for the road was too dangerous to travel every day. They couldn't afford a tutor these days, and anyway there were none to be had. They could hardly afford the school fees. Now James had also gone to stay with Elizabeth, to be with his brother and sister, and to prepare for school. Life on the deserted plantation was no place for a growing boy.

Jass must come home soon, Sally thought. They couldn't manage much longer. She had avoided digging up the small store of gold that Jass had buried at the beginning of the war, until there was no possible alternative. It had lasted surprisingly well because she doled it out as scrupulously as any miser, but it had gone six months ago, and then she had dug up the box in the cellar, and slowly but surely that nest egg was diminishing, and she was nervous of exhausting it. She thought of selling a few acres of land, but the price was rock bottom, thousands upon thousands of acres of prime Southern farming land were on the market, and there were very few buyers. Besides, it was not her land to sell. It belonged to Jass. She couldn't understand why they had not heard from him. The wretched Henderson had made it back, all the way from Virginia, and Jass had been stationed in nearby Georgia when she last heard from him. But for several weeks there had been nothing, not a letter, not a message, not a word. They weren't even sure he was still alive, but no death notice had been delivered, and they could only assume that he was. If only he would come home. If nothing else, he would solve the problem of Queen.

Since the time that she had first raised the subject, Sally had never again suggested that Queen leave; she thought the point had been well made. Nor did she want her to go until the war was over and they could start putting their lives back in order. Until Jass came home, they could not manage without Queen, but when he came home they would not need her. Oh, perhaps for a little while, until they found someone else, or until one of the slaves came back. Sally, like many others, believed it was only a matter of time before several of the ex-slaves realized that life in a known environment was infinitely preferable to life in an alien and cruel world. She seldom went into town anymore—the road was too dangerous—but they had visitors from time to time, and already she had heard the horror stories of the way blacks were behaving in this new South, and even worse stories of how some of them were being treated. Looking for a scapegoat for their defeat, many of the returning veterans were venting their fury on blacks, in dead of night, and all the efforts of the policing Federal forces could not control them. And many of the blacks were vilely abusing their newfound status, treating any white with disdain or impudence, reveling in an orgy of excessive behavior and frequently abusing their former Massas and Missys, while the bodies of those last slain in war were not yet cold in the ground. It was inevitable, Sally thought. Like children in a candy store, they were starting to indulge what could be formidable and dangerous power. She feared for their potential and worried for their safety, and it didn't matter that many of the stories she heard were untrue or greatly exaggerated; she had no yardstick to judge the reality of the situation. Jass would know, Jass would explain everything to her, Jass would—

Yet we must not expect too much of him, she told herself. He will be as lost as we are. But he is a man, and he will know how to cope. If only he would come home.

For Lizzie, especially, the lack of him was unbearable, and yet it had to be borne. She had survived the war with as much grace as she could muster, which wasn't a lot, but now the war was over, and she longed for him. She was not foolish enough to imagine that he would make everything all right again—Hercules could hardly have improved their condition—but his place

634

was with them, to be responsible for the welfare of his family again. He'd played at soldier long enough.

During the last few months of the war, her emotions had taken a helter-skelter ride of despair at their state, fear of the lawless gangs freely roaming the country-side, joy at the small Southern victories, and bitter acceptance of their defeat. She had been in Florence on the day that news of Lincoln's assassination reached them, taking young James to Elizabeth, and like many in the town, she had cheered heartily at the news. Then the occupying Federal troops had swept among them, brutal and ruthless, announcing that the least demonstration of joy would result in the offender's home being burned, and any rejoicing by the townspeople would bring about the destruction of the town. This had forcibly brought home to Lizzie the power that the Federals now enjoyed, and the new constraints that governed their lives. She lived in fear, not only of the outlaws but of the law itself. She simply didn't know how to behave in this strange world of Northern, military rule, and so she kept her mouth shut and her tail between her legs, and prayed for Jass's return.

Above everything else, and what was most astonishing to her, was how very much she missed him. The death of Easter had taken a great burden from her concept of their marriage. She doubted he would ever take another paramour, for Easter had been a special case, and now there were no slaves for him to choose from, or to go to for a single night. So he was hers at last, in a way he had never been before. She found that she wanted him, she wanted to feel the weight of him beside her in her bed at night, and because she no longer had a rival to whom she was being constantly compared, she wanted to explore the physical side of her marriage with a greater enthusiasm than she had ever known. She lived in expectation of the smell of him, the touch of him, the feel of him, and she wanted to give him another baby, no matter how much it hurt, to prove how very much she loved him. If only he would come home.

Then the brat came into the room, and reminded her of so many things she would rather forget. She was the past, and soon she would be gone, like all the other slaves. Good riddance, thought Lizzie, who missed the service that the slaves provided, but was determined to show the world that she could manage without them. And, like Sally and so many others, she firmly believed that many of the ex-slaves would come running home soon enough, when they discovered what they had lost in return for this wretched freedom. When they did, they'd have to beg for a job as far as Lizzie was concerned. Like the brat, whom she simply ignored.

Queen put down the coffee, and stood waiting, not for thanks, for she knew Gabriel's trumpet would come sooner, but for instruction. Her eyes scanned the room, checking on necessary repairs while she waited. But Sally and Lizzie had forgotten their cues, and Queen had to prompt them.

"Wonder what they want for dinner," she said to the fireplace.

Sally, who hadn't realized the purpose of Queen's attention, responded immediately, but not to Queen.

"I wonder what we should have for dinner tonight," she said to Lizzie.

Lizzie shrugged. Who knew what was in the pantry? She never went there, because she didn't want to have to speak to the brat. Or even see her.

"Oh, fried chicken," she dreamed. "I'd love some fried chicken; we haven't had it in so long. With potatoes, and a rich, creamy gravy—"

"She go out and catch me a chicken, I'll fry it," Queen snorted to a portrait on the wall.

"Be realistic, Lizzie," Sally said at the same time.

There was a tiny silence, while they waited for another prompt. Queen left them in suspense for a moment.

"I s'ppose I could make a vegetable stew," she said to the drapes.

Lizzie sighed. "I suppose we'll just have to make do with vegetable stew again," she said. "Again!"

Queen ignored the barb. They had only vegetables, and should be grateful for that. Occasionally, William or Isaac shot a rabbit, but even they were in short supply. There were too many hunters.

"We must count our blessings," Sally said. "I'm sure it will be delicious."

It was done, the charade had been played out one more time, and Queen humphed and left the room. The contrast of Queen's physical presence with the pretense that she was not there had unsettled Lizzie. She put down her tapestry and looked about her at the shabby room that once had been so grand. If only Jass would come. He would solve all their problems. They would have some kind of income again, for Jass would find a way. And he would get rid of Queen. There was no place for her; she could no longer pretend to have a special bond of attachment to the family. She was a nigra, and nigras, who had some value before the war, were less than nothing now. With Queen gone, with all the slaves gone, they would have to start afresh. They would hire new staff, as and when they could afford it, and life would never be the same as it was before, but it would be something, and they would be happy.

She walked to the window and stared out, hoping to see him walking up the drive.

"If only he would come home," she said softly.

Queen scraped and cut the vegetables, and put them in a pot of water to simmer. She'd already cleaned the bedrooms, made the beds, and changed the sheets. Tomorrow she would start on the weekly laundry, and then, if it was a good drying day, she'd scrub the hall floor. There wasn't much more she could do today, but there would be light for at least another hour, so she went outside to hoe the weeds in the little vegetable garden that she tended, but she was sick of working.

She threw aside her hoe and walked to the slave graveyard to see her mammy instead. Weeds covered the grave and she bent to the task of clearing them, but she felt a little sick. Her time of the month was coming, and she prayed it would not be bad, as it sometimes was, because she had too much to do. Tiredness flooded through her, and she lay on the ground beside the grave to rest. Not to sleep—she had no time for that—but just to rest for a little while. She saw a line of ants crawling through the weeds, going to or from their nest, and dreaded to think that perhaps they burrowed into the ground and crawled over her dead mammy, and that made her sad because she knew her mammy wasn't there anymore, but gone, gone, food for worms. Tears trickled from her eyes, as much for herself and her present desperate loneliness, as for sweet Easter.

She had no one to talk to except Isaac and Davy, and they as field hands avoided her, a house nigger. Even William and Eleanor, when they were here, hardly acknowledged her, taught by their mammy and their gran'ma. She had no one to share her troubles with, no one to ease her burden, no one to laugh with and play with, or even to sit with in companionable silence, knowing that they cared about her. All she had was people to shout at, who pretended that they never heard her.

It would be different when her pappy came home. Please, Mammy, make him come home.

"If we goin', reckon we should go," Davy said.

"Reckon we should," Isaac agreed.

Davy was surprised. They'd talked about it so much, and Davy guessed the truth of Isaac's reluctance to leave. He was waiting till the Massa came home, to see if it was all right to go, to get his permission to leave. Old folk were like that; they clung to the old ways.

"Massa ain't never comin'," Isaac said. He wasn't so old, younger than the Massa, but it confirmed Davy's guess. "Reckon he's dead."

They sat in the clearing of the old empty slave quarters. It was a starry, cloudless night, and they'd built a little fire to keep the mosquitoes away. They'd eaten their portions of Queen's vegetable stew, saved some for breakfast, and they made the decision that they would leave the next day. They didn't have any money, but they'd manage somehow. Davy had heard a story that anyone who was prepared to work in or near the cesspits was well paid, and he was ready to do that. Not for long, of course, just till they had enough cash to get them to New Orleans. Or somewhere. Or anywhere.

They sat in pleasant silence, each dreaming his separate dream and their bold new future. After an hour or so, Isaac spoke.

"Best git to bed," he said. "Best be up early, if we gwine go."

"Yeh," Davy nodded in agreement. After another long silence, they went to their separate beds, but Davy couldn't get to sleep for hours. They were going. At last, they were going. At last, he was going to be truly free.

Isaac woke him at dawn. They packed their few belongings and ate the vegetable stew left over from the previous night. It was a lovely morning, fragments of a gentle mist hovering in the air. Isaac looked around at the slave quarters, where he had lived all his life, and which he was not anxious to leave.

"Gwine miss this ol' place," he said.

Davy nodded, hoping he had not changed his mind.

"Gwine say good-bye to the ol' folk," Isaac said, and walked away, in the direction of the slave graveyard.

Queen was also awake early, and had put the old sheets in a big tub, to soak. She gathered three eggs from the few laying hens, enough for Miss Lizzie and Miss Sally if she scrambled them and made a lot of toast. She put hickory acorns in the oven to roast, prepared the breakfast, and served it in the dining room. No one spoke to her. She went outside, scrubbed the sheets, rinsed them, and hung them out to dry, then put the other clothes in to soak. She went back into the big house, got her dustpan and brush, and went upstairs to clean the rooms and make the beds.

So it was that she saw him first. Straightening the drapes, she glanced out of the window, and saw a tiny figure at the distant gateway. She knew it was him before she could see who it was.

Her heart fluttered, and tears spurted to her eyes. He had come home.

She went downstairs and into the sitting room. Miss Lizzie was working at her tapestry, and Miss Sally was trying to read a newspaper, a small magnifying glass to her eye.

"He's comin'," she said quietly. "The Massa's comin'."

For a moment it was as if she had not spoken, or they had not heard her. But they could not ignore her now. Sally put down the paper and turned to stare at Queen.

Lizzie let out a little scream of joy. She threw down her needlework, and ran from the room. Sally pulled herself to her feet, using her cane as help, and followed more slowly.

Lizzie ran onto the veranda, and looked to the drive. She could see him walking up the hill to the house, and she wanted to fly into his arms and hold him to her and never let him go. But something in his manner stopped her. He looked downcast and proud and lost and found, and the empty sleeve hanging at his right side made her heart catch in her mouth. And then she saw those nigras going to talk to him, she never could remember their names.

She could not, must not, go to him, not now. She could almost sense the defeat in him, and the need for things to be as they were, although they never could be. She composed herself, and straightened her hair and her dress, and waited for him as she would have waited for the returning hero.

Davy had begun to think that they would never leave the graveyard. Isaac had spent forever saying good-bye to all his dead relatives, and Davy thought he had seen tears in the man's eyes. He sat under a tree, to wait until Isaac had finished whatever conversations he was having with these folk who couldn't hear, and, because he was tired, he drifted into a light sleep. The next thing he knew, Isaac was prodding him with his foot.

"Time to go," Isaac said, and Davy let out a whoop of joy. They walked down the hill, past the white cemetery, and toward the mansion.

"Ain't gwine say g'bye to 'em?" Davy had asked, worried that ol' Missy Sally would change Isaac's mind.

"Nope," said Isaac. "But I's leavin' by the front gate." They skirted the bottom of the hill on which the big house stood, and made for the drive, and saw the Massa coming home. Davy cursed his luck. Now they would never leave. Not surprisingly, Isaac walked straight to the Massa.

"Welcome home, Massa," he said. "We's glad you's come back safe."

"Isaac," Jass said warmly, and smiled. He looked at the younger man, but could not remember his name.

"Davy," Davy said. No one ever remembered his name.

"I'm surprised you're still here," Jass said. They were free and he doubted they had been paid. Or perhaps Sally had managed the money better than he had thought.

"Mat'a fac', Massa, we was jus' leavin'," Davy said, to forestall Isaac. Jass stared sadly at the empty cotton fields, and nodded his head.

Isaac felt the need to explain. "Thing is, young Davy

ain't ever been off the plantation. Wants to see the world."

Jass nodded again, but did not look at them. "Well, good luck," he said, as if he understood. "If you change your minds, I guess I'll need a couple of hands here." He smiled again, ruefully. "I don't expect I'd be able to pay very much. But something."

"Thank you, Massa," Isaac said. They stood in silence for a moment, not knowing how to end it, not knowing how to say good-bye.

Jass nodded, and moved on toward the house.

"Good luck to you, Massa," Isaac called after him. Jass did not look back, and Davy could hardly believe his good fortune.

"It true!" he cried softly. "We's free! Massa didn't even try an' stop us!"

"Hush yo mouth," Isaac snapped. He never took his eyes off Jass, but watched the sad, lonely man walk on up to the big house. It was a hard homecoming for him, Isaac thought.

Sally was standing beside Lizzie on the veranda, and Queen was a little distance away, mindful of her dubious place. Like Lizzie, Sally wanted to run to him and take him in her arms, and hold him and love him and soothe the hurt from him but, like Lizzie, some evident pain in his manner stopped her. The empty sleeve at his side caused her mother's soul to cry, but she would not allow the tears to flow.

Jass stopped, a little way from the house. He looked at the women, and tried to smile, but could not find sufficient joy in him even to do that. He could have been back days ago, two weeks ago, but he could not come home to nothing, with nothing. Jass took a resonating pride in his war record, in his achievements as a soldier; he had fought hard and well, but the surrender proved that he had not fought hard enough, and now he had to face the consequences of his failure. He had seen the devastation in Georgia, caused by Sherman's army on its march to the sea, and although he knew that his property would not be so desolate, he knew it would be bad enough. Any soldier who had fought for the Confederate cause knew that of his home. They talked about it among themselves, each sharing the other's gloom. Unless they had gold hidden away somewhere, they had nothing, except land. Jass was rich in that, but the land was worth nothing, like his Confederate bonds and his Confederate dollars and his Confederate bank account, and so he was poor, dirt poor, war poor, Confederate poor, like a thousand and a thousand and a thousand others.

He had tried to come back with something, but no one had anything to give. On his long walk home he had visited every friend, every acquaintance, calling in all his favors, in the hope of some scrap of promise for the future, but promises were all he had, and distant ones. Of immediate help, cash help, practical help, he had nothing. He had stopped in Florence the previous night, with Elizabeth, and comforted her for the death of Tom, and loved his children, and heard of the sorry state of affairs at The Forks of Cypress. This morning he had walked from Florence to the plantation, and saw that everything he had heard, everything he had guessed, everything he had feared, was true.

He stared at his mother, and at the empty, silent, bankrupt fields. Everything he had inherited, everything that had been in his governance, everything that his father had charged him to protect, was reduced to nothing.

It broke his heart.

"Mother," he said. "I'm so sorry. I am so very sorry."

Sally knew that it had to be said, knew that he had to say it, but she was never prouder of him than at that moment. Her son was brave. He had fought and fought well, and would, she knew, have given his life for them. But her son was more than brave. Her son was honest.

She moved to him slowly, love for him and pride in him battling in her heart for dominance. The evidence of his bravery, that awful empty sleeve, caused in her emotions she had not felt since he was born, and was whole and complete and healthy, and she loved him for it. Now he was not whole, he was not complete, but he was alive, and she loved him all the more.

"Oh, Jass, my darling son," she said, like a secret between them. "It's wonderful to see you."

She took her wounded child into her arms, and held him as a mother should, to keep him safe from life's storms. He clove to her. The very smell of her that had so sealed itself in his memory on the day he had gone away to war broke open all the other memories of his love for her, and swept aside the bitter remembrances of war, if only for this moment. He did not weep, because he was home, and safe, and there was no need to cry.

Lizzie, aware of some powerful, visceral emotion between them that she was not privy to, moved forward slowly, and now Jass saw her, his wife and love, and he included her in his embrace with his mother. They stood together, the three of them, and spoke not a word, and moved not at all, until each was sure, in their heart, that he would never go away again.

Then Lizzie laughed through her tears.

"Oh, come inside," she said. "You need looking after." He moved with them to the veranda, to the house, to the open door.

He did not even see Queen, standing on the veranda, waiting so patiently for a word, a look, something, anything, that might acknowledge her existence. But there was nothing. Jass, still locked in Lizzie and Sally's loving embrace, moved past her into the house.

As if she wasn't there.

*

644

It was a shattering moment for Queen. She stood stock-still, waiting for him to come back and include her in his embrace, but knew he would not. She did not exist to him. She wasn't there. She was nothing, worse than nothing.

She bit her lip, hard, determined not to cry, but not knowing how to avoid it. She felt the salt taste of blood, her blood in her mouth, and knew she was trembling. She had to get away, and moved from the veranda, across the lawn, somewhere, anywhere; she had no direction or purpose, she only had to get away.

She stopped at the edge of the lawn, and looked down at the drive. Isaac was moving slowly to the gate, trying to keep pace with the whooping Davy.

Davy, looking back at Isaac, saw Queen alone on the little hill, and called out to her.

"Come along with us, Miss Queen," he yelled, wanting to gather the world into his joy. Isaac looked back and saw her, and seemed to understand.

"Ain't nuttin' for yo' here," he cried.

She should, she knew, go with them, because Isaac was right, there was nothing for her here, not even a father's love. She wanted to call out to them to wait for her, to run down to them, careless of clothes or baggage, to be with people who might have liked her, or at least admitted she existed, off together to a bold bright somewhere.

But she could not. This was her place. These people, even if they did not acknowledge it, were her family. The Massa was her pappy, and she would make him love her. She convinced herself, in that moment, that they needed her at least as much as she needed them. She tried to smile, but could not. She gave a little wave to Isaac and Davy, and Davy called something that she couldn't hear, but that might have been good-bye, then danced away. Isaac, after another glance at Queen, followed him more slowly.

Queen watched them until they were gone from the

645

gate and gone from her life, taking her last opportunity of freedom with them. She turned back and looked at the house. Through the open window she could see Jass, the Massa, her pappy, the returning hero, sitting with his family. His white family.

Well, he would be hungry soon, after his long walk, so she had better go to the kitchen and make him something to eat.

She walked away, to the back of the house.

64

Jass spoke to Queen later, in the kitchen when she was cooking. She'd killed a broody hen to make a little celebration dinner for his return, and occupied herself with jointing the bird while he talked, so that he might understand her determination to go on as before, that she expected no special treatment from him, which, of course, she did. He was kind to her and clearly relieved by her domesticity, and her apparent refusal to ask for more than he could give.

Queen had hardly occupied his mind for the last several months, for her place within the structure of his household was special only to her. When he thought of his family, it was of Lizzie and his children by her, of his mother, and then, by extension and lessening concern, of Elizabeth Kirkman and her family, and on through the great network of his white relations. He was fond of Queen, fonder of her than of any other of his former slaves, for she was Easter's child, and a living fragment of the memory of his love. That she was also his own child was a lesser issue, and one of lessening importance to him. Although the war had been over only for a few weeks, his discussions with his friends and associates had concentrated all his attention on the survival of his immediate and legal family in the postwar years.

As foreseen by Sally some time earlier, and Parson Dick before that, white Southern society was already closing in on itself, as protection against the new occupying armies of the North, military or civilian, and that other army of countless numbers of freed slaves, who represented a considerable threat to life as it had been and the life that any of them saw as a viable future. Queen was part of the past. In that past she had a clearly defined role, a child of the plantation, her place understood by the entire society. In this new world, these children were dangerous, less so in the case of girls, but profoundly so in the case of boys, who, if they were given legal standing, might expect some portion of their true parent's estate. Thus the fragile white Southern inheritance might be diluted to a point when those of Negro blood had dominance over great estates. Since this was unthinkable, these children, boys and girls, had to be excluded. This exclusion did not prohibit gentle treatment of them, or even affection for them, but the gentler the treatment and the larger the affection, the more claim they might have to recognition. Intuitively, every Southerner understood this, and each was going to considerable and sometimes brutal lengths to achieve a dispossession of those who had once been admitted, if not nurtured.

Jass had talked with Sally, and she had told him of Queen's resistance to the idea that she should leave. In this, Jass sided with Queen. She was of his blood, however perversely, and he could not bear to make her an outcast. So he came to her, and treated her as a valuable member of his staff. He thanked her for her hard work, and told her of his gratitude.

"'Tain't nuttin'," Queen shrugged.

"Yes, it is," Jass said. "I don't think my family could have managed without you."

He deliberately said "my family," instead of "our family," as part of the process of exclusion. Queen guessed this, but chose to ignore it as a slip of the tongue.

"It's my job, Massa," Queen shrugged.

He smiled. "You don't have to call me 'Massa' now," he said.

But what else could she call him?

"And there's something else," he continued. "I can't afford to pay you very much. Something, but not much. But then when things pick up—"

Queen was shocked. She was being relegated to a staff position. If he paid her, he could dismiss her whenever he chose. That he could have chosen not to pay her, but to send her on her way, did not occur to her.

"I don't want your money," she muttered.

Jass smiled again. "I have to pay you something," he said. "Slavery's illegal now."

He left the room. He had hardly asked after her welfare, had not discussed his own. He had taken on a cook-housekeeper at miserable wages, and had, neatly and effectively, boxed her into a hole from which it would be difficult for her to escape. Queen slumped on a chair at the table, and hid her head in her hands.

"Slavery's illegal, but family ain't," she whispered to God. "And I's family."

And God was kind to her, just for a moment, and sent a tiny ray of hope into her heart. At least he hadn't dismissed her. At least he hadn't told her she must leave, as Miss Sally had. He was letting her stay, and by doing so, he had left open the door of her confining box. Times were difficult for him, but when they got better he would see the error of his ways, and elevate her, if only a little, from her lowly station. In the meantime, she would put on a cheerful face, and make him realize what she meant to him.

648

She smelled something burning. The potatoes had boiled dry. She jumped up, snatched the pan from the stove, venting her frustration in energy.

Her hopes never came true. Slowly, very slowly, inch by inch, day by day, the circumstances of the family improved, although they never regained anything of their former fortune. Jass sold some small parcels of land, and put other acreage out for rent. Encouraged by friends, he allowed them to put his name foward as a candidate for the state legislature, and was elected senator. His reimbursement was not large, and he was required to spend a great deal of time in Montgomery, but at least he had an income, which was more than many of his friends had, and a job that gave him the opportunity to be of some value to his constituency. He brought the children back from Florence, believing that they belonged at The Forks, at their home, no matter how difficult their daily travel to school might be. It was as well that he did so, for Elizabeth, his half sister, died soon afterward. She had never ceased mourning for Tom, and preferred to be with him in some kind of peace, no matter how ethereal, rather than face the difficulties of the world in which they now lived.

Sally wept for her daughter's death, for she would miss her, but she was no stranger to death; indeed she almost seemed to welcome the concept of it for herself. She spent days poring over the obituaries as published in the skimpy daily newspaper, and attended whatever funerals she could. With the small improvement in her diet, her eyesight seemed to get better, or perhaps it was because the war was over, and Jass was home, and, with the end of slavery, a great burden of responsibility had been taken from her. Almost for the first time in her life, Sally had time for herself.

*

649

Lizzie positively flowered. Since there was no longer any point in trying to be a Southern belle, and she was getting a little old for it, she no longer tried. There were few opportunities for glittering social occasions, as in the old days, for no one could afford them and had little to celebrate other than sheer survival. She channeled her formidable energy into the management of her house and the care of family. And her love for Jass. Or her gratitude to him. He had come home when so many had not, and Lizzie could not bear the idea of life as a widow. Although efficient and capable in her own right, she was a woman who believed she needed a husband to enable her to function at her best. Jass was surprised by the change in her, especially when he took her to bed and she welcomed him into her, and gave every indication that the experience, far from being unpleasant to her, as latterly, gave her pleasure. If Jass had been a suspicious man, he might have thought that she had taken a lover in his absence, but he no longer tried to rationalize or examine what was, or what might have been. He dedicated his energy to a better present.

Lizzie even came to an uneasy understanding with Queen, or at least recognized her existence. Now that Queen had an official position within the household, as paid staff member, some edge of anxiety was removed from Lizzie. But she was a tough, relentless mistress, and was not shy of demanding longer hours and harder work from her servant, if that was possible. She still harbored resentment of her, and perhaps hoped that if the job was made unbearable, Queen would leave of her own volition.

But Queen would not go, nor could she think of any reason why she should. If she was grumpy to others, she always presented to Jass a sunshine face, and hid from him any hurt or resentment that she felt. When told that Lizzie was pregnant again, she smiled, and congratulated her Massa, although privately, in her room, she wept. Jass didn't need any more children. He did not fully appreciate one that he already had.

Thus her life became less than it had been when she was a slave. Then, she had been able to persuade herself that she occupied some special place within her Massa's heart and house.

Now she was simply a drudge.

65

Alec Henderson was doing rather better than most. When he arrived back at The Forks of Cypress after his long trek home, he was greeted with surprising warmth by Letitia, and cordially by Sally and Lizzie. As soon as politeness would allow, he went to his cottage alone, and, to his relief, found that his cache of gold had not been disturbed.

He chuckled, and laughed, and hopped an unlikely jig in the empty room. He was rich. Not really rich in the way that landed gentry had been, but compared to almost anyone else in the district, he was a man of fiscal means. He had a meager dinner at the big house where Letitia was now living, and explained to them something of his plans. Obviously, there was no place for him at The Forks. Without slaves, they had no need of an overseer, and could not afford one anyway. He planned to take Letitia away for a holiday to Charleston, to see her family and discover their postwar circumstances. He had not told his wife of this, and she gave a little shriek of joy.

When he took her to bed that night, he made love to her with a vigor and passion that surprised her, and she responded with an enthusiasm that intrigued him. Letitia supposed he had taken other women, whores probably, while he was away at the war and it did not bother her. It was a man's prerogative, and soldiers did that sort of thing. But she would not tolerate that sort of behavior now he was home, and the best way to keep a man happy was to let him know that he was needed and appreciated. She entered into their love-making with energy, although tempered with a mission-ary correctness. She had found no outlet for her own physical needs while he was away, and was surprised to discover that she had desires for him. She caressed him afterward, and they discussed their future. Hender-son thought they would do well with a little farm, for life on the land was all he knew, but Letitia had other ambitions. They could not afford a large holding, nor the hands for a cotton crop, and she had no intention of being married to a tobacco farmer.

She wanted to own a small store, a place of general provisions, and he could maintain his association with the land, and get the produce they sold at bargain prices. She was a shopgirl at heart, and they would do well, because they would give credit to reliable customers.

Henderson was appalled. Credit was a fool's game. They could never be sure of being repaid.

"No," said Letitia. "It is the way of the future. No one has any money now, so they will flock to us, and we will extend ourselves. But things will get better, because they cannot possibly get any worse. Money will be made, and it will be owed to us, so gentlefolk will be bound to us by what they owe, and will continue to shop with us, if only out of embarrassment or gratitude."

Henderson continued to argue, but his was a hope-less cause. Letitia had her mind set on a particular way of doing business, and she was a formidable opponent. She never asked him where he got the money to fund their new enterprise, and she never told her husband of the joy it would give her when those who had previously shunned her, or sneered at her, were forced to come begging for her largess.

They spent a pleasant three weeks in Charleston, and Letitia, who had no fondness for her ungrateful family, gloried in the dire circumstances of her relatives. Her father was dead, killed by drink, and her mother was reduced to taking in paying guests of the lower white classes. Her brother had never volunteered to fight, but had taken the coward's way, run the blockade and gone to sea on Yankee merchant ships. Her sisters were both widowed by the war, and one lived in the attic of her mother's house, while the other had fallen considerably from grace, and received gentleman callers who paid for the privilege. All this misfortune nourished Letitia's moral rectitude, and as the weather got hotter she was content to travel back to Alabama with her husband and look for a suitable shop to buy, secure in the knowledge that she, alone of her family, had a good husband, prospects, and a Christian conscience.

They found a suitable building some two miles from The Forks of Cypress, on the southern side, away from Florence. It was ideal. Folk who did not wish to make the arduous and often dangerous journey to town could now come to them. Including, perhaps, the high and mighty Jacksons. Letitia had no love for her former employers, who were not ardently religious and espoused some liberal ideas. Even though she had sought sanctuary in the big house during the war, it was from loneliness, she told herself now, not from fear, and both Sally and Lizzie had treated her with some disdain, constantly, tacitly reminding her that she was present only as a favor. Nor could she imagine how they could let that bastard mulatta girl, living proof of the Massa's immorality, share the same roof and prepare their food.

Henderson went about the countryside, renewing old

acquaintances and offering to buy their harvests for minimal recompense. The exigencies of the time gave him several reliable suppliers. Letitia employed two nigras to paint and clean the old wooden building. She had a counter made, and shelves, purchased a fine set of brass scales, and, aproned and capped in clean, neat gingham, opened her shop for business.

They did well, but not well enough to expand the store or staff, for they gave credit freely, and bit quite heavily into Henderson's savings. He had fretted about this for some time, but when the first repayment was made on a debt, he relaxed, for at last he could see some potential for return on his outlay. And his was a pleasant life. Letitia required nothing of him but that he keep her shelves stocked, and so he spent his days riding round the country, chewing the fat with friends, and his evenings in the company of like-minded whites, reminiscing about the war, and planning vengeance on Yankees and uppity niggers. Gradually, the store became a meeting place for those young white males who responded to Henderson's genial authority and who believed that the South would rise again in glory, and the niggers be sent back to hell, where they belonged.

Letitia's life was at least as pleasant, monarch of her small domain, and she had a taste of triumph within a week of the store's opening. Jass had come to her, asking for credit to buy food. He was not shy or diffident about it, although it was anathema to him, but Letitia sensed his distaste for the business and for her, and dragged it out as long as possible, extracting every ounce of pleasure from it that she could.

Jass was scrupulous in his dealings with her. Whenever a little money came his way, he would pay something from his bill, although every visit to the bombastic proprietress repelled him. He went himself only when he had money in his pocket. Otherwise, he sent Queen.

*

Queen hated going to the store. She hated asking for credit, and she and Mrs. Henderson conducted their business with mutual loathing. More than anything, Queen hated the white men who were always hanging around outside the shop, lounging, loafing, threatening. On her first visits, with Jass, they had ignored her, although clearly appreciative of her prettiness. One crisp fall day, Jass was in Montgomery, and Queen had gone on her own. Three of these rednecked men were inside the shop, seated, or squatting against the wall, by the small potbelly stove in the corner. Mr. Henderson was with them, and while Queen shopped she was aware of their silent concentration on her. She had to pass close by one young man, dirty and unshaven, to inspect a bag of dried beans, and he did not move his feet out of the way, but leered at her.

"Nice day for it, lady," he said, but it was not pleasant, and Henderson chuckled.

"Don't bother with her," he told his companions. "She's high yalla."

Queen blushed, and the men whistled.

"Could have fooled me," one said. "Don't matter a damn," said another. "I don't mind a little midnight velvet."

They laughed, and stared at Queen, and she changed her mind about the beans, and moved closer to the counter and the comparative security of Mrs. Henderson's presence.

After that, it was always the same. Whether the men were inside or out, they never directly threatened her, hardly spoke to her, but would stare at her as she walked by, and whistle, or snicker, and whisper what they would do to her if they ever found her alone on some dark night. She complained to Jass, but he said there was nothing he could do, and he was sure the men meant her no real harm. She was protected by the law. She tried to avoid going, but no one else would, and it was her duty. Every visit to the store became an

655

ordeal, and she would stop her horse some little distance from the shop, and steel herself for the coming encounter.

The following summer came early, hot days in May that drained all energy. Lizzie was listless, for she was nearly at term, and Sally had taken to her bed with an unseasonable chill, brought on by the sharp change in the weather. Jass had to go into Florence, on state business, and Queen wanted to go with him to shop, but he told her not to be silly. They didn't need much, and he couldn't get credit in town. Queen put off going to the store for as long as she could, until it was late in the day. She might have found reasons not to go at all, until Lizzie demanded fresh tomatoes for a salad, and their own were not yet ripe.

Queen rode down to the store toward sunset. As usual, half a dozen young men were outside with Henderson, and, as usual they leered at her, but let her pass by unmolested. She gave her short list to Mrs. Henderson, and watched carefully as the tomatoes were being weighed, because she had been cheated before.

"Sure don't look like two pound to me," she murmured, half to herself, but loudly enough for Mrs. Henderson to hear.

"Are you saying my scales are faulty?" the aggrieved shopkeeper demanded.

Queen shrugged. A couple of the young men had wandered into the store, aimless, bored.

"You've lost none of your cheek, I see," Mrs. Henderson continued. "Ken your place, girl. I suppose you want this on credit?"

"Massa Jackson's good for it, he pays his bills," Queen retorted, ill temper simmering. "And your prices are high enough."

It was more than she meant to say, but it was enough to provoke Mrs. Henderson, who eyed her carefully.

"Are you sassing me?" she began, and overrode

656

Queen's protestations. "You're accusing me of over-charging you, in front of witnesses."

She nodded at the young men, who moved closer to enjoy the fun.

"Credit doesn't come free, you know," Mrs. Henderson announced righteously. "And if the high-and-mighty Mr. Jackson has any complaints about the arrangement, tell him to come and see me himself."

She paused for a moment, but only for a moment.

"Not send his bastard slave girl."

The young men laughed and muttered agreement. Queen turned on Mrs. Henderson in fury.

"I ain't a slave no more," she cried, but Mrs. Henderson was in exquisite control. She had been wanting to do this for years.

"You're a useless nigra, with no civil tongue in your head for decent white folk," she snapped.

"In the old days she'd a been whipped," one of the young men agreed.

"That's what she needs now," his companion said, advancing on Queen.

"A good spanking, yeh, tan her little nigra tail," chimed the first.

It was as much sport as anything; it was doubtful they would have harmed her here, in public, but they frightened Queen, and she saw no escape but retreat.

"You cain't touch me," she cried, backing out of the door.

The young men followed, calling after her. "Come here, girl—teach you some manners!"

But Queen was gone, out of the store, running to her horse tethered nearby. The men outside were puzzled at first, until their companions appeared, calling to Queen, announcing the dispute. Now they all ran to Queen, jeering at her. One reached her as she mounted her horse and tried to pull her down, but she hit him, hard, across the face, with her stock. At that moment, it changed from a game to a deadly chase.

The man Queen had hit fell back, hand to a bloody gash on his cheek. "Slut!" he cried. His friends caught him, and ran to their own horses. Already it was past sunset, and a couple had the foresight to grab burning brands that had been lighted outside the store.

Queen spurred her horse and galloped away as fast as she dared, but she was not a natural rider, and the very speed of the horse frightened her. She dared not look back, because she could hear the sound of the men in pursuit of her, the pounding of the horses, and their laughing, angry cries of "whore" and "nigger slut," and the loudest voice was Henderson's. The road stretched straight for a clear mile before her, and she knew she could never outride them. Her best hope was to hide or to lose them, and she turned off the road and into the dense wood.

But her pursuers were men of the land, hunting men, and it made little difference to them if their quarry was a frightened animal or a black human being. They tracked her effortlessly into the forest. Queen could not ride fast because of the tangled bushes, and she was scared that her horse would stumble. As she twisted and turned her way through the trees, she could see the flames of their burning brands, dancing, it seemed, all around her, closer and closer, dazzling her, and all she could hear was their taunting voices.

Her horse caught its foot on a broken log and fell, pitching Queen to the ground. Winded and bruised, bleeding from some small cuts caused by brambles, and blind with panic, she scrabbled through the undergrowth, searching for some tree to hide behind. The gloaming was her friend, and, unable to see where she was going, she slid on some rocks and pitched forward into a narrow ditch.

Almost immediately, the men were upon her, sweeping their brands through the air in search of her, the flames almost inches from her face. They milled around, unable to track her in the twilight.

658

"Cain't see her," called one, the fire he carried glittering in Queen's eyes. There was a silence, broken only by the sounds of coming night in the forest, and of her horse crashing through branches.

"Ain't too far, there's her hoss," cried another, and the hooves of his horse knocked some stones down into the ditch, hitting Queen's face. He spurred away and into the night.

Gradually, the sound of them receded.

"I ain't giving up," she heard another shout, but farther away from her, moving away, and she began to feel that she might be safe, for the moment at least, but cowered in the muddy ditch, lest they should return.

She fainted from shock and fear and relief, and when she came to it was night, with only a silver moon to guide her way. Her senses strained for sounds or sight or feeling of the presence of the chasers, but there were none, although the noises of the forest startled and unsettled her. She lay clutching herself until she was sure they were gone, and crawled slowly from the ditch.

Although she knew she could not be more than a few miles from The Forks, she had no idea of where she was, and no sense of direction to guide her. She walked forward, believing that she must eventually arrive somewhere, but as she struggled on, brambles snatching at her hair, screech owls startling her, moss causing her to slip from time to time, despair settled on her.

She was hopelessly lost.

She thought of curling down somewhere, under a tree, to rest until dawn, for she knew she would not sleep, but the woods were alien to her, and almost as frightening as her pursuers, so she trudged on, crying a little, whispering to God to bring her to some safe place.

After she had walked for perhaps a mile, she saw a light among the trees, small flames, and stopped in fear, thinking it to be the brands of her tormentors. She held her breath and stared at the fire, wondering where she could hide, or if darkness was cloak enough, and then she realized that the flames were constant and unmoving, and brighter than any torch.

Cautiously, carefully, she edged forward, trying not to make a sound. As she came closer, she saw it was a campsite, and shivered, for perhaps the men had settled there to wait for her, or dawn. She was exhausted and hungry, and every bone in her body ached, and suddenly she no longer cared what happened to her. She moved a little closer, and saw that the men sitting round the camp fire were not white.

The color of their skin gave her a small sense of security, and she took a few more steps toward them, wondering how to approach them. A twig snapped under her foot and solved her problem, for they heard it, and stood to see what was happening.

"Who dat dere?" a man's voice called.

The familiar slave dialect reassured her, and now she came out of the sheltering trees, and closer to the men.

"Help me, I's lost," she called to them softly, and came closer still, until her face was illumined by the flickering firelight.

"It dat house nigger," another said in surprise.

Three ex-slaves from The Forks of Cypress had made this little clearing their home, preferring this freedom of the forest to their previous bondage or any future dealings with the white man's world. Having been here for some months, they had started to regard the place as their home, and had cleared a large area. They had erected lean-to shelters from branches and twigs, lived off the land that was generous to them. They sometimes imagined that they would build a more permanent dwelling, and, if no one troubled them or claimed the land, they might begin some small farming.

They had no affection for a light-skinned mulatta who

had lived in the big house, had never given them the time of day, and might very well be a spy for their previous Massa, who owned this land, with whom she was always close.

"Help me, please," she said again.

One man grabbed a branch, and held it up, threateningly.

"Get outa here, yalla bitch," he shouted.

Queen had no energy to scream. Any small hope that had been kindled in her heart was extinguished. Not even blacks would assist her. She turned to leave, and then turned back again, to ask them at least to tell her in which direction to go, but as she did so, a light-skinned woman came out of a lean-to.

"Leave her be," she called to the men. She walked to the fire. "Come here, girl," she said to Queen.

The woman, Pearl, had some authority over the two men she lived with, for each wanted her, and neither was prepared to offend her. They moved back a little, to allow Queen to walk to the fire.

Queen stared at Pearl, looking for some trace of sympathy, but the woman's expression was impassive. Still, she was a woman, and had averted immediate danger. She might understand.

"Some white men chased me!" Suddenly the whole story came blurting out, and Queen was close to tears. "I fell off my horse, and got hurt. They wanted to— wanted—"

She couldn't finish. Pearl's unrelenting stare unnerved her. She looked at the moon, raised her arms in supplication, and dropped them to her side again. The men were hostile, and the woman would not help. It all seemed useless.

Still Pearl did not speak, as if deliberating what she would do. Then she glanced at the pot of possum stew, simmering over the campfire.

"Is yo' hungry?" she asked.

*

Jass was worried, and Lizzie, heavy with child, was angry. Queen had not come home from the store; there was no sign of her, no word from her. The children were hungry and Lizzie and Sally made them something to eat. Then Jass came home from Florence, and Lizzie told him that Queen had run away.

Jass didn't believe it. After he had heard the full story from Lizzie, he rode down to the Henderson store, and they denied any knowledge of Queen's whereabouts. She had been to the store, and then had ridden away in the company of a couple of the lads whose company she was fond of. Jass didn't believe that, either. He knew of Queen's dislike of the store and her fear of the men who frequented it, and she would not have gone willingly away with any of them. He rode home looking for some sign of her, but it was dark, and he found nothing.

Lizzie sided with the Hendersons. Surely Queen had run away, like so many other slaves. And it was such a relief. All her married life there had been a barrier between herself and Jass. It had hurt her desperately when he went off to Easter at night, leaving Lizzie to pine for him. It had hurt her more when Jass brought the brat child to live in the big house, to have her nearer to him, and to flaunt his love for Easter in her face. Even after Easter had died, the hurt remained. She wished no harm to Queen, she hoped she wasn't hurt, but she had to believe that Queen was gone for good. Because every time she looked at Queen, it reminded her of Easter, and reminded her that her husband had loved another woman more than her. A nigra.

She was angry with Queen for giving no indication of her intentions, and Jass for worrying about her; she banged pots on the stove as she prepared some food, and prayed that she would never have to see Queen again.

She went to the veranda to tell Jass his meal was ready, and he nodded, and said he'd be in directly.

"Are you going to sit here all night?" Lizzie asked

him. Jass turned to look at her, and Lizzie hated what she saw in his eyes.

"Well, it's on the table when you're ready," she snapped. "Don't blame me if it gets cold."

She went into the house and called Sally to the table. They ate their meal in silence. Sally, like Lizzie, was sure that Queen had run away, and it hurt her that the child had not said good-bye, but she could hardly blame her.

Jass stared at the moon, convinced that some mischief had befallen Queen, but not knowing what to do, or how to begin to find her. In the silence that surrounded him, he heard a sound that was not of the night. It was the clinking of a horse's bridle.

Queen's horse came trotting up the drive to him. Jass went to the animal and held it, felt it for injury, and then looked to the stars.

He took the horse to the stable to give it feed.

Queen ate her fill of the simple stew, and sat staring at the campfire. The black men were still hostile to her. "She ain't stayin'," one said, and Pearl turned on him.

"She's a po' nigger, like us, an' she tired an' scared," she said. "We look after her, like we would any nigger."

The men lapsed into aggressive silence, and Pearl put her arm around Queen.

"Is yo' tired?" she asked, and Queen nodded, suddenly desperately, achingly tired.

Pearl fetched a blanket from a lean-to, and wrapped it around Queen. "Lie down here by the fire," she ordered, and Queen did as she was bidden. "Keep yo' warm," Pearl said, "give yo' light to see. Yo' is safe now. Yo' with yo' own nigger folk now."

Queen tightened the blanket around her, and stared at the flames of the fire.

"She ain't stayin'," she heard one of the men say. "Fust light, she leavin'."

663

Pearl ignored him, and started to sing a soft lullaby. The flames of the fire danced in Queen's eyes. She wasn't wanted here, and would not stay. This was not her place. These were not her people.

But neither was The Forks of Cypress. She did not fit into this world or that. She stared at the flames, and in her mind they became threatening. She thought she could see the burning brands of her pursuers, and those flames would haunt her for the rest of her life.

There was only the night. And the fire. And the soft, sweet lullaby.

66

Jass was up at first light. He took some bread and cheese from the kitchen, saddled a horse, and went looking for Queen. He intended to ask at every house in the district, search every barn if need be, but his first call was to the Hendersons. They had not told him all they knew, he was sure. As he rode, he contemplated offering a small reward for information as to her whereabouts, but wondered if that was fair to her. If she had run away, which he did not for one moment believe, then perhaps she would not want to be found.

He cursed himself for a blind, selfish fool. Lizzie had been angry with him all the previous evening, had hardly spoken to him until they went to bed, and when he tried to caress her, she turned away from him. He'd provoked her to tell him what was wrong, and then all of her frustrations came tumbling out. Jass was astonished, and bitterly regretful. He had never realized how deeply his relationship with Easter had hurt Lizzie, and how much she resented Queen's presence in the big house. He had thought that Lizzie approved of Easter, because her presence reduced his sexual need for his wife, who had not seemed to welcome their love-making. In that sense he was right, but now he understood that it was not the physical side of his relationship with Easter that infuriated Lizzie, it was the love.

"She made you smile, she made you laugh, she made you happy, in a way that I never could," Lizzie had told him through her tears. And it was true.

"But you are my wife," he told Lizzie, "and I love you."

"More than you loved her?" Lizzie asked, and all he could say was that it was different.

He should not have brought Queen into the big house; he should have known that just looking at the child was a slap in the face to Lizzie, for Queen was the embodiment of Easter.

"Easter was just a slave," Jass insisted. "A nigra—"

"Yes!" Lizzie cried. "And you loved her." And it was true.

"I couldn't ignore the child," he insisted again.

"But did you have to love her?" Lizzie cried again. And it was true.

He did love Queen, but not as he loved his children by Lizzie; they were different, flesh of his formal union with his legal wife, his heirs, his darlings. Queen was an enchantment, a toy, a plaything, a little innocent doll that he had created, who gave him pleasure.

"And what about my pleasure?" Lizzie asked him, quietly now, for her crying was done. "Did you ever consider that?"

And it was true. He had not considered her. He had been a good husband and provider, and he had done his duty by their marriage. But he had never considered Lizzie's feelings, she who should have had first demand on him.

"I'll make it up to you somehow, Lizzie, I swear," he promised her, caressing her swollen stomach.

"But you will not forget Queen," she said. And it was true.

He would find her and he would bring her home, if

she wanted to come home, and he had no idea what arrangements he would make for their future so that all could be happy, but although he would respect Lizzie's feelings and be more attentive to her, he would not dismiss Queen.

Queen woke at dawn, bitten by mosquitoes and stiff and sore. The men would not speak to her, but Pearl made her something to eat, and told her how to get back to The Forks, but reluctantly.

"Ain't nuttin' fo' yo' there," she said.

Queen shrugged, not knowing what to say. She walked north through the woods, as Pearl had told her, and two hours later she broke through the trees, and saw the familiar road home. Dirty and disheveled, burrs sticking in her hair, she limped to The Forks, turned in at the gate, and made her way up the drive. She walked to the back of the house and went into the kitchen.

Lizzie was cooking. She heard the door open and saw Queen come in. Her heart sank. She had convinced herself that she had seen the last of Queen, that the girl had run away, like the brat nigra she was, and would never come back. Yet she was back, and Lizzie, after her argument with Jass the previous night, could not imagine how she would cope.

"Where have you been?" she said, evenly.

Queen walked to a chair at the table and sat down. 'I sorry, Missy," she said. "I had some trouble."

"And are you aware of how much trouble you've caused here?" Lizzie asked her.

Queen hardly expected words of comfort or solace from Lizzie, but she had not expected anger.

"No thought for us, no word of warning," Lizzie said. "Just off and away, like the no-account nigra you are. In the old days we'd have set the dogs after you. Get yourself cleaned up and get to work."

Fireworks of anger were starting to explode in Queen's mind.

666

"I sorry, I—" she began, but Lizzie's temper broke before hers. "Your Massa's been out since dawn looking for you, Miss Sally unable to sleep, and me in my condition—"

Queen could not stand it anymore. They'd treat an old dog better than they treated her. She rose to her feet in fury.

"He not my Massa," she said. "He my pappy!"

Lizzie slapped her face hard.

"How dare you say that! How dare you speak to me like that!"

But Queen dared. She would dare anything now, for she had nothing to lose.

"An' how dare you," she cried. "I ain't some animal for you to push around, Queen do this, Queen do that, cook, wash, clean, garden, plant cotton, pick cotton, morning till night, and never a word of thanks! You don't even notice I exist until you want something done! Well, I do exist, Missus, and I've got a right to a little bit of happiness. An' if I cain't find it here, I'll find it somewhere else."

The events of the previous night were the crack in the dam of her frustration, and now it burst, and her loneliness came flooding out. She did not belong in this white world, could not function in this white world, would never be accepted by this white family for what she was, which was one of them. For she was not one of them. She was some curious addendum to their lives, without place or purpose, other than as willing slave, and she didn't want to be a slave anymore.

She didn't want to be a slave to anyone, she didn't want to be a slave to this family, and most of all, she didn't want to be a slave to her love for her father, for it would never be returned in a way that would have any value to her. Simple recognition of her existence was hardly an adequate substitute for love. For the first time in her life Queen realized that her heart was empty, and that she wanted it to be full.

667

Lizzie was shocked by her impudence. "How dare you," she said. "After all we've done for you."

"You ain't ever done nothing for me," Queen responded as she walked out of the room. "An' you won't ever have to now."

She didn't run, because there was nothing to run to or from. She walked slowly up the stairs, repeating in her mind what she had said to Lizzie, elaborating on it, embroidering it, until it became a litany of the woes of her life. She went to her room, washed herself clean, and brushed her hair. As she looked in her little mirror, she repeated her speech to Lizzie again, and it was longer still. She remembered every tiny hurt, every unkind word, every flick of the switch to her behind. She finished on a triumphant note, demolishing the phantom Lizzie, and, anger spent, she giggled. She wondered what Lizzie's face looked like when she'd left the kitchen.

She changed into her Sunday best, and packed a little suitcase with her few belongings. She gave no thought to her destination or to her purse, which was almost empty, for her obsession was to leave. She did think of saying good-bye to Sally, but decided against it. As kind as the old Missy was, she was the one who had first told her to go.

But she did have to say good-bye to someone. She put on her bonnet, picked up her suitcase, and took a last look as her tiny, sparsely furnished room. She went downstairs, hoping she wouldn't run into any of the family, left the house by the front door, and made her way to the slave graveyard to say good-bye to her mammy.

"I got to go, Mammy," she told Easter. "Ain't no place for me here."

The grave was untidy and overgrown. Queen hadn't had time to tend it, and the weeds were flourishing in the warm, spring sun. Queen knelt and pulled at the weeds.

"Pappy don't know yet," she said. "I don't want to see him. I'm going afore he gets back."

It wasn't completely true. Part of her didn't want to face Jass, but perhaps part of her hoped that if she did see him he would say what she had always longed for him to say, and make everything all right again. In her heart she knew it probably wouldn't happen, but she could not dismiss the hope. And having made the decision to go, she was terrified of the consequences of that decision, for some sense of reality had dawned on her. She had no idea where she would sleep that night, or how she would eat. She felt utterly friendless, utterly alone, and it comforted her to sit beside the only friend she had ever had.

Sally came to her. Lizze had told her of the argument, and of Queen's extraordinary outburst of anger and intention to leave, and Sally had worried about the girl. She would not try to persuade Queen to stay, but she could not let the girl go without some knowledge of her future welfare. She had seen Queen walking to the graveyard, and had followed her. She stood in the trees watching the tender farewell from daughter to mother and then moved forward, to say her own good-bye.

"Weren't you going to come to say good-bye to me?" she asked Queen, gently.

Queen was embarrassed, and got to her feet.

"I'm so sorry, my dear," Sally said. "I didn't want it to end like this, but I thought it must."

Queen turned away, feeling some small spark of the anger she had felt when Sally first suggested that she go. Why? Why did it have to end like this? Because she was nigra and they weren't? She only had a little bit of nigra blood in her. Why did that make her black?

Sally might have guessed her thoughts, or perhaps she felt the need to explain why Queen's position was untenable. Not just for here, but for her future, for the

669

girl was impulsive, and had good reason for complaint. She looked white. She was so very nearly white.

"Wherever you go, Queen," she said, "you must remember that it isn't enough to be nearly white, as you are. Even one drop of black blood makes you nigra."

Queen did not understand Sally's purpose, and said nothing. If she was nigra, why had the blacks in the forest rejected her, as the field hands did? Only Pearl had been kind to her, but Pearl, although darker than Queen, was not black.

Sally held out a small purse of money. "I don't want it," Queen said.

"You always were a stubborn girl!" Sally tried to laugh. "Take it. We owe you this much, at least."

Queen saw the truth of it, and took the purse. She had, in all fairness, earned at least this.

"I don't suppose I'll ever see you again," Sally said. "Good luck, my dear."

It was then that Queen realized an extraordinary thing. Miss Sally did love her, in her way, after a fashion. Why else would she be crying? All of her anger evaporated, and was replaced by an enormous sense of loss. She hugged Sally to her.

"Oh, Missus," she said.

They walked down the hill together, Sally using Queen's arm for support, and when they got to the house Sally wished her luck again, and said good-bye again, and hugged her again, and then went inside.

Queen took a last look at the house, and then set off down the drive. She didn't look back, even when she turned out of the gate, but paused for a moment, wondering where to go. It was not a difficult decision. South would take her past the Hendersons, which was unthinkable. North would take her to Florence. She turned left, to go north.

She hadn't gone very far before she heard a horse

riding up behind her, and for a moment she was scared, thinking it might be one of her pursuers come for her in daylight, but there was nowhere to run now, so she turned to face the rider.

It was Jass. He had seen her from a distance away, from behind, and from her clothes and her suitcase he made a guess that she was leaving. But mostly, he was relieved to have found her.

"Queen," he called out. "Where have you been? I've been looking everywhere."

She was pleased to see him and not pleased to see him. Frightened that he would let her go, scared that he would not let her leave.

"I's leaving," she said. "For good."

Jass glanced at his house, where Lizzie was.

"Miss Lizzie?" he asked her, but Queen said nothing, and he knew the answer.

It was for the best; it solved so many problems. Queen was part of his past, part of the South's past; there was no real place for her in his new life. It would solve so many problems for her, too, and make things very much easier with Lizzie. But he would miss her.

"Are you all right? Do you have money?" he asked, and she nodded.

"You can take a horse," he said. "It's too far to walk."

"I'll manage," she replied.

There was nothing else to say. What could he say? Only good-bye.

"I'll miss you," he said.

She almost broke. At that moment, she would have changed her mind, she would have gone back, put up with Miss Lizzie's tantrums and too much work and too little pay, just to know that he loved her, or cared for her, or appreciated her. All he had to do was ask. All he had to do was say one little thing. He didn't say any of them.

"Good-bye, Queen," was all he said. "Good luck."

Suddenly, he spurred his horse and cantered away,

up the drive to the mansion that she had loved, and that she would never see again.

She watched her father ride home to his family, and then, head high, she picked up her suitcase and began to walk away, off on a great new adventure, off to a bold, bright somewhere.

When Jass reached the house, he stopped his horse and looked back for a last glimpse of Queen.

He could see her tiny figure trudging away down the road to Florence, resolute and brave, and for a moment he was filled with a sense of his own failure to her. He wanted to ride after her, call her back, bring her back to the place that was her home, but could not.

He sat on his horse for a long time, long after he could no longer see her, hidden by the trees, and he sent up a little prayer to God that she find some safe haven.

Then he rode to the stables, dismounted and tended to his horse, and went into the big house, looking forward to his supper. It had been a busy day in Florence, and he still had much work to do.

He seldom thought of Queen again. But sometimes a fragment of memory of her came into his mind, and he would smile. And sometimes, when that happened, he would take a leisurely walk to the slave cemetery, and sit beside Easter's grave, and mourn what he had lost.

67

The day was hot, and the sun at its zenith, sapping Queen's energy and resolution. Blisters on her feet, which had begun the previous evening, were hurting her, and she sat on her suitcase at the side of the road, took off her shoes, and nursed her aching feet. Why had they built the house so far from town? How far had she come? How much farther did she have to go?

He could have given her a ride. She could have taken a horse. She'd have said yes if he'd asked her one more time.

She began to have doubts about her enterprise. It would be so easy to go back, to beg Jass's forgiveness and accept the role she had been cast in, but pride, or dignity, or stubbornness, would not let her do that. By her reckoning, she was about halfway between The Forks and Florence, so to go back was as arduous as to go on. Except that there would be a bed waiting for her if she returned, and there was nothing in store for her if she went on. Needing some sense of security, she counted out the little purse of money that Sally had given her.

Twenty dollars! It was an unbelievable sum to Queen, who had never had any money of her own. It made her, in her own mind, rich, and solved many of her immediate problems. She had to find somewhere to sleep that night, even if it meant spending some of the precious cash and staying in the old slave quarters at the hotel, so the sooner she got to Florence, the sooner she could rest. Knowledge of her new wealth gave her renewed energy, and she got to her feet, sweating in the blazing sun, and limped on.

The time came when she had to relieve herself, and she looked around for a suitable bush. She always chose the spot with great care, because once Parson Dick had gone behind the barn and had peed on a hornet's nest. The angry insects attacked him, and everyone had laughed at the sight of the immaculate Parson Dick running from behind the barn, pulling up his pants and being chased by a swarm of angry hornets. She found a tree that looked safe, squatted behind it, and did what she needed to. Again she considered her options—to go on or to go back—but the relief of her bladder made her feel better. She adjusted her clothing and returned to the road, still not entirely sure of her purpose, but trusting that something would happen.

She heard a cart approaching. There had been very little traffic on the road that day, and the few riders passing by had ignored her. She prayed she might be luckier this time.

Andy, the butcher's boy, was surprised to see her. He'd been on his rounds collecting farm-killed meat, and was heading back to Florence when he saw a white lady standing at the side of the road. He reined in the horse, and realized that it wasn't a white lady at all, but that light-skinned mulatta from The Forks of Cypress.

He drew up beside her, and touched his cap.

"Miss Queen, ain't it?" he called cheerfully. "What yo' doin' out here on yo' ownsome? Where's yo' hoss?"

He'd always liked Miss Queen because she was so pretty, and sometimes he had fantasies of her pale body lying beside his darker one, but although he had an outgoing personality, he was shy of women, and unfailingly polite to them. Sometimes he regretted his good manners.

Queen knew she must look odd, out here all alone with her suitcase, and wasn't sure what to tell him. She wondered if a little white lie would matter, and decided on a vague version of the truth.

"It's a long story, Andy," she said. "Y'see, my horse throwed me, and—"

It was as much as he needed. "That ain't no good," he said. "I'm gwine back to Florence, but I could take yo' back to The Forks."

Queen needed no second bidding, and climbed into the cart.

"No. Florence will do just fine, thank you kindly," she said. He took her suitcase.

"Yo' leavin' the Forks, or summat?" he puzzled.

"No, Andy, I's jus'—ah—gwine' visitin'," she lied,

674

allowing her speech to slur into something closer to Andy's dialect.

He helped her up, and made space for her beside him, on the little bench seat. He flicked the reins, and the patient nag began to walk.

"Yo' be careful, Miss Queen," he told her. "Some white folk don't take kindly to niggers on their ownsome."

Queen knew that to be true, but didn't have a worry in the world now. It didn't matter that Andy, sitting uncomfortably close to her, had a problem with his body odor. It didn't matter that the smell of the meat inside the cart assailed her senses. It didn't matter that the seat was hard and uncomfortable. God had sent her a sign, a chariot and a messenger in the form of Andy and his cart. Her decision to go on to Florence had been the right one.

"I's surely grateful yo' came along then," she said, smiling happily. She listened gravely to Andy's tales of the dangers of life on the road, but inside she didn't stop smiling all the way to Florence.

Andy offered her more help when they got to the town, even, he subtly hinted, a bed for the night, but she maintained her fiction that she had people to visit, and thanked him for the ride.

"Anytime, Miss Queen," he told her. "Anything I c'n do, yo' only got to ask."

He flicked the reins and rode away. Queen stood on the sidewalk and looked about her. She hadn't been to Florence since the war started, but it hadn't changed much, except that Yankee soldiers were everywhere roaming the streets, and they frightened her. There were several hours of daylight left, and so she walked away from the main street, looking for somewhere to eat. It surprised her that a couple of older white men, smartly dressed, tipped their hats to her as she walked by, until she realized that they must think her white as well. It made her feel good, and she giggled. She saw the river sparkling in the distance, and walked toward it. It was such a lovely day.

She came to the docks, a wharf and some warehouses, and enjoyed the bustle of it all. A ferryboat, an old paddle steamer, was loading cargo, and fishermen were bringing in their catch. A couple of street vendors were selling fried catfish and boiled crawdaddies, so she bought some food and was treated with considerable respect, and called "Missy." She settled against an old tree on the bank of the river and used her suitcase as a small table, to eat. She giggled to herself again, for she knew that people thought her white. A full stomach and the breezes from the river lulled her, and she dozed for a while in the pleasant place.

The afternoon was waning when she woke, refreshed from her sleep, her feet aching less and her spirits improved. Her prime objective was to find a place to sleep that night.

And once again, Fate, or Chance, or God, decided for her.

"Ferry fo' Decatur leavin' soon," she heard someone cry.

An enterprising trader had bought an old paddle steamer that was used to transport cotton in the season, and whatever cargo they could get at other times of the year. Knowing that many people found travel by road arduous and dangerous in these postwar times, he had some modest cabins made, and began ferrying passengers between Florence and Decatur. The service was mildly popular, especially with women who needed to travel, for they thought the highways unsafe.

Decatur seemed like an excellent idea to Queen. Although she was not well known in Florence, some few, like Andy, might recognize her, and there was always the chance that she might run into Jass or Lizzie if she stayed, which she preferred not to do. Besides, the ferry ride would delay a decision about her resting place.

She bought the cheapest one-way ticket, which did not include one of the four cabins, and walked along the dock to the steamer. Half a dozen passengers were boarding, and their luggage was being loaded. Queen made her way up the gangplank feeling grand. She had never been on a boat of any kind, and experienced that sense of nervous excitement that is common to all first-time sailors, for travel by ship is the most romantic adventure. Even if she wasn't going very far, she was going somewhere, and anywhere had to be better than where she had been. Smoke belched from the stacks, the wheel started to turn, and as the ferry honked its farewell and the lines were cast off, she felt as if she were saying good-bye to an entire old life, and welcoming a new. Wide-eyed in wonder, she stood on the deck watching the dock, the land, recede, until she was surrounded by water.

"No, you stupid darky," she heard a woman's angry voice. "I told you, that goes in the cabin!"

A plump, middle-aged white woman, overly dressed for traveling, was berating a deckhand.

"Yes, m'm," the deckhand said, carrying a large trunk inside. "I's puttin' it dere now."

The aggrieved woman, fanning herself with a hankie, turned to Queen. It was too hot, she'd been traveling for several days, and her stays were too tight.

"You can't trust those darkies to get anything right," she said to Queen, who smiled shyly.

"And you shouldn't be out here by yourself, my dear, a pretty young thing like you," the woman continued, taking a little mirror from her reticule to adjust her hat and hair. "Those darkies would have us away as soon as look at us. If you take my meaning."

The woman, Mrs. Porteous, or portly Porty, as an unkind friend once called her, hated traveling, but had no option. Her husband had recently died, and her son had been killed in the war, so she had sold her house in Natchez and was going to live with her spinster sister in Knoxville. Everything had gone wrong. The weather was hot, there was no reliable coach line from Natchez to Knoxville, and she had to change many times. Service was unheard of these days in the hotels where she spent her nights, and sleep impossible because of those rowdy, occupying, uncouth Yankee soldiers. The bone-crunching carriages, riding on rough, untended highways, had made her sick, and she had stayed in Florence for several days, unable to face the continuation of her journey. She heard of the ferry to Decatur, and at least that was a pleasanter mode of travel, and would bring her a little closer to her destination. She had started out from Natchez with three cabin trunks, but one had been lost in Memphis, stolen, she was sure, by darkies, who were far too uppity these days, and didn't seem to know their place at all. On top of everything else, she had found her various traveling companions to be decidedly unfriendly, and she was a garrulous woman who loved having someone to talk to.

The pretty girl was sweet. Shy, obviously, but sweet. "Such a pretty thing," she said to Queen. "Visiting?"

Queen started to find her voice, but it was not one that Andy would have recognized. It was the voice she used when she was on her very best behavior, in front of Miss Lizzie.

"Yes, m'm," she agreed. "Relatives. In Decatur."

"Such a relief a find pleasant company," Mrs. Porteous said. "So much trash traveling these days. It's the war, it's changed everything. I've been in fear of my life since Natchez."

She stared sadly at the river, as if remembering attempts on her life, rather than the loneliness of her present widowed existence.

Queen was curious. Clearly, the woman thought her to be white, and she wondered how far she could push the pretense. For the first time in her life, the possibility of deceit came to her, but she justified it as a way to survival. She wouldn't lie, but if people wanted to make assumptions about her, Queen was happy to provide corroborating detail.

"You probably haven't heard of my pappy then," she said. "Colonel Jackson, of The Forks of Cypress."

Mrs. Porteous, still staring at the river, nodded absently.

"It is a very famous plantation," Queen added, trying to think of other things that would impress.

"Our glorious veterans, such difficult times," Mrs. Porteous said, turning away from the river. "You must tell me all about yourself. I'll wash up, and then we'll find somewhere to sit, and have a nice, long talk."

It would be a very long talk, Queen discovered later, although mostly one-sided. Mrs. Porteous had a very great deal to tell. She fanned herself away, to find her cabin, and Queen looked at the river.

It was so beautiful. The sun was going down, casting a golden sheen on the water. Life was wonderful to Queen, and she started to giggle again, because everyone thought she was white. Well, she was. She looked white, so she would be white, from now on. It had to be easier than being a nigra.

The giggle turned into a laugh, and she wanted to do something silly, like throw her bonnet into the air, but she was worried it would fall in the water. But she laughed and laughed, and some passengers and deckhands looked in surprise at the pretty white girl standing on the deck by herself, laughing at nothing.

68

All of Queen's hopes for happiness were dashed by the reality of her existence in Decatur.

The once thriving country town had been laid low by

the war, and if life was difficult on the land, it was close to unendurable in the towns and cities. With no industry but agriculture, Decatur, like much of the South, relied for its prosperity on a single crop, cotton, and in good years, and especially at harvesttime, that crop was bountiful. With the fields devastated, the white male population decimated, and the black males fleeing the plantations, the citizens of Decatur struggled simply to survive. Yet the times were rife with opportunity. The armies of reconstruction were slowly moving in, having made their base camps in the larger towns and cities, for land was cheap, the population naive, and everything scarce. A moderately supplied huckster could do well, and barter was the currency. The policing Union Army lacked the moral fiber of its generals. Bored with war, hating the South, longing to be home, the Yankee soldiers made the most of any situation that could be turned to their advantage. So a carnival anarchy prevailed, which suited those of a buccaneering spirit, but proved disastrous for an innocent country girl with optimistic dreams.

Nor did Queen help her own circumstances. Totally unschooled in the ways of the world, she had lived her life within the sheltered confines of a single plantation, with a few occasional forays into Florence under the protective arm of her Massa. She might have done better if she had accepted society's leveling of her, a nigra ex-slave, but she arrived in Decatur with a dangerous self-deception. Denied her heritage, she foolishly believed that she could be what she thought she was, the white daughter of a respected family, with nothing but her own conviction and the color of her skin to support that role. Wary of the black world, she tried to insinuate herself into the white, and while passing acquaintances such as Mrs. Porteous were tolerant of her, sterner judges, such as potential employers, took a harsher view.

The first few nights had awakened her to reality. She

booked into a cheap hostelry, only to discover that her fellow guests, mostly male, were always rowdy and often drunk, and the few females were of careless morality. Her supply of money, which she had thought more than adequate, dwindled to almost nothing with puzzling and frustrating speed. Having no idea of the value of money, for she had never had to handle it, she spent foolishly on food, made some small loans to other women in the hotel who disappeared without repayment, and was considered an easy touch by he unscrupulous. She was robbed of some dollars by a couple of mendacious soldiers. They stopped her because she was pretty, and searched her purse claiming to be looking for concealed weapons, but when they gave it back there was less money in it than before.

She could not find a job. There were few to be had, and fewer still for someone who was neither black nor white. She would happily have become the most menial skivvy, but no one wanted a white girl to do that, and she applied for a job as a shopgirl, but her speech pattern, which was erratic, gave her away, and her deceit made people wary. She looked for lodgings, to reduce her living expenses, but she would not move into a black household, and white landladies regarded her with suspicion. She soon discovered, from the more blatant guests at her cheap hotel, that she had one commodity of value, but the concept of selling what she had never given away free was repulsive to her, and she would not do that. Despair is the mortal enemy of innocence, but while Queen quickly fell into a period of self-pity, she was determined to survive, and that determination became the only weapon in her depleted armory.

But it was a formidable one. Kicked out of her hotel because she could not afford to pay and would not accommodate the landlord in her bed, she found herself a tiny cupboard below some stairs in an abandoned warehouse, and made herself a squalid home. The warehouse was an unofficial dormitory for scores of transient ex-slaves, all going to or coming from somewhere, and all of whom dwelt in the barren land that freedom, despite its promise of riches, had given them. When Queen first found the new home, she walked through silent waves of derision and dislike from her fellow tenants, but penury made her brave. She chose the cupboard because it was the only private space available, and the door had a bolt on it, on the inside, so she could feel safe. She spent some of her last few cents buying a rusty padlock from a secondhand stall to put on the outside of the door. A hefty kick would have smashed the lock, but it made Queen feel more secure, and ensured her tenancy when she was out. She learned to lie with ease and to steal with caution. In the pell-mell nighttime world of the main street, a muffin man, hawking his wares from an open stall, was her unwitting supplier of dinner.

It had first happened a couple of days after she left the hotel. She was hungry, she hadn't had a decent meal in days, her shoes were worn thin, and her clothes were starting to look shiny and threadbare. She was scared to go into the white soup kitchen and had been rejected from the black. She wandered the streets and envied even the lowliest of her fellow citizens. She stared in the window of a provisions store, the display of food making her mouth water, and hated the ringing tones of the muffin man, announcing his wares from his cart.

"Muffins! Get your fine muffins here!"

Two hungry black boys took him at his word, and one distracted the vendor's attention with shouts of injury, while his companion filched a handful of muffins. But the thief was spotted, and a hue and cry began. The boys tried to run, but were collared by some soldiers. In the commotion, Queen, furtive as a tiny sparrow, slipped forward, grabbed two muffins and hid them in her pocket. Heart racing, she turned away, and bumped into a white man who was watching the fuss. Terrified, thinking she had been caught, Queen began an embarrassed explanation, but the man simply smiled at her prettiness, tipped his hat to her, and apologized for not looking where he was going. Queen ran.

Convinced that her guilt must be blazoned upon her for the world to see, she turned into the nearest alley, and stood in the dark for a moment, breathing heavily, astonished by her own audacity, and appalled that she had broken a sacred commandment. The pangs of hunger relieved her conscience, and she wolfed into one of the muffins there in the alley, and saved the other for her breakfast.

As she settled in her uncomfortable cupboard that night, she considered her circumstances. She would not go back. She would not return to The Forks of Cypress and have Miss Lizzie gloat over her. She could not go on because there was nowhere to go, and anywhere else might be worse than where she was. And since things couldn't possibly get any worse here, they must get better. All she had to do was survive, and since survival required food, and the muffins were not sufficient on which to live, she had to go to the soup kitchen. Her experience with the white man in the street had revived her faith in the color of her skin, but the soup kitchen was a daunting prospect, for other than a criminal life, it was her last hope.

Soup kitchens had been set up in many Southern cities and towns, by churches and charitable institutions, to help feed the many who had been made destitute by the war. Despite the equality of the races announced from Washington, they were ruthlessly segregated. Even the most benevolent charity took the view that distressed white gentlewomen would be even more distressed to eat at the same table as blacks, and many of the ex-slaves down on their luck would have been embarrassed to reveal their new poverty in front of their former Massas. The less charitable would not tolerate integration at any level. Queen, who had once been a slave, had gone to a black soup line, but men had jeered her, told her to get her white tail out of there and get to her own kind. Queen had been too proud to tell them the truth. Wary of whites because of her experience with Henderson and his cohorts, she was as cautious of blacks, because of the men in the forest who had rejected her.

Now hunger gave her courage. She went to the Presbyterian Church Hall, and joined a small line of poor whites waiting to be fed. Her nerves quivering, she advanced to the head of the line, and a kindly white woman of her own age was nice to her, and gave her a big bowl of thin stew and some biscuits. Queen kept her head down and scuttled to a corner, where she sipped the delicious broth, which nourished her spirit like manna from heaven.

She went every day at lunchtime, for food was served only then, and existed on that and the occasional muffins that she stole at night. She spoke to no one, and responded to any questions from the kindly white woman with as few words as possible. She would sit alone in her favorite corner, eat her food as quickly as possible, and leave as soon as she could.

On one occasion, her spirit almost failed her. A young woman was in line, just in front of her, and Queen could tell that she was mulatta. A church warden had spotted her too. The mulatta, like Queen, kept her head down, and her eyes to the floor, but the church warden came to her and, gently but firmly, told her to go to her own people. The whites in the line hissed their angry agreement. The mulatta begged, and protested that no one would feed her, she had been rejected from the black soup kitchen, as Queen had been. The warden was moved by her desperate plight, allowed her to eat a bowl of soup outside, but told her never to come back again.

It unnerved Queen. She accepted her own bowl of soup and went quickly to her corner, trying to look inconspicuous. After a few minutes she saw that the white woman who served the food was walking toward her. Queen wondered if she should leave now, rather than face the shame of eviction, but the woman had always been kind, and without this daily sustenance, Queen did not know how she would survive.

The woman sat beside her and watched Queen eat. She said nothing for a while, which disturbed Queen more, and soup spilled from her spoon.

"It's tough, isn't it?" said the white woman in a whisper. "Looking white." And then she added a word that the slave women sometimes used when addressing each other.

"Sister."

Queen was petrified. "Ma'am, I swear—" she began, but the white woman interrupted her.

"It's all right, I understand," she said. She looked around, but no one was near enough to hear them if she spoke quietly.

"Same as you," she said, and smiled. "High yalla, they call it. Dirty white would be better."

It was a trap, Queen was sure. The woman couldn't possibly be mulatta—her features were fine, her skin was flawlessly white, and her hair was soft and wavy. She looked very much like Queen.

"You funnin' me?" Queen asked angrily. The woman, to convince Queen, slipped easily into slave idiom.

"Yo' think I's gwine sit in a room full a whites an' tell yo' I's colored when I ain't?"

It was hardly reassuring to Queen. "Then what you doin' here," she demanded.

The woman laughed. "Chile," she said, "this here's run by the church. Volunteering a few hours of my time each day gives me something that money can't ever buy. It makes me respectable."

She had an enchanting tone of self-knowledge and self-mockery, and Queen relaxed enough to smile. Still she was careful. The trap could be elaborate.

"I'm Alice," the woman told her, "and I was born lucky. I could choose. And who'd choose to be black? Black's hard. Being white is so much easier."

They talked for a few moments, and Alice suggested that Queen help with the washing-up. Queen donned an apron and worked with a will, but still she kept her head down, and avoided speaking to anyone but Alice. They helped the warden lock up, and he smiled at Queen, and thanked her, and gradually Queen started to believe that Alice was not a threat to her.

As they walked down the street on the summer day, another change began in Queen. Men smiled and tipped their hats to the lovely, confident Alice, and some to Queen, and Queen made a conscious effort to hold her shoulders back and her head up, when for the last few weeks she had walked with a stoop, because that made her feel less conspicuous.

They went to Alice's apartment, a spacious room with a fireplace and sitting area, and a big brass bed in one corner. The drapes were burgundy velvet, the carpet heavily patterned, the chairs elaborate and thickly padded. To a clear eye it might have looked a little tacky and worn, but to Queen it looked sumptuous.

"I picked up most of it for a song," Alice said, throwing her bonnet on the fine mahogany table. "You'd be amazed what the old mansions are selling these days, just to get some cash."

"It's beautiful," Queen said, sinking into the most comfortable chair she had ever sat in. "Is you rich?"

"No," Alice said, and laughed, and knew that the truth must come out sooner or later. "But I have some— generous admirers."

Queen sat up straight. The general immorality of the world outside The Forks was still astonishing to her, and repugnant.

"Is yo' a whore?" she asked. Her vocabulary had increased in Decatur.

Alice looked at her, somewhat sternly.

"If you want to pass as white," she said, "you must watch your speech. Nothing gives you away faster than slave talk."

Queen, who was still worried about Alice's profession, was defensive. Her many frustrations came flooding to the surface, in anger and self-pity.

"I don't want to 'pass' as white," she said, all trace of dialect gone. "I am white. And I don't want to be black, even though that's what I am. Little Miss In Between, that's me. One of God's mistakes."

She bit her lip and turned away, because Alice had been kind to her. She got up to leave, thinking she must have offended, but Alice came to her, took her face in her hands, looked into her eyes, and smiled that confident, self-mocking smile.

"Yo' ain't a mistake, chile," she said, in thick dialect. Her hands moved to Queen's straggly, dirty hair, and her eyes twinkled.

"But yo' smell," she said. "Yo' smell baaaaaad!"

Queen could not resist the warmth and generosity of Alice's personality, and she smiled, and hiccuped because she thought she was going to cry, and Alice laughed, and held her for a moment, and told her it was time for a bath.

They went down to the pump and got buckets of water, which they heated on the stove in the outhouse laundry. Alice pulled out an old zinc bathtub, filled it with water, and Queen stripped, a little shy about her nakedness in front of this woman who might be a whore, but who laughed about everything. Queen slid into the tepid water, looked at her feet which were filthy, and was appalled at how slovenly she had become. Alice set to work with soap and a cloth, chattering about slave dialect and proper speech, but Queen hardly heard her. The sudsy water, the sense of being clean again, the presence of another human being who seemed to care about her, and the relief of having a possible friend who understood her peculiar circumstances were all that mattered to her. She even ceased to worry about Alice's possible profession.

Alice was not a whore in the sense that Queen understood the word, although she had some admirers who were generous to her in return for her favors. She preferred to think of herself as a "demimondaine," although society might have had a less tolerant name for it. She had been raised to it, for her mother had been a maid in a fancy house in Atlanta, before the war. Her pappy was a white Massa who had raped her mother and, on discovering the pregnancy, had sold his slave away. Her mammy was bought by the house, and cared for by the whores during her pregnancy. When Alice was born, she was everyone's darling, and some of the regular clients would dandle her on their knees and give her little presents, and whisper into her infant ears that they would look after her when she was a big girl. Her mammy was eternally grateful to the ladies for their charity, loved them and took care of them, worried about them, comforted them when they cried and nursed them if they got sick. She lived in the dependency in back of the house, with the other slaves, and Alice had grown up in that special half world of easy virtue and rewarding vice. Of consistent tolerance for class, race, and creed, and rigid rules of behavior. Of generous benevolence by hypocritical pillars of male society, which was all tinged with the potential for violence that is inherent within a prostitute's life.

Many expected that Alice would grow up into the profession, and handsome offers were made for her virginity in her early teens, but her mammy counseled strenuously against it.

"Take care a what you got," she told Alice. "It's all a girl has got. Don't let it get wore out."

Still, she was a slave, and the time came when she had to do her Missy, the madam's, bidding. Happily, enchanted by her nubile body, the man had broken her into the adult world without too much pain. Her mammy protested vigorously, and so Alice, her deflow-ering having reduced her value, became a part-time whore, allowed to partake in the activities of the house if she wanted to, not if she didn't. Eventually, she fell in love with a handsome young man, and he, besotted with her, swore that he was going to marry her and take her away from all this. After a six-month affair of mutual bliss and reciprocal planning, he stopped coming to the whorehouse and Alice never saw him again. It broke her heart, and she became less generous in her attitudes toward men, and never again believed what they promised. She developed a small but regular clientele of older, wealthy men, who were less likely to make rash promises, and were generous with their presents.

The war came, and the siege of Atlanta by General Sherman changed Alice's life. When the triumphant Union troops swept into the city, the whorehouse was a natural arena for the drunken, rampaging soldiers. All the prostitutes were raped, and when the madam protested, she was beaten so badly she was scarred for life. Alice, cowering in the dependency with her mammy, was found by three soldiers, and when her mammy tried to stop the ravishing of her daughter, they killed her, and raped Alice anyway. The house was burned to the ground with the rest of the city, and the employees scattered to the winds. Alice, friendless and alone, spent days on the road, until she was adopted by a Confederate officer, who fed her and tended her, and gave her money to get to Decatur, and an introduction to one of his friends there.

They met in a hotel, and the friend, George, was as generous to her with his money as she was to him with her body. He set her up in a nice apartment, and visited her from time to time, when he could get away from his wife. It was a perfect arrangement, for George was not jealous of any other male admirers Alice befriended. His wife was a demanding and jealous woman. Keenly aware that secrets were difficult to keep in a country town, Alice kept a low profile, was selective with her favors, and worked hard to achieve an apparent respectability.

Alice tried to explain something of her life to Queen, avoiding the more exotic details, and concentrating on the rape, and her subsequent resolution that any white man who wanted her would have to pay dearly for the privilege.

They lay together in the big brass bed, and Queen, who had never slept in a comfortable bed, sank into the thick feather mattress and nestled her head into the clean down pillow. Alice had burned Queen's ragged old clothes, and had given her a lovely silk nightgown to wear. The window was open to the summer night, and a cool breeze calmed Queen as she listened to Alice's sad story. She tried to come to terms with Alice's admission that she accepted money from men, but had great difficulty with it.

"I couldn't do that," she said, but she didn't want to offend. "And anyway, I'm not pretty like you."

Alice laughed, and looked at her.

"What did they do to you in that big old mansion," she asked. "Didn't anyone ever say nice things to you? Didn't anyone ever tell you how pretty you are?"

Queen stared at the ceiling and remembered her life. No one had ever told her she was pretty. No one had ever said anything very nice about her. Except one person.

"Only my mammy," she said, and the memory of Easter made her sad.

"Well, your mammy was right," Alice told her. She was silent for a moment.

"Mammys always are," she said, and some soft sadness in her voice made Queen turn to look at her. She was staring at the ceiling remembering her own mammy, and a tear was trickling down her cheek.

Queen could not bear to see her new friend in distress. She reached out and gently stroked Alice's hair.

"I miss my mammy," Alice whispered.

She took Queen's hand, kissed it, and held it against her cheek. They drifted to sleep, the pair of them, side by side, each loving the closeness of someone who wanted nothing except friendship, and each remembering her own dead mammy.

69

They were fast friends within days, and the only thing that worried Queen was that she had no money and was completely reliant on Alice's generosity. Alice insisted she shouldn't worry about it, two could live as cheaply as one, and the right job for Queen would come along eventually. In the meantime, they should simply enjoy life. In doubting moments, bewildered by Alice's continuing hospitality, Queen wondered if her new friend had a devious purpose, if Alice was trying to prepare her to accept the concept of giving her favors to gentlemen, and she would become quiet, and sulk for a while, but then Alice would dazzle her with some small kindness that didn't seem to require any return, and Queen would laugh, and be happy again.

The truth was simpler than Queen's occasional imaginings. Alice needed Queen's friendship almost as much as Queen needed hers. The attentions of men came easily to her, for she was a lovely woman, but she was brutally aware of the price they expected her to pay. Despite her circumspection, and her careful cultivation of a respectable image, and despite her devoted hours of charitable work for the church, mild rumors about her virtue were whispered through the town, and no woman of any standing would befriend her. Added to this, she was living a very dangerous lie. She passed for white without question or demur, but if one hint of her true blood was generally known, she could easily have been run out of town, or worse. More sophisticated than Queen, Alice had watched the Southern whites close ranks upon themselves, vigorously and sometimes violently excluding anyone who had even the tiniest drop of black blood or was rumored to have it. Alice cleverly deflected all questions about her past, and developed a vague and tragic story of parents lost in the war if anyone persisted in asking. Which few people did. Some of her wiser gentlemen friends had suspicions of her secret, but kept quiet about it so that they might continue to enjoy her company. Wanted by men only for what they could get from her and tactfully shunned by women, Alice was lonely.

Like calls to like, and when Alice had seen the mirror image of herself in Queen, her need for a friend overcame her usual caution. There was only a small element of risk, for Queen could pass for white at least as well as Alice, and was an eager student, willing to learn the intricacies of behavior that their fragile position demanded. Alice had no desire to lead Queen astray, no designs for some career of immorality for Queen, and no expectation of Queen other than the return of friendship, and in this Alice was amply rewarded. Like sisters separated at birth who had suddenly found each other again, they had similar tastes and ambitions; yet as much as they were alike, they were also different, but these differences complemented each other. Or perhaps loneliness made them blind to how different they really were. Alice was teacher, Queen her pupil. Alice was sophisticated and Queen naive, yet Queen longed to be worldly-wise, and Alice was desperate to know less. Each wanted to be loved and settled in some stable domestic situation, and if Queen was more optimistic about the immediate prospect of this, her simple faith blunted Alice's cynicism. They were united in their determination to live as white, and if Queen was less acutely aware of the dangers of being thought black, it was only by degree.

Alice listened soberly to the story of Queen's life, and smiled at her blind adoration of her Jass. Alice had never known her own pappy, and needed a father figure sorely, and while she distrusted men, she sympathized with Queen's irrational faith.

It amused Alice, who had grown up among paints and powders, that Queen didn't even know how to put makeup on, and they spent a delightful evening subtly coloring Queen's face. When Queen looked at the results in the mirror, she gasped at her own beauty. It intrigued Alice that Queen had no clothes, and she ransacked her wardrobe for gowns that her friend might wear. It enchanted Alice that Queen had never been to a dance, except to watch and serve as a slave, and she wondered how Queen would respond to an evening of simple, uncluttered fun. And it would be an excellent test of Queen's behavior in the midst of the enemy.

Queen was triumphant. She looked lovely in a lilac gown of Alice's, her hair in ringlets, and her face artfully painted. Alice, in blue, laughed at Queen's nervous excitement. They walked into the church hall together on a warm Saturday night, and were immediately cheered as the belles of the ball. Some might have thought the dance a little hick, but to Queen it was a glamorous occasion. The tables and chairs had been cleared to the side, the hall was decorated with lanterns, and a small band played good music badly on the stage.

An older gentleman, George, her old friend, offered Alice his arm, and when they swept away to dance,

Queen panicked at being left alone. She crept to her favorite corner, for this same hall was the soup kitchen at other times, and watched the dancers dance, just as she used to watch balls at The Forks, and swayed to the music, and prayed that someone would ask her to dance and thought she would sink to the floor in embarrassment if anyone did. She saw a tall, moderately handsome man staring at her and glanced away, but as immediately glanced back, and the man winked at her. Queen blushed and looked to the floor, and saw a pair of feet walking toward her. She looked up into the eyes of the moderately handsome young man, who introduced himself as Morgan, and called her gorgeous.

"Sir, I am a lady!" Queen gasped, because she couldn't think of anything else to say.

Morgan grinned. "You're also the prettiest thing in the room," he laughed, and offered his arm. "Shall we?"

Queen saw Alice nodding encouragement to her, and took the plunge. She accepted Morgan's arm, and they moved onto the dance floor. She could hardly believe this was happening to her, when, not so very long ago, she had been destitute. Now she was happy, dancing in a pretty dress with a moderately handsome young man. It was the stuff of dreams.

She was a good dancer and had been taught well, but excitement and nervousness made her clumsy. Morgan winced in pain.

"You may be a lady, but you don't dance very well," he said, and Queen was mortified. She began to apologize, but Morgan was blithe.

"It's all right," he said, laughing again. "I've got strong boots on."

His laughter was infectious, and Queen relaxed and remembered her lessons, and danced the night away, and even allowed Morgan to peck her on the cheek when they said good night.

She danced round the room when she and Alice got

home, and poured out her delight at the evening. She couldn't remember when she'd had such a good time, despite Morgan's wandering hands, which had added delightful spice to the evening.

Alice was pleased. Queen had passed her first public test superbly, and all her friends, especially George, had commented on Queen's beauty and manners. Vibrant with youthful energy, they chatted till dawn about the evening and about men, and then climbed into bed and drifted to sleep in each other's arms, secure and happy.

Queen agreed to a date with Morgan and saw him a few times, but while he was always laughing, his hands were always wandering, and one day, on the riverbank, they wandered too far. Queen told him off, and wouldn't see him again.

This came on top of a scolding from Alice, who was beginning to wonder if her student was learning far too well. She had been with Queen earlier that day, shopping, and a poor black had approached them, begging for money. Queen had snapped at him not to bother her, and called him a nigger. Alice was appalled, gave the man a few coins, and called Queen a little minx. Only weeks ago, Queen had been in the same state as the beggar; now she was all airs and graces, putting labels on herself.

"You'd better be careful," Alice said, "because pride usually comes before a very nasty fall."

Queen flushed, and pouted, but realized she was in the wrong and apologized. Her afternoon with Morgan, however, did nothing to improve her humor. Looking forward to sharing her misery with Alice, she came home to a cold supper waiting on the table, and a note saying that her friend would be out for the evening until late. Queen guessed that Alice was seeing George or one of her other admirers, and, upset by Morgan and this first real evidence of Alice's immorality, she sulked for the evening. She climbed into bed early, and lay waiting for Alice to come home.

Alice had a fine evening. While she was fond of Queen, she had a deep need for the company of older men and the security they represented to her. She had curtailed many of her activities since Queen's arrival, but now it was reassuring to be in George's company, to be dined and wined in a private room at a small hotel, and to be made love to by a man of some experience. And she had some very good news.

When she came home soon after midnight, Queen was waiting for her, tucked up in bed with the sheet pulled securely under her chin.

Queen's eyes darted with anger. "Where you been?" she demanded. Alice was not surprised at her reaction. She knew that Queen had become dependent on her, perhaps overly so, and she was relieved that, if Queen behaved properly, that dependence would soon be reduced.

"Out," she said, taking off her bonnet and checking her hair in the mirror.

"You sleep with George?" Queen demanded again, and Alice shrugged.

"You're nothing but a whore, despite your fancy words," Queen snapped, and Alice snapped back.

"How I survive is my business, Queen," she said. "Don't call me names."

"It bothers me," Queen replied, burying her face in the pillow. Alice came and sat on the edge of the bed.

"That's a pity, because George is a very nice man, and very rich," she told Queen, enjoying the news that she had. "And he has a job for you, if you want it."

Queen looked at her in horror. "I won't do that sort of work!"

"You won't work in a flower shop?" Alice murmured, a smile dancing at the corners of her mouth.

The effect was all she could have desired. Queen stared at Alice, whose smile had broadened into a grin.

696

Suddenly, Queen squealed in delight, and grabbed Alice. The two of them rolled on the bed together, laughing and making great plans.

It was just the job for Queen. Although few folk had much money to spare, flowers were a cheap extravagance; a small bouquet did much to alleviate the stress of reduced circumstances, and those who did still have money were conscious of the social niceties. The small shop was in a building George owned, and was open only three days a week. On the other days, Queen would ride around the country in a cart, gathering abundant summer wildflowers, or buying garden blooms from people who were happy to get a few pennies for what had cost them nothing to grow. On the days when the shop was open, Queen would arrive early in the morning and fashion her harvest into pretty bunches and bouquets, and she soon learned how to make simple wreaths for the dead. Surrounded by nature's artless beauty, she blossomed herself, and was popular with her customers. The fragrance of the flowers and the simple constancy of their perennial renewal seemed to attach itself to her, and she relaxed and lost the edginess that insecurity had developed in her. She didn't even care anymore about Alice's occasional nocturnal expeditions, but was tolerant of all her friend's foibles.

She looked after her customers well, and was sensitive to their requests, often scouring the countryside to fulfill their special orders. And she always made sure she had roses, for there was one customer, a tall, darkly handsome man, immaculately dressed, who came by almost every day, and always bought only a single rose. He had a slight limp in his right leg, and walked with a cane. Intrigued by him, attracted to him, she once asked him if the rose was for a special woman friend, and he turned to her with sad, sorrowful eyes.

"It is for the grave of my poor dear mother," he said.

Queen's heart bounded. She expressed her sympathy, and the man went away with his rose, while Queen fell into a daydream. This melancholy man was her ideal of her prince.

Every day she had his rose ready for him, and every day he paid, thanked her, and left. He never smiled, but sometimes he looked deep into her eyes, and made Queen's legs turn to jelly.

On a hot June day he came into the shop, and Queen apologized for her roses. He always bought white, but Queen had only red roses that day. He looked at the lovely flower, and then into the distance. He paid for the rose, but didn't leave.

"Is something wrong?" Queen asked, and now, for the first time since she had known him, he smiled.

"No," he said. "But this one, I think, is for you."

He gave Queen the red rose; he took her hand and kissed it gently, then left. Queen almost swooned with delight.

Within a week he had asked her to accompany him on an evening stroll by the riverbank. Fireflies danced in the bushes beside the river, and the lamplighter was lighting lanterns on the levee. He introduced himself as Digby, and he was the complete Southern gentleman.

"From the first moment I saw you, surrounded by roses, I haven't been able to get you out of my mind," he told her. "I trust you do not think me forward, ma'am?"

Queen was trying to be the complete Southern gentlewoman.

"Why, no, sir," she said, remembering Miss Lizzie at her simpering best. "I was most pleased when you asked me to accompany you this evening."

"You are not from these parts?" Digby asked her.

Queen hardly hesitated for a moment. The evening was flawless, and she had learned well from Alice. Mystery, Alice had told her, intrigues a man.

"No," she murmured. "My home is—far away—"

"And your family?" Digby persisted, but still Queen did not fret.

"A very old family, sir," she told him. "My pappy—" she cursed herself inwardly at the slip, smiled at him as if she had let loose a pet name, and corrected herself. "My papa was a colonel in the war. He lost an arm."

Digby smiled ruefully and tapped his leg with his cane.

"You fought in the war?" Queen asked him, to deflect attention from her own background.

"It was my duty and my strong and passionate cause," Digby said softly. "Your father is Colonel—?"

Queen fanned herself with her hankie, and pretended she hadn't heard him. "My," she said, "the evening is so warm. I wonder if we might find a cool drink somewhere? I declare I am dying of thirst."

Digby laughed, and offered her his arm. "I cannot have you die, my dear," he said. "I have waited too long to find you."

They walked away toward the town, and talked of the weather. Digby didn't ask about her family again that evening, but spoke of the war, and the chaos of the reconstruction of the South. Queen sighed with relief, thinking she had got out of a difficult situation rather well.

She saw him again the next day, and the next. Each evening they went for a stroll along the river, and he was never less than a gentleman to Queen. She loved his innate good manners and his poetic civility to her, and began to believe that this was how her father must have been, as a young man.

Digby did not push the subject of her family further than Queen thought was tolerable. She admitted she came from Alabama, and that her father was Colonel Jackson, but she never referred to Florence, and spoke only of "the plantation" when talking about her home. She elaborated on her own childhood with stories of

699

her half brothers and sisters as though they were full siblings, and gradually she came to believe her own stories, because they had so much of the truth in them. If Digby's questions became too provocative, she would ask him about his own family, and especially his mother.

"She died from grief, I think," Digby said. "My father was killed in the war, but she accepted that. She believed it was our duty to fight and, if necessary, die for our country. When we lost the war, she lost her cause, and passed away grieving for our vanished world."

The romantic in Queen completely understood, but the survivor in her was confused.

"But she could have lived," she said, thinking of Jass, and Miss Lizzie and Miss Sally. "She could have gone on—"

"In the cesspool that the South has become?" Digby said bitterly. He paused for a moment, as if looking for the words to express his deepest feelings.

"It is against God's law to pretend that the blacks are equal to us," he said.

Queen did not dare turn away, but stared at him as if hypnotized. Her mind was crying, screaming. He could not be so cruel.

"We offended God when we lost the war, and he is visiting a terrible judgment on us. Look what is happening to the country now. Imagine what it will be like when they start electing niggers to Congress."

He looked at the twilight sky.

"I hope God is satisfied," he said.

Queen knew she should say nothing, but she had to say something. She had to defend her indefensible position.

"Do you hate black people so much?" she whispered, and added an outrageous variant on the truth. "I was always very fond of our nigras."

To her surprise, Digby laughed. "I don't hate them; they simply are not our equals," he said. "But they are not to blame for what happened. The Yankees are to blame. It's the Yankees I hate."

Queen breathed a small sigh of relief. She knew she was on the thinnest of ice, but as long as he didn't actually hate nigras, and as long as he never knew the truth about her, they could be happy together. For she hoped that they would be together.

Alice was less sanguine.

"You be very careful," she said. "Sooner or later, he's going to have to know the truth."

They were working in the soup kitchen, preparing food, whispering to each other.

"I already told him the truth," Queen said defensively.

"That your mother was a slave?" Alice asked, in a taunting whisper, and Queen had to admit the truth.

"No, not that part," she said. Why wouldn't Alice leave her alone? Why did she have to spoil it? Digby was the most beautiful thing that had ever happened to Queen. He had asked her out to the theater on the Fourth of July, and Queen had never been to a theater. Everything Digby did was new to Queen, and she loved him for it.

"Oh, I could spank you," Alice said angrily, who had asked George about Digby. He knew very little about the man, but enough. "He's a white Southern gentleman from a good family, and he was an officer in the Confederate Army. How's he going to feel when he discovers he's paying court to a nigra?"

Queen had no answer for her, except her usual, blind response. "If I don't tell him, he won't know!"

Alice pressed her advantage. She wasn't worried that Queen was seeing Digby, she was worried that Queen was becoming much too fond of him.

"Every moment you're with him, you're living a lie, and one day you'll slip," she said. Queen looked at her angrily.

"He's good to me, he looks after me," she retorted. "I feel wonderful when I'm with him. For the first time in my life I feel as if a man cares about me."

She looked so lost and lonely and vulnerable, and yet so alive, that Alice realized she had a hopeless case of infatuation on her hands. She prayed it didn't develop into love, for she remembered her own first love and the pain it had bought her, and she didn't want that same pain for Queen. But alarm bells were clanging in her head, for Digby was an enigma to her, and the unknown frightened Alice.

"Then let him take care of you, but don't care for him too much. Don't let it become love," she said, knowing it was too late. "Love is dangerous for women like us."

Queen, hopelessly, helplessly in love, bridled at the comparison. "I ain't like you," she growled, and turned away to serve food to a woman in the line. The woman, thin and hungry and rattily dressed, much like Queen had been not so very long ago, took her soup and biscuits gratefully. She looked around to make sure no one was listening, and whispered her awful gratitude.

"Thank you," she said. "Sister."

It hit Queen like a thunderbolt. The woman scuttled away to eat, and Queen stood staring after her. How had she guessed? More important, why hadn't Queen known? Was it true? Did you become so secure you got careless? All her self-assurance flooded out of her. She turned away, and saw the flames in the small stove where the soup was kept hot. The flames danced in her mind, jolting her back to a nightmare chase through a dark forest, and a memory of two black men sitting round a campfire who had rejected her when she was in such distress. She felt the hunger she felt then, the need to eat, the need for comfort, the need for protection and reassurance.

She did an odd thing. She snatched a biscuit from the pile and stuffed it into her pocket.

She turned away, feeling guilty and afraid, and saw Alice staring at her.

"What are you doing?" Alice asked in amazement, for Queen had no need to filch food.

"Nuttin'," Queen whispered miserably, slipping into dialect. "Ain't doin' nuttin'."

70

Digby had guessed that Queen had colored blood almost from the moment he saw her, for he was a consummate liar himself and lived a fantasy existence, of his own fabrication. Almost nothing that he told her was true, although some of it had a basis in fact. His father, still living, had not fought in the war, but was a moderately successful lawyer in Baton Rouge, Louisiana, too often distracted by business to pay much attention to his family. His mother, also still living, doted on her only surviving son, and spoiled him as a boy, indulging his every whim. Strong, arrogant, and handy with his fists, Digby had been a bully at school, who delighted in beating up younger, smaller boys, and seemed to get some perverse pleasure from it. His preferred victims were the younger sons of the landed gentry. Digby resented his lowlier station, and despised his father for not having made more of a fortune.

Expelled from two schools, he was sent to a military academy, where, having survived the violent initiation ceremonies himself, he became an expert at inflicting corporal punishment on those who came after him. He was not unpopular with certain of his like-minded peers, for he could present a pleasant face to the world. He learned to cultivate that poetic melancholy that so entranced Queen, ingratiated himself with his tutors,

703

and persuaded them that he could not possibly be guilty of the injuries he was sometimes accused of inflicting. He did not lose his virginity at the military academy; he inflicted it, forcefully, on an unwilling slave girl, in the company of two of his friends. When the girl protested, Digby beat her until she bled, and when it was his turn to have her, the taste of her blood on his lips, the sound of her screams in his ears, were precious to him, and infinitely exciting.

He was asked to leave college after a nasty incident involving another slave girl, whom he had beaten nearly to death. Her Massa had protested to the dean, and Digby was sent home in disgrace. His father despaired of him, but at his mother's urging gave him a job in his own office, as a law clerk. It bored Digby, who preferred to spend his time and his salary cultivating an image of himself as a gentleman during the day, and in taverns and houses of ill repute at night. He was discreet about his nocturnal pleasures, put some rein on his propensity for violence, and was favorably regarded as a scoundrel boy who had sown his wild oats and had rehabilitated himself into an eligible man. Although not welcome in the better country houses, he was popular among the small middle class, the city folk, and especially those parents seeking a good match for a less-attractive daughter.

He told Queen about the first love of his life, but a romantic version of that ill-fated liaison. The young woman in question had fallen hopelessly in love with Digby, and they had become engaged. Then the war came.

"I don't know how or why," Digby said sadly to Queen, "but she changed. Or I changed. Who can tell? I knew she wasn't happy with me anymore, so I even persuaded her—"

He broke off. Queen was sure she saw a tear in his eye.

"Forgive me, my sweet love; I shouldn't tell you this," he said in a tone of infinite regret. "I even let us become lovers, before marriage, thinking that might keep us together, but—there was a captain in the army. She ran away with him."

For it moment it appeared that he could not go on, and Queen touched his hand gently.

"Perhaps she thought him more of a man than I," Digby said ruefully. He indicated his leg.

"I lost the full use of my leg in the battle of Wilson's Creek. I am not a complete man anymore."

The truth was rather different. Digby and the young woman had become engaged, and had become lovers, but against her will. Unable to control his lust, obsessed with finding out what female blood looked like on white skin rather than black, Digby had raped his fiancée, and beaten her violently. She told no one of her disgrace until she became pregnant and tried to kill herself. In the ensuing scandal, her brothers broke Digby's leg with an iron bar. They would have killed him but for their sister's hysterical intervention, and they contented themselves with twisting the fractured leg, to make it difficult to mend. Laudanum became his only comfort. Digby's father gave him a sum of money and promised a weekly allowance if he would never come within a hundred miles of Baton Rouge again. It broke his mother's heart.

Digby volunteered for the army, but although they would not have him at first, as a cripple, they took him later as a quartermaster, and his was a pleasant war, far removed from the front lines. After the surrender, he wandered the South looking for somewhere to live, and had settled in Decatur, a small town far enough away to make rumors of his scandalous past unlikely.

His father's regular remittances averted a need to work, and he spent his days in idleness and his nights at the inn. So it was that he saw a beautiful young mulatta working in a flower shop, and wanted her at that moment, and set his heart upon having her. Queen's denial of her blood and her fabrications about her past amused him, and he played along with them. The more complex the chase, the more intense would be his eventual pleasure, and the more satisfying her pain.

Alone at night, he would laugh at Queen's innocent faith in the success of her deception. Did she really think he didn't know? He could smell a nigra bitch a mile away.

On the Fourth of July, he dressed in formal evening wear, hired a hansom cab, and called for Queen at her lodgings. She was wearing an elegant pink dress that left her lovely shoulders bare, and Digby could hardly restrain himself. He kissed her hand and her arm, and then her creamy shoulders, and the desire to sink his teeth into that exquisite flesh, to hear her gasp in pain, and to see a drop of her nigra blood spring forth was almost irresistible to him. Soon, he told himself. It must be soon, for the old, familiar urges were upon him.

Queen and Alice had taken considerable care with her toilette. Alice had made the gown herself, and gave Queen a string of white beads that looked like pearls as her only jewelry. Before Queen left, Alice repeated her warning, and Queen smiled, and assured her that everything was going to be all right.

Digby's ardent greeting, romantic yet with a hint of something dark and unsettling, awoke curious feelings in Queen. When she felt his teeth bite hard into her shoulder, it disturbed her, and she gasped in pain. Digby looked at her, and his smile was not reassuring. As she rode to the theater beside her handsome beau, Alice's warnings rang in her ears, and she began to worry, for the look in Digby's eyes was one she had seen before, in other men, at other, frightening times.

Independence Day was an ambivalent festival in the

defeated South, but occasions for a celebration of any kind were rare, and society made the most of them. Women brought their loveliest gowns, hardly worn since before the war, and the evening clothes of many of the men gave off a vague smell of camphor, used in storage to repel moths. The street was brightly lighted, and the theater patriotically decorated in red, white, and blue bunting, although there was little evidence of the Union flag. A crowd had gathered outside to enjoy the spectacle of the arrivals, and cheered their favorite local politicians and city fathers, especially those who had been vociferous against the Yankees. Poor women sighed with envy at the silks and satins, the feathers and fans, and the sight of a rare piece of jewelry made them gasp in appreciation. There were beggars and buskers, and food vendors and balloon sellers, and musicians, and a few disabled veterans, staring with envying eyes.

Digby's carriage pulled up, and a footman helped Queen alight. Her simple beauty brought audible response from the excited crowd. A shabbily dressed black man ran to the horse and grabbed the bridle.

"Look after the horses, suh?" he begged, for sometimes he earned a few cents that way, but the coachman told him to get out of the way, and the beggar turned to Digby.

"Please, suh, just a few pennies," he pleaded. The coachman, who was also black, flicked his whip at the beggar.

"You heard the Massa," he shouted. "Out of the way."

The beggar, who had been lashed too often when he was a slave, angrily grabbed the whip, and pulled the coachman from his box.

"Yo' don't whip me," he cried. "I ain't a slave no mo'."

A scuffle developed and a crowd gathered round,

cheering or hissing or just enjoying the sport. Lashing out at anyone, the beggar knocked a bystander against the horrified Queen.

Queen screamed, and Digby struck the beggar hard, viciously hard, with his cane. The beggar roared in anger and launched himself at Digby, who raised his cane again, quite ready to defend himself. His eyes were sparkling at the prospect of the violence, while a little part of his mind wondered what Queen was feeling.

Others, street-rough whites, rushed to Digby's aid and quickly subdued the furious beggar.

"He cain't do that," the beggar yelled. "He cain't hit a nigger no mo'!"

A burly white man disagreed with him. "We can do what we damn well like, coon," he said, slamming his fist into the beggar's face, knocking him senseless. Digby was enjoying himself, the evening was off to a splendid start, but considerations of etiquette were demanded now. He put his arm around Queen and shepherded her toward the theater. There were cheers of approval from some of the white bystanders, and the mayor, who had seen it all, greeted them in the foyer.

"Well done, old man," he congratulated Digby, shaking his hand. "I don't know what the world's coming to."

Digby smiled. "Damn monkeys should be shot," he said. And looked at Queen.

She was miserable. The evening had been so full of promise, but the ugly fight, and the statements of hatred toward blacks, which she had heard often but had not expected on this night of nights, depressed her. She worried that perhaps Alice was right, and she wanted to flee the theater, run home to where she was loved, and have nothing more to do with Digby. She had persuaded herself that his racial intolerance was no threat to her, since he would never know her true blood, but now she was not so sure. She had seen a

708

frightening look of lusty joy in his eyes when he hit the beggar, as when he had bitten her shoulder, and for a dreadful moment she imagined him hitting her as brutally if ever he found out the truth. Yet now he was himself again, charming and gentle, escorting her into the lamplit theater and introducing her to people of rank and honor, and being completely attentive to her. But she could not rid her mind of the bloody face of the beggar.

She had never been to a theater before, and it worked a little of its magic on her. She felt a rush of expectation when the band struck up, the lamps were dimmed, and the curtain rose on a brightly lighted stage. The pretty costumes and gaudily painted scenery distracted her for a while, but when a soprano started to sing "Dixie," the audience rose to their feet to sing with her. Queen loved the song, but she was supremely conscious that she, a mulatta, was alone among two hundred whites chorusing the anthem of the Confederacy, and the strident passion of their voices made her want to cry.

After the show they walked down to the riverbank to see the fireworks. It was a small, cheap show, but glorious to Queen, who had never seen fireworks before. Her fears disappeared in a cluster of rocketing color, and she turned to Digby, her eyes glistening.

"Isn't it wonderful," she cried, but he did not seem to be sharing her excitement.

"Those of us who fought for the Confederation don't find much joy in it," he said.

Queen turned back to look at the fireworks again, her spirits dashed.

"I wonder if your father is celebrating in Florence," Digby asked her casually, softly.

Queen didn't look at him. Fear shimmered down her spine. She had never told him exactly where she came from. But he knew.

"I know all about you," she heard Digby say. "There aren't too many Jacksons of Alabama. I know his

709

plantation is called The Forks of Cypress, and that it is a few miles outside Florence. Not so very far from here."

The image of Digby striking the beggar came into Queen's mind again. She thought she might run, but he would catch her easily. She stood stock-still, staring fixedly at the river.

"I also know that his estate has gone to rack and ruin since the war," he said.

It hadn't been so difficult for Digby to find out, for Florence was not so very far away, and he had many connections. He guessed what was going through her mind, for he had chosen his moment to tell her, and the words, most carefully. It amused him to watch her, too scared even to look at him. A tiny, frightened sparrow, trembling, in the expectation of immediate disaster.

He let the implicit threat drift into the night, and then put a smile into his voice.

"You silly goose. We're none of us what we were." He could see her tension melt away and her beautiful shoulders droop, from relief.

"I've watched my family's fortune fade to nothing but a stash of useless Confederate notes," he continued. "We are all poor now."

She turned to look at him at last. She had been such a fool. He didn't know everything about her; he knew only what anyone could find out. Fear still lingered in her eyes, but it was overridden by her need for reassurance. He touched her sweet soft neck and let his fingers trace up to her chin. Gently, he pulled her face up to his. His mouth was inches from hers.

"Here we are," he whispered. "Two lost and lonely people who have found each other at last."

He kissed her tenderly, letting his lips just brush against hers, and looked into her eyes again.

"I've no right to ask you, and I know I should ask your father first, but I think he will understand," he said. "Will you marry me?"

710

Queen stared at him, in wonder, and dread, and foolishness. She felt faint, and thought she was going to fall, but his strong arms were there to support her. He held her to him and kissed her, and she felt his tongue caress her lips and edge its way into her mouth.

Every rational instinct in her body told her to say no to him, to break away, leave him now, get away from him now, but she was betrayed by all her senses, and her heart and her mouth said yes.

Alice called her a fool, a blind, stupid, dangerous fool, and slapped Queen's face to knock some sense into her. She couldn't marry Digby and keep her blood secret forever. He was bound to find out, by a slip, or a well-meaning acquaintance, or what if she had a baby, and a little pickaninny popped out? At the very least, Digby would want to meet Queen's father, and then he would know that Queen had tricked him, lied to him from the moment that she met him. And then what would he do?

The image of the bloody beggar came into Queen's mind, and she wept, but Alice was pitiless. Queen blurted out the story of the fight at the theater, and told Alice of Digby's frequent statement of hatred for blacks, and Alice stared at her in consternation.

"Then why did you say yes to him?" she asked coldly.

"I don't know!" Queen told her truthfully. She didn't know why. Except that she was fond of him, and wanted to be loved. And the potential for violence that she had seen in him so alarmed her she would have done anything not to offend him.

Alice fought hard to make her see reason, but even if Queen agreed with her, she didn't know what to do.

"Get out of this, girl, as fast as you can," Alice told her. "You've been playing with fire too long."

They argued for half the night. Queen knew Alice was right, but was too stubborn about her own romantic mistake, and too frightened of Digby to tell him the truth. Alice blamed herself, but not in a way that Queen understood. Alice was regretting that she had been stupid enough to take in this foolish girl who was putting everything Alice had worked so hard to achieve at risk.

"Don't you understand? It isn't just you," Alice insisted. "It's all of us who can pass. We all come under suspicion then, just for knowing you."

Finally, Alice delivered her ultimatum.

"If you don't break it off, you will have to leave," she said.

Queen could not believe her ears, could not believe her friend was saying this, but it had its effect. Caught between the devil and the deep blue sea, Queen could only choose the lesser of the two evils. Even if Digby hit her, as he had hit the beggar, it could not be worse than losing the only security she had, her friend and her home.

Emotionally exhausted, Queen slept badly and late. She dressed soberly, and made her way to Digby's lodgings. She tapped on the door, and when he opened it, he smiled and expressed his pleasure and surprise, but wondered if they should go out, for they would be alone in his apartment. The lack of a chaperone did not bother Queen. It did not affect what she had to do.

She had never been to his apartment before, and was surprised at how untidy the sitting room was. She had thought him a man of neat habits. Perhaps she was seeing him with clearer eyes, for suddenly he didn't seem to be quite as handsome as before, but fitted into his seedy surroundings. The drapes were drawn against the midday sun, and papers were scattered over the floor. Through the open door she could see into his bedroom. The bed was unmade, and there was a smell of dirty clothes in the air. He hadn't shaved yet, and his shirt was unbuttoned and the sleeves rolled up. She could see his muscular arms, and he made no attempt to put on a jacket, or disguise his body from her. His smile, which had made her heart melt only a short few days ago, now seemed to be leering, and a little contemptuous. She was very frightened of him. The air in the room was close and stuffy, and when he asked why she had come, she thought she might faint. She looked very pale, and he sat her on a chair and brought her some brandy. She choked on the strong drink, and he laughed, and assured her it was completely medicinal. She could not resist the feeling that he was enjoying her discomfort.

He came close to her, sat beside her, and stared at her. His look was unnerving, for she could see no trace of his usual kindness in it.

"I wrote to your father today," he said.

The room spun about her, and Queen fell to the floor in a swoon.

Digby picked her up, carried her into the bedroom, and laid her on the bed. He didn't bother to tidy up the covers. He didn't need neatness for what he planned to do.

Queen was not insensible for long, and when she woke she was disoriented for a moment. Then she remembered where she was, and clutched at her clothes, but he had not molested her. He was not in the room, and she got up to leave. Perhaps he had gone out, and she could get away and come back some other time to do what had to be done, but then she thought of Alice, and lay back on the bed in despair.

There was a tap on the door, and Digby came in, carrying a small bottle and a glass.

"Wide awake?" he asked. She nodded, and wondered how long she had been asleep.

"Only a few minutes," he said, sitting on the edge of the bed beside her. "Now, drink this. It will make you feel better."

He poured a little clear liquid from the bottle into the glass, and gave it to her to drink. Queen knew from the

713

smell it was laudanum, and she didn't want it, but he insisted. Reluctantly, she swallowed a little of the drug. She was surprised that he took a sip of it too.

He stroked her face and told her how pretty she was, and how naughty they were to be alone in his bedroom. His hand caressed her neck and her shoulders, and she tried to pull away, but she felt lazy, and warm, and nothing seemed very important. His voice was so soothing.

"Relax," he crooned, "let the drug do its work. Don't you feel better? Don't you feel good? Don't you feel as if you're floating on a fluffy pink cloud?"

Queen nodded slowly, for she did feel like that. He told her he took the opium to relieve the pain of his war wounds, but he had not been wounded in the war, and had been addicted to laudanum for some years. His voice had no sense or meaning to her; she was drifting in a timeless mist and nothing mattered anymore. It didn't matter when his hand moved down to her breasts and he fondled them with gentle but increasing urgency. It didn't matter when his hand moved down to her hips and down her leg and pulled up her dress and lifted her petticoat. It didn't matter when he kissed her full on the mouth and forced his tongue into her. It didn't matter when she felt his hand move up inside her leg, or that she could feel his hard manhood pressing against her. She was lost in an erotic heaven, and his lulling voice, speaking of his love for her, was the music of angels.

But now something else began to happen. Perhaps she had not taken enough of the opium to surrender to him. The rough stubble on his chin grazed her cheek, and when he kissed her, he chewed on her lips, until it became unpleasant to her. He started to pull at her camiknickers, and when she tried to stop him, he became more forceful and pushed her back on the bed. The fear of his increasing violence battled with the drug, and she struggled against him, which made him laugh. He pinched her hard, and slapped her rump, and it hurt her. She cried out, and her cries of pain mingled with his cries of lust. He hit her again, and there was nothing playful in it, and she saw that same look in his eyes as when he hit the beggar. She tried to twist away from him, but he grabbed her by the arms and dragged her back to him. He ripped her petticoat and her knickers and forced himself between her legs, mauling her breasts, slapping her face, biting her shoulders. He wrenched at the buttons on his pants, and pushed her head down to his groin. When she screamed, he hit her again and told her to do it to prove that she loved him.

He thrust himself into her mouth, and pushed her head down onto him. Queen gagged and gasped and pulled herself free, and screamed at him the one thing she thought might stop him.

"I's nigra!" she cried.

But he only laughed.

"You stupid slut," he said. "Do you think I didn't know?"

She stared at him, unable to believe him. How could he have known?

"It was a game," he said. "A funny, delightful game. I wanted to see how far I could go before you told me. Did you really think I would marry a slut like you?"

Her last defense was gone, and all she could do was try and get away. He might do anything to her now.

"Now the game's over and you lost," he said. "So you have to pay."

She tried to run from the bed, but he caught her, and hit her with all his might. She screamed and fell, blood running from her mouth. The sight of it brought a terrible new intensity to his already frightening urgency.

"Bitch," he yelled, and hit her again. "Cheap, nigra bitch." He smiled an awful smile.

"You'll get what cheap nigra bitches deserve."

He forced himself into her mouth again, thrust himself into her while she gagged and cried. He hit her rump, a dozen times, each time harder than before. When she tried to pull free from him again, he smashed his fist into her face. He tore open her bodice and bit her breasts until he drew blood.

He twisted her over onto her face, and locked her arm behind her back with his hand until she thought he must pull it from its socket. With his other hand he pulled up her dress and forced himself into her from behind, like a dog. Yet he was careful. Even at the pitch of his frenzied desire, a greater passion ruled him, and at the time of his climax, he spilled his seed onto her and not into her, for there were enough nigger bastards in the world already.

Pain was searing through her like lightning. She screamed, and begged God to save her, and eventually God could not bear to see her in so much agony, and delivered a merciful oblivion unto His tormented daughter.

71

He kicked her out when he had finished with her, toward dawn. Beaten and bloody, she staggered through the quiet streets to her only sanctuary. Her mind refused to remember what she had been through, and all she understood was the pain of the present. Her clothes were torn, and she pulled her coat tight around her, as if to cover her shame. Walking was difficult for her, and some of her wounds were still oozing blood.

The stairs to Alice's apartment daunted her, and she sat for a while, halfway up, and tried to find some reserves of strength. But she was so close to home, so close to help, so close to someone who might understand what she had been through, that she pulled herself up, and went to the apartment.

Alice had not slept. She was still fully clothed, staring at the empty fireplace. When Queen came into the room, Alice saw her sorry state, but felt little pity for her. Violence toward women was not uncommon in the world in which Alice had grown up, and what Queen had done was worse than any physical beating.

"You told him," she said. It was not a question, but Queen nodded, puzzled by the coldness of her friend.

"We're not going to be married," she whispered, and sank into a chair. She wanted Alice to come to her, hold her, caress her, and tell her that she was loved. Alice did something else instead. She went to the window and pulled back the drapes, to reveal a pane of shattered glass.

"How could you tell him?" she asked.

Queen's head swam. She had done what Alice wanted. Why was she so angry?

Alice picked up a small rock from the floor. A note was tied to it, and she gave it to Queen to read.

Some words had been roughly penciled on the note: "All nigra bitches will die."

Alice shrugged. "Him, or his friends," she said. "They'll all know by now."

She turned on Queen in anger. "How could you tell him? You knew you were playing with fire. How many warnings did you need?"

Queen hung on desperately to the only truth she knew. "He raped me," she whispered piteously.

It made no difference to Alice. Rape was part of a woman's destiny to her. Survival was all, and Queen had put their survival at perilous risk. Word would spread like wildfire, a couple of mulattas successfully passing as white, and the consequences of that public knowledge were too hideous to imagine. Queen's whispered admission of her blood was a hurricane that tore

717

down Alice's elaborate house of cards. She guessed what had happened.

"And you told him, to try to save your precious virginity?" Alice said, in amazement. She had no concept of what virginity might mean to a girl like Queen.

Queen nodded miserably. "It was all I had," she said. And then anger, ignited by Digby's cruelty and Alice's cynicism, exploded inside her.

"And no one got the right to take it away from me, without my say-so," she blazed. "No matter what the cost!"

The little tirade cost her dearly, sapping the last of her energy. She slumped in the chair again, caressing her beaten body. Her mind was numb as she listened to Alice's plans. Queen would have to leave, get out, get away, somewhere, anywhere, Huntsville, Savannah, North, to the devil, for all Alice cared. Alice would lie low, and wait until any hue and cry had died down. She would spread the word that she had kicked Queen out when she discovered she was mulatta. Her admirers would help, and perhaps she might survive. She set about writing a note to George, ignoring Queen, as if she had already gone.

Queen did not even beg to stay. She knew it was useless, and she didn't want to remain in the same town as Digby. Or even Alice. She cleaned herself up as best she could, and tended her injuries. She had no plan for the future and dared not remember the past. There was only what she had to do now. She wanted to take nothing of Alice's with her, she wanted to leave as she had arrived, but simple public decency demanded at least a change of clothes, and she put another cheap dress into a bag. She didn't bother saying good-bye to Alice, for she knew there would be no response.

She avoided the center of town because she didn't want to run into anyone who knew her, but made her way to the river. She stood on the bridge looking down at the Tennessee River, and thought how simple it would be to end it all, to let herself slip, fall into the fast, flowing water and welcome oblivion.

She didn't slip, she didn't fall. She had no idea of where she would go, or what she would do, but she would go somewhere and she would do something, because she could not believe that God intended anything else for her.

She picked up her bag and walked across the bridge, a distant memory ringing in her ears. The talk she used to hear among the slaves was her drumbeat.

North. North. North.

North was the promised land to a slave, and if she could get to the North, her troubles would be magically, mysteriously, over.

The road to the North led to Huntsville, and Queen trudged along, a weary pilgrim making her lonely progress.

It was hot. Heat haze shimmered on the road, and dust from the passing carriages sprayed into her hair, into her wounds, calming them, binding them, but no one who passed by offered a ride. Blacks thought she was white, and whites thought she was trash, and the only person she had to talk to was God, but she cursed her friend now, for what He had brought her to.

She walked slowly and rested at the roadside frequently, because every step was painful, and by the end of the day, she had only covered a short distance. As a bloodred sunset swept the land, she couldn't go on anymore, and when she saw an old barn by a deserted farm, abandoned in the war, she went to it, to find some little corner in which to rest.

Others, a few blacks, were there before her. In these postwar, postslave days, thousands had become drifters, searching aimlessly for the fulfillment of the promise of freedom. Any barn, any deserted building, any roof that offered shelter for the night was temporary home to an aimless community of stragglers.

719

A group of men sat round a fire, and a woman was boiling some roots and a rabbit. Queen limped toward the group, uncertain of the protocol. She looked for some separate shed in which she could hide, and be alone, and lick, like a dog, her bruised body and battered heart.

The blacks stared at the new arrival in contempt, because she was not black. A white woman here was dangerous, but Queen stood her ground.

"I need somewhere to sleep," she said.

No one spoke for a while, and then a man jerked his head toward the old pigsty. Queen was not shocked by such a lodging, or ashamed to accept it, and the animals were long gone. As she walked toward it, she heard the blacks whispering among themselves, and some women giggling.

She walked into the pigsty and almost fell to the ground, too exhausted to go on, now that she had found her haven. She rested her head against the wooden pen, and dozed for a while. When she woke, it was dark, and the blacks at the camp fire were eating. The smell of the food made her realize how hungry she was. She stood unsteadily, and walked a few paces toward them.

The woman who had made the stew looked at her. Her face was expressionless, showing neither compassion nor contempt.

"Is yo' hungry?" she asked, and Queen nodded her head, thinking the woman might be kind, as Pearl had been to her, in the forest.

But the woman was not Pearl. She looked at the plate of food in her hand, and again at Queen, and she hurled the plate to the ground.

"Eat that, whitey," she sneered. The simple gesture contained all her anger at the things her Massa had done to her when she was a slave. She hated white folk.

Queen was beyond insult now, and accepted what

720

the world had to offer. She saw a couple of pieces of bony meat in the mess at her feet, picked them up, brushed the dirt from them, and went to the pigsty to eat.

She heard the women laughing at her distress again, and the men talking in frightened whispers of things she did not understand, and the woman who had thrown the food was being told off.

"Shoulda bin mo' friendly," she heard a man's voice say. "If'n dey come tonight and she tell 'em what you done, could go bad fo' you."

"Here, girl," he said, and threw some half-eaten corn husks into the pigsty. Queen did not understand his change of heart, nor did she care. She gnawed on the food until it was gone. She found some old straw, fashioned it into a rough bed, and lay down to sleep.

They came while she was asleep, the three white men, on horseback, with scarves tied around their necks and pulled up to hide their faces. They carried burning brands, and rounded up the blacks who had been sleeping in the barn, chased them with fire, and made sport with them.

Queen woke to the screams of some of the women. Tucked in a corner of the pigsty, she peered out and saw a white man ride up to the barn and throw a burning brand at it. The old dry wood of the building caught fire like tinder, the hay in the stalls speeding the progress of the flames. The blacks left inside scrambled for safety, and the night rang with their screams.

One woman didn't get out fast enough, and was engulfed in flames. All this Queen saw from her hiding place, as in a daze, a perverted dream, a nightmare of horror. She saw the white men round up the blacks and force them from the property. The blacks begged for mercy, but the white men were resolute. The blacks were not welcome here. They had wanted freedom and they'd got it. But not here.

Satisfied with their night's work, the white men galloped away. The blacks, scared to return to their camp, and having no reason to now, stared at the burning barn and then drifted into the night to find some other shelter.

Queen was transfixed by the fire. The flames of the burning barn merged with the fire of the campsite in the forest and the brands of her pursuers, and she heard Henderson's laughter again, and the insults of his friends.

The firelight glittered in her eyes, flames that would haunt her forever.

In the day she walked on toward Huntsville, without any sense of direction except the elusive North. It was harder this day. Her bruises had developed, and her injuries were sharp and scraped at her body like razors. The small energy that had come to her with her determination to get away from Decatur had deserted her with her night's rest. The sun beat down on her, and her lips were dry. Every step was an achievement.

She could see the city in the distance, but it gave her no joy, for she couldn't imagine that it held any promise for her. She began to believe that she could not go on, and that there was no point. Still she didn't stop. Scattered farms gave way to scattered houses, and there was more traffic on the road, but no one stopped for her.

She thought that even God must have deserted her, and then she heard a choir singing a hymn, and saw a little church in the distance. It was a rough-and-ready building of unhewn timber, hastily put together, but a small steeple surmounted by a wooden cross announced its purpose. Queen could tell it was a black church from the sound she heard; whites never raised their voices like that. She expected to be evicted from it if she went in, but she had no choice. She could not survive the parching, noonday sun.

The Preacher was a dedicated man, who had honed his sermons at services held in the open cotton fields that some Massas used to allow their slaves to attend. He had developed a stentorian voice, and could make his sermons ring to the open sky that had been the roof of his makeshift churches. His ministry was to bring hope to his people, not in this life but in the glorious peace that was to come.

"Our troubles in this mortal world can last a day, or a year, or a lifetime," he shouted at his congregation, and they vociferously agreed.

"But they cannot last forever," he told them. "Forever is eternal, and our mortal misery is but a moment in the blinking of God's eye. And when that moment we call life is done, we will be taken up into the bosom of His sweet love, in glory, and our troubles will be banished forever."

The congregation roared its agreement, and no one noticed a tiny white woman sneak into the church through the open door, and fall against the wall at the back.

"Taken up in Glory!" the Preacher yelled again. "We will dwell in the eternal sunshine of God's love, in Glory! And we will forget our agony, and we will forget our pain, and all the misery of our human days, because we will live in His eternal Glory!"

The crowd was clapping now, and cheering him on. The woman at the old pedal organ looked at the ecstatic congregation, her heart awash with the love of Jesus. But she was puzzled to see a little white woman, bruised and dirty, leaning against the wall near the front door of the church.

"Not just for a moment," the Preacher cried. "Or a day, or a year, or a lifetime. But fo'ever. And fo'ever. And fo'ever! In Glory!"

"Hallelujah," the people sang, raising the roof. "Oh, glory hallelujah!"

"Let us pray," the Preacher exhorted them. His flock

723

fell silent, and the Preacher noticed the strange white woman near the door. He stared at her, because white women didn't come into black churches. Gradually, the congregation turned to Queen, until every eye in the building seemed to be staring at her.

She had to do something to make them understand; she had to let them know how much she needed help; she had to say something to stop them from throwing her out, for here was her only salvation. But it was so hard to say. Despair and defiance struggled in her heart, and she was shaking with emotion. When she spoke, it was in a whisper that only those close to her could hear.

"I's nigra," she told them. And when no one responded, she said it again, louder now.

"I's nigra!" And louder again. "Nigra! Nigra! Nigra!"

Only the Preacher replied.

"Hallelujah, sister," he said. The crowd chanted and clapped its approval.

The simple relief that flooded through Queen astonished her. She felt as if she had found home, after years lost in the wilderness.

72

Joyce, who played the organ at the church, was a motherly woman, and took charge of Queen. She took her to her ramshackle home in the black shantytown on the outskirts of Huntsville, ordered her children to clean up the shed and make up a rough bed for their new guest, and told them that they were not to bother Queen. She tended Queen's injuries, bathed her bruises and bound her wounds. She made Queen sit in an old rocking chair on the rickety porch, and fed her hot soup. She didn't ask how Queen came to be in such a state, for she knew the girl would tell her in her own good time. What she needed now was to be alone in caring company. The tribe of children obeyed their mother, but were curious about their visitor. Two of Joyce's girls sat in the yard pretending not to stare at her and, at their mother's suggestion, watching out for her welfare. Although Queen never guessed it, for the time she stayed with Joyce she was seldom out of someone's sight. Abram, Joyce's husband, came home in the evening, and was told of Queen and introduced to her, and politely offered her the hospitality of his home. He had been a slave, like his wife, and was an expert blacksmith. After the war his former Massa, appreciative of his skill, set him up in his own business, and Abram worked seven days a week to provide for his large family and pay off his loan.

After a rowdy family meal, Joyce took her to the shed where a comfortable bunk and a clean blanket awaited her. She undressed Queen, checking her injuries and clucking her disapproval of whatever had caused them. She tucked Queen into bed, as Easter used to do, and stroked her pretty hair, and hummed a soft, sweet lullaby, as Easter used to do. Her undemanding charity and patient care broke Queen's reserve. She turned her head to the wall and began to weep, but Joyce took her into her arms, and held her while she cried, as a mother holds her child. As Easter used to do.

Joyce was a simple, honest woman who had found a simple honest man to love. Their life on the plantation had been hard, but now, as their own Massas, they were determined to reap all the benefits that the precious freedom offered. They tried to find goodness in everything about them, and because they sought it, and recognized it when they saw it, they found it more often than most, and praised it, and ignored or dismissed the bad. The children were following in their parents' footsteps, for Abram was a stern but fair father, and Joyce a generous mother who shared her love equally, and set a firm moral tone for her offspring.

Their second son, Wash, was not their own, but a light-skinned quadroon who had been born with a crippled leg. His real mother had died when he was little, and Joyce had adopted him, and loved him. When Wash's father, who had never had much time for his son, ran away from the plantation at the start of the war and was never seen again, Abram simply accepted the boy's temporary presence in his house as a permanent fact and Wash could not remember that he had ever had other parents.

The family, with its easy, raucous familiarity and overtly displayed affections, was a revelation to Queen, who had never known such simple treasure. Within days she became part of the household, appreciated by all of them, and they in return gave her the simple gifts of uncomplicated laughter, of sibling bickering that vanished as quickly as it arose, and the understanding and support that came from mutually shared problems. Each evening the family sat together on the porch, Joyce and Abram in rocking chairs, and the children squatting on stools or on the ground, and discussed their day, with its joys and its dilemmas, and counseled each other, wisely or badly, but with care and affection.

Queen would join them and she heard with increasing awe the squabbles and discipline, the jokes and the advice, the gossip and the news, for this was how she wanted her life to be. No one cared if she was white or black, but all were solicitous of her welfare.

One warm evening she was alone with Joyce on the porch. Abram was working late, and the children had been allowed to go to a sock hop. Joyce rocked gently, knitting for the coming winter, and Queen sat in Abram's rocker, watching the moths dance around the lamp, and listening to the sounds of the shantytown night. Music and laughter and sometimes a distant, angry voice. And mothers singing lullabies. She began to talk, softly, slowly, haltingly, of her experience in Decatur, until the whole awful story tumbled out. Joyce

726

said nothing throughout, but went on knitting, and nodded from time to time, to let Queen know she was listening. When she finished, Queen was surprised that she wasn't crying. She had relived the nightmare of Digby's rape in every bloody detail, and it caused her much pain, but she didn't want to cry. She told the story of Alice's rejection of her, from a slightly different point of view, with some sympathy for Alice's predicament.

Joyce made no comment on the story, but put her knitting away, and suggested they pray for the forgiveness of those who had treated Queen so badly. Queen smiled and shook her head, an intolerable burden lifted from her shoulders. She might pray for Alice, but never for Digby.

Queen prayed often and fervently these days. She went regularly to the church of her salvation with Joyce, and was encouraged by the Preacher to believe that her footsteps there had been divinely inspired.

"Yea, though I walk through the valley of the shadow of death, I will fear no evil," the Preacher intoned, "for Thou art with me. Thy rod and Thy staff, they comfort me."

And Queen agreed.

What surprised Queen most was how easy it had been. She had spent her life denying she was black because she believed herself to be white, and wanted Jass and all her white relations to admit that fact, but it had only brought her unhappiness, and rejection by some of darker skin.

In Decatur she had tried to pretend that she had no black blood at all, and that had brought her misery.

Here she had accepted her blood, and had allied herself to people with whom she felt a sense of kinship, and it was giving her a rare and welcome sense of belonging. She began to understand that her rejection by the field hands was because of mutual insecurity and fear, hers because she didn't want to be one of them and thought herself different, theirs because they didn't understand her ambitions, and thought her different.

The sadness was that it could not last. Abram and Joyce would not ask her to leave, but Queen knew she was an additional small strain on their meager resources. Nor did she want to live the rest of her life as part of their family. She wanted a family of her own.

Joyce found the job for her, through the Preacher, who had contacts with some of the white missionaries in town. At the appointed hour, Queen, soberly dressed, went with Joyce to a sprawling, gracious house with a large and untidy garden. A tall, frail woman of late middle years, her hair pulled back in a fierce bun, answered the door to them, and introduced herself as Miss Gippy. She looked at Queen appraisingly and then led them to the sitting room.

Her sister, Miss Mandy, conducted the interview, for she ran the house, but Miss Gippy frequently chimed in, usually with a quotation from the Bible that had some relevance to what was being said. Queen, who was in a happy frame of mind, even though neither she nor Joyce was invited to sit, almost giggled at one interruption, and thought that Miss Gippy must know the Good Book backward.

Miss Mandy was rounder and less frail than her sister, of similar years and sterner stuff. She listened to Queen's qualifications, and explained their circumstances. Originally from New Hampshire, they had come South after the war to minister to the souls of the newly freed blacks. They had lived here for a year, and were in need of a housekeeper. The several girls they had employed had been either flighty or lazy, and all had left. Miss Mandy admitted they were strict taskmasters, but were fair, and Queen would get her pay, her board and her keep, and one afternoon off a week. In return she was to run the house to the sisters' instructions.

"If any would not work, neither should he eat," Miss Gippy droned sanctimoniously.

Queen said the conditions were acceptable, and waited while Miss Mandy walked around her, inspecting her as if she were a slave on the block. A tiny smile fought its way to Queen's lips, and she dared not look at Joyce. But she did look at Miss Gippy, and the smile disappeared to where it had come from.

Finally, Miss Mandy pronounced herself satisfied. "Excellent. And lovely teeth," she said. "When can you begin, Queen? Such an odd name."

It was agreed that Queen could begin immediately. She would collect her few belongings from Joyce, and return to prepare supper. They were about to depart, when Miss Gippy coughed.

"We should say a little prayer first," Miss Mandy said, and knelt. Miss Gippy knelt beside her, and Queen and Joyce followed suit.

"Man goeth forth unto his work, unto his labor," Miss Gippy prayed. "O Lord, how manifold are Thy works. In wisdom hast Thou made them all."

The wretched smile that Queen had fought so hard to subdue struggled to her lips again.

It was hard work, for the sisters had not had help for several weeks, and there was much to catch up on, but slowly Queen brought it all under control. She was provided with two black dresses, white aprons and caps, the cost of which was deducted from her wages, and she worked from early morning till late at night, but usually took some hours off in the afternoon, or didn't hurry home when she went shopping. Miss Mandy had been honest with her—both sisters were strict taskmasters, but very fair, and frequently helped in the kitchen. They seldom went out, and Queen saw little evidence of their missionary work, other than their mild discouragement of her continuing friendship with Joyce.

"Obviously," Miss Mandy said to Queen, "you have

729

had a good education. Women like Joyce have not, and are only a few steps from the jungle. That is why we have a mission to them."

Queen bit her lip and didn't answer back, didn't defend Joyce, because she had come to understand that what the sisters called their mission was an excuse, a rationale for what otherwise would be an empty existence. They were deeply religious, and Queen's day was punctuated by calls to pray with the sisters, or hymns sung to a pounding accompaniment by Miss Gippy on the pump organ.

"They're a pair of dragons," she told Joyce, as they walked together to church. "But their fire is pretty old now."

Sunday was not Queen's day off, but she was expected to attend church in the morning. To the sisters' chagrin, she always went with Joyce to the black church, because it marked an important turning point in her life, and she loved the rousing sermons and hearty, heartfelt hymns. Sometimes it all got so exciting she would get carried away, and chant and shout with the best of them, and sometimes she was sure the Spirit moved within her, and she went into a trancelike state of ecstasy.

She was baptized one late fall day, just before the cold weather of winter set in. The service was held at the riverbank, where the congregation gathered and sang their joy in Jesus. A number of whites collected nearby, to watch the niggers have their fun, for it was a colorful occasion.

The Preacher stood up to his waist in the chilly water, with some deacons and Joyce beside him. Three or four celebrants stood in a line before them, teeth chattering with fervor and cold. The preacher put his arm around Queen and roared to heaven.

"O Lord, we beseech Thee, receive now this child, Queen, that she may be born again, into Thy sweet grace. Just as Saint John baptized Thee, we now wash away her sins in the water of love, and dedicate her to Thy glory fo'ever."

He held his hand over Queen's mouth and nose, and dunked her in the river. The choir was at fever pitch. When Queen bobbed up, her eyes shining, her spirit vibrant, there was clapping and cheering.

"I know it! I know the Lord now!" Queen shouted to the world. "I feel his great love!"

Truly, she felt wonderful, and even if it was only by contrast to her earlier misery, that was enough, for she genuinely believed that God was directing her life.

The sisters strongly disapproved of the way blacks worshiped the Lord, and every Sunday they told her she should come with them to their own church, and contemplate the wonder of His works in calm and quiet.

"Those rowdy sermons, 'The earth am flat, the sun do move,'" Miss Gippy sniffed. "Dangerous stuff, Queen."

"Clapping and dancing and singing, and dunking people at baptism," Miss Mandy agreed. "This is heathen behavior, idolatry!"

"Voodoo and African ritual," Miss Gippy went further. "You are not in the jungle now. You have to be civilized, even in worship. Especially in worship."

Queen nodded her head seriously, for she had become quite fond of the old biddies.

"Maybe the Lord moves in mysterious ways, m'm," she said. They sighed, and nodded sadly, and agreed with her, and sent her off to prepare their dinner. Just as Queen had become fond of them, they felt surprisingly affectionate to her, both for herself and for what she represented to them.

Miss Gippy had been christened Gypsophilia, a tiny flower, by sober Lutheran parents, merchants in New Hampshire, who had hoped that the good Lord would send them a son. It was not to be. They named their

731

second daughter Amanda, and even though they prayed with all their hearts and worked strenuously at their physical union, they were not blessed with any more children. They raised their daughters with discipline tempered by as much love as their austere religion allowed them to show, and prayed for good husbands for both of them. Again, their prayers were not answered, and the parents began to believe they had offended the Lord in some way. Materially they prospered, and could provide a good dowry if any young man had the sense to take either daughter in wedlock, but no one took the opportunity.

Both girls were plain, each loved the other, and both were devoted to their church. Occasionally, men crossed their paths, and both had mild and inconclusive flirtations, but by the time she was twenty-five, Gippy understood that she had been left on the shelf, and ceased to be anxious about men, because she had Jesus. Mandy, who had a more rebellious spirit, was not so accepting of potential spinsterhood. As Gippy's interest in men declined, Mandy's became avid, and she sought out the company of any eligible bachelor with increasing desperation. As a child she adored her dolls, and as she grew up she transferred that affection to other people's children. It wasn't so much that she wanted to be married; it was that she wanted children of her own, to love, and to mother and protect, and she could not bear the prospect of being barren. She became something of a joke, and then an embarrassment, among the young men of the town, for she sought them out and threw herself at them, but when they asked for more than she was prepared to give outside of marriage, they rejected her, and she became hysterical.

She met a young man, a shady salesman from Boston, who learned of her financial security, but not her reputation, and, to secure his own prospects, asked for her hand in marriage. Mandy overwhelmed him with her gratitude, and he began to have doubts about his neurotic fiancée. Her parents had larger doubts about the union, for he was not religious, and inquiries in Boston told them that the salesman was not to be trusted with money, and was out for what he could get. Mandy would hear nothing against her love, and so her parents offered the salesman a sum of money to remove himself from the district. He left for California the next day, to make his fortune in gold.

It broke Mandy's heart. She took to her room, and when she came down a few days later, she had donned a chaste composure, and settled to a life of loneliness with her sister, Gippy, and devotion to charity. They became pillars of the local church and espoused all the liberal causes, especially abolition, although neither had ever met a black person. Their parents died and left them well provided, and they continued to live together, for they could not imagine a life apart from each other. Humorless, austere, and devout, they were their only friends. As they grew older, the northern winters became harder for them, and they talked of moving to a more temperate climate, but would not live in a slave state. During the war, they dedicated themselves to the cause of the Union. They attended recruitment meetings and handed out flags and patriotic pamphlets to those who enlisted, wrote countless letters to the newspapers protesting the latest Southern outrages, and made a few, very small donations to those missionaries who were helping runaway slaves. They heard lectures from those same missionaries about the appalling plight of the blacks, slave and free, their passionate faith in a form of God, and their curious style of worship.

It gave them the cause that they needed. Their hearts were appalled, although their actions were limited to supplying their church with fresh flowers. At the end of the war, they would move South, and by example and patient instruction, by simply living as good Christians, they would bring the newly freed slaves to their unforgiving God. They sought a quiet city for their gentle lives, and settled on Huntsville, where they bought a splendid house at a bargain price with their good Yankee dollars. They found a quiet church that suited them, with a minister of ascetic authority, and looked forward to their new lives with some anticipation.

Almost immediately, they realized that persuading blacks from their wild forms of worship was an impossible task, and as immediately, they became intolerant of most black people, whom they thought primitive, irresponsible, and immoral. And, in the case of their maids, lazy. They despaired of their rambling house, and closed off most of the rooms. Miss Mandy struggled with the garden, but the verdant, unpredictable Southern horticulture defeated her, and no gardener would tolerate her imperious directions. The only reason they didn't sell up and go back home was because the weather suited them both beautifully, and they could not face the prospect of a long, dark winter again.

Then a young woman came to work for them who suited their purposes exactly. She was nigra but pale, and obviously her white blood had calmed her pagan genes. She was the product of a fall from grace by her father and her mother, and so was ripe to be saved. She was an excellent worker, who seldom complained. And she was young, and brought some sunshine into their crimped lives, just as the lovely Southern weather eased their rheumatic bones. That she gently resisted their attempts to bring her to their purifying, Protestant angst did not concern them. She was malleable, and they had nothing else to do. For the rest of their lives.

It was a healing time for Queen. Her new church gave her friends and unbounded joy, the sisters gave her companionship and something to complain about, and the community who had so lovingly adopted her gave her a sense of place. That Christmas was the happiest she could remember. She made presents, silly, sweet things, for all her friends, and gave Miss Mandy and Miss Gippy little lavender bags that she had stitched and filled herself. They, in turn, gave her prayer books and a new Bible. She spent a cheery Christmas morning at her church, singing the joy of Christ reborn as lustily as anyone present. She served an excellent dinner of ham, gravy, and creamed potatoes to the sisters, and ate her own food alone in the kitchen, where she took all her meals. A few days later, in that same kitchen, she wished herself a very happy New Year, and had every reason to believe it might be true.

Thursday afternoons were her own. With the nudging of spring, she would stroll in the park, or shop with Joyce, and they would go to a little café and have big slices of rich peach pie, covered in cream. It pleased Joyce to see Queen so happy, and she told her so.

Queen laughed. "I love being me," she said. "I tried being on the other side, and now I love being black."

"But you white as snow," Joyce laughed.

Queen shook her head. "This black blood must be a powerful thing. One little drop of it, and you can't be white. It's all or nothing for them."

She looked down and fiddled with her pie, remembering the bad times, the white times. Joyce took her hand.

"Seems to me there's only one thing you need to make yo' life complete," she said, her meaning perfectly clear, for she said this to Queen every time they met. Part of Queen agreed with her. She wanted very much to have a man in her life, but the awful memory of Digby still lingered, and she was too suspicious of men to feel comfortable with them if they showed any romantic interest in her. Her caution was easing with time, and she was trying to convince herself that Digby was exceptional, but she was not ready to test the theory.

Men who made her laugh, and who represented no

serious threat to her heart or her body, were different, like the smart young man loping toward them, his eyes glinting with delight at Queen.

"Charles real sweet on you," Joyce hinted.

"He isn't for me," Queen said.

"Yo' need a man in yo' life," Joyce insisted.

Charles joined them, dapper, dandy, and colorfully clad. He doffed his hat.

"Miss Queen, Miss Joyce," he greeted them, but hardly looking at Joyce. He was real sweet on Queen. "What a very sublime pleasure."

Joyce got to her feet. "Sit here and talk to Queen," she told Charles. "I see a friend over there."

Queen laughed out loud at the unsubtlety of it, and Charles slid into Joyce's seat.

"Yo're looking radiant, Miss Queen," he beamed, on his very best behavior. "An' what a fine big dish o' pie. But then you just a little ol' itty-bitty thing, and yo' need feedin' up."

Queen laughed again, and hid her face in her hands. If nothing else, Charles was funny.

Charles knew people laughed at him, and used that to his advantage. Tall, thin and scrawny, and a born survivor, he had an unthreatening impudence and a cheeky personality and a silver tongue. He made the most of every opportunity, and created opportunity where none existed. No one was exactly sure how he made his living, because he made his living at so many things, but he was obviously doing well for himself. A house nigger before the war, freedom saw him flower. In the ill-supplied South, Charles could usually supply anything anyone wanted, given enough notice and if the price was right. His customers ranged from a Union general who was collecting fine antiques from impoverished mansions, to a Confederate colonel who liked to drink imported brandy at domestic prices, and scores of simple people, black and white, who knew that Charles could provide a few simple luxuries and more necessities, at unmatched prices. If an ex-slave needed a cheap plow for his few sharecropping acres, Charles could find it. If a Federal soldier wanted souvenirs of the war, Charles would talk a veteran Rebel into parting with his promotion orders signed by Robert E. Lee. If a Southern woman wished to sell, discreetly, a piece of jewelry to pay her bills, Charles was her man. The only thing Charles would not do was trade in human flesh. Asked by drunken youths if he could find them female companionship for a few hours, Charles would smile, shake his head, and extricate himself from their company. The concept of a human being selling her body to another, however willingly, reminded him too strongly of slavery.

He dressed to the height of his concept of fashion, in smart suits of eccentric colors, and to the surprise of many who knew him only slightly, Charles was deeply religious, and attended the same church as Queen. He was smitten by her from the first moment he saw her, and lived in the vain belief that one day she would come to her senses and realize what he was offering her. In the meantime, he courted her with irrepressible enthusiasm.

Joyce's encouragement of his hopes, and the fact that Queen was never actually rude to him, sustained his hope, and he was constantly thinking up new ways to convince her of his ardor.

Queen sat in the church the next Sunday, listening intently to the Preacher's sermon, and she became aware that something was being passed from hand to hand among the congregation. It was a note, and it eventually came to her, with her name on the outside of it. Joyce beamed at her, and Queen opened the note. It said: "May I call on you?" The fact that it was unsigned didn't confuse her; she knew exactly who it was from. She looked up, and saw Charles, a few rows away, grinning at her. She threw her eyes to heaven and then glared at him, but that didn't stop him from grinning.

She heard a knock on the front door the next afternoon, and was sure it was Charles. As she moved down the hall, she could see the dark shape of a man through the stained glass, and made up her mind that she was going to end this business once and for all.

She opened the door angrily. "Charles!" she barked. "I told you—"

She knew it wasn't Charles the moment she saw him, even though he had his back to her and was staring at the garden. He turned and looked at her with brown velvet eyes.

Queen caught her breath. He was probably the most handsome man she had ever seen.

"I'm sorry," she said, feeling foolish. "I thought you was someone else."

"I's looking for work," he said, taking off his hat. "An' yo' garden's a terrible mess."

She didn't know what to say, and thought she must have stood silent for several minutes, although it was only a second or two. She could hear the clock ticking in the hall, and the sound of her own heartbeat.

She found her voice at last.

"Wait outside," she said. "I'll fetch the Missy."

He nodded slowly, but didn't take his eyes off her. She closed the door and leaned against the wall for a moment, then recollected herself, and went upstairs to call Miss Mandy, who was having a nap.

When she looked out of the window at the top of the stairs, the man was already at work in the garden. He had found a scythe, and was cutting the overgrown grass.

She forgot her errand, and stood watching him, until Miss Mandy came out of her room, wanting to know who was at the door.

73

His name was Davis, and Miss Mandy hired him after only a small negotiation. Told that a strange black man was working in the yard, Miss Mandy, who dreamed of a formal garden, felt a small jolt of fear. But donned a righteous wrath, went down to him, and demanded that he leave.

"Who told you to do that? Who gave you permission?" she asked him sharply. Queen hovered behind her, at a safe distance.

Davis did not stop scything. He had an easy, swinging stroke, and already he had cleared a large area.

"I took it on my own authority," he said. The sight of the vast black man with a lethal weapon in his hands made Miss Mandy quail, but she stood her ground.

"Get out of here at once," Miss Mandy ordered. "Before I call the law." It was an empty threat. There was no guardian of the law within sight or earshot. There were very few guardians of the law in this rambunctious South.

Davis agreed that she had every right to do that, but her garden was a mess, and he was looking for work. He rested on his scythe, and spoke calmly to Miss Mandy.

"If you could see yo' way clear to employin' me, I'd work fo' you right hard," he told her. "If not, or if you cain't afford me, I'll give you this afternoon fo' free, coz I hates to see a garden so."

He looked sadly at the wilderness that was the front lawn. "But if'n you want, I'll leave," he added.

He had an extraordinary, quiet power about him. Miss Mandy, with little evidence to hand, was sure she could trust him.

"You're very sure of yourself, young man," she said.

Davis smiled. "Cain't see a reason not to be." He stared at Miss Mandy, and she blinked first. She accepted his offer of a free afternoon's work, and if he was satisfactory, she would consider more regular employment. Davis thanked her, touched his cap, and went back to his scything. Miss Mandy watched his easy grace for a moment or two, and then went back to the house.

"I will be watching you, young man," she called to him, as she went inside.

"Yes, m'm," Davis replied, and looked at Queen.

Queen was astonished by him. He had handled the situation with charm and grace, and had got himself a job. And when he looked at her, she, like Miss Mandy, thought she could trust him with her life. It was too disturbing to her, and so she tried to put him in his place.

"Them roses need pruning," she ordered, pointing to the untidy, rambling rosebushes.

Davis looked at the roses. "Yes, they do," he agreed. "But not now. Wrong time of year."

He looked at her again, and she was sure he was laughing at her. Smiling at her, anyway, and there was something else in that smile, something provocatively unsettling. Queen scuttled back to the house, bristling with indignation.

He worked hard and well all afternoon, to an unseen audience. Miss Gippy, who had learned to fear black men from her few female acquaintances at their church, peered out at him from the comparative safety of her bedroom window, and prayed that she would be raped. Miss Mandy watched from the sitting room, and it delighted her to see the dramatic improvement to her garden that happened before her very eyes. He raked and hoed and cleared, and what had been chaos became order, and visions of an English garden, of formal lawns, colorful borders, and sweet smelling roses, encouraged Miss Mandy to employ him on a weekly basis. She went out to him, to tell him so.

Queen watched from the kitchen window as Miss Mandy talked to Davis, and tried to work out what made him so attractive. It was not that he was so very handsome, she decided now; her first impression had been wrong, his features were a little irregular. He was black, black as ebony, had a superb body, she could see, for he had taken his shirt off and was working in his vest, but the sheer magnitude of him was, in itself, daunting. Yet somehow the complete man added up to more than the sum of his separate physical parts, and it was his eyes, Queen thought. Those dark, magic, melting eyes, like liquid amber. No, it was his voice, deep and warm, like molasses. Or perhaps it was his personality. When he looked at her, she felt he was exposing his soul to her, while still keeping some private anguish hidden. His embracing personality, gently commanding and totally reassuring, made her want to tell him the secrets of her heart, as if he would absorb her sorrows into his own.

"The devil finds work for idle hands, Queen!" Miss Mandy had come into the kitchen. Queen had not heard her, and was startled by her voice. She shook herself from her reverie, and felt stupid. How long had she been staring at Davis? And why? He was only a gardener. She also felt a little guilty.

"Sorry, Missy," she murmured, and hurried to the sink. Miss Mandy guessed the secret, for she was party to it herself. She would never admit it because it was dangerous, disturbing; she was too old, she had no carnal needs, and desire for a black man was unthinkable. But it was there, like a little imp, nibbling at her conscience. Davis thrilled her, and she thought of him in the basest terms, as a magnificent, untamed animal.

"Why don't you take some lemonade out to that man in the garden?" she suggested to Queen. "He's a good worker, and it's a hot day."

Queen nodded, and busied herself with lemonade. Miss Mandy stared out at Davis.

741

"He seems to be a fine young man," she said. "Does he know he has a friend in Jesus?"

For suddenly she had a new cause. She would bring this lion of the jungle to the rocky, redeeming slopes of Calvary, and prayed that some other missionary had not reached his soul first.

He was fixing some trellis when Queen brought the lemonade to him. Queen set the tray on a box, and poured a glass of lemonade from the jug.

"You can have a break," she said, and to persuade him, she added her authority. "Miss Mandy said."

He didn't respond, but worked on. Queen was a little miffed that her gracious order was ignored, but her speech lapsed from its formal vowels, and adopted some of his less cultivated pattern.

"You doin' a good job," she said. "Miss Mandy said."

Still, he ignored her. What was the matter with the man? Queen wondered, temper rising a little. He didn't even look at her, and men usually looked at her in considerable appreciation, even if she ignored them.

"I c'n give you dinner in the kitchen when you done, afore you go home," she said. "Miss Mandy said—"

His work on the trellis done, he turned to her. He liked to finish one job before starting another.

"Better do what she says, then." He smiled, and her heart went pit-a-pat. She would make him a lovely dinner.

The meal was as frustrating as anything she could remember. He washed up in the laundry, and took off his muddy boots before he came into the kitchen. He sat at the table, accepted the food she gave him, and was impeccably polite. Queen had prepared a fine dinner; she even saved the knuckle of the roast leg of lamb for him, because she remembered it had been her father's favorite. She piled his plate with potatoes,

742

pumpkin, and cabbage, and he ate everything she put in front of him, but in silence. Queen did her best to make conversation, but he responded to her with polite and noncommittal monosyllables. He had three pieces of her good apple pie, and when he was done, he stood and thanked her.

"That was a fine dinner, ma'am," he said. "I thanks you kindly."

He walked to the door, but Queen could not let him go.

"You know—" she began, but stopped because she couldn't think of anything to say.

He turned and looked at her with those velvet eyes, and she found her only possible lifeline.

"—you have a friend in Jesus," she said.

He considered this and nodded, but absently, as if he could not imagine that he had any friends. Then said he would see her tomorrow, and left. She came to the door and watched him put on his boots and walk away down the path, into the night.

She walked out into the garden. The sky was clear, the stars were bright, and the silver moon illuminated the work he had done that day. She went back inside, washed the dishes, prepared the trays for breakfast, and went upstairs to her attic room.

She went to sleep and had sweet dreams that night. She was on a hill looking toward a distant city, and she could see Jesus triumphantly approaching Jerusalem. He was wearing white robes, riding on a donkey, and was surrounded by waved palm fronds. She walked to the city, but He never seemed to come any closer to it, and soon she was close to Him. When He turned to look at her, His face was full of quiet pain. And black, like Davis.

743

74

The pattern was quickly set. He came to work each day, and his hard labor and the bursting spring brought tranquility and a sense of renewal to what had been disorder. Miss Mandy, desperate to find some justification for a fruitless life, saw it as a metaphor for the South, her own small contribution to reconstruction, and infinitely more successful than that directed by the Federal government. Good Christian example and discipline was what these blacks needed. Queen and Davis were the living proof of that, not the flagrant and unjustified equality that Washington was trying to inflict upon them.

Queen and Davis. She began to think of them as an inseparable pair, and she cherished the idea of a possible union for them, a good and happy marriage, with herself as instructing governess of their delightful children. She was sure her ambition was shared by Queen, for the girl positively blossomed whenever Davis was around, and was scratchy and unpredictable on his day off. When he came back to work, his boundless composure calmed her irritability, and she, in turn, was the only one who could make him smile.

Davis built a pleasant arbor for the sisters, sheltered from the sun, and planted climbing roses. The sisters sat there for hours on the warm days, reading their Bibles, or doing their embroidery, or simply watching the lovely garden grow. Occasionally, Miss Mandy would find reasons to speak to him, first about plants and then about the love of God, and he would listen to all she had to say solemnly, and nod his head, and tell her it was much to think about. She was content with this. She was in no hurry to speed his conversion, for then what would she have to do?

During the day, he never came to the house, but Queen would bring him cool lemonade, and sit with him for a while, and admire his handiwork. Each evening he took his dinner with her in the kitchen, and appreciated her good cooking. She would chatter to him endlessly about her day, and he would laugh or sympathize or offer a few words of advice as the occasion demanded, but he would never talk about himself. He always seemed a little distracted, as if he were cogitating matters of important and insoluble moment, and sometimes Queen was embarrassed that her gossip was distracting him from his unknown purpose. He seemed to understand this, and would smile at her, and compliment her on her pie, and she would serve him another generous helping.

She didn't know where he came from or where he lived, or what his intentions in life were, nor did she care. She was still wary of a relationship, but the fact that this man to whom she was so attracted never did anything to disturb her peace of mind was like a balm to her hurtful experiences with other men.

As the weather grew hotter, she convinced herself that his appetite for the lemonade increased, and her visits to the garden became more frequent.

She came to him one hot day when he was working on the roof of the garden shed, to fix the leaks. He was stripped to the waist, and when he climbed down and turned away from her to get his shirt, she saw that his back was a mass of scars. She gasped, although she knew the cause of them.

"Who did that to you?" she cried. He shrugged, and put on his shirt.

"Massa," he said simply. "In the old days."

He accepted the cool drink, and changed the subject to roses.

That night at dinner, she tried to get him to talk about his bondage.

"Why they whip you that bad?" she asked.

He shrugged again. "Ran away," he said, without a trace of bitterness. "Caught me. Whipped me. Ran away again. Same thing."

Queen had never been whipped, but had seen it often enough. She closed her eyes, to block out the image of the lash striking Davis.

"How many times?" she whispered.

"Often as I could," he said calmly. "I didn't want to be a slave, I never asked, wasn't my idea of my life. Jus' coz they white, how come they had that power?"

Queen had no answer, but put her faith in the future.

"That's all over now," she said, to comfort him, but Davis stared at her as if he didn't believe her.

"Mebbe," he said. He paused for a moment, but she could see he had something more to say.

"Ain't changed much. I's free, but I cain't seem to find my place in life."

It's here, right here, you've found it, Queen wanted to tell him, but she said nothing. He seemed to be battling with some inner demon, and suddenly words flooded out of him as if a dam had burst.

"Ain't gwine find it in the South, I reckon," he said. "Slavery's gone, but white folk still think like the ol' days. I don't want to dig gardens all my life. I don't want to be treated like a jungle nigger. I don't want to live in a place where I ain't ever gwine be given the chance to better myself, free or not free. I don't want to beg for change from the white man's pocket."

He spoke quietly, but his voice thundered in Queen's ears, and his magnetic personality filled the room. At that moment she would have followed him to the ends of the earth.

He relaxed then, and seemed embarrassed by how much of himself he had revealed. He smiled, and shrugged again. "North, mebbe," he said as a coda. "They reckon a man can find his self up there."

He stood up, thanked her for his dinner as he always

746

did, and left. Queen sat on a chair, her hand shaking a little. The power and intensity of his speech, and the loneliness and anger that provoked it, had frightened her a little, for she remembered herself, when she had been in her times of greatest distress, which were not so very long ago.

He didn't refer to the conversation when he saw her again, and resisted her mild questioning of his eventual aims in life. But he surprised her a few days later when he asked her if he might accompany her to church the following Sunday.

Queen was only too happy to agree, but asked why he wanted to go. He chuckled and said that it might stop Miss Mandy's endless preaching at him.

The men had enlarged the church somewhat over the last few months, as more and more blacks, disillusioned with the hardships of their reconstructing society and the failed promises of freedom, sought solace from a higher source. A small choir had been formed, and Queen, with her sweet soprano voice, was part of it. A fervent believer, she sang in her most pure voice that Sunday, and she had eyes for only one man in the congregation. She was determined that she would be the bridge between him and his spiritual well-being, and she prayed that the simple songs would transport him on angels' wings to the embracing love of Jesus.

As they walked home, she asked him what he thought of the service. He walked a few paces, as if putting his thoughts in order, before he replied, and when he spoke it was with his accustomed reserve and apparent lack of involvement.

"I thanks you kindly, ma'am," he said. "Fo' showin' me that good thing. It gives me much to think about."

She was disappointed that he was not more enthusiastic, but he went to church with her regularly every Sunday after that, and while he never prayed or joined in the hymns, he would listen to the sermons with rapt attention, and discuss the meaning of them afterward as they walked home. He became good friends with several of the men, even Charles, his erstwhile rival, and spent considerable time with Abram. Joyce told Queen later that Davis spent his days off at Abram's workshop, helping him with the fire and forge, and ceaselessly questioning him about working conditions, and the role of black men in the world.

He wrenched his shoulder one day, grubbing a stump of an old tree in the garden, and when she came to him with his refreshment, she found him in the potting shed trying to rub oil onto himself.

"Let me do that," she said. He made no demur, but sat on a box, and let her massage his arm and shoulder. It felt good, and he told her so.

"My mammy taught me," Queen said, pleased. "She said it was my pappy's favorite thing."

She put more oil on her hand, and caressed his injured muscles. She could not resist staring at the scars on his back, the hideous imperfections on his otherwise flawless body. The shed was hot and quiet, and she worked in silence, but she knew she gave him pleasure. Her hands inched toward the scars, attracted to them, repelled by what had caused them. She touched them and caressed them, and soothed them with oil, and he groaned softly, the broken twisted nerves close to the surface, and sparklingly alive.

"Did it hurt?" she whispered, and was surprised to hear him chuckle.

"Waren't you ever beaten?" he asked her in surprise, and Queen felt almost guilty that she, a slave, had not suffered as other slaves.

"Not really," she said, as if apologizing. "I got the switch a few times."

Davis nodded. "Then you was lucky," he said. "It hurt."

And yet he did not believe he had the words to tell

748

her how much it had hurt, for what words could describe that agony? They said you didn't feel it after the first few lashes, that your body and mind went numb, you fell unconscious, but that wasn't true. You felt every sting of it, or he did, and assumed he was not alone. It cut like a razor across your back, and went on cutting and cutting, like acid eating into your flesh, until you could not stop yourself crying out in agony, no matter how strong you were. And still it went on, pain without end, ceaselessly, unimaginably. You couldn't even count the number because it went on and on, and all you could feel was this terrible pain, and a dreadful anger that someone had the power to do this to you for no other reason than because you were black.

If you were lucky, you fainted, but still it went on until you thought you must die.

Then, wonder of wonders, suddenly it stopped, and they cut you down, and let you go. You pulled yourself up, struggled to your feet, somehow, anyhow, just to try to hang on to some last thread of your dignity, your self. You walked away, staggered away, feeling the blood pour out of you, running down your back and your legs, and squelching out of your boots, if you were lucky enough to have boots. And you hated them with every ounce of your being for doing this to you, just because you were black, and you swore to yourself a most sacred, solemn vow, by whatever God you believed in, or nothing if you did not believe, that someday, somehow, somewhere, you would make them pay for what they had done to you. Because you were black.

"It hurt like the very devil," he said to Queen again.

He could not believe it. The power of her gentle hands had sharpened the memory of his distress, and he felt that churning, irrational anger again, and a desperate, aching sense of injustice. But beyond everything else, he felt lonely. He felt tears well up inside him, and fought like the tiger he was to control them.

"I hate them fo' what they did," he said, his voice choking with unreleased and indescribable emotion.

The depth of his emotion, his profound distress, pierced Queen's heart. She moved her hands around him, and held him close to her, careless of the oil that glistened on his back, careless of her modesty, careless of everything else in the world but the single driving need she felt to alleviate his sorrow.

"Don't hate," she whispered in his ear. "There's no need to hate now."

"It's all there is," Davis said, for hate had become the reason for his existence. He lived only for revenge— shapeless, formless revenge—against a target he could not define. Someday, somehow, somewhere, someone would pay for what they had done to him, but he was patient, for he wanted that revenge to be as intense as the pain that had been so casually inflicted on him.

"No," Queen said. "There is love."

He nodded gently, as if he were considering what she had said, when in fact he was battling an urge to do something he believed must destroy him, for if there was not hate, if there was only love, what would he have to live for?

He lost the battle. His need to be not alone was so overwhelming that he turned his face to Queen and put his lips to hers, and devoured her into him, and she gave her mouth willingly to his, and her body unfolded to him, like a lotus to the sun.

But even as she surrendered to him, she resisted him. As much as she trusted him, she could not believe he would not hurt her. He sensed that she was not ready, and stopped, and looked into her eyes.

She nodded her head. She loved him so, she was prepared to endure any pain he might cause, but he knew the moment had gone, and that she was not ready.

"I will not take what you cannot give," he said. He moved gently, and lay back on the floor, and nestled

750

his strong arm around her. She wanted to cry, but did not know why, there was no reason to cry. She rested her head on his shoulder, and luxuriated in the closeness of him, the feel of him, the smell of him. She drifted into a contented sleep, and when she woke he was still there.

He lay on his back, staring at the roof, conscious only that the sweet thing lying asleep beside him was a gift more precious than any he deserved.

75

Nothing seemed to change between them, but Queen believed that something had. Their lives continued as before, with the ritual they had established, but whenever she brought him his refreshment in the garden, he was always outside, and Queen thought he engineered it deliberately, so he would not be alone with her in the shed again. To let him know how much she cared for him, and how very much she appreciated his tact and unselfishness, she would touch his hand sometimes, when they sat together in the sun. He would respond, and hold her hand for a while, but he never gave any indication, by word or deed, that he wanted more from her. These were the most pleasant times for her, and puzzling too, for she wanted their relationship to be more than it was, but did not want to sacrifice the simple beauty of what they had.

He still ate with her in the evenings, only now he would talk a little more freely to her, and sometimes offered ambiguous clues to his background. She knew he had been a slave, and she knew he resented that bondage with a deep and abiding bitterness, that endured even now, when it was over. She knew he had been truculent, and knew he had run away several times, only to be caught and lashed for it, and that in itself confused her. He was a clever and resourceful man, and she found it hard to believe, given his resolute determination in all things, that of his many escapes none had succeeded for more than a day or two. It occurred to her that perhaps he had not actually wanted to get away, that he escaped and allowed himself to be caught again, and endured his punishment as if he believed that one day even his Massa must be appalled at the torture that had been inflicted on him, and would say enough. It would have been a mighty triumph if that had happened, it would have destroyed the system from within, but it was an impossible dream, which never came true. The fact that he was prepared to suffer such torment for such an unattainable ideal made her love him even more, and gave him, in her eyes, the stature of a saint or a martyr. She sensed his aching loneliness and his feeling of detachment, of isolation, from other people, and she believed it was her bounden duty to bring him to peace with his brethren and himself. She was certain that his place in heaven was secure, even though he was a nonbeliever, for God could not exclude such a good and caring man. What was not secure was his place on earth, and she started to think of herself as his salvation, that she, as a woman, had a redemptive power that would ease his hurt and calm his soul.

She wondered about the history of his heart. She knew he had never been married and that he had no children, but otherwise he never spoke of women. It was possible he had never been in love before, and while Queen didn't know if he loved her, she was sure that she loved him. It was a generous love, that wanted little for herself, only the knowledge that she had, in some way, made him happy. Her faith in her love was so strong that she was sure that when she exposed him to it, it would be returned a hundredfold.

Yet she had failed him. She had rejected him because of her own fears of physical hurt, and the change she saw in their relationship was that since then he had avoided any situation where she might reject him again.

She had no idea how to achieve her goal, for she was too shy to tell Davis of her love in simple terms, fearing he would not understand the depth of it. It shocked her to realize that she had never had the occasion or the opportunity to tell anyone, except her mother, how much she loved them, and no one except her mother had ever said it to her. Whatever school there was for love that other people attended, Queen had been excluded from it.

She tried to talk about it with Joyce, but it was difficult, for how could you ask anyone what love is? They sat on the porch one afternoon when the rest of the family was about their business, rocking in unison, and Queen wondered, vaguely, about men.

Joyce knew the intention behind the question, and made a little speech about men, so big and strong and thinking they could rule the world, but really completely reliant on women. She stressed the virtues of married life, with its joys and difficulties, but stressed the joys and minimized the difficulties, for she had another objective. She cared for Queen dearly, and didn't entirely trust Davis. While she liked the man, admired him, she saw too many dark forces in him and too much of the wandering soul in search of some masculine goal, to believe that Davis was ready to settle down with one woman. And she didn't want Queen to be hurt. Or get into trouble.

"Still steppin' out with Davis?" she asked casually, in the little silence that followed her talk about matrimony.

Queen nodded, although she didn't know if it was true. They went together to church on Sundays, but otherwise they never saw each other outside the house. They had different afternoons off, and he never asked her out. Joyce didn't care if they were actually courting or not, they were constantly in each other's company, and she knew how much Queen loved the man. She could read it in her shining eyes.

"Ain't doin' more than steppin' out with him?" Joyce asked her.

The question irritated Queen, and she shook her head.

"I don't even know where he lives," she said, as proof of her evidence.

"Down yonder a ways," Joyce told her, nodding her head in the direction of the river, but being deliberately vague. "He got a li'l shack by the river, Abram say. 'Tain't much of a place, but Davis say it good enough for him."

She could not resist a word of caution to her friend.

"Be careful, missy," she said. "Don't let him get too close. The man don't even love himself. He cain't love anyone else."

But Queen didn't want to hear that.

The following Thursday she made herself as pretty as could be, and left the house late. She went to see Abram and asked him exactly where Davis lived, claiming she had a message to deliver from the sisters. She found her way to the shack, intending to wait outside until he came home, but it was warm, and she wanted shelter. She tapped on the door, and saw that it was not locked or barred. She opened the door and called out his name, but no one was there. Feeling both excited and guilty, she went inside.

It was what she might have expected, a sparse and spartan room, furnished with only a rough bed, a chair, and a broken table. There was a small trunk that was locked and she guessed that was where he kept his few clothes. Although he was always clean and tidy, for Queen did his laundry, he didn't have many clothes, and seemed uninterested in them. There was a tin plate and mug and a knife, and some bread and cheese in a small meat safe. Beyond that, there was nothing to indicate that anyone lived there.

Yet it was redolent of him. The sense of his presence was almost tangible to her, and she lay on his bed and put her face to the blanket, and was sure there was a lingering smell of him. Or if there was not, it didn't matter, because she could believe that there was. Tingling with anticipation of him, she lay waiting for him to come home.

When she heard footsteps approaching, she got up from the bed. She went to the small, rectangular hole that was the window, pushed aside the sack that covered it, and stared at the nearby river. When the door opened, she turned to greet him, but did not smile.

He looked at her, and if he felt any surprise, he did not show it. He came in, shut the door, and put a small brown bag of provisions on the table. He moved close to her, and touched her hair, but then dropped his hand to his side, as if waiting to be told what to do. She took his hand in hers, drew it to her mouth, and kissed it tenderly. She moved his hand to her neck, and traced it down over her body, and put her free hand to his neck and traced it down over his chest. She turned her face up to him and looked deep into his wondrous eyes, to let him know that she was ready to give him whatever he wanted to take.

Still for a moment he did not move. Then he leaned down to her, for he was so tall and she so tiny, and gently kissed her lips and let the tip of his tongue discover the taste of her. His mouth moved to her eyes, and he kissed each in turn, gently, and she closed them, as she knew he wanted her to do.

He picked her up, carried her to the bed, and laid her gently down. He sat on the edge of the bed for a while, stroking her hair and neck, and then lay beside her and kissed her, and opened his mouth to her, to let her know that he would be passive and not force himself upon her. She let her tongue caress his, and his mouth yielded to her, and seemed infinite. As she kissed him, she stroked his body with her hands—his neck, his shoulders, his chest. Carefully, she undid the buttons at the neck of his shirt, and pulled the garment free from his pants, pushed it upward and upward, until she had to break the kiss, and now he helped a little by pulling the shirt over his head and off, but lay down again. He moved his hands to her blouse and repeated the actions she had done to him, a mirror image of her need, not his. When her breasts were free, he stroked them, staring at them and at her, and delicately kissed her nipples.

She was suspended in time. The lack of urgency in him released her inhibitions, and it was she who directed his hands to where she wanted them to be. Naked now, they lay for an hour, touching, kissing, caressing, until his manhood became a friend to her, and she welcomed that friend into her body. They lay side by side, joined as one flesh, he hardly moving until a soft thrusting of her hips told him that it was time to do so. Never dominant, never assertive, he concentrated all his attention on her pleasure, as if his own were irrelevant. In the days and nights to come he would pay more attention to his own needs, but this time was for her.

It was exotic, languorous love to her, bringing her a pleasure she had not even imagined existed. Holding him close to her, deep inside her, her hands stroked the welts on his back that were the focus of her love, for she believed she would heal his heart, and leave it clear and unscarred, unlike his back, no matter how deep the wounds there.

When it was done, they lay together, like naked, pagan children, and tiny tears of love appeared in Queen's eyes. Davis leaned over her.

756

"On the plantation I swore I would drink the tears of every black who ever cried," he told her softly.

Her put his mouth to her eyes and drank her tears.

"It would be an ocean," he whispered.

He worried that it had been bad for her, that he had hurt her, but she shook her head, and laughed away his concerns. She nestled into his powerful embrace, touched his lips with her fingers, and asked why he did not smile. So he smiled for her, and held her hand, and could not tell her the depth of his love, for he had never found love in the world before, and his could not match her own.

She came to him every Thursday, and brought little comforts for the shack, but nothing that would make him feel that she was trying to tame him. They made love every Thursday, and he never betrayed her trust in him, and never took more from her than she could give.

Fall came, and the first chill of winter. He fixed some old glass into the open space that was his window, and bought a stove so that they might be warm. He celebrated Christmas at church with her, and then walked her home to the sisters, for she had to serve their dinner. She gave him her gift, a new shirt, and he was embarrassed, because he had nothing for her. He had never given anything to anyone, because he had never had anyone to give anything to. She laughed, and told him it didn't matter. His love was all the present she needed. Yet she wanted something more.

"I want yo' baby," she whispered to him one night when they lay in each other's arms, and she thought he was asleep. She wanted to feel his seed quicken inside her, and swell and grow big in her belly, until she exploded with the product of his love.

Davis was not asleep, but he did not stir, did not open his eyes. He did not want her to know he had heard her, for he did not know how to explain to her that he would not bring a child into this world.

From his earliest memories he had been consumed with bitterness at his enslaved state. A dark and rebellious boy, he had grown into a darker, more rebellious man, and he viewed with contempt those other slaves who seemed prepared to tolerate their imprisonment, or make the best of it, for Davis saw no good to be made of it. He was known only by his given name, because he refused to take the surname of his Massa, as was common practice on the plantations, and would not answer to it if called. He had a strong need for women, but avoided them, and deliberately chose an ascetic life, shunning human contact. He wanted no consolation or condolence for his plight, and no simple comfort that might ease it. Much as he pined for a wife and children, he would not bring a child into this world, born into bondage. All he wanted was his freedom and when he had it he would be his own man and until then he would not belong to anyone.

Not even his Massa. He did as little work as he possibly could, was the bane of the overseers, and felt the frequent bite of the lash. He ran away at the first opportunity, and thought himself, for a moment, free. He was exultant, but the reality that his freedom was a myth soon became clear to him. As able and resourceful as he was, the chances of being able to get from southern Alabama to the northern side of the Mason-Dixon line were virtually impossible, and he did not know how to contact anyone on the Underground Railroad that might have eased his passage. Slave catchers and dogs came after him, and within days he was back at the plantation and was given a hundred lashes. Since he could not escape to any secure freedom, he set his mind to breaking his Massa's will. He ran away whenever he could, fully expecting to be caught, taken back, and lashed. Eventually, he thought, they

758

must see reason, eventually they must understand that he would not stay, and then they would let him go. Or kill him. Like Cap'n Jack before him, he thought slavery irrational and he could not understand why rational people tolerated it. In this, like Cap'n Jack, he profoundly underestimated the society he was dealing with. His Massa would willingly have killed him rather than let him be free, for to let one slave go simply because he didn't want to be a slave was to undermine everything the society was built on, and stood for, and aspired to.

Marked as a persistent and dangerous troublemaker, when the war came Davis was kept in leg shackles, so that he would not escape, for then he might have made it to sanctuary. When he was released from those shackles with emancipation, it was almost anticlimactic to him. Having fought against one thing all his life, now he had nothing left to fight for, and he did not know what he wanted to achieve. Being free, he discovered, was not enough for him.

He traveled northward and what he saw appalled him. The vaunted equality of reconstruction was turning into a jungle of survival by shameless opportunists and many good and decent men were trampled in the rush. Segregation was rampant, and they could not even ride in the same streetcar as whites. Although some black men with property could vote, how many black men had that much property? The merits of a few, a very few, were being recognized, but that was mostly patronage, crumbs from the white man's table. And it would always be like that. Always and always and always. No white man would ever give real power to a black man, or real freedom. It had to be taken.

When Queen told him that she wanted his baby, his soul blenched. There was nothing for a black boy in this world, and it was even worse for a black girl.

He loved Queen as much as he could, but not as

much as she loved him. Her love collided with his hate, and it made the pain worse than any white man's lash, and sweeter than any honey.

Queen never told him again that she wanted his baby, because there was no need. He had already given her the gift that she wanted from him.

76

She told no one about it until it was inevitable. She didn't believe it herself until it was inevitable. When she missed her time of the month in late November, she wasn't unduly concerned, for she was not always regular, but as the days dragged through December she began to worry, and before Christmas she was sure. She was lethargic and often unwell, and even though she tried to pretend it was because of winter chills, every morning she looked in the mirror and held her stomach to see if it was growing, if her secret was starting to show. Then the Preacher gave a sermon about lust and fornication, and the plight of the poor innocents brought into the world by those who could not, would not, avoid temptation.

"Fornication, and all uncleanness, let it not be named among you; let it not be once named among you, as becometh saints!"

Queen believed the words were directed exclusively to her, and cried a little, for she thought what she did with Davis was beautiful, and not unclean, but blessed in the sight of the Lord. And He had rewarded her with this precious gift, which would be hers and hers alone, and which she would love. She fought the guilt the Preacher made her feel, and became resentful, for the angel had called Mary blessed, and she was so in awe of the process of creation, of the miracle of this tiny thing growing inside her, that she believed it divine.

"From fornication, and all other deadly sin; from all the deceits of the world, the flesh, and the devil, good Lord, deliver us."

She flushed, for she had been deceitful. She had deceived Joyce and the sisters by not telling them about her baby. She had even deceived Davis by telling him that she wanted his child and not telling him her wish had been granted. But she did not believe she had sinned.

"Deliver us, O Lord, deliver us. Hallelujah!"

The rising shouts of the congregation, in full-throated agreement with the Preacher, made her despair, and she began to worry about the future of her child, if he should be fatherless, for she had already decided it was a boy. She despaired for herself, for what would people say to her, do to her, when they found out? She looked at Davis, who was sitting beside her. He took her hand and squeezed it gently. Queen wondered if he had guessed already, but knew he had not.

Someone else had guessed. Joyce kept her eyes on Queen during the sermon, and saw the guilt, the eyes cast down to the floor. She saw Queen look at Davis, saw him take her hand, and saw the great need that Queen had for him. Joyce sighed, and prayed she was wrong, but knew she was not. She would deal with it when it had to be dealt with, and until then she could only pray.

Someone else had guessed as well. Miss Gippy had sharp ears, sharper eyes, and a fervid imagination. She had no experience with pregnancy, but had a fascination with fallen women, being so far from the precipice herself. In her younger days she had spent much time in Boston, lecturing to those who had strayed from the straight and narrow, and had questioned them avidly. She thought she knew all the classic symptoms, even if that knowledge was superficial. When she heard Queen being sick a couple of times in the morning, she smiled smugly to herself, and make a wild, but utterly correct, guess as to the reason. Miss Gippy said nothing to her sister. She preferred to wait and see what developed and take advantage of those developments to save the sinner from hell. Disillusioned with the life the Lord had assigned her, Miss Gippy had an occasional maliciousness about her, which her sister did not share.

Miss Mandy, who should have been the first to guess, never did, and had to be told. And finally it was too choice a secret for Miss Gippy to keep to herself.

Queen had developed a curious habit. Plentifully supplied with food from the sister's pantry, she began to steal food. It was no great crime, because the odd thing was that she took only what she could have had for free. It didn't happen very often, but occasionally, when she was depressed or agitated, concerned for the future welfare of her boy. She would filch a piece of toast from Miss Gippy's morning tray, or snatch a cake from the afternoon tea stand. She served breakfast one morning—crisply fried bacon and poached eggs, toast and butter and jam—and she stood waiting at the table as the sisters said their prayers. She always had to wait until the prayers were done, in case they needed anything more once they began to eat, and she was expected to pray with them.

Miss Mandy's eyes were firmly closed, as it was her turn to lead the prayer. Queen, who knew she could not keep her condition secret much longer, had her eyes firmly open, and fixed on the basket of toast.

"O Lord, we thank Thee for Thy precious bounty," Miss Mandy intoned. "And for Thy many blessings on these Thy humble servants."

Sure that no one was watching her, sure that the sisters' eyes were closed in prayer, Queen, quickly, furtively, grabbed a piece of toast from the table, hid it under her apron, and stuffed it into her pocket.

"Queen, what on earth are you doing?" Miss Gippy said sharply. Her eyes had been only partially closed, and watching Queen.

Queen flushed, and prayed that the floor would open up and swallow her.

"Nuttin', Missy," she said, lapsing into dialect, as she always did when she was nervous. "I ain't done nuttin'."

Miss Mandy looked up, wondering what the fuss was about.

"I saw you take that piece of toast," Miss Gippy admonished. "Don't we feed you enough, that you have to steal from our very table?"

Queen couldn't think of anything to say, and looked at the floor.

"The eighth commandment, girl!" Miss Gippy snapped. To Miss Mandy, the situation was completely confusing, but she understood there had been a puzzling crisis, and discipline was needed.

"I think you'd better go to your room," Miss Mandy said, longing to be alone with her sister, to find out what the matter was.

"After you've put the toast back," Miss Gippy added.

The miserable Queen took the toast from her pocket, put it back in its basket, and scurried from the room. Miss Mandy waited for some word from her sister, but Miss Gippy was enjoying herself far too much. She buttered a piece of toast, spread it liberally with apple jelly, and took a bite from it.

"Well?" Miss Mandy asked.

There was another little silence while Miss Gippy chewed her food. It was not good manners to speak with your mouth full. She took a sip of tea and sprinkled salt on her eggs.

"Nesting," she said casually, and tucked into her breakfast.

It was as well that she did so, and thus could not see the look on her sister's face. Miss Mandy stared at her, first with amazement, and then with something very close to hate. At that moment, she hated Gippy, she hated Queen, she hated the world. It was her dearest wish in life to have a child, and now even the physical possibility of it was gone. She was consumed with envy. She had been so good all her life, and loved the Lord, and He had denied her this simple reward. Yet Queen, immoral, illegitimate, nigra Queen, had been providentially blessed. The reward for chastity was emptiness, and the wages of sin were glorious. It simply wasn't fair, and her only defense was to denounce the animal propensities of all blacks.

"Pagans," she whispered harshly.

Miss Gippy nodded her agreement, a tiny drop of egg yolk dribbling down her chin. She picked up her napkin and wiped it away, entirely satisfied with her morning.

Queen sat on her bed, rocking gently, and keening, pity for her own distress and a lullaby for her unborn child.

She had no alternative now. She had to tell someone, ask someone for help. But it would not be Davis.

"I warned you," Joyce said angrily. "Don't let him get too close, I said!"

"Well, I did!" Queen blazed back. "So there ain't no point in makin' speeches about it!"

She turned away, her flash of anger quickly spent and dejection its immediate successor.

"What am I going to do, Joyce?" she cried. Joyce moved quickly to her, and held her.

"Hush, girl, no use cryin'," she said. "Ain't no use in cryin' now."

But she let Queen cry, and then dried her eyes, and told her it was only proper that Davis should know. It was his baby. She did not understand why Queen was

764

so reluctant. It was unlikely that Davis would hit her, and it was right that he share the burden. Maybe, if they were lucky, Davis would do what he should; certainly he would if Joyce had anything to do with it.

Queen could not explain to Joyce that she was sure Davis would not marry her, because she was scared to admit it to herself. In the end she agreed to tell him, but only if Joyce went with her.

Davis stared at her, and those eyes that she loved so seemed full of reproach. In this she was right, but he was not angry with her. Only with himself.

Joyce was impatient. "She say it's your'n, and she ain't a liar, so what you gwine do about it?" she demanded.

Davis said nothing, and Queen could not bear his silence.

"I's sorry," she said, and to her relief and amazement, Davis smiled.

"Guess I's gwine have to marry you," he said. Queen closed her eyes, and told her heart to be still, but it would not. When she opened her eyes again, he was still there, and still smiling. She got up, to fly into his arms, but Joyce had a few things to say first.

"Not so fast, missy," Joyce commanded, and Queen stayed where she was. Joyce turned her attention to Davis.

"She weren't gwine tell you, coz she didn't want to force you to marry her," Joyce told him, to Queen's surprise. She had not told Joyce this, Joyce had guessed.

"But she don't want if yo' jus' marryin' her coz you must," Joyce continued. "She don't want you if'n you don't love her." Queen hadn't told Joyce this either, but it was close to the truth.

The smile had faded from Davis's lips. He listened to what Joyce had to say, and then turned and looked out of the window at the moonlight on the river. He could not lie; he could only tell them the truth. He adored Queen; he respected her and admired her. He thought

765

she was the dearest thing he had ever met, filled up with love, and she deserved a fine man, and boundless happiness. By rights, that man should be him. The child was his, and Queen loved him. He would fulfill his duty, and marry her, if that was what she wanted, for he couldn't bear to think of her raising his child in this dark world on her own. But if loving her was the test, then he failed, and he could only be honest.

"I don't know if I loves you," he said. "I don't think I know what love is."

He saw the sadness wash into Queen's eyes, and guilt attacked his conscience. He could not do this to her.

"But if'n I's gonna find out from anyone, I reckon it's you," he said. "And I will try and love you."

The effect on Queen was miraculous, and it seemed to satisfy Joyce.

"I surely hope so," she said. "Coz if'n you don't, if you don't look after this child and cherish her like she deserves, I will come fo' you wherever you are, and I'll fix you so you cain't never give any po' girl a baby again."

She stressed her point, to be sure that he understood.

"Y'know I will," she said.

"I know y'will," Davis agreed.

Joyce had done as much as she could. She looked at Queen.

"Now you c'n go to him," she said. And when she saw the love shining out of Queen's eyes, her heart melted. Queen moved into Davis's arms, and he held her close to him, and hated himself for what he had done.

Queen stayed with him that night, and they made their plans. Davis said he would do whatever she wanted, and they could stay if that was her wish, but he thought the sisters would make things difficult, that Queen's condition would offend them, and they would sack either or both of them. It was better they go somewhere else.

For himself, he did not want to give up on all his plans. He'd always wanted to go North, because if there was any future for black people, it was there. And they should go soon, before the sisters found out, and while they still had the chance to set up a new life before the child was born.

"Anywhere," Queen told him. "Anywhere in the whole wide world that you want to go, I will go with you."

Then she laughed, and corrected herself. "We will go with you."

Davis put his hand on her stomach. He couldn't feel anything but the warmth of her flesh, and he envied the child, cozy and safe inside her, secure from the travails of the world. Just for a moment, he regretted that he had ever been born.

"Don't love me too much," he whispered. "All I ever do is make people cry."

But his warning came too late. She loved him too much already.

They would leave on Thursday. It was her afternoon off, and would arouse no suspicion from the sisters. He would leave work early, saying he had to buy plants, and would meet her at the coach depot.

The change in Queen was blatantly apparent to Miss Mandy, but she attributed it to the wrong reason. She thought Queen's radiant happiness was due to her pregnancy, and her envy of her servant's condition magnified. She wanted to confront Queen, call her the baggage that she was, and kick her out, and that animal man with her, and she begged the Lord for forgiveness of her sin. To her surprise, the Lord answered her prayer, and her jealousy gave way to her blissful realization that soon she would have a little baby in the house, to love as her own. From then on, her happiness

767

rivaled Queen's, and she was solicitous to Queen, and constantly on guard for her welfare, while still not admitting that she knew the child was coming.

But the baby was not the only reason for Queen's mood. Much as she already loved the tiny thing, her real joy came from the fact that soon the child would have a proper home in which to be born and to grow and to be loved, and a mother and father to do that loving, which she had never had. It did not matter that Davis did not love her as much as she loved him. He loved her more than anyone else had ever done.

On Thursday afternoon, she packed a few things in a small case, and waited until the sisters went to their rooms for their afternoon nap. She crept down the stairs and into the kitchen, and let herself out by the back door. She saw Davis working in the front garden, and waved to him happily, but did not go to him in case either of the sisters was looking out of the window. She left by the back gate, and walked quickly down the lane, and again down another lane, until she was a few blocks from the house. She sat on a park bench at peace with the world, until she heard the clatter of horse's hooves that signaled the approaching streetcar.

She went to Joyce's house to say good-bye. Joyce gave her a small posy of flowers, and wished her well. The women hugged, and cried together for a while, tears of happiness and loss. They sat in the rockers and talked of nothing until it was time to leave.

Queen made her way to the coach depot, and got there early. She waited patiently for Davis, and she was never sure exactly when she knew he wasn't coming. Nor was she exactly sure when she realized that she had always known he wasn't going to come. Perhaps that was why she had been scared to tell him about the baby.

Perhaps she had known it when she did tell him, and had seen that look of reproach in his eyes, that she now understood had not been directed at herself. Perhaps she had known it when they lay together and made their plans, and he told her of his ambition to go North. He had included her then because he felt that he had to, but now she thought it had been his way of telling her he was leaving.

She wasn't angry with him; she was angry with herself for being foolish enough to dream that she could bind him to her. There was something he had to do with his life that precluded her and a child, and it was important to him, and because it was important to him, it was important to her.

And anyway, she had a part of him, growing inside her, the best of him. All that mattered to her now was his child.

She left the little posy that Joyce had given her on a seat at the depot. If by chance she was wrong, and he had been delayed, he would see the posy if he came to the depot, and would know it was from her, and would know where to find her.

She didn't realize she had waited for him for five hours past his appointed time.

77

Queen gasped at the shock of the pain again, pushed as hard as she could, to Miss Mandy's naive instructions, and grabbed on to the bedposts for leverage. It had been going on for some hours, the contractions coming with increasing frequency, and the birth was imminent. It was as well, for Queen felt as if she were trying to push a giant watermelon through her loins. Past all inhibition, she yelled to the rafters. Miss Mandy shouted at her, but happily, for she was in her element.

Miss Gippy was leaning against the wall in a state of shock, muttering for guidance from Jesus, trying to block her ears to Queen's cries, and uselessly insisting that they fetch help. No one heard her. Miss Mandy was determined to bring the child, which she had already come to think of as her own, into the world herself, and Queen had no other thought than to see him safely delivered.

Queen had not been devastated by the loss of Davis for she thought it inevitable. She was angry because he had not been brave enough to tell her the truth. She missed him, she was lonely. But mostly she was scared for the future.

She had dreaded the scene she knew must happen with the sisters when they were told of her plight and her condition. She had gone to Joyce for advice, and both agreed that Miss Mandy and Miss Gippy were her best chance. Joyce did suggest one other alternative, but getting rid of her baby was inconceivable to Queen, as Joyce knew it would be. Queen had never had anything that was truly her own before. Some clothes, which were usually other people's hand-me-downs, and a few trinkets, most of which she had misplaced. But the child inside her was hers, not to be shared with anyone, not even, now, with Davis. The baby was part of her body and all of her love, and the only person who could ever take him away from her was him. She didn't know what she would do if her baby didn't love her; it didn't even enter her thinking, for she could not imagine that he would not.

Joyce had gone with her to the sisters, and had told them the news. The reaction was exactly predictable, at least at first.

"A wicked, naughty girl, that's what you are!" Miss Mandy told her. She'd been wanting to say it for some time, but had refrained because she didn't want to lose Queen, wasn't prepared to risk Queen's running away before the child was born. Now that Queen was safe with them, for the term of her pregnancy at least, Miss

Mandy gave full flood to her moral rectitude, chorused by her sister.

"A sinner damned to hell," Miss Gippy triumphed. "The seventh commandment!"

Joyce protested Queen's innocence, but Miss Mandy had other plans for her.

"How dare you speak to me like that." She glared at Joyce.

"I'll speak to you any way I wants, you dried-up ol' prune," Joyce responded as angrily, playing right into Miss Mandy's hands. "This child need help, not yo' sermons."

This was heresy to Miss Gippy. What was a sermon but a path to divine assistance? She ordered Joyce out of the house, but Miss Mandy was more careful. Where was Queen to get this help, if not from them? It fell to the sisters to bear the burden of Queen's sin.

Queen was curiously detached from it all, and played no part in the proceedings. Her mind was remembering Davis and thinking of her son. The sisters might very well throw her out. Miss Gippy was intent on it, although Miss Mandy was less determined. If they did throw her out, she would survive. She had a little money saved, and Joyce would help.

"I'll take her with me," Joyce told Miss Mandy, and it was as good as done to Miss Gippy.

"Out of the house, the pair of you," she commanded again. Queen accepted the order, and moved toward the door with Joyce, but a still small voice stopped them.

"Not so fast," Miss Mandy said softly. "There are other things to consider here."

Everyone looked at her, and she looked at Miss Gippy.

"Such as the child's immortal soul," she said. "Queen is lost to us; all the prayers in Christendom could not save her now. But the child is something else."

A clear, shining path to Jesus revealed itself to Miss

Gippy. Allow the little children to come unto me. They would allow the unborn babe to come to Him; indeed, they would push him along. They would take him by the hand and deliver him to Calvary. It was why they had come South, to save the souls of the innocents.

"A precious burden," she whispered, in awe of the inspiration. "An innocent babe."

Miss Mandy turned to Joyce. "I will not let the child go into your care," she said. "He needs the advantage of a proper Christian upbringing."

Joyce was still angry with her. "I's Christian," she affirmed, but Miss Gippy, stirred by true missionary zeal, shouted about paganism, and heathenism and false prophets, which made Joyce even angrier.

"I ain't lettin' her stay," she snapped, but Miss Mandy was ruthlessly reasonable.

"How will you stop it? Queen is in our employ, in our care, and I doubt that the authorities would consider you more suitable than we are. And where would she find another job, in her condition?"

It was inarguable. Whoever these authorities were, secular or religious, they would undoubtedly be sympathetic to a white woman of faultless civic standing, and would scarcely listen to the pleadings of a black, no matter how reasonable. It was also logical. As generous as Joyce was, she and Abram did not have the physical room or the financial resources to care for Queen for an extended period of time. They would have found a way, but it would have been hard for them, and Queen would indeed have trouble getting another job. So while Joyce still resisted the sisters, it was less stubbornly now.

"She ain't stayin'," Joyce said, without conviction.

"I have to," Queen said quietly.

It was the simple truth, and everyone breathed a small, silent sigh of relief.

"A fairly graceless response, Queen," Miss Mandy chided, entirely satisfied with it. She laid down her

772

rules. Queen would continue to work for them as her condition allowed, and would be paid, and given her board and lodging. She would be well looked after and given whatever medical help and advice was necessary. When the child came, Queen would continue her employment. Miss Mandy asked only one thing in return, that Queen forsake her rowdy, nigra church, and worship with the sisters. Joyce tried to protest, but lamely, and Queen agreed to the terms. Joyce was told to leave, and it was indicated that she was not welcome in the house anymore, although Queen could continue to see her occasionally, as a friend. Joyce said a private good-bye to Queen, assuring her of any help she needed, and alternative sanctuary if conditions with the sisters became intolerable, and left. Miss Mandy sent Queen to her room, for it was already quite late, reminding her that they would have prayers at seven in the morning.

Queen sought simple mercies in her prayers that night. She prayed for Davis, that he be blessed and protected wherever he was, and that he be granted a little happiness. He shouldn't have run away, or at least he should have told her good-bye, but she understood why both were impossible. She asked a similar blessing and protection for her child, that he be born whole and complete, and that he come to love her. She asked nothing for herself, except that the old dragons not be too hard on her.

She climbed into bed, missing Davis, missing his protective arms around her, and worrying about where he slept that night, and what the future held in store for him, who had known so much suffering. But he was gone from her now, and someone else needed the attention of her heart. Quietly, sweetly, softly, sadly, she sang the song of her unborn baby.

Miss Mandy sang that song too. Through the weeks and months of Queen's pregnancy, Miss Mandy lived it with her, as if the child had two mothers. While Miss Gippy expected Queen to fulfill all her household duties, Miss Mandy wanted daily reports as to her welfare and that of the child. She looked to all the mothers at her church for guidance, and fussed about Queen's diet and the baby's health. As Queen's stomach filled and rounded, Miss Mandy insisted on increasingly long periods of rest, and even Miss Gippy joined in the spirit, and cosseted Queen, for the closer Queen came to term, the more Miss Gippy stood in awe and fear of the processes of creation. Queen became quite fond of them—their many attentions made her feel secure, and their delight in imagining the child as an infant was touching. On the warm summer days Queen would sit in the garden with Miss Mandy, while Miss Gippy fussed with warm, unnecessary rugs and welcome, cool refreshments. They had a new gardener now, an older man, but he came only twice a week, to maintain what Davis had done. It pleased Queen to sit in the pretty arbor, surrounded by the fragrant roses, and survey the handiwork that her man had made.

"And though I bestow all my goods to feed the poor, and though I give my body to be burned, and have not Charity, it profiteth me nothing."

Miss Mandy was reading from her Bible. Miss Gippy was fussing with a tray.

Prospective motherhood became Queen, and she looked wonderful.

"Charity suffereth long, and is kind. Charity envieth not. Charity vaunteth not itself, is not puffed up."

It pleased Miss Mandy to sit here on these pleasant afternoons, close to maternity, and she vaunted herself a little, and puffed herself up at her own charity to Queen, which is why she read the good words of instruction, to be delivered from vanity and pride.

"It's getting a little chilly," Miss Gippy said. "Don't you think you should go inside, Queen?"

It was a very hot day. Queen smiled, and Miss Mandy was cross.

"For heaven's sake, Gippy, don't fuss," she told her sister. Miss Gippy was a little put out. She was only thinking of Queen's well-being, and the baby's. The way Mandy carried on, anyone would think the child was her own.

"I'm only thinking of the boy," she sniffed, and picked up the tray.

"Why you so sure it's going to be a boy?" Queen wondered, to placate her and include Miss Gippy in a process from which Miss Mandy seemed determined to exclude her.

Miss Gippy did something very odd. She giggled, and was embarrassed by her own frivolity.

"Well, of course, I don't know," she twittered. "How could I know?"

She moved away toward the house.

"Don't sit out here too long," she said, to spite Miss Mandy. Queen adjusted her position on the chair. She was almost to term and could never sit comfortably in one position for very long. Miss Mandy put down her Bible and stared at the garden.

"She's convinced it will be a boy because she wants it to be a boy," she said quietly. "We both do."

She wondered why. Men were deceitful, distrustful, and disloyal. Look what her fiancé had done to her, all those years ago. Look what Davis had done to Queen. Why should she want to bring such a creature into the world? She was honest enough to admit to herself that she adored men, for all their imperfections, and a boy child could be fashioned into the image of a perfect man. A boy child could be made to understand the nature of women, and be kind to them when he grew. He could be schooled not to hurt women, and not to make promises to them that he did not intend to keep. A boy child could learn of women's pain, and become

775

the image of the husband she, Mandy, had never had. She did not want to bring a girl child into this world, for who would wish a woman's life on a poor babe? Yet she knew she would be happy with whatever Queen gave her.

"How does it feel?" Miss Mandy asked quietly.

"Heavy," Queen said, adjusting her weight again. Miss Mandy was always asking her how she felt. But presently, Miss Mandy's mind was on other matters. Her thoughts were metaphysical.

"No, I mean how does it feel in your heart?"

Queen considered the question carefully, but it was so difficult to describe the complex emotions that engulfed her. She had never, for one moment, regretted the pregnancy, and when the physical difficulties of it made her irritable or tired, or when she felt ill, or when she couldn't do her work properly, she would sit somewhere, and talk quietly to her child, and would caress her belly so that he would learn the gentle touch of her hands. She wished she were a poet, or had been schooled better, so that she could communicate the pure wonder of it. The only words that came to her were simple ones, but honestly spoken, directly from her heart.

"I feel—full up with him," Queen said. "Complete with love for him." She smiled.

"There now, I think he's going to be a boy, too. I feel him growing inside me, kicking inside me, and I never want him to leave me. No matter how big he gets I will always think he's too little for this world."

Miss Mandy blinked in the sunlight, and glanced at her Bible.

"And now abideth Faith, Hope and Charity, these three, but the greatest of these is Charity."

They sat in silence for a moment. Bees hummed. Crickets sang. Butterflies danced by.

"I envy you so much," Miss Mandy whispered. Queen looked at the old woman, and felt a surge of sorrow for her, for her aura was abject loneliness. She wanted to give Miss Mandy a gift, in return for the charity she had shown.

She took Miss Mandy's hand and held it against her stomach. They didn't have to wait very long. The child was getting anxious to be born. When Miss Mandy felt the movement of the kick against her hand, a golden smile suffused her face, and a sharp pain stabbed her heart. The child kicked again, a slight, dull thump, and Miss Mandy pulled her hand away.

"Don't make it worse for me," she said.

So it was perfectly reasonable to Queen that Miss Mandy be her midwife, and in any case Miss Mandy would tolerate no other. Miss Gippy was far from convinced. What if something went wrong? What if the child had problems? And who was going to clean up the mess?

"We're nearly there!" Miss Mandy cried, and Miss Gippy's eyes popped out in amazement. Queen had given a shameless yell and an almighty shove, and the head of the baby appeared. Miss Gippy fell to her knees, and prayed for assistance or deliverance.

"Get up off your knees, woman, and get me a towel," Miss Mandy ordered. Queen yelled again, and pushed again, and so it was that a child was born, to three lonely women, who had no experience of such wonder.

"Bless my cotton socks," Miss Mandy whispered, in awe. "It's a boy."

The words lulled Queen, like a benediction. She lay back on the bed, in exhaustion, and elation, and triumph.

"Let me see him," she said.

Miss Mandy and Miss Gippy were fussing over the tot, doing the things that had to be done.

"In a moment, Queen," said Miss Mandy. "We have things to do."

"Let me see him," Queen said again, but Miss Mandy

didn't even reply. The baby was so darling, and so fragile, and yet she had to be brutal with him, to ensure his survival. She cut the cord herself, and cleaned him, and spanked him to make him cry, so that she was certain he would live. And there was so much else. She had to make sure he was complete, that all his tiny toes were there and his dear little fingers, that his ears were well formed, and touch his tiny, fluffy hair. And he wasn't really black at all, just a sort of milky coffee, and anyway, perhaps he would lighten a little as he grew. And she had to hold him to her, hold him to her breast, so that he would know that no matter who fed him, this was where he was loved. What on earth was Queen making such a fuss about?

"He's my baby!" Queen was shouting now. "He's mine. I want to see him."

Every fiber of her was pleading for this part of her body to be returned to her.

"Don't be so ungrateful, Queen," Miss Mandy said sharply. Oh, he looked lovely, wrapped in clean swaddling clothes of palest blue. This was how the darling baby Jesus must have looked, and Miss Mandy's soul magnified the Lord.

"I want my baby!" Queen cried. "Give me my baby!"

Miss Mandy sighed, but came to Queen with the child, for he was whimpering, and might be hungry, and he was never going to be hungry, or want for anything. Miss Mandy would see to that. With maternal care, she put him into Queen's arms at last, and Queen stared at the tiny thing, and vowed she would never let him out of her arms again. She freed her breast, and put the child's mouth to it. Of all the pleasures life can give, this was the finest feeling, for she, who had given him life, was sustaining him. She could not isolate any of the thousand emotions that were punching at her heart, and as she stared at her son, she tried to see his future, and knew she would do everything in her power to make it blessed.

"He's a very fine, very handsome boy," she heard Miss Mandy say, and nodded in agreement. "We must think of a very special name for him."

Queen didn't even bother to look at Miss Mandy, for the matter was already settled. He would be called David, which meant Beloved.

"I don't think that's entirely suitable," Miss Mandy said. Queen didn't respond, because there wasn't anything to say. His name was David, and she was feeding him. She wished the sisters would go away, so that she could be alone with him, and welcome him in private, as mothers should, but Miss Gippy was saying something, about King David, and Bathsheba, and adultery.

"We thought Abner," Miss Mandy said.

"Abner," Miss Gippy agreed. "A fine, biblical name."

Queen was puzzled. This had nothing to do with them. She was very grateful to the sisters for their many kindnesses, but the name of the baby was not their business.

"His name is David," she said.

Miss Mandy thought she was being very difficult. She had taken Queen in, when many might have thrown her onto the streets. She had looked after her and delivered her baby. The very least Queen could do was to let her choose the boy's name, and yet she seemed insistent on a name that remembered his philandering father. Oviously, Miss Mandy sensibly decided, nothing was to be gained by discussing it now. Queen was tired, and in an emotional state. Miss Mandy had plenty of time, Abner didn't have to be christened for several weeks, and Queen would see reason after some rest.

The sisters went about their business, to put sheets and towels in the wash to soak, and then to say their separate private prayers, thanking God for his many blessings, and at last, Queen was left alone with her boy.

He was asleep, safe in her loving arms, and she

promised him she would do her best by him, always. She told him how sorry she was that he didn't have a pappy, but his pappy had important things to do in the world, and she would be Mammy and Pappy for him.

And then, from somewhere deep in her soul, sweet music flooded forth from her, wordless music that was her lullaby.

Six weeks later, in a simple, private ceremony arranged by the sisters at the Lutheran Church, Queen watched with uplifting pride and listened with a certain ambivalence as the minister sprinkled water on her baby's head and christened him Abner.

78

Miss Mandy was trying to steal her baby. Queen was sure of it; there was no other explanation. It hadn't been so obvious in the early days, the first few weeks. There was the trouble over his name, but Queen had not put up too much of a struggle about that. She didn't want to appear ungrateful for everything the sisters had done for her, and if it pleased them to call him Abner, it was only a name. Queen had compromised, in her own mind, that he was Abner David, but as the weeks went on, common usage prevailed, and now he was simply Abner.

From the very beginning Miss Mandy had been obsessive about the boy, worrying about his health, his feeding times, and his food. She asked questions that Queen thought were far too personal, about her diet, to be sure that Abner was getting good milk. She would sit holding him for hours while Queen worked. She talked to him endlessly about Jesus, and told him Bible stories, even though he was too young to hear. She fretted about him if he cried, and rocked him gently when he slept. She even changed his soiled linen.

She would call for Queen when she thought Abner was hungry, and make Queen feed him in front of her, which Queen didn't like. She had protested the first time it happened.

"He's starving, Queen," Miss Mandy said. "Where have you been?"

"Pro'bly just got the burps," Queen replied. "He been fed."

Miss Mandy referred to her notepad.

"That was four hours ago," she said. "I have it written down."

Abner did seem to be snuggling into Miss Mandy's breast, as if he were hungry. Queen felt the milk moved in her breast. Miss Mandy tickled Abner's chin, and made goo-goo eyes at him.

"Poor little baby's hungry, isn't he?" she clucked. "Nasty Mammy won't feed him."

"I ain't nasty," Queen chided. She took Abner and made to leave the room.

"Do it here, Queen," Miss Mandy ordered. "You know I like to watch."

Queen knew that. In the first few days, while she was still in bed, Miss Mandy had hardly left her room, fascinated by the boy, everything he did, and everything that was done to him. It hadn't seemed to matter then, to feed the baby in front of her. It was starting to matter now. She was being allowed less and less time alone with her son.

"'Tain't fittin'," Queen said. "It's private business 'tween me and him."

Miss Mandy laughed. "It can't do him any harm. And it pleases me."

Queen, who had been trained all her life to obey orders, did not know how to avoid the instruction. She sat in a chair by the window, opened her blouse and bodice, and took out her breast.

781

Abner fed happily. Miss Mandy nodded her head as happily, and started to sing a hymn.

It happened every mealtime from then on, except at night, and sometimes even then. Miss Mandy would come into her room, without knocking, to check that Abner was comfortable. She would adjust the blankets in his cot, or make sure he was not wet, or rescue the pacifier she had bought him from the place on the mantelshelf where Queen had put it, and give it to Abner to suck.

She washed him and weighed him. She dressed him in clothes of her own choosing, relegating the few that Queen had bought to the trash. She came home one day with an expensive perambulator, and every afternoon she would take him for a stroll in the garden while Queen worked, chatting to him, or singing hymns. She began to teach him. She would point things out to him, and say the name of them over and over again, and was sure his gurgles signified recognition. Sometimes she would take him in the pram for longer walks, down the street, to introduce him to the new, wider world that awaited him. She did all the things a mother would do, and left very little for Queen.

Sometimes Queen protested, and then Miss Mandy would look aggrieved, and say that she was only trying to keep Abner happy while Queen was working. Queen's work was the excuse for everything, and Queen thought they deliberately found more things for her to do to keep her away from her baby.

Queen grieved for her lost hours with her son. What she had thought would be hers, and hers alone, was hardly hers at all. Except at night, when Miss Mandy had gone to bed, and then Queen would take her child from his cot, and lie on her bed holding him to her, trying to make up for all the time she had missed.

Curiously, Queen thought that Miss Gippy was on her side. Miss Gippy was quite fond of Abner, but his crying distressed her. She often complained of being wakened in the night. On several occasions she suggested that Miss Mandy should give the boy to his mother. Sometimes when she came into the kitchen to tell Queen that Miss Mandy wanted Abner fed, or be looked after in some way, Queen would say it had been done, or that she was busy, and Miss Gippy seemed to understand.

"I know," she said, "but you'd better go see what she wants." She, not Abner.

On one occasion, Miss Gippy had told Miss Mandy that she was spending too much time with Abner, and was neglecting her prayers and Bible studies. Miss Mandy was angry then, and told Miss Gippy she didn't know what she was talking about. Then she had even wept, and said that no one understood what she was trying to do for the boy.

As Abner grew, the situation became worse. What was most difficult for Queen to accept was that Abner seemed to prefer Miss Mandy to her. For all the attention she gave the boy, Miss Mandy seldom disciplined him. If he was fretful and crying, Miss Mandy would get irritated with him, and call for Queen. It was Queen who had to introduce Abner to the word "no," not Miss Mandy. Because Queen was so often tired from her work, she said "no" to Abner rather more than she wanted, even though he was too little to fully understand the word. Miss Mandy made jokes about it.

"Be careful, Abner," she would say, "or I'll send for nasty Mammy."

Queen lost her temper.

"I ain't nasty," she flared, not for the first time. "An' why don't you let me decide what's best for my boy?"

"Because you don't have a very strong sense of responsibility, Queen," Miss Mandy replied smugly. "If you did, Abner wouldn't be here, would he?"

Slowly it dawned on Queen that Abner always laughed and looked happy when he was with Miss

Mandy, and was always whimpering and difficult when he was with Queen. It was more than she could bear.

On her afternoons off, Queen was allowed to take Abner with her on short walks about the garden or down the back lane, but never into the streets or into town, if Queen had to go shopping. Queen wanted to take Abner farther afield, to the park, to be in the open air with her son, and had put him in the pram once, but Miss Mandy stopped that.

"I cannot have you parading the proof of your sin in public, Queen," she said.

"You parade him!" Queen shouted. "You take him everywhere!"

"That's different," Miss Mandy said. "He isn't my sin. I am saving his soul."

That salvation was more like thievery, and that was when Queen decided Miss Mandy was trying to steal her baby from her. She became frenetic with Abner, clutching him to her in her room, hugging him, holding him, whispering to him, begging him, desperate for some proof that he loved her. It disturbed the boy, and made him cry even more. Queen was distressed because she didn't understand what she had done to make him cry so, and would shout at him. Sometimes Miss Mandy heard her, and came in to see what the fuss was about. Then Abner would stretch out his arms to Miss Mandy and cry to go to her, and when she took him he would quiet down. On more than one occasion, Miss Mandy threatened to move Abner's cot into her room if Queen couldn't look after him better. They would argue about that, and Queen would shout at Miss Mandy, and that made Abner cry even more.

Yet sometimes, when she was not so tired, she would sing lullabies to him, and he would smile and laugh at his mother, and stretch out his tiny hand to her face, squeeze her nose gently, or pull on her hair, and it was sweet and lovely to her.

*

She had to talk to someone about what was the happening, but had few friends. She never went to her own church, by agreement with the sisters, and seldom saw Joyce, as the sisters had commanded. Now she missed Davis. If he had stayed, she would not be in this predicament; he would have put Miss Mandy in her place. Or if they had run away together, Miss Mandy would be only a distant memory. Now she realized the depth of her love for Davis, for any kind of life with him was preferable to any kind of life without him, for the sake of their son. Now she was angry with Davis, for the boy needed a father. He had mothers enough.

She went to Joyce. It had been three months since they had met. Joyce hadn't changed, and was delighted to see Queen. Her warm, motherly embrace brought all of Queen's frustrations wrenching to the surface, and she held on to her friend for dear life, and wept. Joyce was astonished at the flood.

"Chile, chile, whatever's wrong?" she comforted. Queen gulped away her tears, and told Joyce the sad story.

"I ain't his mammy no more," she cried.

Joyce calmed her down, and stroked her hair.

"You gotta tell her, girl," she advised. "She cain't steal yo' baby."

"That's what she's doin'," Queen agreed.

They talked it through, and Joyce decided Queen must leave the sisters' employ, and find another job. She could come and stay with Joyce and her family. Queen resisted mildly, for she knew she and Abner would be a burden, but Joyce would have none of it. They were welcome for as long as they needed. So Queen agreed.

"I'm leavin', quittin'," she told Miss Mandy, who was nursing Abner. "Me an' Abner's goin'."

It was a wonderful moment. She thought she saw fear in Miss Mandy's eyes. Miss Gippy, who was reading her Bible, looked up in surprise.

"And why is that?" Miss Mandy asked carefully.

"Coz you tryin' to steal my baby from me," Queen snapped, believing her case to be impeccable, and delighted to be having her say at last.

But the fear she had seen in Miss Mandy's eyes was replaced by something else, something more like relief.

"Don't be ridiculous," Miss Mandy said.

"I ain't ridiculous!" Queen answered. "I never gets to see him no more, he's always with you. You wash him, change him, play with him, take him out. You'd feed him if you could, only you's all dried up so you cain't!"

And the relief was replaced by a flash of anger.

"So we's leaving," Queen said again.

"I can't imagine you'll find another job very easily." Miss Mandy seemed almost calm.

"I don't need another job; friends is lookin' after me." Queen was defiant, but a little unsettled.

"Joyce, no doubt," Miss Mandy guessed, and knew from the look on Queen's face that she was right.

"If you leave our employ after all we have done for you," she said, "I shall go to the authorities and have you declared unfit to be a mother."

Queen reddened. She was frightened of the authorities. It was the chink in her armor, for her earliest training was her downfall. As a slave, she'd seen that white Massas had all the authority they needed. She wasn't certain that anything had changed. "They wouldn't do that," she said.

"Oh, yes, they would," Miss Mandy told her. "Look at it from their point of view. You would be walking out on a good, well-paid job, and taking your illegitimate son from a safe and secure home, where he is loved and provided for, to bring him up in shantytown. All because you have some silly idea that I am trying to steal him from you."

Queen shifted uncertainly. It didn't sound so simple when it was put like that.

"Because you stealin' him!" she insisted.

Any charity that Miss Mandy had ever felt toward the black race seemed to disappear for a moment.

"Why would I want to steal your nigger baby?" she asked, steel in her eyes. "I am white. Or had you forgotten?"

Queen was horrified, believing what she was told. No white authority was going to listen to her side of the case, and all authority was white.

"Now I suggest you go to your room, and forget all this silly nonsense about leaving," Miss Mandy said. She sat, and cooed at Abner. Queen moved forward to take the boy, but Miss Mandy held on to him.

"Abner can stay with me for a while," she said.

Queen was almost blind with impotent rage. All she could see was her darling son in the white woman's arms. She ran forward and grabbed Abner from her.

"You give me my baby," she shrieked. "You cain't have him! I'll kill you first!"

The vehemence of it shocked both sisters, and Miss Gippy hissed in disbelief.

"Harlot. Jezebel," she murmured, but for the moment, Queen had won. She ran from the room, clutching Abner to her.

She sat on the floor of her room rocking Abner in her arms, desperately calling to God for some answer to her distress. She'd lighted a little fire to keep them warm, and was staring at the flames of it, and the flames licked and danced in her mind, and reminded her of other awful fires, at other times, in other places.

The door burst open, and Miss Mandy swept in, followed by Miss Gippy. They ignored Queen, and went to Abner's cot.

"I have decided to move Abner into my room," Miss Mandy told Queen. "Take that end, Gippy."

The sisters moved to the cot, and Queen jumped to her feet.

"You leave that be!" she cried.

787

"I believe it is best for Abner," Miss Mandy said calmly. "You are a fallen woman and he can't stay with you. It puts his soul in danger."

"Harlot. Jezebel," Miss Gippy hissed again. She had been deeply shocked by Queen's outburst downstairs, and any sympathy she had for Queen's plight had disappeared at that moment.

Queen begged the sisters not to be so cruel, but Miss Mandy was adamant, and called her hysterical. If Queen did not control herself, Miss Mandy would call on the authorities first thing in the morning and tell them Queen was mentally unbalanced. She had a witness, Miss Gippy, who had heard Queen threaten to kill her.

"The sixth commandment," Miss Gippy chimed in.

It was true. At that moment, Queen was mentally unbalanced. And the flames of the fire, the flames of her torment, lighted some dark corner in her mind. The only way to escape fire was to run away from it. She calmed herself, and seemed to accept what Miss Mandy was telling her. But she asked to be allowed to have this last night with Abner. Faced with an apparently more rational Queen, Miss Mandy relented. The sisters left the room.

Queen stared at the fire again. The flames glittered in her eyes, in her mind, frightening her but making her determined on survival. She would run away from the fire. She would run away from the sisters. She would take Abner with her to someplace where no one would ever find them, and they would be safe.

There was nowhere in Huntsville. She couldn't go to Joyce, for the sisters would hear of it, and find her, and take Abner away from her. She couldn't even tell Joyce that she was going, for Joyce might try to talk her into staying.

South, perhaps. Everyone expected nigras to go North, so maybe if Queen went South no one would find her. But exactly where she would go was a decision for later. She had a little money in her purse, saved from her wages. They could go anywhere. The most important thing was to get away. She was sly as any vixen. She turned down her lamp, so that Miss Mandy might think she was asleep. She put Abner in his cot and lay on her bed, and waited until the distant clock struck two, and she was sure the sisters were asleep.

She turned up her lamp a little so that she could just see. She put a few things for herself and Abner into a bag, and wrapped the boy in a blanket.

Quietly as she could, she opened the door. The house was dark and silent. She walked carefully, Abner on one arm, her bag and her shoes in the other hand. She crept softly down the stairs into the hall. The front door was in front of her. They were only yards from freedom.

A floor board creaked. Queen froze, but Abner stirred in her arms.

"Hush now, chile," Queen whispered. "You love yo' mammy, you hush, you hear?"

Miraculously, Abner heard his mammy, and hushed.

When she was sure no one had awakened, Queen moved slowly to the front door. She turned the key in the lock with infinite patience, trying to avoid the merest squeak.

She opened the door, stepped out into the night, and softly pulled the door shut again. She walked more quickly now, but still with caution, across the veranda, down the steps, and onto the lawn, avoiding the gravel path. Quicker again, across the lawn and to the front gate. She opened the gate, moved out of the property, and began to run.

She ran in her stocking feet, as fast as she could, weighed down by her child and her case. At the end of the street her shoes fell to the ground, and she stopped for a moment to slip them on.

Then she ran again, and ran and ran, until she was

panting for breath, but she would not stop. Abner was awake now, and burbling happily at the unexpected adventure.

As she ran, she whispered joyously to her boy.

"We free!" she told him, in triumph. "We free!"

But she kept on running, away, into the night.

Free.

79

Although Queen went South, she wanted to avoid Decatur, and she took the easterly road and crossed the river at Guntersville. Anxious to conserve her small purse of money, she slept where she could, in barns and outhouses. Sometimes she asked at farms for shelter, and sometimes she was invited in and fed, or allowed to sleep in the milking shed and have good, fresh, creamy milk for Abner.

Abner, fat and healthy, throve on the wandering life. Now that his mother was his only constant friend, he came to depend on her, to need her, and to adore her. At last he gave her the return of love that she so sorely needed, and had come so close to losing to Miss Mandy.

Poorly dressed but cheerfully optimistic, she encountered occasional hostility from whites, but nothing she was not used to, simply a casual intolerance of free blacks, and every small act of discrimination was repaid by another of some small courtesy.

She was fascinated by the difference in attitude to her that she encountered. When she had been traveling by herself, she had been perceived as an unlikely white woman, trash or mulatta, and ignored by many whites, reviled by some blacks. Having Abner on her hip defined her. Clearly the mother of the darker-skinned child, she no longer looked definably white herself, and many took pity on her because of her baby. Farmers in carts on their way to market would stop for her, and give her a ride to their destination, or to their homes, where their wives would welcome her. She might even work for them for a few days, to repay their generosity, and was sometimes rewarded with a few pennies for her pocket, as well as her keep.

The gossip that she heard intrigued her. She was told extraordinary stories of the black determination to take Washington at its reconstructing word, and grab for equality. She heard of strikes by city workers, or by field hands protesting their pay. She heard of riots and even small armed rebellions against civic authorities who were reluctant to put the new Federal laws into effect. She heard one story of an overseer in Georgia being forced off his rice plantation by the hands, who would not work for him. Queen hardly believed the story, and laughed, because she could not imagine Henderson being forced off The Forks of Cypress by the slaves.

She was offered friendly advice and told to avoid the larger cities, where segregation was rampant. Generally, she learned, the attitude of urban Southerners toward the blacks was even less benevolent than before the war, although a few civic leaders had publicly devoted themselves to the black cause. Whenever anyone asked her where she was going, she became vague, and murmured something about finding her husband in the South. Often, when she was alone, she asked herself where she was going, and what she would do with her life, because she knew she couldn't roam forever. Her faith kept her going, and she had the absolute conviction that God was directing her footsteps, and would bring her, surely and safely, to her promised land. Abner was her dear companion, and his company assuaged her on those few lonely nights when even her spirit failed her, and she questioned herself, and her travels, and her life.

It was her inconclusive story of her missing husband,

told to a cheerful, militant ostler and his family, that gave her news of a man who might be Davis.

There was a trade-union leader, she heard, a fine and passionate orator, who had some skill as a black-smith, and who was dedicated to the cause of black equality. He went around the country making passionate speeches about the rights of blacks, and had been in Gadsden, where she was now, and he had persuaded some restaurant workers to form a guild. He had moved on, but her hosts were not sure where. Georgia, they thought, to the low country. He had often talked of the appalling conditions on the plantations there.

Queen hardly slept that night, her mind full of Davis. It all fitted in: He had learned smithy skills from Abram, and had forged his convictions about the circumstances of the newly freed blacks at the anvil. He had tried to talk Abram into forming a guild in Huntsville, and had the internal fire of a fine speaker. There was a chance that it was not Davis, but her need for some direction in her life, and her need for him, were so great that she could not allow herself to doubt. If he had found his mission in life, he would surely have room for her.

At last she had a goal and a destination. She would go to Georgia, and find Davis.

80

The day was unbearably hot, stiflingly humid. The coach rattled and creaked over the rough road, the horses sweating, and the almost useless springs unable to ease the bone-crunching ride. Every stone or furrow made the coach jolt and jerk, jarring Queen's bones. Abner, in her arms, was fretful, crying constantly, and Queen prayed for the journey to be over. She was traveling on the box with Micah, the coachman, and with one hand she held on to the small rail, to stop herself from being thrown to the ground, and with the other clung to Abner.

She yelled at Micah to slow down, but he only grinned a toothy grin, and lashed the horses. Queen began to wonder if he was driving her to hell. It was hot enough.

Mrs. Benson, her Missy, was inside the coach with her husband and her baby boy, William, to whom Queen was nanny and wet nurse. The oppressive heat of the South Carolina low country caused Mrs. Benson as much distress as Queen. Although she rode in slightly greater comfort, the tight stays and heavy petticoats, the formal dress and elaborate bonnet that her position in society demanded, caused her to curse this inhospitable land, and she longed for the cooler mountains of Georgia, which were her home.

She did not regret her decision to accompany her husband, for he had important work to do, and she was a good wife. She believed in his cause, and always stood by his side. They had been on the road for several days, but at least the nightmare journey was nearly over. They would reach their destination by late afternoon, and perhaps the hotel would be halfway decent, and William would get a good night's sleep. The journey was making her infant son fractious, but he couldn't possibly be hungry, Queen had fed him when they stopped for lunch only an hour ago. She gave a small prayer of thanks that Queen had been sent to her, and stared out at the depressing landscape.

They were passing through flat farmland, edged by scrubby vegetation. The fields were untended, and empty of farm hands. The world seemed deserted, and Queen began to think they were traveling nowhere, endlessly moving, suspended in time.

A small line of field hands appeared on the horizon, walking in the same direction. The coach lessened the distance between them, and Queen could hear the men singing lustily, a work song. As the coach passed by, the men cheered Micah and Queen, and called out for food, or money, but Micah did not slow down.

Mr. Benson put down his newspaper and looked out at the men.

"Scum," he said, almost to himself, and Mrs. Benson, distracted by the heat and William, nodded absent-mindedly. She always agreed with her husband.

"Where they goin'?" Queen asked Micah.

"Beaufort. Same as us," Micah told her. "Dey on strike."

Queen turned back to look at the men. She had never seen a striker before, black or white, but they looked no different from other men. She felt a thrill of excitement because she could equate the little she knew of strikes with the little she knew of Davis, and hoped that he might be one of the men. But he was not.

"Why they strike?" she asked Micah again.

"Money." Micah grinned his toothy grin. "Dey sick of workin' for pennies, to make dere Massa rich. Dey want better pay."

Micah spoke in a thick, old-time, slave dialect, which fooled many people into thinking he was ignorant. In fact, he was a knowledgeable man, and took a keen interest in the world. His position with the Bensons made him privy to a broad spectrum of news. He knew exactly why they were going to Beauford.

They were some distance ahead of the strikers now, and Queen craned her head back to see them.

"I ain't never heard of it," she said, her voice taking on some of Micah's dialect, which was reassuring to her. "Black folk, on strike."

"I don't like it, Missy Queen." Micah grinned again. "Gwine be trouble."

Queen could not imagine what trouble he meant, for she had no experience of trade unions and bosses, only slaves and Massas. All she wanted to do was find Davis.

She had heard of him again, in a small town south of Atlanta, this charismatic union man who could fashion a horse's shoe as well as any blacksmith. She asked if anyone knew where he was, but heard only guesses that it might be the low country. Unions, she was told, were sorely needed in the low country; there had been trouble there since the end of the war. She kept traveling east, and everywhere she went she asked about him, but heard no more, but she did hear stories of constant racial trouble in the coastal rice-growing districts.

A farmer had given her a lift into a country town near the Georgia border with South Carolina, and Queen sat in the pretty square for a while, not quite sure where to go next. It was the middle of the day, and she asked Abner if he was hungry, because she was. Abner, staring at a flock of crows in the trees, gurgled agreement. There was a general store across the road with a café attached to it. Queen went to it, and looked for a back entrance, but could find none. She went inside.

The store was large, but gloomy. The shelves were stocked with produce and provisions, and there was an eating area for whites, a few tables, with not very clean clothes. A well-dressed woman was sitting at one of the tables, trying to feed warm milk to a baby on her knee. Queen went to the counter.

"Where c'n I eat?" she asked the server.

He looked at her in mild surprise, and then saw Abner, and understood.

"Niggers in back," he said, nodding to the back of the store. Queen began walking there, but the woman at the table spoke, sharply and clearly.

"She may sit here, with me."

The server was alarmed, but he could tell from the

woman's accent and attitude that she was not to be trifled with.

"Ma'am, she cain't," he said. "She's nigra."

"We are all equal now. Or had you not heard?" the woman said to the server, but Queen didn't think she sounded generous. The woman turned to Queen. "Come here, girl."

Like the server, Queen was not anxious to argue with the woman. Very few people, she was to discover later, ever did, and anyway, Queen was intrigued. She walked to the woman's table. The woman examined her carefully, and Abner.

"Extraordinary," she said. "If it were not for the child—"

Queen knew she meant that no one would guess her color. She felt quite pleased. The woman picked up a menu.

"What will you have?" she said. "There's—"

Queen thought she might fight back a little, so that this imperious woman did not get the wrong impression of her.

"I c'n read," she said. The woman smiled, passed her the menu, and invited her to sit. She turned her attention to her own baby, and Queen sneaked a few glances at her, over the menu. The woman looked up, and caught Queen's stare. Queen dropped her eyes to the menu, and the woman smiled to herself.

"How old is he?" she asked of Abner.

"Ten months," Queen said.

"Is he weaned?"

Queen was shocked. She thought it a very personal question for such a short acquaintance, and she shook her head. The woman nodded, and thought for a moment.

"I don't suppose you're looking for a job?" she asked Queen, who wasn't sure how to reply. She could use the money, but she wanted to find Davis.

"I's going North," she responded ambivalently.

"This would only distract you for a while," the

woman said. "A few weeks at most, until I get back to Atlanta. I cannot feed my boy, William."

She smiled at the baby on her lap, and put a spoon of warm milk to his mouth.

"I have a wet nurse," the woman continued, "but she's uppity, and her milk's a little sour. Anyway, William doesn't like it. I pay quite well."

Queen was astonished by her frankness, and found herself attracted to it. She was wary of employers, but the presence of the boy child alleviated some of her caution. Some, but not all. She thought about it for a moment. If the woman paid well, she could save some money, and if she was only wanted for a few weeks, it would not unreasonably delay her search for Davis. She was tempted to say yes, but had to be careful.

"'Scuse me for asking, ma'am," she said politely. "But is you very religious?"

The woman thought the question impertinent, but liked Queen's spirit.

"It's none of your business, but yes, I believe in the Lord."

That worried Queen.

"Is you on a mission to black folk? Savin' their souls?" she inquired carefully.

The woman was incredulous. She stared at Queen for a moment, and then laughed, in open derision.

"I don't believe you nigras have souls," she said.

That was a considerable relief to Queen. She understood people who thought like that—she had been brought up with them—and she preferred that attitude to Miss Mandy's missionary zeal. She laughed with the woman, but for different reasons.

"That's all right," she said. "We could work for you. Fo' a little while."

"Good," the woman said, puzzled by her, or at least by her laughter. "I think I'm pleased. I am Mrs. Benson. Can you start immediately? We are traveling to Beaufort, and have stopped for lunch."

Queen agreed that she could, and gave her name. Mrs. Benson sent her to the nigra tables, telling Queen to order what she liked, she would pay for it. Queen was pleased, and as she walked to the back of the store, she whispered to Abner that they had just got lucky.

Mrs. Benson was pleased too; it solved a very difficult problem. She had not told Queen the exact truth. A wet nurse, Plick, had been with her when they started out from Atlanta, but she didn't have one now. Plick had a six-month baby of her own, and was difficult, uppity, forever making speeches about the new equality of blacks, and demanding her rights. William didn't like her. Nor did Mr. Benson, who had demanded her dismissal. It had all come to a head that morning, and Plick had left in high dudgeon, leaving Mrs. Benson stranded in the middle of nowhere with an eight-month-old baby to feed. The situation was so desperate that Mrs. Benson thought she might have to desert her husband, even though he needed her sorely, and return to Atlanta. She'd come to the café to be alone while her husband met with some associates, and this white creature had come in with an unweaned, nigra child, and was looking for a job.

"The Lord moves in mysterious ways," Mrs. Benson said to William.

William was completely satisfied with the new arrangement, and snuggled happily to Queen's breast before they resumed their journey. Abner wasn't jealous, Mrs. Benson was pleased, Micah was friendly to Queen, and Mr. Benson ignored her. The only unpleasant thing was the humidity, which was completely enervating. Shortly before they reached Beaufort, two days later, a blessed rain shower cleared the air, but it was still hot.

As they rode into the town, Queen began to share some of Micah's apprehension, for there was an atmosphere of tension and potential violence. Small groups of strikers stood on street corners, singing and chanting, and shouting their grievances. Other groups of white men harangued them, and once a scuffle broke out between the two groups. A couple of armed sheriffs ignored the fray. Beyond that the streets were deserted, as if the good citizens of the town were staying inside, to avoid trouble, or perhaps the weather.

Micah guided the coach to the hotel, which appeared deserted, but as soon as they arrived bellhops came running out to handle the luggage. Micah helped Queen and Abner down from the box, while Mr. Benson jumped out and went to greet a couple of businessmen who had come out of the hotel. Queen and Micah helped Mrs. Benson and William from the carriage, and Mrs. Benson looked at the town.

She didn't seem impressed by what she saw, but gave William to Queen, squared her shoulders, and organized the bellhops, calling out instructions for the luggage. There were some shouts from across the street, and another fight. Two black strikers were beating up a white redneck, and again, no one interfered.

Mr. Benson watched the fight, and seemed to be appraising the situation. As he turned back to his associates, he caught Queen's eye, and she shivered, for the look on his face frightened her. He said something to his friends, and then told Mrs. Benson to see the rooms while he talked with his friends. The men walked away, deep in conversation. Mrs. Benson told Queen to come along, and swept into the hotel, which was the best the town had to offer. Queen, carrying Abner and William, followed.

Inside, the manager himself greeted Mrs. Benson, and the formalities of checking in were quickly attended to. The manager led the way upstairs, Queen followed with the boys, and Micah, who was directing the bellhops, and Queen began to think that Mrs. Benson must be a very important lady.

The suite was spacious, a sitting room and two bedrooms. Mrs. Benson came in with the retinue of staff and the obsequious manager, who was telling her how splendid the rooms were. Mrs. Benson was not impressed, and the heat made her tetchy. Queen waited to be told what to do, and Abner began to cry.

"If these are your best, they'll have to do," she told the unhappy manager, "but they're not what we're used to." She looked into the master bedroom.

"Our finest suite, ma'am," he insisted, but Mrs. Benson ignored him and ran a gloved finger over a table.

"Filthy," she snapped, "hasn't been dusted in weeks. I want maids in here now."

She looked into the second room. "And my nigras?" she asked the manager.

"Tolerable accommodations in back, ma'am," he said, wishing she'd go away. He had a headache from the heat.

Mrs. Benson pointed to the room that was to be the nursery and turned to Queen. "Get William settled in there," she said.

"Abner's hungry, Missy," Queen began, but Mrs. Benson wasn't interested in Abner's problems. Or Queen's. Or anyone else's.

"Then Abner will have to wait," she said. "William comes first, at all times. You know that."

She went into the bedroom, commanding the manager to follow her by the sheer tone of her voice.

"I will need a baby carriage for my son, and good supply of clean towels" was the last Queen heard. She took the boys into the nursery room, and laid them on the bed. She changed William's linen, got him ready for bed, and offered to feed him, but he wasn't hungry. She did not dare feed Abner while Mrs. Benson was in her present mood.

She ran to Mrs. Benson's orders for an hour, and then one of the bellhops showed her to her tolerable accommodations, which were intolerable, and had been the old slave quarters, tin shacks at the back of the hotel. The waning afternoon had not relieved the heat, and Queen's room was an oven. Like everyone else, Queen was on the edge of her temper, for the weather was unbearable, and Abner was still crying.

She opened a tiny lid in the roof that was the only ventilation, grumbling about Mrs. Benson's commands, and then sat on the bed to feed Abner.

"Bossy ol' bitch," she said to herself about her employer, as her son took his fill. She looked about the awful room.

"Hotter'n Hades," she said. "How's a body s'pposed to sleep?" She rested her head back against the wall, and sang a little lullaby to Abner until he was done, and then she changed him, and settled him on a pillow on the floor. She thought she might feel better if she had a wash, and opened the door to find the black washhouse, when Micah came to her.

"She want you, Missy Queen," he said. He looked tired and frayed, for his Missy had been difficult. "She gwine shoppin'."

Queen began to understand why the other wet nurse had left Mrs. Benson's employ. She wondered what to do about Abner, but would not leave him on his own, so, toting him on her hip, she went to find Mrs. Benson, who was in the lobby complaining about the quality of the soap.

The world, or the hotel, had jumped to Mrs. Benson's command. A baby carriage had been found for William, and Abner was allowed the use of it. Once the boys were comfortable and the matter of the soap resolved, Mrs. Benson went out onto the street, with Queen following, pushing the carriage. Micah went with them, although Queen wasn't sure why, but he helped her with the baby carriage.

There were very few people about, just some strikers

walking as if with some purpose to somewhere else, and three or four white bystanders, jeering them. Queen saw a couple of sheriffs, with their guns, moving quickly to someplace in the town, and there were shouts and cheers coming from that direction.

Queen would have walked the other way, but to her surprise Mrs. Benson walked toward the distant noise, looking for a shop that suited her list. As they crossed the street, a black beggar approached her.

"Spare some change, Missy," he pleaded with Mrs. Benson. "I ain't et in a week."

"Then get back to work," Mrs. Benson told him briskly, without breaking her stride. "Lazy nigras," she said to no one in particular, and Queen flushed. Abner and William were asleep, side by side, in the carriage. Mrs. Benson stopped to look in the window of a provisions store.

"I want good milk," she told Queen. "I don't trust that hotel. And fresh fruit—there must be some fresh fruit somewhere."

Queen looked in the window. There was a display of fine peaches.

"Here," she suggested, but Mrs. Benson glanced at the name on the sign above the store.

"No," Mrs. Benson said. "Not here. They are Semitic."

She walked on. Queen glanced back at the sign, but the name painted on it meant nothing to her.

"What's Semitic?" she asked Mrs. Benson.

"Jews," Mrs. Benson said. "Semites. We do not give them our business. I'm sure there's somewhere else."

They walked on, and came closer to the shouting and cheering. Queen could see a large group of men gathered, having a street meeting. Mrs. Benson found a store that suited her, and made her purchases. There was no respite from the heat, and inside the store was hotter than outside. Shopping done, Mrs. Benson came out with Queen to check her list. Abner had wakened, and Queen picked him up and rocked him while she waited for Mrs. Benson. As she did so, she watched the men at the meeting, and wondered what it was all about. A black man had climbed onto a box, and was making a speech to the strikers.

Sheriffs stood watching, guns ready. White workingmen jeered the speaker.

"You all know our cause," the speaker told the strikers. "Decent pay fo' a decent's day work."

The strikers cheered.

"Cash money, instead of checks that can only be redeemed at plantation stores," the speaker shouted, and the strikers cheered again.

Mrs. Benson glanced at the speaker, and then went back to ticking things off on her list.

"They're the ones that should be shot," she said absently, to Queen. "The ringleaders."

But Queen was not listening. She was fascinated by the voice of the speaker.

"They promised us better things in better times, but those better days never come," the speaker proclaimed. "And I am overflowing with their unkept promises."

It was Davis; Queen was sure of it. She could not see his face clearly, but his voice was as familiar to her as her own. She had found him at last, and her heart was beating fast, while her shoulders sagged in relief. She listened to the words pour out of him, in impassioned oratory.

"I don't care what they say they will do," Davis told his rapt audience. "I judge them only by what they have done. And until now they have done nothing. So from now, we take. But we take only what is rightfully ours, what is rightfully due to us, only what we have been promised."

He was a beautiful and eloquent speaker. All the deep anger and passion that had churned within him for so many years had finally found its outlet.

Queen's eyes sparkled with pride and pricked with

803

tears. She moved a little closer, off the sidewalk, onto the road to see him better. She wanted to run to him. But she could not do that here, in public. Her business with him was private.

And there was something else, something more important, to do. She held Abner up, high in the air, as high as she could, so that he might see the man and hear his voice.

Mrs. Benson looked up from her list, and was puzzled to see Queen standing in the road holding her son in the air.

"Come along, Queen, don't dawdle," she called, but Queen did not hear her, or if she did, she did not respond. Mrs. Benson clucked in irritation, and moved closer to Queen, to fetch her.

Queen had eyes only for Davis and mind for Abner.

"It is now!" Davis cried, and the strikers cheered him louder than ever.

Oblivious to everything but her boy and his father, Queen cried out to Abner. "Look, boy, it's yo' pappy!"

Abner was not the only one who heard this news. Mrs. Benson heard it too, and smiled a small astonished smile of curious excitement. And the look in her eyes was triumphant.

81

Queen wanted to stay, to try to make some contact with Davis, but the cheering strikers led him away, and Mrs. Benson was anxious to be gone. As they walked back to the hotel, Mrs. Benson chatted happily with Queen, and did not discuss what they had seen, or anything about the strike. As they were about to go into the hotel, she casually asked if Queen knew the man who had been speaking. Queen wasn't quite sure what to say. She recognized that her actions with Abner

804

must have been puzzling to Mrs. Benson, and admitted that she thought she had met the man once, a long time ago, but was mistaken. Mrs. Benson seemed satisfied, and they went into the hotel.

Queen's nerves were jangling, with anticipation because she was so close to Davis, and dread that he might not want to see her again. She tried to work out her feelings toward him, but she was too excited to be rational. She loved him still—she was sure of that—loved him even more perhaps, for his speech had inspired her, and she was so proud of him it made her heart sing. She could not imagine what he would think of her, or of Abner, and she fretted that he might resent the boy. She felt a spasm of anger then. Even if Davis did not want to accept parentage, Abner was the reason he had left Huntsville and traveled on the road to his true vocation, so he should be grateful for that, at least. Then she remembered the courtesy and kindness that Davis had always shown her, except once, and she was sure he must love his son. How could he not?

Queen bathed William, and sat in the nursery room feeding him, while Abner sprawled on the bed, irritable because of the heat. Queen was determined to find Davis, but could think of no way to achieve her goal. There was the possibility that she might run into him in the street, but she didn't want to leave anything to chance. When William was satisfied, she put him to bed in his cot, and then took Abner downstairs, to eat her own meal in the kitchen, with the hotel staff. The bellhops and kitchen staff were talking about the strike, in complete sympathy with it, and full of praise for this man Davis, who had come to town when the men first walked off the job, and had inspired them to their present defiant stand. Filled with pride, Queen wanted to ask them how she might find this man, but dared not. This was too public a place, and she was already aware that some element of danger attended Davis. After she had eaten, she found Mrs. Benson, and asked if she might be allowed to have a few hours rest, she was not feeling well. Slightly to her surprise, Mrs. Benson was fussily concerned for her welfare, and agreed to her request. Queen went to her room and waited until she was sure Mrs. Benson would be having her dinner with her husband, for they always ate at the same time. She put Abner on her hip and slipped out into the night to find Davis.

She wandered the empty streets hoping that by chance he would appear, but he did not. She went back to the scene of the afternoon's meeting, looked around for some clue to his whereabouts, and saw a small, lighted tavern across the road. Some men were drinking outside, squatting against the wall, and she recognized a couple of them as strikers she had seen that afternoon. She went to them, but although they gave her appreciative whistles, they were wary of her, and ignored her. Adjusting Abner's shawl so that his colour could be clearly seen, she summoned her courage and spoke to one of the men, and told him she wanted to find Davis. They shrugged and tried to send her on her way, but she said she would make a scene if they didn't help. She put on a fine performance, claiming that Davis had promised her marriage but had dumped her, leaving her with his baby, and she wanted to give him a piece of her mind.

Which was true. In her frustration with him—at his departure, at the difficulty of locating him, and now the difficulty of getting to him—Queen felt a genuine anger rising inside her. It convinced the men, but still they resisted her, until Queen's voice rose, and she threatened to call the sheriffs if they didn't help. The men begged her to silence and had a whispered conversation among themselves. One went into the tavern, and came out a few minutes later with another, older man, who questioned Queen, and looked carefully at Abner. Her story or her indignation, or both, convinced him, and he jerked his head to indicate that Queen should follow him. He and the striker who had called him led her to the back of the tavern, where the horses were tethered. They mounted, and the older man pulled Queen up behind him, while the younger rode with Abner in his arms.

They rode for a couple of miles into the night, the moon lighting their way, until the farmland gave way to woods. About a mile into the trees, by a small body of water, a river or an inlet, there was a shack, guarded by two or three armed strikers. Queen could see at least two other black men, with guns, watching them from the trees. The guards at the shack accosted them as they brought their horses to a halt.

"She say she know him," the older man told them. The guards looked at Queen doubtfully.

"White bitch?" one murmured. Queen was still on her horse, and reached out her hand to Abner.

"This here my boy," she said.

The younger striker offered Abner for the guard's inspection, and they looked from him to Queen. One of them told her to get down and wait, and he went into the shack. Queen dismounted and took Abner. She stood waiting in the hot, humid night, a little frightened by the guns, and thrilling in anticipation.

After a few moments, the door of the shack opened, and Davis came out. He stared at Queen, and emotions rose within her that were too complex for her to begin to understand, for his face was filled with amazement, and then with pain.

Then he smiled, a sweet smile.

"Is it you?" he said.

Queen nodded, not trusting herself to speak. And then a furious, blazing anger began in her belly, surged through her body, and burst out of her.

"Yes!" she cried. "And this is your boy!"

She marched up to Davis and thrust Abner at him.

"Didn't you even want to see what he looked like?"

If Davis was surprised by her fury, he didn't show it.

He stared at Queen, then looked at Abner, and, gentle as a shepherd with a lamb, he took his son from her, and held him close. Tears stung in his eyes.

"I knew he would be beautiful," he whispered softly to Queen. "Like you."

Queen saw his tears and almost started to cry herself, for his reaction to his son was more than she had ever hoped might be possible. But still she was angry with him, and loved him, all at once.

"I had enough of yo' sweet talk to last me a lifetime," she said, and turned away from him. It was then that she saw that the strikers and the guards were smiling at her, laughing even, and her anger churned. She rounded on Davis.

"You got any idea what it's like for a woman, stuck on her own with a baby, no man to turn to?" Like a festering boil, all the disappointments and deprivations of her life, the loneliness and injustice, the hurt and the misery, came to a hot and angry head, and were lanced by his tears. She was yelling at him now, and at the guards and strikers, and at all men.

"I trusted you," she cried. "But, oh, you men, you gets what you want, and then the hell with us women. You could have told me. You could have written, but not even a word, or a letter—"

"I cain't write, you know that!" Davis said, trying to control his temper. He had not expected her wrath, and he was hurt by it, and guilty.

"Could've sent a paper with yo' mark on it," Queen retorted. "That would have been something—"

Suddenly he couldn't control his temper. His men were laughing almost openly, and his anger raged within him, and matched her own. He gave Abner to a guard, marched to her, grabbed her and kissed her violently, harshly, beautifully, on the mouth, but she pulled away from him.

"That's my mark!" he cried. "You had that! You got that!"

He would not let her go, and kissed her again. And this time she responded to him, and kissed with all the passion that a life of frustration and a year of missing him, of loving him, and wanting him, and not having him, had engendered within her.

The shack was small and sparsely furnished, one room with a sleeping area separated from the rest by a curtain. He brought her inside and dismissed the strikers. They sat together for a while hardly talking, content to be with each other. He rocked Abner to sleep on his lap, and the boy was secure in his father's arms.

"He's a fine boy," Davis said.

"He's yo' son," Queen nodded.

He had not asked what had happened to her while they had been apart, but now he did.

"Has it been hard for you?"

Queen thought for a while before responding. It had been hard, but she had borne it, and now she had her reward.

"'Tain't been easy," she said softly.

"I's sorry," he said. He looked at the sleeping Abner, and Queen understood that it was time for something else to happen. She found a blanket and made a rough bed for her baby, then faced her man. She went to him, leaned up to him, and kissed him. He responded, but then stopped her.

"No," he said. "Do nothing. I owe you love."

He picked her up, carried her to the bed, and laid her down. With infinite care, singing her soft crooning lullabies, he touched her, stroked her, kissed her, and each time she tried to respond, he told her no. Slowly, taking forever, he freed her from her clothes, and himself from his own. When she lay naked before him, he traced his tongue over her entire body until he tasted every inch of her, and with his fingers caressed her hair, her eyes, her mouth, her chin, her breasts, until she thought she must faint from the beauty of it. He lay beside her, and the warmth and hardness of him pressing against her was wonderful. She opened her body to him, and her heart and her soul, and when they were joined as one flesh she felt complete again, and whole, and all the trammeling care of her life disappeared into a blaze of happiness that engulfed her.

Afterward, they dozed together for a while, and when she awoke he was still there, it had not been a dream. But a sadness had settled on him.

"I cain't ask you to stay," he whispered. "It ain't safe."

"I don't care," she cried softly.

"I care," he told her. "I will not have harm come to you. Or him."

She shivered in fear for him, and he held her close.

"Should I be scared for you?" she whispered, and he could not hide the truth from her. Too much was at stake.

"Why not?" he said. "I scared for me."

He wanted to rid her of her immediate fear, and explain the high, bright future that he saw.

"This is where it begins," he said. "This is where the black man draws the line, and says enough, no more. This is where the promise that was made must be fulfilled."

She believed him, and would have followed him to the end of the earth.

Morning mist lazed over the river. The steel gray of dawn crept into the sky, and filtered through the window of the shack. A new day was beginning, but still they lay together.

"I gotta get back," Queen said.

"She be mad, yo' Missy?" he wondered.

Queen expected that Mrs. Benson would be mad as hell, but she didn't care. A moment with Davis was worth a year of her anger. He made arrangements for her safe return to Beaufort, and watched her ride away into the morning with his son.

Davis had been shocked by his decision to desert Queen, although he could never exactly pinpoint the moment when he had made up his mind to do it. It might have been when she first told him of the child, it might have been as they lay making plans for the future, or it might have been as the day of leaving approached and the call that he heard to do something else got stronger and stronger. He was ashamed at what he was doing to her, but did not believe he had any alternative, for the general good was greater than her particular need. Queen, he guessed, or knew, or persuaded himself, would survive, and while it would be hard for her, she had a friend to turn to in Joyce. He also hoped that the sisters would be kind to her, as it seemed, in general, they had been.

He also believed himself to be worthless, and therefore not worthy of her. Filled up with rage against the world, which rage he contained when he was with Queen for he could find no outlet for it, he believed that one day that hate must explode into some form of action or violence, and he did not want her to be hurt by it. On the appointed day, he left the sisters' house early, as had been planned. He went to his shack, put some things in a bag, and began walking, away from Huntsville, away from Alabama, away from Queen. He cursed himself as he walked, and tried to console himself with the concept that she had his seed inside her, the best part of him, but did not convince himself. He made a vow that he would change his wretched ways, that he would actively seek some effective role in life, rather than passively accepting what life threw at him. Later, when he found that role, he blessed Queen, for it was she who had provoked him to it, and he thought of her fondly, and his heart ached to see the product of their love.

He went to Atlanta, and got himself a job assisting a blacksmith, as Abram had taught him, and was persuaded by the smithy, who was politically militant, to join the local guild. So it was that he found his voice, for the sense of brotherhood he obtained in the union was miraculous to him. For the first time in his life he felt he was not alone, that his grievances and anger were not unique to him. The shared sense of purpose, the bloody-minded determination to take what was rightfully, morally theirs, by combative action if necessary, thrilled him. The words that he had kept contained inside him because he saw no point in saying them burst out, and he became, in a short space of time, an admired and respected orator, and a considerable asset to the fledgling union cause.

It was the union that sent him traveling, to centers of industrial unrest, and it was he who voiced the frustrations and ambitions and dreams of his black brethren. Many of the slaves had been dispossessed from their only homes, which were the plantations, they had few skills to earn a living in this new world of freedom, and, if they had the skills, they were cheated and abused by their new Massas, the bosses.

He took the high-minded words of the government to heart, and equality had genuine meaning for him. He wanted no more than that for his brothers, but he was determined to achieve at least that, and to take it forcibly if it was not given. He also understood something that set him apart from his peers, and gave him a purer sense of purpose, a purer power, and a purer ability to achieve his goals. He understood that it was not simply a matter of black versus white, but of worker against boss. While his speeches were directed primarily to blacks, he had the vision to include disgruntled, unemployed whites in his embrace, although most rejected him.

The low-country plantations of Georgia and South Carolina grew rice and fermented trouble. In this swampy land of tidal rivers and intolerable summer weather, of disease and racist attitudes, the working conditions of the field hands were intolerable. It was in Brunswick, south of Beaufort, that the hands had revolted, as Queen had heard, and refused to obey their martinet masters, many of whom were veteran Confederate officers to whom the concept of free niggers was intolerable. Race riots had ensued, and units of the national guard were called out. The end of slavery, the end of an abundant supply of free labor, had revealed that many of the plantations were not economically viable, and so the hands were employed in vile conditions that bordered on paid slavery. Instead of being given their meager wages in cash, the hands were given checks that could be redeemed only at plantation stores, and so they were feudally bonded to their employers. Without specie, cash money, they could not survive, as there were few other jobs for unskilled men, and for most of them, the land was the only labor they knew. Davis had come to Beaufort to try to improve their conditions, but the plantation owners were completely resistant to change, claiming they could not afford it, and even more resistant to unions and a leader from somewhere else who incited their niggers to rebel, or inspired disturbing ambitions.

Davis was no revolutionary. He did not want to overthrow the system; he wanted the working black man's place within the system to be recognized. It was a fine distinction, which many whites who heard him speak refused to recognize, and to many he represented a potential for intolerable violence. The horrors of the French Revolution, the destruction of an entire class system and its egalitarian aftermath, were the foundation of the fears of the white ruling class, and the winds of industrial and social change that were sweeping through Europe fanned those fears into fires of burning resentment against anyone who spoke of equality, of race or class.

Yet there was hope. A black man in Beaufort, encouraged by Davis, was determined to stand for mayor, and given the preponderance of newly enfranchised black voters, he might very well win. This prospect was deeply shocking to the whites, and, desperate as they were to find some focus for their rage, some scapegoat, Davis was increasingly and unrealistically seen as the single engine of black ambition. Davis laughed at the attention, for no one man was responsible for these surging changes; they were the consensus of the many. But he knew he could direct the general mood to particular ends.

He also knew it was dangerous, and that the bosses, and many of the white working class, could not let the situation in Beaufort continue. A showdown was approaching, and Davis was ready for it, and did not fear its possible consequences.

Until Queen came to him.

When he saw Queen standing in the moonlight outside his shack, his child in her arms, his heart sank. She was part of his past, the other him, and was safe there from danger. There was no place for her in his new life, because that might bring harm to her, or the boy, and he could not bear the thought of anything happening to her. She had suffered enough, and partly because of him. His sense of responsibility to her was so profound that he wanted her gone, even though her going would pain him as no fire ever could.

But she was there, and he could not resist his heart. He had taken her to him, and loved her as well as he could because he owed her so much. But now he had to find some way to get her away from here, out of his life, and away from the possibility of harm, which loomed so large on his horizon.

The striker who took Queen back to Beaufort delivered her to the back of the hotel. Queen went to her room, and wondered how she could face Mrs. Benson. She

814

knew her Missy must be furiously angry, for she had missed at least one feeding time for William, and although she had claimed sickness, Mrs. Benson must surely have checked her room, and found her gone. Yet the maternal side of her also worried for William, who seemed so helpless when he lay in her arms, so dependent on her milk, on the sustenance she gave him. She felt guilty about what she had done, but was inspired by Davis, and so she went to Mrs. Benson's room, ready for anything.

She heard William before she saw him, because the boy was yelling as if he had never been fed. Queen's spirit sank, but she tapped on the door and went into the room.

"There you are at last!" Mrs. Benson cried.

Mrs. Benson was certainly angry, but it was not quite the wrath that Queen expected. Although the words were harsh, and the tone, there was also a tinge of relief in her voice. William was on her knee, and she was trying to feed him bread soaked in warm milk, but he didn't want that. Queen started an apology, but Mrs. Benson had to have her say.

"The boy's been awake all night long," she complained. "I haven't had a wink of sleep, nor poor Mr. Benson, with so much on his mind."

The room was a mess, for it was true: Mrs. Benson had been up half the night, trying to calm William, and change his linen, and at the same time assure her husband that all was well. It was another hot day, and she was cross with Queen for causing this interruption to her domestic arrangements, but not for anything else.

"I's sorry," Queen apologized again. She had expected to be sacked, but now she didn't think that was going to happen, or not until William had been fed. She went to the boy, who quieted immediately and sought her breast through her blouse. Queen smiled at him, and told him to be patient. She sat on a chair and

815

fed him, while Mrs. Benson made vain attempts to clean up the room, which smelled of baby.

"Aren't you going to tell me where you've been?" she demanded of Queen, and rang the bell to summon servants.

Queen was puzzled. Although tetchy, Mrs. Benson was almost friendly to her, as if she'd been a naughty girl who had done some silly trivial wrong, and, the crisis over, was expected to share her naughty secrets. She tried to think of some lie that would satisfy Mrs. Benson, but none came to her.

"Then let me guess," Mrs Benson said, and sat at the table. "You've been with Abner's father, perhaps?"

Queen did not look at her, but concentrated on the feeding William. She felt a rush of fear, because she did not know how Mrs. Benson knew of Davis or what her reaction would be. She blushed, and kept her head down.

"Oh, don't be silly, Queen," Mrs. Benson laughed. "I saw you in the street yesterday, the way you looked at that wretched union man and told Abner he was his father. I know you lied to me when you told me you didn't know him."

Queen's fear gave way to relief, for now she understood how Mrs. Benson knew, and it didn't seem devious.

"Yes, m'm" was all Queen said.

There was a knock at the door, and a maid appeared. Mrs. Benson ordered a tray of breakfast for two, and busied herself at the washstand. She chattered about nothing and everything while she waited for breakfast, and Queen began to think that the woman was trying to make some girlish, foolish contact with her. She felt kindly toward Mrs. Benson, and relieved that someone else knew her secret.

The staff arrived, and Mrs. Benson had breakfast set out on the table, while Queen changed William and put him down. When she came back from the nursery, Mrs.

Benson was sitting at the table and another place was laid. For Mr. Benson, Queen assumed, but again, Mrs. Benson surprised her.

"Sit down here with me," she said, "and have some breakfast, I'm sure you're hungry."

Queen was very hungry; she'd had nothing to eat since her dinner the previous night. She pulled out the chair, sat on the edge of it, and took a piece of toast.

"That's not enough," Mrs Benson said. "We have to look after you, for William's sake."

She piled a plate with eggs and toast, passed it to Queen, and began to eat herself.

"Now," she said when Queen had relaxed sufficiently to feel comfortable. "Tell me about Abner's father."

Still, Queen was cautious, and Mrs. Benson giggled.

"He's so very handsome," she said, like a schoolgirl with a crush. Queen smiled too, and told her a little of Davis. Not much, just trivial, womanly things, and Mrs. Benson's eyes were bright with gossip and she shared a few secrets of her own married life. When they were done, Mrs. Benson took her shopping, but said they should be off the streets that afternoon for she had heard that there was to be a big strike parade and there could be trouble. It was best for the women to keep out of the way.

Queen was entranced by her consideration, and felt herself warming to Mrs. Benson as the day went on. From the hotel windows, they watched the parade of strikers through the street in the early afternoon, with Davis being carried on the shoulders of some of the men. Queen was filled with pride, and pointed him out to Abner. White workers lined the streets, jeering the procession, and there were some fights.

Mrs. Benson made a lot of complimentary comments about Davis, and tutted about the violence, and Queen forgot that she had said that the ringleaders ought to be shot. Queen saw Mr. Benson standing in the street with some other businessmen, watching the parade, and she asked why he was not with his wife. Mrs. Benson said something vague about business, and suggested that Queen must be tired and should have a nap.

Queen was very tired; she hadn't really slept since yesterday. She took Abner to her room, lay down with him on the bed, and fell fast asleep with her son in her arms, dreaming of the boy's father.

She awoke, some hours later, at sundown, to an urgent tapping on the door, and she heard a fierce whisper.

"Queen!" It was Mrs. Benson. "Wake up—!"

She roused herself, blinked the sleep from her eyes, and opened the door. Mrs. Benson slipped into the room and shut the door. She was agitated, apparently frightened.

"You must go to him, Abner's father," she whispered, her eyes wide with fear. Queen, still fuddled by sleep, did not quite understand.

"Get him away," Mrs Benson said urgently. "They know where he is, and he is in danger."

Queen was awake now, and caught Mrs. Benson's sense of fear but didn't know what to do. She looked at Abner.

"I'll keep Abner safe with me till you return," Mrs. Benson assured her.

Still it didn't make sense to Queen; she went to Abner, picked him up, gave him to Mrs. Benson, and looked about the room, pulled at her dress.

"Quickly, take a horse from the stable," Mrs. Benson said, with more urgency than ever. She clutched Queen to her.

"There will be terrible work done this night," she whispered.

"It is the Klan."

For a split second that might have been an eternity, Queen was petrified. She knew of the Klan. She had seen the dark seeds of it outside Decatur when the masked men had burned the barn, careless if any died

818

in the conflagration, as one woman did. She first heard the formal name on her journeys, this avenging servant of Lucifer, and she was told the rivers of the South held countless bodies of those secretly done to death, and the earth held the unknown graves of those who had been burned from life.

She panicked for Davis. Reassured by Mrs. Benson as to Abner's welfare, she ran to the stables, saddled and mounted a workhorse, and rode into the twilight, the gloaming.

She did not know that she was followed by a masked white man, who had bound his horse's hooves with cloths to deaden their sound.

82

They gathered in the forest at night, for darkness was their friend, and what they did could not withstand the glare of the sun, for it was obscene to God. They claimed divine inspiration for their work and that they stood on the right hand of the celestial throne, but, like the archangel Lucifer, they had fallen from grace, never to rise again. Their symbol was a cross, but it burned with the flames of hell, from whence it had come. Their robes were black, as befitted their satanic origins, but they wore white hoods, to keep their faces hidden from the angels. Their trumpets were clarion calls to violent death.

In the bright light of day they might have seemed like ordinary men, far too mild for the work they did, and they needed anonymity to make them brave. Often they knew their victims well, and had grown up with them, and, cowards, could not kill their helpless friends without the mask of night. They took strength from their numbers, which were spread wide throughout the land, a huge and hideous secret society whose leaders traveled far from their own homes to spread their demon seed.

So a man had come to them from far away, and stood before them now, in front of the cross of fire. They chanted prayers and sang loud hymns, and did not know that the cacophony made heaven weep.

"This is our land," the speaker roared at them. "White man's land, given to us by God's covenant. But the vile nigger would steal it from us, and we must fight and kill, for if we do not stop them now, where will it end?"

They loved their country and had fought for it honorably in the war, but in defeat they would not surrender their cause. Killing became their creed.

"I am not ashamed to be a white American. I am not afraid to die in defense of my country and my way of life. I am not afraid to kill to defend my country and my way of life. It is my sacred duty."

They claimed they did not hate the nigger just because he was black.

"Miscegenation is our destruction. The African black was a harmless, docile animal, happy in the place that the Bible had allotted him. But liberal Yankees and the lecherous Jew have inbred with the creature, and created a new and impure race who think themselves our equal. They would take the very food from out mouths, and the land from our people."

Most of all, they feared one thing.

"And rape our women!"

And had one solution.

"They must be chopped out root and branch, if the tree of white hope is to survive."

The leader stopped, and a lone voice cried the response to the catechism.

"Let them burn! Let them burn!"

All the voices took up the cry, until the night resounded with the chanting.

"Burn! Burn! Burn!"

"Let the nigger burn in hell!"

83

To Mrs. Benson it was all so simple she could not understand why there was any dispute. It was a covenant with God, and anyone who disputed it was blasphemous and heretic. Initially, her fury had not been directed at the nigras, for they were ignorant animals, led piteously astray by atheists. The Republican party was to blame, and its monstrous leader Lincoln, who, with Satan's help, had devastated the South, freed the slaves, and brought anarchy to what had been Eden. When Lincoln was struck down by an avenging angel who acted under divine direction, Mrs. Benson fell to her knees in awe of what her Maker had wrought. But the damage to the South had been done, and must be corrected. They bore Lincoln's lieutenant, Johnson, with ill grace, but when the butcher Grant ran for the presidency, Mrs. Benson and her husband had vowed to do everything in their power to defeat him and his party.

They were not circumspect in voicing their opinions, nor alone in their feelings. Politically active, they had been introduced to some charming people who were members of a social club, originally founded in Tennessee, that was dedicated to the glory and supremacy of white America. That the activities of the club included occasional nighttime violence toward blacks was not distasteful to the Bensons. After the indignities that defeat in war had heaped on them, the men had to have some outlet for their energy and loss of honor, and the women cheered them on. The coming election gave specific focus to their ideals and their wrath. Wearing black robes and white masks to disguise their faces, they broke up Republican meetings and parades, and on election day itself had successfully prevented many from voting. Grant won in spite of this, by margins that appalled them, and the Bensons believed that while they had done well, they had not done enough. It also became clear to them that the most potent way to achieve their aims was to rid the land of the pestilential black.

When she was little, her parents, devout Protestants, instructed her diligently. They taught her that the Bible was the unedited manuscript of God, and the foundation of all their lives. That Jews were the sons of Cain and had murdered Christ. That niggers were the sons of Ham who had mocked his father, the patriarch Noah, and God, in revenge, had taken his soul. That Catholics were idolaters who worshiped graven images, who bought their way out of damnation, and who gave to a man, the Pope, the omnipotence of the Almighty.

As a girl growing up in southern Georgia, she never met a Jew, and she had never actually despised the nigras for they were not worthy of it. They were simply nigras and slaves and she had enjoyed the company of many, as she would enjoy the company of a pet dog or cat. As she grew older, she came to fear black men, convinced she was an object of their sexual desire, and she lived in mortal fear of being raped. She might survive the rape, but could not bear the taint of it nor any issue from it, and would kill herself and the fetus before she gave birth to a mulatto.

Shortly before the war, and partly because of the Northern belligerence, she married a very eligible young merchant from Atlanta whom she had met at her coming-out ball, and who shared her ambitions and attitudes. Both were formidable overachievers and planned an exemplary life. They believed devoutly in God and as devoutly in the Confederation, and detested abolitionists, emancipationists, and all who could not understand the simple truth. White Christians were born to rule and all others to serve. America would be a wasteland inhabited by naked savages if it were not for white vision, white industry, white intelligence. The blacks had been rescued from the jungle and brought to this country to share the white man's bounty, and should be grateful for it. But, like the senseless animals they were, nothing was ever enough for nigras; the more you gave them the more they expected, and the only discipline they understood was the lash.

When the war came, Mrs. Benson's husband enlisted immediately and was killed in the battle of Antietam.

It broke Mrs. Benson's heart. She never forgave Lincoln, she never forgave the Yankees, and she never forgave the nigras, who were the cause of it all.

She went back to live with her parents in the country and wore widow's weeds for the rest of the war. Convinced she would never marry again, she devoted her life to charitable causes, but longed for a man in her life. At a social event she met a prosperous businessman from Atlanta whose health had prevented him from enlisting in the military. He had done what he could as a civilian, supplying munitions to the Confederate government, and his patriotism had been rewarded with excellent profits. Thanks to his poor health and judicious investments in California, he had survived the war in good shape, physically and financially. His intolerance of Yankees and nigras was greater than her own, and he fueled her new hatred, and mended her broken heart. He informed her of the insatiable sexual habits of the decadent, animal nigger, and conjured up a potential nightmare world of miscegenation, in which the blood of good, industrious whites would be sullied and abased, and the progeny dragged down to the level of the jungle. He also told her of the Jewish conspiracy to rule the world and destroy all Christians just as they had killed Jesus.

They married two years after the war, and devoted their lives to the single-minded belief that the South would rise again. His zeal and sense of duty made Mr. Benson a well-respected member of their club, and they traveled the state together, forming new chapters, encouraging new members, and doing the violent errands that they believed would restore them to God's favor. In all things they were a partnership, and Mrs. Benson attended meetings with her husband, wore their uniform with pride, was never far from her husband's side.

Except tonight. She could not be with him tonight. She had done her night's work, and she sat in the hotel sitting room, rocking William on her lap, and waiting for his nurse.

Queen rode fast to Davis, unaware that she was revealing his location to a masked white man who was silently following her. Guards took her to him when she got to the shack, but she could not persuade them to leave.

"But they know where you are," she cried, for she believed what Mrs. Benson had told her.

Davis was silent, and Queen believed he was considering a decision, but he was not. He was accepting his fate.

"Then let them come," he said. "We cannot run forever. I will not."

He had never tried to avoid the consequences of his stubborn convictions; indeed, he almost seemed to embrace them. When he ran away from the plantation it was so that he would be caught, returned, and punished, even unto death, in a vain attempt to shame his Massas.

"It's the Klan!" Queen cried again. "They'll kill you!"

But he had guards and guns, he told her, and would be safe. She begged him to go, pleaded to be allowed to stay with him.

"No," he said. "Go to the boy. He is the future."

He hugged her and kissed her, and forced her away from him, and then he gathered his few men and made preparations for their coming visitors.

*

Queen would not allow herself believe that she had said a final good-bye to him, could not believe he would die. She dreaded what this night would bring, but took the duty he had given her as a solemn charge. Whatever else happened, Abner had to be protected. At the hotel, she ran quickly up the stairs and went to the Bensons' suite. She knocked, but the door was open and she went in. The sitting room was empty, so she went to the nursery, calling for Abner.

William was asleep in his cot, but Abner was not there. Her heart began to worry for him, although her mind told her he was safe, with Mrs. Benson. She went back into the sitting room, and saw that Mrs. Benson had come from the main bedroom and was locking the door to the suite.

"Where's Abner?" she cried.

Mrs. Benson put the key in her pocket and turned from the door. She smiled at Queen, for she was content, and happy.

"Abner isn't here," she said. "He is doing God's work tonight."

There was something in her manner that caused in Queen the primal urges that only a mother can know, when she is sure her offspring is in mortal danger.

"Where is he? Where's my baby?" she asked apprehensively.

"He is with his father," Mrs Benson said. "Whether he lives or dies depends on what his father does."

Queen did not, could not, understand the complexity of the relationships in which she was entangled; she knew only blind fury and cold hate. She screamed and ran to Mrs. Benson, to fight with her to get the key, to get out, to do anything, but Mrs. Benson was ready for her and struck her hard across the face, and then again, and Queen fell to the floor, moaning.

The guards waiting in simple ambush in the trees near the shack thought they were ready, but they had the

825

disadvantage of fear. Although there was no official membership of the Klan in Beaufort, they all knew what it meant, and knew the cause had many sympathizers. It was as well they did not know that Mr. Benson had enlisted some of those sympathizers since he had been in Beaufort, and given them purpose, direction, and collective strength through unity, for if they had known, their fear would have been magnified. Or perhaps it didn't matter what they knew, for the robed men came bursting out of the trees, on horseback, carrying brands, and several had military training. It was a short, sharp battle that the guards lost because they did not believe they could win. Two died instantly, one was fatally wounded, and two ran away into the night.

Davis fired from the hut, but he was not a trained shot, and the men on horseback kept beyond his range as they rode in circles around his fortress, calling on him to come out. Davis roared at them to rot in hell, but one night rider who seemed to be the leader shouted out to him.

"Come on out, nigger," he shouted. "We have your boy."

Davis looked at his gun, which was useless to him now. He peered out of the window and saw that the leader had spoken the truth. A brand illuminated one of the riders who was holding Abner.

Davis was scared, but not to die, he almost welcomed that. He had courted death too often to be afraid of it, and it had become his ultimate friend. He was scared for his son, whom he hardly knew.

"Come on out, or the boy burns first," the leader shouted again.

Davis thought that if his life had any purpose or meaning, it was now. If he could do anything to save his son, it was worth any sacrifice, for he believed what he had told Queen. The boy was the future. Davis had lived in negativity all his life, and his life was meaning-less to him. Then a simple woman had loved him without limitation, and had borne his child, and he had found a purpose at last. Not to be father to the boy, but to try to create a better world for that boy to live in.

And he had succeeded. The work he had done had helped build the foundations of something that he knew he would not see complete in his lifetime, no matter how long he lived. But he had seen a wrong and tried to right it, and, like the ever-widening, rippling circles from a pebble thrown into a pond, the righting of that wrong would continue, for endless generations, for the righting of wrongs was an endless task. He had achieved what he had set out to do, for the world that his son would inherit would be better, if only by an infinitesimal degree, than the world that Davis had been born into, and that, no matter how small, was much. He knew the boy's mother would communicate to him what his father had done, and the boy would be proud, and hold his head high, and know that his father had helped to change the world.

Suddenly, the immensity of human existence and experience astonished him. His ancestors had been brought unwillingly from Africa, and kept, like the Israelites in Egypt, in bondage. But, like the children of Israel, they had survived their ordeal and been freed from their chains. Faith and hope had sustained them, and they had taken their first few footsteps in a vast and uncharted territory that beggared the imagination, for it was without border or boundary. As long as the human race existed, the greed of some would battle the charity of others. In his life, he had seen a great wrong righted, because some good men, white men, he realized with a wry smile, had sought to redress what other white men had instituted. He had taken advan-tage of the freedom that they brought to him, and carried on the fight, because he had hope for the future.

827

Queen had given him that, and faith that he could make some change, no matter how tiny. In God's eye he must be smaller than any ant, but he had contributed to the hill.

Queen had been right all the time. Hate was meaningless, negative. Love was the sublime driving force, for what was love but faith and trust in another person, and hope for the future. And the greatest gifts a father could give his son were faith and hope and love.

The boy must live.

They threw a rope over a branch on a tree, and put the noose at the end of the rope around Davis's neck. They kicked the horse he sat on, and he felt a sharp and sudden pain and a choking in his throat, and he jerked and jolted at the end of the rope, by instinctive reaction, because his body fought to breathe. His eyes grew dim, but his mind and his heart did not fight against the coming of the dark angel, but welcomed it, because suddenly he saw a great, golden light and as it flooded over him it revealed, for a moment, the most beautiful land he had ever seen, a land of untold promise as viewed from the highest mountain, and he knew he had found home at last.

They doused his body with paraffin and set brands to it, and as the flames engulfed him, the man who was the leader held Abner up to see the burning body.

"Watch him burn, boy, and remember!" the leader said. "Watch your pappy burn."

Queen had crawled into a corner, into a fetal ball. She was clutching herself, moaning to herself, but her mind was numb, and she did not hear the explanation that Mrs. Benson gave her.

"It is for William, you see, and all the little white children of America. It is our sacred, bounden duty to ensure that they inherit a world of peace and order. A clean and pure America, unsullied by animal blood. It is God's law."

She was hugging William to her, caressing him with

maternal love, oblivious of the maternal pain she had caused to another human being, for she did not believe that being was human. The creature had been useful, her milk nourished William, and thankfully milk was not blood. She could still be useful in the glory days to come when the true kingdom of God was established in this bounteous land, for she had been sent by Providence to aid their night's work. But she thought a visit to the doctor was in order for Queen, to make sure she bred no more bastards.

There was a tap on the door. Queen cried out and scrabbled into the corner in fear. Mrs. Benson went to the door and unlocked it, and Mr. Benson came in. He nodded at his wife.

"Now God be praised, who has brought us to this hour," she prayed. Oh, but she longed to be part of it, to be present at the killing, for she knew the effect it had on her husband, and, vicariously, on her. Mr. Benson grabbed her and kissed her lustily. Then he saw Queen.

"Get her out," he said huskily.

"My baby, where's my baby," Queen moaned. Mr. Benson came to her, dragged her to her feet, and pushed her out of the room.

"He's with his father," he said, to be rid of her. He slammed the door, and turned to his wife, his sexual energy charged to fever pitch by murder.

Queen did not take a horse, because she had no mind to think of practicality, and did not want to arrive at where she had to go. She did not dare imagine what she would find when she got to the shack, but she had to go there, because that was where they were. Moaning and crying, clutching at her dress, grabbing at her hair, she staggered through the night, oblivious to all around her, flames of torment filling her mind, holding on by a slim, silken thread to sanity, which thread might break at any moment.

It was dawn when she got there, and mist lazed across the river and the land.

She saw the charred body of Davis swinging gently from the tree when she was still some distance away, but she didn't cry out, for it was what she had been expecting. Moaning still, she stumbled toward him, and then she saw Abner lying motionless on the ground beneath his father.

She screamed to heaven then, and fell to the ground, at her lowest ebb of self. Grief flowed upon grief, and still more grief, and pain, and fury at the unfairness of life so prematurely taken.

"What have we ever done to them, Lord?" she cried. "Why do they hate us so much?"

She swooned, in abject wretchedness.

And God, as if ashamed of what He had wrought, relented.

A gentle rain started to fall.

It woke Abner up, and he began to cry.

PART FOUR

A WIFE AND
MOTHER, LOVED

Beyond the years the soul shall find
That endless peace for which it pined,
For light appears,
And to the eyes that still were blind
With blood and tears
Their sight shall come all unconfined
Beyond the years.

Paul Laurence Dunbar

84

Rain drizzled down on the mighty Tennessee River at Savannah. Alec Haley steered his ferry, a small, flat-bottomed steamboat, from the northern shore to the south. It was late afternoon, a busy time of day, with people anxious to get to their homes. His passengers had their coats pulled up over their heads as shelter from the rain, or old newspaper or blankets to protect their hats. It had been raining for days, and there was very little conversation among the passengers; the weather had dampened their spirits.

As Alec guided the ferry to the small jetty, new passengers were sheltering under trees, waiting to make the journey north.

Alec tied a line to the wharf and the passengers disembarked, calling thanks or farewell to him, and made their way up the muddy track, which led past the Cherry mansion on the hill and on into town. The new passengers dashed from the shelter of the trees and took their places on the boat. They greeted Alec as cheerfully as the depressing weather would allow and Alec took their fares, exchanged greetings, and looked around for any latecomers. It was then that he saw the woman.

She was tiny and light-skinned, with a darker child on her hip, wrapped in a thin blanket. She was poorly dressed, her coat was worn and sodden by the rain, and she had cardboard tucked into her shoes. She stood under the trees, apparently oblivious to the weather, and stared at nothing, as if she were lost. Alec was puzzled. He assumed she wanted to cross the river—there was no other reason for her to be waiting there—but she made no move toward him.

"Comin' on?" he called.

It broke the woman's reverie. She looked at him as if she did not know where she was, and was surprised to see him. She walked slowly to the jetty, then stopped again, uncertain of something. Some few of the passengers on the boat were already grumbling at the delay she was causing, but Alec guessed the reason.

"It's a nickel," he said.

The woman opened her small, tattered purse and counted out a few pennies, obviously down on her luck. Alec watched, intrigued by her light skin and her darker child.

"Where you headin'?" he asked her.

She looked at him with vacant eyes.

"North," she said. She gave him the money, climbed onto the boat, and settled on a bench. She pulled the blanket closer around the boy, her coat tighter about herself, and waited with patience for the journey to begin. She had nothing else to do.

"C'mon, Alec!" a passenger shouted. "I's gettin' soaked."

Alec grunted and cast off the line. "Make y'hair grow," he said to the complainant, Fred, who was was bald. He started the engine, and the ferry chugged north.

The weather didn't bother Alec. He loved his ferry, and, together with the twenty acres of farmland he owned, it gave him a good living. He was settled and secure, his own man, and owed nothing to anyone, except a sense of gratitude to Massa Cherry, who was not, and never had been, his Massa.

Following the common custom among slaves, Alec had taken the name Haley from his true Massa, although his real father's name was Baugh. William Baugh was an overseer on the Haley plantation in Marion County, Alabama, who had sometimes taken his pleasure with a slave woman, half black, half Cherokee, called Sabrina. It was a casual relationship, and when a son, Alec, was born, he became a child of the plantation, owned by the Massa. An honest and industrious boy, he grew up in the protection of the extended family that slave life provided. His several surrogate fathers taught him well, and by the time he was a young man he could turn his hand to almost any job that the plantation required. He accepted his slavery only because he had known no other life, but he deeply resented his lack of freedom, his inability to choose his own life, and be his own Massa. The fact that he was never whipped did not reduce his hostility; it was injustice enough that he was not free.

But he was cheerful and energetic, and looked for the best in all other aspects of his life. Shortly before the end of the war he fell in love with a tiny slave called Teenie, and married her when freedom came to them. He could have stayed on the plantation because Massa Haley respected his ability, but Alec had a young man's zest for adventure. He and Teenie set off to discover the world with their new daughter, Minnie. He took work where he could find it, as a farmhand, or driving cattle to the railroad, but times were hard in Alabama. Looking for opportunity, they headed North. They never got farther than Tennessee. In Savannah, Alec, looking for work, had been engaged by Mr. Cherry, and after proving his skill on the land, was given some acres to sharecrop. It was a hard life but a rewarding one. They were blessed with a son, whom they called Freeland, for this was the land of their freedom, and another daughter, Julie, and Teenie modified her name to Tennie, in honor of the state that was their new home.

Tragedy struck when Tennie died in childbirth. Alec grieved for her sorely, and for a time lost his appetite for life. Mr. Cherry, perhaps as a form of solace for Alec, whom he liked and admired, purchased a boat to institute a ferry service across the river, and offered him the management of it. It was the balm that Alec needed. He loved the river life. He loved the river on sunny days, when the sun sparkled on the water, and the paddle steamers chugged by. He loved the river on cloudy days, when the fishermen came out in force, sitting for hours in the hope of a bite, cogitating the world, and calmed by their own unhurried pace and the reluctant appetite of the fish. He loved the river in the summer mornings, when mist obscured the shores, and he loved it on winter days, when the crisp cold gave him something to complain about. He loved the fall, when the changing colors of the leaves delighted his eye, and he loved it in the spring, when he was filled with a sense of the renewal of life. He still farmed his acres, with the help of George, a local lad, an orphan who was like a son to him, but the river was his obsession. Apart from a few itinerant travelers, he knew most of his passengers by name, and much of the detail of their lives, and he basked in their endless, idle gossip and chatter. He was kind to those in need of assistance, stern with those who offended him, and did his best to provide his children with a good home life. In many ways his life was full, but an important part of his heart was empty. He missed Tennie sorely, and he was lonely.

He looked at the thin, frail woman sitting on the bench, her child held firmly in her protective embrace, and guessed that North was an ambivalent destination for her, an ideal to cling to because she had nothing else, and wished he could help and give her some other purpose. He had seen an endless procession of freed slaves head North, only to return weeks, months, years later, with nothing in their pockets but broken dreams. And for all those who came back, he knew ten times that number stayed, in disillusion.

He wondered where the woman would sleep that night, or what she would eat. He had seen that her purse was almost empty, and seized the moment. They were about halfway across the river.

"That girl of your'n still looking for a job?" he called to Fred, the bald passenger, who was an old sparring partner.

Fred stared at Alec in surprise. "She ain't lookin' fo' a job," he said. His daughter had a job, a good one, nanny to a white family.

"Well, if'n you hear of anyone . . ." Alec shrugged. "Massa Cherry's been looking fo' help this past two month, and no fool girl's got the sense to apply."

Although it was said to Fred, he spoke loudly, above the rain, so that the woman would hear.

"Good job fo' someone," he continued. "Room and board and good eatin'. And you know Dora, who cooks for Massa Cherry, she c'n make mean victuals. Her hog ribs with barbecue sauce—oh, man, that's eatin'."

He knew he had struck home, because he saw a flicker of interest in the woman's eyes, and pushed his point.

"An' her pumpkin pie, and her peach cobbler—"

But the mouths of the other passengers were watering too. It was late in the day; they were on their way home and looking forward to a good dinner. They shouted him down with aggrieved announcements that they hadn't eaten yet, or were hungry, or that their Missus could make the best peach pie in the country. The woman didn't respond to the din.

"Jus' sayin'." Alec shrugged again. "You cain't get a good hog up North. They all skinny ol' things up there."

He docked the ferry at the northern jetty, and the passengers crowded off, bidding him farewell, hungry for their dinners. The woman quit the ferry with them, and stood on the shore for a moment as if wondering which way to go. New passengers began crowding on, jostling each other and complaining of the rain. Alec, who had been busy tying up the line, looked up to take the fares, and could see no sign of the woman. He shrugged and returned to his business.

They sailed south again, and Alec could not get her out of his mind, an itty-bitty thing, who carried such a sense of hopelessness with her. He had done all he could; he had planted a seed and it hadn't taken. He wished her well, wherever she was, and fell into conversation about the grasshopper plague in the west.

Freeland was waiting for him on the southern side, and dashed from the trees to help his father tie up. Fresh from school, which he hated, Freeland loved to work on the ferry with his father. School was a pain in the you know what. He helped passengers off and new ones on, and was allowed to take the fares, because he was good at counting.

"Y'c'n count good, an' you never had much schoolin'," he said to his father, and barked an unnecessary order to the passengers. "All aboard!"

"I still have trouble countin' past ten," his father grinned, and cast off.

To Freeland, it was all grossly unfair. He could count past ten, he could count to anything, he did most of the money counting for his pappy, and he wanted to leave school and work on the farm, like George, his hero. He never missed an opportunity for stressing his case to his father, especially on the ferry, and did so now, as they headed north. But Alec was adamant.

"You stayin' till you done sixth grade," Alec told him sharply, as he did almost every day. "It's what yo' mammy wanted."

It was the habitual end of the argument, and Freeland sighed, stared at the river, and dreamed of being as old as George, who was sixteen.

Alec was sympathetic to his son's ambition. He'd never had much schooling, but had done well enough in life. He thought education was a waste of a boy's time, but counting was important, and he'd made a promise to Tennie. Besides, the discipline wouldn't harm Freeland, and he was still too small to be much use on the land.

He guided the ferry to the northern jetty, and was surprised to see the woman standing under a tree, her child still clutched to her. He felt a small sense of satisfaction. She had risen to his bait. Now she had to be hooked. He nodded a greeting to her, but she didn't respond. Freeland helped the leaving passengers off and the new ones embark, took the fares and saw Queen.

"Y' comin' on, lady?" he called. "Only a nickel."

Everyone was staring at her, because she was holding up the departure. Queen hesitated. She wanted to go back south, she wanted the job the ferryman had talked about, she wanted food for herself and her boy, and she wanted a warm dry place to sleep. There was only one problem.

"I ain't got a nickel," she cried out suddenly. "I ain't got one red cent. I ain't got nuttin'!"

It was passionately spoken, and everyone looked at her in astonishment, mingled with some small pity for her plight, and annoyance, because they wanted to be on their way. Alec took charge.

"Now I cain't hardly charge you fo' takin' you back where you came from," he called. "Only don't tell all these other niggers, else they'll all want a free ride."

The passengers laughed. They knew the woman would ride for free, because Alec was a kind man and she looked so poor, and they knew they'd all pay their own fares without hesitation, but with considerable, vocal complaint. It added a spark of interest to an otherwise ordinary ferry crossing.

Queen, angry at having to reveal her poverty and furious at their laughter, made her way to the boat. She wouldn't take charity, she told Alec grumpily. As soon as she got a job, as soon as she got back on her feet, she would repay him. Alec smiled, and agreed that was the best solution. Queen settled on the bench and glared angrily at the other passengers.

"Y'all quit staring at me, y'hear?" she shouted. "What

you think I am, white trash? I's black like you, so you keep yo' eyes off me."

Everyone looked the other way and pretended they hadn't heard. Except Alec, who couldn't take his eyes off her.

"An' that goes for you too," she shouted at him now. "You and all men, y'all got just one thing on your minds, and I ain't got no time fo' none of you!"

Her fury was formidable, and her performance spectacular. It drew murmurs of agreement and appreciation from the other passengers, who variously assured her that they heard her and wouldn't look at her.

Except Alec, who simply watched her, and she, perhaps embarrassed, changed Abner to her other arm, and stared at the river.

Freeland was wide-eyed in wonder.

"Glory be, Pops," he said. "That is one mean-tempered woman."

"Ain't she just," Alec agreed, clearly impressed by her. They sailed south. Queen's temper was almost permanently mean these days, for she wore her troubles, her deep anger and her heartbreak, about her like a shroud, and the world responded to her in kind.

She had never gone back to Mrs. Benson, but some strikers, aware of her relationship to Davis, took pity on her, and gave her shelter. They had little else to give her because they had so little themselves, and when the strike was broken, only days later, they had even less. But their spirits, unlike Queen's, were not broken. They had not succeeded this time, but Davis had given them a sense of purpose and unity, and a belief in the future. Three years later they would strike again, and this time they would succeed, but Queen was not there for their victory. She hated Beaufort, for it reminded her of Davis, and she set off on her journey again, with no idea of where she was going, except to find some small elusive peace. She did not go North, for if she had gone there and found unhappiness again, where else was left to her? Without clearly understanding what she was doing, she headed east, back to Georgia, to Alabama, and to Florence. If she had thought about it, she would not have believed that The Forks represented any kind of sanctuary, but she didn't think about anything anymore; her only concern was for Abner's survival, and, to a lesser extent, her own.

Without direction, without ambition, she existed, rather than lived. Her temper quickened and her speech coarsened. She accepted rides from strangers, but would not talk to them, only to her child. She hardened her heart against the world, because she had lost all sense of trust in other people. She took charity, gracelessly, where she could find it, and begged or borrowed or stole when there was nothing else. Abner was her only consolation, and the only contact she made with anyone was for his welfare. He settled into an extraordinary acceptance of their circumstances. He stared out at the world with round, open eyes, received gratefully all that it offered, and cried only if he was hungry and they had no food, or if he was tired and they had no bed for the night. She took jobs if she could find them, only to be dismissed because of her short temper. And yet the world was kinder to her than she allowed it to be. Folk took pity on her, perhaps because she was so desolate, or for the boy's sake, and she survived. She avoided anywhere that she might be known, such as Huntsville or Decatur, and tried to avoid anywhere she had been.

After a year of wandering, she came to the outskirts of Florence, and was forced to make a decision. She could go back to The Forks of Cypress and beg some shelter at least, from Jass, or Missy Sally, or she could go on. Since going back to an unhappy past was almost worse than her surviving present, she chose to go on, but to where she did not know. She followed the river and eventually she came to Savannah. She took the ferry north, and when the ferryman talked of a job and food, her mouth watered, for she had not eaten in two days, and her body craved for shelter, for she had not slept in a bed for a week. When she got off the ferry, she walked for a few hundred yards on the northern shore, well aware of her empty purse and her hopeless position, and then turned back, to throw herself on the mercy of the ferryman.

It was the last run for the day. Soon it would be night. As Alec docked, he looked at Queen.

"Wait there," he said, nodding to the trees. Queen did as he bade, not knowing what he had in mind, but put herself in his hands because she was beyond making a decision for herself. If he proved as venal as all men, she would defend herself, and she would survive somehow, but at that moment, she did not know how, or for what reason, except Abner.

Alec tied up the ferry and sent Freeland home. He offered to carry Abner, but Queen would not part with the boy. He led her up the muddy path to the Cherry mansion, took her in the back way, and introduced her to Dora, who was cook and housekeeper to Mr. Cherry.

Dora was mountainous and magnificent, of brisk manner and immense heart. She took one look at the sodden sparrow clutching her boy to her and gathered them up and cared for them as if they were her own. She made warm milk immediately, then took them into her own bedroom, next to the kitchen, and found warm dry clothes for Queen and a fresh, dry blanket for Abner. She poured a big basin of hot water for them to wash, and went back to the kitchen while Queen changed. She heated up a pot of thick stew and talked to Alec, who had made himself comfortable by the fire. Both guessed at her circumstances without reaching any conclusions, and Alec told her that he had mentioned the job to the woman.

"Time enough fo' that later," Dora said to Alec, as Queen came nervously back into the kitchen. She felt a little silly in the enormous dressing gown, and still held Abner close to her, as she was wont to do in a house of strangers, however well-intentioned they appeared to be. Dora sat her at the table and put a big plate of stew in front of her, and cut some slabs of bread. Queen mushed up some meat and vegetables and fed them to Abner, making sure he was satisfied before she attended to her own hunger. She would not speak, and only answered questions with a grunt or a monosyllable, which made Alec a little cross. Thank you was not such a hard thing to say. But her devotion to the boy impressed him, and he glanced at Dora. She flicked her head at the door, suggesting he leave, for she thought Queen might respond better if she was alone with a woman. Alec took the hint and made his goodnights. He had to be home to his brood, and see what problems the day had brought. Queen did not acknowledge his leaving.

It was clear to Dora that Abner had eaten as much as he needed, and Queen very little.

"The chile's done eatin'," she said. "I'll hold him while you finish up."

But Queen would not let Abner go.

"Don't touch him," she said.

Dora was puzzled and concerned.

"Lord, girl, what you think, I'm gwine steal him from you?"

Queen shrugged. Too many people had tried to take Abner away from her already, but she had no way of explaining that.

Dora busied herself with pots and pans, and asked about her qualifications. Queen responded less curtly, and her answers satisfied Dora, who agreed she could have the job for a week, on a trial basis. It was long hours and hard work, but Mr. Cherry was a fine, fair man, and if Queen proved suitable she would be asked to stay on. There was no response, and as Dora turned from the stove, she saw Queen filching some bread

843

from the table and stuffing it into her pocket. Again, Dora was intrigued, but made no comment about it. She saw that Abner was asleep.

"Look at that boy, fast asleep in his mammy's arms," she said. "Sweetest sight in all the world."

She sat beside Queen, to try to find some way to communicate with her.

"Is you still hungry?" she asked, and Queen shook her head. She was staring down at her plate, as if her head was too heavy to hold up upright.

"Is you tired?" Dora asked. For a moment there was no reply, but then Queen looked at her and tears were streaming down her face. She hadn't cried since the death of Davis—there was no point in it—but now in this warm kitchen, in the company of a kindly woman, with a job and not hungry anymore, a year's worth of tears found their release.

"I never been so tired in all my life," she said. She held on to Abner and wept. She could not go to another human being for comfort, because she had been too long alone, so Dora went to her. She put her embracing arms around the unhappy woman, and held her to her bosom while she cried. As mammies do.

Dora let Queen cry until she was done, then dried her eyes and told her everything was going to be all right now. She might have taken her up the back stairs to her room, but she wanted Queen to have some appreciation of the job she had been offered, and led her through the main hall of the house, and up the sweeping staircase.

The hall was elegantly appointed, and fine portraits hung on the walls, reminding Queen of The Forks of Cypress. She walked up the stairs feeling as if she were back where she started, and remembered herself climbing stairs similar to this, many years ago, in the company of a woman who didn't love her, taking her away from her mammy, who did.

"Massa won't mind Abner being with me?" she asked Dora, who laughed.

"Do his heart good to have a chile in the house again," she said. "This ol' place has been all echoes and shadows since Massa Cherry's chillun done leave home."

She was anxious to learn what she could of Queen's background, and pried gently.

"Don't s'ppose you ever seen the like," she said, referring to the magnificent hall, and the splendid portraits.

Queen's mind was filled with ghosts.

"Oh, yes," she nodded. "My pappy was a great man. I lived in the big house."

It wasn't much, but Dora thought it was a considerable breakthrough.

"Where yo' pappy now?" she asked, as they moved across the upper hall to the second stairs. "He passed on?"

She didn't react when she heard a soft, sad voice behind her, but the words stung her heart.

"No," Queen said. "He didn't love me. Because I am black."

Her room was small, but comfortable, and blessedly warm. She made Abner comfortable under the blankets, his head on a pillow, and Dora told her to sleep in the dressing gown.

"First thing tomorrow, we get you some decent clothes," she said, thinking nothing of it. This was too much generosity for Queen, who was used to begging for it, and stealing it.

"I don't want no charity," she muttered angrily.

Dora was concerned. She needed help in the house and Queen had the qualifications, but under normal circumstances, she would have preferred someone with a happier personality. She had been kind to Queen because she was a kind woman and Queen needed help, but her first loyalty was to Massa Cherry, for whom she had worked, slave and free, all her life. She also thought that too much kindness might not be the best thing for Queen.

"You listen to me, Missy," she said sharply. "If you gwine work here, you gotta dress nice and look nice and be nice. You say you was raised proper and got good manners—well, you start showing it. Massa Cherry don't want some mean-tempered skivvy running round the house."

Queen turned away, sulking.

"If'n it'll make you feel better, I's takin' the cost of yo' new clothes out of yo' wages."

She thought she had been stern enough for the moment, so she relaxed a little.

"Coz you don't look so good in my hand-me-downs," she added, with a twinkle in her eye and her voice.

Her warmth of tone and commanding personality reassured Queen, who needed someone to tell her what to do.

"I's sorry," she whispered, and Dora laughed. She helped Queen into the bed and tucked her in. As mammies do.

The crisp, clean sheets felt wonderful to Queen, and she snuggled Abner to her, and thought she never wanted to wake up. Dora sat on the edge of the bed, and stroked her hair.

"Don't have to worry no more," she said softly. "You safe now."

Queen could not accept that. She turned her head away, to look at the wall.

"Don't belong nowhere," she murmured.

Dora could only guess at what had happened to Queen to bring her to such desolation, but she was beginning to understand something of the forces driving her, and what she needed.

"Glory be, chile," she said. "Everybody belong some-

846

where. Jus' takes some folk a while to work out where it is."

Still she stroked Queen's hair, and thought of her own children, married now, with families of their own. She thanked God that she had never seen any of her girls in a state as wretched as Queen's.

She began to hum a gentle lullaby, which slowly formed into soft, loving words.

Queen drifted to sleep with Abner in her arms, while Dora sat with her, and lulled her with childhood songs.

As mammies do.

85

When Alec got home that evening, it was to the usual domestic chaos. He employed a girl, Little Bit, as part-time housekeeper, but she was a foolish, dreaming girl, lazy and difficult, and far too young to be surrogate mother to Alec's children. For although Minnie, his eldest girl, was useful around the house, Freeland was too full of youthful energy to be anything but a nuisance, and Julie was not old enough to help anyone. George, who lived with them in the shed at the back of the shack, did his best, but was young himself, and often tired from his long hours on the farm. No matter how much love Alec tried to show his children, no matter how many speeches of mutual cooperation he made, no matter how much authority he gave Little Bit over the household, she was hardly older than her charges, and there was constant bickering and general unhappiness. Tonight, the dinner was late.

"Lord sakes, Little Bit," Alec said tetchily, "they should have et an hour ago."

Little Bit thought she had worked hard, and resented his constant griping.

"I cain't do everything," she complained as she always did. "I bin here fo' hours cookin' and cleanin', an' I's dog tired."

Although she wasn't too tired to look forward to her date that night with her new boyfriend. Rather than argue with her, Alec gave in, for it had been a long day.

"All right, Little Bit," he said. "You go on home. I'll see to everything."

Little Bit needed no second bidding, and grabbed her hat and coat.

"Time you had a new wife to slave for yo'," she sniffed as she walked out of the door.

Alec's presence and Little Bit's departure calmed the children, and Minnie organized everyone in helping with the dinner. She and Alec served the meat and beans, and cooked the turnip greens, while Freeland and Julie laid the table, and George did his best to tidy up, but he was tall for his age and got in everyone's way. As they ate their dinner, the youngsters complained of Little Bit, giggling that she was a little bit worse than useless, until Alec told them to shush. They sat together as a family for a while and told their father their stories of the day, and then one by one, Alec dispatched them to bed. Minnie and Julie slept in a small room at the back of the shack, and Freeland shared the shed with George. Alec said prayers with the young ones, tucked them in, and kissed them good night.

He looked at the shack and shook his head. The children were right, Little Bit was a little bit worse than useless; the place looked like it hadn't been properly cleaned in weeks. He thought sadly of Tennie, who had kept the little house in such apple-pie order. He was too tired to tackle the mess, and went outside to sit on the porch with George, as was their evening ritual.

The rain had eased and it was a pleasant night. Alec sat in his old rocking chair, and puffed on his pipe. George was comfortable on the steps. There was another, empty rocker next to Alec, but no one ever sat in that, for it had been Tennie's chair.

They talked for a while about George's day, and the prospect of a plentiful crop that year, then lapsed into reflective silence.

"Dey's need a mammy," George said after a while, and Alec nodded.

"An' you need a wife," George said after another small silence.

Alec knew that was true, but wasn't quite ready to admit it yet.

"Watch yo' mouth," he told George, affectionately cross.

George grinned. Alec was more than his employer, his boss; he was like a father to George, who had never known one.

"Y' cain't leave it fo'ever," he said, untroubled by Alec's admonition. "You's gettin' old, an' one day you gwine wake up and be too old."

"Hush yo' mouth, I said," Alec told him again, for George had hit a raw nerve. "Y'ain't so big I cain't whump you."

George grinned again, for he was already bigger than Alec. "Like to see you try," he said. He got to his feet, said his good-nights to Alec, and went to the shed.

Alec sat alone, puffing on his pipe and staring at the night. It was bad enough that Dora was always telling him to find another wife, and Massa Cherry, and most of his friends, but now even George was on about it.

The image of a tiny, frightened woman with a child on her hip came into his mind, and he felt protective toward her, and intrigued by her, and wanted to know more about her.

"Dadgummit," he said softly.

He saw her the following afternoon, back from a shopping expedition into town with Dora, to buy new clothes, and he smiled and waved, but she ignored him. Dora looked at him knowingly and shook her head. Alec decided not to speak to Queen for a few days, until she was in better temper, but he thought about her often when he was steering his ferryboat across the river, and once was in such a reverie that he almost forgot to slow down the boat and came close to smashing into the jetty. Only the shouts of his passengers brought his attention back to the business at hand.

Mr. Cherry returned from a business trip to Memphis, and was introduced to his new housemaid. Usually his wife handled all the domestic matters, but she was visiting relations in New York. Wearing a smart black dress and white apron and cap, Queen looked lovely, fit and rested, but she was still suspicious of kindness and generosity. Mr. Cherry bade her welcome to his house, and hoped she would be happy with them. If she worked hard and well, she could be with them for a long time.

"Oh, I ain't staying," Queen said, to Mr. Cherry's surprise. "No, sir, Massa. Soon as I's back on my feet, I's going North, to start a flower shop."

It was the dream that she clung to, her defense against the world.

"I understood from Dora that it was to be a more permanent situation," Mr. Cherry said, slightly offended by her manner.

"No, sir," Queen insisted. "I ain't planning to be a kitchen skivvy all my life."

The edge to her manner was so sharp and dismissive, she managed to rile even the tolerant Mr. Cherry. He nodded as if in approval of her ambition, but sent her back to work.

"Be that as it may," he said, "I'm paying you as a maid, so perhaps you should be about your business."

"Yes, suh!" Queen snapped impudently. "I's going now, suh!"

Mr. Cherry very seldom lost his temper, but he came close to it, briefly. He went into his study and rang for

Dora to find out if the new maid was always so bad-tempered.

She was. She worked hard and well, but no one, except occasionally Dora, could get a smile from her. She snapped at everyone else for imagined slights, and spent her free time in her room with Abner. She kept him there when she was working, and sat him on her knee when she was eating her meals in the kitchen. Gradually, she began to trust Dora sufficiently to keep an eye on the boy, but otherwise she would not let anyone near him. Especially not Alec.

Alec found some pretext to call at the house almost every day, to discuss business with Mr. Cherry, or gossip in the kitchen with Dora. He tried hard to find some conversation with Queen but was always rebuffed.

"You lookin' better," he said to her, as he often did, for he could not think of any other opening.

She would sniff and find something else to do, or walk away, and if Abner was near she would pick him up and remove him from Alec's vicinity. Her exclusion of them began to get on everyone's nerves.

But Abner excluded no one. A quiet and reserved child when he first arrived, he blossomed into a happy, chubby boy, had a smile and a laugh for everyone, and was especially fond of Alec.

He accepted his mother's absences at work, but was happiest when he was near her, or anyone. One warm day, he was sitting on a rug in the garden, while Queen put carpets over the line and beat them, to get the dust out of them. The sun was shining, the gardener was working in the vegetable plot, and Abner was playing happily with a toy that Dora had given him.

Only Queen was immune to the general goodwill, and thwacked the carpets vigorously, as if she were beating everyone who had ever done her harm.

Alec had been working on his land, and was on his

851

way home for the midday meal. He had stopped in the kitchen to deliver some fresh beans to Dora, and when he came out he saw Queen. He decided to vary his ritual approach.

"Pretty day," he said, for it was the prettiest of days.

Queen didn't respond.

"How's the job?" Alec asked. Queen was fed up. It was a pretty day, but she had to work, and didn't want to be reminded of it.

"If'n you're looking for me to say thanks fo' getting me the job, or summat," she said, still hitting the carpet, "you can forget it. I'd have managed, somehow."

"Sure you would," Alec agreed, but did not leave. He couldn't work out why he felt so protective toward this wretched, ill-mannered woman. His continued presence irritated Queen even more.

"Ain't you got a ferry to run?" she called as she beat.

"Saturday, George and my boy Freeland do it. I work the land," he told her. "Ain't the biggest block of land, but with the ferry, we get by."

"How well you do or how well you don't do, ain't nothin' to do with me," Queen snapped, refusing to be drawn by him. Because she wouldn't look at him, she didn't see that Abner had toddled over to Alec, and was tugging on his jacket for attention. Alec looked down at him.

"Well, now, young fella," he said, picking Abner up, "what's your name?" He knew Abner's name but had not been introduced, and wanted to make contact with the boy.

Queen turned and saw her beloved son in Alec's arms, and she panicked. She dropped the carpet beater and ran to Abner, grabbed him from Alec.

"You leave him be!" Queen shouted at Alec. "He's mine, and no one ever going to take him away from me."

Alec was astonished by her ferocity, and Dora, who

852

had come out to talk to the gardener, looked on in amazement.

"Lord, woman, I was jus' askin' his name," Alec protested, but Queen hardly heard him.

"He ain't no business of your'n," she cried, and took Abner into the house. Alec was baffled and hurt by Queen's reaction, and looked at Dora.

"Abner," Dora said calmly. "The chile's called Abner."

Alec nodded, for he knew that. "Fine name fo' a boy," he said. "Biblical." He walked home to his shack puzzling at the depth of Queen's unhappiness, and while part of him wanted nothing more to do with her, part of him was determined to discover the reason for her distress. He lost his temper with Little Bit, who had taken it on herself to spank Julie for some trivial naughtiness, and he sacked her.

Dora, who was as puzzled as Alec by Queen's behavior, took the gardener to task for the scrawny carrots he had picked.

"Yes, m'm, Miss Dora, dey's the biggest I c'n find," the gardener said to placate her. He was used to her.

But Abner cried, and Queen could not comfort him. Abner didn't understand why his mammy had dragged him away from the nice man. But then Abner was luckier than Queen. Abner knew he was home.

"She's been hurt bad," Dora told Alec. They were sitting in the kitchen, shelling peas. "She got a bellyful of anger against the world."

Alec nodded, popping more peas into his mouth than into the pan.

"But Massa Cherry like a happy house," Dora cautioned. "She carry on like this, she won't have a job."

She slapped Alec's hand, for eating too many of the peas.

It came to a head at a formal dinner party that Mr. Cherry gave. A gregarious and hospitable host, he kept a fine table, and enjoyed good conversation. Because of his position in the county, his guests were of some standing, though not necessarily of good manners.

Queen was serving, and a female guest snapped her fingers and demanded water. Perhaps it was the finger snap that grated on Queen, or perhaps she was tired, but when she poured the water, a little of it spilled on the woman's dress.

The woman shouted at Queen impatiently, demanding cloths to clean up the mess, and turned to the other guests.

"These nigras!" she said disparagingly. "Nothing's been the same since the war."

The thoughtless comment made Mr. Cherry angry, and he was about to chide his guest, but Queen got there first.

"I ain't a nigra!" she exclaimed. "My pappy was white, and his pappy afore him, all the way back to Ireland."

Her explosion caused a startled silence at the dinner table, and in the silence Queen felt her frustration rising. It was true that she had as much Irish blood in her as black blood; she didn't feel Irish, and she wasn't treated as Irish, but why was she considered more black than Irish? She knew she'd said too much already, but she couldn't stop herself from saying more.

"Just because I got an itty bit of black blood in me, you think you can snap yo' fingers at me like a dog and have me dancing to yo' beck and call." She was shouting now, unstoppable.

"Well, if you take yo' family tree, you'll mebbe find you've got an itty-bitty little bit of black blood in you," she told the amazed woman. "And even if you ain't, that don't give you the right to call people names."

"Queen, that will do!" Mr. Cherry told her sharply. "Since you cannot control yourself, go to the kitchen, and send Dora to serve."

It was a hard, sharp order, and Queen stared at him

854

for a moment, still angry and unapologetic for what she had done, but understanding that she had gone too far. Although she would admit it to no one, she had come to respect and admire Mr. Cherry, and was furious at herself for having embarrassed him. Pride would not let her apologize, and she did as she was told.

Dora was as angry with Queen, and would have sacked her if she had not needed the help. She went into the dining room, where Queen's outburst was the main topic of conversation, and the insulted guest was demanding Queen's dismissal. Mr. Cherry promised that he would have strong words with Queen, and looked at Dora, but another guest managed to calm things down.

"She could be right though, Daphne, old girl," he said happily to the victim of Queen's wrath. "You never know what your father or grandfather might have got up to with those slave girls."

A few others chuckled, and the atmosphere calmed down a little, but Daphne was doubly insulted now, for it was true. Her grandfather had got up to some nonsense with a slave girl. It was the shame of her family.

"Don't be vulgar, Charles," she said.

After his guests had gone, Mr. Cherry called Queen to him, and gave her a stern lecture.

"She insulted me," Queen said sullenly.

"Be that as it may, it is not your place to berate my guests, no matter how they behave," Mr. Cherry insisted. "Unless you can keep your temper under control in future, I shall have to make other arrangements."

Which is what Queen had thought would happen from the moment she got the job. It had happened to her so many times before, and she was ready for the inevitable.

"That suits me jus' fine," she said, and left the room.

*

Dora was ready to go after her and give her a piece of her mind, for she could not tolerate ingratitude, but Mr. Cherry stopped her. As always, his heart got the better of his common sense, and he, despite all appearances to the contrary, liked Queen, and had admired the logic behind her outburst, if not the way she had done it.

Edgar Cherry's position had always been something of a paradox, even to himself. Raised in the South, he had owned slaves, and they had helped him make his fortune, but he had enjoyed a liberal education in the North, and despised the practice. He could not understand why any human being could believe others inferior simply because of their race, or the color of their skin. He was good to his slaves, and gave several their freedom, but believed that only wealth and influence could bring about change, and the slaves were the key to his fortune. Like Queen and so many others, he puzzled constantly that it only took one tiny drop of black blood to set someone apart from their peers, and Queen's claim that she was actually as much Irish as black had amused him greatly. He had become a devout abolitionist, working to subvert the system from within, to bring his fellow Southerners to an understanding of the terrible injustice they were inflicting on the black race, but made little headway against the pervasive, ruling system. The war gave him the chance to put his ideals into action. He welcomed the Union troops, allowed his house to be used by their officers, and sent some of his slaves behind Rebel lines, to act as spies. He freed his slaves with the announcement of the Emancipation Act, and it pleased him that many chose to stay with their former Massa. It depressed him that the attitude of most whites had not been changed by the war, but while he applauded Queen, he could not tolerate her rudeness, for he believed that such behavior encouraged intolerance, not diminished it.

*

Queen sat in her room, shaking with tangled emotions, and rocking Abner, who sensed his mother's distress, and cried. His distress only added to her own, for he would not be comforted, and Queen could find no way to alleviate her own distress. Her life was following its usual pattern, and she believed it was only a matter of days before she would be dismissed and on the road again. To heaven knows where.

What distressed her most was that she did not want to go. Somewhere deep inside herself she understood that this job, this house, and this place represented the best chance for some small security in her life. The possibility of that chance being snatched away from her, largely by her own intemperate actions, caused her mind to cringe in fear for the future. But she did not understand that she could change that future, for she did not know how to change herself.

She stared at the empty fireplace, and suddenly flames exploded in it, and burst into life, flames of the torches of relentless pursuers, and flames of a burning barn, and flames engulfing the body of the man she had loved, who was father to her son.

86

Dora had her say the following morning, when she took Queen into town to shop. As usual, Queen brought Abner with her, and her obsessive refusal to be parted from the boy began to annoy Dora. He would have been quite happy back at the mansion, in the care of one of the gardeners, but when she mentioned it, Queen became sullen again. Expertly driving the small gig, Dora flicked her whip at the horse to relieve the frustration she felt with this obstinate woman.

"Gwine have to let go of the boy some day," she said,

and saw Queen's face redden. "He cain't go through life thinkin' his mammy is his only home."

"I'm all he's got. I'm the only one who loves him," Queen muttered.

Dora saw her chance, and turned on Queen.

"Now you may not know who you are, missy," she said, "black, white, yalla, or sky-blue pink, and it don't matter a hoot the color of yo' skin, because I know what you are. If'n you think you c'n keep that boy in a glass case the rest of his life, then you are a fool, girl. The biggest dang fool on this earth, that's what you are."

Queen was equally angry. "Abner the only one who love me," she cried. "No one going to take that away from me."

"It's high time you worked out who your friends are, missy," Dora snapped, her frustration with Queen flooding out. "Massa Cherry's a good man, who's been kind enough to give you a job and a home. Well, home is where you are loved, and there's folk here would love you, if'n you gave them a chance. So it's high time you let go the pain that's eatin' you. It's time you let someone love you."

She brought the gig to a halt outside the butcher's shop and the boy came running out to hold the horse's head.

"You wait here," Dora said to Queen. "Y'ain't good company today." She heaved her vast self out of the gig, and turned back to Queen for a parting shot.

"Y'ain't good company too many days," she said, and went inside.

Queen sat in the gig and pulled Abner closer to her. If everyone was going to be angry with her all the time, it might be better to leave the job now, of her own volition. But she didn't want to do that. If she had to go, she'd rather be sacked, for that would feed her resentment and her pain. But, oh, she wanted to be rid of the pain.

858

She glanced at the boy holding the horse's head. He was very light-skinned, and could have passed for white, but Queen guessed that he was not. Two middle-aged women passing by didn't have such good eyesight.

"I'll never get used to it," one said to the other. "White boys holding horses, and white girls working as mammies to pickaninnies."

It was said loudly enough for Queen and the boy to hear, and it was meant to hurt. But it had the opposite effect. The butcher's boy glanced at Queen and smiled, for he knew her blood was similar to his own. She smiled back at him, as if they both shared a great secret. Then both of them started to giggle, and to laugh.

Dora, waiting for the butcher to select his choicest cuts, glanced out of the shop window and saw the happy Queen.

"Lord a' mercy," Dora said to no one. "She almost pretty when she laugh."

She told Alec about that laughter when he called in for his usual Saturday visit. He was tired. Keeping house without Little Bit was only marginally more difficult than keeping house with Little Bit, but he needed someone, and couldn't find anyone to take her place.

"You need a wife," Dora said. "Yo' chillun needs a mammy."

She'd said it before, a thousand times, and would go on saying it until he did something about it.

"The silly thing is," she added, as if the idea had only just occurred to her, "I know a l'il boy that needs a pappy. An' a woman that needs a man."

Alec stared at her. She couldn't mean Queen, that mean-tempered, moody, no-account critter who wouldn't give him the time of day. But he knew she did, and for all Queen's faults, the idea was not completely alien to him.

859

"I ain't in the market, I tol' you," he said, apparently dismissing the subject, but actually wondering what Queen looked like when she smiled.

He didn't convince Dora. "Uh-huh," she groaned. "You tol' me a thousand times, an' I still don't believe you."

Alec lost his temper. "She don't even give me the time of day!"

"P'raps you ain't asked her right." Dora was very smug. She'd only thought of the possibility of a union between Alec and Queen as a bolt from the blue, but having had the idea it made absolute sense to her. "Lovey-dovey stuff ain't gwine get to her. She needs someone as mean-tempered as she is."

She looked at her friend with enormous affection. She thought of him as a gentle grizzly bear.

"An' Lord knows, you can be the meanest-tempered man in this county."

Alec snorted in derision, and then smiled, because he knew he could be irascible. Even if he dismissed the idea of Queen as a potential wife, she might make an excellent housekeeper, especially if a small part of the love she directed so completely at Abner could be at least partly shared with a few other children. His children. He had no idea how this could be achieved.

Abner solved the problem for him. It was a warm day, and Queen had put him in the garden, on the rug. She thought him safe, for even if he could toddle to the garden gate, he couldn't unlatch it, so she went back in the house to finish some chores. She did not intend to be gone for very long, but she was gone for long enough.

Alec walked through the garden on his way home, and Abner saw the nice man that he liked, and toddled after him. Alec opened the gate and told Abner to go home to his mammy, but Abner wouldn't be told. He took Alec's hand and walked with him through the gate. Alec looked at the house, in two minds what to do. He knew that Abner's absence would make Queen even angrier than usual, but there would be nothing unusual in temper. He believed that the boy needed to get away from his mother's apron strings, and Abner seemed to be of the same opinion. And if Abner was absent for a while, and then was found, it might persuade Queen that other people could be trusted to look after him. On balance, and with a lot of rationalization, he decided that no harm could come from it, and perhaps a little good. He would send Minnie to tell Queen, or Dora, where the boy was. Still, he left the decision to Abner. He began walking slowly down the track, and Abner stayed with him, chattering to himself in a language that only he could understand.

But a mile is a long way for a toddling boy, especially when there are so many interesting things to see, and a nice man to talk to. He inspected every tree and looked at every flower, and after a little while he got tired, so Alec picked him up and carried him the rest of the way home.

Queen came out of the house and saw that Abner wasn't on his rug. Immediately, her heart beat a little faster, and she went searching for him through the garden, calling out his name. When she couldn't find him, she went back to the house and burst into the kitchen, calling for Abner. Dora had not seen the boy, and was concerned on his, and Queen's behalf.

"Cain't be too far away," she said, and went out with Queen into the garden to continue the search. Queen ran through the property crying out his name, and begging him not to play games with his mammy. When she saw that the back gate was unlatched, her heart almost stopped, for the path beyond the gate led to the river. She saw the gardener coming up the path, and called out to him, but he scratched his head; he hadn't seen the boy. Queen was sure that something untoward had happened to Abner. If he'd wandered down to the river, he might have fallen in, and he was only little, he couldn't swim.

"Oh, sweet Lord, no," she begged, and ran down the path to the river. There was no sign of Abner anywhere. She saw George helping passengers onto the ferry, and called out to him and them.

"My little boy's lost!" she cried. "Has anybody seen him?"

George and the passengers shook their heads, and fell into a discussion about what might have happened to the child, and everyone looked at the river. Queen was becoming frantic; she ran up and down the shore calling his name, and passengers tried to help her and calm her. They promised to organize a search.

Then Minnie appeared at the top of the hill, and George asked her if she had seen Abner.

"I see'd him," Minnie confirmed, and Queen ran to her, grabbed at her, and begged where.

"At my pappy's place," Minnie said, surprised at the commotion. Abner had come home with her pappy, and was perfectly all right. She'd been sent to tell Queen and Dora where the boy was.

With the news that Abner was safe, Queen's emotion changed. She became immediately suspicious.

"What's he doin' there?" she asked, but Minnie was slightly frightened by the fuss, and shook her head.

"Don't rightly know, m'm," she said. "But he there, safe as can be."

Abner was indeed safe and happy and having the best time. He was sitting on the nice man's knee, on a chair that rocked backward and forward, and the nice man was telling him a story. Abner didn't understand what the story was all about; he didn't know what a tortoise was, nor a hare, but it was fun. Alec had given him lemonade, and played with him, and then settled to tell him fables. He was at the end of the one about the tortoise and the hare when he heard a furious yelling of Abner's name in the distance, and Queen appeared, running down the track.

Queen hardly paused when she saw Abner, but ran to him, and grabbed him from Alec's lap.

"Jus' tellin' him stories," Alec said calmly.

But Queen didn't want him to tell Abner stories; she wanted him to keep away from her boy, and demanded to know how he had got here. He couldn't have toddled all this way on his own.

"He's here, ain't he?" Alec said, filling his pipe with tobacco. His resolute calm in the face of what had been, to Queen, a considerable crisis, infuriated her. She lost her temper, said she was sick of the whole world knowing what was better for her child than she did; she was sick of this place, and as soon as she had enough money saved, she would be on her way. With Abner. With that, feeling she'd had the satisfactory final word, she stomped away.

"How much do you need?" Alec asked quietly, and that made her madder still. She rounded on him, because she'd told him before that she didn't want charity, and if he was still worried about the nickel she owed him for the ferry ride, he'd get it back with interest. This riled Alec, but he did not forget his purpose.

"We'll all be right glad to see the back o' yo' bad temper," he snapped. "An' if'n it'll get you on your way a little quicker, I need someone to work for me."

Queen laughed in derision. She wouldn't work for him if he was the last man on earth, but what did it involve? Alec shrugged that he needed a part-time house-keeper for his children.

"Tho' why I'd wish yo' mean ol' ways on them, I surely don't know."

Queen had stopped walking away, but she wasn't sure why. She didn't want to stay in Savannah, but she didn't want to leave. She was suspicious of Alec, but she didn't know why. She was sure there was more to Abner's disappearance than he was telling her, but he had been kind to her, and found her the job with Massa Cherry. She had no intention of working for him, because she didn't need a job, she had one. But she still cherished the fantasy that as soon as she was back on her financial feet she could move on, and a few hours part-time work would speed that day. And she wasn't sure how long she would keep her job with Massa Cherry, for she knew she was on trial with him. She was doing her best to be pleasant to him, but she wasn't sure how long she could keep that up.

"How much?" she asked cautiously. They negotiated in anger, and settled on a figure that was sufficient but not large, and agreed on a starting time, which was now. Queen had a few conditions of her own.

"But I don't want to talk to you, 'cept when I have to," she insisted. "An' you keep away from my boy."

"Suits me fine," Alec agreed.

Queen looked at him for a moment, deciding if he could be trusted, and reached a positive conclusion. She went into the house, and had things summed up in a trice. She put little Julie in charge of Abner, and when Minnie came home, somewhat nervously, Queen put her in charge of Julie and Abner.

Alec sat rocking on the porch, puffing on his pipe, wondering what he had got himself into.

87

Within days, Alec's children adored her. She was careful and cautious with them, but firm and kind. It was an enormous relief to Minnie and Julie to have a woman to talk to, and they almost swamped her with an accumulation of love, and adored Abner, and played mother to him. George accepted her happily and willingly, for she represented a longed-for maternal figure in his life, and only Freeland resisted her presence, but not for long.

Dora was pleased by the new arrangement, and gave it her blessing, provided it did not interfere with Queen's duties at the mansion. Queen assured her it would not; she would work evenings and Saturday afternoons for Alec, and work doubly hard to make sure her duties at the mansion were attended to. Mr. Cherry was a mildly dissenting voice, worried that Queen would not be able to do the two jobs, and that she would not have any time to herself, but the almost immediate change in Queen's attitude persuaded him not to interfere.

"Good Lord," he said to Dora. "She's almost pretty when she smiles." Dora nodded smugly.

Her relationship with Alec took longer to improve. She kept her word, and spoke to him only when she had to, and he kept his part of the bargain, except at night, when she left the shack to go home, and he always spoke to her first.

He sat on the porch every night, puffing on his pipe and rocking in his chair. Queen came out of the house, and he thought she looked tired.

"Take the weight off yo' feet," he said, indicating the other rocking chair. Tennie's chair.

Queen was very tired and very tempted, but she wasn't ready to relax with him, and refused.

"Jus' askin' you to sit!" he grumbled. He wasn't going to bite her; he was just asking her to sit for a while. Or was she too scared of him to do that?

The truth of it hurt Queen, and she began to lose her temper for the first time since she had started working for him, so she sat on the very edge of the rocker.

"Happy?" she said angrily.

"At least you sittin'," he said.

There was silence.

"What you want to talk about?" Queen demanded.

865

"Nuttin'," Alec said gruffly.

They sat in silence and talked of nothing, and Queen relaxed, and leaned back in the chair. They rocked together in silence, and it was pleasant to both of them. Then Queen got scared because it was too pleasant. She got up to leave.

"How's the savings goin'?" Alec asked her.

"Getting there," Queen replied steadily. "I'm getting there."

The hours were long and the work was hard, but it was rewarding in ways that had nothing to do with money. Queen's heart went out to the motherless children, and she identified with them, for she remembered her own desolation and loneliness after Easter died. She understood why Freeland resisted her, and she did nothing special to try to win his love, but treated him with scrupulous fairness, as she treated the others. It was not that Freeland didn't like her, but he was shy of this new authority figure in his life, who was not his real mammy. He longed for love from her, but did not know if she could give him what he needed, because he perceived her as hired help, not as family, and was frightened of opening his heart to her. She might leave, as his real mammy had done. He played challenging games of discipline with her, to try her, and to his surprise she always passed his tests. The longer she stayed, the more he trusted her, and the more he tried to work her into the fabric of his heart, but he was still confused. He didn't understand why he had to have a bath in front of her, for example.

It was bath night, Friday night, and Queen was soaping Abner in the big old bathtub. Minnie and Julie were done, and tucked up in bed. George was fixing a broken chair—his bathtime was later—and Freeland was slowly removing his clothes.

"Why cain't I have a bath on my own, like George?" he asked, reluctant to take off his pants.

"Coz George is older," Queen told him. "He's a man."

"I's nearly a man too," Freeland insisted, and Queen understood his problem.

"I guess you nearly are," she said sympathetically, although Freeland was still some way from puberty. "All right. I'll turn my back."

She turned away from him, and the grateful Freeland dropped his pants and slipped into the soapy water. Queen turned back and lifted Abner out to dry him. Freeland still felt the need to confirm his manhood to Queen.

"Couple of years, I'll be old enough to work on the farm," he said. "Then no mo' school. I hates school."

George, working on the chair, chuckled, and Queen was surprised.

"I sorry to hear that, Freeland," she said. "Why you hate it?"

"Jus' coz," he shrugged.

"Jus' coz he ain't too good at it," George murmured, the devil in him, and Freeland flicked some soapy water at him.

"Am too," he muttered.

Queen, drying Abner on her lap, chatted to him about school. She suggested he play a game with school, and Freeland was intrigued. He liked games.

"'Stead of going to school thinking you're going to hate it," Queen suggested, hoping she didn't sound as if she were preaching, "why not go wondering if there's anything interesting you can learn? Will you do that for me?"

Freeland shrugged. It wasn't the most exciting game, but he'd give it a try, even if only a halfhearted one.

"Good boy," Queen said. "And in return, I'll let you bathe yourself, and stay up later each night, like George." Freeland thought that was a pretty good bargain.

She tucked him into bed, in the shed, kissed him

good night, and came back into the main room of the shack. George had finished the chair and was testing it.

"Freeland ain't never gwine like school." He smiled at Queen. She sat with him, and found out the way of it. Boys went to school because they had to, up to fifth grade, or sixth grade at most, and then they left and worked the land, sharecropping for their fathers, or entered a trade.

"What if he's good at school?" Queen wondered. "What if he likes it? What if he ain't good at farming?"

"Don't happen," George shrugged. "Be a terrible waste of a good pair of hands."

Queen's primary concern was for Abner. She had no idea what he would be when he grew up, but she was determined he was going to have a good education. She remembered Cap'n Jack, and how he had taught her, and she regretted she had not had the opportunity to learn more.

She said good night to George, picked up Abner from the cot, and went outside, to go home.

Alec was sitting on the porch as he always did at night, puffing on his pipe and staring at the stars. Queen came out to him and sat in Tennie's chair, as she always did. They rocked in unison, and talked of the children, and of the farm. It was going to be a good season.

"You work hard for it," Queen said.

Alec nodded. "I do," he agreed. He looked at Queen. "So do you."

She nodded her agreement.

They talked of Massa Cherry, and Dora, and the mansion and the town, and then Queen got up to leave.

"Best be on my way," she said.

"How's the savings going?" Alec asked her.

"Getting there," Queen said steadily. "I'm getting there."

*

Christmas came and it was the most wonderful festival she had ever experienced. For the first time in her life she had a family who loved her to share her Christmas with. She gave presents to everyone, and they gave gifts to her, and she cried a little at the mutual generosity. Minnie and Julie helped her cook a special Christmas dinner, a fine big turkey with all the trimmings, and everyone helped wash up. Abner fell asleep on Alec's bed, and Queen didn't see the point of waking him up to go home, so she tucked him in with Minnie and Julie. She went outside and sat with Alec.

"Where's Abner?" he asked her in surprise, and she told him that there didn't seem to be any point in waking the boy, that Minnie and Julie would look after him until tomorrow. Alec nodded in satisfaction, for he knew this was a major step for Queen.

"How's the savings going?" he asked her, to make her feel secure. Queen looked at the stars, and nodded her head slowly, but she did not speak.

It was odd to go home without Abner, but she knew he was in good hands, at home. She laughed, and thought that she had two homes, a little room in the mansion where she slept, and a wooden shack down the road where she lived, and was loved. She began to think that one day she might have to make a decision as to which was her real home, but thought perhaps she already knew. The immensity of that decision and its ramifications frightened her, and suddenly she wanted to run back to the shack, snatch Abner away, and bring him home to his mammy, but she didn't. She consoled herself with the thought that it was all out of her hands. She was happy with her life as it was, and unless Alec did something to disturb that, she didn't have to make a decision of any kind. If anything were to change, she still had her escape. The lifeline that he threw her every night by asking about her savings, which indicated that he accepted she would one day leave, was her salvation. Even if she knew it was a pretense.

She glanced at the little fire in the grate, and the flames were steady and calm, and did not leap into her mind. She knew that the fire demons inside her were not dead, only sleeping, but that, in itself, was a considerable advance.

The cold days of winter gave way to spring, and now Queen was such a permanent fixture in Alec's shack, her working positions were reversed. She worked full time for Alec, and part time for Massa Cherry. To an extent she maintained her job with Massa Cherry so she could keep her room in the mansion, for that, like Alec's constant questioning about her savings, was an escape from something she was not yet ready to commit to.

She loved to take the children shopping on Saturdays, for then they seemed like a real family. Alec changed the work schedule so that Freeland could have the day off, with George, while he ran the ferry. They'd buy the weekly provisions, and talk with all their friends in town, and Queen would take them all out to tea, or find them a treat. Candy apples were their favorite, and although Queen could make them better, buying them from the store was a favorite, tiny extravagance. On the Fourth of July she took them all to the fair, and Alec gave her a special allowance, so they could go on all the rides. They had a splendid day, although Abner was sick from eating too much, and in the late afternoon they headed for home, to eat with their father and then come back to see the fireworks.

Scores of carriages and carts were lined up outside the fairgrounds, with people coming and going, and suddenly there was a cry for help.

Someone had let off some premature firecrackers, and a frightened horse had broken loose and was dragging its young white rider with it, the boy's foot caught in the stirrup.

People were screaming and running out of the way. Without a moment's hesitation, George ran at the horse, grabbed its reins and hung on, trying to drag the terrified animal to calm. The horse, bucking and rearing, smashed George against a fence, but he held on.

Others came running to help, subdued the horse and rescued the boy, who was scared and bruised, but otherwise unharmed. Queen's only thought was for George. Followed by her children, for she thought of them all as her own, she ran to him. He was lying on the ground, grimacing in pain, his leg broken.

The white boy's hysterical mother had found her son, and was clutching him to her. He, shaken by his adventure but rather proud of it, insisted he was all right.

"That nigger saved me," he said. His mother came rushing to Queen, and thanked her profusely, asking after George's welfare.

"I think his leg's broke," Queen said. The mother, more interested in her son's welfare than George's, drifted away, calling for help for the poor nigger. Other, kinder, black men volunteered their help and their advice. Someone had a cart, and carefully they laid George into it, to take him and his family home.

At the shack, they carried George inside, while Queen organized the children. She sent Freeland to tell his father, and told Minnie and Julie to take Abner to Dora, at the mansion.

But Freeland did not go. He was staring at the shack, and tears were rolling down his cheeks. Queen put her arm around him.

"He gwine be all right, Queen?" Freeland stammered through his tears, for George was his hero. Like any good mother, Queen folded him into her embrace, and dried his tears, and told him to go fetch his pa. She would look after George, and he would be all right. She promised.

George was lying on Alec's cot, sweating and

moaning gently. One of the black men who had brought him in offered to go for his brother, who could set bones. Queen shook her head. She could do it. She sent the men to find pieces of wood and cloth, and sat with George.

She stroked his forehead, and he smiled that it was bad, and apologized to her, but held on to her hand.

"No need to be sorry," Queen assured him gently. "That's what I'm here for."

She smiled, and kissed him tenderly.

"That's what mammys are for."

George knew it was a lie, for she was not his mammy, but it was sweet to him. The men had found suitable pieces of wood and cloth, and Queen told George that it would hurt, but she had nothing to give him, there was no liquor in the house.

George nodded, and the men held him down while Queen felt his fractured leg. She found the break, and caressed it for a while, crooning softly to George, who gritted his teeth. Suddenly, and with a strength and sureness that surprised the men who were watching, she set the bone.

Alec came home with Freeland and it was all done. George was asleep, his leg in makeshift splints. Dora came by to see if she could help, and took Freeland back to the mansion to eat with the others, as a special treat. Queen made a scratch meal for the men who had helped her, which they ate gratefully, and after some small conversation, they drifted off to their homes.

Queen sat rocking on the porch with Alec. The sun had gone down; the night was clear and the moon full. They rocked in silent unison for a while, with Alec puffing on his pipe, and it felt good to both of them. Although she understood much of the complexity and depth of her relationship with Alec and his family, she had never thought of him as a husband or bed partner. She had come to love him, but not in the way that she had loved

Davis. It was a different sort of love, with mutuality as its basis, mutual trust, mutual loneliness, and mutual need. She admired him and respected him, and believed he felt the same about her. She knew that Alec would protect and cherish her, defend her and provide for her, and she would respond in kind. If passion was missing from the equation, perhaps that was no bad thing, for in its place was something of infinitely greater value to her.

She regarded her new family as one of misfits: the orphan George, who had become like a son to her, the motherless children of Alec, the widowed father, and she, the dispossessed black who looked white, and mother to a boy whose father was dead. The mutuality of need extended beyond herself and Alec; it embraced all of them. The puzzle now was the next step. Would it be more than it was, or was that enough? Was this as much as God gave? It was almost as if Alec was not prepared to test that limit, and Queen was not anxious that he should, lest she lose what she had.

"You got another pipe?" Queen asked him eventually.

Alec was only mildly surprised, and reached for a corncob pipe from the window ledge behind him. He gave it to Queen, and she sucked on it. He offered her his tobacco, but she shook her head. It was fine as it was.

They rocked some more in silence, and Alec was moved by what had happened that day, and deeply grateful that this woman had come into his life.

"Ain't nobody sat in that chair since Tennie died," he said. "It was her chair. They all know it, an' they don't sit in it."

Queen nodded, knowing that she did not have to move.

"Didn't think I'd ever find anyone to take her place," Alec said. "Didn't think anyone would sit in that ol' chair again."

Queen nodded again. It was a good chair, a comfortable chair. It was home.

"How's the saving goin'?" Alec asked her softly, and Queen shook her head.

"Not so good," she said. "Not real good at all."

It wasn't true. She was saving well, but even if she saved all the fortune that her grandfather had once made, she would never have enough money to leave here.

Alec stretched out his hand to her. She reached to him and put her hand in his, and he grasped it hard.

"That's all right, then," he whispered, and his voice was gruff with affection.

They were married in the local church, and it seemed to them that all of Savannah came to their wedding. Minnie and Julie were bridesmaids, George was best man, and Dora looked after Freeland and Abner.

Queen looked wonderful in white, and Mr. Cherry gave her away, because she had no pappy to do this for her.

When the service was done, Alec kissed her, and then Dora and George brought a broom, and placed it in front of them. Alec and Queen joined hands and jumped over the broom into the land of matrimony, as thousands of their forebears, slaves, had done.

They were free, and were proud of their freedom, and cherished it, but not ashamed of their days of slavery, for it was not of their choosing and they had survived. Free, they jumped over the broom in remembrance of all those who had not survived, and in remembrance of the small traditions that had helped so many endure the long years of their bondage.

Free, they jumped over the broom, and were married, and turned back to the cheers of the applauding congregation. And when Queen smiled at Alec, it was with a smile that might break your heart.

874

88

Her father was dead, killed in an accident to his carriage caused by a runaway wagon.

Mr. Cherry himself told her the news, in the quiet of his study. He had read it in the newspaper.

Queen was surprised that she was not more distressed. She nodded her head, thanked Mr. Cherry, left the house, and walked down by the river, trying to remember Jass, who had once been the most important person in her life. She had thought about him occasionally in the years of her marriage to Alec, but only occasionally, and then as some fond memory of some other life that did not matter to her now. Her new family occupied the totality of her heart, and Alec had become husband, father, and lover all rolled into one. She had given him two children, Annie and Conway, fine healthy babies who were growing into fine small people whom she loved as much as any of the others, certainly not less than Abner and perhaps only a little more than those who were not of her own body. Abner was still her darling, for he was her firstborn son, and had shared a suffering with her that the others had not known, but how do you divide and quantify love?

She felt some need to come to terms with at least some of her past. There was an epidemic of yellow fever, the black wind as it was called, in Alabama and some of the other Southern states, but against Alec's strong advice, and she seldom went against him, she decided to go to Jass's funeral, and to take Abner with her. It was proper that he be present at the burial of his grandfather.

They took a coach to Florence, riding on the outside because they were nigra, and Abner thrilled to the journey, for he had no memory of anything outside Savannah. They booked into a cheap lodginghouse, and the following day Queen dressed in black, and hired a cart and driver to take her to The Forks.

As they rumbled down the old familiar road that was not familiar to her anymore, Queen looked desperately for things she might recognize, but found nothing, not even a few distant memories. She tried to recall where Andy had picked her up in the butcher's cart, but could not. Every bend in the road looked the same as any other. The driver of the cart, Jonson, an old black man who had been a slave, talked of The Forks of Cypress and how famous it once had been, and how sad it was that Massa Jackson was dead. She learned that Jass had never regained anything of his former fortune, but had enjoyed a settled life as state senator. She learned that he was no great friend to black people, and had voted, in the state legislature, against several measures that might have improved their lot. Of the surviving family she learned very little, other than that Miss Lizzie had died some years ago, perhaps about the time that Queen had arrived in Savannah.

Then suddenly they broke through the trees, and the mansion stood before them on the little hill. Queen gasped at the flood of memories that surged through her, but she felt no pain, and began telling Abner of the days of her youth. This was why she had come, for it was important that he know something of his past. Abner, who was ten, listened attentively to his mammy, but found it difficult to imagine why this house, splendid as it was, so occupied his mother's mind.

She did not want to be too early for the funeral, so she told Jonson to drive on past the house, farther down the road. When they came to the old Henderson store, it was locked and abandoned, the windows boarded up. Jonson did not know what had happened to the people who had owned it.

They rode back to The Forks and Jonson let them off

at the main gate, and said he would come back for them that afternoon. Queen took Abner's hand and walked with him up the drive. The racecourse was long gone, overgrown with weeds, and only a few fences left to suggest what it had once been. Queen could hardly remember what it looked like.

"And over here," she said, pointing to the other side of the drive, "were cotton fields, as far as the eye could see."

Abner tried to imagine cotton fields to the horizon, but all he saw was untended grass on a few acres, and edged by encroaching trees. They approached the mansion. The lawn was pretty and well kept, and the magnolia tree was enormous now, and filled with huge, creamy blossoms. But the house was not quite as large as she remembered, not quite as magnificent, and the twenty-one lovely columns were sorely in need of a coat of paint.

They didn't go inside, for they had not been invited, but made their way to the back of the house, and down the track through the empty, derelict slave quarters, most of which had been pulled down. Through the trees Queen could see that the weaving house was still there, but she avoided it.

She was filled with a sense of nature reclaiming its own, for the path to the graveyard was overgrown, and the trees lining it were crowding in, as if they were walking through a forest.

"Man that is born of woman hath but a short time to live, and is full of misery. He cometh up, and is cut down like a flower. He fleeth as it were a shadow, and never continueth in one stay."

The preacher stood at the grave, surrounded by many mourners, for Jass had been an important man. All were white. Queen stayed back, at the edge of the graveyard, holding Abner's hand. She looked for faces she might recognize, but saw none, except a frail old lady with white hair, wearing thick pebble glasses, who was supported by a younger man she did not know. William, perhaps? James?

"In the midst of life, we are in death. Of whom shall we seek succor but of Thee, O Lord, who for our sins art justly displeased."

Queen became aware that someone had noticed her, and smiled to herself, for the color of Abner's skin was the confusion. All the mourners were white, as she looked to be, but the darker Abner told the truth.

"Yet, O Lord God most holy, O lord most mighty, O holy and most merciful savior, deliver us not into the bitter pains of eternal death."

One of the mourners whispered to another, and pointed to Queen. The man who had been spoken to detached himself from the group, and walked quietly to Queen. He asked who she was, and what she was doing there. Queen sensed his antagonism, and told him that she had been a slave at The Forks, and had come to pay her last respects to her old Massa. The man told her she could stay as long as she behaved her nigger self, but she was to keep away from the family. He walked back to the funeral, and Queen bowed her head and prayed.

"We therefore commit his body to the ground, earth to earth, ashes to ashes, dust to dust, looking for the general Resurrection in the last day, and the life of the world to come, through our Lord Jesus Christ, at whose second coming, in glorious majesty to judge the world, the earth and the sea shall give up their dead."

Queen moved back into the trees and stood with Abner watching as the family made their way from the graveyard. Sally, supported by the young man she didn't know, walked by, and for just a moment Queen wanted to run to her and hold her and comfort her. But she didn't think Sally would know who she was.

When they were gone, she took Abner to the grave, and said a small prayer for her father. She led her son up the hill to the slave cemetery, and looked for her mother's grave, but could not find it. There were some few mounds in the earth, but no markers, and nothing to indicate that the dead lay here. It didn't matter, Queen thought. Easter was somewhere happier.

They wandered back to the slave quarters, and sat on the grass under an old oak tree. Queen had some sandwiches in her bag, and they made a picnic lunch.

"This is where the slaves used to live," she told Abner. She could feel the ghosts of them now, and marveled at the fortitude with which they had endured their bondage for so many years, with so little hope.

"Was you a slave?" Abner asked her, and Queen nodded, and pointed to the weaving house.

"I was born over yonder." She could not avoid it; she had to go there.

It was abandoned, almost derelict. Dust and cobwebs had claimed it for their own. Abner explored the nooks and crannies, while Queen stood in the middle of the room and wondered why this house had ever seemed so important to her.

Then Abner brought her some treasure. A few old cards, handmade and painted, of the alphabet. The dam that had been blocking her memory broke, and she remembered how Cap'n Jack taught her the ABCs from these cards, and Easter's disapproval, and she put them in her purse, and kept them for the rest of her days. She remembered the awfulness of her mother's death, and she remembered hearing Jass tell Easter that she, Queen, was to live in the big house.

She went outside, to free herself of the nightmare that was sneaking into her mind, for the big house reminded her of things she would rather forget, of Lizzie, and of the Henderson store, and of being chased through the woods, and flames, and a burning barn, and more flames, and the body of Abner's father, and she wept a little for what had been.

She held him close to her, and the sun and the daylight eased the grief.

"We gwine go to the big house, Mammy?" Abner asked, for he was anxious to see inside it.

Queen shook her head. There was nothing for her here anymore. Whatever relationship she had with this place was over, buried with Jass.

"No, chile, we're going home," she told Abner.

For home is where you are loved.

89

Simon came to her late in life. Another little girl was born to them, Emma, after Annie and Conway, but Emma died when she was three. She had been playing on the kitchen floor, and drank some lye, while Queen was hanging washing on the line. She died in great pain, and Queen blamed herself for what had happened, and for a while they worried for her mental state, but then she became pregnant again.

She had thought her childbearing days were over, and she believed Simon to be a gift from God, to take Abner's place, for recently he had demanded his right to his own life, and had left home. Abner had grown into a handsome, strapping young man, with a young man's energy. He worked hard and well on the farm, but he pined for a wider world, for adventure, and he heard the siren song of the big city.

He tried to explain it to his mother. "I'm twenty-one, an' all I ever seen of the world is Savannah. I wants to know what the rest is like."

But his mother would not listen. He was still her baby. She had to protect him from the cruel world.

"What you going to do, end up in a gutter like half the other nigger boys up North?"

He grumbled because he didn't want to go far, only to Memphis, and only for a year or two, to see what it was like, and he wouldn't end up in a gutter, he'd get a job.

"Ain't much call for sharecroppers in Memphis," Queen snapped.

"I's going, Ma," he insisted. "No matter what you say."

She tried to get Alec to talk some sense into him, but he listened to what Abner had to say, and nodded as if in agreement.

"All my life, I's done what other people tol' me," he explained. "You an' Ma, and ev'ryone. Nobody ever done ask me if I wanted to be a farmhand, I jus' did it, coz I was tol'."

Alec accepted that, and it made Queen increasingly nervous.

"All right. I'll ask you now," Alec said. "What do you want to do?"

Abner didn't know, but he wanted to be more than what he was, doing the same thing day in, day out, coming home every night with cotton tufts in his hair, going to the same places, seeing the same people.

"I don't want to end up with my guts busted from throwin' cotton bales, and never knowin' what else was out there."

He looked at his mother, who was fiddling with her dress.

"It don't mean I don't love you, Ma," he said softly.

Alec didn't want him to go to nothing, and it was agreed he could visit Memphis on weekends and look for employment. If he found a job, he could take it, with Alec's blessing.

"No!" Queen shouted. They looked at her in surprise. She was snatching cookies from the table, and stuffing them into her pocket.

"You don't listen to him on this," she told Abner. "He ain't your real pa. You listen to me!"

She stopped in horror, appalled by what she had

said. She pleaded with Alec to forgive her, but he was bitterly hurt. He got up and left the shack. He sat in his old rocking chair, puffing on his pipe, furious with Queen, for he had never done less than his best by Abner. To his surprise, Abner came and sat with him, on the step. He wasn't quite sure what to say. Nor was Abner.

"She didn't mean it, Pa," Abner said eventually. "She's upset, coz of me."

"I know it," Alec agreed.

"I won't go if'n it's gwine cause trouble," Abner said, and he meant it, Alec knew, but it cost him dear.

"You go, if'n you want," Alec said. "If'n you c'n find a job. You cain't live yo' life tied to yo' mammy's apron strings. She gotta let go, one day."

In the kitchen, Queen tried to do the dishes, but she was bitterly disappointed in herself for what she had so unfairly said to Alec, and she was terrified for Abner, who had so nearly been taken from her by fire when he was little. Those fire demons crept up on her, and burned themselves into her mind. She went out into the night, to be free of them, but no matter where she went, she could not find peace.

They found her two hours later down by the river, wandering up and down the bank, clutching at her skirts, and crying out.

"They're after me," she cried, for all she could see was flame. They took her home and Alec fetched the doctor, who recommended care and rest, and constant attention. He walked outside with Alec, and suggested that if she was not better in a few days, he might want to consider having her put in an institution for a while, for examination.

Alec was appalled. "She ain't mad!" he insisted. "She jus' a l'il bothered about her boy."

He paid the doctor and went back into the shack. He sat with Queen, holding her hand, and stroking her

882

forehead. He slept beside her at night, and stayed with her in the day. He fed her and washed her and changed her, and slowly the fire eased in her mind. Abner did not mention leaving while she was ill, but he went to Memphis on his weekends, and eventually found a job that suited him, in the cattle yards. He did not know how he was going to tell his mother.

To everyone's surprise, Queen accepted Abner's news well. Her brush with her demons had frightened her, and by now she knew she was pregnant with Simon. She took it as a sign that she should let Abner go, and in any case was persuaded that his going was inevitable. She kissed him sweetly, and wished him Godspeed.

"Wherever you go, whatever you do," she told him on his last night with her, "if you don't find what you're looking for, or if you got troubles, or if you lonely and cain't manage no more, remember no matter how far you've traveled, it ain't such a long road home."

He kissed her, and told her he would not forget, but she was not happy.

Yet as she had hoped, her last-born son healed the rent in her heart caused by her first. Simon was a blithe and serious child, light-skinned, and with a gentle, caring manner. He was also a quick study, and by the time he was four he knew his ABCs. Queen taught him, using Cap'n Jack's old cards and others she made herself in place of those that were missing. When he was five, she delivered him to school and felt a pang of loss, but it was not as sharp as that caused by Abner. Simon did well at school, and was his teacher's delight. By the time he was in sixth grade, the teacher had developed an ambition for Simon that she knew was unrealistic, but she could not bear to see his mind go to waste. She went to see Queen, and said she wanted Simon to stay on at school, until eighth grade, at least. Queen was all in favor of it, but had learned something from her experience with Abner. She spoke to Simon, to find out what he really wanted to do, before tackling the man who had the final decision.

"No," Alec said. And to make sure Queen understood, he said it again. "No!"

"I heard you the first time," Queen said calmly, sucking on her empty pipe. They rocked their chairs in the peace of the night.

"He's leavin' school," Alec said firmly. "That's what boys do in these parts. I need him on the land."

It wasn't true. George was married and had a few acres of his own, but Freeland and Conway were all the help Alec needed, and Simon had never been much use in any practical sense, on the farm. Still, Alec couldn't imagine an alternative career for him.

"You hear me?" He was angry now.

"I hear you." Queen nodded calmly. "Cain't believe what I'm hearing, though."

Alec sighed. He knew he was in for a hard time.

"Dadgummit!" he muttered.

Queen had her arguments beautifully marshaled, and went through them point by point. She wondered what they had worked so hard for all these years. They'd built the farm up to a hundred and fifty acres, and didn't need any more. They weren't rich, but they surely weren't wondering where their next meal was coming from. It had been hard, and she and the children had worked hard, and Alec, but it had been good because she thought it had been for a purpose. Now she wondered what it had all been for.

"It's been fo' us," Alec said, "an' fo' our children. So they'd have a better day to look forward to than we did."

"That's what I thought," Queen agreed. "Obviously, I was wrong."

Alec said "Dadgummit" again, but more softly, knowing she wasn't done.

She wanted to know where the better day was for

Simon. He worked hard, as hard of any of them, was in sixth grade while most boys of his age, black or white, were in fifth, and now he had to throw it all away because his pappy was so pigheaded he saw only a life on a farm for a boy, no matter whether the boy was suited for that life or not. Did he want the same thing to happen to Simon as had happened to Abner, so frustrated with life in this narrow community he left it rather than stay?

"I thought you were more of a man than that," she said. "I thought you were somebody who could afford to waste a boy, just one, and let him follow his own star. Obviously, I was wrong. Obviously I've been working my po' fingers to the bone all these years for no reason."

She stopped talking and lapsed into aggrieved silence. Alec didn't speak for a while, but something she had said had amused him.

"Wastin' a boy?"

Queen knew she had won.

"If schooling's a waste of time, that's what it would be."

Alec was tickled pink by the idea of "wasting" a son, and surely he could afford it. He owned a hundred acres of good bottomland now, and two other small farms, of five acres each, one of which he rented to George.

"Wastin' a boy," he chuckled again.

Queen nodded, but was sly, and didn't let him see her smile.

"Ain't too many men in the district can afford to do that."

They sat in silence again, and puffed on their pipes and rocked on their chairs, and then Alec delivered his ultimatum.

"But I ain't payin' fo' all the books he'll need," he announced. "Those books cost me a fortune."

They rocked together.

"Uh-huh," said Queen.

Inside the house, Simon, who had been listening through the open window, did a little silent sock hop of joy.

He got work to pay for his books. He did odd jobs at the Cherry mansion. He was a delivery boy for the general merchant, he tended gardens, he chopped wood in the winter and sold lemonade in the summer. Queen thought that he did all this with his nose in a book at the same time, for his grades were excellent, and even Alec was impressed by Simon's industry. He took great pride in telling his friends on the ferry that he was "wasting" a son, until a few of them, thinking he must be wealthy, started asking him for small loans.

On a warm Saturday in late spring, Queen was alone in the shack, and decided it needed a thorough cleaning. Alec was running the ferry; Conway and Freeland were working the land. Simon was selling home-made lemonade, somewhere down the road. She dragged the rugs outside, threw them over the line, and as she beat them, she plotted what she would say to Alec when she had to persuade him that Simon should go on past eighth grade, for she, Simon, and his teacher were determined that he should.

She saw Simon coming up the path and was surprised.

"You sold all that lemonade already?" she asked him. He didn't reply. His expression was forlorn, and he had a bloody handkerchief to his nose.

She dragged the truth out of him, although he was reluctant, for it was his own battle. Some boys, bigger than he, poor white trash, had offered to buy his lemonade, drunk it, and then refused to pay. There was a fight, and Simon got the worst of it.

A spark of fire exploded in Queen's mind. She dragged him, unwillingly, to the poor-white part of town, and found one of the boys who had beaten up Simon. She demanded payment for the lemonade, but he jeered at her, told her she was a nigger fool, and it had nothing to do with him.

So Queen hit him, slapped his face hard. The boy yelled and called for his pa, but it was his ma who came out to deal with the crazy nigger woman who was hitting white boys. Others gathered to watch the fun, and Queen, who was becoming hysterical, stood her ground and demanded payment for the lemonade. A sheriff arrived and tried to make the peace, but Queen would have none of it. To try to shut her up, the sheriff threw some coins at her from his own pocket, but she smashed them to the ground.

"I don't want yo' charity," she cried. "I want what's rightfully mine. You think I'm some po' nigger you can beat up on and cheat and lie to?"

She hoicked up her skirts, to show her leg.

"I is white, you hear me? Whiter than most of you!" She pointed at the bystanders, who were amused by her, or angered by her. The fires raged in her head, and she danced across the border of insanity, into the country of the mad. She raved at them, a long, rambling speech of her grievances, but she kept coming back to her central point.

"I don't want yo' damn white charity. All I want is what's mine! What is due to me!"

Suddenly, she stopped, her body rigid. It was as though suddenly she had stepped outside of herself, and saw what was happening to her.

"For God's sake, give her the money," the sheriff said to the boy's mother in the silence that followed. "The woman's mad."

Simon, who had been ashamed of his mother's behavior, and concerned for her, sprang to her defense.

"She ain't mad!" he shouted at the sheriff. "She just suffered, is all. We don't want your money. We got money."

He turned to his mother and took her gently by the hand. "Come on, Ma," he said gently. "Let's go home."

He led her away, and the crowd parted for them in silence, although he heard at least one snicker about damn crazy niggers.

Queen stared at the empty fireplace. The flames in her mind were quiet again, and had been replaced by an awful fear. Alec sat with her, holding her hand, trying to bring her back from whatever awful place she had gone to.

"I'm here," he said, again and again. "Ain't nuttin' fo' you to be afraid of. I'll always be here."

She shivered. "I so scared," she whimpered.

Alec would have given everything he owned to know what it was that frightened her so, but he had to give nothing, because she told him.

"I scared of me," she whispered.

Perhaps that is why he protested only mildly when Queen told him that Simon wanted to continue his education. Or perhaps he had seen it coming. Or perhaps he was just getting old.

"Nigger boy goin' to high school," he scoffed. "I ain't never heard the like."

Simon had been accepted by Lane Institute, in Jackson, sixty miles away. Queen was so proud of him. "If that's your final words on the subject—" she began, but he was ready for her.

"That's my final word!" He didn't give her a chance to finish, but it wasn't the last of it.

They sucked their pipes.

"He cain't go," Alec roared, infuriated by the silence.

"Uh-huh," Queen said.

Simon would go. He had to go. It had become her dearest dream. They had been slaves, and now they were free, but in many ways they still thought like slaves. They had done well with their lives, but they still accepted a subsidiary place in society, and that was

888

how it would always be, unless they changed their thinking. But, oh, there was more, there had to be more. The words of Davis rang in her ears, like a clarion call. They had to start taking what they could get, not simply accepting what they thought they were allowed to have. She wouldn't do it in her life, and Alec wouldn't do it; they were old now, but the young, they could do it, if they were given the chance, and the key to that chance was education. She thought of Cap'n Jack, and his dreams. To live in freedom was not just a basic right, it was also a precious gift that should be appreciated and nurtured. It had been denied them for so long that not to take every possible advantage of it was immoral.

But she knew her man. It was not fair to push him, who was so generous, further than he could go.

"Uh-huh," she said again.

Alec wished she would argue at least, so that he could lose his temper, and then it would all be over. Perhaps. But she wouldn't even discuss it. "Uh-huh" was all she would say to any argument he put forward.

"Dadgummit," he muttered.

Simon was on tenterhooks about Alec's decision, but Queen had no good news for him. He turned his face to the wall.

"Tain't fair, Mammy," he said. "I can do it. I know I can."

He was filled with self-pity, but there was something more to his distress, for he had a young man's dreams, a young man's zeal, and a young man's belief that he could change the world, and make life better for his people. He watched his father's friends work the land, using the old ways, the ways they had learned from their fathers, and their fathers' fathers before them, resisting change, resisting new ideas. But there were new ideas, and new ways to farm, and better ways to raise crops and make the farms more productive. Black folk wouldn't do any of these things unless the white

889

folk did them first. Surely it was not enough to take only what the white folk were prepared to give? They had to start learning for themselves, finding their own ideas, their own solutions. And maybe one day, they would start teaching the white folk, in return.

"Tain't fair," he said again.

"I know, boy, I know." Queen stroked his hair. "And it ain't over yet."

It took Alec a week to change his mind. He talked about it with some of his friends on the ferryboat, and while none of them had ever heard of a nigger boy going to high school, they were all impressed that Simon had the chance.

He talked about it with his other children, with Minnie and Julie, who were married and starting families of their own, and they thought he was being an old stick-in-the-mud.

He talked about it with Freeland, who had hated school, but was right proud of Simon, and thought he'd be useless on the farm anyway—his head was always stuck in some book.

He talked about it with George, who thought it was a fantastic opportunity. George had no learning, but admired those who did.

He didn't talk about it to Mr. Cherry when they went fishing, because he wasn't sure that Mr. Cherry would be on his side, but he couldn't get the matter off his mind, and the fish weren't biting.

"Dadgummit," Alex muttered in frustration. "I must be gettin' old."

Mr. Cherry knew exactly what the matter was. Dora had seen to that.

"Yes, you are," he said. "Old and crotchety, and you've no idea what the modern world is coming to. I feel the same way."

He bided his time, because he knew it was a momentous decision for Alec.

"Black boy going to high school," Mr. Cherry said. "I never heard the like. It'll be college next."

The words struck home to Alec. He hadn't thought that far ahead, but it was obvious once it was said.

"But then again," Mr. Cherry added, "if he can do it—why not?"

Alec had no argument against that.

"Dadgummit," he said.

He called Simon to him, but would not let Queen be present. She sat outside on her rocker, and heard every word through the open window.

Alec wasn't sure where to start. He adopted what he hoped was his most commanding presence, and made a little speech about Simon being way past the age when he should be working, and he wasn't working and he should be.

"Yes, Pa," Simon said dutifully, with no idea where it was going.

"You'd pro'bly be useless on the farm anyway, with your head always stuck in a book," Alec continued, finding his stride, and Simon dared to hope.

"But we gotta do somethin' with you, so I'm sendin' you to high school whether you like it or whether you don't," Alec announced, as if it was all his idea.

Simon closed his eyes, and breathed a silent prayer of thanks.

"Yes, Pa," he said, very carefully, anxious not to offend his father, in case he changed his mind. "Thank you, Pa."

Alec grunted. It was done. For better or worse, it was done. He made a fatherly speech about Simon being young and a long way from home, and not to get into any trouble with girls.

Then he took fifty dollars from his pocket. It was the biggest sum of money Simon had ever seen.

"Only the good Lord knows what this thing is gwine

cost," Alec said, "an' I ain't made of money. I'm giving you fifty dollars, an' that's it, there ain't no more. You've got this durned scholarship thing, so I ain't spendin' one cent more than this fifty dollars. Anythin' else you need, you're gwine have to work for it."

He put the money in a little purse and gave it to his son. Simon could hardly contain his joy, and tears of gratitude sparkled in his eyes.

"I'll work hard, I promise, Pa," he swore.

Alec sent him out to tell his mother, and turned away. When he spoke to the empty room, his voice was gruff.

"Most fool thing I ever did."

Queen was puffing on her pipe, rocking in her chair, when Simon came out to her, a grin as big as Texas on his face.

"Oh, thank you, Ma!" he said.

"Nothing to do with me," she said. "I don't approve. You're too young to be so far away from home."

Simon was puzzled. He had thought she would be pleased.

"Why should I be pleased?" Queen demanded, trying to blink away the tears. "My little boy going off alone in the world, and only the good Lord knows what evils are lurking out there to snare you."

But she lost the battle, and the tears ran.

"Of course I'm pleased; you think I'm touched in the head?" She held out her arms to him, and he moved into her embrace. She clung to him for a moment, then sent him on his way to tell his friends.

"And don't be late home," she warned, wiping her eyes with her hankie. "I ain't got long with you."

"No, ma'am," he laughed, and ran off into the night. Just before he disappeared into the shadows, he leaped high in the air, and let out a great whoop of joy. Then he was gone, and there was silence.

Alec came out and sat in his rocker, beside his wife. They puffed on their pipes and looked at the stars.

And there was silence.

Alec drove them in the buggy to the little train depot at Sarsparilla, seven miles down the road. Simon was bursting with excitement and nervousness. He was very smart in his freshly pressed suit, but Queen thought he looked far too young to be setting off on such an adventure. There were several people waiting for the train, and as it chugged toward the depot, the white flagman waved it down. Simon had never seen a train before, and it thrilled him, and gave him the sense that now, truly and at last, he was on his way.

He offered to shake Alec's hand, but to his surprise, his father embraced and hugged him hard, and wished him well. Then Simon turned to his mother. She straightened his collar and tidied his hair, and said little private things of love to him, and then it was time to go. He pulled away, as choked up as she.

He climbed into the packed Jim Crow car with the other blacks, and a red-capped porter helped him aboard. He felt so grown-up, and proud, and he felt a brief rush of anger that he could not sit in the other cars, with the whites. But his transcending emotion was joy at his bright adventure, and the great days of his future that lay ahead.

Queen couldn't bear to see him sitting there with all those grown-ups, and she almost changed her mind.

"He cain't, he's too young," she cried out, but the train whistle drowned her voice, and only Alec heard her, and he put his arm around her.

The train began steaming away. Simon leaned out of the window to wave farewell to his parents, and waved so much and leaned out so far that he nearly fell out. His traveling companions pulled him back in, and laughed at his happiness, for it was infectious.

The train chugged away, and Queen watched it go until it was lost to the horizon, and only a column of smoke suggested where it had been.

They rode home in the buggy against a lowering sky, for rain was in the air. They both felt a sense of loss, for this, the last of their children, had left home, and now all they had was each other.

"You'll miss him," Alec said, knowing he would too.

"Uh-huh." Queen nodded. She reached out to her husband and took his hand, in a simple gesture that might, she hoped, let him know how very much she loved him, and appreciated him.

"Just have to make do with you, won't I?" she said.

90

He couldn't fail. It wasn't possible for him to fail. It wasn't fair of God to let him fail.

Queen's hands were shaking. She was in the kitchen trying to prepare a meal, using the simple domesticity to calm herself down, to come to terms with the news about her boy.

For Simon was failing. He had scraped through Lane Institute by the skin of his teeth. To a large extent, this was because of his financial situation. In order to pay his way, he had taken a multitude of part-time jobs. He waited tables in the student dining room and helped at a home for wayward boys. He worked in a greenhouse. In the winter he persuaded four white homeowners to pay him a dollar a week each to come into their homes at dawn and build fires for them, so that they might wake up to a warm house. He was almost permanently tired and often fell asleep as he was eating his meals. He became the butt of student jokes, although there was one girl, a pretty dark teenager, Bertha Palmer, who was kind to him. Their friendship ripened and developed, and was a blessing to Simon, for Bertha was a ray of sunlight on his otherwise clouded horizon.

He had almost no time to study. His grades in English and agriculture were good, but low in every other subject. At the end of twelfth grade, his average was just good enough for him to transfer to A & T College in Greensboro, North Carolina. There he had to reconstruct his exhausting work schedule, and his studies suffered. He survived his freshman year, but in his last sophomore semester the professor of a course for which he couldn't afford the books told him he was going to fail him. It was almost a relief to Simon, for he didn't have the energy left to fight. He had applied for a summer job with the Pullman company as a porter, and when he received a letter informing him that he had been accepted, he made his decision. He would work on the train for the summer, save enough money to buy a mule and plow, and go home to Savannah, his tail between his legs, to work the land.

Much as Queen longed to have her son home with her, her heart bled for his distress and his thwarted dreams, and for the sense of failure that, in his letter to her explaining his decision, was almost palpable.

Queen's mind ran like glycerin. There had to be some way she could help him. She was sure it was not a question of his ability, only of his circumstances, and if those circumstances could be changed, he would triumph yet. They had a little money; they could give him an allowance, but she doubted her ability to persuade Alec, or even Simon, to see the wisdom of that. Both men, father and son, were stubborn, and even if Alec gave, would Simon accept? In any case, she had to face the reality, that his professor was going to fail him. There was nothing she could do about that.

She felt old and tired, for the battle had been long, and instead of victory, she was staring at defeat. She opened the door of the stove to put more wood in, and the flames danced and sparked. She stared at the flames and they ate into her mind, burning her brain, bringing back awful memories she hoped she had forgotten.

She saw the fiery brands of men chasing her through the woods, and a burning barn, and a woman on fire screaming as she tried to escape. She saw a burning cross, and the burning body of a man she had loved. She turned abruptly away from the fire, as if to block the flames from her mind, but knocked against a pan on the stove, with hot fat in it. The fat caught fire and she grabbed the pan, to move it to the sink, but some of the flaming fat spilled on her dress, and her skirt began to burn.

Hysterically, she beat at the flames, but could not get them out.

She had escaped from it all these years, but now the fire had caught her at last.

Screaming for help, she ran from the shack and threw herself to the ground, rolling over and over in the dirt to try to douse the flames.

All the passengers on the ferry knew that Alec was in a bad mood, but could not work out why. He grunted when spoken to, complained if he had to give change for the fares, and would not tell anyone his problem. Fred, who was on the ferry, tried to get a spark out of his old sparring partner.

"How's that boy of your'n doin'?" he asked innocently, for surely Alec was proud of Simon. Everyone else in Savannah was. To his surprise, Alec gave only a minimal response.

"Fine," he muttered. "Jus' fine."

If Fred had been more aware of Simon's true circumstances, he might have dropped the subject, and let Alec simmer in his own dilemma for a while, but Fred couldn't do that, because he didn't know.

"We's all mighty proud of him," he continued, rushing in like an angel intent on healing. "Ev'ry nigger in Savannah's gwine have a party the day he graduate."

It was true. Simon represented a bright ray of hope for the future to this community of sharecropping ex-slaves, for whom life was hard. But Alec would not be cheered.

"All them niggers best not count their chickens," he grunted. He was surprised that he was so depressed by Simon's failure. Having resisted, so obstinately, the plans for Simon's higher education, he had become, faced with the fact, extraordinarily proud of his son. Now it had all come to nothing, as Alec had predicted it would, but he found no pleasure in being proved right. He was grumpy and miserable, but could not blame the boy for he had already achieved so much more than Alec had ever imagined possible. He cursed himself for not giving the boy a proper allowance, and swore that somehow he would make amends to his son, but he could not think of anything that would mend a broken dream. The knowledge that the dream was collective, and shared by so many more than those directly involved, depressed him even more.

He guided the ferry to the southern landing stage, and saw Minnie running down the hill, shouting at him.

"Pappy!" Minnie cried. "Ma's run off, and she cain't be found!"

Alec guessed immediately what had happened, and why, for there was a history of it, and he cursed himself again for not realizing that Queen would have taken the news about Simon so hard.

Minnie had come to visit Queen that afternoon, as she did two or three times a week, to bring preserves and spend a pleasant time chatting about the world, and the difficulty of raising a family, and seeking advice about those difficulties. She went into the shack without knocking, and knew that it was empty. She called out for Queen and went into the kitchen. She saw the pan lying on the floor, and the charred patches of wood where the flames had caught and died, and began to worry. She looked all through the shack and the shed, and searched the surrounding property, but there was no sign of Queen. She went to the mansion and alerted the gardeners, but they had not seen her, nor had Dora. Like Alec, Minnie guessed that there had been a crisis, and ran down to the wharf to tell her father.

Word quickly spread, and all the family gathered to join in the search for Queen. The gardeners from the mansion helped, and several of the passengers from the ferry, and other farmers and their sons, for Queen and Alec were well known and respected. They scoured the fields, and sought through the bushes on the riverbank. They looked in barns and outbuildings, and asked everyone they met, but no one had seen Queen.

At evening they lighted torches to continue the hunt, and the night air echoed with the sound of her name being called.

There was no sign of her.

Alec came home at midnight. He was weary and worried, but there was no point in looking anymore until daylight. Julie had come to keep Minnie company, and they had cooked a meal for the searchers. When Alec came in, they looked at him hopefully, but he shook his head. They sat him down and fussed over him, and told him to eat, but he could not, knowing Queen was out there somewhere, hungry and alone.

He fell to his knees and prayed that she be safe. He was not an overly devout man—he believed in God in a general way, not as an active participant in their lives—but he had no one else to turn to. When God did not answer his prayer the next day, he became bitter, and despaired for his wife. He sat in his rocking chair that night and would not go to bed. He hoped, against all common sense, that in a little while he would see her walking along the path toward him, and she would come to him, and sit in her rocking chair, and puff on her empty pipe, and never go away again. As the night wore on, he could not even bring himself to look at the

898

empty chair beside him, for it reminded him too painfully of what he had lost.

As the steel of dawn edged into the sky, he fell asleep in his chair, still waiting for her to come home.

A couple of miles away, in that same early morning light, a sharecropper and his son made their way down the lane to their few acres, and heard a scrabbling sound in the ditch that edged the fields. They thought it was an animal who had been hurt and went to find it, to put it out of its misery.

It was Queen, covered in mud, brambles stuck in her hair and her dress, cowering in a hole she had dug with her bare hands. She was muttering, and stared at the sharecropper with vacant eyes. He knew she was the ferryman's woman, and reached out his hand to her, but she backed away from him, frightened, whimpering her fear.

"Fetch yo' ma, boy," the sharecropper told his son. "This be woman's work."

The sharecropper sat near Queen to keep an eye on her, and she seemed to accept his presence, but would not move out of her hole. His wife and two daughters came, and were gentle with Queen, and coaxed her from her hiding place with woman's words, and led her home.

They brought the deranged Queen to Alec, at his shack. He stood on the porch watching her return, with Minnie and Julie, but did not go to her, because she did not seem to know him, or where she was.

"This here's yo' wife," the woman said.

Alec's heart exploded. "She low sick?"

"She touched in the head," the woman said, simply, just as it was, without comment or criticism. Alec moved to Queen and put his arm around her, but she did not seem to know him. He offered food to the woman and her daughters, but she said there was no need.

"I'm right sorry to see her this way."

Alec led Queen to the house, telling her she was safe because she was home, but she did not hear him, nor did she recognize her daughters.

91

Simon tried to make himself comfortable in the cramped porter's cubbyhole as the train rattled through the night from Buffalo to Pittsburgh. It was two in the morning, and all the passengers in his compartment were tucked into their berths. Sleeping, Simon thought enviously, which he could not do. He was tired, depressed about his future, and worried about his ma.

He had been writing a letter to Bertha, but the movement of the train jarred his hand, and his writing looked scratchy. Or so he told himself, when really he knew that he could not tell Bertha of his mother's plight, for he was worried she might not understand. Queen had been institutionalized because of her mental breakdown, and to the uncaring mind that equated with mad, and he did not want anyone to think that of his mother. He screwed up the paper and threw it in the bin. He would have to tell Bertha—she had to know—but he would do it tomorrow, when he was thinking clearly. He settled on the stool, his back against the wall and his feet on a shelf so he could rest his head on his knees, and closed his eyes to rest.

He enjoyed his job as a Pullman porter, but he found it difficult to adjust to his nighttime schedule. He spent very little of the money that he earned on himself, and what he had saved from his wages, together with his tips, had given him sufficient money to dream about college again. He wouldn't have minded his failure if he believed that he did not have the ability to do well, but he was sure his low grades were because of his several part-time jobs, and he was loath to abandon his academic ambitions entirely. He wanted at least the chance to compete on a level field, to see if he was right, and he had begun to wonder if he could go back to A & T for one last semester. The money he had saved meant that he would not have to work for that time, and he would be able to devote all his energy to his education. Then he had received a letter from his brother Conway, telling him of Queen's plight, and Simon felt his place was in Savannah, with his mother.

He woke suddenly, a few minutes later, to the insistent ringing of the bell. One of his passengers was awake and wanted something. Simon blinked the sleep from his eyes, and pulled himself to his feet. The bell rang again, and it irritated Simon.

"Yes, suh, Massa. I's a-comin', Massa," he muttered angrily at the bell, in fair imitation of slave dialect. "Hold yo' hosses."

He splashed water on his face, and hurried to answer the summons. He presented a pleasant face to the passenger, an elderly man in silk pajamas and a fine dressing gown. His wife couldn't sleep, and he wondered if warm milk was possible.

Simon was warming the milk on the stove in the serving cubicle when the passenger appeared in the doorway. The cubbyhole was small, and two was a crowd.

"Something else, sir?" Simon inquired politely, but the passenger shook his head. He was a night owl, and did most of his thinking, and most of his work before his retirement, at night. Now he was wide-awake, and wanted someone to talk to. He kept his voice low, because others were asleep.

Simon didn't know what to talk about, and busied himself with the milk.

"Good job?" the passenger asked him.

"'Tain't my dream," Simon shrugged.

901

The man smiled, and wondered what Simon's dream was. So Simon told him, and told him of his plan to go back to the farm.

The passenger raised his eyebrows. "You don't want to graduate?"

"I wish," Simon said, shrugging again, and saw no reason not to tell the truth. "My grades are terrible."

"Ahhh," said the passenger, and that made Simon mad.

"Ain't no 'ahhh' about it," he said, rather more sharply than he intended. "I could do it, I know I could, but I never got the time to study."

He explained something of his circumstances, and the passenger nodded gravely, but his only comment was that it seemed a pity to waste all his hard work.

Simon nodded politely, but seethed inwardly. What could this rich white man know of a young black boy's problems? Simon was guessing that he was rich, but his dressing gown was luxurious, and his manner courtly.

"Milk's ready, sir," he said, to be rid of the man. The passenger took the tray and went back to his wife, but returned a few minutes later as Simon was settling to doze again.

"Sorry," he said. "I forgot to introduce myself. I'm Mr. Boyce. What's your name?"

Simon gave his name, and they talked for a while of the world and its problems. The man seemed more interested in Simon's general knowledge and eventual ambition, rather than his specific educational achievements. He talked of world events, and of the possibility of war in Europe. The United States would not be involved, but Mr. Boyce wondered how Simon would feel if his country ever did go to war.

"Reckon I'd enlist," Simon said.

Mr. Boyce nodded and smiled. "Even though your country has not exactly treated your people well?"

Simon didn't want to get into an argument about race relations. It was too late and he was too tired.

"Be a sight more exciting than working on the farm," he said.

Mr. Boyce nodded again. He checked his watch, and apologized for keeping Simon from his duties. He smiled.

"Or your sleep," he said, and bade Simon good night. Simon settled into his cubbyhole and closed his eyes, but all he could think of was his mother.

On the platform at Pittsburgh the next morning, Mr. Boyce sought Simon out and introduced his wife to him. He thanked Simon for the interesting conversation of the previous night and gave him a five-dollar tip.

"Don't give up on your dreams too easily," he said. He and his wife wished Simon well, and went on the way.

Simon put the five dollars in his pocket and finished up his duties. Mr. Boyce had annoyed him a little but had spurred him as well. As he worked, he came to a decision about his future.

At the end of the summer, he went home for a week to see his family. Alec met him at the depot, and greeted Simon warmly.

"How's Ma," Simon asked.

"Not too good, boy," Alec told him. They climbed into the buggy, and as they drove Alec explained what he knew of Queen's mental state.

"Profoun' dementia, that's what they said." He wasn't sure he'd got it right. "I think that's what they said."

Alec had called a doctor to Queen after her breakdown, and he had recommended she be institutionalized. He did not think Queen was dangerous to anyone else, but believed that she could do harm to herself. Alec resisted him strongly, but when Queen's condition did not improve to any great extent, he put aside his prejudices about mental illness and committed her. He almost changed his mind when he took her to the institution; it was a nightmare place, a house of the mad, and Alec did not want to admit that Queen was mad. The doctors persuaded him that they could help Queen, and, however reluctantly, he agreed to let her stay.

She was getting better, but he hated what they were doing to her. They had some water treatment they used on her, to flush the fire demons out of her, they said, but Alec thought it was something from a manual of torture. They strapped her to a chair and poured a headlong rush of water on her, from above, from a fireman's hose, sometimes for up to half an hour. He couldn't imagine how the frail woman who was his wife could endure it.

But she did seem to be getting better.

"The thing is," he told his son, "I keep wonderin' if'n she's in there coz of me."

He blamed himself bitterly for Queen's condition, but couldn't see what more he could have done to help her. He visited her as often as he could, and tried to provoke her to health.

"I ain't mad," she said.

Alec was gentle with her, but firm. He had to be firm, for both their sakes.

"You here," he said. "Must be somethin' wrong."

She didn't want to hear that, and turned away.

"I keep wondering what I did wrong," he said. "I tried to make a good home fo' us, I tried to be a good husband to you, I tried to be a good pappy to our chillun . . ."

He remembered her distress when Abner wanted to leave home, and what she had said to him then.

"I think I tried hardest with Abner," he said, "because he weren't mine. He was some part of you I could never reach, and I thought if'n I could reach him, I could reach that part of you. An' I cain't work out what I did wrong."

If there was one, single moment when Queen began

to see the light that would guide her back to sanity, it was then. She could not bear to see him castigate himself, for he had done nothing wrong. She reached out to him and touched his hand.

"Not a thing, I promise you," she whispered. "Not one single thing."

But he would not relent. In his heart he believed that she would only get better when she wanted to get better, and he had to give her that will.

"I wants you to be well an' happy," he said. "But if'n you cain't be well, I wants you to be happy, an' if'n you cain't be happy, I wants you to be well."

The tiny light that Queen could see in the distance grew stronger. All sorts of things that had never made sense before suddenly became clear to her.

She didn't know how to be happy. No one had ever taught her. As a child she was expected to serve and obey, but no one ever cared about her happiness. She had been happy, briefly, in Decatur, but it was some other she, the white side that the world rejected, and she had lived a lie, so the happiness was a lie. She thought she'd been happy with the sisters in Huntsville, but when Abner was born she realized that the sisters didn't really care about her at all; they were using her for their own selfish needs. She tried to be happy with Davis, but he was too concerned with the pain of the world to be able to alleviate hers.

All her life she'd been trying to work out where she belonged, all her life she had tried to fit in with what other people expected her to be, but no one had ever asked her what she wanted. No one had ever asked her if she was happy.

And then she realized that wasn't true. One man had asked her that question.

"I loves you with all my heart," Alec said.

And she began to get better.

*

"She be pleased to see you," Alec said to Simon, as they pulled up outside the institution. "She be better now you home."

It was the perfect opportunity for Simon to tell his father of his plans, but he could not do it until he had seen his mother. He looked at the ugly building where his mother was incarcerated, and shivered slightly, but his father would not take him inside.

"'Tain't fittin'," he said. "'Tain't a good thing fo' a young man to see."

He arranged to have Queen meet her son in the garden. Simon waited patiently under a tree, and tried to avoid looking at the few inmates who were allowed outside to exercise. Their clothes were filthy, and their hair matted, and one of them talked soundlessly to someone only she could see, and another called on Jesus to deliver her. Simon felt pity for them, but could not imagine his mother in the company of these unfortunate souls.

He saw Alec leading Queen to him. Her appearance shocked him, for she seemed so old and frail, and so unlike her old self in this dull garb. He wanted to snatch her up, and take her away from here, and never let her out of his sight, and protect her always. He moved quickly to her, and when she saw him, her eyes lighted up with joy, and she was, for a moment, herself again.

"Oh, Ma," Simon cried.

She hugged him hard, held on to him, and moaned a little with the love of him. Then she told him her secret,

"I ain't mad," she said.

Alec went and talked to the doctors, to discover Queen's progress, and to give her the chance to talk to her son. Queen and Simon walked together in the pretty garden, and he told her things that he thought might make her happy, silly, trivial things, and made her smile, and laugh. Then, carefully, he told her of his plans.

He was going back to A & T, just for one semester.

He had money saved from his summer job, and he would not have to do any part-time work to sustain himself. He could devote all his time and attention and energy to his studies. He believed he would get good grades, and wanted to prove to himself that he could. Just for one semester. Then he could come home to the farm, but he could not come back in failure.

It was better than the best Christmas she could remember. It was what she wanted to hear from him, needed to hear from him, and it made her heart sing.

"You can do it," she said, her eyes shining with pride. "It was meant to be."

There was something else to tell her. He wasn't sure if now was the moment, but she was his ma, and she deserved to know. Just as Bertha had deserved to know the truth about Queen's condition, and he had told her, and she had responded with care, and affection, and concern. He had been very wrong to doubt that she would.

"I've met a girl, Ma," he said.

For a moment, he thought he'd done the wrong thing. Queen's eyes narrowed.

"And what's her name?" Queen demanded. "What she call herself, this girl who's stealing my baby away from me?"

"Bertha," Simon said meekly. "Bertha Palmer."

Queen was silent, staring away from him, at something in the distance. Then Simon realized something odd. She was laughing. She turned to him, and she was laughing.

"Not my baby?" she said. "Not my little baby boy?"

He laughed with her. "Quite a big boy now, Ma," he said.

It wasn't so hard for Queen to let Simon go. She'd had to let go of Abner, and that had pained her, but she had learned from it. And Abner had not lied to her; he still loved her, and was more attentive to her now, from far away, than ever he had been when he was home.

So she let go of Simon, and all she prayed for was that he be happy. Because now she understood a simple truth. There was one man who loved her more than anyone else in the world, and to expect more love than that from life is simple greed.

Simon visited her every day for the week he was in Savannah, and on the last day when he went to say good-bye, she hugged him and wished him Godspeed and good luck.

He went back to Greensboro, and settled to his studies. He wrote to Bertha regularly, and gave the good news of his progress, and of his excellent grades. Then one day he was summoned to the president's office. It made him nervous, because he could not imagine what he had done wrong.

But the president was fulsome in praise of his work, and gave him some extraordinary news. A certain Mr. Boyce had written to ask the cost of one full year's tuition, and then sent a check. It covered everything: tuition, dormitory, meals, and books. Simon was speechless. Why had someone he didn't know done this extraordinary thing? He hardly heard what the president said after that, because all the dark clouds had lifted from his horizon, and in his future he saw nothing but unbounded joy.

When he left the president's office, he walked across the lawn trying to work out who his benefactor was.

Then the penny—or rather, the five dollars—dropped, and he remembered a courtly, elderly man on a train, whose wife couldn't sleep.

He let out a whoop of exultation that shocked the students near him, and leaped several feet into the air.

At about the same time, Alec drove his buggy to the institution to bring Queen home. A nurse escorted her from the forbidding building and delivered her to her husband. Alec put his arms around her, and hugged her hard, then helped her into the buggy. They didn't speak very much on the journey home, because they never spoke very much about the things that were important.

It was a hot and dusty day, and when they got to the shack all was quiet. Queen stared at the little house, loving it, loving being home.

"Dunno where's the family," Alec wondered. "They said they'd be here, to meet you."

But Queen shook her head.

"It don't matter," she said. "This is all I need."

He helped her down, and held her arm, and took her into the quiet house. Inside, as if from nowhere, there was a burst of color, and noise, and people. Streamers flew around her, and all her family were there to welcome her. Minnie and Julie with their husbands and children, and Freeland with his wife and sons. George was there, with his family, and Abner, who had tired of city life, and had come home for good.

Queen stood among them all, surrounded by their love, and could not keep from crying.

That night she sat with Alec on the porch, rocking in their chairs, and puffing on their pipes, as if she had never been away. They laughed about the day, and gossiped about the family, and Queen thanked him for all he had done for her.

"'Tain't nuttin'," he said.

But it was something, she wanted to tell him, it was something of enormous importance to her, but she did not know how to say it. She realized something that shocked her. In all their years together, she had never actually told him how much she loved him. She had always assumed that he knew, but it was thoughtless to make such an assumption. She sought for a way to tell him what was in her heart, and an odd memory burst into her mind.

"Years ago," she said, "when I was a little girl, I lived in the big house, my pappy's house, with my half

909

brother William. We slept in the same room, only he had a big four-poster, and I had a pallet at the foot of his bed. We'd lie in bed and dream of our futures."

She was lost in memory.

"I always said that I was going to marry a prince on a white horse, and William would laugh at me. 'Who's going to marry an itty-bitty slave girl like you, Queen?' he'd say."

She looked at Alec, and saw his gray hair, and knew that her own was at least as gray, and her face lined, and her figure full, and that they had grown old together. But that didn't matter, because in his company she was a girl again, dreaming of the man she would marry, and he was a young ferryman, who was kind to her.

"He shouldn't have laughed, because he was wrong. The only thing is, how could I possibly have known that when I did find my prince, he wouldn't be on a white horse. He'd be riding on a ferryboat, across a mighty river."

Alec nodded gently. They sat together in silence, puffing on their pipes and rocking in their chairs. Then he put out his hand to her. She reached to him, and put her hand in his, and he grasped it hard, and when he spoke, his voice was gruff with love.

"That's all right, then," he said.

92

Simon graduated from A & T College, and when World War I came, he enlisted in the U. S. Army. He was sent to France, where, in the Argonne Forest, shortly before the end of the war, he was gassed. After treatment in a hospital overseas, he was returned home and mustered out of the army.

He received his master's degree at Cornell University, and went on to have an outstanding career as Dean of Agriculture at AM & N College, in Arkansas.

He married Bertha Palmer, and they had three sons. After Bertha's death, Simon was married again, to Zeona Hatcher, and they had a daughter.

The grandchildren of Queen Haley by her son Simon were:

George, who became a lawyer.

Julius, who became an architect.

Lois, who taught music.

And Alex Haley, who became a writer.

AFTERWORD

Alex was often asked how much of *Roots* was fact and how much fiction. I have been asked the same question, and my answer is similar to his, although less emphatic.

Most of the lineage statements in this book can be documented, except the most critical one. I do not have in my possession written evidence that James Jackson, Jr., fathered Queen, and I think it is unlikely that such evidence exists. Queen believed it. Alex believed it. It was accepted, in my presence, by several of the white descendants of the Jackson family. Alex was welcomed by them as a cousin, and several of them journeyed from Alabama to his farm in Tennessee to give him a memento of The Forks of Cypress, and to welcome him, officially, into the family.

There is a major genealogical error, however, concerning the Jackson family, and to them I apologize. In all my discussions with Alex, my concern was for Queen and her direct lineage, and the early research provided to me suggested that James Jackson, Jr. ("Jass"), was the first-born son of James and Sally Jackson. After Alex's death, when I began work on the book, I uncovered later research that documented the birth of an earlier son, Andrew Jackson Jackson ("A.J."). Obviously, Alex was aware of this, but none of his notes for the novel gave me any indication of how he intended to incorporate A.J. into the story. In trying to find a path through the clutter of this nineteenth-century family, and because A.J. hardly affected

Queen's life, I have invented an untimely death for him. In fact, he lived to a good age.

Beyond that, almost all the people are where they should be almost all the time, although I have given a couple more years of life to Pocahontas Perkins than she actually enjoyed, and her daughter, Lizzie, is born a tad earlier than in life. Uncle Henry in Ireland and Uncle Hugh in Philadelphia have been combined into one character.

I doubt that young James was ever called Jass, but as he, his father, and his grandfather were all called James Jackson, I thought some clarifying nickname was necessary.

I have also been asked how much of the book was written by Alex and how much by me, and I find this impossible to quantify. I have a seven-hundred-page outline provided by Alex, boxes and boxes of his research are available to me, and some finished pages for the book, but my major resource was Alex himself. His head was full of the stories that constitute this work, and I spent two of the happiest and most informative years of my life listening to those stories and debating them with him. Some scenes we wrote together, around the kitchen table at his farm, on a banana boat to Ecuador, and during journeys of exploration to the South.

I am aware that some historians dispute some of Alex's conclusions. Given certain constraints of time, I have done my utmost, and have employed staff, to verify his research. In the mass of reference works we have consulted, some few stand out: the several volumes of *A People's History* by Page Smith; *Reconstruction* by Eric Foner; Michael Paul Rogin's *Fathers and Children*, and specifically for Andrew Jackson, *The Border Captain* by Marquis James. The diaries of Mary Chestnut were invaluable for confirmations of the society's attitude to relationships such as that of Jass and Easter, as were several reference works about Thomas Jefferson and his thirty-nine-year relationship with his slave mistress, Sally Hemings.

I am keenly aware that this is not the book Alex would have written. Like *Roots*, this was to have been a personal history of his family, and he told it to me as such. But it is not my history, my family, or my people, black or white. When Alex died, I had to move into new and unfamiliar territories. Not a historian, I had to piece this history together, and it is a period of high definition for many Americans. I am sure some will be offended by my assumptions, and to those offended I can only shrug my shoulders and say sorry.

Alex wrote the following statement about his intentions:

"This book will convey visceral America. For our land of immigrants is a testimonial to the merging of the cultures of the world, and of their bloodlines."

I am not American, but for me, the overriding achievement of *Roots* was as a spectacular metaphor for the travails of every black family in this country and their journey through history. In that sense *Queen* is also a metaphor, a representative woman for the thousands upon thousands of children of the plantation who were dispossessed of their families and their heritage. I can only be grateful for this extraordinary opportunity to pass on what Alex left behind, and grieve with all my heart the circumstance that brought it about.